Praise for David Oshinsky's *A Conspiracy So Immense*

"[Oshinsky is] a great storyteller; he has done some terrific research, and best of all, he knows how to handle the drama of the era without getting too preachy."

—*The New York Times Book Review*

"Oshinsky's elegant and comprehensive biography . . . can now lay its own claim to being the finest account available of Joe McCarthy's career."

—*Reviews in American History*

"The objectivity and scholarship of *A Conspiracy So Immense* should make it a standard treatment . . . a vivid account of the Senator's progress from demagogue to grand inquisitor."

—*The New Leader*

"Professor David Oshinsky's *A Conspiracy So Immense* is the finest book on the period I have read."

—Patrick J. Buchanan

"A staggeringly successful and rare new book of history . . . . It is hard to tell in the space of this column why *A Conspiracy So Immense* impressed me so much. Of course, it has something to do with the excellent writing, which may set a standard for crisp, witty historical prose . . . . It has something to do with the extraordinary thoroughness of Oshinsky's research. His footnotes are historical gold mines. [Above all] Oshinsky shows that in that evil time, even the purest of motives were soiled. He shows us what man is. That is what makes great history, which is what *A Conspiracy So Immense* is."

—Ben Stein, *Los Angeles Herald-Examiner*

A
Conspiracy
So Immense

The World of Joe McCarthy

David M. Oshinsky

OXFORD
UNIVERSITY PRESS

OXFORD

UNIVERSITY PRESS

Oxford University Press, Inc., publishes works that further
Oxford University's objective of excellence
in research, scholarship, and education.

Oxford   New York
Auckland   Cape Town   Dar es Salaam   Hong Kong   Karachi
Kuala Lumpur   Madrid   Melbourne   Mexico City   Nairobi
New Delhi   Shanghai   Taipei   Toronto

With offices in
Argentina   Austria   Brazil   Chile   Czech Republic   France   Greece
Guatemala   Hungary   Italy   Japan   Poland   Portugal   Singapore
South Korea   Switzerland   Thailand   Turkey   Ukraine   Vietnam

Copyright © 2005 by David M. Oshinsky

Published as an Oxford University Press paperback, 2005
198 Madison Avenue, New York, New York 10016
www.oup.com

First published by The Free Press, a Division of Simon & Schuster, Inc., 1983

Oxford is a registered trademark of Oxford University Press

Library of Congress Cataloging-in-Publication Data
Oshinsky, David M., 1944–
A conspiracy so immense : the world of Joe McCarthy / David M. Oshinsky.
p. cm.
Originally published: New York : The Free Press, 1983. With new pref.
Includes bibliographical references and index.
ISBN-13: 978-0-19-515424-5 (pbk)
ISBN-10: 0-19-515424-X (pbk)
1. McCarthy, Joseph, 1908–1957.
2. Legislators—United States—Biography.
3. United States. Congress. Senate—Biography.
4. Internal security—United States—History—20th century.
5. Communism—United States—History—20th century.
6. Anti-communist movements—United States—History—20th century.
I. Title.

E748.M143O82 2005   973.921'092—dc22   2005010664

1 3 5 7 9 8 6 4 2
Printed in the United States of America on acid-free paper

*For my brother Stephen—a man of extraordinary courage
and compassion, a pillar of the family,
a perfect friend.*

Contents

Preface

IN THE PAST TWO DECADES, the subject of American Communism has become a cottage industry for writers of every discipline and point of view. Hundreds of books have appeared from across the political spectrum, spinning familiar stories, pleading shopworn cases, and settling long-forgotten scores. Until recently, these volumes have largely endorsed the portrait of Senator Joe McCarthy as a headline-hunting goon who helped turn the pursuit of Communists into a reckless national crusade. Almost every major bookstore today has a shelf—sometimes an entire section—on the so-called McCarthy era, bearing titles such as *Scoundrel Time, The American Inquisition, and Washington Gone Mad*. The term "McCarthyism," coined in the 1950s to describe the Wisconsin senator's odious behavior, has become part of our political lexicon. Indeed, the current edition of *Webster's New World Dictionary* defines the term this way: "noun [after Joseph McCarthy], the use of indiscriminate, often unfounded, accusations, sensationalism, inquisitorial investigative methods, etc., as in the suppression of political opponents portrayed as subversive."

The senator's legacy seemed set in cement. Even his most ardent supporters admitted as much. Their hero was a pariah, they agreed, a figure so hated and disgraced as to rule out any attempt to seriously reexamine his career. How did one restore the reputation of a man whose very name had become a pejorative, linked to the worst excesses of a deeply troubled time?

The answer came in the early 1990s, with the stunning collapse of communism in the Soviet Union and Eastern Europe. For the first time, historians from the West were given access to the KGB records and to the papers of the American

Communist Party (CPUSA), which had been secretly smuggled out of the United States. Meanwhile, following decades of silence, the National Security Agency released a portion of the Venona Cables, a supersecret military code-breaking operation that had traced Soviet intelligence traffic during World War II. The impact of this new information was dramatic, to say the least. It revealed not only the impressive size and scope of the Soviet spy operation inside the United States during the 1930s and 1940s, but also the key role played by the CPUSA in supplying most of the recruits.

Venona was particularly instructive. Running to more than 5,000 pages, its decrypted cables proved how deeply the federal government had been penetrated by communist spies during Franklin Delano Roosevelt's three-plus presidential terms. Thousands of workers had been needed to staff a huge bureaucracy created by FDR's New Deal and the nation's entry into World War II. With virtually no security system in place, communists found it relatively simple to form spy cells in some of the government's most sensitive places: the State Department, the Treasury Department, and the Manhattan (atomic bomb) Project, to name a few. These cells, wrote one analyst, provided the Russians "with a cornucopia of policy and technical secrets from the United States." Among the key Soviet agents described in Venona and the KGB archives are Alger Hiss, Julius Rosenberg, and Harry Dexter White.[1]

For McCarthy supporters, such disclosures equaled vindication. The senator, they insisted, had been right all along. Writing in 2000, historian Arthur Herman blamed assorted "liberals" and "intellectuals" (this author included) for dishonoring a patriot who had dared to tell the truth. Ann Coulter agreed, accusing the left-wing "blabocracy" (this author again included) of destroying Senator McCarthy in the hope of silencing his vital anti-communist crusade. "Only a small number of the intercepted Soviet cables have been decoded," she writes in *Treason*, her recent account of "liberal treachery" in modern America. "But even that much proves McCarthy was absolutely right in his paramount charge: The U.S. government had a major communist infestation problem. It is treated as a mere truism that McCarthy was reckless, made mistakes, and was careless with his facts. It can now be said that McCarthy's gravest error was in understimating the problem of Communist subversion."[2]

Well, not exactly. For the great majority of historians, including those most familiar with Venona and the Soviet archives, these documents tell a strikingly different tale. They speak to domestic subversion at a unique time in our history—from 1933 to 1945, the heyday of American communism—when radicalism was in vogue, the Russians were seen as allies in the fight against Hitler, and spying itself was rationalized by traitors like Hiss and Rosenberg as essential to the coming socialist revolution.

---

[1]Allen Weinstein, *The Haunted Wood,* 1999, p. 340; Harvey Klehr and John Earl Haynes, *The Secret World of American Communism,* 1995; Harvey Klehr and John Earl Haynes, *Venona: Decoding Soviet Espionage in America,* 1999.

[2]Arthur Herman, *Joseph McCarthy: Reexamining the Life and Legacy of America's Most Hated Senator,* 2000, pp. 1–18, 321–27; Ann Coulter, *Treason: Liberal Treachery From the Cold War to the War on Terrorism,* 2003, p. 37.

But then the Cold War descended, and domestic communism collapsed. As the crimes of Stalin became undeniable to all but a pathetic handful of party fanatics, and the federal government began a major crackdown on the CPUSA and its leadership, a mass defection occurred within the ranks, denying the Soviets the loyalists they needed to support their once-thriving espionage cells. "By the close of the 1940s," states the U.S. commission report that accompanied the release of Venona, the KGB had been "reduced to recruiting thieves as spies." It is no coincidence that the two spectacular espionage cases following World War II involved spying that occurred in the 1930s (Alger Hiss) and the early 1940s (Julius and Ethel Rosenberg). Indeed by 1950, when McCarthy made his first charges about hundreds of communists and subversives currently "shaping the policy" of the State Department and other agencies, the communist threat in the United States was all but over.[3]

New accounts of McCarthy's career must take careful note of the key role played by the American Communist Party in what historians now call "the golden age" of Soviet espionage. But such accounts must also describe the ways in which McCarthy shaped and manipulated this issue in the early 1950s—the era that still bears his name. It is my hope that readers of *A Conspiracy So Immense* will come away with a feel for the personal qualities that shaped the senator's career as America's premier Red-hunter, as well as the political forces that fueled his erratic anti-Communist crusade. Few politicians in our history have had the emotional impact of a Joe McCarthy—his power to terrify, to fascinate, and, ultimately, to divide.

---

[3]Quoted in Weinstein, *The Haunted Wood,* p. 340.

Acknowledgments

I BEGAN RESEARCHING this project in 1975. Many people helped along the way. Gerd Korman intensified my interest in McCarthy; John Roche and Leonard Levy kept that interest alive. James Martin, Maurice Lee, Richard L. McCormick, and Steven Whitfield read parts of the manuscript and made valuable suggestions. Robert Amdur and William O'Neill labored over the various drafts; their kind and creative assistance can hardly be exaggerated. Robert Rutter and David Schmitz served expertly as research assistants. I am deeply indebted to the librarians and archivists at the Truman Library, the Eisenhower Library, the Kennedy Library, the Princeton University Library, the Mundt Library, the Library of Congress, and the Wisconsin State Historical Society. In particular, I would like to thank Tom Soapes and David Wigdor for their personal interest in the project.

My editors at The Free Press were skillful and supportive. Charles Smith displayed more patience than I deserved. His interest in the project was contagious. Joyce Seltzer read the manuscript with great care. Her comments and insights made for a much better book. George Rowland was both a critic and a friend. I relied on him every step of the way.

A
Conspiracy
So Immense

CHAPTER ONE

Beginnings

A SMALL KNOT OF PEOPLE, perhaps fifty strong, has gathered on the far edge of St. Mary's cemetery in Appleton, Wisconsin. They stand on a lovely tree-shaded knoll above the Fox River, waiting for the memorial service to begin. It is May 4, 1975.

The Reverend Hugh Wish has come up from Milwaukee to deliver the eulogy. He tells the participants—local folks, mainly, from Grand Chute and Appleton—that the turnout is getting smaller every year. Too many Americans have somehow forgotten what a patriot this man was. His graphic warnings about Communist treason and conspiracy, as valid today as ever, are no longer heeded. "The fall of South Vietnam," Wish claims, "is clearly attributable to the fact that people failed to take his advice."

The mourners nod in agreement. "A saint is buried here," says one. "He truly gave his life for his country." A woman holding an infant presses closer to Reverend Wish. "I want my baby to see this," she whispers, "and to remember this man and what he stood for." The priest seems pleased. If the new generation can learn the truth about him, he answers, the country will soon pass into safer hands. After a silent prayer, Father Wish heads down the knoll, leaving behind a few women to say their personal goodbyes and to decorate the site with flowers.[1] The lengthening afternoon shadows partly obscure the gravestone's simple inscription:

JOSEPH R.
McCARTHY
UNITED STATES SENATOR
NOVEMBER 14, 1908   MAY 2, 1957

OUTAGAMIE COUNTY, in northeastern Wisconsin, lies along "the great water highway" between Lake Winnebago and Green Bay. It was settled in the early nineteenth century by French Canadians and New England Yankees, who bought and cheated the Fox and Winnebago Indians off their land. In the following decades thousands of German immigrants, attracted by the cheap, fertile soil, moved into the area. They were followed by a smaller number of Dutch, Belgian, and Swiss farm families. By 1900 about one in three Outagamie residents spoke German, and one in ten some other foreign tongue.[2]

In the 1850s the local residents began to see the potential of their waterways for industry and shipping. They formed the Fox and Wisconsin Development Company, which built a series of locks and canals around the town of Appleton. Most of the heavy labor was done by the newly arrived Irish, who settled in southern Outagamie, near Lake Winnebago. When the project was completed, some stayed to tend the locks, but most acquired small farms in the outlying areas. One cluster, the so-called Irish Settlement, was in Grand Chute, a small village on the outskirts of Appleton.

There were two Catholic churches in the area: St Joseph's, which served the German, Belgian, and Dutch worshipers; and St. Mary's, poorer, less influential, and exclusively Irish. The congregations rarely mingled. For reasons of preference, or perhaps prejudice, the Irish kept to themselves, farming the cheaper land and sending fewer of their children to the public schools. They were, however, acknowledged to be the best workers around. The Irish Settlement, noted one local resident, "was known all over the county for its productivity. The farms were clean and efficient. And if you hired an Irish kid you were assured a fair day's work. People respected them for that."[3]

The first McCarthy to settle in Grand Chute was Joe's grandfather, Stephen. Born in Tipperary, Ireland, in 1821, he had fled to upstate New York as a young man to escape landlords, famine, and grinding poverty. "There he spent ten years in faithful work," wrote the historian of Outagamie County, "and in addition to sending money home to his mother . . . he accumulated enough to purchase a tract of wild land . . . and came here with a team of oxen, a wagon and other crude necessities, to try to wring a livelihood from the soil." Why he chose Grand Chute is a mystery. He may have known some people who had settled there, or he may have moved where the farms were cheap and the farmers were Irish. His deed, recorded on March 23, 1859, shows that he paid $600 for 160 acres. The land was bought unseen.[4]

In 1862 Stephen hurdled Grand Chute's ethnic barrier to wed Margaret Stoffel, the daughter of Bavarian immigrants. Their life together proved bountiful. They raised ten children—six boys and four girls, two of whom became nuns—and did well enough for Stephen to bring his mother over from Ireland and settle her on the adjoining property. Before they died, the McCarthys purchased additional land to spread among their offspring. One portion—"143 acres more or less, according to Government Survey"—was passed on to son Tim in 1896. Margaret, who evidently was illiterate, signed the warranty deed with an "X."[5]

Tim must have been at home on the land. Surrounded by his brothers and sisters, he settled down to farm with his wife, Bridget, a member of the neighboring Tierney clan. Like most Grand Chute residents, the McCarthys lived in a simple log cabin, hand-plowed their fields, raised strong horses, and watched over a small herd of cows. By the time Joseph Raymond, their fifth child, was delivered by a midwife, Tim and Bridget had moved into a new white clapboard house. It, too, was simple, with no electricity or indoor plumbing.

Though physically unimposing, Tim was well suited for the hardships of rural life. One neighbor described him as a "jaunty little Irishman. . . . He wanted to be a no-nonsense farmer, and that's what he was." His life was well ordered and ordinary. He spent fifteen hours a day, seven days a week, running his spread. "Tim worked all the time," said one townsman. "And he expected his boys to do the same. He was a serious fellow."[6]

Bridget McCarthy—Bid to her friends—was a large, stocky woman with "fine Irish features." Portrayed as "kindly," "plain," "uneducated," and "fiercely religious," she supposedly had a soft spot for Joe, her "favorite child." According to the McCarthy legend, the boy won his mother's attention and sympathy because of his shy, introverted manner and his odd physical appearance. As a "gawky ugly duckling," he was bullied and ridiculed by his older brothers. When Joe could take it no longer, the story goes, he would challenge them to fight, take a beating, and retreat to the comforting arms of his mother. Tim would then scold Bid for coddling the boy.

McCarthy's childhood has been described in very bleak terms. Unattractive, tormented by his brothers, he was a constant source of friction between a doting mother, who saw him as uniquely gifted, and a surly, rough-tongued father, who felt he was ordinary, quite like the others.

Withdrawing into himself, the story goes, Joe longed for the day when he might escape those hostile surroundings. Once he left, he never looked back. The memories were simply too painful.

Actually, such generalizations are based on guesswork and wishful thinking, nothing more. With one exception, McCarthy's previous biographers did no primary research; and the exception, an inveterate McCarthy-hater, was determined to portray his subject in the worst possible light. Yet these generalizations have been repeated so often that few people question their veracity. Among the skeptics, however, are those who knew Joe best, his childhood friends and neighbors. They remember him as a vigorous, extroverted, ruggedly handsome boy. And they bristle at stories of family friction. "The McCarthys were very close," says Jim Heenan, a retired Grand Chute farmer who lived adjacent to Tim's spread. "They always looked out for each other. All this stuff about Joe's feuding with his father and his brothers is a lot of bunk. I know. I was there."[7]

Heenan's recollections are corroborated by other neighbors. The McCarthy boys did play rough, they contend, often teasing each other and battling with their fists behind the barn. But that was the way differences among children were generally settled in Grand Chute. And Joe, who was big and very powerful for his age, could more than hold his own. Contrary to the belief that he learned to box in college, he had a local reputation for taking on all comers, particularly the German boys who lived down the road. "Joe wasn't a bully, but he did like to scrap," a friend recalled. "And he never went crying to Bid. That just wasn't done around here."

Students of Irish-American culture have long contended that Irish-American males, in particular, learn to control their feelings of warmth and love through brawling and external ridicule. In his provocative essay, *That Most Distressful Nation*, Andrew Greeley has written:

> Ridicule is the matrix for many presumably intimate relationships in Irish-American families. . . . It is constant and incredibly nasty. Some Irish-Americans begin it when they encounter those they "love" and keep at it mercilessly as long as they are in each other's presence. It is as though the most cruel verbal viciousness is absolutely essential for survival in intimate relations.

But he concludes that the Irish have a much higher level of sibling loyalty than other American populations:

> We cannot be indifferent or apathetic on the matter of our siblings. We fight with them, quarrel with them, sometimes don't speak to them for years, but when they are in trouble, we rally fiercely around them. We may have spent

a lifetime in conflict with them, yet we are nonetheless overwhelmed with sorrow when they die.[8]

There is, of course, no way of knowing how well this model fitted the McCarthy family. But Joe's neighbors, who recall their brotherly brawling, are quick to note that the McCarthy children never lost touch with one another. After Joe left the farm, he remained in close contact with his siblings, attending family parties, giving money and support, and returning home to lend a hand at barn raisings and other functions. Despite his later success, he always found time for the likes of Steve, a factory worker; Bill, a truck driver; and Howard, a farm auctioneer. He was, in every respect, the dutiful brother.[9]

Joe's "hostile" relationship with his father has also been challenged. "You must understand," said Heenan, "that Tim was a nothing-for-frills kind of person. But he was very loving when it came to his children. When Joe was grown, he would visit with his parents every chance he got. Tim was proud as hell of that boy." * John Ellenbecker, a childhood friend who would later serve as McCarthy's undertaker, offered this opinion: "Joe was an agreeable kid. Anything Tim asked, it was always, 'Sure thing, I can do it.' Tim worked him hard, the same as all the boys. But there was plenty of time for fun, and Joe was always in the middle of it. . . . To say that Joe was picked on or abused is ridiculous."[10]

If anything, neighbors claim, the reverse was probably true: Joe may well have been Tim's favorite, a status he earned by toiling longer and harder than anyone else. He was strong, energetic, and anxious to please: in short, a valuable economic asset. "Joe worked like the devil," a local farmer recalled. "I remember one day when he was helpin' Tim load hay into the barn. We was usin' a team of horses and a rope and pulley to hoist the hay up. Joe's job was leadin' the horses. He had to lead them across the yard and through a ditch and clear to the road. The ditch was near fulla water, but Joe plowed right into it, up to his knees, leadin' them horses. Never even slowed down. One of his boots came off in the mud, and I remember he didn't go pick up that boot till all the hay was in."[11]

Why did he work so hard? For one thing, Tim expected it. He supervised his sons carefully and stood for no nonsense. For another, the ability to do backbreaking labor was part of Grand Chute's passage to manhood. It was the primary standard by which a father judged a son,

---

* Friends and acquaintances who went along with McCarthy on his frequent visits to the family farm were struck by the genuine affection between Joe and his parents. Invariably, when McCarthy was ready to leave, Tim would take him aside, put his arms around him, and remind him to say his prayers. Interview with Urban Van Susteren, October 22, 1977; Bob Schwartz, "The Junior Senator: Early Life," unpublished manuscript in the *Robert Fleming Papers*, Box 4, Manuscripts Division, Wisconsin State Historical Society.

and a son established his masculine credentials. "When a farmer spoke of his boy," mused one native, "it was mainly in terms of how useful the boy was, how much he could do and how well he could do it. Today sports and school are important. But not then. That was a different time." [12]

It is possible, too, that Joe was a hyperactive child. He is best remembered as someone who "couldn't sit still." He gulped his food, ran from place to place, labored incessantly, and slept a good deal less than his brothers and sisters. "Joe was like any other kid," said his brother Howard, "except he was generally three steps ahead of them." [13] In later years people would be similarly impressed by his nervous energy, his twitchy manner, and his ability to work and carouse for days without rest. Invariably, this brutal pace left him susceptible to all sorts of physical ailments. Illness, both real and imagined, would plague him throughout his life.

Had the McCarthys lived closer to Appleton, the children would have gone to parochial school. But the trip was an hour by wagon in good weather, and the bitter winters made daily travel impossible. So they attended the local Underhill School, a cramped one-room structure that housed eight grades and a lone teacher. By all accounts, Joe was an excellent student. He learned fast and was blessed with extraordinary recall. His problem, typically, was not knowing how to keep his mouth closed. Often, when the teacher drilled her older pupils with problem sets, young McCarthy, though several grades behind, would cause a stir by blurting out the right answer. It got to the point where the teacher had no choice but to let him sit in on the advanced lessons. Finally, with Bid's consent, he was allowed to skip a grade. [14]

Bid was probably disappointed when Joe quit school at fourteen to join Tim and the older boys full time on the land. She realized that he was more precocious than his brothers and sisters, that he had an unusually sharp, retentive mind. But a high school education was rare in Grand Chute, and Joe was not excited by the prospect of earning one. He saw no future for himself but farming—an attitude his father did little to discourage. If there was any parental friction, it probably surfaced at this point. Tim believed that the time had come for the boy to get on with his life's work. Bid, who had long pressed Joe to "get ahead" and to "be somebody," may have wanted more for her child than simple farming. [15]

Joe did not last long at his new job. He worked hard enough, but the routine was too monotonous for him. "Like all of us," recalled his sister Anna May, "he had chores around the farm . . . but they never seemed to satisfy him. He wanted—something else—something special." At sixteen Joe decided to go into business for himself, raising chickens. After earning a few dollars as a part-time laborer, he went to his father and asked for the use of some land. Tim rented him a spare acre at the going rate. He warned his son not to expect the family's help.[16]

Joe didn't want it. This was his big chance, and he plunged forward with the same bursts of raw energy and enthusiasm that characterized so many of his endeavors. Within a year he had a thriving little business with 2,000 hens, 10,000 broilers, a large chicken house, and a battered truck. His diligence, neighbors say, "was both a family pride and a family joke—he was known as the only man who could go out to the barn on a cold winter night wearing two coats and come back with chicken droppings all over the outside coat and the inside one as well."[17]

As legend has it, the boy's finest moment came when he persuaded Bid to accompany him on one of his long selling trips. "To show his mother how he stood in the world of men," a biographer has written, "Joe put her in his truck and took her to Chicago with him: a sixteen-year-old boy, driving a man's truck, doing a man's job, taking his mother across Wisconsin state line for the first time in her life." The tale is dramatic but probably untrue. Bid McCarthy was deathly afraid of machines. It is doubtful that Joe could have coaxed her into his broken-down truck for a ride to Appleton, much less Chicago, and unlikely that he ever tried. In Grand Chute the very mention of this incident brought skeptical looks and one loud guffaw.[18]

Neighbors do recall, however, that Joe "played the gambler" and "took really big risks" with his business. He was forever loading more and more chickens into his truck until, finally, the crates were piled higher than the side panels. Once, rounding a bend near Kenosha, the truck tipped over, scattering chickens, feathers, and broken crates all over the highway. Joe survived the accident, but his fortunes sagged the next year when he contracted a serious case of influenza. His stubborn pride, combined with Tim's warning, kept him from seeking the family's assistance. Instead, he took on a few local boys who knew nothing about chickens and proceeded to destroy the flock. By the time Joe recovered, his little empire had vanished.

He tried for a time to rebuild it, but his enthusiasm for poultry had cooled. One day, while peddling eggs door to door, he learned that the Cashway grocery chain was looking for someone to run its new outlet in Manawa, a small farming community northwest of Appleton. After bombarding the district manager with tales of his business knowhow, Joe was given the job. At twenty he began a new career as Manawa's county grocer.

Joe left Grand Chute with mixed emotions. Like many young adults, he was attached to his surroundings but eager to press beyond them. Fortunately, his parents understood those feelings and encouraged him to move on. "Go out and be somebody," Bid would tell her son. "Take a chance. Nobody starves in America."[19] And Tim, despite earlier misgivings, proved equally supportive. Having once encouraged his son to leave school, he would soon be lending him money for college.

It is difficult, of course, to speculate about the way family, religion, and physical environment shaped the senator's personality. He did not talk much about these years, and the recollections of friends and neighbors are always suspect. Besides, we have little knowledge of other influences that may have been at work. The Irish, for example, were a minority in Grand Chute, surrounded by people who often viewed them as less than equal. The McCarthys were very provincial; when Joe went to Appleton, friends remember, the children would tease him about his bib overalls, bringing tears to his eyes. And McCarthy's boyhood included the war years 1917–18; ethnic tensions were high in town, and vigilante action against the "disloyal" was all too common.

What can one make of those years? McCarthy's biographers have painted a depressing picture, assuming, perhaps, that someone as "dangerous" and "destructive" as Joe McCarthy could not have had a "normal" childhood. They may well be right, but their analyses are poorly researched and marred by personal bias. The best *available* evidence, admittedly superficial, points in another direction: McCarthy was an outgoing, physically aggressive boy, quite willing to take risks in the name of self-improvement. He knew that hard work brought attention, admiring words, and the prospect of future gain. And he was surrounded by plain, frugal, religious family members who understood, however vaguely, that he was a cut above his peers. Unfortunately, the inner dynamics of his youth—his dreams and fears, his deepest feelings about Tim and Bid, and theirs about him and themselves—will never be known.

━━━━━━━

MANAWA, WISCONSIN, has not changed very much in the past fifty years. Its population of 700, mainly Danish- and German-American, still farms the land or works in the stores and restaurants on the single main street that runs for three blocks and then disappears into a blacktop county highway. Its social life revolves around its school, its churches, and its fraternal clubs. When folks talk about Manawa's contribution to America, they proudly mention Senator Joe McCarthy, their "adopted" son.*

* Of the many people I met during my stay in Manawa, only the former postmaster had a bad word for McCarthy. I asked him why, but he refused to explain. "I can't understand why anyone in his right mind would want to write a book about *him*," he sneered. Before I could utter another word he turned and walked away.

The year that McCarthy spent in Manawa was among the most important and productive of his life. He came as a brash young man, full of bluster and ambition, determined to set the town on its ear. And he succeeded. His exploits were so extraordinary that older residents still recall them with genuine astonishment. "I never saw anybody so steamed up," said one. "He just couldn't ever relax; he worked at everything he did. He was pushing all the time."[20]

Joe's business methods were unorthodox, but quite successful. He advertised the Cashway by walking the streets and country roads, introducing himself to everyone in sight. When the town's chicken population took sick, he went from farm to farm offering his special talents free of charge. He was the only grocer to keep his store open after sundown. Before long business was booming. The Cashway, one observer remarked, was "usually as crowded as a county fair. Other grocers felt so lonely that they came over in the evenings to help handle the crowds. It got to be a hard task to get people out at midnight." Of Cashway's twenty-nine stores, the "Manawa Madhouse" was smallest in size but greatest in cash volume.[21]

Joe spent the year in the home of Mrs. Frank Osterloth, across the street from the high school. According to Minnie Osterloth, a daughter who lived nearby, he "just appeared at the front door one day and asked if he could stay. Mama was very lonely. All the children were grown and Papa was logging up near Lake Superior. He didn't come home for months at a time. The house was empty and she was sick for company. Joe had the run of the house, and Mama cooked most of his meals. They were very close."[22]

It was Mrs. Osterloth who persuaded Joe to return to school. Uneducated herself, she admired the young man's gumption and sensed that his intelligence was well above average. After hours of motherly coaxing she got him to ask Leo Hershberger, the local principal, for permission to enroll at Little Wolf High School. Hershberger was understandably hesitant about putting a rawboned twenty-year-old, standing almost six feet tall and weighing 170 pounds, in the same room with kids half his size. But he finally agreed to let McCarthy attend classes and "proceed at an accelerated pace."[23]

Accelerated indeed. Joe completed his freshman and sophomore course work during his first semester, and his junior and senior requirements in the second. He had, in other words, finished Little Wolf in a single year, a feat the current Manawa denizens recall with prideful smiles. How did he do it? In 1929 the high school used a system in which each student, working alone, could choose to fulfill the lesson requirements for a grade of A, B, or C. ("Joe always tried for an A," Hershberger noted.) Everyone worked at a different pace. Some might take a week to complete the lesson; others could knock it off in a day. This allowed

McCarthy to move way out in front of his classmates. He was older, better motivated, and far more mature. And he possessed a sponge-like mind that quickly ingested material from the printed page. Only one course troubled him: intermediate algebra. He would often slip out of the Cashway and walk down to the furniture store, where Ada Nye, a recent high school graduate, offered free tutoring and advice.[24]

McCarthy's consuming interest in schoolwork eventually cost him the Cashway job. His sister Olive came up from Grand Chute to help mind the store, but it wasn't enough. Joe was the main attraction, and with him gone the customers drifted away. He seemed too busy to notice. Rising at five each morning to prepare his lessons, he put in a nine-hour school day and worked nights as an usher at the local movie house. By June he had lost twenty-five pounds and begun wearing eyeglasses. "Joe had more 'stick-to-itiveness' than anybody I ever met in my life," said Hershberger. "He nearly killed himself that year."[25]

According to one source, he nearly killed a few of his classmates as well. In order to work off an excess of energy, we are told, Joe gave boxing lessons to the children and reportedly beat them to a pulp. Anderson and May assert that "the younger students grew tired of being used as punching bags and stopped showing up."[26] No doubt this vivid portrait of McCarthy as an incorrigible bully was intended to help us "understand" his cruel political behavior in later years. It simply isn't true. Those who knew him then say that he treated his classmates with compassion and restraint. "Everyone liked him," Hershberger insists. "The kids just couldn't leave him alone."

People *were* fond of Joe in Manawa. And very good to him, offering friendship, security, and a chance to make something of his life. By most accounts, however, his human contacts were peripheral: a friendly greeting, a quick handshake, a conversation on the run. One Manawa resident gave this assessment of him: "We all liked Joe. He'd always stop everyone on the street, say hello, and ask how they were doing. But he rarely stayed to listen to their answers. People didn't resent this. They knew how busy Joe was. I believe he was really concerned about us. He just didn't have the time to get close."[27]

Leaving Manawa was easy. Joe had gone as far as he could there. His horizons were expanding, and he wanted very much to attend college. But he took a valuable lesson along with him that year: When ambition and raw energy confront established rules and traditions—like those governing high school attendance—it is often the rules and traditions that give way. The lesson was brought home again when he applied to Marquette, the well-known Jesuit college in Milwaukee. Its questionnaire asked whether the applicant had attended four years of secondary school. Rather than have Joe lie, Hershberger filled out the form himself.[28] "I just left that question blank," he said, "and I told Joe he didn't have to go around Marquette bragging that he had gone through high school in one year." *

McCarthy's only regret, it seems, was leaving Mrs. Osterloth. Like Bid before her, she gave Joe comfort and support, while helping to channel his energy in a positive direction. Their final meeting that year, as described by daughter Minnie, was filled with sadness and tears. "Joe kept hugging her, saying, 'I won't forget you, Mother,' over and over. They were both crying. Joe always remained close with Mama. He wrote her from Washington. And whenever he was in Appleton he would call her on the phone to say hello. She felt more for him than for her own sons. . . . She really loved her Joe."[29]

━━━━━━━

McCARTHY ENTERED COLLEGE in the fall of 1930. He chose Marquette for religious and financial reasons. The Depression was in full swing, and few working-class or farm-bred students had the money to go out of state. This left two real choices: the University of Wisconsin at Madison or Marquette. The latter, situated in a larger city, offered better employment opportunities. Most of Joe's classmates paid their tuition by working in gas stations or by washing dishes at the local beaneries. Furthermore, Marquette was a Catholic school that stressed religion, while Madison was not. "There was a strong feeling in my home that the state university was a godless place, filled with atheists and Communists," noted Richard Farrell, now a county judge in Green Bay. "You send your kids there, my parents believed, and they wouldn't go to church any more. Marquette was the place for good Catholics. McCarthy was a good Catholic."[30]

That is true. Throughout his life Joe remained close to the Church. He went regularly to confession, observed meatless Fridays, gave generously to Catholic charities, and rarely missed Sunday Mass. Those who traveled with McCarthy in Wisconsin's north country say he would drive for hours to attend services. An acquaintance who met him on a senatorial jaunt through Ohio wrote of the experience: "An amazing thing to me was that after a Saturday night lousy drunk, and having bedded with one or more gals, as he called 'em, he would get up early the following morning to go to Mass." In his excellent study of McCarthy and the

* Upon learning that he would not be penalized for his abbreviated high school career, Joe went public in typical McCarthy fashion. In 1930 the Marquette student newspaper carried a big picture of him hard at work at his desk. The caption read: " 'Can't' is not in the vocabulary of Joseph McCarthy, freshman in the college of engineering, and he proved this by doing the almost impossible task of going through high school in one year." In 1931 the newspaper carried another story on the subject: "Joe McCarthy, promising Marquette boxing candidate, disproves the assertion that brawn, not brains, makes good boxers. Joe made his high school credits in one year of study so that he could enter Marquette." See Marquette *Tribune*, October 30, 1930; March 26, 1931.

Catholic Church, Father Donald Crosby noted that the senator "seems to have given hardly a passing thought to the more philosophical . . . aspects of religious belief." Yet, he concluded, "if McCarthy thought that going to Sunday Mass (as well as getting baptized, married, and buried in the church) was what Catholicism was all about, it was nevertheless true that he observed these functions with a fidelity that would have brought joy to the heart of many a Catholic pastor."[31]

As an entering freshman at twenty-one, McCarthy took a room in a nearby boarding house filled with Marquette law students and got to know the lady who ran it, Mrs. John Kuhn. She was an older woman—stocky, gentle, and motherly. She cleaned his room, cooked some of his meals, and fussed over him in a way that caught the attention of the other boarders. Before long Joe was calling her his "second mother," but she was never as close to him, or as vital to his development, as Mrs. Osterloth had been. For one thing, his success in Manawa had left him more independent. And the living arrangement—a house filled with male boarders and Mr. John Kuhn, a burly, eccentric Prussian who stomped about in military garb—was hardly conducive to a close friendship.[32]

After a brief stint in the college of engineering, McCarthy switched to law. His freshman grades were average—C's in Chemistry and English, B's in Algebra and Drawing—but the course load bored him to death. Engineering was precise, mechanical, and mathematically demanding; law required a good memory, a good tongue, and the chance to work with people. His best friends were already studying law. Many were "boisterous, congenial and garrulous like himself."[33]

McCarthy joined Delta Theta Phi, the law fraternity, and served as bailiff in 1934–35. His membership was important, for it widened his circle of friends and afforded him access to the canned briefs and study sessions that kept his head above water. According to Tom Korb, a college classmate, Joe's "cramming" ability was legendary at Marquette. "He would often work sixty hours a week at odd jobs," Korb remembers. "I'm not exaggerating. He'd go to classes in the morning and then work a twelve-hour shift as a grease monkey. About two weeks before finals, he'd sit in on the review sessions at the fraternity. He'd cram a year's work into a few days of study. He didn't have the money to buy books, so he'd use the library when he could. By the time Joe left those cram sessions he knew as much as anybody else."[34]

Few students worked harder than McCarthy outside the classroom. He washed dishes, ran elevators, worked as a parking-lot attendant, short-order cook, and boxing coach. In 1933, while managing a Standard Oil service station, he won the company's annual tire sale contest. Charlie Middleton, a friend who accompanied him to Milwaukee, says that Joe was at his very best when he had something to sell. "He called me up one day and asked if I wanted to make a few dollars," Middleton recalls. "He had bought a caulking gun and was going door to door telling people that their homes were leaking. I went around with him for a few hours, but I couldn't take the abuse. The Depression was on, and folks weren't too friendly to salesmen. But Joe had a way with them, especially the ladies. He was a big, brawny guy, but he came on like a choir boy. Real earnest and polite and friendly. Once he had his foot in the door they were goners."[35]

Another source of income was gambling. McCarthy played poker the way he played everything else: no holds barred. He raised the stakes so high and so fearlessly that opponents invariably folded with better cards. "One should play poker with him to really know him," a friend wrote, "but in case you do, it would be my advice to play table stakes or get some big bank to back you. He raises on poor hands and always comes out the winner." Joe played often in the back rooms of Milwaukee's neighborhood taverns, but his biggest killing was made at the expense of several Marquette alumni on a football trip to Pittsburgh. It reportedly covered his bills for an entire semester.[36]

Hustling work and playing hard-nosed poker were two aspects of an exaggerated masculinity that marked Joe's behavior. Older and gruffer than his classmates, with thinning hair and a five o'clock shadow, he looked and played the part of the two-fisted man about town. He'd give public demonstrations of his virility by sharpening a straight razor on the palm of his hand. He'd arm wrestle anyone for money. His favorite entertainment in Milwaukee was the burlesque show. "He went when he could," laughed Middleton. "It was expensive but about six of us would chip in for one ticket and give it to Joe. He would walk in legal and open the back door for the rest of us. He had more guts than we did. And he liked the show better. Going was always his idea."[37]

He also boxed at Marquette, where the intramural bouts were major social events. His first fight, before 900 fans, went rather well. The Marquette *Tribune* reported that his "pile-driving lefts and rights . . . battered Al Razor to the canvas three times in the first round and allowed him to coast to victory." The following month, however, he lost to a veteran fighter who chose to box rather than to brawl. "Frank Didier fought a clever battle and was content to remain in the foreground and occasionally gave his Irish playmate a clout across the ear."[38]

While McCarthy trained hard, he never learned the finer points of self-defense. He was a crowd-pleasing slugger, nicknamed "Smiling Joe" for his ability to take enormous punishment in stride. His final fight was typical enough. He came out swinging, dropped his opponent for a count of nine, took several right hands "that started on Thirteenth Street," and won the decision going away.[39]

Those who knew McCarthy at Marquette remember him fondly. The

Jesuit Fathers claim he was humorous, outgoing, and deferential toward the clergy. His friends recognized his faults—the hustle, the masculine bluster, the demand for recognition—but insist there was a personal side to him that has been generally ignored or distorted. "Joe was actually an insecure person," says Korb. "He came from a very humble, very provincial background. He was always concerned about what people thought about him. He wanted so much to be accepted that he tended to go overboard. He was a little too friendly, and he was an excessive flatterer. Deep down he really liked people, and he wanted to be liked by them, too." [40]

His friends were also impressed by his close family ties and the way he faithfully obeyed his parents' preachings about religion. And their stories of his kindness and genuine concern for others are quite believable. In his private life, surrounded by people he trusted, McCarthy was a different person—quieter, less aggressive, far more relaxed. In the "outside world" he saw no friends, only potential adversaries who might oppose his ambitions or frustrate his will.

Take, for example, an incident that occurred during Joe's final year at Marquette, when he decided to run for class president. He had been telling everyone about his political plans after law school, and he assumed that the election would be a good barometer of future success. McCarthy conducted a vigorous campaign, but in order to keep it from getting too rough he and his opponent, Charles Curran, agreed to vote for the other come election day. As luck would have it, the two candidates wound up in a dead heat. When Curran suggested a simple cut of the cards to determine a winner, Joe refused. He wanted another ballot. Curran relented, and the next tally gave McCarthy the presidency by two votes. "Joe," asked Curran suspiciously, "did you vote for yourself?" "Sure," came the quick reply. "You wanted me to vote for the best man, didn't you?" Curran was outraged by the betrayal, but years later he added an interesting footnote to the incident. "My father died in 1933, while I was in school," he recalled. "Just before the funeral, Joe drove all the way to our house in an old Model A he'd borrowed. He cut classes, left his job, and borrowed money to get there. He did that for me, and he'll always be my friend." [41]

The point here is not that McCarthy was often a concerned and loving fellow, but that he was capable of being unscrupulous yet loyal, cruel yet understanding, destructive yet generous to the same people, without showing a conscious sense of personal confusion. He seemed consumed by two conflicting forces: a frightening drive for recognition and for advancement, and a compulsive need to be liked, to be a "good fellow." This led to a startling role dichotomy, public man versus private man, which ran like an unbroken line through his adulthood. To the public McCarthy, life was a game in which no quarter was asked and none given. His approach was so primitive, so cynical, so devoid of commitment to any goal but personal success, that few opponents had the will or the stomach to fight him on his own terms. After all, who wants to lock horns with someone who obeys no rules and will do anything—absolutely *anything*—to get what he wants?[42]

Once the public battle had ended—or the cameras clicked off—a Jekyll–Hyde transformation took shape. In what seemed a pathetic attempt to disown responsibility for his behavior, McCarthy would go out of his way to meet the victim and express heartfelt concern for his welfare. This ritual occurred with such frequency that almost everyone who knew Joe more than casually has felt the need to describe it. After viciously attacking Senator Douglas during the 1954 campaign, McCarthy was the first to greet him upon his return to Washington. "Rushing up, he shook hands heartily and assured me that he was delighted by my reelection," Douglas remembered with some bewilderment. "Joe was that kind of fellow. He was like a mongrel dog, fawning on you one moment and the next moment trying to bite your leg off." At a cocktail party in Washington, McCarthy ran into an old drinking buddy whose name he had muddied at a public hearing. Within earshot of a roomful of startled guests, Joe asked the man why they hadn't gotten together recently. "Jeanie was talking about you the other night," he said "How come we never see you? What the hell are you trying to do—*avoid* us?"[43]

Francis Werner, a Wisconsin attorney who knew Joe well and admired him, was struck by the way this behavioral problem affected McCarthy's personal relationships. He recalls: "One time when Joe was a circuit judge, a bunch of us took a short vacation with him in the north country. Something was bothering him, I don't remember what, but on the way home he kept stopping at roadhouses to grab a drink, which was rare for Joe. In one of these places, near Antigo, I told him that either I drive or we weren't getting back into the car. He was in no mood to be challenged, so he said, 'Fine, screw you,' and just drove off, leaving us stranded in the middle of nowhere. All our baggage and our house keys were in the car. It took us hours to hitch home, and even then we were locked out. Well, my wife and I just wrote him off. This was not our idea of friendship.

"A few days later, Joe called and talked us into meeting him for dinner at a restaurant in Appleton. When we got there, the table was filled with wine and flowers. Joe was like that. He'd do something nasty and then make it up to you. He couldn't stand to have people stay mad at him. It upset him no end."[44]

AFTER GETTING HIS LAW DEGREE in 1935, McCarthy moved north to Waupaca, a small county seat near Appleton. His plan was to set up a one-man practice, get to know the people, and then run for political office. Having little money, he sought out an acquaintance from his Manawa days, Dr. William Remmel. "Joe came up here with a brand new car and fifty cents in his pocket," said the former dentist, obviously enjoying his reminiscence. "He came to our house and asked about staying for a few weeks, till he got an apartment. Before we knew it, Joe had moved into our upstairs bedroom, lock, stock, and barrel. He lived with us for the rest of his stay in Waupaca."[45]

McCarthy did his legal business from a single room in the Loan and Abstract Building on Main Street. (He reportedly won a desk, filing cabinet, and two chairs in a card game.) What kind of lawyer was young Joe? The local attorneys say he had "hustler" written all over him. "He was what you'd call an ambulance chaser," said one. "He'd do things no other lawyer in town would think of doing, like shading you out of a case, talking behind your back to your own client." Another remembered McCarthy as "a big friendly guy, always talking and joking with everybody. But he was out for himself, a real opportunist. He made no bones about it."[46]

Remmel asserts that much ill will was generated by McCarthy's insensitivity to the needs and standards of the community. "One day in the Loan and Abstract Building," he said, "I passed the door of Lloyd Smith [another lawyer]. There was a woman I knew in his office, and she was asking him to begin a divorce proceeding. Well, Lloyd really turned on her. I'm paraphrasing, of course, but he said, 'Stop bitching to me. Go home and work this thing out. You've been married too long to stop talking now.' All the lawyers did this. They would not take cases that they felt would upset the town or could be resolved out of court. But Joe was different. He would have taken the woman's retainer and begun divorce proceedings in five minutes. I remember once he strung a lady along for five months before she got up the courage to tell him she really didn't want a divorce. He even had her doing his laundry as part of the fee. People didn't like that at all."[47]

The portrait of McCarthy as someone who had little respect for community values crops up time and again. On occasion, when it suited his purpose or when he felt comfortable in the surroundings, he could behave with proper deference to established tradition and authority. But more often he played the opposite role—the lawless, unsocialized fellow who elbows his way to the center by overwhelming his rule-bound neighbors. What he lacked, it seems, was a sense of inner restraint, the mechanism that serves to check one's darker aggressions. "I've always felt that Joe lived in a different moral universe," one Waupaca attorney mused. "He asked himself only two questions: What do I want and how do I get it. Once he got rolling, you had to step aside. It was every man for himself, sort of what anarchy must be like."[48]

Times were rough in Waupaca. With the Depression in full swing, legal work was hard to come by. Characteristically, Joe kept his head above water by playing poker for big money. He spent more time in the back room of Ben Johnson's Roadhouse than he did in his law office. Irving Hanson, owner of the Loan and Abstract Building, recalls that McCarthy always paid his rent on Monday with the poker winnings from the previous weekend. "Funny thing, though," Hanson remarked, "Joe used to leave the lights in his office burning at night. He told me that he wanted people to think he never stopped working." According to Remmel, McCarthy once "broke the bank" at Ben Johnson's and used the money to pay off a slew of back debts. "He came to me and asked to borrow $150. He even offered to put up his car for collateral. He said he was going down to the Roadhouse to play some serious poker. 'I'll nurse my drink till one o'clock,' Joe told me. 'My head will be clear and the other guys will be on the way down. If my money can hold out I'm gonna make a bundle.' " The next morning, as the Remmels were leaving for church, McCarthy strode in waving an enormous roll of bills. He gave Remmel five dollars and told him to drop it in the collection plate. "I won't be coming with you today," he smiled. "But I do want to express my appreciation to the Lord. He was awfully good to me last night." [49]

Playing poker became an obsession with him. On one occasion, accompanied by a young woman from Milwaukee, he joined Ed Hart and his wife for a few drinks at the Roadhouse. Upon learning that a card game was in progress, McCarthy entered the back room for "a look-see" and never returned. "It was impossible to get him out of there," said Hart. "He stood up his date, a good-looking lady, leaving her to find her way home." [50]

There was one other thing the townspeople remembered about Joe: He was sloppy and disorganized. Finding something in his room or his law office, they recall, was a major project, like searching for the proverbial needle in the haystack. Books, papers, clothing, and food wrappers were scattered everywhere. (His room at Marquette looked the same way, "as if an army had camped there," said an old college friend. "I always assumed he was too damned tired to clean the place up.") Joe could hardly keep track of his clothing, his possessions, or his monetary dealings. "He was forever wearing my ties and handkerchiefs," Remmel says. "His own were lost somewhere under the bed or behind the bureau. And he was loose with money. If somebody needed a loan, Joe gave it to him and often forgot to ask for repayment. Money went through his hands like water. He would give you his last dime and expect you to do the same. Since I usually had more money than he did, I must say I resented this a little. But I knew if the situation were reversed, Joe would come through." [51]

For political as well as social reasons, McCarthy joined the local softball team and the Junior Chamber of Commerce, sold tickets for the annual President's Birthday Ball Against Polio, and took on the chairmanship of the Lions Club Harvest Day Committee. More significantly, since Waupaca was a solid GOP bastion, where political advancement was controlled by the town's established Republican leaders, he decided to make his mark as a Democrat. In Waupaca, Remmel remembers, "Joe became a flaming New Dealer. I can't say that he really believed in what Roosevelt stood for, but he sure was pushing that line."[52] *

IN 1936 OPPORTUNITY CAME KNOCKING in the form of a job offer from Mike Eberlein, a prominent attorney from nearby Shawano. Joe accepted at once, knowing that the chance to work in a larger town would improve his political visibility. The partnership was oddly supportive. Eberlein needed someone to help with the heavy work load. And McCarthy's New Deal image neatly balanced Big Mike's conservative Republicanism. According to the Waupaca *County Post*, a local prankster warned the Shawano townsfolk about their new lawyer's "radicalism" by secretly filling his briefcase "with a couple copies of the *New Masses*, a recent edition of the *Daily Worker*, and a vest-pocket-sized *Das Kapital*."[53]

As Eberlein's right-hand man, McCarthy gained instant status and respect. And he got to know the residents by joining more clubs and addressing more meetings than anyone in Shawano's collective memory. It is difficult to picture him telling a Lions breakfast about the "problems of rectifying miscarriages of justice," but he did. Try to imagine him showing slides of his Canadian vacation to the local Rotarians. ("He praised the hospitality of the Canadians and spoke well of their road conditions," said the Shawano County *Journal*.) Or describing "the rise and fall of civilizations which flourished along the great rivers of the world" to the Shawano Junior Women's Club. It was all in a day's work for a budding small-town politician.[54]

Furthermore, with the Democratic Party almost extinct in Shawano, McCarthy had no trouble rising to the top. Before long he was treasurer of the county organization, chairman of the Young Democrats of the Seventh Congressional District, and a leading fund-raiser for FDR. During the 1936 campaign he stumped hard for Roosevelt and his "great, noble, unfinished task." Breathlessly, he debunked the Republican–Landon platform as "brainless, half-baked, cockeyed . . . harebrained, illogical, and senseless."[55]

* McCarthy's affinity for the New Deal was not unusual. The Irish in Outagamie County were strong Democratic supporters. Joe's father and his uncles were Democrats. Furthermore, the Roosevelt landslide of 1932 had broken the Republican grip on Wisconsin and led many ambitious politicians into the ranks of the traditionally inept state Democratic Party. See below, pp. 37–39.

In 1936 McCarthy announced his own candidacy for district attorney on the Democratic ticket. He came to the voters as "a militant New Dealer" and "an authority on poultry raising"—meager credentials to be sure. But he had a catchy issue: placing the district attorney on a part-time schedule and cutting his salary in half. The county wouldn't suffer, Joe insisted, because there wasn't much legal work to be done. The problem lay with the incumbent, who pocketed $4,600 each year while holding down another job."* As usual, McCarthy asked his opponent not to take these attacks personally. "Regardless of the outcome," he purred, "I hope I can still number the district attorney . . . among my friends."

Joe knew that he had no chance of winning. He was in the race for the experience and the publicity it would bring him. So he set out to convince the voters that he was a principled young man who, in the words of one skeptic, "didn't mind losing so long as the county gained." His big campaign speech, delivered to the enthusiastic patrons of Joe Casetta's Bar, called on the candidates to "help every voter to base his vote upon facts and reason, rather than unreason and fallacy. If, when the morning of November 4th dawns, I know that I have in any way helped the voters to cast a vote based upon the facts as they are—distorted neither one way or the other—then the question of whether or not I personally am elected will, in my mind, fade into insignificance." The question of McCarthy's election, of course, was never in doubt. He was swamped by the incumbent.[56]

For the next two years Joe occupied himself with the business of small-town law and carefully plotted a comeback. In 1939 he set his sights on the circuit judgeship, a nonpartisan office that would allow him to run free of party affiliation. But Mike Eberlein, his friend, mentor, and law partner, had long expressed an interest in the same job. Joe was in a quandary. Having privately agreed to support Eberlein, he felt that his boss had no chance of upsetting the powerful incumbent. "You know, Mike has one of the finest legal minds in the state," he liked to say. "But he's probably the world's worst politician."[57]

Maybe so, but Eberlein, a domineering man, had been awfully good to him. He saw to it that McCarthy met the right people and he tried to smooth some of his partner's rough edges. When Joe announced his candidacy *first*, leaving Big Mike no choice but to deny his own judicial

---

* McCarthy did not say what this other job entailed. He simply raised the issue and hoped for the best. The district attorney, a man named Louis Cattau, was getting an additional $40 a month as secretary of the Shawano County Fair, a job he did in his spare time. This may, in fact, have been illegal, for the district attorney was not allowed to engage in any outside practice of law. Furious—and no doubt alarmed—Cattau took out an advertisement in the local paper to answer the charge. "Why he asked, "wasn't Mr. McCarthy fair and state the fact in his pamphlet rather than insinuate some other connection?" See Shawano *Evening Leader*, November 2, 1936; also Michael O'Brien, *McCarthy and McCarthyism in Wisconsin*, 1980, p. 21.

ambitions, there were many raised eyebrows in Shawano. It is possible that Joe truly believed he was doing the noble thing by saving his friend from a humiliating defeat. After all, people do have a way of hiding their baser instincts, even from themselves. But this sort of charity was hardly characteristic of his public behavior. More than likely, he saw a good opportunity and grabbed for it. Eberlein just happened to be in the way.

McCarthy later made amends for his actions. ("He couldn't stand to have people stay mad at him. It upset him no end.") As a senator, he helped Eberlein win that same circuit judgeship.[58] In 1939, however, relations between the two men were badly strained, although Joe seemed too busy to care. There were important things to consider, like the coming race against a judicial fixture named Edgar V. Werner.

CHAPTER TWO

═══════════════

G. I. Judge

EDGAR WERNER, the circuit judge for Langlade, Shawano, and Outagamie counties, had been dispensing justice since the days of Woodrow Wilson. When he decided to stand for reelection in 1939, his constituents assumed there would be little or no opposition. That was the way it had always been. The man was honest, independent, above partisan attack. In Edgar Werner, the *Post-Crescent* editorialized, "This district has a judge of unassailable integrity. . . . The people . . . should be in no mood to reject the services of one who has proven so dependable for so long."[1]

All of which meant nothing to Joe McCarthy. One of the marks of his political genius was a knack for sensing when a supposedly unconquerable figure—a Bob LaFollette or a Millard Tydings—had reached the point of vulnerability. Edgar Werner was at that point, a fact McCarthy saw first. "I told Joe he was crazy when he went after that judgeship," laughed Richard Farrell. "We all did. No one thought he had a prayer."[2]

Despite Werner's impeccable credentials ("a distinguished jurist with an unblemished record," as one McCarthy biographer put it), he was not popular with the local attorneys, particularly the younger ones. McCarthy knew this, and he sensed the damaging implications. In the outlying communities, Werner's reputation was based largely on what the lawyers told the town folks. And the lawyers had soured on him. "He was a good man and we respected him," said one. "But he took it as an insult if you questioned his authority in any way. We felt he could have been a lot more flexible." According to Cliff Mullarkey, Werner often made up his mind at the outset of a case and rarely found the need to change it. "The man was too old for the job," he asserted. "When Joe brought him down most of us were delighted." Ed Hart described Werner as "a bull-headed Dutchman, a really stubborn judge." But he added an interesting afterthought. "Werner was an honest man. Joe went after him in a way that was unconscionable. Maybe that's what he had to do to win. I don't know. But it's a hell of a price to pay. You've got to live with yourself."[3]

Hart's feeling is shared by all of McCarthy's biographers. In their eyes, Werner was a fine judge whose career was shattered in one sickening campaign. McCarthy ran a dirty race, they say, filled with lies about the incumbent's age and his salary. When it ended, Werner was a battered hulk who had no idea what hit him. He was, in short, the first real victim of McCarthyism.[4]

As legend has it, Joe centered his campaign around Werner's impending senility. He "hoodwinked" the voters by claiming that the judge was born in 1866 (making him seventy-three), when, in fact, it was 1873 (making him sixty-six). "It was a matter of record," writes Richard Rovere, ". . . that Judge Werner was not seventy-three . . . but sixty-six. The ordinary, unliberated liar would not have attempted anything quite so bold, if for no other reason than that he would have feared being trapped in untruth. After all, Judge Werner's real age was verifiable—a matter of public record."[5]

In fact, it wasn't this simple. The judge had the "best" evidence—his birth certificate from 1873—but the challenger, ever diligent, produced some evidence of his own. It consisted of the *Martindale-Hubbell Law Directory*, which listed Werner's birth year as 1866, and an old biographical sketch in the Shawano County *Journal*, which gave 1870, not 1873, as the date of birth. Had Joe been a gentleman, he would have accepted Werner's figure and let the matter drop. But he was an underdog scratching for an issue—any issue—that might damage the incumbent's standing with the voters. The age question was perfect, for it allowed him to exploit discrepencies that *were* part of the public record. Furthermore, the judge could not cry foul without highlighting his age—as well as the suspicion that he had lied about it in the past. Cleverly, the challenger said: "I want it definitely understood that I take no issue with Werner as to when he was born. As far as I am concerned, his word is final on this question." A month later, he added: "Two of the three claims as to his age must be wrong. . . . Certainly I cannot know which if any of them is correct."[6]

What about the salary issue? In one newspaper spot, McCarthy paid tribute to his "seventy-three-year-old-opponent" and reminded the voters that Werner had "served over thirty-five years in public office . . . at a total income of $170,000 to $200,000 and it might be well for him to retire voluntarily." Averaged over a lengthy career, encompassing three decades, Werner's salary was quite modest; but the lump sum figure conveyed an *impression* of wealth and entrenched power. Was the ad misleading? Of course, and intentionally so. But before roasting McCarthy, one must admit that politicians generally consider such trickery to be "part of the game." This doesn't make it right or proper, but it does place McCarthy's behavior in a more realistic perspective.[7]

More significantly, these issues were peripheral to the race. McCarthy won because he put in the time that victory demanded. By election day, Farrell recalled, Joe had spoken to almost every eligible voter. "I visited with him once in 1940. He knew every field, every signpost, every darn tree in the area. Joe had unbelievable stamina and a great memory. I was *very* impressed." A local resident, who thumbed a ride from McCarthy, had a similar experience. The two men struck up a conversation about Bear Creek, the hitchhiker's town, and Joe amazed him by rattling off the names and occupations of the residents. He had been there only once, on a campaign trip.[8]

What was remarkable, a reporter noted, was that Joe's law practice "had been nothing to get excited about. . . . The public demand for his election to the bench was wholly inaudible." McCarthy, in fact, created the demand by seeking out the voters and talking not of legal issues or job qualifications, but of neighborly things like crop prices, children, and the weather. As one farmer recollected, a campaign visit from the young challenger went something like this: "He didn't know me from Adam. But somehow he had learned my name, and my wife's name, and our kids' names, and our dog's name. By the time I got to the front door, he was handing my daughter a lollipop, and then Indian-wrestling with my boy. . . . He wanted to know if I'd let him milk a cow; said he wanted to keep his hand in. He milked good."[9]

Before leaving, McCarthy would get all the information he could about the farmer down the road—where the act would be repeated. "Most of these people had never laid eyes on Werner," said one of Joe's friends. "He had never leaned over a fence to find out how things were going. McCarthy was someone they could identify with—real warm and informal. Even after he took office, it was always, 'Call me Joe.' Never any of this 'Your Honor' stuff."[10]

McCarthy loved to tell an anecdote about the campaign that concerned a tribe of Indians near Lake Winnebago. After taking great care to win over the elders, he got word that things were "safe." The Indians were all behind him. Sure enough, when the votes were counted, Joe won all but a handful. Overjoyed, he called the elders to express his thanks and jokingly asked why he hadn't "swept" the reservation. "Because," they replied, "a couple of stubborn bastards decided to mark their own ballots." The story is apocryphal, but his visits to the reservation were very real. Unlike Werner, who hated to campaign, Joe worked to win every vote he could, any way he could. In the end, he got 4,000 more than he needed.[11]

Following his defeat, Werner retired from the practice of law and died shortly thereafter. Not surprisingly, his family was certain that McCarthy had hastened his passing. Years later, Werner's son wrote privately that Joe "not only drove my father to his grave but turned long-standing friends against our whole family. . . . It was amazing how one man could wreck the reputation of another man so loved and honored in his community."[12]

This allegation is understandable. McCarthy certainly treated the judge with less respect than had any previous adversary. But it is also true that Werner, after twenty-four years on the bench, had come to demand a kind of deference that was politically unrealistic. "He saw himself as an institution," claimed one lawyer. "It was almost an insult to oppose him." The real issue here was not that Joe took a few cheap shots, but rather that he had the gall to run for circuit judge in the first place. Werner would have had trouble accepting defeat at the hands of any challenger. Losing to a pushy novice like McCarthy added a touch of humiliation that was impossible to swallow.

━━━━━

McCARTHY'S JUDICIAL CAREER was surrounded by controversy from the beginning. At the age of twenty-nine, the youngest circuit judge in decades, he inherited a bench with a backlog of 250 cases and worked around the clock to clear the docket; during his first two months in office, he kept the courtroom open after midnight on twelve separate occasions. The prestigious Milwaukee *Journal* noted that "never one to stand much on red tape, Judge McCarthy's court innovations slash musty tradition to eliminate delays and speed hearings." Anderson and May had a more critical impression: "He tried five cases for every one his colleagues tried; divorce trials were sometimes knocked off in five minutes; manslaughter trials took a little longer. Justice took off her robes and put on a track suit." Before long, Joe was so far ahead of schedule that he began traveling around the state to help other judges decrease their caseloads—a maneuver carefully designed to attract publicity, widen his circle of friends, and line up political allies.[13]

The Anderson and May portrait is based on old newspaper stories, which claimed that McCarthy had granted "quickie divorces" to friendly Republican politicians. Supposedly, he began the proceedings while bounding up the courthouse steps:

"Are you the lawyer for the plaintiff?" McCarthy asked one of the attorneys striding alongside him.

"Yes," the lawyer answered.

"And are you the lawyer for the respondent?"

"Yes."

"Are these stipulations correct?"

"Yes."

"Is there anything anyone wants to say before we proceed?"

"No."

And within minutes the proceedings were over. The plaintiff looked up in surprise as she was told she could leave the courtroom. "Am I divorced?" she asked. "Yes," Judge McCarthy announced, "you're a free woman." "But is that all there is to it? I thought there would be a court trial." "We're efficient around here," Joe said. "You wanted a divorce and now you have it." The woman walked out of the courtroom bewildered. "I don't *feel* divorced," she said to her lawyer. "I thought it would seem more official."[14]

This story may well be accurate. It is true that McCarthy was more lenient than other state judges in granting divorces. And one can logically assume that he did try to curry the favor of GOP leaders. But the charge made by some biographers that his courtroom was a divorce mill for the rich and powerful is extreme. The number of these "outside cases" was never very large; and in each case the couples had wanted a divorce, had reached agreement on terms, but had seen litigation stalled in other Wisconsin districts. There were some lawyers who viewed McCarthy's divorce record in positive terms, as a service to unhappily married couples. "To get a divorce at that time," said one, "a husband had to grab his wife by the hair, whirl her about his head, and splatter her against the far wall of the judge's chambers. Even then it would take a couple of years. Joe gave these people a break. I think he was ahead of his time."[15]

There was a more serious controversy at the Appleton courthouse. Known as the Quaker dairy case, it involved a local company that had run afoul of a state law designed to set "price floors" on the sale of milk. The dairy, a price-cutting outfit, was popular with consumers and unpopular with farmers and rival distributors, who expected the law to be enforced. Following numerous complaints, the state filed suit against the dairy in McCarthy's court.

At first Joe went along. Under pressure from Gilbert Lappley, the contesting counsel, he issued an injunction to keep the dairy from violating the law. But this led to pressure from the other side. The owner appeared, insisting (correctly, it turned out) that the law in question would be allowed to expire at the end of the year. The owner begged McCarthy to suspend the injunction—which McCarthy did on the

rather remarkable grounds that the enforcement of this "lame-duck statute" would work "undue hardship" on the violator. Lappley was flabbergasted. The law was the law, he said, and it *had* to be enforced. Lappley
demanded a trial; McCarthy refused, calling it a "waste of the court's
time." He dismissed the case instead.

Lappley did not give up. He petitioned the State Supreme Court for
a writ of mandamus, compelling Judge McCarthy to "support and uphold
the laws of Wisconsin." When the Court wired Appleton for the case
records, the clerk sent them along—minus McCarthy's remarks about
the need for a new trial. The high bench demanded an explanation, of
course, and McCarthy replied that parts of the stenographic record—the
parts *he* deemed "improper and immaterial"—had been destroyed.*

Chief Judge Marvin Rosenberry was furious. In a blistering opinion,
he noted that McCarthy had been wrong in suspending the law, wrong
in judging the materiality of the notes, and wrong in ordering their
destruction. "In this proceeding," he observed, "*this* court is the judge
of the materiality of the notes." Furthermore, "the destruction of evidence under these circumstances could only be open to the inference
that the evidence destroyed contained statements of fact contrary to the
position taken by the person destroying that evidence." Citing his "abuse
of judicial power," the Court ordered McCarthy to restore his injunction
and to hear the case again.

Now McCarthy was furious. He held the hearing but his verdict was
never in doubt. The dairy won—and so, too, did the judge who had been
censured by the State Supreme Court. Using the "rules of common
sense," he emerged as the champion of the consumer and the enemy of
Gilbert Lappley and the price-fixing bureaucrats in Madison. According
to the best account of the case, "McCarthy's decision . . . was the most
favorable he achieved as a judge. . . . The Appleton *Post-Crescent* carried his decision on its front page, including his ringing defense of 'poor
consumers, the unrepresented, and the inarticulate.' " Put simply, he
"had snatched a triumph of publicity from the jaws of a judicial defeat."[16]

Gilbert Lappley did not fare as well. He tried to appeal but his superiors said no—enough was enough. Here Lappley lost control. He took
the ruling as a personal defeat, and he bought radio time to tell his side
of the story. A few weeks later, he was out of a job.

This seamy side of McCarthy's judicial record is well known. What is
generally hidden, though, is the fact that Joe was a popular judge, recognized by lawyers and laymen alike as fair, innovative, and generally

---

* The court reporter, Pat Howlett, recalled that McCarthy came over and ordered him
to "tear out the remarks." Howlett refused, saying, "There's the book. You tear [them] out
if you want to." At this point, McCarthy grabbed the book and ripped out a page. Howlett
could hardly believe his eyes. He had never seen a judge do that before. See Michael
O'Brien, *McCarthy and McCarthyism in Wisconsin*, 1980, p. 36.

compassionate. "He was very well-liked," said one attorney. "He went out of his way to convenience us rather than himself. He traveled all over. You could call on him any time if you had a problem. Joe was full of vitality, piss, and vinegar. He opened the courtroom windows and let in a little fresh air." [17]

His speedy disposition of cases, moreover, was unanimously applauded in the Tenth Judicial District. McCarthy virtually abolished the regular court schedule and told the lawyers that he would travel to their towns when *they* were ready for trial. Upon arrival, he refused to tolerate legal delays. And he relied heavily upon the pretrial conference, in which attorneys entered his chambers to see if the case could be settled out of court. At his urging, most of them were. [18] *

McCarthy's personal style, free of pomp and solemnity, was tailor-made for his small-town constituency. He was on a first-name basis with the farmers, the merchants, the shoppers along Main Street; blessed with an incredible memory and a huckster's sense of when to josh and when to flatter, he could turn a two-minute conversation into a memorable event for these people. And his lively courtroom sessions—"Bill, if you want to win a case here, put out that cigar"—left the distinct impression that justice dispensed with humor and plain good sense was far superior to the kind that came out of thick, musty law books.

Joe seemed relatively subdued in Appleton, the district's administrative center. For one thing, his job did not stress competitive behavior; unlike a freshman legislator, he was not forced to jockey with ambitious colleagues for publicity, choice committee assignments, or political influence. For another, he was in familiar territory, surrounded by relatives and friends. This left him more relaxed and secure. He bought a small house, visited his parents' farm when he could, and spent many nights at the home of his sister Olive and her husband, Roman Kornely. There was sadness, too. Bid McCarthy, who had been ailing for some time, died in 1941, at the age of seventy.

The judge's personal routine remained largely unchanged. He stayed close to the church, attending Mass with unerring regularity. Catherine Wyngaard, a long-time friend, remembers an argument she had with McCarthy after she refused to drive him to services in a distant town. "He gave me a hell of a lecture," she laughed, "and said I ought to be

---

* According to Urban Van Susteren, McCarthy made up for his inexperience by demanding precise briefs from the contesting attorneys and then relying heavily upon them. Pat Howlett, the court reporter under Werner and McCarthy, claimed that "Joe was the sharpest on legal evidence of any judge I have ever worked for . . . and I have worked for about forty at one time or another. Joe could get to the root of a case faster than any judge I ever knew." It is significant that McCarthy had a relatively low percentage of reversals by the Wisconsin Supreme Court. Interview with Urban Van Susteren; also, Anderson and May, "Rough Notes," in the *Files of the National Committee for an Effective Congress,* Washington, D.C.

ashamed of myself." A friend in Milwaukee, who often had Joe as a house guest, recalled a more bizarre incident. One evening he entered McCarthy's darkened room to close a window and tripped over a huge obstacle on the floor. It was the judge, kneeling at the foot of his bed in prayer.[19]

Joe was known around Appleton as a practical joker, a guy who'd do anything for a laugh. Oddly, his favorite prank involved pouring water down the pants of his male companions. He loved to take a running hose, put it in someone's pocket, and wait for the frenzied reaction. "At the first party I ever attended in his house," a newsman recalled, "he was busy trapping innocent victims into a game in which a marble was dropped from the forehead into a funnel tucked into the belt. At the appropriate moment, water poured down the funnel." When asked about the implications of such behavior, the newsman just shrugged his shoulders. McCarthy, he said, "was a big kid who never grew up."[20]

The heavy gambling continued. Joe placed large wagers at Appleton's notorious Club Tavern until he supposedly welched on one and had his account closed out. Often, on weekends, he and his best friend, Urban Van Susteren, traveled north to play the roulette wheel at Lonnie Powell's Jack O'Lantern, near Antigo. "He'd bet on anything," said Van Susteren. "Cards, dice, horses, the stock market—it didn't matter. He'd call me up and say, 'Van, I've got a tip.' Then he'd tell me to buy soybean futures or Canadian rye or some uranium stock. Everything was 'good as gold,' except they always wound up costing him money."[21]

Mostly, though, the game was poker, played in the back rooms of Appleton's fraternal clubs. Gambling was illegal, but no one paid much attention, least of all the circuit judge. Those who played with McCarthy remember the experience well. "He would sit quietly counting his chips," said one, "then suddenly shove them into the pot and say, 'I'll bet $104.75.' Many men who would bet $100 against him would fold rather than bet $104.75—partly because he was betting his whole pile, partly because they didn't want to count it out. If anybody did bet him, possibly raising him a quarter to $105, McCarthy would come back and raise him another $104.75, using money in his pocket." Since the judge would do this without even looking at his hole cards, the game took on a nerve-racking air. "You got to the point where you didn't care what he had in the hole," a player recalled. "All you knew was that it was too costly to stay in the game."[22]

It was a standard joke in Appleton that McCarthy hired good-looking young women for his office and spent more than a few nights entertaining them. According to one friend, "all of Joe's girls in Wisconsin were (a) pretty and (b) poor." Another contended that his courtships followed a monotonous pattern: "They begin with a big rush, and each new candidate is convinced that this time he means it. Invariably, this period is followed by a progressively cooler relationship. At some point in this phase, nine out of ten of the girls demand to know where they stand. So McCarthy tells them. A short time later a new courtship begins with another girl."[23]

Joe often claimed that marriage did not interest him. "I can't work at politics," he would say, "if I have to call home every half hour." Yet in 1941 he proposed to a young woman who worked at the courthouse. "She was lovely," Van Susteren remembered. "When Joe joined the Marines, people told her not to wait for him. It was good advice. After Joe got back he felt that a wife would be like extra baggage, so he broke the thing off. He did love her, I suspect, but politics came first."[24]

Politics *always* came first. But the fact that McCarthy got engaged is significant. It was a startling aberration from his pattern of chasing loose and pretty women—"floozies," as his friends called them. His fiancée has been described as competent, warm, responsible, and "sparkling Irish"— the very traits reminiscent of Bid McCarthy, who had just died. It is noteworthy that Joe remained close with this woman after their engagement ended. He seemed genuinely pleased that she married a local resident, raised several children, and settled into the kind of domestic routine that he knew he was incapable of providing.[25]

Gambling, carousing, politics, more politics, a nightly prayer—these were the main ingredients of McCarthy's Appleton existence. Unlike his cronies, he had little interest in sports. He didn't own a rifle, a fishing rod, a bowling ball, a tennis racket, or golf clubs. He bought skis but hurt his leg, telling everyone he had fallen from a taxi. Moreover, despite his quick intelligence, he seemed remarkably uncurious about the world beyond his immediate ambitions and physical needs. He knew nothing about history, literature, music, art, or science. And he had no real desire to learn. "As far as I know," said Van Susteren, "Joe looked at only one book in his life. That was *Mein Kampf.*"[26]

"I wouldn't make too much of this," he added. "Lots of people read *Mein Kampf* in Appleton. Hitler had support here. But Joe, I think, was more taken by the tactics, by the means and not the end. He had no use for Hitler or for anything the Nazis did. But when he looked at *Mein Kampf*, it was like one politician comparing notes with another. Joe was fascinated by the strategy, that's all."[27]

Predictably, the judgeship soon bored McCarthy to tears. He viewed himself as a politician, and he told everyone within earshot of his desire to seek "real" political office. His plans were sidetracked, however, when the Japanese bombed Pearl Harbor. Like many office-seekers, he knew the value of a war record, and he told Van Susteren that he must enlist at once. Van Susteren remembers advising him: "Look, if you've got to be a hero to be a politician, join the Marines." McCarthy agreed. Early in 1942 he entered a "leatherneck" recruiting office in Milwaukee and signed on the dotted line. Thus began the saga of "Tail-Gunner Joe."[28]

JOE MCCARTHY DID NOT HAVE TO GO TO WAR. His job was important enough to exempt him from military service. It would be nice to say that he volunteered for the best of reasons: a strong sense of duty, a hatred of fascism. It would also be untrue. To his thinking, front-line action was an essential prerequisite for young politicians. There was but one rule to remember: One had to survive in order to exploit it.

The news that a circuit judge had traded in his robes for a helmet and rifle traveled quickly through Wisconsin. And Joe helped the story along by implying that he wanted no special favors. He'd join up "as a private, an officer, or anything else you want me to be." In fact, McCarthy had already written a letter on court stationery requesting an officer's rank. He was sworn in as a first lieutenant.[29]

McCarthy did not resign his judgeship. He agreed only to waive his judicial salary during military service. Under Wisconsin law this meant that the state could not appoint someone to replace him. On the contrary, the other judges would be forced to assume his caseload. This arrangement so disturbed the chief of judicial circuits that he sent Joe a letter urging him to remain on the bench. The patriotic thing, he wrote, was to stay in Appleton where he was needed. McCarthy thought otherwise. On August 4, 1942, he began his tour of duty in the Pacific.

Most servicemen would have been perfectly happy to come home from the war with McCarthy's military achievements. For almost three years he served as an intelligence officer at Bougainville, debriefing combat pilots who returned from bombing runs over Japanese-held islands. By all accounts, he did a creditable job; his assignment, while hardly dangerous, was vital to the fliers who took the risks and got most of the glory. In his spare time, Joe played poker and acted as the island's "procurer"—not of women, but of such things as liquor and exotic food. One Christmas he rounded up a few pilots and flew to Guadalcanal, where the men bartered for medicinal brandy, canned turkeys, pineapple juice, and other luxuries. Upon returning, he held an open house, passing out free food and drink to those who happened by. "He was always liberal with the stuff he scrounged," a buddy recalled.[30]

But Joe was not about to be viewed as a small cog in a big machine. Not when his political instincts told him that those who came home with military honors would be rewarded at the ballot box. Before long, stories about his military exploits began filtering back to Wisconsin. In 1943 the *Post-Crescent* printed the following dispatch:

Guadalcanal—Every evening the "judge" holds court in a dilapidated shack just off a jungle air strip deep in the South Pacific combat zone. The folks in

Wisconsin might be a trifle shocked at his lack of dignity now. He stands barechested before his bench, an ancient table reeling on its last legs, and opens court with: "All right, what kind of hell did you give the Japs today?"[31]

That was only the beginning. News reached Wisconsin that Joe had become a tail gunner, flying dangerous missions and spraying more bullets (4,700 in one sortie) than any Marine in history. How did it happen? "I was dissatisfied with the high-altitude photography," he said. "I squawked about [it] so much that one day the C.O. called me in and told me to get a volunteer who was rated on radio, gunnery . . . and photography. The C.O. knew darned well that we didn't have anyone with such a rating. So in about thirty minutes I had to learn how to operate a camera and when I found myself in that dive bomber plane, heading for the Jap strong points in a raid, I said to myself, 'McCarthy, what in the heck are you doing here?' "[32]

Brave, humble, humorous, unassuming—McCarthy carefully molded his image for the folks back home. In the process, his daredevil exploits grew ever larger. In 1944 he spoke of fourteen bombing missions; in 1947 the figure rose to seventeen; in 1951 it peaked at thirty-two. He requested—and received—an Air Medal, four stars, and the Distinguished Flying Cross, awarded for twenty-five missions in combat. His campaign posters pictured him in full fighting gear, with an aviator's cap, and belt upon belt of machine gun ammunition wrapped around his bulky torso. Honors poured in from the American Legion, the Gold Star Mothers, and the Veterans of Foreign Wars.[33]

In 1949 the Madison *Capital-Times* received a letter from Marine Captain Jack Canaan, a flyer who was stationed with McCarthy at Bougainville. It claimed that Joe's only combat experience had been two missions in one day. "He told me that he did it for publicity value," wrote Canaan. "In fact, in a hospital in the New Hebrides he personally showed me the Associated Press clipping about firing more rounds than any gunner in one day. . . . I believe on the day he fired them, the Jap planes at Rabaul were all dead." Canaan advised the newspaper to check McCarthy's "official jacket in Washington." It would, he thought, "expose the guy for the fraud he is."[34]

The *Capital-Times* did not pursue the tip, but other reporters got wind of it and started their own inquiries. Before long the real story of Joe's Pacific exploits had emerged. In 1943 his squadron was assigned to Henderson Field, Guadalcanal. The work varied—from routine "spotting" flights on New Georgia to bombing runs over Rabaul. Sometimes, to ease the boredom, the pilots would try to break every flight record on the books—most missions in a day, most ammunition expended, and the like. According to one marine, "Everyone at the base who could possibly do so went along for the ride on some of these missions—it was hot, dusty, and dull on the ground, and a ride in an SBD was cool and a break in the monotony. It was also quite safe—there weren't any Jap planes or anti-aircraft gunners around."[35]

Apparently Joe wanted to break the record for most ammo used in a single mission. So he was strapped into a tail-gunner's seat, sent aloft, and allowed to blast away at the coconut trees. As a matter of routine, the public relations officer gave him the record and wrote up a press release for the Wisconsin papers. A few weeks later, McCarthy came into the fellow's hut waving a stack of clippings. "This is worth 50,000 votes to me," he said with a smile. The two men then had a drink to celebrate the creation of "Tail-Gunner Joe."[36]

All told, McCarthy made about a dozen flights in the tail-gunner's seat. He strafed deserted airfields, hit some fuel dumps, and came under enemy fire at least once. His buddies recalled that he "loved to shoot the guns." They gave him an award for destroying the island's plant life, and they laughed hysterically when he lost control of the twin 30s and pumped bullets through the tail of his plane.

It was on one of these missions that Joe claimed to have been wounded in action. In his Senate campaigns he would walk with a limp, saying that his plane had crash-landed or that he carried "ten pounds of shrapnel" in his leg. When pressed for details, he would refer to a citation from Admiral Nimitz: "Although suffering from a severe leg injury, [Captain McCarthy] refused to be hospitalized and continued to carry out his duties as an intelligence officer in a highly efficient manner. His courageous devotion to duty was in keeping with the highest traditions of the naval service."[37]

Citations like this were easy to come by. In McCarthy's case, he apparently wrote it himself, forged his commanding officer's signature, and sent it on to Nimitz, who signed thousands of such documents during the war. What bothered some newsmen was the fact that Joe had never been awarded a Purple Heart. Could it be that his wound was not war-related? "Maybe he fell off a bar stool," mused Robert Fleming, the Milwaukee *Journal*'s crack reporter, as he began piecing together the incident. Fleming soon discovered that McCarthy had been aboard the seaplane tender *Chandeleur* on the day the injury occurred. It was June 22, 1943, and the *Chandeleur*'s crew was holding a "shellback" initiation as the ship crossed the equator. During the hazing, Joe was forced to attach an iron bucket to one foot and run the gauntlet of paddle-wielding sailors. He slipped, fell down a stairwell, and suffered three fractures of the metatarsal (middle foot) bone. That was the extent of his war wounds.[38]

The Fleming exposé was a journalistic bombshell that demolished both the tail-gunner and the war-wound fabrications. Typical of McCarthy, he disputed the story without expressing any ill will toward its author. Publicly, he labeled Fleming and his newspaper "pro-Communist"; privately, the two men maintained a warm relationship. "I consistently find McCarthy very cordial," Fleming noted. "He laughs when I say I dislike seeing him before a meal because it spoils my appetite. He knows of my work on his past and mentions it . . . but never angrily."[39]

It is not unusual for someone, particularly a politician, to exaggerate his war record. Nor is it the sort of falsehood that generally hurts the feelings or the reputations of others. Why, then, the controversy over "Tail-Gunner Joe"? The question can be answered in several ways. For one thing, McCarthy's puffed-up gallantry was not an isolated instance of deception, but rather an example of the way he *consistently* misrepresented his actions. This makes it harder to ignore. For another, Joe used his war record to shameless advantage. He thought nothing of attacking political opponents as cowardly slackers or of claiming the exclusive right to speak for crippled veterans and "dead heroes." This makes it harder to forgive. Finally, like some compulsive braggarts, McCarthy seemed increasingly unable to differentiate fact from fancy. He lied so often and so boldly about his exploits that he himself came to accept their veracity. His friends insist that Joe always stuck by his war record, even in private. When Van Susteren once asked about the wound, McCarthy rolled up his pants, exposed a nasty scar, and growled, "There, you son of a bitch, now let's hear no more about it." One can only wonder about these blood-and-guts fantasies. Were they merely vote-getting ploys? Or were his insecurities such that he was driven to masquerade as a tough and brave and heroically virile character? Perhaps they served both ends.

━━━━━━

Two other Pacific episodes helped to shape McCarthy's political future. The first was a chance meeting with a young Navy lieutenant named John F. Kennedy. According to Joe's account, Kennedy nurtured their friendship by taking him for rides on his PT boat and even letting him play with the machine guns. This friendship, however, was always more real to McCarthy than to Kennedy. It is true that Joe did have intimate dealings with the Kennedy family. He hired Robert as a staff member, dated sister Pat on occasion, and became something of a hero to Joseph Kennedy, the clan's volatile patriarch. It is also true that John Kennedy was the only Democratic senator to remain consistently neutral on McCarthy (and the only one to attend both his wedding and his funeral). But they were hardly close friends. A Kennedy aide once described McCarthy as "the *other* type of Irishman that Jack tried so hard to disassociate himself from." McCarthy, said another, was "the kind of gross and uncultured fellow that Kennedy was bound to dislike." Other family members, particularly Robert and Joseph, Sr., were cut from different cloth; they had fierce Catholic loyalties and a stronger taste for alley fighting. John Kennedy was smoother: style and manners were important to him. His relationship with McCarthy was based on practical politics, not friendship.[40]

The second episode was related to Joe's immediate ambitions. For months he had talked and joked about his plans to go to Washington; the jeeps at Bougainville were plastered with signs reading "McCarthy for Senator." In the spring of 1944 he stopped joking and got down to business, the business of opposing incumbent Alexander Wiley for the GOP senatorial nomination.

No one is certain when Joe decided to become a Republican, but it seems likely that he abandoned the Democratic Party after his defeat for district attorney in 1936 and opted for the GOP when he decided to seek major political office. One Shawano Republican told Senator Wiley that "this fellow [McCarthy] was never active in the political activities of this county and he has generally been considered a New Dealer."[41]

It would be an understatement to say that Joe entered the race as a long shot. He was, after all, a political novice residing some 9,000 miles from Wisconsin. And his hastily fashioned campaign platform consisted of two vaguely worded statements about "job security for every man and woman" and "lasting peace throughout the world." Still, the very thought of a two-fisted Marine running for political office was both novel and patriotic. In a matter of days, the Committee to Elect Joseph McCarthy U.S. Senator was open for business. It included his relatives, his college pals, his poker buddies, and a handful of friendly editors, such as John Riedl of the Appleton *Post–Crescent* and Rex Karney of the Wisconsin *State Journal*.[42]

There was a complication. According to Wisconsin law, judges can "hold no office of public trust, except a judicial office, during the term for which they are elected, and all votes for any office, except a judicial office . . . shall be void." Was McCarthy violating the law? The secretary of state thought so, but the attorney general took a more liberal approach. McCarthy could run, he decided, and the courts could untangle the mess if he happened to win. Of course, McCarthy did not expect to win. He was in the race for the experience, the publicity, and the chance to position himself for a serious run in 1946. With the campaign in high gear, he got a thirty-day leave and returned to a hero's welcome. "When Joe set foot on Main Street this morning," wrote the Shawano *Evening Leader*, "he did not have to walk far to find a friend. It was 'Hello, Joe,' left and right, to the young judge who left a seat on the bench . . . to take another . . . behind the rear guns of a dive bomber."[43]

The most puzzling aspect of the 1944 campaign was its financing. With few real contributors, the McCarthy committee listed expenditures of $20,000, but the true figure was at least twice that high. In the waning days, the committee sent two and one-half million flyers to 88,000 families—the largest direct mail campaign in Wisconsin history. Where did the money come from? Mostly, it seemed, from McCarthy's relatives—$4,000 from father Tim and $10,600 from brother Howard. Remarkably, Howard's reported 1944 income was $3,700, while Tim's was $1,433.[44]

Several years later, a Senate report would disclose that Captain McCarthy had parlayed a $2,200 investment into a stock market windfall of $40,000. (His reported income was $5,336 in 1942 and $5,527 in 1944; in 1943 it reached $42,353.) Always the gambler, Joe had opened a margin account with Wayne Hummer and Company of Chicago. The report stated:

> McCarthy made a profit . . . in excess of $40,000 in 1943 and withdrew most of these profits in 1944 prior to the August 14 primary election. . . . Although the figures are not conclusive, it is singular that on or about the dates that McCarthy's campaign committee received amounts from the relatives of Senator McCarthy that he withdrew stock market profits somewhat in excess of the amounts reported by the committee.[45]

Why did McCarthy funnel the money through his relatives? The answer is simple. Under Wisconsin law, a candidate could not contribute more than $5,000 to his own campaign.

To make matters worse, McCarthy filed no state tax return for 1943. "I spent no time in Wisconsin," he told the tax authorities. "I had no property in the state and received no income from within the state, having waived my salary as circuit judge." Since Joe filed tax returns in 1942 and 1944, his explanation seemed curiously self-serving. He finally paid the $2,459, plus $218 in interest.[46]

Joe did not defeat Wiley, but he did run second in a large field with a respectable 80,000 votes. Even better, he captured the three counties within his judicial district. Upon returning to the Pacific he applied for another leave, claiming that his judicial duties had been too long overlooked. When it was denied, he resigned his commission and obtained his official discharge in February 1945.[47] While the war was far from over, the "fighting judge" had other things on his mind. A major national election was only a year away, with another Senate seat up for grabs. That it belonged to Robert M. LaFollette, Jr., a figure of heroic proportions, meant little to McCarthy. Less than a month after his discharge he was busily preparing for the 1946 political campaign.

CHAPTER THREE

Gunning for the Senate

A FIRST-TIME VISITOR to the handsome capital city of Madison would have little trouble identifying Wisconsin's most celebrated family. The imposing domed statehouse, with its many statues and commemorative plaques, is virtually a LaFollette museum. The marble-columned State Historical Society bulges with memorabilia documenting one LaFollette triumph after another. The two great intellectual landmarks, *The Progressive* magazine and the University of Wisconsin, are essentially LaFollette creations. It is as if every major undertaking in the state's illustrious history had somehow been initiated by a relative of the ubiquitous LaFollette clan.

There is a grain of truth in this Olympian notion. From 1900 until 1946, at least one family member sat in the Wisconsin governor's chair or in the United States Senate. Along the way, the LaFollettes transformed their conservative dairy state into a vast laboratory for progressive ideas. Railroad regulation, the direct primary, a corrupt-practices act— the list goes on and on. Many still view the LaFollettes, not the Roosevelts, as the founders of America's modern reform tradition.[1]

The dynasty was begun by Robert Marion (Fighting Bob) LaFollette. After serving three terms as governor, he was elected to the United States Senate in 1906, where he remained until his death nineteen years later. (During World War I, the Senate almost ousted LaFollette for his "dis-

36

loyal stand" against American involvement; in 1957 it named him one of the five outstanding men ever to sit in that body.) Backed by a remarkable coalition of small farmers, intellectuals, and city workers, he ruled the state Republican Party with an iron hand. His GOP opponents, the right-wing Stalwarts, were little more than a voice in the political wilderness. What kept them together was an overwhelming hatred of the senator and everything he represented.[2]

LaFollette expected his two sons, "Young Bob" and Phil, to devote their lives to public service. Phil relished the idea; he was handsome, extroverted, and self-assured—a natural leader. Bob was none of those things. Quiet, humorless, ill at ease with strangers, he shunned the publicity that surrounded his active family. In addition, a series of childhood illnesses had left him a hypochondriac, and he feared the debilitating routine so common to public figures. Still, as the older son of a political legend, Bob could not escape his calling. In 1925 he campaigned for his father's vacant seat, won handily, and became the youngest U.S. senator since Henry Clay a century before.[3]

Phil had been too young to run for office that year. But he captured the governorship in 1930 by promising to aid the victims of the Great Depression. His platform was simple: soak the rich to help the poor. With true family spirit, he rammed through a progressive income tax, a public-works program, and the nation's first unemployment compensation law. At a time when President Hoover seemed oblivious to human suffering, LaFollette demonstrated that the state could work to ease it. "Many of the best things that were part of the New Deal," wrote David Lilienthal, ". . . came out of the minds and imaginations of the men and women who were around Phil in Madison."[4]

Following Roosevelt's landslide victory in 1932, the LaFollettes fled the GOP to create a new political entity, the Progressive Party of Wisconsin. They had little choice. The Republican label had become an albatross, reminding millions of Hoover and Depression. It was no longer appropriate for a family accustomed to winning office. The Democrats were still building in Wisconsin; their time had not yet come. The obvious solution was a third party, based on the liberal principles of Fighting Bob LaFollette. And what better time for it than the early 1930s, when unemployment and poverty gripped the land?[5]

At first, the LaFollette brothers maintained a working relationship with FDR. In return for Bob's support of New Deal programs, the President allowed them to distribute federal patronage throughout Wisconsin. This arrangement pleased Bob no end. He had grown fond of the Senate, but he hated to campaign. Now, with Roosevelt's political blessing, he could remain in Washington with little concern about getting reelected.

Phil was more suspicious of the President. He viewed him as an opportunist who hadn't the will to crack down on big business. What America really needed, he felt, was a more dynamic leader—a man, quite frankly, like Phil LaFollette. In 1938, amid steel-helmeted national guardsmen and a red, white, and blue cross and circle (resembling, some thought, a "circumcised swastika"), he launched the National Progressives of America. The dream ended quickly. Phil was easily defeated for reelection as governor of Wisconsin.[6]

Bob was appalled by his brother's stupidity. He knew that a national third party could not hope to overcome FDR's great popularity. And he feared that a Roosevelt–LaFollette donnybrook would cost him his job by splitting Wisconsin's liberal vote. Yet he blessed the NPA for reasons of family loyalty, nothing more. "Bob always followed Phil," a Progressive leader recalled sadly.[7]

Relations with FDR were never the same. Although Bob, a strong isolationist, supported the administration after Pearl Harbor was bombed, he frowned upon Roosevelt's bid for an unprecedented fourth term in 1944. As a result, he lost both his presidential endorsement and the favor of many Wisconsin voters who identified with FDR's tough stand against Hitlerism. By war's end, the state Progressive Party was in shambles, Philip's political career was over, and Bob was up for reelection. His prospects did not look good.[8]

SHORTLY BEFORE THE 1946 WISCONSIN PRIMARY, the senator told his closest friends that he "might be happier" out of public office. He loved his work but feared that his deteriorating health could not stand the rigors of a tough campaign. Bob was scared. He had spent most of the war in Washington, returning home for short, infrequent visits. It was common knowledge that he had lost touch with the grass roots. Friend and enemy alike knew that his consuming interest in national problems had alienated many constituents. He seemed distant, aloof, and bored with local matters.[9]

Worse still was the collapse of Wisconsin's Progressive Party, a collapse that stripped Bob of his traditional vehicle for reelection. The time had come to bury it and to join forces with either of the major parties. From an ideological standpoint, the Democrats offered the more comfortable alternative. During the late 1930s, when the Progressive coalition withered under the strain of Philip's presidential bid and FDR's strong defense posture, Wisconsin liberals had begun joining the Democratic Party in large numbers. By 1946 the Democrats were on the move; while clearly weaker than their GOP counterparts, they had become a respectable force in state politics.[10]

Furthermore, the Democrats *wanted* LaFollette in their party. His political presence, they felt, would unite liberals under one banner, their own. The state chairman publicly welcomed Bob, even assuring him of the party's senatorial nomination. And pressure was exerted at the national level, with Harry Truman and Henry Wallace urging the senator to "come to the party of Roosevelt rather than the party of Hoover." [11]

LaFollette's second option was to rejoin the Republicans. But that would not be easy. When he bolted the GOP in 1934, the Stalwarts had assumed control. Convinced that Bob was a troublemaker who had packed the Statehouse with radicals and Jews, they were in no mood to welcome him back. The very thought of a LaFollette attempt to recapture the GOP was enough to stiffen the most flexible of Stalwart spines. On this issue there would be no compromise. [12]

The Stalwarts were led by Tom Coleman, a wealthy Madison industrialist, who had served as chairman of the powerful Republican Voluntary Committee.* Coleman had known Bob and Phil for most of his life, and his hatred of them was legendary. "Boss Tom," as some called him, loved to reminisce about the time he and other children "built a winter slide on a Madison hill and the LaFollette boys . . . who had not helped to make the slide, came along and used it." This was typical, he would say, for the brothers had "lived off some other person's work all their lives." Coleman readily admitted that his goal was to run the LaFollettes out of government. To his thinking, 1946 would be a banner year if the Stalwarts were to trounce Bob while losing every other office on the ballot. [13]

Despite this hostility, LaFollette still favored the GOP. He knew that it now offered him exactly what it could not in 1934, the greater chance for victory. As Harry Truman stumbled through his early months in office, 1946 seemed to all observers a Republican year, especially in Wisconsin, where the Democrats had not yet reached maturity. "I, for one, won't pretend that [our] desire . . . to rejoin the Republicans is anything but opportunistic," wrote one LaFollette supporter. "Bob can't afford to suffer from ideological squeamishness now." [14]

Most Progressives went along. At a statewide convention called to decide the party's future, they voted to return to the GOP. Still, this rank opportunism infuriated some delegates, who were unwilling to sacrifice their principles for the benefit of one individual, even Bob LaFollette. They left determined "to back some good liberals who would make the race for the Senate on the Democratic ticket." [15]

━━━━━━

TOM COLEMAN HAD SPENT MOST OF HIS ADULT LIFE trying to end Bob LaFollette's political career. Having come close at times, only to have

---

* The RVC, organized in 1925 to combat the LaFollette influence, had become the Stalwarts' vehicle for nominating and supporting conservative candidates.

victory snatched away, he no longer made optimistic appraisals. But Coleman could sense the promise of 1946. The Progressives were dead, LaFollette's support was shaky, and the nation's mood was decidedly conservative. For Bob to be reelected, moreover, he would have to face the Stalwarts in their own backyard, in the hostile Republican primary. This was the moment Coleman had waited for, the chance to grab La-Follette by the throat and choke the political life from him.

The Stalwarts were ready to do battle. They were disciplined, well financed, and conscious of the need to back a *single* candidate against LaFollette. The problem, of course, was finding the *proper* candidate, no mean task in a party filled with ambitious politicians. But one individual, a circuit judge in Marine garb, kept popping up throughout Wisconsin. Young McCarthy was a political dynamo, crisscrossing the state in an old sedan, trying to impress Republican leaders with his popularity, or at least his endurance. During the early months of 1946 he visited seventy-one GOP meetings, gave hundreds of speeches, and reorganized the dormant Young Republicans under the leadership of a few loyal supporters. His frantic pace upset some observers, who viewed it as a sign of political weakness. "For a while it appeared McCarthy was making some headway," wrote one skeptic, "but he was overcampaigned and has run smack-dab into the law of diminishing returns."[16]

Joe disagreed. He was a long-shot candidate with a lot of ground to make up. His instincts told him to go all out, to work twice as hard as his opponents, the way he had always done. But he was also a realist. He knew that Stalwart politics had long been dominated by money, influence, and family name. A few prominent clans usually put up the winning candidates in important primary contests. To succeed, he would have to discourage just that sort of competition.

There were two early favorites for the nomination: Julius Heil, a hard-drinking, roly-poly ex-governor, and Walter Kohler, Jr., a member of Wisconsin's most influential conservative family. Both had money to burn. Heil controlled a huge financial empire based on the production of heavy machinery; Kohler, son of a former governor, was heir to one of the largest industrial fortunes in the Midwest. As expected, Joe began with Heil, a notoriously obtuse politician. On the eve of the RVC's nominating convention, a dozen McCarthy supporters purposely engaged him in small talk. When Heil asked how things looked on the convention floor, each replied (with minor variations): "God, Julius, I'm all for you . . . but among my delegation I can't make any headway. I don't know what it is. They're all going for that darn fool McCarthy." Heil panicked. He withdrew the next morning.[17]

Joe was more direct with Kohler. By his own account, he barged into the candidate's office, reminded him of his (Kohler's) recent divorce, and hinted that such distasteful matters attracted heavy media coverage during a political campaign. Although Kohler swore that McCarthy had never directly threatened to raise the divorce issue, he did drop out of the race following their mysterious confrontation. (Several years later, Kohler, then Governor of Wisconsin, warned a *Time* magazine correspondent that Joe was devoid of scruples. "He strikes me as a mediocre lawyer with an easy conscience," the governor remarked sourly.) [18]

There was one final obstacle, Boss Tom Coleman. In his view, McCarthy was a liability—a novice, a Democrat-turned-Republican, a Catholic in a predominantly Protestant state. Their first meeting in 1945 had ended abruptly when Joe rejected Coleman's advice that he wait before seeking high office. ("Tom, you're a nice guy and I like you," he had responded. "But I got news for you. When that convention is over next year, Joe McCarthy will be the Republican-endorsed candidate for U.S. Senator.") Their second meeting a few months later had only made things worse. It was held at the posh Madison Club, which required male visitors to wear a coat and tie. When McCarthy appeared in a soiled Marine shirt, open at the collar, he was denied admittance. Coleman solved the problem by finding his guest the proper attire. But he understood that the candidate's rumpled appearance was meant as a clear gesture of defiance. [19]

In the end, Joe won over Coleman by doing what he did best— outbluffing him. He told him that he was going to run in the senatorial primary with or without the RVC's "official" endorsement. If the Stalwarts blessed another candidate, McCarthy warned, they would face the certainty of a three-way race (and a probable LaFollette victory). Although Coleman did not often receive, much less respect, ultimata from small-town politicians, he took this one seriously. For one thing, La Follette's defeat had become an obsession with him. Nothing, but nothing, could be allowed to stand in its way. For another, he believed that Joe would do *anything* to get what he wanted. The threat, therefore, had to be taken at face value. Coleman agreed to support the McCarthy nomination.

The RVC soon followed suit. But its convention delegates were hardly enthusiastic. In fact, while they applauded politely when Joe rose to make his acceptance speech, no attempt was made to give him the traditional standing ovation. Most political observers were startled by the selection. "Coleman is too intelligent to believe that McCarthy . . . can carry the Republican Party to victory," wrote one. "Boiled down to minimum essentials, Coleman laid an egg." [20]

Some Republicans found the nomination impossible to swallow. Walter Goodland, Wisconsin's popular eighty-four-year-old governor, could not bring himself to remain in the same room with the candidate. McCarthy, he warned, was a political plunger who lacked the decency, the bearing, and the conscience to hold major political office. When Coleman tried to pacify the governor by telling him that Joe was "an excellent campaigner," Goodland simply exploded. According to Coleman's rough notes of their conversation, "Goodland said that he would under no circumstances vote for McCarthy and that if McCarthy became our candidate he . . . would vote for LaFollette. . . . I asked the Governor . . . on what information he based his antipathy. He said it wasn't anything but prejudice. . . . He just didn't like him." Coleman was being less than honest. He knew that Goodland could not understand why the GOP was capitulating to a young hustler like McCarthy.[21]

Even more damaging was the blow delivered by Wisconsin's two major dailies, the Milwaukee *Journal* and the Madison *Capital–Times*. Once the campaign began, they roasted McCarthy for remaining on the bench. Citing both the state constitution and the American Bar Association's Code of Ethics (which forbids judicial officers from engaging in political activities), they demanded that he resign his judgeship or withdraw from the race.[22]

McCarthy did neither. Although tired of his judicial duties, he was unwilling to face the prospect of unemployment should LaFollette trounce him. ("I can't afford to quit," the judge told one Stalwart gathering. "My job is my means of support.") Of course, he was not about to blow the chance of a lifetime either. LaFollette was vulnerable; the opportunity to bring down an incumbent of his stature did not come along very often. So he asked the State Supreme Court to decide the legal issue, and he simply ignored the moral one. "I'm not a member of the Bar Association," Joe dead-panned, "and therefore not subject to its restrictions."[23]

The high bench upheld his candidacy, ruling that a state could not set qualifications for federal office-seekers. But three years later, with McCarthy safely domiciled in Washington, the Wisconsin Board of Bar Commissioners urged the court to void his license as a practicing attorney. Their private correspondence was harsh and to the point. One commissioner felt that, while Joe had a legal right to run for federal office in 1946, "he had no moral right to continue to draw his judicial salary . . . when he was obviously rendering no service." Another chastised him for displaying "a complete lack of morality" and for bringing judges "generally into disrepute." The court did censure McCarthy, but it rejected disbarment because he had "never previously been derelict in his duties."[24]

This was untrue. Joe *had* been reprimanded eight years earlier in the Quaker State Dairy case. Privately, Chief Judge Marvin Rosenberry claimed to have gone lightly on him for three reasons: He was now a U.S. senator; his offense was not likely to be repeated by others; and, standing alone, "it didn't seem like a matter worth disbarring him over."

In one sense, the incident was oddly reassuring to McCarthy. It demonstrated again that the penalties derived from a defiant and clearly unethical course of action are often outweighed by the personal gains. He mocked Rosenberry's opinion ("it was illegal—Joe was a naughty boy, but we don't think he'll do it again"), and called upon the commissioners to resign at once. Their actions, he proclaimed indignantly, "are a disgrace to every honest, decent lawyer in the State of Wisconsin."[25]

———

JOE WAS STILL IN DEEP TROUBLE. Opposition to him was so widespread that GOP leaders met secretly to reconsider his candidacy. But Coleman stood firm. Any last-minute change, he argued, would only split the party. And he felt sure that the voters would not condemn a genuine war hero for such a minor indiscretion. One McCarthy supporter put the "moral issue" more cynically: "Arguments about political ethics," he wrote, "are too fine and subtle to make much impression upon the mind of the rank and file."[26]

The Stalwarts fell into line. They may not have liked McCarthy, but he still seemed like the best bet to defeat LaFollette. They therefore made every resource available to him, including a public relations firm, a campaign staff, and an enormous capital outlay. The Committee to Elect Joseph McCarthy spent more than $75,000 during the race. The LaFollette figure was about $13,000. Given Joe's poor standing, this money became the great equalizer.

Much of it was used to produce a slick brochure ("The Newspapers Say") with pages of photographs and short favorable quips from the local press. The reader learned that McCarthy was a man with small-town, working-class roots; a self-made man, free of inherited wealth and privilege; a robust man who had been a farmer, a boxer, a tough Marine gunner. It was an exceptional piece of work, emphasizing the very qualities that set him apart from LaFollette. Joe loved the brochure. Most people, he told Van Susteren, "vote with their emotions, not with their minds. Show them a picture and they'll never read."[27]

Much of the literature played strictly upon McCarthy's war record. Combat veterans have always done well at the polls, and 1946 was a fine year for patriotic chest-thumping. His newspaper spots were misleading but effective. They explained how he turned down a soft job EXEMPT from military duty; how he joined the MARINES as a PRIVATE; how he fought on LAND and in the AIR; how he and millions of other Joes kept Wisconsin from speaking Japanese. And they all ended the same way: "TODAY JOE McCARTHY IS HOME. He wants to SERVE America in the SENATE. Yes, folks, CONGRESS NEEDS A TAIL-GUNNER."[28]

Joe then zeroed in on LaFollette's failure to enlist. (The senator, forty-six years old when Pearl Harbor was bombed, remained in Washington with virtually all of his congressional colleagues.) "What, other than draw fat rations, did LaFollette do for the war effort?" asked one campaign flyer. Another called Bob a war profiteer, a charge that McCarthy pressed with great relish. The senator, it seemed, had invested in a Milwaukee radio station and was rewarded with a $47,000 profit during 1944–45. Noting that the Federal Communications Commission licensed the station, Joe alleged that LaFollette had made "huge profits from dealing with a federal agency which exists by virtue of his vote."[29]

The charge was absurd. All stations are licensed by the FCC, and McCarthy never tried to prove that collusion occurred. But it did awaken liberal voters to the fact that LaFollette, a long-time spokesman for the regulation of excess profits, had made a financial killing on a limited investment. "Bob had no business with that ownership of WEMP," said one Progressive. "Coleman was right. . . . No man can get involved in that way and still be with the common people." This allegation did irreparable damage in working-class areas. Bob's image as the archenemy of privilege had begun to wear thin.[30]

McCarthy said little about his own platform. He supported veterans' pensions and the creation of an all-volunteer army—issues he knew to be popular with returning veterans and their families. His speeches on foreign affairs were laced with generalities that appealed to isolationists and internationalists at the same time. His main theme, for example, was that America had the duty either to lead the world or to play no part in it at all. He never did say which alternative he favored.[31]

McCarthy's big foreign policy address was delivered to the Young Republicans at Eau Claire. Promising to "take today's world picture and subject it to the cold, searching light of reason," he began with the "so-called Far East," which, he said, was no longer far. "We find that all of the causes of war which were there five, ten, and fifteen years ago still exist. All the festering cancerous sores are there, but growing ever larger. It is crystal clear that unless they are removed and the sores washed out . . . then just as certain as the sun is to rise out of the east in the morning there shall be another war." At no point, however, did McCarthy attempt to transcend these generalities. Was he referring to the future threat of Japan when he talked of "festering cancerous sores"? Did he mean the battle for China? Soviet designs on Manchuria? Further speculation is impossible, for this was *all* he said about the issue. Having disposed of the Far East in four sentences, he proceeded to turn the "cold searching light of reason" on the problems of Europe.[32]

Issues, then, were hardly the backbone of the McCarthy campaign. GOP strategists relied instead on expensive packaging plus a heavy dose of the candidate's imposing personal assets—his driving ambition, his enormous physical stamina, his insatiable thirst for victory. The campaign had a curiously manic air about it, dominated by a figure who would say anything, threaten anyone, go anywhere to achieve his objective. No town was too small or isolated for a whistle stop; in one four-day swing Joe visited twenty-seven hamlets with names like Mondovi, Chetek, Bloomer, and Neillsville. He'd enter banks, general stores, barber shops, and pool halls, grabbing for every hand, making the same boisterous pitch: "I don't want to lose your vote, sir. My name's McCarthy; I'm running for the United States Senate—against Bob LaFollette, you know." On one occasion he cut a 250-mile swath across the state in fifteen hours, personally fixing three flat tires, junking his automobile, hiring a cab and then two private planes to make a final late-night appearance near Lake Superior.[33]

Before long, Joe had worn out the newspapermen assigned to cover him. "The evening rally in Beloit should have been the end of any campaign day," lamented the Milwaukee *Journal*'s weary reporter. "But no—candidate McCarthy had yet to visit the American Legion clubroom, the Eagles Club, and the Veterans of Foreign Wars. There were votes there, and the judge worked until midnight to gather them." Catching a few hours' sleep, he made Janesville in time to meet the shift change at the local automobile plant. All the while, LaFollette remained sequestered in Washington.[34]

Joe was also optimistic about his chance to win "by 5 percent, maybe more." This made him an ideal candidate since he believed he was working toward an *achievable* goal. The skepticism expressed by the political "pros" never filled him with panic or self-doubt. He kept plugging away, ever hopeful that his murderous schedule would pay off. McCarthy's confidence was unflappable, as Phil LaFollette discovered when the two men accidentally crossed paths during the campaign. Sidling over to the ex-Governor, Joe warned him about his new secret weapon: "We've got thirty-five guys who are built like Bob and who have rubber masks which look exactly like him. They are going to travel the state, walking down main streets and bumping into people, asking them who they are, bumping into a United States Senator." Phil shot McCarthy a quizzical look and turned away, convinced that his brother was running against a crazy man. Like most of Bob's supporters, he did not take the judge seriously until the votes were in and counted. By then the laughter had turned to despair.[35]

———

BOB'S POLITICAL DILEMMA was enormous. On his right flank were Coleman, McCarthy, and the Stalwarts—hard-nosed, determined, spoiling for a fight. They undoubtedly posed the major reelection threat. But there was also trouble on the left. In the past decade, many former Progressives had begun joining the Democratic Party. While they still found much to admire about LaFollette, they were not about to follow him into the Stalwart-dominated GOP. This meant that the senator would have to challenge McCarthy in hostile territory—the Republican primary—without a solid bloc of supporters behind him. The prospect was hardly appealing.

To make matters worse, the Democrats seemed determined to punish LaFollette for ignoring their overtures. Their own senatorial candidate, Howard McMurray, had worked tirelessly to coax him into the Democratic fold. When Bob opted for the Republicans, McMurray swore revenge. "I won't get elected," he told one Progressive leader, "but I'll see that Bob doesn't either." This was no idle threat; following his selection, McMurray set out to destroy LaFollette's candidacy. Although running unopposed in the Democratic primary, he wanted to pile up as many votes as he could, thereby denying Bob the support *he* needed to beat McCarthy in the GOP contest.* [36]

McMurray was a former U.S. congressman who taught political science at the University of Wisconsin. He liked to think of himself as a scholar in a world of politicians, a man of intellect, not prejudice; of integrity, not expedience. But he had run a strong campaign for the Senate in 1944, and he was known to get very rough when he had to. Before long, McMurray was accusing Bob of everything from political indifference to pro-Nazi bias. "LaFollette spent five years before the war voting for Hitler," he said of the senator's isolationist record. "If a man had to sell out his civilization to get votes he should not represent free people in a democratic society." [37]

McMurray spent most of his time in the industrial counties of Milwaukee, Kenosha, and Racine, where the unions used their considerable resources to promote his candidacy. The labor press pictured him as a wise and compassionate New Dealer. LaFollette, on the other hand, was portrayed as a turncoat who had forsaken his ideals for personal gain. "Bob must be a lonely man these days," sniped the Racine *Labor*. "We can just picture him lying awake at night, tossing in his scorching bed, wondering how he ever came to be in there with so many reactionaries." In Kenosha, the labor councils registered more union voters than in any past off-year election; in Racine and Milwaukee, Democratic candidates addressed packed gatherings as a result of massive labor publicity drives. That effort was vitally important, because LaFollette counted on urban working-class votes to offset Stalwart strength in the rural areas. By 1946, however, his hard-core support had largely vanished. [38]

Certainly the most controversial aspect of the campaign was the role

---

* Wisconsin has an open primary, meaning that a voter, regardless of political affiliation, can choose to enter either the Republican or the Democratic primary. Once he makes the choice, however, he has to stay within that primary. Therefore, someone who entered the Democratic primary to vote for Governor or Sheriff could not then switch over to the GOP primary to vote for McCarthy or LaFollette.

played by a group of Communist labor leaders in LaFollette's defeat. As the years passed, and McCarthy evolved into America's premier Red-hunter, the theory that he was brought to power by the forces he allegedly despised gained widespread acceptance. The Communists "were out for LaFollette's hide," noted one McCarthy biographer, "and the exhaust explosion of their negativism blew Joe . . . right into the United States Senate." Another wrote: "Though many factors contributed to the defeat of LaFollette, the final turning edge was supplied by the Communists; they had elected their own nemesis." [39]

The theory goes something like this: In 1946 the Communists ran the Wisconsin CIO and dominated its 75,000 members. They had generally ignored LaFollette until the previous year—when he began criticizing Stalin's expansionist policies. In a fit of anger, the *Wisconsin C.I.O. News* labeled Bob as pro-Nazi and anti-Russian. Headlines like "La-Follette Shields Role of Reactionary," and "Pro-Fascist Groups Support Bob," appeared regularly in the newspaper. [40]

Judge McCarthy had taken a more ambiguous stance toward the Russians, the theory continues. For virulent anti-Communists, he related a sordid tale of "American appeasement in foreign affairs." But for Soviet sympathizers, he offered a different line: "I do not subscribe to the theory that a war with the Russians is inevitable. . . . Stalin's proposal for world disarmament is a great thing and he must be given credit for being sincere about it." When a reporter asked Joe about the CIO's election role, he allegedly replied, "Communists have the same right to vote as anyone else, don't they?" * Sensing McCarthy's political opportunism, CIO leaders viewed him as the lesser of two evils. [41]

The popularity of this theory is understandable. After all, who among McCarthy's liberal detractors would not *want* to believe that he was

---

* Although McCarthy hotly denied ever making this remark, it was to plague him for the rest of his life. The quote was first printed by Anderson and May in their 1952 biography, *McCarthy*, p. 104. It was picked up by many writers and still appears in the most recent works about the senator's career. (Cook, *The Nightmare Decade*, 1971, p. 104; Thomas, *When Even Angels Wept*, 1973, p. 44.) Surprisingly, no one has ever been able to pin down exactly when or where or to whom McCarthy said it. In 1953 the public relations director of Americans for Democratic Action made a frantic attempt to document the quote after ADA vice president Joe Rauh used it during a televised debate in Washington. She went first through Anderson and May's rough notes but found nothing. She then wrote to Robert Fleming of the Milwaukee *Journal*, Wisconsin's resident expert on McCarthy, for help. His reply: "Your letter . . . inquiring about a McCarthy quote indicating tolerance or acceptance of Communist support caused our library staff to do intensive work. The result: nothing. Several of us have known of the quote and have read it often in recent times, but when our people tried to find it . . . they failed. Our librarian went through all our Mc-Carthy material as well as clips of the 1946 campaign but found nothing." (Susanna Davis to Robert Fleming, December 2, 1953; Fleming reply to Davis, December 7, 1953; both in Box 39, Legislative File, Papers of the *Americans for Democratic Action*, Wisconsin State Historical Society.)

I, too, have looked carefully for the quote but have never been able to find it. My feeling is that McCarthy was correct, that he never uttered such a comment.

elected by Communist votes? Unfortunately, the theory has ignored a mass of evidence pointing in the opposite direction. The Communists, for example, were hardly unique in attacking LaFollette's anti-Soviet position. Following his criticism of Stalin, Bob was subjected to withering rebukes from all over Wisconsin. The liberal Milwaukee *Journal* wondered "if Senator LaFollette's purpose is to sabotage the U.N. . . . and enthrone the isolationism which became so tragic a failure after the First World War." The conservative Wisconsin *State Journal* opined, "Probably the major reasons in Russia's sometime lone-wolf role are performances like . . . LaFollette's which still draw alarming applause." It was not until a year or so later, when the Cold War became an established political reality, that Bob's hard-line position was readily accepted in America. By that time, of course, he was no longer sitting in the Senate.[42]

More significantly, it seems doubtful that many CIO members were influenced by the anti-LaFollette diatribes of their leaders. In fact, the Communists were in the process of being removed from office by rank-and-file insurgents representing about 90 percent of the CIO's membership. And one of the key issues in their demise was "the outrageous pro-Soviet attitude of the *Wisconsin C.I.O. News.*" By the end of 1946, Communist influence in the state CIO had been virtually eradicated.[43]

In short, while the Communists controlled much of the CIO's organizational machinery during the primary, there is no evidence that they dominated the minds or votes of many CIO members. The workers, for the most part, were Democrats, not Bolsheviks. "I do not think the Communists should be blamed for Bob's defeat," said one of LaFollette's old cronies. "Labor made up its mind . . . long before . . . that they must fight their battles in the Democratic Party. It was stressed to Bob . . . that labor would not go into the Republican primaries and that he would be fighting in an arena where his friends would not be able to help him." The anti-Communist unions agreed. "No, we did not desert Bob," remarked the *Kenosha Labor.* "It was the other way around—Bob deserted us."[44]

———

CONSIDERING THE FACTORS working against LaFollette—the Progressive dissolution, the tough Stalwart campaign, and labor's alliance with the Democrats—there was every reason to assume that he faced an uphill fight. Yet Bob seemed oblivious to the danger. He had no effective campaign organization, spent little money, and returned to Wisconsin only ten days before the election. Some of his friends have maintained that he stayed in Washington for the best of reasons, to ensure passage of the Congressional Reorganization Act. "This bill had been Bob LaFollette's baby for years," said one. "Nobody cared about it; certainly not you; certainly not I; certainly not his constituents. The important thing, you and I said, was to come home and get reelected. But Bob LaFollette was performing the purest kind of public service. He got his bill through and he lost his job."[45]

There is some truth to this contention. LaFollette was, by all accounts, a dedicated public servant. Yet this is only part of the story, a rather small part. Originally, Bob's supporters had been quite anxious about his chances for reelection. But McCarthy's selection by the RVC calmed them considerably. "I have yet to hear a single one of the scores with whom I talked say that McCarthy has a ghost of a chance," one wrote cheerfully. "The invariable reply, translated for family consumption, is: 'Hell, nobody can beat LaFollette this year.' " This unwarranted optimism made sense to the senator, because he *wanted* to remain in Washington, away from the campaign trail and the petty annoyances of his constituents. Why return home when the opposition was running such a mediocre candidate? The election, he felt, was already in the bag.[46]

The final tabulations showed McCarthy with 207,935 votes; La-Follette with 202,557; and McMurray, who ran unopposed, with 62,361. Needless to say, the primary marked a major turning point in the lives of both Republican candidates. For McCarthy it meant a giant step on the road to international prominence—and notoriety. His friends claim that the victory over LaFollette was his fondest political memory. For Bob the road led quickly downhill to loneliness, depression, and suicide. There were rumors after the election that President Truman would appoint him Ambassador to the United Nations, but nothing ever came of them. LaFollette decided to stay in Washington, where he worked for various industrial concerns. But poor health and the humiliation he felt in defeat combined to destroy his fragile self-confidence. One morning in 1953 he called his wife Rachel and told her to return home at once. Before she arrived, Bob took a loaded pistol, put it into his mouth and pulled the trigger. He died instantly. He was fifty-eight.

═══

AS HISTORIANS HAVE LONG NOTED, the 1946 general elections were greatly influenced by the onset of the Cold War. Republican candidates, in particular, freely attacked their Democratic opponents for encouraging domestic radicalism and failing to confront the Soviet threat in Europe. GOP National Chairman B. Carroll Reece insisted that "the choice which confronts Americans this year is between Communism and Republicanism." Senatorial hopeful James Kem of Missouri claimed that President Truman was "soft on Communism." In Wisconsin, GOP candidates Charles Kersten ("Put Kersten in Congress and Keep Communism Out") and Alvin O'Konski ran on their promises to rid the federal bureaucracy of "New Deal Communists." In Nebraska, Senator Hugh

Butler told his supporters that "if the New Deal is still in control of Congress after the election, it will owe that control to the Communist Party in this country." GOP Stalwart Ken Wherry made the point most clearly: "The coming campaign is not just another election. It is a crusade."[47]

Oddly enough, few historians have attempted to study McCarthy's political behavior during the 1946 senatorial race. By assuming that he stumbled upon the Communist issue in 1950, they have all but ignored his earlier Red-baiting episodes. This is a mistake, for the evidence suggests that, even by the vigorous mudslinging standards of 1946, he took a back seat to no politician in his exploitation of this theme.

McCarthy began his senatorial campaign with a visit to, of all places, Chicago. It was billed as a short vacation, but the judge was in no mood to relax. He was there for a meeting with Colonel Robert "Bertie" McCormick, publisher of the Chicago *Tribune*. McCormick, who equated the New Deal with "Russian-loving Communists," had formed a new group, American Action Incorporated, to finance right-wing congressional candidates. Taking an immediate shine to McCarthy, he offered to support him in the senatorial race. Joe readily accepted, saying he needed all the help he could get.[48]

Back in Wisconsin, Howard McMurray received a far more embarrassing endorsement. It came, unsolicited, from the Wisconsin Communist Party, and it became a cause célèbre in the state's powerful Republican press. "Does Mr. McMurray repudiate the Communists who have infiltrated into the New Deal political machine in this state?" asked the Green Bay *Press–Gazette* and the Appleton *Post–Crescent* in identical editorials. "Or does he crave political success so deeply that he would accept any support disregarding its origin and sinister purpose?"[49]

McCarthy went a step further. When questioned, at an open forum in Milwaukee, about his connections with AAI, he responded that "if it is organized to help fight Communism, as they say, then I welcome their help in defeating Communists and those who are Communistically inclined like Howard McMurray." This inflammatory remark–so very similar to those he would employ four years later—brought McMurray instantly to his feet.

> McMURRAY: I have never had a responsible citizen—I say responsible citizen—challenge my loyalty to America before. I am sure my friends and my students in my political science courses of past years will not challenge my loyalty. This statement is a little below the belt. I'll leave the answers to the voters.

> McCARTHY: I said that for the benefit of Howard McMurray. But I also want to ask him, does he not welcome the endorsement of the *Daily Worker*, which referred to him in a recent issue as a "fellow

traveler," according to quotations in the Appleton *Post–Crescent* and the Green Bay *Press–Gazette?*

McMurray: I welcome that question. I have not seen the reported statement in the *Daily Worker,* nor the comments of those two reactionary newspapers in Appleton and Green Bay. I certainly repudiate that paper [*Daily Worker*] and their whole tribe.[50]

Joe continued to hammer away at the "disloyalty" of the opposition party and its candidates. During a speech in Appleton, he claimed that the Democrats were controlled by men "with foreign inclinations, yes, foreign obligations. I, too, have responsibilities," he said, "but mine are to the people of this country." It was more of the same in Janesville, where McCarthy told a partisan crowd that "all Democrats are not Communists. . . . But enough are voting the Communist way to make their presence in Congress a serious threat to . . . our nation." At Eau Claire, he promised to make every effort "toward removing the vast number of Communists from the public payroll." One columnist warned that "this phony business Judge McCarthy is pulling . . . is an excellent clinical study of how Red Scares are manufactured."[51]

By November, McMurray had been buried under a sordid pile of allegations and innuendoes. The *Press–Gazette* claimed that he was "in favor of the enemies of our country." The Oshkosh *Daily Northwestern* warned its readers not to vote for a man endorsed by the Communists. Worst of all, perhaps, was the behavior of the *Post–Crescent,* which called McMurray "a noisy, blatant, unbearably egoistic gentleman upon whom the American editor of the *Moscow Pravda* slobbered."[52]

McCarthy also took a more conservative line on domestic issues. The reason was simple. He knew that, while he could not win the votes of many LaFollette supporters, neither could McMurray. ("Whatever we feel about McCarthy," said one Progressive leader, "we will always remember that it was McMurray who knifed Bob in the back.") This meant that a huge bloc of liberal voters would probably ignore the senatorial election. For Joe to win, he had only to ensure a strong turnout among the state's regular Republicans. He did this by attacking the New Deal.[53]

To many people, but particularly a Midwestern Republican, the New Deal had come to symbolize all that had "gone wrong" with America: the rise of big government and big labor; the elevation to power of urban and foreign types, haughty bureaucrats, and intellectual misfits; the demise of cherished concepts like free competition, individual initiative, and local control. It is doubtful that Joe felt much sympathy for this view; if he did, he never mentioned it prior to 1946. But, like many politicians, he was perfectly willing to exploit these resentments for his own ends. Witness the following McCarthy ad in the Stevens Point *Daily Journal:*

Tired of Being Pushed Around? Do you like to have some government bu-
reaucrat tell you how to manage your life? Do you enjoy not being able to
buy the food your family needs to eat and the things your home needs to
make it comfortable? Who's to blame for all this? Nobody but the New Deal.[54]

The election results were a foregone conclusion. By identifying himself closely with Republican interests and issues in a predominantly Republican state, Joe carried seventy of seventy-three counties and won by
a margin of almost two to one. His political career had taken him (op-
portunistically, if not ideologically) from the New Dealism of his early
days in Shawano clear across the political spectrum to the regular Republicanism of Tom Coleman and the RVC. Joe McCarthy went to the
Senate as an anti–New Deal conservative—a position he was to maintain
until his death a decade later.

CHAPTER FOUR

The Pepsi-Cola Kid

BOW YOUR HEADS, folks, conservatism has hit America. All the rest of the world is moving Left, America is moving Right." So wrote *The New Republic's* T.R.B. in his grim postmortem of the 1946 national elections. The Democratic collapse, analysts agreed, had been breathtaking in scope: fifty-four House and eleven Senate seats lost; solid GOP control of Congress for the first time in eighteen years; humiliating defeats at the state and local levels. Styles Bridges, a rock-ribbed New Hampshire conservative, put it best: "The United States is now a Republican country."[1]

Not just Republican, he might have added, but right-wing Republican as well. The newcomers to Washington—John Bricker (Ohio), Richard Nixon and William Knowland (California), Bill Jenner (Indiana), "Molly" Malone (Nevada), Harry Cain (Washington), Zales Ecton (Montana), and James Kem (Missouri), to name a few—constituted the "Class of '46." They were determined to rid the government of Communists, perverts, and New Dealers, get tough with Joe Stalin, crack down on labor unions, and dismantle the Office of Price Administration. Some observers compared them to small-town rotarians; others joked about the resurrection of Calvin Coolidge. But all agreed that it was quite some time since this many like-minded conservatives had massed at the Capitol gates.[2]

In the midst of such company, one could easily mistake Joe Mc-

Carthy for a political centrist—or even a liberal. Little was known about him. His campaigns against LaFollette and McMurray had been mudslinging efforts that carefully skirted the paramount issues of foreign relations and domestic reconversion. Since no one was sure what, if anything, Joe stood for, the Milwaukee *Journal* interviewed him at length:

> In talking with McCarthy, one gets the impression that he will make a record as a liberal Republican, and that he will be closer to Republicans of the type of former Governor Harold E. Stassen of Minnesota and Senators Wayne Morse of Oregon and Joseph Ball of Minnesota than he will be to Senator Robert Taft of Ohio, the apparent conservative choice for President in 1948.

Joe nodded approvingly. "I feel that all of the new and younger men in Congress," he said, "will serve as a nucleus for a really forward-looking Republican Party—one geared to 1948, 1952, and 1956 rather than to the 1920s."[3]

In falling prey to this rhetoric, the *Journal* overlooked the surest barometer of future action, McCarthy's conservative political base. Even if the senator were serious about working to liberalize the GOP, he could not have done so without cutting his own throat. The Stalwarts were the dominant political force in Wisconsin, and they were in no mood to accept a "closet liberal" as their junior Republican senator. The ground rules called for a conservative, someone who would push for tougher labor laws, smaller federal budgets, and an end to price controls. McCarthy didn't mind. He was a soldier of fortune, not an ideologue. Voting conservative, voting liberal—it hardly mattered to him. But he knew that it mattered to Tom Coleman and his Stalwart friends. He was not about to let them down.

For reasons of necessity, then, Joe McCarthy threw in his lot with the "Class of '46." He talked tough, voted conservative, and socialized with the Bill Jenners and the Molly Malones. But even in those early days there was something that set him apart from the others. It was, in the words of the historian Robert Griffith, "his continual violation of the rules, customs, and procedures under which the Senate operates." Every time he took the floor to speak, trouble seemed to follow. Harried colleagues accused him of lying, manipulating figures, playing fast and loose with the Senate's most cherished traditions. At first the established heroes and villains of the late 1940s—Douglas MacArthur, Alger Hiss, Albert Einstein, John L. Lewis—combined to overshadow this bizarre newcomer. Most senators viewed him as a minor irritant, someone to be avoided whenever possible. It was only after McCarthy had hit the big time in 1950 that many would kick themselves for not dealing with him earlier, when it required neither great courage nor a full-scale public explanation.

JOE MCCARTHY CAME TO WASHINGTON with a good bit of fanfare. He was, after all, the fellow who buried the LaFollette dynasty. At thirty-eight, ten years younger than the average senator, he was a "comer," a man who bore some watching. The *Saturday Evening Post* called him "The Senate's Remarkable Upstart." *U.S. News* lauded his "hustling, whirlwind" style. Even *Life* took notice with a pictorial special about McCarthy's first day in office. When the photographer asked for his initial impression of Washington, Joe got serious. "I stepped down from the train," he recalled, "took a look around and said, 'Hell, it's raining!' "[4]

Like most newcomers, McCarthy had trouble finding a place to live. His dilemma became the focus for yet another story ("Bachelor Senator Who Can Cook, Needs an Apartment"). The Washington *Post* reported that Joe, having mastered the culinary art while slinging hash in beaneries around Marquette, was interested in renting space with a good kitchen. Before too long he took a room in the Anacostia flat of his office manager, Ray Kiermas. "Nothing fancy," said McCarthy with the proper dash of farm-boy modesty. "Just a place to hang my hat."[5]

Joe had no intention of finding an apartment. With the exception of his home in Appleton, which he used infrequently and sold after the 1946 election, he spent most of his life in rented rooms. An apartment meant, in the most general sense, roots, a kind of physical attachment to the community. "He was like a stray dog," said Van Susteren. "He'd stay three days at one place, three at another, and four at another. He'd sleep on the couch, on the floor, on the porch—it didn't matter at all to him." McCarthy seemed to thrive in this transient atmosphere; its lack of permanence meshed well with his irregular life style and his alienation from Washington's established order.[6]

He did buy some new clothing. After checking on the sartorial habits of his colleagues, he began sporting $45 double-breasted suits, snap-brim hats, and dark, sober ties. But his outfits were ill-fitting, poorly coordinated, and rarely pressed. The pockets, friends noticed, bulged with handwritten notes, scraps of paper he could never find, and pieces of broken comb and pencil. One reporter said he looked "like a football coach," while a staff member acknowledged that "his ties and socks would match his suit only on a lucky day." A Wisconsin chum who visited Joe's room in Washington found balled-up suits everywhere and ties lining the floor. "He's also got a lot of hats. There are hats all over the place. But they all look like hell." McCarthy, it seemed, was in the habit of getting undressed as he walked from one end of the room to the other, leaving garments where they dropped from his body. Often he never bothered to collect them. After every road trip, the hotels he frequented mailed large packages of forgotten clothing back to his office.[7]

Joe continued to gamble. He spent many afternoons at Bowie, Laurel, and Pimlico, often in the company of J. Edgar Hoover. When he told his secretary, "I'm going to Bethesda, to the Naval Hospital," it meant, "I'm heading for the track, see you later." He occasionally sat in on the Senate's poker games, but his presence was never encouraged. He played "the wildest, weirdest game of poker I ever saw in my life," said New Mexico's Clint Anderson.[8]

The Senate's big gambler at that time was Bob Kerr, the gregarious Oklahoma Democrat. Since Kerr played gin rummy, a game Joe knew little about, their early matches were quite one-sided. To equalize the odds, McCarthy pored over gin rummy manuals and asked Oswald Jacoby, the card expert, to give him lessons. Jacoby declined but sent along the name of someone who could. Before long, Joe was taking Kerr for large sums and bragging about it all over Washington.[9]

The senator dated a good deal in those years, but his relationships with women seemed predatory and superficial. A friend offered this rather typical account of McCarthy's behavior:

> To say he was a rough diamond was a misnomer in the sense that he was never a diamond. He was rough. . . . He would fairly often get disorderly. He brought a succession of floozies, usually, out with him. If he didn't, he was making passes at everybody in the house, including my sister.[10]

At one dinner party, the man recalled, McCarthy appeared with a buxom young woman, "disappeared upstairs and screwed her on the hostess' bed. . . . He didn't even take the damn counterpane off. The hostess said she was never going to have him in her house again."[11]

The only dramatic change from Appleton to Washington concerned his drinking. Where McCarthy had rarely indulged before reaching the Senate, he did begin consuming large quantities of alcohol once there—encouraged, no doubt, by the new pressures and the absence of family and close friends. Another factor may have been the death of his father in 1946. When Tim passed away, at seventy-nine, Joe blamed the local doctors. At the last moment he even rushed in a specialist from Milwaukee. Viewing the death as premature, he took a long time to get over it.

A Washington reporter who socialized with McCarthy once wrote: "The thing to remember . . . is that he is a country bumpkin—a small-town, would-be bigshot who made it. He is ignorant, crude, boastful, unaware of either intellectual or social refinements." McCarthy was, in many ways, a captive of his provincial environment. His interests were narrow and self-centered. When not working, he gambled, chased women, talked politics, and watched Westerns. He spent a lot of time in the back room at Harvey's, where he could drink, relax, and order up an overcooked steak. "Cremate it," he'd tell the waiter.[12]

There are others, however, who would argue that McCarthy was less a country bumpkin than a shrewd manipulator of small-town and lower-class resentments, that his disdain for "intellectual and social refinements" was assiduously cultivated to set him apart from the educated Protestant order—"the striped-pants crowd." He therefore *encouraged* reporters to feature his lowbrow pursuits. The man's bread and butter, some have speculated, was his carefully groomed image as a tough-talking, crap-shooting, womanizing ex-G.I. Why else would he burst into a hearing room, breathless and disheveled, claiming to have had "quite a night . . . and breakfast in bed"? And who else would loudly instruct his committee counsel to get the address of a pretty young witness "for the record," and "her telephone number for me"?[13]

Yet these assessments are not mutually exclusive. McCarthy was a man who loved his vices and saw how they could be used for political advantage. They were, he believed, the vices common to rugged American males, the very things that set him apart from his colleagues. He was always proud that, unlike a Bob LaFollette, he did not have to hold his nose when he campaigned on a Grand Chute dairy farm or in the grimy taverns of South Milwaukee. He could talk hog prices, swap war stories, down a few beers, and ogle the women without really compromising himself.

In 1948, when the Senate recessed after weeks of tedious overtime, McCarthy did not head for a mountain resort, or Bermuda, or the Maryland shore. Instead, he and a friend signed on anonymously as field hands for the North Dakota wheat harvest. According to Senator Milton Young, who got them the jobs, "Both . . . made me promise on a stack of Bibles that I wouldn't tell who they were, as they wanted to work as ordinary harvest hands, and not receive any special consideration."

The two men took a bus to Appleton, picked up Joe's car, and drove 1,000 miles to Dickinson, North Dakota, where they got work on the farm of Jake Lafore. Toiling from dawn to dusk, McCarthy refreshed his sagging spirits. He ate German food, drank beer, cracked bad jokes, and gained everyone's respect. When Lafore finally discovered his guest's real identity, he told Young: "It was a fine thing for him to do. I wish more of these high officials in Washington would do something like that and see our problems . . . at first hand."[14]

On a personal level, McCarthy never felt comfortable in Washington. At the capital's better parties, he invariably played the primitive, the tough guy, the two-fisted Irish Marine in the midst of eggheads and softies. He must have felt odd mixing with guests from the world of private schools and clubs, who exchanged tips about restaurants, resorts, and bestselling fiction. Their strengths were obviously his weaknesses. "I wonder what these people would think," he remarked at one posh gathering, "if they knew I raised chickens."

But McCarthy felt that the reverse was also true: His strengths were *their* weaknesses. He was a self-made man, braver and tougher than they. So he told them he was a boxer, a war hero, a man of great physical prowess. From the moment Joe arrived in Washington, he seemed obsessed by the need to publicize his masculine virtues while demeaning his critics as weak and effeminate.

At the same time, his day-to-day relationships with those who did not patronize or threaten him, who did not compete with him for headlines or political gain, could be remarkably warm. He went out of his way to learn the names of the blue-collar workers at the Senate Office Building, and he encouraged them to call him "Joe." According to Ruth Watt, chief clerk of the Government Operations Committee, McCarthy was the most agreeable politician she ever came across. "He was extremely friendly," she recalls, "and very concerned with our feelings. If I made a mistake, it was always, 'Don't worry about it, Ruthie. It's no big deal. Don't let it bother you.' No one, absolutely no one, was better to us." [15]

A Wisconsin priest gave a similar account of McCarthy's behavior. While studying in Washington, he noticed that the senator took a special interest in seeking out visiting priests, conversing with them, and making them feel at home. This, he observed, was in marked contrast to the behavior of other Catholic politicians, including young John F. Kennedy, "who never went out of [their] way to greet the clergy, and who even seemed embarrassed by the presence of priests." [16]

Columnist Jack Anderson, one of Joe's early Washington friends, was often flabbergasted by McCarthy's "unsenatorial" posture. "Once," he remembered, "Joe and I bumped into a woman with two small children in front of a supermarket. The woman wanted to go shopping, but she couldn't because her kids were acting up. So Joe said to her, 'Look, you go inside and shop and I'll watch your kids for you.' There he was, a United States Senator, babysitting for people he had never met before. I can't think of too many others who would have done that. He was a democrat with a small 'd.' " [17]

Story follows story of Joe's benevolent nature. Upon learning that an elevator operator had no place to spend Thanksgiving, McCarthy made arrangements for him to have dinner with a local family. When Christmas came around, he always shared his gifts with the less fortunate building workers. The lamest hard-luck story would bring a twenty-dollar bill from his wallet. Apocryphal or not, these reminiscences are consistent with Joe's behavior. He was often a concerned friend, he wanted very much to be liked by those around him, and he could show great kindness in noncompetitive situations. [18]

━━━━━

WHAT DOES A NEW SENATOR DO on his first day in Washington? Sleep late? Check the mail? See the sights? McCarthy called the President. He wanted to talk about John L. Lewis and the coal strike that was paralyzing the nation. The White House politely turned him down. Perhaps the two men could meet, it suggested, when Congress reconvened in January.[19]

Joe did the next best thing. He called a press conference. A handful of reporters showed up. There was not much political action that December, and some of them were curious about his motive. They could not remember the last time a senator-elect had done such a thing on his second day in town.

> "Mr. McCarthy, what makes you think you're important enough to call a press conference?"
>
> "Now, let's get down to business. About this coal strike. I've got a solution. The Army should draft the striking coal miners. That would solve the problem."
>
> "What about John L. Lewis?"
>
> "Draft him too."
>
> "And what if they refused?"
>
> "Then they could be court-martialed for insubordination and you know what that means."
>
> "You mean you would line up men like John L. Lewis and have them shot?"
>
> ". . . Lewis should be directed to order his miners to mine coal. If he does not do that, he should be court-martialed. We should go straight down the line. . . . All this talk about you can't put 400,000 miners in jail is a lot of stuff. They won't go to jail. They will mine coal first."[20]

The proposal was hardly unique. Harry Truman had used similar threats to end the railway strike seven months before. Although clearly unconstitutional, the ploy had won the overwhelming approval of a nation fed up with labor disruptions and spiraling wage demands. It was this anti-union sentiment that McCarthy hoped to exploit.

He did get a couple of headlines. The New York *Times* and the Washington *Post* covered the press conference, as did the *Army and Navy Bulletin,* which criticized Joe for turning a "noble calling" into a "vast penal institution." But his suggestion was quickly buried when Truman went on radio to demand that the miners return to work at once. They did, coaxed along by a federal judge who fined their union $3,510,000 for criminal contempt. The President's victory over Lewis was one McCarthy must have envied. It involved the surrender of a man who had never before admitted defeat in public. ("When Harry walked back to the mansion," a White House aide remembered, "you could hear his balls clank.") But Joe didn't come away empty-handed. He had, after all, made a few waves *before* being sworn in. As a gesture of appreciation, he sent several wheels of Wisconsin cheese to the National Press Club Bar. "When you want me," he told reporters, "don't hesitate to call me, night or day."[21]

It didn't take long for McCarthy to establish himself as an arrogant and wildly unpredictable colleague. Assigned to the Committee on Expenditures in the Executive Departments, he became a one-man demolition squad, savaging Democrats and Republicans with equal abandon. No subject was beyond his expertise, as a group of Californians learned when they lobbied for a new aqueduct near San Diego. By day's end, Joe had overwhelmed their spokesmen, among whom was Sheridan Downey, California's senior U.S. senator.

At issue was whether San Diego really needed the project. The Californians, contending that it did, came loaded with charts and facts and figures. McCarthy was not impressed. Using the same charts and facts and figures, he calculated that San Diego could endure a two-year drought and still have enough water for eight hundred additional days. Downey jumped up in protest. "I just want to state to the committee that I am *sure* that the Senator's conclusions are totally wrong," he said. And San Diego's water expert looked puzzled and worried. "My calculations do not bring me out to quite that long a time," he told McCarthy.

Well, said Joe, it was all quite simple. "If your present facilities could take care of 30 million gallons per day, could take care of the evaporation, and could build up 59 billion gallons reserve, we must assume that if the weather is normal over the next six and a half years, the present facilities will still take care of 30 million of evaporation. . . . I can't arrive at any other figure."

When challenged closely, Joe would scribble a bit on his pad and come up with a new set of numbers. "Your rainfall gives you roughly 30 million gallons a day," he lectured one wide-eyed expert, "and if you have got a backlog in your reservoirs of 39 billion gallons of potable water, that would mean, according to my arithmetic, that you are getting a flow of 56 million a day, so you are depleting your reservoirs by 20 million gallons a day. With a backlog of 39 billion gallons, that would mean you can go for nine thousand days before you exhaust the potable water supply. . . . It seems like simple arithmetic."

Simple or not, it was too much for the opposition. The experts had now lost faith in their figures, and the politicians had lost faith in their experts. It was left to poor Mayor Knox of San Diego to save the day, but he fell victim to a flurry of questions about stream control and reservoir capacity. "You get down to the Lower Otay," said McCarthy, "and you took a 15-percent loss on the amounts in all of the reservoirs. You would be in excess of 28 billion. However, we do not take a 15-percent loss from the 12 billion gallons in the Lower Otay because it is already there. Right?" Knox sat frozen in place. "I did not understand that," he frowned. Joe responded with a broad, sympathetic smile. The battle had become a rout, and his interest was quickly waning. So he expressed his regrets—"I hate like the devil to leave at this point"—and headed for the door. "In your absence I can probably do a lot better," Knox replied. "I am afraid you will," said McCarthy to the delight of the hearing-room crowd.[22]

In the following weeks, Joe battled committee witnesses at every turn. Was Arizona exaggerating its tick infestation? Was hoof-and-mouth disease a serious problem in Mexico? Were there enough government veterinarians? McCarthy spoke with characteristic assurance, and he rarely tolerated dissent. ("Just answer the question, Doctor. Don't give me a speech.") For sheer arrogance, however, nothing quite matched his performance during a routine session on the disposal of a federally owned magnesium plant in Henderson, Nevada. Since Nevada was interested in buying the plant, it had recruited its senior senator, the crusty Pat McCarran, to testify in favor of the sale. Within minutes, McCarthy had caused a stir by asking his colleague to define the limits of Nevada's borrowing power. McCarran hemmed and hawed. Given his reputation, he was not expecting pointed questions. "Senator," Joe lectured his elder, "if you are to be of any value to us at all when you come in and tell us the State of Nevada would like to buy the property, we must know what the borrowing power is. . . . As of now you cannot tell us."

McCarran was insulted. This sort of grilling was clearly beneath him. Yet McCarthy persisted, spurred on by the love of verbal combat. "Were you a lawyer at one time, Senator?" he asked. "I do not know whether I was or not," McCarran shot back, "but I tried to be." The grilling continued. At one point, when McCarran angrily pulled rank, Joe cut him off, saying, "Will you do this for me, in answering? Will you try and stick to the question, and then if you want to make a speech afterward, make it?"[23]

———————

LIKE MOST INCOMING SENATORS, McCarthy searched for an issue to call his own. Initially, he became the defender of America's fighting men. Following World War II, the nation was looking for ways to repay its gallant soldiers. And Joe was one of them, a "decorated" veteran who had experienced the pain and hardship of combat. His favorite speech— delivered to a national radio audience in 1947 and repeated at least fifty times thereafter—was a sensation at legion halls and church breakfasts:

> The whole picture of an early morning is painfully clear before my eyes at this instant. Let me paint it for you. It was before one of our first and roughest bombing attacks on the airfields and shipping in the Rabaul area. All of the pilots and gunners of our dive-bombing squadrons had been crowded into their ready tents. After the briefing had been finished . . . my skipper . . . turned to the chaplain and said, "Chaplain, we know that some of us shall die today. Might you have a few words to say?"
>
> As the chaplain rose, no other sounds could be heard. That chaplain's

body today lies on the floor of a vast moon-swept, wind-tossed Pacific, but his words I know are burned deep into the hearts and minds of each of those young pilots and gunners who still live, and this is what he said:

"If each of you young men shall remember two fundamental truths . . . that there is a God who is eternal, and second, that each of you has a soul which is immortal, then regardless of whether you die within the next few hours or live for another fifty or sixty years, you shall serve yourself, your country, and your God to the last full measure."[24]

When many women were present, he would slip in a paragraph about his heartbreaking task of "writing home to the young wives and mothers. If, as was often the case, I had to explain why the body, having been lost at sea . . . would remain forever unmarked, I might try to tell that unfortunate young woman that the greatest headstone any fighting man could desire would be the vast moonswept, wind-tossed Pacific Ocean." It was very touching, and unreal. McCarthy's unit—VMSB–235—suffered no fatalities and but one injury (a broken arm) in its 8,000 man-hours in the air.

Still, this wartime fantasy might have served some purpose had he really tried to lobby for the veterans. But he didn't. His early proposals were either so self-serving (a bill to preserve the soldiers' wartime tax exemptions) or such publicity grabbers (wheeling paraplegics into the Senate anteroom to lobby for a free home for every crippled veteran), that no one took them seriously. On the substantive issues—price controls, public housing, and federal education benefits—Joe parted company with the veterans' groups. Soon he had moved on to greener pastures. It was impossible to lobby for his comrades, he realized, without supporting all sorts of social-welfare programs that were anathema to conservatives. And this he was unwilling to do.

Yet McCarthy made it *seem* as though his measures were needed to overcome Washington's habitual indifference to the enlisted man. His aim was not to produce remedies but to make the Army and the Congress look bad while establishing himself as a patriotic sort who felt duty-bound to protect the common soldier's welfare. This was an important theme, one that provided a foundation for the senator's later investigations. Joe McCarthy's job, he liked to say, was making sure that decent, God-fearing people were not deceived and abused by the insufferable bureaucrats, the morons, and the traitors who ran America's most powerful institutions. It was a dirty, thankless job that pitted one man against the nation's sacred cows—the State Department, the Army, the labor unions, even the Republican establishment. But what better man to do it than a tough Marine gunner who had risen from the ranks, who had always fought for the rights of the little guy? What better man than Senator Joe McCarthy?

THE "CLASS OF '46" ENTERED the Senate during the period of reconversion, the painful and confusing switch from war to peace. The problems facing Congress seemed endless. Which should be repealed first, price or wage controls? What could be done about labor strikes? How long should the rationing of consumer goods be continued? Would there be enough jobs for the returning veterans? Could a Depression economy made healthy by military production sustain itself once the fighting ended? As expected, Capitol Hill was soon bursting with labor leaders, consumer advocates, and business lobbyists who pressed their conflicting solutions upon the burdened legislators.

One of the first reconversion battles centered on the commodity known as "white gold"—sugar. Like so many consumer goods, it had been strictly rationed during the war. By 1947, however, a combination of interests, led by the soft-drink lobby, was pushing for decontrol. The Administration was eager to oblige, but it wanted to be sure that enough sugar was available to meet the enormous demand. If the commodity remained scarce after rationing ended, its market value would skyrocket, allowing the giant firms to corner the supply and pass on the high cost through hefty price increases, a vicious blow to the average consumer.

The Senate was split over the issue. Those from regions where sugar consumption was unusually high (like New England, with its home-canning tradition) were pitted against colleagues from the sugar-producing states of Louisiana and the upper Midwest. The "consumers," led by Republicans Charles Tobey of New Hampshire and Ralph Flanders of Vermont, wanted a gradual decontrol that ensured equal amounts for industrial users and housewives. The "producers" demanded a quick decontrol with the commodity going to those who could pay the highest price. Since Wisconsin had a large beet-sugar industry, it was natural that McCarthy would support the producers. He did, with a furious display of energy that baffled other Senate members. Before long, word had it that Joe was fronting for the beverage industry. He even picked up a nickname, the Pepsi-Cola Kid.

It was no secret that soft-drink companies were funding the decontrol battle. In desperate need of sugar, they hoped to convince Congress that postwar rationing was unnecessary because no shortage existed, a contention they knew to be false. The company lobbyists were searching for a Senate coordinator, someone to spread this notion while furnishing the obvious legislative remedy. McCarthy was a logical choice. For one thing, he was seen as a hard-nosed politician, the type who would gladly bend the rules or step on a few toes to get things done. For another, he was rumored to be in the sort of trouble that Pepsi-Cola could easily rectify. He was supposedly on the verge of financial collapse.

The rumors were true. When McCarthy returned from the Pacific, he had borrowed large sums to play the stock market, using the stocks themselves as collateral. In 1945 he wrote his friend Matt Schuh at the

Appleton State Bank: "In making my request for a loan of approximately $75,000 in which I will put up as security certain stocks, I am fully aware of the fact that you may find it necessary . . . to dispose of the stocks to protect this loan. If and when that situation should arise, obviously there can be no objection on my part."

By 1947 "that situation" had become a reality. The senator was in over his head. His stocks kept falling in value, lowering both his collateral and his ability to pay the back interest on the loan. As the months passed, moreover, the letters from Matt Schuh, the friendly bank president, grew increasingly desperate in tone: "I would like to hear from you . . ." "Something must be done immediately . . ." "I am really on the spot."

In a state approaching panic, McCarthy contacted Russell Arundel, a Pepsi lobbyist, and obtained a financial transfusion. Arundel endorsed a note for $20,000 to be used as collateral against the senator's loan.* There was nothing illegal about this. Arundel claimed that he was helping a friend, albeit a new friend, and McCarthy insisted that he was serving the interests of the beet growers back home. In 1952, however, a Senate committee would conclude that McCarthy's "acceptance of a $20,000 favor from a Washington representative of the Pepsi-Cola Company at the very time he was attacking the Government for its manner of handling sugar control makes it difficult to determine whether he was working for the best interests of the Government, as he saw it, or for Pepsi-Cola."[25]

It must be noted that politicians frequently receive compensation from the business lobbies. Inside tips, free vacations, the use of company planes, and secret contributions are all part of the game. To single out McCarthy, as many have done, is a bit unfair. It also misses the point. The extraordinary aspect of his role in the sugar controversy was behavioral, not financial. Once he got going, logic and decorum gave way to threats, personal attacks, and multiple distortions.

Joe began by claiming that there was no shortage at all. In a letter to his colleagues, he accused federal authorities of hoarding sugar and "creating planned scarcity." The letter was vintage McCarthy—overblown, self-serving, conspiratorial in tone. His opponents "freely admitted" their errors or made "rather fantastic claims" that were "not only unnecessary but ridiculous." McCarthy, on the other hand, had "spent a great deal

---

* Owner of several Pepsi bottling plants, Russell Arundel, the self-proclaimed Prince of Outer Baldonia (an island he owned off Nova Scotia), was known around Washington for his lavish ways. One stag party he threw for 300 Democrats, including President Truman, was described by the Boston *Herald* as a "two-day frolic which made the Biblical feast Belshazzar look like a White Tower feed." Ironically, the Appleton State Bank eventually rejected Arundel's note, claiming that the lobbyist had few liquid assets. To rectify matters, McCarthy was forced to have his office manager, Ray Kiermas, dip into his own savings account to cover McCarthy's outstanding debts.

of time studying the sugar problem" and was thus in a position to place "a few uncontradictable facts" on record.[26]

During the floor debate, Tobey and Flanders pressed their colleague for proof. Was he sure that enough sugar was available? Joe told them not to worry. According to his figures, the Cuban sugar crop was really 6,137,000 tons, not the 5,000,000 that everyone expected. Now, subtracting 350,000 short tons for Cuban consumption and 300,000 tons of "export free" sugar to Latin America, plus 1,600,000 more to Europe and Japan, America would get the whole Cuban crop, minus 2,250,000 tons. However, the Cuban increase, plus bumper crops in Brazil and Argentina, which canceled out the 300,000 "export free" tons, not to mention the big Hawaiian harvest, "give us 791,000 tons of sugar which we had not counted."[27]

Senator Flanders, a meticulous man, sensed that something was terribly wrong. "The senator from Wisconsin has raised questions so fast," he complained, "that I am having difficulty in keeping up with him." Tobey agreed. "Mr. President," he objected, "I ask the senator to wait a moment. He talks too fast." Faced with mounting suspicion, McCarthy played his trump card. Only moments before, he said, he had received word from the Department of Agriculture that twenty extra pounds of sugar would be allotted to housewives for the canning season. The government was in complete agreement with him: "The sugar is here."

While McCarthy rambled on, boasting of record sugar crops around the world, Tobey slipped from the chamber to phone the Secretary of Agriculture. Had the Secretary authorized McCarthy to state that more sugar was available for home canning? Certainly not, he responded. In fact, the reverse was true; the shortage seemed worse than ever. Tobey returned to the floor in an angry mood:

> The Department of Agriculture's announced position was misrepresented by the senator from Wisconsin today. Here is the answer which came from Secretary Anderson just three minutes ago . . . : "I authorize you to state that I have not, at any time, made a statement that we can give more sugar for home consumption now. . . . There is no more sugar available. . . ." That is Secretary Anderson's statement, and it refutes the statement which has been made by the senator from Wisconsin.

McCarthy had been caught in a lie, which was bad enough. Even worse, a fellow Republican had refused to take him at his word. It was one thing for a senator to question a colleague's interpretation of the facts; it was quite another for him to go behind that colleague's back for their immediate verification. Those present in the chamber were a bit surprised. Charlie Tobey was known as a man who played by the rules. It wasn't like him to get quite this rough.

Joe had no such reputation to protect. He took the floor with one thought in mind, getting even. Having just used Secretary Anderson to firm up his case, he now debunked him as an unreliable source. ("I don't give a tinker's dam what . . . Anderson says about the matter.") McCarthy then turned on Tobey and Flanders, charging that they had personally told him of their intention "to introduce some type of fictitious amendment which . . . will do nothing more nor less than deceive the housewife." Bedlam followed. Flanders rose from his desk, but a red-faced Tobey grabbed the floor "on a matter of personal privilege." "I heard the statement by the senator from Wisconsin," he said. "My hearing is fairly good. . . . He charged that my amendment is deceptive and fictitious. I take exception to his derogatory remarks. His statement, I submit, far contravenes the truth, to put it plainly."

McCarthy's colleagues were dubious of his allegation. Many suspected that, having been caught in one falsehood, he was trying to redeem himself with another. And it was common knowledge that his statistics were coming straight from the soft drink lobby, a group determined to prove that a surplus existed. Unfortunately, most senators were tired of the whole issue. Joe may not have been a believable advocate, but he was pushing a cause that Pepsi-Cola and a majority of Americans seemed to want—sugar decontrol, the sooner the better. They therefore supported his "compromise" amendment, which brought an end to sugar rationing five months earlier than had been anticipated.

Tobey was furious.

> The speculators are being put on notice that the doors are ajar. The flood-gates of speculative profit are open to greedy hearts. . . . I want the country to know where the blame lies. It lies with a group in my own party, in the Republican Party, who have been trying to sabotage this measure at every possible opportunity.

Although Joe had won a limited victory, he emerged from the fracas with a tarnished image. "The observance of Senate folkways," one historian has written, "requires patience, restraint, and moderation."[28] Younger members, especially, are expected to abide by the rules, show loyalty to party, courtesy to elders, and deference to the established customs. McCarthy's behavior toward Tobey, Flanders, McCarran, and Downey was hardly in that tradition. He seemed brash and restless, incapable of patient waiting or sober public dialogue. Though he had been in the Senate for only a few months, his colleagues began to mark him as a troublemaker. And Joe was only warming up.

———

WHEN THE WAR ENDED and millions of servicemen returned to civilian life, America discovered a new reconversion headache, the housing shortage. Washington, D.C., reported 25,000 homeless veterans, Chicago more than 100,000. In Atlanta 2,000 people answered a single rental notice. An Omaha newspaper ad read, "Big Ice Box, 7 by 17 feet. Could be fixed up to live in." North Dakota veterans took to living in converted grain bins. One returning serviceman bitterly summed up the feelings of his buddies: "It's the same old story. You fight a goddamn war and you finally come home and everybody slaps you on the back and tells you what a wonderful job you did and all that crap, but when it comes to really doing something, then nobody's home. All you get is words."[29]

Conservatively speaking, about 5 million families were seeking homes in 1945, although 75 percent of them could not afford more than $50 a month in rent or $6,000 for a house. When President Truman removed controls on building materials, a construction boom did occur. The problem, as Housing Expediter Wilson Wyatt noted, was that it resulted in "a rash of race tracks, mansions, summer resorts, bowling alleys, stores, and cocktail bars. Yes, it was a fine building boom, except nobody much was bothering to build any homes that veterans could afford." To remedy the situation, the Senate passed the Taft–Ellender–Wagner bill, which provided 1.25 million new housing units per year for the next decade. It called for easy loans for veterans, incentives for private construction, slum clearance, and 500,000 public housing units.[30]

As expected, the real estate lobby was dead set against the bill. Using its enormous influence in the House of Representatives, the lobby helped to bury the bill there. In an effort to reach some sort of compromise, a joint congressional committee was created to study the housing problem "from A to Z." Among its members was the man who had suggested the idea, Wisconsin's Joe McCarthy.[31]

The senator made no secret of his plans to run the committee. Its chairman and vice chairman, he knew, would travel throughout the nation, garner tremendous publicity, and work closely with the rich and politically powerful real estate interests. "Seldom has a freshman senator been presumptuous enough to demand the chairmanship of a joint congressional committee over the heads of his seniors," wrote one Washington columnist of Joe's early maneuvering. "But that is what bumptious Senator McCarthy is trying to do when it comes to investigating housing." There was only one obstacle, New Hampshire's Charlie Tobey. As the committee's ranking Republican, he was theoretically entitled to the chairmanship. Still smarting from the sugar battle, Tobey was not about to let his abrasive junior colleague push him aside.[32]

So Joe concocted one of the most ingenious power plays of the Eightieth Congress. It began when Tobey returned to visit his ailing wife in New Hampshire. In his absence, McCarthy polled the committee members about a date for the initial meeting. He discovered that on August 19, six days hence, several public-housing supporters would be out of town. Acting on his own authority, he notified the House members that a date had been agreed upon—August 19. He then informed Tobey that the House members were expecting to meet on August 19, and he suggested that the Senate members be notified as well. Joe's letter was quite conciliatory, even offering to postpone the session at Tobey's request. ("Obviously if you desire to be here for the original and all important spade work, none of us will desire to hold the meeting without you.") But it intimated that everyone was *expecting* to meet on August 19.[33]

Tobey was trapped. He did not want to leave his wife. Her condition was critical. But he did want to be chairman, and he assumed that the decision to meet so quickly represented the committee's collective will. Reluctantly, he returned to Washington.

The "all important spade work" was the matter of choosing the chairman and vice chairman. Arriving in Washington on August 18, Tobey collected the proxies of several committee supporters who could not attend the meeting. This assured him of the chairmanship, or so he thought. The next day, McCarthy outflanked him by moving that all proxies be rejected. "Outrageous," bellowed Wright Patman of Texas. Why, every joint committee for the past twenty years had accepted them. And Tobey could hardly control himself. "This comes with little grace from you," he yelled, pointing an angry finger at Joe. "You, who dared to use proxies time after time during the sugar controversy, sometimes when you didn't have them and got assent afterward."[34]

McCarthy refused to budge, and his motion carried by a small margin. Representative Ralph Gamble, an obscure New York Republican, was elected chairman, while Joe graciously accepted the vice chairmanship. Outside the hearing room, Gamble confessed surprise at his good fortune. "I didn't have the remotest thought of being chairman," he admitted. "I certainly didn't seek it. It was thrust upon me, you might say."

McCarthy was elated. After telling reporters that Tobey would have made a poor chairman, he rushed over to shake his hand. Tobey refused. "You have the chairmanship by a minority vote," he fumed. "This child is born as a result of malpractice." Joe said nothing, but a week later, when Tobey's wife died, he sent his colleague a warm and no doubt heartfelt note of condolence.[35]

Gamble turned out to be a figurehead. The committee's staff, its activities, and its hearings were directed by McCarthy. Traveling more than 30,000 miles, he waged a relentless campaign against public housing. His committee sessions were loaded with real estate lobbyists, private builders, and prefabricated housing experts, whose testimony about the evils of federal intervention received fawning attention. The few public-housing advocates were treated with outright hostility. Before long, letters of protest began filtering back to Washington. "I wish to document the un-American manner in which Senator McCarthy conducted the housing probe in Pittsburgh," a woman wrote to Tobey. "He left no doubt that he is opposed to the T-E-W Bill. . . . He was gracious with the Real Estate and Building Representatives, but unfair and arbitrary to those who tried to present the real problems in housing here and the means with which to remedy the situation." [36]

No one was surprised. By that time Joe had already blamed public housing for broken homes, more divorces, and an increase in juvenile delinquency. Its supporters, he claimed, were mainly "left wingers and extremists." In Rego Park, New York, he visited a public-housing project and called it "a breeding ground for Communism." The place, McCarthy told reporters, "was built over a garbage disposal area. Wives of veterans were wading in mud up to their ankles to hang out the washing. I, myself, saw four dead rats." [37]

On several occasions, he accepted large fees ($500 plus expenses) to speak at real estate conventions. According to the man who invited him to address the Association of Building Standards in Columbus, Ohio, the visit was like nothing he had ever experienced. Having been in town for less than an hour, McCarthy was already borrowing money to shoot craps in his hotel room.

> It was a disgusting sight to see this great public servant down on his hands and knees, reeking of whiskey, and shouting, "Come on babies, Papa needs a new pair of shoes." He did stop long enough between rolls to look over the gals his aides brought to him: on some, he turned thumbs down, but if one suited his fancy, he'd say, "That's the baby, I'll take care of her just as soon as I break you guys." The baby in question sat patiently on the bed, awaiting her chances for a ten-dollar bill. I overheard McCarthy tell one aide to keep a couple of others around just in case. If these statements are denied, one or more of the gals who were there are eager to testify as to what they saw. Be that as it may, Mr. McCarthy was up bright and early on Sunday morning, looking none the worse for wear and tear, and inquiring about the best route to the nearest Catholic church. [38]

When Joe returned to Washington, he, Congressman Gamble, and some experts from Bell, Jones, and Taylor (the real estate lobby's public relations firm) sat down to write the committee's final report. The result, a twenty-page diatribe against public housing, was judged unacceptable by the other members. "Why, you'd think only Rabbis, Priests and Communists had any use for public housing," one senator remarked. After a toned-down version was again rejected, Tobey, Flanders, and Wagner rammed through a majority report, recommending 500,000 public housing units, local slum clearance projects, and the formulation of a national housing policy. This massive act of insubordination so disturbed Gamble that he reportedly broke down and wept. [39]

McCarthy refused to give up. Instead he published his "Individual Views" on the subject, which ignored slum clearance but supported the idea of public housing for "low-income groups"—those who could not afford to purchase a prefabricated modular home. In addition, McCarthy stressed the need for easy mortgage money, lighter corporation taxes, and land grants to builders who entered the middle-income field.

The Senate supported the Majority Report; the House opposed it. Faced with the prospect of no bill at all, Congress passed the McCarthy substitute, a carbon copy of his "Individual Views." President Truman reluctantly signed it into law on August 11, 1948. "Because it will be of some help in meeting the critical housing shortage, I am giving it my approval," Truman said, "but the people of this country should understand that it falls far short of the legislation which could and should have been enacted."[40]

Had this been the end of the story, one might be content to portray McCarthy as a close friend of the real estate lobby. There was, on the surface, nothing illegal or even unusual about his activities. They were part and parcel of the warm and depressingly normal relationship between lobbyists and politicians. But the story was only beginning, and the more it unfolded the seamier it became. Early in 1949 the senator called a press conference to announce that an article he had written on the housing shortage had been purchased by the Lustron Corporation, a manufacturer of prefabricated homes. The author's fee, he told reporters, was "embarrassingly small. Besides I have split it with ten people who helped me."[41]

When Lustron declared bankruptcy the following year (squandering $37 million in government credits), the Senate Banking Committee began a full-scale investigation. Among its findings was a canceled check for $10,000 made out to Joe McCarthy. The senator, it turned out, had approached Lustron President Carl Strandlund about the possibility of marketing his article in pamphlet form. Since Strandlund was then negotiating a multimillion-dollar federal loan, he readily accepted the proposal. McCarthy's article was not "in publishable form," but a contract was signed whereby Lustron agreed to print 10,000 copies, sell them for 35 cents each, and give Joe a dime for every one purchased. As an advance on royalties, the senator was given the "embarrassingly small" sum of $10,000. In the end only 20,000 copies were printed, and most were distributed free of charge. Lustron lost $8,412 on the venture.*[42]

---

* It turned out that Strandlund had also cashed checks for McCarthy at race tracks in the Washington area. "It was just an accommodation and I didn't even know the senator." Strandlund said. "I probably wouldn't have cashed his checks, but his colleagues were also a little short of funds, so I volunteered. . . ." At the time, McCarthy was the vice chairman of the Joint Committee on Housing and a member of the Banking subcommittee that was reviewing the federal loans to Lustron. See U.S. Congress, Senate, 81st Cong., 2d sess., Senate Committee on Banking and Currency, Subcommittee on the Reconstruction Finance Corporation, *Study of the Reconstruction Finance Corporation, Lustron Corporation*, 1950, pp. 198–208.

The investigation turned up another interesting fact: McCarthy had not written the article. The real work—the research, writing, and editing —was done by employees of Lustron and the Federal Housing Authority. Nor, for that matter, had McCarthy split the fee with the "ten people" who helped him. A check of his tax returns showed the full $10,000 listed as earned income.[43]

This money was important to McCarthy. He had promised it to the Appleton State Bank, which was dunning him for more margin and demanding the back interest on his notes. "I will naturally be glad to assign the book royalties to the bank," he wrote the weary Matt Schuh in 1949. "I assure you that any monies received . . . will be immediately applied in full measure to improve the picture."

But McCarthy did not use this money to clear up his loan. Instead, he sent in to Wayne Hummer and Company as partial payment for 2,000 shares (at $22 per share) of the Seaboard Airlines Railroad, a company that owed the government millions and hadn't paid a dividend in eighteen years. In 1951 he sold 1,000 shares for a net profit of $35,600 but held on to the rest. By 1953 Seaboard was quoted on the New York Stock Exchange at 113. In this instance, at least, the senator's "tip" had paid off handsomely indeed.[44]

McCarthy's involvement with Lustron was in some ways similar to his dealings with Pepsi-Cola. In neither case did he violate the letter of the law or waver from the established conservative line. (Most Republicans were opposed to public housing and to continued sugar rationing.) What made him unique, however, were the reasons for his devotion to these causes and the manner in which he championed them. The driving force behind young McCarthy was, to some extent, financial. He needed money to cover his debts and his insatiable desire to gamble—at cards, at the track, in the stock market. But he was motivated as well by a need to confront established authority in a way that made *him* the center of attention. Where freshman senators usually seek the favor of influential colleagues with gestures of caution and respect, McCarthy took them on in raucous, often insulting public spectacles. Where freshman senators readily accept the ground rules—the creaking seniority system, the notions of courtesy, formal procedure, and team play—he went it alone, bowing to them when they served his purpose, trampling on them when they did not. Where *all* senators play up their familial attachments or remain discreet about their private lives, he accentuated his vices in ways that offended some colleagues and certainly baffled the rest. While this odd behavior may have aided his early successes, it also isolated him and established his reputation as a renegade. By any standard, his future prospects did not look good.

CHAPTER FIVE

Rock Bottom

By 1949, AFTER TWO YEARS IN THE UNITED STATES SENATE, Joe Mc-Carthy had reached a dangerous political crossroads. His early career could not have been more promising. The son of farm people, he had worked his way through high school, college, and law school. From there, he had pulled off an "astounding upset" to become the youngest judge in the history of the Tenth Judicial Circuit. After a well-publicized hitch in the Marine Corps, he returned home to engineer "the political coup of '46," a remarkable primary victory over Robert LaFollette, Jr. His horizons seemed unlimited. He was young, bright, hard-working, and frighteningly ambitious. Even the hostile Milwaukee *Journal* acknowledged his potential in a postelection editorial: "Joe McCarthy has it in him to be a good senator. . . . He is possessed of great vigor and personal charm. He is where he is today because of the efforts of Joe McCarthy and should be beholden to no man. . . . If he will use his talents and his experience . . . he can have a bright future in the U.S. Senate." [1]

But McCarthy's record in the upper chamber was disappointing. His scuffles with Tobey, Flanders, and McCarran had marked him as an "outsider" who could not work well with fellow members. In a damaging assessment, columnist Drew Pearson mocked Joe's early accomplishments. "He came to the Senate with more publicity build-up than any colleague, but fizzled faster. He worked hard for Pepsi-Cola sugar decon-

72

trol, preached aid to veterans but consistently voted with the real estate lobby against them, talked more and did less constructive work than any new congressman except Ohio's John Bricker." Even worse, Senator Burnet Maybank, a conservative Democrat, demanded that McCarthy be removed from the Banking and Currency Committee. "He's a trouble-maker, that's why I don't want him," snapped the South Carolinian, in attempting to strip Joe of his only major committee assignment. "I told [Majority Leader] Scott Lucas that I don't want McCarthy on any com-mittee that I was chairman of and that if he wanted me to be chairman, not to put McCarthy on it."[2]

Maybank got his wish. When the committee assignments for 1949 were announced, Joe was dropped from his Banking and Currency post and reassigned to the lowly District of Columbia Committee. He re-sponded by firing off an angry note to Senator Hugh Butler, Republican chairman of the Committee on Committees. "I feel it was unreasonable to the point of being ludicrous," he complained, "that a senator with three important committees . . . is given a fourth as against a senator who does not have any." When no remedial action was taken, he asked Robert Taft to intervene. "I am the only Republican singled out for no major committee which . . . will be extremely embarrassing to me in my state," wrote Joe, in a letter that was, for once, almost pathetically def-erential. "I know it is needless to tell you . . . I shall certainly appreciate it." Taft refused to lift a finger. In 1949, at least, he saw no reason to help a junior colleague with a big mouth and a knack for making powerful enemies.[3]

McCarthy was clearly rankled by the failure of right-wing Republi-cans to come to his defense. Despite his abusive behavior, he felt that he had been a good party man. His voting record on domestic legislation, for example, was one of the most conservative in the Senate. During this period he consistently supported tax cuts for the wealthy, restrictive labor legislation, and smaller federal budgets. On the other hand, he voted against federal aid to education, public housing, and public power appro-priations. Of the seventy-five senators who remained in continuous ser-vice from 1947 through 1949, sixty-six had more liberal voting records (according to the Congress of Industrial Organizations). McCarthy was tied with Taft, both being ninth from the bottom. Joe viewed that record as the true mark of party loyalty, and he expected to be rewarded for his efforts. When the opposite occurred, he complained that the Republican establishment had sold him out.[4]

What would have happened, one might ask, had the GOP leadership been more conciliatory and attempted to straighten out McCarthy by involving him in committee matters, party policy decisions, and the like? Rather than chastising his rude behavior, might they have been better off trying to woo him through a series of political rewards? Perhaps, but the evidence suggests that Joe rarely modified his public stance in the face of harmonious gestures. He was brash and defiant before his Senate rebuke in 1949, and he would remain that way long after he was rewarded with a committee chairmanship in 1952. It seems unlikely that any manner of accommodation would have radically altered the man's behavior. But neither did the punishment meted out by Hugh Butler and Burnet Maybank. To strip a colleague of his major committee assignments, they reasoned, was one sure way of curing him or, at least, of containing his ability to commit mayhem. This strategy backfired; McCarthy's behavior got worse, not better, in 1949, and his disrespect for the Senate's traditional folkways increased dramatically. In fact, it set the stage for the most outrageous episode of Joe's early senatorial career, the Malmedy Massacre investigation.

━━━━━

DURING THE BITTER EUROPEAN WINTER OF 1944, the German armies on the western front had begun their last offensive of World War II. In the midst of the desperate Battle of the Bulge, an elite battalion of the German First S.S. Panzer Division captured several hundred American soldiers near the Belgian village of Malmedy and brutally mowed them down with machine guns. Following Germany's surrender, seventy-three S.S. troopers were convicted by an American war-crimes court for their participation in the massacre, and forty-three were sentenced to be hanged. After a series of legal delays, the condemned men petitioned the U.S. Supreme Court, claiming that false confessions had been beaten out of them by sadistic American prosecutors. Simultaneously, a new investigation by the Office of Judge Advocate discovered that the prosecutors, while eschewing physical torture, had engaged in certain questionable practices. It recommended that the death sentences be commuted to life imprisonment.[5]

These revelations caused a minor sensation on Capitol Hill. A few senators with vocal German–American constituencies expressed concern for the condemned soldiers. Several more demanded that the butchers of American POWs get their full measure of punishment. Before long, the Senate Armed Services Committee agreed to have a look at the controversy. It formed a three-man subcommittee, chaired by Connecticut Republican Raymond Baldwin, and including Democrats Lester Hunt of Wyoming and Estes Kefauver of Tennessee. Baldwin routinely encouraged all of his colleagues to participate in the deliberations. But only one took the offer seriously, Wisconsin's Joe McCarthy. As a gesture of courtesy, the chairman allowed Joe to submit a list of prospective witnesses and to cross-examine those called by the subcommittee. It was a gesture he would long regret.

Historians have often wondered why McCarthy took such an interest in the hearings and, particularly, why he chose to defend the condemned soldiers. There are no simple answers, just speculations. The senator came from a state with a large, wealthy, and politically conservative German–American population. In many areas, it formed the backbone of the Stalwart Republican movement. While most German–Americans were undoubtedly sickened by Malmedy, a goodly number felt that a new investigation—particularly one by a committee partial to the U.S. Army—would serve to inflame anti-German feelings in America and anti-American feelings in Germany. On the eve of the hearings, Alexander Wiley, Wisconsin's senior senator, warned Baldwin to "watch out for this fellow McCarthy." After thanking Wiley for his concern, Baldwin asked the obvious question: Why was McCarthy so interested in the Malmedy affair? "Ray," Wiley told his colleague, "there are an awful lot of Germans in Milwaukee."[6]

According to some accounts, McCarthy was pushed into Malmedy by members of the wealthy Harnischfeger family, which manufactured heavy machinery and prefabricated homes. A nephew, Frederick von Schleinitz, had strutted around the University of Wisconsin, telling of his family's great admiration for Hitler and proudly exhibiting a copy of *Mein Kampf* that the Fuehrer had autographed for him. Walter Harnischfeger, whose company was cited for refusing to employ Jews and blacks, had lobbied for a negotiated peace with Germany during World War II. In 1948 he denounced the Nuremberg Trials as "worse than anything Hitler ever did. It beats Dachau." A *Capital–Times* reporter wrote to Abe Fortas in 1950:

> For some time, McCarthy's patron in Wisconsin among the big industrialists has been Walter Harnischfeger, a prominent Milwaukee Republican. Harnischfeger has very close connections with elements in Germany that were very close to the Hitler crowd. . . . I attended a meeting here in Madison at which he [Harnischfeger] spoke two years ago urging help for the German people. In the course of that speech, which he made in a state of rather advanced intoxication, he made reference to the fact that Germany was in a desperate plight because it was "once again being turned back to the masses . . ." I have heard from various sources of his affinity for the Nazi ideology.[7]

Joe's relationship with Harnischfeger is difficult to assess. Having won him over during the LaFollette campaign, McCarthy had kept his trust by voting properly in the Senate and doing what he could to serve the industrialist's needs, particularly in the field of prefabricated housing. In return, Harnischfeger had responded generously whenever the senator needed his help. ("I have made complete arrangements with Walter Harnischfeger . . . to put up sufficient collateral to cure both our ulcers," he wrote the Appleton State Bank in 1947.) Still, the evidence linking Harnischfeger, McCarthy, and Malmedy is circumstantial at best. As the hearings began, Thomas Korb came to Washington to help Joe "reorganize" his office. Korb was an old friend from Marquette. He was also Harnischfeger's attorney.[8]

It is possible, too, that McCarthy's recent humiliation by the Committee on Committees led him into the Malmedy affair. Bitter at the loss of his committee assignments ("a foul deal," he complained to Taft), he was determined to strike back at his tormentors. The Armed Services Committee was a natural target. As a prestigious body, manned by dependable party regulars like Baldwin, it existed mainly to support the whims of the Pentagon and to uphold the military's popular image. Its role in the Malmedy investigation would be predictable enough: play up German atrocities, ignore American abuses, protect the Army's good name. Anyone who took the opposite position was bound to upset the Senate leadership and to make a few headlines. Apparently, Joe was in the mood to do both.[9]

One of McCarthy's more remarkable traits, it had been noted, was an instinct for detecting, and then exploiting, the political weaknesses of his opponents. This was clearly the case with the Baldwin subcommittee. Its members, Joe sensed, could not easily cope with a sustained attack from the outside. The two Democrats were virtually useless. Kefauver, a bright and normally diligent senator, seemed uninterested in the Malmedy affair. He attended only two of the first fifteen hearings. Hunt came to nine, but his innocuous contributions added little substance to the debate. Baldwin, on the other hand, was extremely knowledgeable about Malmedy, having followed it from the beginning. The only trouble with him, as McCarthy divulged in public session, was that a member of his Connecticut law firm had been one of the Malmedy prosecutors. When an embarrassed Baldwin offered to relinquish his chairmanship, the full Armed Services Committee gave him a strong vote of confidence. Baldwin agreed to remain, but the "conflict of interest" charge hampered his ability to run an effective hearing.[10]

Backed by the likes of Walter Harnishfeger, spoiling for a fight with the Senate establishment, looking to make a few headlines, sensing the vulnerability of the Malmedy probers—the motives for Joe's bizarre defense of S.S. troopers seem rather plausible. But there is one nagging question, a question that McCarthy's critics have generally avoided asking. Is it possible, just *possible*, that the senator came to the defense of those soldiers because he believed they were being denied due process? Is there a chance that his motives were in the best tradition of American justice?

A careful study of the Malmedy transcript shows that they weren't. Throughout the hearings, McCarthy bullied witnesses, made scores of erroneous statements, exaggerated his evidence, and turned almost every session into a barroom brawl. At the same time, however, he demonstrated that Baldwin and Hunt were no more interested in an impartial investigation than he was. Their manners were better, their tone more subdued, but they were determined to exonerate the Army at all costs, just as Joe was determined to prove its culpability.

The gist of McCarthy's argument went something like this: When the war ended, the U.S. Army rounded up as many First S.S. Panzer Division soldiers as it could and charged them indiscriminately with taking part in the massacre. Confessions were obtained through force: Jaws and teeth were broken by rifle butts, men were permanently disabled by kicks to the groin, and mock trials were held in a style reminiscent of the Ku Klux Klan. This was hardly surprising since most of the prosecutors attached to the case were "39ers," Jewish refugees who had fled the Nazis and who "intensely hated the German people as a race." Those prosecutors were not the real villains, however. They were men with overwhelming grievances against the Nazis, men whose bitter memories had been shamefully exploited by their military superiors. Needless to say, the confessions they obtained were worthless. "I assume that you and I would agree," Joe lectured one witness, "that an innocent man will scream about as loudly as a guilty man if you are kicking him in the testicles, and an innocent man will perhaps sign the same confession that a guilty man will if you kick him long enough and hard enough." * 11

McCarthy came at his adversaries from every possible angle. At times he was open and friendly, cutting through those tedious formalities that burden all Senate hearings. He used first names when he could, apologized profusely for his sinus condition, and twice offered to bet Chairman Baldwin "the best steak dinner he can order" when they clashed over obscure bits of testimony. But those were exceptional moments. Since Joe was trying to prove that the prosecutors had covered up their own criminal acts, he had to shake their testimony by portraying them as pathetic liars. His demeanor, therefore, was necessarily belligerent. He complained that witnesses were "hedging" on him, giving evasive and untruthful answers. "Be very careful and give us the facts," he warned

---

* Most of McCarthy's "evidence" came from the Catholic bishop of Munich, who heard secondhand of the alleged abuses; a mentally unstable German dentist, who treated the S.S. troopers; an American judge, of German extraction, who made serious allegations of mistreatment in a magazine article and later claimed, under sharp examination from Senator Baldwin, never to have written the piece; and the Malmedy troopers themselves. This information was collected by the National Council for Prevention of War, a Quaker-run group and a tireless advocate of American isolationism. It later came to light, much to Joe's embarrassment, that one of the NCFPW's key German sources, Rudolf Aschenauer, was probably a Communist agent, using the Malmedy affair to drum up anti-American sentiment in Germany. Joe swore later that he had no direct contact with Aschenauer. How much he knew about the man at the time of the hearings is not known. See U.S. Senate, 81st Cong., 1st sess., *Malmedy Massacre Investigation*, pp. 225–69; 860, 981, 1432–66; Anderson and May, *McCarthy*, pp. 162–63; Edward L. Van Roden, "American Atrocities in Germany," *The Progressive*, February, 1949, pp. 21–22.

one of them. "I'm going to get this from you if I keep you here a week," he said to another. "I think you are lying," he told a third. "I have been a judge so long that it makes me rather sick down inside to hear you testify about what you think is proper and improper," he lectured a fourth.[12]

McCarthy's language was shrill and exaggerated. Events were "fantastic," "unbelievable," "incredible," and "phenomenal." The condemned soldiers got progressively younger during the hearings. Joe claimed that many were "eighteen and seventeen," then "sixteen and seventeen," and finally "young fifteen- and sixteen-year-old boys, many of whom never even went through grade school." The military courts in Germany were run by "brainless" and "imbecilic" American judges. ("I think this committee should see what type of morons—and I use that term advisedly—are running the military courts over there.") Still, despite his limited resources, he was slowly unraveling the coverup. ("I don't have any staff of investigators; all I do is get reports from interested parties.") And the American public was responding enthusiastically. ("Also, Mr. Chairman, I've been getting a tremendous amount of mail.")

This was not the worst of it. At one point Joe described the 39ers as "non-Aryan refugees." At another point he asked a witness, "If you were a German would you feel that you would be willing to have a matter of life and death decided by this man Rosenfeld?" A bit later he attacked the American judges at Nuremberg who had sentenced Baron Ernst von Weizsacker, a prominent Nazi official, to seven years in prison for "war crimes" that included the deportation of thousands of French Jews to the death camps in Poland. McCarthy called von Weizsacker "our prime listening post in Britain in 1936 . . . our No. 1 spy"—a claim that must have astonished the Baron, who offered not a hint of such behavior in his otherwise self-serving memoirs published in 1951.[13]

Baldwin was furious with Joe, viewing his behavior as an attempt to exonerate sadists at the expense of the Army's good name. The two clashed repeatedly, with McCarthy scoring the more potent blows. In one exchange, Baldwin insisted that the Army had acted "with malice toward none and charity toward all," and asked "what chance for an appeal and review the men had who gave their lives at the Malmedy crossroads and were shot down in cold blood." Joe's response: "I assume you [Baldwin] would have difficulty persuading those sixteen- or seventeen-year-old boys who were kicked in the testicles, crippled for life, that the 39ers were operating with malice toward none and charity toward all. One thing the Army has proven so far is that it acted with the utmost malice."[14]

McCarthy brought the hearings to a climax by demanding that the Malmedy prosecutors be given lie detector tests. "I have the utmost confidence in them," he declared. ". . . If these men under a lie detector show they are telling the truth, as far as I am concerned, I do not think we need to go any further." Of course, should Baldwin refuse this demand, the American people would know that the hearings were a sham, a complete "whitewash" of the Army. Baldwin took the bait. He promised to take up the proposal with the Armed Services Committee at once.[15]

That was precisely what Joe wanted. He knew that the full committee, loaded as it was with military supporters, would never allow such tests to be administered. In the first place, the lie detector was relatively new, and its findings were inadmissible in most American courts. Besides, if any of the prosecutors flunked the test, the credibility of all would become suspect. To no one's surprise, the committee issued a flat rejection, thereby strengthening the charge that Baldwin and his cohorts were out to protect the Army at all costs.

The next day Joe announced his decision to withdraw from all future sessions. It was simply impossible, he lamented, to overcome the prejudice that dominated the subcommittee's thinking. Baldwin was livid. His words of rebuttal came out at the slow-motion rate of a man struggling to regain his composure. He regretted that McCarthy had "lost his temper and with it the sound impartial judgment which should be exercised in this matter." And he thought it reprehensible that a colleague should accuse American soldiers of lying, while blandly "accepting and espousing the affidavits made by convicted German war criminals some two years after completion of their trials."[16]

Joe made no attempt to interrupt, although the attack against him lasted for perhaps fifteen minutes. When it ended, though, he could not resist a quick parting shot. Rather than shouting across the room, or matching insult for insult, he cleverly magnified Baldwin's anger by thanking him for his courtesy. "The chairman is so fair and honest," he purred, "that the day will come when he is going to regret this deliberate . . . attempt to whitewash. I think it is shameful . . . and inexcusable. Goodbye, sir." He then scooped up his papers and walked sternly from the room, his face a mask of righteous indignation.[17]

Richard Rovere collared Joe in the outside corridor that afternoon and followed him up to his Senate office to see "why he was in such a stew." Once there, McCarthy began feeding him an unending series of affidavits, photostats, and news clippings related to the "coverup." When Rovere commented that they seemed like rather routine documents, proving little if anything about the case, Joe nodded in vigorous agreement. "You're certainly right about that. Don't get me wrong, now. I didn't mean you'd find the *whole* story there." Another flood of documents would follow, equally irrelevant, equally obscure. Finally, Rovere asked the senator if he could *prove* that it was the Americans, not the Germans, who were lying. Joe flashed a knowing smile. "You've put your finger on it. Those are precisely the facts that Baldwin and the Administration don't want me to bring out. That's why I walked out of that hearing. They're concealing all the evidence." Rovere left the office with an uneasy feeling, the kind that comes when one misunderstands a simple conversation and blames himself for the communication gap. "I was not aware then," he admitted, "of having been switched, conned, and double-shuffled by one of the masters." [18]

Joe was not quite finished. On July 26, 1949, he took the Senate floor to accuse Baldwin of whitewashing the Army prosecutors in order to vindicate his law partner. Other senators—including Hunt and Kefauver —loudly protested McCarthy's violation of the upper chamber's rule against personal attacks on fellow members. And in an unprecedented move, the Armed Services Committee passed a resolution expressing confidence in the way Baldwin had conducted the hearings. ("We, his colleagues, take this unusual step . . . because of the most unusual, unfair, and utterly undeserved comments . . . that have been made concerning Senator Baldwin and his work as chairman of his subcommittee.") It was signed by some very powerful members, including Democrats Lyndon Johnson, Richard Russell, Millard Tydings, and Republicans Styles Bridges and Leverett Saltonstall. [19]

As expected, the Baldwin subcommittee *did* exonerate the Army. While condemning minor judicial abuses, it concluded that the German soldiers were tried fairly and given every possible opportunity to appeal. (The Army eventually commuted all the remaining death sentences.) According to most accounts, the Malmedy episode so upset Baldwin that he decided to quit the Senate in favor of an appointment to the Connecticut Supreme Court. Actually, he had announced his resignation before the hearings started. But he did say later that the drubbing he took from McCarthy had reaffirmed the wisdom of his decision to resign. [20]

MCCARTHY'S ODD SENATORIAL BEHAVIOR was also reflected in a noticeable loss of popularity back home. Although he had been helpful to certain groups in Wisconsin—the fur industry, the sugar beet growers, and right-wing German–Americans—most constituents viewed him with indifference or disdain. The Stalwart community took his conservative voting record for granted, claiming that he was only doing what was expected of him. But it was clearly disturbed by his abusive public assaults and by the way other Senate conservatives like Taft and Butler openly shunned his company. Worse still, a series of quick hammer blows—the income tax controversy, the Supreme Court censure, and the "divorce mill" stories—had served to portray the senator as a shady character, a man with real ethical problems, none of which spoke well for the folks who elected him. "How long" fumed the *Capital–Times*, "is this fellow McCarthy to be permitted to toy with . . . the prestige and majesty of the great state of Wisconsin?"[21]

Not long at all, experts agreed. Most viewed Joe as a sure loser in 1952. A pro-McCarthy journalist expressed the common belief that the senator "has slipped badly. . . . Always a plunger and rarely discreet, he has been marked off by some . . . politicians in the Republican organization." A *Capital–Times* reporter claimed to be "frightened at the fury with which some of Joe's old champions denounce him. Things have come to such a pass that I have found myself on rare occasions uttering a word in his defense." One GOP senatorial hopeful boasted that he could probably "take Alexander Wiley in 1950, but I'll wait for the easy one in 1952." The "easy one," of course, was Joe McCarthy.[22]

The senator reacted angrily to this criticism. It was unfair, he thought, for Stalwarts to sit on their hands, while moderate and liberal types gleefully assassinated his character. Indeed, he wrote a friend, his public reputation as a hustler and a "reactionary bastard" was the work of irresponsible newspapers like the *Capital–Times*. The letter exemplified the level of McCarthy's frustration, for it contained an uncharacteristic racial slur ("lower than a darky with a shovel and hoe") and concluded that the Communist Party was somehow responsible for the nation's ills—a notion that often surfaced when Joe smelled trouble. He even fired off an angry letter to the University of Wisconsin's student newspaper, *The Cardinal*, after it mocked him in a fictitious interview with "Mr. Joe Frump." "Although you obviously did not intend your readers to take 'his' remarks as an earnest discussion of important matters," he wrote, testily refuting this feeble attempt at satire, "his statements could well have misled some students." Attached was a tedious three-page letter outlining McCarthy's legislative accomplishments.[23]

Undoubtedly, Joe's most irritating critic was the *Capital–Times*. In 1946 it had tried to block his senatorial nomination by raising the "judge-in-politics" issue. During the McMurray campaign, it had broken the "quickie divorce" story. When he went to Washington, it had initiated the censure and disbarment proceedings against him. Joe was itching to get even, and in 1949 he did just that by attacking the newspaper for its "pro-Moscow slant" and by calling its city editor, Cedric Parker, a "Red." Once again, McCarthy had decided to test the murky waters of political anti-Communism.

It should be stressed here that, contrary to popular opinion, the senator did not "discover" the Communist issue in February 1950. He had used it effectively against Howard McMurray in 1946, and he continued to employ it with some regularity during his early Senate years. On a superficial level, McCarthy would get an occasional headline by claiming that the supporters of public housing were Reds, or by arguing that fur imports from Communist-bloc nations were subsidizing Russian spy op-

erations in America. On a more serious level, he became a strong advocate of bills to register subversive organizations, and he helped to direct
the congressional movement to force the Communist Party off the ballot. "I do not think the Communist Party is ever legal," Joe told Warren
Magnuson, the Washington Democrat, in one Senate exchange, "and I
submit that any man who joins the Communist Party, knowing that it is
dedicated to the overthrow of the government by force, is guilty of treason the minute he joins it."[24]

In 1947, on the nationwide radio show "Town Meeting of the Air,"
McCarthy argued this position with a mixture of Catholic philosophy
and canned schmaltz. "Now when I hear or read of the Communist
concept that human life is valueless, that there is no human soul," he
said, "I cannot help but compare that concept with the American concept of life, so ably and briefly stated by a Marine Corps chaplain before
dawn one morning on the island of Bougainville." Joe then shifted into
his routine about the boys in the ready tent, the chaplain's final words,
the bodies lying unmarked in the "vast moon-swept, wind-tossed Pacific,"
and the comforting final thought that there is a God who is eternal.
"That, ladies and gentlemen, is the American concept of life, a concept
so foreign to the Communist concept, a concept preserved over the years
by the expenditure of blood and flesh and steel. That concept of life we
must preserve. That concept of life we shall preserve." The studio audience responded with loud applause.[25]

McCarthy was also one of the few Senate conservatives to support
the cornerstones of America's postwar containment policy—the Truman
Doctrine, the Marshall Plan, and the North Atlantic Treaty Organization (NATO). Unlike Robert Taft, who saw these programs as too provocative and too expensive, Joe believed they were needed to halt Soviet
expansion. "It must be borne in mind," he wrote to a constituent in 1949,
"that the world, unfortunately, has already been divided into two camps
—Communist-controlled nations and non-Communist nations. . . . I
am firmly convinced that Stalin is no more bluffing in his promise to take
over the entire world than was Hitler, when he proclaimed his plans of
world domination in *Mein Kampf.*" In fact, the senator claimed that
Truman's policy was too weak and inconsistent—"just the opposite of
Theodore Roosevelt's policy of 'speak softly and carry a big stick.' . . . If
under the North Atlantic Pact we continue to talk tough and act weak,
the Pact will be a dismal failure and a waste of money. Yet I think . . .
that it is worth trying."[26]

McCarthy, then, was no stranger to the Communist issue by 1949.
And he was shrewd enough to realize that an assault upon a longtime
Stalwart enemy, the *Capital–Times*, might serve as a vehicle for reelection. With this thought in mind, he told a gathering of Madison Shriners
that Cedric Parker, "a known Communist," was working to pollute their

city with a foreign ideology. "One of the major aims of the Communist Party," Joe declared, "is to locate members in important positions in newspapers—especially in college towns so that young people will be getting daily doses of the Communist Party-line propaganda under the mistaken impression that they are absorbing 'liberal' and 'progressive' ideas."

McCarthy said he was taking a great risk by condemning Cedric Parker. But, luckily for Madison, he was willing to suffer a few blows in order to spotlight the enemy. ("When the time comes that I quit exposing things because I might bleed a little, I promise you gentlemen, I will resign from the U.S. Senate.") After then comparing the *Capital–Times* with the *Daily Worker*, Joe asked the Shriners to consider a boycott of their local paper:

> There is no law which prevents the *Capital–Times* from following the Communist line right down to the last period. It is for the people of Madison . . . to decide whether they will continue by advertisements or subscriptions to support this paper in view of the facts which I have set forth in this documented statement.[27]

That speech was the prototype for those he would deliver in later years. There was the inference that exposing Communists was a bloody business, demanding especially virile men; the comparison of an unfriendly newspaper with the *Daily Worker*; the suggestion that economic boycotts could somehow retard the spread of subversive ideas; and the reference to a "documented statement" that unequivocally proved his case. It was a virtuoso performance, cleverly blurring all distinctions between fact and fiction. Parker *had* once belonged to several Communist fronts. But to jump from there to a charge that his employer followed the "Moscow line" was perverse. Joe knew that the *Capital–Times* was anti-Communist; but he also knew that the Stalwarts would be tickled by the charge. True or not, it was something they *wanted* to believe.

The response was dramatic. McCarthy's allegations, said the Republican press, were right on target. Headlines like "McCarthy Quotes Record to Show How *Capital–Times* Follows Reds" and "McCarthy to Welcome Libel Suit on Red Charge" blanketed Wisconsin. For the first time in three years, his career seemed to be moving in a positive direction.

Like any politician—but particularly one who has struck pay dirt after a series of disastrous misses—McCarthy took full advantage of his good fortune. For the next two months he stumped Wisconsin, warning the locals about the growing Red Menace. The *Capital–Times* was bad enough, he claimed, but as a United States senator he had a responsibility to look for traitors in higher places. Soon he was telling the Kenosha Young Republicans that the State Department was "honeycombed and run by Communists." Then it was on to Marquette for an address before his Jesuit teachers. "The picture of the current 'war' between the Communist and atheistic world and the Christian nations," he said, "is becoming more and more dangerous not every month or year but every minute. We are losing at a tremendous pace." Blaming the State Department for America's "world demise," he promised to weed out the subversive elements when he returned to Washington. The date was December 6, 1949, still two months before his fateful swing through Wheeling, West Virginia.[28]

CHAPTER SIX

The Red Bogey in America, 1917–1950

In ATTEMPTING TO DOCUMENT the origins of McCarthyism, historians have traditionally limited their studies to the early Cold War era, the years 1945–49. While interpretations abound as to whether this phenomenon resulted from a Republican plot to recapture the White House, a Democratic desire to "play tough" with the Russians, or a "status revolt" by affluent but unappreciated Americans, there is general agreement that the onset of the second Red Scare *predated* McCarthy's famous Wheeling address of February 1950. As a result, the senator's rise to power has generally been explained as a reaction to the events of the preceding four years.

There is much to be said for this approach. It is impossible to comprehend the rise of McCarthy without analyzing the growth of anti-Communism in the late 1940s and the way that issue was used by groups and politicians to further their own interests. The one shortcoming of this approach is that it ignores the question of whether anti-Soviet and antiradical prejudices were already fused in the American mind before the Cold War began. Few attempts have been made to study the Cold War era in light of our knowledge of the first Red Scare (1919–20) or to find out whether the hysteria of this earlier period left behind a strong undercurrent of anti-Communism that could easily be exploited when, and if, Soviet and American interests came into conflict.

FOR MOST AMERICANS, the rise of Bolshevism was an unexpected and unwelcomed event. Only months before they had witnessed the "real" Russian Revolution when Tsar Nicholas abandoned his throne in favor of a provisional government which promised to promote the cause of constitutional democracy. At that time America's response had been overwhelmingly favorable. Theodore Roosevelt rejoiced "from my soul that Russia has ranged herself on the side of ordered liberty," while the Washington *Star* observed that a "free people naturally wants all the other people of the world to be free." Less than a week after the anti-Tsarist forces took control, President Wilson called for recognition of the new regime.[1]

There was, of course, another reason for America's support. It was commonly believed that Russia's poor military showing against the Germans had been due to the people's hatred of the Tsar. Now that this burden had been lifted, the Russians would redouble their efforts to protect the freedoms they had recently won. What Americans failed to understand was that the Russian people were not about to tolerate the war's continuation under any regime—a lesson the provisional government would learn in short order. As one historian put it, the American people "could not believe that the majority of Russians would heed the Bolshevik cries for peace; to American ears, these cries sounded like the 'traitorous' and 'pro-German' appeals of pacifists in the United States."[2]

Even after the Bolsheviks overthrew the provisional government in November 1917, many Americans hoped that Russia would continue its participation in the war. Within a few weeks, however, the Bolsheviks shattered this illusion by withdrawing completely and proclaiming a worker's revolution to destroy the international capitalist order. In response, the American press portrayed Lenin and Trotsky as German agents who had subverted the will of the Russian people by suing for peace.

The stories quickly got worse. It was claimed that the Soviets had an electric guillotine that chopped off hundreds of heads an hour; Bolshevik leaders drove around in fancy automobiles while businessmen were starving to death; and Russia had nationalized women by requiring them to register at "bureaus of free love." The message was always the same: the Bolsheviks were hated by the people and represented only themselves. It is not surprising that between 1917 and 1919 the New York *Times* reported on ninety-one occasions that the Bolsheviks were about to be overthrown, four times that Lenin and Trotsky had fled the country, three times that Lenin was in prison, and once that he was dead.[3]

Most Americans believed these stories. They were frightened by Bolshevism and puzzled by its success. To their thinking, it could only be categorized as the direct antithesis of everything for which America stood. A group of prominent New Yorkers described Bolshevism as "the assault of greed, ignorance, and brute force upon values that Americans have learned to hold most sacred. It destroys liberty, property rights, law, order, marriage, the home, and education. . . . Its loot enriches a few black-hearted and red-handed leaders and beggars everybody else."[4]

As historians have noted, the Bolshevik bogy was the main component of the Great Red Scare (1919–1920). By exploiting traditional fears of immigrant radicalism, the government, in conjunction with patriotic groups and employer associations, began to stifle dissent, deport foreign "troublemakers," and restrict the flow of immigrants into the country. The main focus of this period was a negative one—to preserve the *status quo* by excluding or destroying those "foreign influences" that might subvert it. After returning from a visit to the Soviet Union, William T. Ellis recommended the exclusion of all immigrants, but particularly Russians, because "self-preservation is America's first and highest duty to world-wide democracy." Mrs. George T. Guernsey, president of the Daughters of the American Revolution, demanded the deportation of Russian aliens on the grounds that "nothing will save the life of this free Republic if these foreign leeches are not cast out." And the newly formed American Legion called for a revival of "100 percent Americanism," which, the Legion explained, meant *opposition* to Bolshevism, anarchy, and disorder.[5]

According to most accounts of this era, the federal government, led by Attorney General A. Mitchell Palmer, used the Bolshevik bogy as a pretext for smashing dissent and agitation across the board. Palmer carried out "the greatest executive restriction of personal liberty in the history of this country" and "tore up the Bill of Rights at the first flash of red in the western sky." What is generally overlooked, however, is that Palmer came into the Cabinet determined to return the nation to its senses. Early in 1919 he had released 10,000 enemy aliens from parole and attempted (unsuccessfully) to end the Justice Department's illicit relationship with vigilante groups like the American Protective League. Even after his home was fire-bombed by suspected radicals, Palmer remained skeptical about reports of a Bolshevik plot to overthrow the government.[6]

Many thought otherwise. Irate citizens flooded the Justice Department with mail, while prominent newspapers chided the Attorney General for his "leniency." The U.S. Senate passed a resolution urging Palmer to arrest and deport radical aliens. Even fellow cabinet officers agreed that this "was no time to be timid . . . to remain passive . . . when faced with such an inveterate enemy of the present social order."[7]

The pressure was too much, especially for a man with strong presidential ambitions. In the summer of 1919, Palmer ordered the Bureau of

Investigation to compile dossiers on radical groups and individuals. By 1920 a young agent named J. Edgar Hoover had established a huge card-index system with 200,000 names. To make sure that Hoover's work did not go unnoticed, the Attorney General sent letters to the press. "My one desire," he wrote, "is to acquaint people like you with the real menace of evil-thinking which is the foundation of the Red movement."[8]

In the autumn of 1919 federal agents initiated a series of alien round-ups, one of which, a raid on the Russian People's House in Manhattan, allegedly uncovered some explosives. On December 21 the government placed 249 aliens on an Army cargo ship (dubbed the "Soviet Ark") and shipped them to Hango, Finland, for their final train ride to Russia. Although the vast majority of deportees had never been indicted for criminal activity, public opinion was virtually unanimous in support of the expulsions.

On January 2 and 6, 1920, the government carried out a second series of arrests known as the Palmer Raids. Acting without warrants, federal agents "entered bowling alleys, pool halls, cafés, club rooms, and even homes, and seized everyone in sight." The raids were aimed primarily at foreign members of the infant Communist Party; they wound up netting thousands of innocent people. At first, the public applauded. State legislatures passed resolutions supporting the raids. The Washington *Post* demanded more action and less talk about constitutional rights. ("There is no time to waste on hairsplitting over infringements of liberty.") And politicians competed with one another to determine who could be tougher on radicals. "If I had my way," proclaimed Massachusetts Secretary of State Albert Langtry, "I'd take them out in the yard every morning and shoot them, and the next day would have a trial to see whether they were guilty."[9]

These mass roundups marked the crest of the Great Red Scare. In the following months, as the immediate threat of Communism subsided, lawyers, judges, and clergymen expressed their misgivings about the raids. (Many had recently read "Illegal Practices of the U.S. Department of Justice," a pamphlet written by Harvard Law School Professors Felix Frankfurter, Zechariah Chafee, and Roscoe Pound.) The war was over, the "radicals" were silent, the labor movement lay in ruins. Political dissent in America had suffered a blow from which it would not quickly recover.

The Red Scare ended in 1920. The effects lasted for years. "Continued insistence upon ideological conformity, suspicion of organized labor, public intolerance toward aliens, and a hatred for Soviet Russia were but a few of the more important legacies," wrote historian Robert Murray. From 1919 through 1933 four successive presidential administrations refused to recognize the new Soviet regime. Secretary of State Bainbridge Colby said in 1920 that "we cannot . . . hold official relations with, or give friendly receptions to the agents of a government which is determined and bound to conspire against our institutions." A year later the new Secretary turned down a Soviet trade offer with the explanation that Russia could not possibly meet its obligations. (Why not? Because it had abolished private property and ignored the sanctity of contracts.) In addition, the State Department gathered reams of information to "prove" that radical activities throughout the globe were directed by devious Kremlinites. In 1933 this information was leaked to the press in a final attempt to sabotage America's recognition of the Soviet regime.[10]

On the domestic scene, the government still made life for suspected radicals as uncomfortable as possible. With few notable exceptions, Presidents Harding and Coolidge refused amnesty for political prisoners of the Red Scare era. (Pardons for German sympathizers were more common, because the Attorney General considered them "less dangerous" to the nation.) In the 1920s the Army quietly entered the field of antiradical surveillance. Its Military Intelligence Division formulated a "war plan" to cope with radical uprisings and to develop courses in antirevolutionary warfare. The Army also persuaded many state legislatures to reestablish their national guards.[11]

Equally disturbing were the roles played by the FBI and the local police. Throughout the 1920s the Bureau coaxed large appropriations from Congress by portraying the Communist threat in ominous terms. "Bolshevism is becoming stronger every day in this country," declared FBI Director Frank Burns in 1924. "I dare say that unless we become thoroughly aroused concerning the danger of this radical element . . . we will have a serious situation." With its $3-million-a-year budget, the FBI routinely infiltrated reform movements and handed out "subversive lists" to employer groups and patriotic organizations. On the local level, many cities established "Red Squads" to keep tabs on radical gatherings. In a 1924 Survey (*What 88 Police Chiefs Think and Do About Radical Meetings*), the American Civil Liberties Union concluded that the majority of law enforcement officials did not believe in protecting the rights of political dissidents. In what seemed a representative opinion, the police chief of Hot Springs, Arkansas, promised that if radicals decided to meet in his city, "we would certainly see that they were *put out P.D.Q.*"[12]

Before long, "Bolshevism" and "Communism" had become catchwords to discredit movements with which Americans disagreed. Advocates of Prohibition argued that those who disobeyed the Eighteenth Amendment were guilty of "practical Bolshevism." Leaders of the antievolution fight blamed their troubles on "Communists" from New York City. And the DAR branded the Sheppard–Towner Maternity Act as a "special Red weapon" for brainwashing housewives about the virtues of birth control and the evils of child labor. It was no coincidence, moreover, that the 1920s saw the first loyalty oaths for teachers and the mass production of patriotic observances—Flag Day, Constitution Day, Preparedness Day, and the like.[13]

To a great extent, then, the anti-Communism of the 1920s was produced by a combination of factors: an inherent distaste for domestic radicalism, a desire to preserve the *status quo*, and a distorted perception of Soviet objectives. The first two factors were hardly new in American history; what distinguished the 1920s was the addition of the third—the foreign threat. From World War I onward, radical and progressive movements would often be equated with Russian Communism. And those who led them would often be viewed as the agents of a foreign power.

————

IN 1929 THE AMERICAN COMMUNIST PARTY was small, weak, and under constant attack. Harassed by public officials, pummeled by vigilantes and Red-baiting newspapers, it claimed a grand total of 7,000 members, mostly immigrants who lived in and around New York City.

Some of its wounds were self-inflicted. In 1928 the Sixth Congress of the Communist International expressly forbade collaboration between Communists and all others on the left. As a result, when the Great Depression paralyzed America in 1930, the Communists picked up members and momentum, but very few allies. They made headlines by preventing the eviction of rentless tenants. They led bloody but unsuccessful strikes in Minneapolis, Toledo, and New York. They won the allegiance of writers—including John Dos Passos, Erskine Caldwell, and Granville Hicks—who prepared a manifesto urging the election of William Z. Foster as President of the United States in 1932. But Foster received only 103,000 votes; Norman Thomas, the Socialist candidate, polled seven times that amount.

In 1935, as the Nazis began their domination of Europe, the Seventh World Congress ordered Communists everywhere to forget about revolution and ally themselves with *all* enemies of fascism. This reversal was not without its humorous moments. In Louisiana, the Party told its members:

> May we remind you that this is Americanism Week. The Communist Party of Louisiana declares its steadfast loyalty to our Nation's democratic institutions, pledging ourselves in word and deed to fight any "ism" of any clique, group or minority from within the country or from abroad that would destroy or undermine our democratic institutions.

In New York City, when the local chapter of the DAR overlooked its usual anniversary salute to Paul Revere, the Young Communist League hired a horse and rider, in colonial garb, to trot down Broadway bearing the sign: "The DAR Forgets But The YCL Remembers."[14]

The Communists made great strides in the late 1930s. They joined new organizations, penetrated old ones, and created many of their own —the Communist fronts. Bearing humanitarian titles, like the American League for Peace and Democracy, these fronts appealed to people who admired the Soviet achievement or feared the rise of Fascism, but who were left cold by the rigidity of Party life. Some who joined may have been unaware of the Communist presence; others simply accepted the Communists as partners—and leaders—in the fight for a "safer world." As Freda Kirchwey wrote in *The Nation*:

> With all their faults, the Communists perform necessary functions in the confused struggle of our time. They have helped to build up and run a string of organizations . . . which clearly serve not the cause of "totalitarianism" but of a more workable democracy. And the value of these organizations lies largely in the energy and discipline and zeal of their Communist elements.[15]

Communists also entered the federal government during this period. How many, and how much damage they did, are questions that would dominate the political arena for years. In his superb book on the subject, Earl Latham wrote that "there does not seem to have been a planned and premeditated 'infiltration' of the federal agencies, certainly not at the start." He estimated (along with Whittaker Chambers) that there were seventy-five Communists scattered throughout a bureaucracy containing a half-million federal employees. And he concluded that the *primary objective* of these Communists was not espionage, but rather the promotion of "left tendencies" in the agencies for which they worked.[16]

———

THE 1930S WERE MARKED by a lessening of tension with Russia and the growth of the American Communist Party. Traditional fears of Soviet expansion declined, the result of Stalin's well-publicized victory over the Trotskyists. Still, the American people did not appear to alter their views about the *evils* of Communism or its *potential* dangers. Public opinion polls revealed a strong distrust of Russia *per se*, a nagging fear of domestic Communism, and solid support for legislative attempts to "expose" subversives in and out of government.

Those who analyzed the polls often pointed to the unfavorable treatment the Soviets received in the press and the public schools. American textbooks emphasized Russia's "Mongolian characteristics"; the phrase "scratch a Russian, find a Tartar" was used in several high school texts. Soviet men were portrayed as illiterates or revolutionaries, while Soviet women were characterized as "Amazons" or undersexed Marxists. Small wonder that a study of high school students in 1927 revealed a majority who categorized Russians as inferior people, or that a national opinion poll in 1939 showed Russians to be "bad risks" for American citizenship. "Thousands upon thousands of people are . . . trying to get out of that country and into America," one congressman complained. "And when they get here all they want to do is overthrow our government." [17]

Although most Americans did not consider the Soviets to be dangerous rivals in the 1930s, they did express a greater hostility to Stalin's Russia than to Hitler's Germany. And their fears about domestic Communism were very real, indeed. In poll after poll Americans portrayed the Communists as evil people and supported extreme measures like their deportation to Russia. Even in 1944, when the Soviets were wartime allies, a study in the *Public Opinion Quarterly* concluded that "domestic Communists" were thought "to be the single greatest menace to our way of life." [18]

GIVEN THESE SENTIMENTS, it was inevitable that the Communist *issue* would become a vital force within the political system.* And that issue took root in the late 1930s, when the House of Representatives created a special Committee on Un-American Activities. Chaired by Martin Dies, a Texas Democrat, it included several members—indeed a majority— who opposed New Deal reforms and often equated them with treason. Chairman Dies contended that the Communists and their dupes did not need to overthrow the government because they already controlled it. J. Parnell Thomas, a New Jersey Republican, said that New Dealers had "sabotaged the capitalist system." Joe Starnes, an Alabama Democrat, warned that they intended to "mongrelize" the races. (Starnes, a former school teacher, once told Earl Browder that, unlike the Russian Revolution, the American Revolution had involved no killing; later, on hearing a witness refer to Christopher Marlowe, he said, "You're quoting from this Marlowe. Is he a Communist?") [19]

In short order the committee listed 640 organizations, 438 newspapers, and 280 labor groups as possible Communist fronts. The list included obvious targets like the American Civil Liberties Union, and less obvious ones like the Boy Scouts and the Campfire Girls (which had come under suspicion for attempting to "increase international understanding"). Even little Shirley Temple got a reprimand. Why? Because her manager had sent a routine letter of congratulations to the French Communist newspaper *Ce Soir* on its first anniversary. [20]

The committee was not shy about "naming names." In 1939 it obtained the mailing list—not the *membership* list—of the American

---

* Earl Latham and others have made the very real distinction between the Communist *problem* and the Communist *issue* in America. The former involved the Communist infiltration of the government and the way in which official agencies attempted to deal with it. The latter involved the fear of Communism (including domestic subversion) and the way in which that fear was exploited by partisans for partisan ends. See Earl Latham, *The Communist Controversy in Washington*, 1965, pp. 3–4.

League for Peace and Democracy, a suspected Communist front. The list contained the names of 463 federal employees, who may or may not have been members. The committee didn't know—or care. It published the list with the explanation that "if there are . . . names on the list who are not members, it is not the mistake of the Dies Committee, it is the mistake of the . . . League." A few months later the committee charged that 1,121 government workers were either Communists or "sympathetic with totalitarian ideology."[21]

As historian Robert Griffith has noted, the Dies Committee was responsible for "the whole spectrum of slogans, techniques, and political mythologies that would later be called 'McCarthyism.' " It was Dies who popularized the concepts of prescriptive publicity and guilt by association.* It was Dies (and other members) who used phrases like "coddling Communists," "soft on Communism," and "I hold in my hand." Finally, it was Dies who demonstrated the enormous appeal of anti-Communism and who wielded it like a club against the Administration then in power.[22]

Dies became a national celebrity. His charges were spread and supported by the Hearst syndicate, the American Legion, and the McCormick newspaper chain. Public opinion polls revealed that most Americans were familiar with, and sympathetic to, the committee's work. Political analysts credited Dies with the defeat of several New Dealers in 1938. Sam Rayburn announced that "Martin Dies could beat me now in my own district."[23]

In 1939 Congress passed a law making loyalty to America a condition for peacetime employment in the United States. Known as the Hatch Act, it prohibited government workers from belonging to "any political party or organization which advocates the overthrow of our constitutional form of government." A year later, as war raged in Europe, Congress passed the Alien Registration or Smith Act, the first peacetime sedition law since 1798. Aimed at the Communist Party as well as the German–American Bund, it forbade *all* Americans to "knowingly or willfully advocate, abet, advise, or teach the duty, necessity, desirability or propriety of overthrowing or destroying any government in the United States by force or violence." The Smith Act had the reluctant support of President Roosevelt. It passed the Senate by voice vote and the House by 392–4. One congressman remarked during the debate:

> The mood of the House is such that if you brought in the Ten Commandments today and asked for their repeal and attached to that request an alien law, you could get it.[24]

---

* Prescriptive publicity was a form of extralegal punishment whereby individuals named before congressional committees as Communists, fellow travelers, radicals, security risks or even nonconformists would be ostracized by the communities in which they lived. For McCarthy's use of the device, see below pp. 339–41.

The Smith Act was passed against the backdrop of war and totalitarian aggression in Europe. In the summer of 1939 the Soviet Union astonished its American admirers by signing a neutrality pact with Nazi Germany. A few months later it undermined much of its remaining support by invading Finland and bombing the city of Helsinki. "By this brutal assault," the *New Republic* lamented, "the Soviet Union has unleashed the dogs of hate that were already straining to tear it to pieces. It has made defense of its actions impossible . . . and provided a strong moral case for those who wish to destroy Communism and all its works." * [25]

By 1941, however, this assessment had been swept aside by the rush of world events. In short order the Germans moved on Moscow, the Japanese bombed Pearl Harbor, and the United States allied itself with Britain and Russia against the Axis Powers. As a result, American attitudes toward the Soviet Union changed with remarkable speed. In many newspapers and magazines the "treacherous Reds" became the "brave Russians." *Life* described them as "one hell of a people" who "look like Americans, dress like Americans, and think like Americans." It even portrayed the NKVD as "a national police force similar to the FBI." [26]

On the other hand a number of publications remained hostile to Russia and suspicious of collaboration in any form. The list included *Collier's*, *The Saturday Evening Post*, and the New York *Daily News* (which boasted thereafter of its foresight in denouncing "Bloody Joe.") Equally suspicious were the leaders of the American Catholic Church, who maintained a steady stream of anti-Soviet propaganda during World War II. Father James Gillis warned that Stalin could never be trusted because "he is largely Mongol, and for unscrupulous cunning the Mongol is superior even to the Chinese." On a higher plane, the Jesuit weekly *America* foresaw an "inevitable clash" between Communism and Catholicism in Eastern Europe. "The fate of Catholics becomes a particular

* On the eve of the Nazi–Soviet Pact, a number of writers and intellectuals wrote an open letter to *The Nation* expressing their complete faith in the peaceful and progressive intentions of the Soviet leadership. It read, in part:

1. The Soviet Union . . . works unceasingly for a peaceful international order.
2. It has eliminated racial and national prejudice . . . and made the expression of anti-Semitism . . . a criminal offense.
9. The Soviet Union considers political dictatorship a transitional form and has shown a steadily expanding democracy in every sphere. Its epoch-making new constitution guarantees Soviet citizens universal suffrage, civil liberties . . . and equality of all races and nationalities.

The letter was written after the forced collectivization of peasant farms and after the Moscow purges in which millions of Russians were slaughtered or sent to concentration camps in Siberia. Furthermore, it was *published* after the news of the Nazi–Soviet Pact had reached America. The letter was signed by Max Lerner, I. F. Stone, and several individuals who would later become McCarthy targets: Frederick Schuman, Dashiell Hammett, Harvey O'Connor, and Corliss Lamont. See "To All Active Supporters of Democracy and Peace," *The Nation*, August 26, 1939, p. 228.

source of anxiety," it wrote in 1944, "as the Russian armies advance into territories where millions of Catholics live."[27]

According to public opinion polls, this sort of anxiety was not limited to Catholics alone. On the contrary, the American people seemed intent on maintaining good relations with Russia yet fearful that it would make "unacceptable demands" once the war had ended. One survey asked: "With which of these four statements do you come closest to agreeing?"

It is going to be very important to keep on friendly terms with Russia after the war, and we should make every possible effort to do so.	22.7%
It is important for the U.S. to be on friendly terms . . . but not so important that we should make too many concessions to her.	49.2
If Russia wants to keep on friendly terms with us . . . we shouldn't discourage her, but there is no reason why we should make any special effort to be friendly.	11.3
We shall be better off if we have just as little as possible to do with Russia after the war.	9.3
Don't know	7.5

Clearly, friendship and suspicion were walking hand in hand.[28]

IN THE FALL OF 1945 a prominent journalist observed: "There is no use dodging what is now plain: A serious cleavage has developed between Russia and the Western democracies. There had been predictions for months, even years, that when the war ended 'those strange bedfellows' would fall out . . . but such differences were ignored in the drive for victory."[29]

These were prophetic words. The wartime alliance had been just that —a *wartime alliance.* It began to unravel, in American eyes, at the first sign of Soviet aggression in Europe. The takeover in Poland, the mass arrests in Hungary, the coup in Czechoslovakia, the Berlin blockade— all added fuel to the fire. Meanwhile, the American press began to play up the astounding—and generally accurate—reports of Soviet brutality in Russia and the occupied lands. American Catholics protested the imprisonment of Cardinal Mindszenty in Hungary and Archbishop Stepinac in Yugoslavia. Patriotic societies called for military action to stem the Red advance. And the Gallup Poll showed more and more Americans agreeing that Russia was aggressive, imperialistic, and determined to rule the world.

Equally disturbing were reports of espionage and subversion by Communist agents in the West. On March 11, 1945, security officers from the Office of Strategic Services (OSS) broke into the Manhattan head-quarters of *Amerasia*, a pro-Communist publication, and discovered thousands of classified government reports. In the following months FBI agents staked out the building and seized the stolen material. Six people were arrested, including editor Philip Jaffe, a longtime supporter of Communist causes; Emmanuel Larsen, a member of the State Department's Far Eastern Division; and John S. Service, a foreign service officer who had recently returned from China.* At first the federal prosecutors appeared to have an airtight case; then they discovered that the OSS agents had never obtained a warrant for the raid. After long negotiations, Jaffe pleaded guilty and Larsen pleaded *nolo contendere*, but neither man went to jail.[30]

How important were the *Amerasia* documents? Most were mundane reports about Far Eastern policy that had no business being classified. A few were marked "top secret," however, and dealt with subjects like the strategic bombing program for Japan. Although the government could not prove that any of these documents had reached a foreign power, it was later revealed that Jaffe had visited the Soviet Consulate, the home of Earl Browder, and the headquarters of the American Communist Party during his three months under FBI surveillance.

In Canada, meanwhile, the defection of Igor Gouzenko, a code clerk at the Russian Embassy in Ottawa, led to the arrest of twenty-two people for passing secret documents to the Soviet Union. In some ways the Canadian spy case was more dangerous—and revealing—than the *Amerasia* affair. For one thing, it *proved* that a successful Soviet spy ring was operating in Canada and the United States. (Soviet agents had accumulated extremely valuable information, including, it seemed, the top-secret plans for the proximity fuse.) Furthermore, these agents had worked closely with Canadian Communists, thereby reinforcing the notion that groups like the American Communist Party were deeply involved in espionage and subversion.

There was undoubtedly some truth to this, though scores of politicians and government officials would comb every detail for partisan advantage and personal gain. Their leader was J. Edgar Hoover, whose expertise in such matters was accepted by virtually everyone but the Communists themselves. In 1946 Hoover claimed that "Red Fascism" had become a major force in unions, newspapers, magazines, book publishing, radio, movies, churches, schools, colleges, fraternal orders, and the government itself. Always fond of statistics, he noted that America had one Communist for every 1,814 people in 1947—a truly ominous ratio considering that Russia had had only one Bolshevik for every 2,771 people in 1917. "The disloyalty of American Communists is no longer a

---

* For more on the case of John S. Service, see below, pp. 128–29.

matter of conjecture," Hoover declared. They were traitors, pure and simple, and they had to be dealt with accordingly.[31]

Most Americans seemed to agree. Their fears about Communism and Soviet intentions were deeply ingrained, easily aroused, and, by 1947, *understandably acute.* The Great War had not made their world a safer place in which to live. Soviet aggression had robbed them of the fruits of victory. One form of totalitarianism had been replaced by another. At home, Communist conspirators were working to undermine everything that Americans held dear. The FBI director said this, and so did the Attorney General of the United States. "There are today many Communists in America," he warned. "They are everywhere—in factories, offices, butcher shops, on street corners, in private businesses—and each carries with him the germs of death for society."[32]

President Truman played a role as well. In mobilizing support for his "containment" of Soviet expansion, he sounded at times like the Red-baiting alarmists whom he thoroughly despised. And in attempting to defuse the explosive issue of Communists-in-government, he established a federal loyalty program that scared civil libertarians half to death. The program called for extensive background checks on all civilian workers in the Executive branch. The criteria for dismissal included "reasonable grounds . . . for the belief that the person . . . is disloyal to the government of the United States." And the criteria for disloyalty included everything from espionage to "sympathetic association" with groups deemed to be "totalitarian, fascist, Communist or subversive" by the Attorney General.

The program provided minimal safeguards for the accused. It did not differentiate between sensitive and nonsensitive jobs, and it hopelessly confused the concepts of loyalty and security in the public mind. As one historian explained:

> A man too reliant upon the bottle, or having suspicious relatives, or in other ways vulnerable or indiscreet, might be fired on security grounds; the program's workings left the unjustified but nearly certain implication that his allegiance, too, was in question. A suspect could be charged by anonymous accusers whom he was not allowed to confront. . . . Loyalty boards questioned employees on a wide variety of topics—like race relations—which were unrelated to loyalty. It appeared that thought, not just overt acts, would be penalized, and the enforcers of government purity had rather far-reaching notions of what constituted dangerous ideas.[33]

Even worse, the loyalty program did not defuse the issue of Communists-in-government. If anything, it stirred up the congressional Red-hunters by conceding the possibility that a serious problem existed. The assault was led once again by the House Committee on Un-American Activities, chaired now by J. Parnell Thomas, and including John Rankin of Mississippi, a notorious anti-Semite; John Wood of Georgia, a Ku Klux Klan supporter; and Republicans Karl Mundt of South Dakota and Richard Nixon of California. Warming to its task in 1947, the committee held a series of spectacular hearings on the Hollywood film industry. It reported, before the hearings even began, that "some of the most flagrant Communist propaganda films were produced as a result of White House pressure" during World War II. And it heard from a host of "friendly" movie stars, including Robert Taylor, Gary Cooper, Ronald Reagan, and the dapper Adolphe Menjou, who declared: "I am a witch-hunter if the witches are Communists. I am a Red-baiter. I would like to see them all back in Russia."[34]

In 1948 the committee returned to more familiar ground. On the eve of the presidential campaign, it unveiled the "Blond Spy Queen," a plump, middle-aged Vassar graduate named Elizabeth Bentley. At a public hearing Bentley claimed to have been a Soviet courier who transported secret documents from Washington officials to Russian agents in New York. Her list of "traitors" was impressive: Lauchlin Currie, an administrative assistant to President Roosevelt; William Remington, a foreign trade expert in the Commerce Department; and Harry Dexter White, a former Treasury Department official who directed the International Monetary Fund.*

A few days later the committee summoned another ex-Communist, Whittaker Chambers, to corroborate Miss Bentley's allegations. Chambers had joined the Communist Party in 1924. He had worked as an underground agent from 1930 to 1938, when he left the Party and warned New Deal officials about a spy ring in Washington—to no avail. After that, Chambers recalled, he had "lived in hiding, sleeping by day and watching through the night with gun and revolver within easy reach." Reappearing in 1939, he had taken a job at *Time* and worked his way up to senior editor at a salary of $30,000 a year.

Richard Nixon described Chambers as "short and pudgy. His clothes were unpressed; his shirt collar was curled over his jacket. He spoke in a rather bored monotone and seemed . . . a reluctant witness." Reluctant or not, Chambers backed up most of Bentley's testimony and added nine names of his own. One of them was Alger Hiss.[35]

At first Chambers made no mention of espionage. He simply alleged that Hiss, a former State Department official, had been a close friend and fellow Communist in the 1930s. Hiss testified two days later, denying

---

* There was a grim footnote to Bentley's charges. Remington denied them and even filed a libel suit against his accuser. However, he was convicted of perjury (lying about his membership in the Communist Party) and sent to prison, where he was killed by a fellow inmate. White appeared before HUAC to deliver an emotional (and apparently convincing) rebuttal. He died three days later, the victim of a massive heart attack. Currie was no longer in government when the charges against him were made. His case did not arouse much interest and he eventually moved to South America.

that he had been a Communist or that he had known Whittaker Chambers *as Whittaker Chambers.** Obviously one of the men was lying, and Hiss dared Chambers to repeat his charges away from the hearing room, where the rules of congressional immunity would no longer apply. When Chambers took the dare on the radio program "Meet the Press," Hiss sued for libel in a federal court.

Chambers struck back hard. At a pretrial hearing he produced dozens of State Department documents which, he claimed, had been stolen by Alger Hiss. Suddenly the ground had shifted to espionage, a far more serious charge. And when the committee demanded more evidence, Chambers led HUAC investigators to a pumpkin patch on his Maryland farm, where he retrieved some microfilmed summaries of State Department reports which had been typed on a Woodstock typewriter owned by Alger Hiss. On December 14, 1948, a grand jury indicted Hiss on two counts of perjury. (The statute of limitations on espionage had run out.) The first trial ended with a hung jury—eight for conviction, four opposed. The second trial would send him to jail.

A student of the Hiss case once observed that a generation was on trial at the federal courthouse in Foley Square. His point was well taken. Hiss was the quintessential New Dealer—young, intelligent, sophisticated, Ivy League. He had gone to the best Eastern schools—Johns Hopkins (Phi Beta Kappa) and Harvard Law School (*Law Review*). A protégé of Professor Felix Frankfurter, he had clerked for Justice Oliver Wendell Holmes before accepting his first New Deal post in the Agricultural Adjustment Administration. After that he had worked for the Nye Committee, the Justice Department, and the State Department, where he rose quickly through the ranks. In 1944 Hiss had supervised the Dumbarton Oaks Conference, which laid the groundwork for the United Nations. The following year he had served as an adviser to President Roosevelt at Yalta, and the year after that he had presided over the first U.N. Conference at San Francisco. In 1947 Hiss resigned his post to become president of the Carnegie Endowment for International Peace. He had been recommended by John Foster Dulles, one of the Endowment's leading trustees. He was forty-two years old.

In Alger Hiss, conservatives from both parties found the perfect symbol for all that they distrusted and despised. Impeached with Hiss were not only his intellect and his Eastern connections but also the liberal-internationalist philosophy that had guided the Democratic Party for a decade and a half. President Truman understood this—and lashed back in typical Truman style. Responding to a reporter's question, he called the Hiss case a political "red herring," cooked up to divert public atten-

---

* In a face-to-face confrontation set up by the committee, Hiss did concede that he recognized his accuser as George Crosley, a deadbeat journalist whom he had befriended many years before.

tion from the failures of the Republican Congress. Not surprisingly, the public disagreed. A Gallup Poll in 1948 found overwhelming support for congressional spy probes; in fact, three out of four *Democrats* in the survey believed that HUAC was on to something important, and not just "playing politics."[36]

Still, Truman was hardly alone. Many journalists, public officials, and liberal activists supported Hiss on instinct, nothing more. This was certainly understandable. They could not do otherwise—however convincing the evidence that Chambers presented—without conceding an enormous victory to the Red-baiting opportunists who ran the House Committee on Un-American Activities. Furthermore, Leslie Fiedler was probably correct when he wrote that many liberals had been conditioned to accept the paradox "that (a) there were really no Communists, just the hallucinations of 'witch hunters,' and (b) if there were Communists, they were, despite their shrillness and bad manners, fundamentally on the side of justice."* On the day Hiss was indicted by the grand jury, Eleanor Roosevelt declared: "I am going to believe in [his] integrity until he is proved guilty." As it turned out, Mrs. Roosevelt—and many others —continued to believe in Hiss after he *was* found guilty and shipped to the federal prison at Lewisburg, Pennsylvania.[37]

———

IN 1949, AS HISTORIAN ERIC GOLDMAN HAS NOTED, a series of new and devastating shocks "loosed within American life a vast impatience, a turbulent bitterness, a rancor akin to revolt." The first one occurred in March, when FBI agents arrested Judith Coplon, a Justice Department employee, during a rendezvous with a Soviet official in New York. Coplon was obviously engaged in espionage; she had been providing the Russians with confidential FBI reports since 1946. Convicted on two separate occasions, she nevertheless went free because an appeals court threw out the wiretap evidence that conclusively proved the government's case against her. This time, at least, no prominent liberal rushed to Coplon's defense.[38]

August brought another shock: the release of the State Department's 1,054-page White Paper on China, conceding that the world's largest country was about to fall into Communist hands. "The unfortunate but inescapable fact," said Dean Acheson, the new Secretary of State, "is that the ominous result of the civil war in China was beyond [our] control. . . . Nothing that this country did or could have done within rea-

---

* Leslie Fiedler, "Hiss, Chambers, and the Age of Innocence," *Commentary*, December 1950. Fiedler added: "American liberalism has been reluctant to leave the garden of its illusion; but it can delay no longer: the age of innocence is dead. The Hiss case marks the death of an era, but it also promises a rebirth if we are willing to learn its lessons." As we shall see, the Hiss case would haunt political leaders and government officials for years to come.

sonable limits . . . could have changed that result. . . . It was the product of internal Chinese forces. . . . A decision was arrived at within China, if only a decision by default."[39]

The situation in China had been deteriorating steadily since 1946, when Chiang Kai-shek and his Nationalist (Kuomintang) forces began an all-out offensive against the Communist forces led by Mao Tse-tung. Chiang had counted heavily upon his American ally. He assumed that the government in Washington was locked into a policy of total support. After all, he was fighting Communism; he had powerful friends in Congress; and his image as China's Christian savior had been carefully crafted by his idolators in the press, especially Henry Luce.

The Administration had other ideas. President Truman and his advisers were far less interested in Asia than they were in Western Europe or the Middle East. On the scale of American priorities, "saving" China ranked very low indeed. Truman, Acheson, and George Marshall understood the limits of American power. They were not about to be trapped into an open-ended commitment in Asia, certainly not by Chiang Kaishek, who ran a corrupt, unpopular, and hopelessly incompetent regime. From 1946 to 1949 the Administration gave the Nationalists about two billion dollars in military aid—enough, it was hoped, to satisfy Chiang's American friends without seriously affecting the more important build-up in Europe. (Most of the weaponry was discarded by fleeing Nationalist troops; it soon wound up in Communist hands.) By year's end, Mao's Army had gained complete control of China. Chiang and his supporters had fled the mainland for the island of Formosa, where a government in exile was quickly established.[40]

Acheson was correct in announcing that America could have done nothing "within reasonable limits" to alter this result. In 1949, however, his White Paper read more like an excuse than an explanation. Americans were angered and bewildered by Chiang's demise. William Manchester put it well:

> The China they knew—Pearl Buck's peasants, rejoicing in the good earth— had been dependable, democratic, warm, and above all pro-American. Throughout the great war the United Nations Big Four had been Churchill, Roosevelt, Stalin, and Chiang. Stalin's later treachery had been deplorable but unsurprising. But Chiang Kai-shek! Acheson's strategy to contain Red aggression seemed to burst wide open. . . . Everything American diplomats had achieved in Europe—the Truman Doctrine, the Marshall Plan, NATO —momentarily seemed annulled by this disaster in Asia.[41]

The news kept getting worse. In August an American spy plane returned from Asia with photographs revealing strong traces of radioactive material. The conclusion was obvious: Russia had exploded an atomic device. America's nuclear monopoly had come to an end.

On September 23 President Truman broke the news in a one-sentence statement to the press: "We have evidence an atomic explosion occurred in the USSR." The reaction was severe. Americans had been conditioned to believe that Russia was scientifically inept, that it could not possibly develop the bomb before the mid-1950s, if ever. This could only mean one thing: espionage. The Russians had stolen the biggest secret of all. On September 26 Congressman Harold Velde (a future HUAC chairman) echoed the words of Karl Mundt, J. Edgar Hoover, and other "experts" in the field:

> The Russians undoubtedly gained 3 to 5 years in producing the atomic bomb because our government from the White House down has been sympathetic toward the views of Communists and fellow travelers, with the result that it has been infiltrated by a network of spies. . . . Plainly Congress must act now unless we want to welcome a second Pearl Harbor with open arms.[42]

BY 1950 THE SECOND RED SCARE was well under way. The events of the postwar era had revived the Communist issue with a vengeance. It had become the focal point for Republican attacks upon Democrats, conservative attacks upon liberals, and congressional assaults upon the Executive branch. At the same time, as we shall see, the Communist *problem* had been almost eradicated by the strenuous—and sometimes questionable—efforts of the Democratic Administration. There would be only one major case of espionage after 1949, and that one, the Fuchs–Rosenberg case, concerned a spy ring which had operated during World War II. Furthermore, the Communist Party had been battered by mass desertions, the jailing of its leaders, and the scrupulous attention of the FBI. Despite the warnings of J. Edgar Hoover, it was no longer a force in American life.

CHAPTER SEVEN

Wheeling

FOR MANY AMERICANS, 1950 was a difficult and depressing year. In January they watched their President wrestle with the decision to construct a hydrogen bomb. February brought the arrest of a British scientist for passing atomic secrets to the Russians. March, April, and May were filled with congressional testimony about Communist influence in the State Department. June witnessed the North Korean attack across the 38th parallel. July saw the arrest of Julius Rosenberg. In August his wife, Ethel, joined him in prison. Throughout the autumn months Congress debated and finally passed the Internal Security (McCarran) Act, an extraordinarily repressive measure. In December word reached home that American troops in Korea were in full retreat before an advancing Communist Chinese army.

The first month set the pattern to follow. The big issues—Hiss, China, and the Bomb—were as politically combustible as ever. Speaking to the National Press Club on January 12, Dean Acheson insisted that the only way to halt Soviet expansion in Asia was to support "progressive forces" there—a clear slap at Chiang Kai-shek and his American friends. President Truman went a step further. After stating that the U.S. would not defend Chiang in the event of a Communist assault, he refused to spend the $75 million that Congress had already earmarked for Formosa. "I've still got [the money] locked up in the drawer of my desk," the President remarked, "and it is going to stay there."[1]

The response was predictable. Conservative Republicans accused Truman of shortsightedness, cowardice—and worse. Herbert Hoover called for immediate naval action to protect Chiang's island fortress. Senate Minority Leader Kenneth Wherry condemned Truman's "determination to go forward with blundering policies that please the Communists." When one Republican advocated the military occupation of Formosa, Democrat Tom Connally took the Senate floor to demand that GOP critics "put up or shut up." "You can't occupy Formosa with a few tourists," he exploded. "Where is the senator who wants to send an army?" No one responded.[2]

By this time, however, there were too many critics and too few Tom Connallys. On January 14 Governor Ernest Gruening said that Alaska was virtually defenseless against a Soviet attack and could be "taken tomorrow." Addressing the American Legion, Karl Mundt portrayed Harry Truman as a blundering leftist and called for "vigilante action to combat Communism through . . . grass-roots committees in every American town." Most disquieting of all was J. Edgar Hoover's claim that the United States harbored at least 540,000 Communists and fellow travelers. In the event of war with Russia, he warned, their destructive potential was almost limitless. "I am flabbergasted," said Indiana's Homer Capehart. "It is the most alarming thing I've heard in a long time."[3]

On January 22 a New York jury found Alger Hiss guilty of perjury. The verdict was a blow to the Administration, of course, and Dean Acheson compounded the damage by telling the press: "I should like to make it clear to you that whatever the outcome of any appeal . . . I do not intend to turn my back on Alger Hiss." As reporters dashed for the telephones, Acheson sent word ahead asking for a meeting with the President. "I drove to the White House and told Truman the story," he wrote, "adding that my resignation was at his disposal."*[4]

It was easy for a nation experiencing the stress of a Cold War to misunderstand—or purposely misconstrue—the charitable intent of this remark. Right-wing newspapers, like the Chicago *Tribune* and the New York *Journal–American*, came close to calling Acheson a traitor. The moderate dailies were simply appalled by his judgment. "Acheson's remark," wrote the Washington *Star*, "has served only to stimulate the energies of that little band of Republican senators who are bent upon

---

* Acheson had been involved in the Hiss defense from the very beginning. At his press conference on January 25, 1950, he told reporters that his feelings about the case were summed up in the 25th Chapter, verse 34, of the Gospel according to St. Matthew: "Verily I say unto you, in as much as you have done it unto one of the least of these my brethren, ye have done it unto me." During an interview with Alger Hiss (March 7, 1978) I asked him whether he was surprised by Acheson's remark. "No," Hiss said, "I would have been surprised if he hadn't made it." Hiss claimed that, after the remark was made, he sent Acheson a word of thanks through his brother Donald Hiss, who was still friendly with the Secretary. After that, Hiss and Acheson never communicated again.

probing for some political advantage among the ruins of the career of Alger Hiss."[5]

What made the incident worse was the Secretary's low standing on Capitol Hill. Even congressmen who supported his policies were put off by his haughty manner. They saw him as a "smart-aleck," a "striped-pants diplomat," an "overdressed, overeducated wise guy." Maury Maverick, the popular Texas Democrat, actually met with Acheson to tell him so. "I'm not going to be polite," Maverick began. ". . . I'm tired of hearing about you and Harvard and Yale and that you're witty. I've never heard you say anything funny." Acheson laughed sheepishly, noting that he couldn't help it if he'd gone to Yale. But Maverick cut him off: "If Harold Ickes got caught in a whorehouse at three A.M. killing a woman, a lot of people would bail him out. But not you, you've got no friends."[6]

One of the few politicians who did stand by Acheson was Harry Truman. Five years before, in a similar incident, the President had been roasted for attending the funeral of "a friendless old man just out of the penitentiary," Kansas City's political boss Tom Pendergast. Truman admired the Secretary's remark and understood its true meaning. But his public support served only to stimulate the Republicans, who taunted Acheson when he next appeared before Congress. In one exchange, New Hampshire's Styles Bridges asked him if "a *friend* of a person convicted of perjury in connection with a treasonable act" was a potential security risk. Acheson's embarrassed response—"It's a matter I'd have to look into"—brought snickers from the audience. Afterward, Hugh Butler of Nebraska wrote to a crony, "I think if we keep piling it on him as we have lately, he will soon resign of his own accord."[7]

On January 26 Richard Nixon charged the Administration with suppressing evidence of Hiss's Communist connections. This did not mean that Truman was disloyal, Nixon said, but it did raise the question of whether he was fit to be President. Concluding with a rhetorical flourish, the congressman defined presidential misconduct in terms almost identical to those his own critics would employ some two decades later:

> It is customary for any Administration, be it Republican or Democratic, to resist the disclosure of facts which might be embarrassing to that Administration in an election year. Because President Truman treated Communist infiltration like any ordinary political scandal, he is responsible for this failure to act against the Communist conspiracy, and has rendered the greatest possible disservice to the people of this nation.[8]

On the heels of this "disclosure" came word that the Administration had decided to begin construction of the hydrogen bomb. Opinion polls showed a generally favorable reaction. Most Americans, it seemed, were frightened by the weapon and terrified by the thought of not possessing it. Truman would be "shirking his responsibility," said the Washington

Post, "by leaving the United States one fine day to face a stand-and-deliver ultimatum from a Soviet Union armed with an H-bomb."[9]

Almost simultaneously, a British physicist named Klaus Fuchs was arrested in London for violating the Official Secrets Act. He soon confessed to "the crime of the century"—funneling A-bomb plans to the Russians. Then J. Edgar Hoover said that Fuchs, a veteran of the Manhattan Project, had probably transmitted H-bomb secrets as well. Although no evidence was presented to support that contention, the press took Hoover at his word. Both the Washington *Post* ("Hydrogen Bomb Secrets Feared Given Russians . . . Implications Grave") and the New York *Times* ("British Jail Atom Scientist—He Knew of Hydrogen Bomb") simply assumed Fuchs's knowledge of the H-bomb, as did most political leaders. Lost in the hysteria was the fact that the Soviets were quite capable of making advances in nuclear weaponry without stolen blueprints from the West.[10]

The belief that Russia was on its way to building a "super bomb" accentuated fears of a nuclear holocaust. In New York City school officials began distributing metal "dog tags" and holding practice drills in which youngsters were taught to dive under their desks and shield their eyes from an atomic blast. (One first-grader explained his tag this way: "That's if a bomb gets me in the street, people will know what my name is.") In Washington, D.C., real estate agents put ads in the local papers reading, "Small farm—out beyond the atomic blasts," or "An estate in Belle Meade, Virginia—a safe 58 miles from Washington." Toledo's Mayor Michael DiSalle tried to calm worried residents by joking that he would build large neon signs directing Russian pilots to Cleveland and Detroit. The most extreme reaction came from William Loeb's Manchester *Morning Union*, which advocated an immediate nuclear strike against the Soviet Union:

> We cannot sit idle and wait for Armageddon and destruction. We must forestall such a catastrophe and the only way is to strike a proposed aggressor before he is ready to strike. A preventive war . . . will be the greatest agency for peace in the world today, as well as our only salvation from impending destruction. We cannot delay longer.[11]

Standing alone, the Fuchs arrest would have been fuel for any campaign; following so closely behind the Hiss case and the fall of China, it was political dynamite. As the Republicans prepared for their Lincoln's Birthday speaking engagements, they were determined to push a common theme: subversion in government. "There are other spies and there will continue to be," fumed Homer Capehart, "as long as we have a President who refers to such matters as 'red herrings' and a Secretary of State who refuses to turn his back on Alger Hisses."[12]

FEW STORIES IN MODERN AMERICAN HISTORY have been as frequently recited, or as widely accepted, as the one documenting McCarthy's "conversion" to anti-Communism. Like Teddy Roosevelt at San Juan Hill or Warren Harding in the Blackstone's smoke-filled room, Joe's dinner meeting at Washington's Colony Restaurant has become part of American folklore. It was there, we are told, that the senator was spoon-fed the issue that resurrected his sagging career and helped start the nation down the road to political repression and hysteria.[13]

As legend has it, McCarthy dined on January 7, 1950, with Father Edmund Walsh, dean of Georgetown's School of Foreign Relations; Charles Kraus, a political science instructor at Georgetown; and William Roberts, a tough-talking Washington attorney. In deep political trouble, Joe was searching for a reelection issue with "some real sex appeal." After kicking around a few possibilities—old-age pensions and the construction of a St. Lawrence Seaway—the men adjourned to Roberts's law office, where Father Walsh suggested his own favorite, "Communism in government." McCarthy jumped at the idea. "The government is full of Communists," he is quoted as saying. "The thing to do is hammer at them." After a lively discussion, as reported by Jack Anderson and Ronald May,

> . . . his three fellow Catholics went away with the feeling that the sincere McCarthy would do his country a service by speaking out against the Communist fifth column. They little realized that a day would come when they would all have to repudiate the young man who started his Big Show with their basic idea.[14]

There is no question that the meeting took place. But the participants have always disagreed about what was discussed. Drew Pearson, who broke the story, claimed to have gotten it from Roberts, a supposedly impeccable source. Yet Walsh insisted that the evening's conversation was light, taking in the weather, personal anecdotes, and other such topics. He even tried to get a retraction from Pearson but finally gave up in disgust.[15]

Regardless of whose version one accepts, it would be wrong to assume that those men were responsible for McCarthy's "conversion." The senator was well acquainted with political anti-Communism. He had used it against Howard McMurray, public housing advocates, and the Madison *Capital–Times*, among others. His Red-baiting career did not begin at the Colony.

Furthermore, if "Communism in government" was discussed that evening, it made little impression upon McCarthy. In the following weeks, he barely touched the subject. Aside from a speech on Alger Hiss, he spent his time talking about the evils of organized crime, the need for pension reform, and his hope for a well-nourished America. "There's something wrong with destroying food when people are going hungry," he told the Washington *Post*.[16]

When McCarthy journeyed to Wheeling on February 9, he was not yet a one-issue politician. He chose to speak there on Communists in government for several reasons: It was the burning issue of the day, something he had exploited in the past, and the subject that most Republicans intended to use. Only a few days before, Joe had hired a Washington newsman named George Waters to write the speech for him. Needing assistance, Waters had approached Willard Edwards of the Chicago *Tribune* and said, "The senator wants a speech on Communist subversion. Can you help me?" Edwards was the right man to ask. Having just completed a series of articles on the subject, he gladly turned over his notes to Waters. "I didn't know McCarthy very well then," Edwards admitted. "All I knew was that he was looking for some information that I could easily provide. I was glad to help him out."[17]

Joe hadn't the faintest notion that his life was about to change. A letter to a friend, dated February 7, spoke of the coming trip in ordinary terms, as a political chore. He made no attempt to tip off the press or the Republican Party. The Wheeling papers assumed that he would speak about aid to the elderly. And the GOP gave him dismal bookings— Wheeling, Salt Lake City, Reno, Las Vegas, and Huron, South Dakota. McCarthy, it seems, was anticipating a rather dull weekend.[18]

───

THE WHEELING SPEECH, delivered to a dinner meeting of the Ohio County Women's Republican Club, was pompous campaign oratory, designed for an unsophisticated audience. Much of the background material was taken from Richard Nixon's recent address to the House of Representatives. "The great lesson to be learned," Nixon had said, "is that we are not just dealing with espionage agents who get thirty pieces of silver to obtain the blueprints of a new weapon. . . . This is a far more sinister type of activity because it permits the enemy to guide and shape our policy." McCarthy's Wheeling description: "One thing to remember . . . is that we are not dealing with spies who get thirty pieces of silver to steal the blueprint of a new weapon. We are dealing with a far more sinister type of activity because it permits the enemy to guide and shape our policy."[19]

The theme of the speech was rather simple: America, the strongest nation on earth, the center of "the Democratic Christian world," was losing the Cold War, and losing badly, to the forces of "Communist atheism." Why? Because the Department of State, led by Dean Acheson —"this pompous diplomat in striped pants"—was filled with dupes and traitors, men and women who *wanted* the other side to win. "The reason why we find ourselves in a position of impotency," the senator explained, "is not because the enemy has sent men to invade our shores, but rather because of the traitorous actions of those . . . who have had all the benefits that the wealthiest nation on earth has had to offer—the finest homes, the finest college educations, and the finest jobs in Government we can give."

McCarthy named several names: Harlow Shapley, John Stewart Service, Gustavo Duran, and Mary Jane Keeney. Then, according to several witnesses, he said: "While I cannot take the time to name all of the men in the State Department who have been named as members of the Communist Party and members of a spy ring, I have here in my hand a list of 205 . . . a list of names that were known to the Secretary of State and who nevertheless are still working and shaping the policy of the State Department." *

McCarthy had no list, of course, but the figure 205 was not hard to track down. In 1946 Secretary of State James Byrnes had written to Congress about a preliminary loyalty screening of 3,000 federal employees. Byrnes noted that damaging information had been uncovered in 284 cases. As of July 1946 only 79 had been discharged. This left 205 still working at State. Joe had no idea how many more had been fired in the intervening years; nor did he know whether those individuals were Communists, Fascists, alcoholics, sex deviants, or common liars. As a gambling man he was simply raising on a poor hand, searching for an ace or two before his bluff was called.[20]

According to Willard Edwards, the Wheeling address was typical of McCarthy, who had a habit of tinkering with prepared speeches until they became unrecognizable to the writer. On one occasion, Edwards noted, several of Joe's staffers came to him with information about "Communist influence" within the National Labor Relations Board. "If we give this to the senator," they told him, "you know what he will do. He will blow it up to proportions which cannot be supported. We thought you might write a speech for him based on what we have, and presenting

---

* Two points should be made here. *Point one:* McCarthy denied uttering these words, and there is no accurate record of exactly what he did say. His speech was recorded by radio station WWVA, but the recording was accidentally erased. While his rough notes did, indeed, contain the words quoted above, he reworked the speech in his hotel room that afternoon; and that evening he spoke extemporaneously, sometimes roaming the platform without notes. McCarthy admitted that he had used the number 205, but only, he said, to list the number of "bad risks" in the State Department. His key sentence, he added, was "I have in my hand 57 cases of individuals who would appear to be either card-carrying members or certainly loyal to the Communist Party."

Point two: McCarthy knew nothing about Gustavo Duran, John S. Service (whom he called John W. Service), Harlow Shapley (whom he called Howard Shipley), and Mary Jane Keeney (whom he called Mary Jane Kenny). In the coming weeks he would present nine public cases to a Senate Committee—including those of Service, Shapley, and Duran. He would say nothing more about Keeney. This was ironic, for she would have been a fairly strong case. She had been friendly with Earl Browder, head of the American Communist Party, and she had entertained Soviet espionage agents, such as Gerhardt Eisler and Nathan Gregory Silvermaster, in her home. After resigning from the State Department in 1946 (in order to spare herself the notoriety of being dismissed as a security risk), she had obtained employment at the U.N. In 1951 she was dismissed from her U.N. job.

him with the finished product. He might deliver it as given to him without putting in his own embellishments."[21]

Edwards agreed to write the speech. It was, by design, a conservative document which began, "Mr. President, I rise to inform the Senate of evidence which, I believe, establishes that Communist influences are working to affect the judgments of the National Labor Relations Board." Edwards's strategy was sensible. Let the opposition think that McCarthy had a weak case. Then, after the customary cries of "false charges," Joe could counter with his best evidence. Edwards recalled:

> I turned over the speech. After a few days, I inquired about its fate and was told, "The senator is working on it." I feared the worst. I was in the Senate gallery when, without warning, McCarthy rose and uttered this opening: "Mr. President, I rise to inform the Senate that I have indisputable evidence establishing that the National Labor Relations Board is honeycombed with members of the Communist Party." This charge was totally unprovable and the counterattack of "false charges" was unanswerable.[22]

AT FIRST, THE WHEELING SPEECH attracted little notice. It was, after all, delivered by a relative unknown in an out-of-the-way place. But McCarthy was persistent. When his flight to Salt Lake City touched down briefly at Denver's Stapleton Field, he offered to show a few curious reporters a list of "207 bad risks" employed by the State Department. After rummaging through his briefcase, he remembered that he had left the list in his baggage on the plane. Unfortunately there was no time to retrieve it. The Denver *Post* took him at his word, printing both the allegation and a big photo of Joe looking earnestly through his briefcase, with the caption: "Solon Left Commie List in Other Bag."[23]

In Salt Lake City the senator came up with a new figure. "Last night," he said, "I discussed Communists in the State Department. I stated that I had the names of 57 card-carrying members of the Communist Party." Yet, as if to compensate for the smaller number, he made these "Communists" a bit more important. They were "no ordinary espionage agents," he told a gathering of local Republicans, but rather "men in the $5,300 or higher income bracket—the shapers of American foreign policy."[24]

How did Joe come upon the number 57? In much the same way he "discovered" 205—by lifting it from an old document. In 1948 the House Appropriations Committee had been allowed to peruse the State Department's loyalty files. Led by Robert E. Lee, a former FBI agent, its investigators found 108 past and present employees who posed "security problems." As of 1948, 57 were still working there.

By 1950, of course, this number was invalid. Only about 40 of these suspects remained on the job. And the "derogatory information" in their files was quite subjective, ranging from charges of Communist activity to association with minorities. "A number of informants have emphasized that she entertains Negroes and whites, both men and women, in her apartment," the dossier of case 104 said. Other suspects were described as "a bit Leftist" and "somewhat left of center." One was alleged to be "a heavy drinker and promiscuous," while another was seen playing bridge with members of the Soviet Embassy. Very few could accurately be labeled as "card-carrying Communists."[25]

When Joe got to Reno, the press was there to greet him. His charges had now reached Washington, where things were heating up. The big newspapers were curious; politicians were concerned; the Administration was angry. What everyone wanted was proof. Who were these card-carrying Communists, and how, exactly, had the senator learned of them? McCarthy wouldn't say, although he wired the President demanding that the State Department's loyalty files be reopened at once. "Failure on your part to do so," he warned, "will label the Democratic Party as being the bedfellow of international Communism."[26]

McCarthy's speech that night was almost identical to the one he delivered in Wheeling. The newspapers said it was well received, drawing gasps and even a few tears from the Republican faithful. But one patriotic listener was clearly disappointed. The commander of the Nevada American Legion wrote to his Wisconsin counterpart:

> Your man McCarthy came to Reno and made a splendid talk on subversive elements in the State Department, but when called upon to provide details I fear he fell down in so doing. This, of course, hurts the cause . . . and in the opinion of many people he has gotten himself out on a limb.[27]

After several more stops, Joe returned to Wisconsin. He spent one day in Milwaukee, lunching with local reporters. "We pressed him about his information," Robert Fleming recalled. "I remember his words well. He said: 'I've got a sockful of shit and I know how to use it.' But he didn't give us a thing—not a damned thing."

The next move belonged to the Administration. It could respond to these allegations or dismiss them as partisan rhetoric. Neither alternative was appealing. The first could serve to legitimize McCarthy, to show that the Democrats were concerned enough to respond. And the second had the trappings of a cover-up, like Truman's "red-herring" remark a few years before.

To compound the problem, Administration officials had no idea that Joe was relying on outdated public documents or that he was changing their meaning to suit his purposes. At the White House, presidential aide George Elsey sat down to assess the situation. His handwritten notes for February 13 are most revealing:

205 or 207? State Department can't find the names; we assume McCarthy doesn't have them either.

57? Said by McCarthy to be Communists. We don't know whether McCarthy has a list. He says he does. We don't know to whom he refers.

The important question: Does State know if McCarthy has anything the House of Representatives didn't have two years ago?[28]

Truman was furious. He vented his anger in a personal letter to McCarthy that went unsent. Spotted, perhaps, by a horrified assistant, it read: ". . . Your telegram is not only not true . . . it shows conclusively that you are not even fit to have a hand in the operation of the Government of the United States. I am very sure that the people of Wisconsin are extremely sorry that they are represented by a person who has as little sense of responsibility as you have."[29]

What bothered the Administration was the *specific* nature of these allegations. McCarthy was not making vague charges about socialist tendencies or left-wing bias; he was claiming to have the names of card-carrying Communists. Would a United States senator go this far out on a limb without hard evidence? Would he dare to make fraudulent charges that could so easily be unmasked? These were the big questions as Washington prepared for McCarthy's return.

<hr>

ON THE AFTERNOON OF FEBRUARY 20, Joe McCarthy took the Senate floor to discuss "the extent to which Communists have infiltrated into the State Department and are shaping its policy." When he began talking, the chamber was crowded with members who had anticipated a long session on a cotton quota bill. But Scott Lucas passed the word that no important business would be decided that day. His plan was to empty the Senate, thus minimizing the impact of McCarthy's remarks, deflating his ego, and denying him a quorum all in one fell swoop. Because of the lateness of the hour, many Republicans filtered out with the Democrats. By 5:00 P.M., there were perhaps a dozen senators left on the floor.[30]

McCarthy quickly withdrew his charge about the 57 card-carrying Communists. He would speak about "81 loyalty risks," he said, adding, "this list includes the 57, plus additional cases of less importance." At first he admitted that his material was really not new. "It has been there a long time. If . . . anyone . . . had expended sufficient effort, he could have brought this to the attention of the Senate." But he then changed his mind, saying that only an enterprising sleuth with extraordinary contacts could have obtained it. "I know that the State Department is very eager to know how I have secured this information. I know that the jobs of the men who helped me secure it would be worth nothing if the names were given."

For more than two hours, the senator and a few supporters fought a rear-guard action against the handful of remaining Democrats. It was an ugly spectacle, filled with shouting matches and political slurs. At times, Joe infuriated his opponents by posing as an expert on Communism. Were people aware, he lectured, that "practically every active Communist is twisted mentally or physically in some way"? Or that Communists believe "there is no Supreme Being"? At 7:30 he asked for a quorum call. When fewer than forty-nine senators answered the bells, Lucas called for a recess. The motion was defeated, and the sergeant at arms was instructed to "compel" a quorum—a measure that had last been employed in 1945.

It took almost thirty minutes to fill the chamber. This done, McCarthy rose to continue his case-by-case analysis of the 81 "loyalty risks." Relying upon the outdated Lee List—a fact which eluded the curiously unprepared Democrats—he paused time and again to embellish his "evidence." One suspect on the list was described as "inclined towards Communism"; Joe called him "a Communist." A "typist at the Soviet Embassy" was magically transformed into "an assistant editor." A "friend of someone believed to be a Communist" became "a close pal of a known Communist." One dossier noted that the suspect had "a report dated July 7, 1949, showing that his health is uncertain"; McCarthy alleged that "a report, which is dated July 7, 1947, shows that his *mental* health is unstable."[31]

These discrepancies were relatively minor when compared with McCarthy's handling of other dossiers. The following list shows some of the more significant falsificatons.

Statement from Original Dossiers	*McCarthy's Interpretation*
An individual with her husband's name was a Communist Party election petition signer. Apparently to date, no effort has been made to identify the above election petition signer as the suspect's husband although the information has been on hand for several months.	Her husband signed a Communist Party election petition, stating that he was a member thereof.
A report of December 31, 1946, reflects that witnesses describe her as being: "liberal," "pink," "no more of a security risk than many others if kept under proper supervision." She has been quoted as	A security report dated December 31, 1946, describes her as being "pink" and as advocating that we substitute conditions in Russia for those in the United States.

saying, "Everyone in Russia has equal rights" and that in this country minority groups are persecuted.

The informant also advised that a brother of the subject was a member of, and active in, the Jackson Heights, Long Island, Branch of the Communist Party in 1944. Further information was obtained to the effect that the subject himself has been a member of the Communist Party.

His brother, who either was or is in the State Department, was a member of the Jackson Heights branch of the Communist Party. . . . The file indicates that this man is not only very active as a Communist, but is a very dangerous Communist.

The senator took almost eight hours to misrepresent his evidence. With few exceptions—Mundt, Wherry, Ferguson, and Brewster—the Republicans sat quietly as the drama unfolded before them. "It was," Robert Taft said later, "a perfectly reckless performance." The Democrats, of course, tried desperately to blow holes through McCarthy's presentation. But their lack of preparation made an effective counterattack almost impossible. At 11:43 the Senate adjourned, leaving its members confused, exhausted, and not yet grasping the enormous political significance of what had just transpired.

CHAPTER EIGHT

Battle of the Billygoats

Scott Lucas rose early the next morning and spent a long day mapping strategy with his Democratic colleagues. They all agreed that a carefully controlled investigation of McCarthy's charges was now imperative. It was too late to ignore them; they could, however, be neutralized by a well-orchestrated power play. As Lucas saw it, the Democrats might call for a special subcommittee, limit its investigative scope, and pack it with hard-nosed Administration loyalists. On February 22 he asked the Senate that such a body be empowered to study "whether persons who are disloyal to the United States are employed by the Department of State as alleged by the Senator from Wisconsin (Mr. McCarthy)."[1]

The Republicans were skeptical. While few were then prepared to support McCarthy's allegations, none was about to let him or the anti-Communist issue be buried prematurely by the opposition. Before accepting the Lucas proposal, they demanded the addition of two crucial amendments: The resolution must be broadened to cover previous charges of State Department subversion, and the subcommittee must have access to the "complete loyalty and employment files and records of all government employees against whom charges have been made."[2]

Lucas capitulated. He wanted it clear that the Democrats had nothing to hide. What worried him, of course, was the inevitable confrontation over the files. Since Truman remained firm in his refusal to allow congressional inspection, it was possible that a Democratic-led committee would be forced to cite a Democratic President for contempt. As Senator McMahon noted, the Republicans seemed less interested in perusing the files than in forcing Truman to keep them closed.[3]

Still, Lucas was optimistic about his chances. What encouraged him —and others—was the fact that a man of McCarthy's meager accomplishments would be leading the fight. At the State Department, a senior officer grumbled, "I've got the son of a bitch and I'm going to let him have it." Another joked that the Republicans were about to break a cardinal rule of politics: "Don't put your wrong senator forward."[4]

This rule held for the Democrats as well. They were determined to stack the committee with heavyweights, men like Millard Tydings, Maryland's conservative senior senator. Tydings was a good party man, not a lackey. As chairman of the Armed Services Committee, he had established strong anti-Soviet credentials. On a personal level he was well respected though not always popular. Known for his excessive vanity, he had once punched a photographer, yelling, "You guys wait until I'm picking my nose before you shoot!" A list of the "Ten Most Powerful Senators" described Tydings as "elegant, sarcastic, with a mind like a rapier." Connally and Lucas begged him to head the committee. After twice turning them down, he finally agreed. What worried Tydings was that he was up for reelection in November.[5]

The other Democratic members were Theodore Green and Brien McMahon. At eighty-three, Rhode Island's Green was a man of charm, energy, and intelligence. An ardent New Dealer, he was best known for his unwavering defense of civil liberties. In the face of stern pressure from his blue-collar Catholic state, he stood almost alone in voting to sustain Truman's veto of the Internal Security (McCarran) Act of 1950. Unlike Tydings, moreover, he treated his Senate colleagues with good humor and respect. He was one of the few Democrats who chose to attend McCarthy's wedding in 1953.[6]

Connecticut's Brien McMahon was an ambitious Irish Catholic who chaired the Joint Congressional Committee on Atomic Energy. Nicknamed "Senator Atom," he had led the successful campaign to wrest control of the arms program from the Pentagon and give it to civilian planners. According to one journalist, McMahon was "deeply partisan, untroubled by philosophic hesitations and not at all deterred by excessive scruples from hitting a Republican, in the political sense, over the head with any odd bit of plank or masonry that happens to be lying about." On previous occasions the Democratic leadership had used him as a "hit man" against selected GOP tormentors. This undoubtedly was to be his role on the committee. Like Tydings, he was up for reelection in 1950.[7]

The two Republican members, Henry Cabot Lodge of Massachusetts and Bourke Hickenlooper of Iowa, personified the bitter split within GOP ranks. Lodge was a patrician, the very epitome of the Eastern Establishment. He was committed to internationalism and to many New Deal domestic reforms. For reasons of principle and breeding, Lodge was repelled by McCarthy. Their only bonds were party affiliation and the strength of the Communist issue itself—bonds that were to prove stronger than most observers predicted.[8]

Hickenlooper, on the other hand, was the perfect caricature of the hayseed in Congress: dull, plodding, always ready with the ill-timed non sequitur. His odd handling of witnesses during Senate hearings had led columnists to joke of "pulling a Hickenlooper." Conservative, suspicious of all attempts at international cooperation, he was to be McCarthy's only real ally on the committee.[9]

WITH THE HEARINGS SCHEDULED for March 8, Joe had little time to prepare his case. He knew that his early charges were sure to be shredded by Tydings and McMahon. (He could probably hear them sneering, "How many are there, McCarthy? 205? 57? 207? 81?") Needing fresh information quickly, he took a room at the Library of Congress, where his staff began the tedious process of sifting through old congressional hearings and reports.

Joe's investigative unit was headed by Donald A. Surine, a ten-year FBI veteran who had just been fired for involving himself with a prostitute during a white slavery investigation. Hoover was fond of Surine and quite sorry to see him go. He recommended the ex-agent to McCarthy, who hired him at once. It was Surine's job to work as liaison between Hoover and McCarthy and to milk the contacts he had made during his decade in the Bureau. Edward Morgan, a top FBI official, recalled a visit he had from Surine shortly after the Wheeling speech. "You know the State Department . . . as well as anyone," Surine said. "Can you tell us one man who can give us a case? He'll be taken care of, either financially or politically." Morgan was outraged. "Had not Surine been a former agent," he confessed, "I'd have thrown him out of my office."[10]*

Joe spent many hours pumping friends, colleagues, and natural allies. He got Richard Nixon to let him see some of HUAC's secret material. He persuaded Jack Anderson to let him peruse Drew Pearson's files. And he begged William Randolph Hearst, Jr., to help the "cause" by helping Joe McCarthy. "Joe never had any names," Hearst recalled. "He came to us. 'What am I gonna do? You gotta help me.' So we gave him a few good reporters."[11]

Most of McCarthy's information came from a network of right-wing

---

* Edward Morgan would serve as the majority (Democratic) counsel to the Tydings Committee. Robert Morris would serve as the minority (Republican) counsel.

propagandists who had been pushing his line for almost twenty years. The group included J. B. Matthews, the former staff director of HUAC; Alfred Kohlberg, the mysterious "China Lobby Man"; Robert Morris, a well-known loyalty-security investigator; Louis Budenz and Freda Utley, a pair of ex-Communist informers; Willard Edwards and Walter Trohan of the Chicago *Tribune*; Frederick Woltman of the Scripps-Howard chain; and George Sokolsky, Westbrook Pegler, and Howard Rushmore of the Hearst syndicate. A few, like Woltman, a Pulitzer Prize winner, were serious anti-Communists who preferred research to rumor. Others, like Willard Edwards, were opportunists who viewed the controversy in terms of their careers. ("McCarthy was a dream story," Edwards remembered. "I wasn't off page one for four years.") Still others were zealots who smoked out—and fabricated—all kinds of stories linking the New Deal with Moscow.[12]

According to McCarthy's friend Robert Morris, the senator did not have to seek out these people. After Wheeling they came to him.

> Freda Utley called up and volunteered her services. Matthews and Kohlberg opened their files. Sokolsky couldn't wait to meet him. I mean, here was a United States senator saying the same things they had been saying for years. They just embraced him.[13]

Matthews was the leader, "the guts of the operation." A man of extremes, he had been an energetic fellow traveler before jumping the spectrum to become a right-wing oracle. "It was J. B. Matthews's curse," a critic noted, "to be unable to survive except in extravagant company. He looked at America and saw nothing between Earl Browder and Martin Dies." Matthews's value lay in his contacts and his voluminous files on domestic subversion. "To me a letterhead of a Communist front is a nugget," he liked to say. His biggest nugget was "Appendix Nine," a list of 22,000 supposed fellow travelers that had been suppressed by HUAC but never recalled from his New York apartment. It would serve as Joe McCarthy's bible.[14]

Other documents were supplied by Alfred Kohlberg, owner of a prosperous import company dealing in Chinese embroideries. Fascinated by the Orient, Kohlberg had read up on its history and become active in the Institute of Pacific Relations (IPR), an organization devoted to the study of Asian affairs. In the 1930s he had urged swift American action against the Japanese, who were then overrunning China. In the 1940s he had warned against the Communists—in China, the State Department, and the press. As a friend and supporter of Chiang Kai-shek, Kohlberg was determined to save the Generalissimo from his "slanderous detractors." Anyone who spoke ill of the Nationalists was obviously a Red. There was no middle ground.[15]

In 1947 Kohlberg had leveled this charge at the IPR's Board of Trustees. When it was rejected by the full membership, he quit in disgust. By 1950 Kohlberg had become a central figure in the "China Lobby." Never monolithic, it included those who saw Chiang as the best hope for a democratic China, others who felt he was vital to America's security, and some who joined for political gain. What made Kohlberg so important was the new element—treason—that he and his supporters brought to the controversy. Chiang was not defeated on the battlefield, they contended. He was "sold out" by a cadre of scholars, writers, and State Department officers.[16]

Like J. B. Matthews, Kohlberg had compiled a mountain of information about his specialty. Some of it was the product of his own research; he had spent the greater part of 1946 reading works on Asia at the New York Public Library. The rest came from informers like Utley and Budenz, from the files of the Chinese Nationalist secret police, and from a well-placed clerk in the federal bureaucracy. "We learned later," said Donald Hanson, a White House aide, "that a woman employed at the Loyalty Review Board had sent FBI reports on . . . government employees to a man named Kohlberg."[17]

At first, this information was passed on to various Republican senators, including Styles Bridges and Ken Wherry. But after the Wheeling speech, Kohlberg found his ideal conduit. Hopping a plane to Washington, he joined McCarthy and his assistant Jean Kerr for a "super cram session." "Joe asked me to give him the story of the China sellout step by step and in chronological order," Kohlberg recalled. "This I did during a two-hour dinner. Jean Kerr took brief notes. . . . and the following week . . . the senator would tell the story . . . just as I had told it to him there, almost without error."[18]

━━━━━

THE MARBLE-COLUMNED SENATE CAUCUS ROOM was standing-room-only on the morning of March 8. For weeks stories had circulated about a Democratic "first-round knockout" strategy. Tydings, it was rumored, had decided to flatten McCarthy before he could generate any momentum. "Let me have him for three days in public hearings," the chairman had boasted, "and he'll never show his face in the Senate again." Since Joe was the leadoff witness, the Caucus Room hummed with the electricity that often precedes a bloodletting.

As expected, the Democrats came out swinging. When McCarthy tried to read a prepared statement, Tydings cut him off with a pointed question: Would the witness care to name the State Department officer who he claimed was responsible for clearing case #14, a "flagrant homosexual"? Tydings already knew that the man in question was one Joseph Panuch, and that on the evening of February 20 McCarthy had warmly praised one State Department officer and roundly condemned another without realizing that they were the same person—Joseph Panuch.*

Joe backpeddled furiously. He asked for permission to read his full statement before responding to questions. He mixed up case #14 with case #57 in an attempt to demonstrate the futility of dealing with specifics so early in the hearings. He even invited Tydings up to his office, where "I will dig that case out and give you all the names in the files, all the information you want." But the chairman kept tightening the noose.

TYDINGS: We do not want to go to your office. We are conducting a hearing.

MCCARTHY: You will have to wait, then, until I get the information over here, Mr. Chairman.

TYDINGS: Do you or do you not know the name of this man? Do you know it?

MCCARTHY: At this point, Mr. Chairman, I could not give you the names of half of these people.

Senator Lodge jumped into the fray, demanding that McCarthy be allowed to proceed without interruption. Green objected: "It seems to me that it is important to continue in this unusual manner. . . . The question is whether the witness knows the name or whether it is imaginary." Bourke Hickenlooper took up Lodge's argument, prompting McMahon to speak up for Green. Within minutes, this partisan exchange had dispelled any illusions about the possibility of an impartial or decorous investigation.[19]

The first skirmish went to the Republicans. Sensing that his behavior was alienating Lodge, a potential ally, Tydings backed off. His behavior had been overbearing; he had, in fact, displayed more interest in discrediting McCarthy than in listening to his testimony. There was little to do now but let him proceed.

After a few preliminary remarks, Joe dropped a folder on the table and began listing the evidence against his first "security risk," Dorothy Kenyon. The galleries, the press, and the five senators looked puzzled. No one, it seemed, had ever heard of the woman. Later that day, upon learning of the charges made against her, Kenyon asked a reporter, "Who is McCarthy?"

The confusion was understandable. Kenyon was not among the Lee List cases that Joe had presented to the Senate—an oversight he chose

---

* Panuch was a darling of the right who had supposedly been fired by the State Department for being too anti-Communist. When Panuch learned that McCarthy had raised questions about case #14, he told reporters: "The man was neither a homosexual nor a Communist. . . . McCarthy must be crazy if he is raising that case."

to ignore. What he did tell the committee was that Kenyon held "a high State Department position" and belonged to "at least twenty-eight Communist front organizations," nine of which had been cited by the Attorney General. The case did *seem* imposing.[20]

But not for long. On closer inspection, McCarthy's verbiage outran his evidence. He provided "documentation" for twenty-four fronts (not twenty-eight), of which four (not nine) had been cited by the Attorney General. And his testimony was filled with ominous and misleading statements. While claiming that Kenyon was a security risk, not a Communist, he would say: "Here again we have this prominent State Department official . . . crying aloud in her anguish for a *fellow Red.*" How was it possible, Joe wondered, for the State Department to clear someone with Kenyon's subversive background?

The answer was simple: Kenyon had never undergone a loyalty check. Whether this was due to carelessness, willful negligence, or something else is hard to say. Most likely the Department felt she wasn't worth the effort. After all, her position—a delegate from 1947 through 1949 to the U.N. Commission on the Status of Women—was an honorary one, far removed from the decision-making process at Foggy Bottom.

Ironically, had Kenyon been checked, the result might not have been unfavorable. She was, by any standard, remarkably casual about lending her name to new groups and causes. But she was rarely an active participant, and in only one instance—the National Council for Soviet–American Friendship—did her membership postdate the Attorney General's subversive designation.

She was, moreover, in good company. After examining the NCSAF's letterhead, Theodore Green ticked off the names of other "paper" members, including four United States senators and the scientists Albert Einstein and Harold Urey. Joe admitted that "some fine people" had been duped into joining a Communist front or two but contended that no person "of normal intelligence" could innocently belong to twenty-eight. "I personally would not be caught dead joining any one of them," he said testily.

McCarthy's credibility was further undermined by the appearance of Ms. Kenyon. She proved to be an effective rebuttal witness, fielding questions with skill and playing the role of innocent-though-gravely-wounded victim. As "an independent, liberal Rooseveltian Democrat," she freely admitted giving her name to several organizations that were later classified as Communist fronts. At the time of her membership, Kenyon noted, those groups seemed to be engaged "in activities of which I could and did approve." Upon discovering their true objective, she had resigned. Now, a decade later, her past had been distorted and her good name ruined. "Literally overnight," Kenyon remarked, "whatever personal and professional reputation . . . I may have acquired has been seriously jeopardized, if not destroyed, by the widespread dissemination of charges of Communist leanings that are utterly false."

Kenyon's case was aided by McCarthy's curious absence from the proceedings. Not only did it appear that he was ducking a confrontation, but the task of cross-examining the witness fell to Hickenlooper, who dredged up all sorts of trivial indiscretions from her past. (Had she not described herself as a radical in the Smith College *Class Book* of 1918?) This mindless probing allowed Kenyon to restate her strong *anti-Communist* beliefs. She spoke of her disgust with the Hitler–Stalin Pact and her public statements about "Russian slavery." Hickenlooper threw in the towel. There was no evidence, he told Kenyon, pointing to subversion or disloyalty on her part.

The press was generally appalled by McCarthy's performance. *Life*, a paragon of anti-Communism, praised Kenyon as "a convincing witness" with "a look of deadly and impressive seriousness," while *Time* called her accuser "loudmouthed" and "irresponsible." McCarthy, it speculated, "has probably damaged no reputation permanently except his own." The Washington *Post* published a Herblock cartoon of Joe hiding in the Senate cloakroom as Kenyon testified. On his hands and knees, he was whispering to an incoming senator, "Pst—Is She Gone Yet?"[21]

The Kenyon debacle was undoubtedly the product of last minute haste and confusion. McCarthy did not learn of the woman until the day before the first Tydings session, when her name was plucked from Appendix Nine. According to Willard Edwards, this was "standard procedure," since Joe "never knew at 9 P.M. what he would be doing at 10 A.M. the next day." The senator, of course, provided a different explanation. He had chosen this case carefully, he said, "not because Kenyon herself was important, but . . . to show just what it meant to be cleared by a Loyalty Board." McCarthy somehow forgot that *he* had called her important, and that no loyalty board had cleared her. But he did provide a curious reason for his drubbing: "Unfortunately, it happened to be the case of a lady."[22]

IN THE MIDST OF HIS ATTACK ON KENYON, McCarthy had taken a backhand slap at United States Ambassador-at-Large Philip Jessup. It was no more than a passing reference, noting the diplomat's "unusual affinity . . . for Communist causes." What made it newsworthy was Jessup's high position in government and his close association with prominent Administration officials like Dean Acheson. His name was familiar to millions of Americans. On March 14 the Washington *Times–Herald* ran the eight-column headline, "Jessup Pal of Reds—McCarthy."[23]

In the late 1940s Jessup had emerged as something of a Cold War hero. A well-respected professor of international law, he had left Columbia University to become America's delegate to the United Nations. There he had been forced into direct and bitter conflict with the likes of Yakov Malik and Andrei Vishinsky, his tough-talking Russian counterparts. Jessup had done well. He was calm, good-humored, and fast on his feet. (When Malik poked fun at the failure of American pollsters to pick the winner of the Truman–Dewey race, Jessup responded, "Perhaps Dr. Gallup should transfer his activities to your country. It would be much easier to predict the results there.") Later, as an international trouble-shooter, Jessup had been credited with helping to end the Berlin Blockade on terms favorable to the American side.[24]

Jessup's primary interest, however, was the Far East. He had been for many years an influential member of the IPR, serving as chairman of the Institute's American Council and as a member of the Board of Trustees. In 1947 he had signed a letter that dismissed Alfred Kohlberg's charges as "inaccurate" and "irresponsible." Kohlberg had responded in spades, calling Jessup "the initiator of the smear campaign against Nationalist China and Chiang Kai-shek and the originator of the myth of the democratic Chinese Communists."[25]

Kohlberg had no proof, only a flock of dubious assumptions. It was true that the IPR housed a number of Communist sympathizers, and equally true that its publications were often hostile to Chiang Kai-shek. Since Kohlberg equated loyalty to the Generalissimo with loyalty to America, he naturally assumed that all criticism of his hero was treasonous, the work of disloyal minds. Thus Philip Jessup—IPR leader, friend of Acheson, critic of Chiang *and* Kohlberg—became central to the conspiracy.

There were other black marks against Jessup. He had been accused of "fellow-traveling" by the House Committee on Un-American Activities; he had edited the controversial White Paper on China; and he had served as a character witness for Alger Hiss, a formality that was purposely distorted by some Republican senators. Well before Wheeling, Karl Mundt had accused the ambassador of a "sell-out" in China, adding, "One can wonder . . . how much Alger Hiss may have influenced the thinking of Professor Jessup." And Styles Bridges had asked his colleagues, "What confidence can we have in a man who testified as Mr. Jessup did?" *[26]

McCarthy's accusation, then, was only the latest in a series of con-

---

* As noted earlier, Walter Trohan and Willard Edwards of the Chicago *Tribune* had supplied McCarthy with much of his early ammunition. On August 9, 1949, Trohan wrote in the *Tribune:* "The ambassador-at-large Jessup, who directed a staff of 80 experts in the preparation of the Administration's defense for failure to halt the communization of China, was an associate of Alger Hiss and testified for him in the perjury trial which grew out of Hiss' Communist associations. Jessup was cited four times in the files of the House Committee on Un-American Activities in its investigation of subversive propaganda in the United States."

servative Republican attacks. Jessup learned of it while in Asia on a fact-finding trip. He caught the first plane back to Washington, noting that his abbreviated journey had been marred by criticism from another source as well: "While I was in the Far East I was attacked by two sources —*Izvestia* and Senator McCarthy. Anyone who believes in the concept of guilt by association might draw some startling conclusions from this fact."[27]

The articulate Jessup proved to be his own best ally. His testimony before the committee combined the right blend of humility, wounded pride, and concern for the national interest. The attack upon his loyalty, he surmised, was a regrettable episode that would probably do him no harm. The injury done to America's foreign policy, however, could not be so easily repaired:

> It may be relatively unimportant whether the character of a single American citizen is blackened and his name brought into disrepute, but in the present serious situation of international relations . . . it is a question of the utmost gravity when an official holding the rank of Ambassador at Large of the United States of America is held up before the eyes of the rest of the world as a liar and a traitor. I am aware, Mr. Chairman, that Senator McCarthy has not used those words. But if his insinuations are true, those words would certainly be appropriate.[28]

Like Kenyon, Jessup bludgeoned the committee with evidence of his strong anti-Communism. His trump cards were letters written in his behalf by Generals Marshall and Eisenhower, two supposedly unassailable public figures. Marshall had lauded Jessup's firm "opposition to all Soviet and Communist attacks and pressures," while Eisenhower had commended his "devotion to the principles of Americanism." Here, to be sure, was a classic example of *innocence* by association, and Tydings made the most of it by slowly reading the full text of both letters into the record.

McCarthy was present throughout Jessup's testimony. He even asked for permission to cross-examine, which Tydings denied. Once again, the mantle of prosecutor fell upon the unsteady shoulders of Senator Hickenlooper. With McCarthy feeding him an occasional question, he quizzed Jessup about his testimony at the Hiss trial and his alleged membership in several Communist fronts.

Jessup fielded these thrusts with ease. He had testified only about Hiss's public reputation, not about his guilt or innocence. That was the role of a character witness. As for the Communist fronts, he noted that only one of them, the American–Russian Institute, had ever been listed by the Attorney General. In that case, he was one of many celebrities who sponsored a dinner the group held in the 1940s. At no time, he insisted, had he belonged to the organization. Hickenlooper did not press the matter.

When Jessup had finished, the Democrats crowded around to congratulate him. They had waited impatiently for Hickenlooper to conclude, wrote one skeptic, "studying the arrangement of the furniture with an eye to being the first to wring the Ambassador's hand when his ordeal was over." Green won the race, lauding Jessup for having "so thoroughly cleared up these so-called charges." Close behind was Brien McMahon, who told the witness he was "entitled to the thanks of all our people for the magnificent job you have done. I join with Generals Marshall and Eisenhower in paying tribute to you." This partisan display lowered the stature of the hearings yet another peg. Having decreed that neither McCarthy nor his charges merited serious attention, the Democrats had taken to providing his victims with instant vindication.[29]

DURING HIS TESTIMONY, McCarthy had produced seven more names—Esther Brunauer, Harlow Shapley, Frederick Schuman, Gustavo Duran, Haldore Hanson, John S. Service, and Owen Lattimore. Only one, Ms. Brunauer, had appeared on the Lee List, and her case was typical of the way McCarthy distorted his evidence. Brunauer, a liaison officer between UNESCO and the State Department, had been charged by a "reliable informant" with Communist Party membership. In addition, her husband, Stephen, a Navy chemist, had admitted joining the Young Workers' League some twenty-five years before. That was hardly news, having been disclosed by a Senate committee in 1941 and by HUAC in 1947.[30]

McCarthy's case was pathetic. He not only embellished the old documents, he seemed to *create* the new ones. Ms. Brunauer, he claimed, was "the first assistant to Alger Hiss in the San Francisco Conference. This is set forth in her biographical sketch issued by the State Department." But the State Department register had no such listing, and the senator never produced the supporting evidence. He did say, however, that "this is one of the most fantastic cases I know of"—thereby placing it in the same "unheard of," "fantastic," "incredible," and "unbelievable" category with about 90 percent of his discoveries.[31]

And so it was. Following McCarthy's attack, the Navy Department concluded that Stephen Brunauer had security problems and suspended him. Esther fared no better. Despite a previous loyalty check, she was dismissed from the State Department in 1952—as a security risk.

Harlow Shapley (Harvard) and Frederick Schuman (Williams) were college professors who belonged to numerous front groups. Both had been cited by HUAC as fellow travelers. "Read side by side," sniped William F. Buckley, "[their] cases suggest a personal contest between the two to see which of them could help the Soviet Union more while hanging on to his academic reputation."[32]

There was, however, a ticklish problem: Neither man "worked" for the State Department. Despite McCarthy's claim that Schuman was a regular lecturer at State, the professor had given only one talk there, in 1946, and he had done so without pay. Shapley had been a member of the National Commission for UNESCO, but his appointment by the Secretary of State was a formality. He had been *nominated* for the post by the American Association for the Advancement of Science. Desperate for names, McCarthy seemed to throw out these two in the hope that their impeccable left-wing credentials would overshadow their dubious status as government "consultants."

The case against Gustavo Duran was not much stronger, but it would earn McCarthy big headlines and cost his victim dearly. Duran was a naturalized citizen who had fought on the Republican side during the Spanish Civil War. Although U.S. military intelligence reports listed him as a member of the Spanish Communist Party and, possibly, of the Russian Secret Police, he had obtained State Department work in 1943, shortly after coming to America. In 1946 Duran quit the Department to head the U.N.'s Survey, Research, and Development Branch, located in New York City.[33]

What made the case so curious was that the military intelligence reports were based largely on information received from the state-controlled press of Franco Spain—a malicious and wildly inaccurate source. Since Franco had powerful friends in Washington, Duran soon found himself under bitter congressional attack. In 1946 several Republicans, including Wherry and J. Parnell Thomas, urged a State Department probe. This was done; Duran was cleared of the charges but resigned to take the U.N. post. A year later Congressman Alvin O'Konski, a friend of McCarthy, called Duran "one of the most notorious international Communists the world ever knew." But this seemed like a parting shot. The hunters had lost interest, and the case soon faded from public view.[34]

Its resurrection by McCarthy was a desperate act. After all, Duran no longer worked at State, and the charges against him were old and murky. But the senator pressed forward, claiming that Duran still associated with leftists and that his job at the U.N. was more sensitive than people had imagined. Was the committee aware that Duran's brother-in-law was none other than Michael Straight, "the owner and publisher of a pro-Communist magazine called the *New Republic*"? Or that Duran's new job had him "screening refugees in connection with our Displaced Persons program"? McCarthy provided no proof of this, and, surprisingly, the committee asked for none.[35]

Duran hotly denied that he was or ever had been a Communist. He did claim to have fought with the Loyalists and to have headed their military intelligence service for about three weeks. "I may have naively repeated in conversations some of the superficialities and false illusions about Russia that were then generally accepted," he said later.

After 1950 Duran's life became a nightmare of grand jury probes, loyalty hearings, and vicious attacks from McCarthy. He was finally cleared of all charges in 1955 and allowed to continue his career at the U.N. One of the charges was ironic indeed: "That on at least one occasion you said you were sorry you had become an American citizen."[36]

McCarthy saved his heavy ammunition for Haldore Hanson, a State Department administrator who worked on the Point Four Program. Hanson's job was important; he was chief of the Technical Projects Staff, one of the several groups that conducted Point Four. Yet, as if by reflex, the senator moved him up a few notches and put him in charge of the whole operation. "Here," he added, "is one of the cleverest, one of the smoothest men we have in the State Department. . . . Here is a man with a mission—a mission to communize the world."[37]

Put simply, the case rested on a book Hanson had written at the age of twenty-eight, which chronicled his firsthand account of Chinese Communist guerrilla activities against Japan. By any standard, the book was sympathetic to the Reds—a fact that Hanson readily acknowledged. But it was written in 1939, he explained, at a time when the Communists and the Nationalists were united against a common enemy. "To deduce . . . my attitude toward the Chinese Communists eleven years later, in the midst of a cold war," was, Hanson suggested, a bit unfair.[38]

McCarthy disagreed. "Keep in mind," he warned the committee, that "Hitler's *Mein Kampf* was published ten years before he started putting each and every paragraph into action." While quite sensational, the comparison lost something when McCarthy admitted that he could not remember the name of Hanson's book:

SENATOR McCARTHY: I think it is in here. If it is not, I will have the name for you in just a minute.

SENATOR McMAHON: It is not here, Senator.

SENATOR McCARTHY: It may not be here. . . . I might say, Mr. Chairman, that this is my own filing system—

SENATOR TYDINGS: Take your time.

SENATOR McCARTHY: And, perhaps, not the best one. The name of the book is *Human Endeavor*, Mr. Chairman. . . . Sorry I have to hold the committee up this way.*

---

* Actually the book was titled *Humane Endeavor*, and McCarthy misquoted numerous passages—a fact that escaped the committee members who obviously had not seen the book themselves. William Buckley and L. Brent Bozell agree that Joe paid "scant heed to the rules of scholarship." However, they conclude, "to condemn McCarthy on the strength of these rules is to judge him by unusual standards; it is to demand of McCarthy a norm of behavior not subscribed to by other politicians and, for better or for worse, not expected of them." William Buckley and L. Brent Bozell, *McCarthy and His Enemies*, 1954, p. 90.

Hanson was less than amused. He told an interviewer that after McCarthy's charges were made "a man who feeds cattle on my farm in Virginia was asked why he continued to work for 'that Communist.' One neighboring farmer began to refer to me last week as 'that Russian spy.' " In 1953 the State Department dismissed Hanson by reason of a "reduction in force."[39]

The case of John S. Service was vital to McCarthy's indictment of the "China hands"—an elite group of State Department officers, including John Paton Davies, John Carter Vincent, and O. Edmund Clubb. The son of missionaries, Service was born in China, educated at the Shanghai American School, and later at Oberlin College. After earning a B.A. degree, he returned to China, where he was commissioned as a Foreign Service officer in 1935. Thorough and scholarly, he was fluent in Chinese and knowledgeable about the country's history, its customs, and its laws. In 1942 his superior at the Consulate wrote, "He is the outstanding younger officer who has served me in my thirty-six years of service."[40]

During World War II Service had called for a reevaluation of America's China policy. Convinced that civil war was at hand, he needed no crystal ball to determine the outcome. Chiang's regime, weak, corrupt, and unpopular, had little chance of beating back the Communists. What Service wanted, therefore, was a more even-handed approach. As long as Chiang had America's exclusive support, he would see no reason to compromise or to begin the saving reforms. And the Communists, when they ultimately gained power, would have every reason to hate and fear the United States.

Service was not alone in holding these views. They were supported by every political officer at the American Embassy in Chungking. What made him vulnerable, however, were his numerous reports on the Chinese Communists, his favorable assessments of their strength and their reforms, and his involvement in the sensational *Amerasia* affair. Upon returning to Washington in 1945, Service had met with Philip Jaffe, editor of the left-leaning *Amerasia*, and given him copies of classified memoranda he had written while in China. To say that Service used poor judgment would be understating the case. But his objective was not espionage; it was rather to publicize an alternative position on China through a news leak.* Service was arrested, but a grand jury voted unanimously against his indictment.[41]

By the time McCarthy got around to the case, it had been simmering

---

* Some scholars have compared the *Amerasia* case to the release of the Pentagon Papers, implying that the actions of John Service and Daniel Ellsberg were indiscreet though certainly well-intentioned. (See, for example, Joseph Esherick, *Lost Chance in China*, 1974, xix.) Needless to say, this sympathetic view does not include Joe McCarthy, who would use much the same logic as Service and Ellsberg in leaking classified information of his own.

for almost five years. Because of *Amerasia* and the stepped up attacks by right-wing journals, Service had undergone departmental loyalty hearings in 1946, 1947, and 1949. He had been cleared each time. McCarthy added no new information, only a series of misstatements. He charged, for example, that Service "was consorting with admitted espionage agents" and that "a number of members of the grand jury, but not the required twelve," had voted for his indictment. Surprisingly, though, the senator ended on a cautious note. He did not call Service a Communist. He concluded only that he "is not a sound security risk today." [42]

Service's days in government were numbered. In 1951 the Civil Service Loyalty Review Board declared him a loyalty risk, and Acheson quickly dropped the ax. The reason, ostensibly, was the *Amerasia* affair. But that was a smoke screen. In the following months other China hands, who had nothing to do with *Amerasia*, were also dismissed. What they had in common was a vision that Chiang would lose in China and that America would be wise to adjust its policies accordingly. When Chiang *did* lose, his supporters raised the angry cries of "sellout" and "treason." In Joe McCarthy, they found the perfect instrument of revenge.

Postscript: McCarthy knew nothing about Straight. He attacked him because Straight and the *New Republic* had been attacking McCarthy. It came out later that Straight, a Communist during his college days in England, had known for years about the treasonous activities of Guy Burgess, Donald Maclean, Anthony Blunt, and other Soviet "moles" in the British diplomatic corps. Straight had refused to turn them in, despite the enormous danger they posed to his own country's security. Straight eventually told the FBI his story —long after Burgess and Maclean had defected to Moscow. See "The Honourable Schoolboy," *Newsweek*, January 10, 1983, p. 22.

CHAPTER NINE

Stand or Fall

Until 1950 Senator McCarthy had gone his own way, asking little of his party and giving little in return. His major battles, in fact, had pitted him against other Republicans like Raymond Baldwin, Ralph Flanders, and Charles Tobey. But that was before Wheeling, before he had latched on to the party's best campaign issue—subversion in government. Now McCarthy was a Republican under attack, making partisan charges and drawing heavy Democratic fire. He was doing the GOP's dirty work, and he expected its support. More was at stake, after all, than the career of a lone Republican. If the senator was discredited, the party's big issue would suffer too. And most Republicans, he felt sure, were not about to let that happen.[1]

At the very least, McCarthy could expect the backing of the Senate's conservative–isolationist bloc, totaling perhaps two dozen Republicans and one or two Democrats. Foremost among them was Kenneth Wherry, the GOP's colorful floor leader. A licensed embalmer, known as "the merry mortician," Wherry was, by all accounts, the Senate's champion talker. During the 80th Congress he had set a record by speaking on 398 different subjects. And each and every address, it seemed, was punctuated with at least one memorable gaffe—or Wherryism. He spoke of Vietnam as "Indigo China." He recognized Wayne Morse as "the Senator from Junior" and Spessard Holland as "the Senator from Holland."

He railed against "the Chief Joints of Staff" and "the anti-Sherman Trust Law." He offered a colleague "opple amportunity" for debate. He referred bills to "the Rules and Illustrations Committee." He often prefaced his remarks with, "It is my unanimous opinion . . ." When Ken Wherry got up to speak, his colleagues usually stayed around to listen.[2]

Yet Wherry was no buffoon. On the contrary, he was regarded as a good salesman and a shrewd judge of character. His job was not to make party policy; that belonged to more cerebral Republicans like Robert Taft. Instead, Wherry mobilized support for Republican bills and led the fight against those coming from the Administration. By doing this job well—and fairly—he had earned the respect of senators on both sides of the aisle. As Connecticut's William Benton, a liberal Democrat, remembered:

> Ken Wherry was the kind of man who inevitably owns half the business in a small town and who inevitably earns the confidence of his fellow townspeople. . . . His outlook reflected his Nebraska background and it was something I understood because of my boyhood in Minnesota and Montana. I was opposed by conviction—and not by party loyalty alone—to virtually every political stand Wherry took. Yet I trusted him as a person.[3]

Wherry's conservatism was legendary. One journalist called him "the noisiest and most persistent spokesman for the extreme right of the Grand Old Party." Another saw him as "Washington's leading symbol and rallying point of die-hard conservatism." In domestic affairs, Wherry opposed everything the liberals and moderates had to offer—public housing, minimum wage, slum clearance, public power, and federal aid to education. Fearful of all foreign entanglements, he had voted against the British loan, the Marshall Plan, and NATO. At one Washington cocktail party, the story goes, a man bowed politely to a woman who didn't recognize him. "You remember me," the man said hopefully. "I'm the most reactionary fellow in Washington." "Why, Senator Wherry!" the woman beamed. "How are you?"[4]

Wherry's early support of McCarthy went a lot deeper than party loyalty. He liked Joe, understood his ambition, and was pleased by his seeming indifference to big city ways. He saw in his junior colleague a reflection of himself—a small-town booster determined to root out the crooks and cranks and Communists who had made life so troublesome for ordinary Americans. When McCarthy singled out Dean Acheson for special abuse, Wherry was positively gleeful. After all, he had voted against Acheson's confirmation as Under Secretary of State in 1945—the tally was sixty-nine yes, Wherry no—and had directed the bitter fight to deny Acheson the secretaryship four years later. Wherry and McCarthy would remain close until the end of 1951, when the Nebraskan succumbed to abdominal cancer.

On the whole, McCarthy's Senate allies were less distinguished than Ken Wherry. They were men who despised the New Deal, saw the U.N. as a Red front, and opposed foreign aid that did not flow directly into the pockets of Francisco Franco and Chiang Kai-shek. Some of them—including James Kem, Hugh Butler, John Bricker, Styles Bridges, Bourke Hickenlooper, and William Knowland—supported McCarthy's charges without actively seeking his favor in return. "Joe," Bricker once told him, "you're a real SOB. But sometimes it's useful to have SOBs around to do the dirty work."[5]

There were others, however, like William Jenner, Owen Brewster, and Herman Welker, who relished the label of "McCarthy supporter" and went out of their way to secure it. Jenner, young and handsome, had come to the Senate from Indiana in the landslide of '46. Big things were expected of him, but his views were so provincial, his rhetoric so extreme, that insiders quickly wrote him off as hopeless. Ironically, Jenner had attacked McCarthy's best targets—George C. Marshall, Dean Acheson, and Drew Pearson—long before McCarthy got around to them. What he lacked was his colleague's toughness, his knack for publicity, and his great manipulative skill. Jenner was a follower—but a loyal one.

The Washington press corps saw Jenner as the epitome of rural ignorance, a Li'l Abner in shoes. One newsman commented that he was "devoid of influence among his colleagues and partisan to the last brain cell." Another wrote, "Senator Jenner returned to Washington today and gave the whole world twenty-four hours to get out." In 1949 a poll of 211 national correspondents ranked him as the "second worst senator" (Taft was voted the best, Bricker the worst).[6]

Herman Welker, a rough-and-tumble ex-miner, was elected to the Senate from Idaho in 1950. Known as a sports fanatic, he had once threatened an investigation of professional boxing when a light-heavy-weight he admired was denied a title shot by the "Eastern boxing clique." In his spare time Welker scouted baseball prospects for major league teams and even landed a few, including slugger Harmon Killebrew. "I never saw a ballplayer who was a Communist," he remarked proudly. Fearful that his nation had gone soft, that it was now ruled by "Red Rats," perverts, and snobs, he saw McCarthy as the rallying point for America's virile, liberty-loving majority. "That fighting Irish Marine," said Welker of his hero, "would give the shirt off his back to anyone who needs it—except a dirty, lying, stinking Communist. That guy he'd kill."[7]

On the fringe of this pro-McCarthy bloc stood Robert Taft, the Senate's most powerful Republican. To some observers, Taft's early support of McCarthy was both disturbing and unexpected. He was, after all, a man of reason and order, a logical man who liked to play by the rules. Unlike many conservatives, he did not crusade to limit the rights of dissidents; and he was genuinely upset by tirades against the Soviet Union, viewing them as provocative and harmful to peace. "I see no reason for the President and the Secretary of State and everybody else calling the Russians names on every occasion," he wrote to Socialist leader Norman Thomas. "I realize that they are impossible to deal with, but I really do not believe that they intend to start a third world war."[8]

Still, Taft was a partisan who felt that incidents like the Hiss case should be played to the hilt. In 1948 he had urged a congressional aide to "make every possible issue" of Communism in government. But it was the fall of China that pushed Taft into McCarthy's waiting grasp. Like many Republicans, he believed that Chiang's collapse was due to State Department stupidity and treason. Since Truman had refused to dismiss the responsible parties, the GOP had no choice but to do it for him.[9]

Under ordinary circumstances, McCarthy's crudeness would have offended Taft's sense of fair play. By 1950, however, Taft was out to dismantle the State Department's high command; the means were irrelevant. So began a working relationship that was to plague him for his remaining years in the Senate.

Following McCarthy's wild performance on February 20, Taft was inclined to dismiss the charges as "nonsense." What changed his mind was the strong grass-roots support that his colleague had generated. By late March he was telling Joe to keep punching—"if one case doesn't work out, bring up another." Several witnesses overheard a Taft–McCarthy conversation in early April that ended with a backslapping, "Keep it up, Joe." There is also evidence that Taft was secretly feeding information to his colleague. On May 2 he sent him the name of a State Department employee who merited "special attention."[10]

Despite this encouragement, Taft bristled when news stories linked the two men in any way. On one occasion he ran into Doris Fleeson, the liberal columnist, and said, "The trouble with you reporters is that you have a mania about McCarthy." Taft was more than upset, Fleeson recalled. He was "almost berserk." In one breath "he'd say that McCarthy was unimportant and in the next that he was right. . . . He said that 90 percent of the senators agreed that McCarthy had something. . . . He got brick red and yelled, 'You smear me and try to destroy me. . . . There are 96 senators. Why pick on me?' "

Fleeson did not publish these remarks. She simply included them in a long, thoughtful memo to herself. "These notes," she said, "are written by me immediately after the conversation. If they err, it is on the side of not reporting the senator's views as extravagantly as he yelled them at me." Fleeson added: "I can understand at least part of what ails him. He is in trouble with those who wish that the Taft legend of honor and integrity were not tarnished by his ties with McCarthy and his apparent indifference to the McCarthy methods."[11]

This ambivalence was felt by other Republicans as well. At a series of strategy meetings—attended by Taft, Wherry, and Bridges—an interesting consensus emerged. McCarthy, they agreed, was not the best man for the job. He obviously had guts and the ability to absorb punishment without flinching. But he was undisciplined, prone to exaggeration, and difficult to control. What was needed, therefore, was a way to separate McCarthy, who was expendable, from the anti-Communist issue, which was not.[12]

In the following weeks a coherent Republican strategy was developed. The party would downplay McCarthy while quietly giving him all the help he needed. If his case panned out, Republicans could embrace him and share in the political rewards; if it failed, they could easily disown him. Like the proverbial boxing manager, said *Newsweek*,

> . . . the Republican Party was right behind . . . McCarthy urging him to get in there and fight. . . . He stood in the center of the ring, wide open . . . with his chin hanging out, hoping to connect with a lucky punch and knock the Administration cold. If that happened, the GOP was thoroughly prepared to collect. . . . Of course, if Joe . . . got his ears cauliflowered, Republican candidates . . . could be expected to say: "That bum? We never heard of him."[13]

There was a good deal of silent GOP opposition to McCarthy, centered largely in the party's moderate Eastern wing. It was common knowledge that Republican leaders had difficulty finding a moderate who would agree to sit on the Tydings committee. Henry Cabot Lodge consented only after Alexander Wiley and New Jersey's H. Alexander Smith had refused; and Lodge avoided active participation by absenting himself from many of the hearings. Other moderates chose to suffer in silence. Charles Tobey, who had often clashed with McCarthy over consumer issues, now said little about his colleague in public. In private, though, he told a friend: "Confidentially, I think McCarthy is irresponsible and has got himself out on a limb which will collapse in due time." To a constituent who claimed that McCarthy was "augmenting prejudice, distrust, and hysteria," Tobey responded, "You are dead right in your conclusions."[14]

No Republican was more distressed by Joe's allegations than H. Alexander Smith. Fair-minded, meticulous, distrustful of those who shot from the hip, Smith had never thought much of his junior colleague. Now he had a personal grudge as well: Philip Jessup was his very good friend. On March 12, Smith wrote in his diary that McCarthy was "wrong to make public the names of people who may be innocent." The next day he went to Joe's office and was told that three or four "promising cases" had been developed, including Jessup's. At first, Smith was determined to make a speech defending his friend's loyalty and highlighting

"McCarthy's mistaken approach" to the security problem. But he soon had second thoughts. "My trouble," the senator confided, "is with Jessup's Hiss . . . connection. Yet I am sure of his complete loyalty and his fine public service." [15]

Smith spent the next few days soliciting the advice of Washington's inner circle. He lunched with columnist Stewart Alsop, who urged a public defense of Jessup and Acheson and a condemnation of McCarthy. Anything less, Smith was told, would destroy his chance to succeed the ailing Arthur Vandenberg as Republican leader of the Foreign Relations Committee. Heartened by what he heard, Smith went to Vandenberg's home for dinner. To his dismay, he was warned against supporting Jessup or Acheson. Vandenberg, it seemed, was worried that McCarthy might soon produce damaging information against them. That would leave their defenders holding the bag. That evening Smith wrote anxiously, "I had a strenuous day . . . and I am going ahead with the speech. I have taken both Acheson and Jessup out of it. God will guide me on the floor. It is important not to make a controversy but to make an appeal for a united front." [16]

His address, delivered on March 27, was a model of restraint—and political evasion. Calling upon the Tydings Committee to conduct its investigation without "partisanship or prejudice," Smith *seemed* to save his strongest criticism for McCarthy. He deplored name-calling and condemned those who failed to differentiate between "disloyalty and honest difference of opinion." Charges of treason, he continued, "should never be confused with charges of mistaken policy. It is entirely possible for a loyal official to hold tragically mistaken views." Unfortunately, Smith prefaced these words with a truly baffling statement:

> In nothing that I am about to say do I want it to appear that I am not in full support of the objectives and purposes of the Senator from Wisconsin. . . . In my judgment he is rendering a patriotic service and is performing his obvious duty. I regret the attacks on him, and the attempts to discredit him in the eyes of the public. . . . He should have our wholehearted support in his endeavors to get to the bottom of these matters.

The speech, remarked one Democrat, was akin to condemning Nazi atrocities while exonerating Hitler and the High Command. [17]

When Smith had finished, Senator Clinton Anderson brought up the Jessup case. If Smith supported McCarthy's objectives, Anderson wondered, did he also support McCarthy's attack upon his close friend, Dr. Jessup? "No, of course not," Smith shot back. "I definitely criticize it." Would Smith then be willing to publicly affirm Jessup's loyalty? Smith hemmed and hawed. "I do not think that is quite fair to emphasize that," he replied. But Anderson would brook no diversions. "I am sorry that the Senator from New Jersey is not prepared to stand by Jessup. . . . I want to say to him that if his name had been on McCarthy's list . . . every Senator on the floor would have jumped up and denounced the accuser."[18]

Smith had given his speech with the best of intentions. He wanted only to bring the spirit of reason and compromise to an explosive issue. Yet his message got lost somewhere in the translation. The Republicans weren't sure whether the speech was a thinly veiled attack upon McCarthy or a pathetic attempt at praise. And the Democrats saw it as a surrender to the forces of reaction. "I find myself depressed," Smith wrote in his diary, "because of the misrepresentation of my Monday speech. It is interesting to note that I had planned to leave McCarthy out of it and leave Jessup and Acheson in. My final revision left Jessup and Acheson out and McCarthy in. This gave the press the picture that I had endorsed McCarthy." Smith vowed to steer clear of the controversy in the future. It was, he complained, just one big headache.[19]

―――――

THIS GENERALLY SYMPATHETIC REPUBLICAN ATTITUDE was based on a number of factors: a belief that the Cold War was going badly and a feeling that the fall of China had been preventable, that security risks *were* loose in the government, that Truman was hopelessly incompetent, and that McCarthy, by raising these points, was performing a public service—and a political one as well. But GOP patience was hardly inexhaustible. Pressure was already mounting for the senator to produce a more menacing specimen than Philip Jessup or Dorothy Kenyon. While attempting to oblige his allies and appease a growing number of skeptics, Joe dredged up a most unlikely villain. His name was Owen Lattimore.

On March 21 McCarthy informed the press that he was about to unmask "the top Russian agent," the "boss" of Alger Hiss. Flabbergasted by the remark, Tydings assembled the committee for a closed-door session, in which Joe fingered Lattimore as the culprit. "Look, let's go off the record for a moment," he told the members. "I am willing to stake my whole case on this man. If I'm wrong about him, then I am discredited as a witness." The next day, without mentioning Lattimore by name, the senator said he was "willing to stand or fall on this one."[20]

Although McCarthy and the committee members were sworn to secrecy, the very idea of keeping Russia's "top agent" under wraps was more than they could bear. According to the columnist Doris Fleeson, they spread the name around Washington with such gusto that "people whose curiosity was killing them could probably pick it up in the course of a thirty-cent taxi ride from Union Station to the Capitol." Yet the press, fearing a libel suit, refused to make the name public. On March 26 Joe personally broke the logjam by giving the "official story" to Jack Anderson, who told his boss Drew Pearson, who broadcast it over national radio. (McCarthy also tipped Anderson that four Soviet agents had landed in America by submarine and gone directly to Lattimore's home for their instructions. Pearson decided to pass on that one.) As *Newsweek* reported: "Washington newspaper editors were kicking themselves . . . for letting . . . Pearson break the story. Every reporter covering the Tydings sessions knew the name that McCarthy had submitted and wanted to print it. But the editors . . . conferred with libel lawyers until too late —the news was out."[21]

Owen Lattimore, director of the Walter Hines Page School of International Relations at Johns Hopkins University, was well known in academic circles but virtually anonymous in the great world beyond. The author of many books and articles on Asia, he had spent much of his adult life there, studying its people and politics. In 1941 President Roosevelt had chosen him to serve Chiang Kai-shek as a political adviser. He had spent much of the war as head of Pacific Relations for the Office of War Information. Throughout the late 1940s, he had lectured to foreign service officers and had taken part in government-sponsored symposia on Asian–American relations. Although the final *Tydings Report* took great pains to show that Lattimore was never "in any proper sense an employee of the State Department," he had worked closely with its personnel, and his opinions were carefully scrutinized by those who helped formulate Far Eastern policy.[22]

Like Service and Jessup, Lattimore had been a longtime target of Alfred Kohlberg and his supporters. They charged that as editor of *Pacific Affairs*, an IPR journal, he had consistently pushed the Soviet world view. And here, at least, they had a fairly strong case. In 1938 the professor had lauded the infamous Moscow Trials, noting that they "sound like Democracy to me." A 1974 study of IPR, with no ax to grind, concluded that Lattimore had purposely toned down the vocabulary of Marxist contributors in order to get their message across more effectively. One scholar aptly portrayed Lattimore this way:

> A self-assured amateur politico and inveterate busybody whose views extended over a wider area than his knowledge and who, while transparently not of the temperament to accept a "line" from the Communists or anyone else, was more often than not to be found advocating positions on Far Eastern policy with which the Communists were in accord.[23]

Lattimore's real sin, however, was his belief that China could not be won for Chiang Kai-shek, and that America's continued support—or "subsidized turpitude"—was both morally wrong and politically unwise. Furthermore, when Chiang did lose in 1949, Lattimore called for a "more flexible policy" in Asia. He claimed that Washington was wrong to portray the Chinese Communists as Russian puppets, wrong to deny them diplomatic recognition, and wrong to support junior versions of

Chiang Kai-shek in South Korea, Indochina, and elsewhere. "China is a fact," he wrote in *The Nation*. "The Chinese Communists are a fact. . . . A new American policy in Asia must start with the admission that these facts cannot be conjured out of existence."

In 1950 the right-wing offensive against Lattimore intensified. Kohlberg barraged Congress with letters of condemnation. The Washington *Times–Herald* and the Manchester *Morning Union* published all sorts of material documenting Lattimore's "treachery." And Senator Knowland attacked the professor for calling South Korea "an American liability." Indeed, McCarthy himself had named Lattimore as one of his original nine loyalty risks; but he really had no idea who the man was or what he stood for.[24]

Richard Rovere once wrote of the Lattimore affair: "I have always been convinced that when McCarthy first talked about his 'top espionage agent,' he hadn't the slightest notion which unfortunate name on his list he would single out for this distinction." This is probably true. It seems clear that Joe knew little more about Lattimore on March 21 (the day he made the "top agent" charge) than he did on March 13 (the day he listed the professor as a security risk). Once the more serious allegation was made, however, McCarthy returned to his office for some heavy cramming. Working in shifts of sixteen to twenty hours, the senator, four staff members, and two stenographers pieced together "the Lattimore puzzle." Predictably, Kohlberg arrived on March 23 to offer his expert assistance.[25]

Joe did his best to enliven an already bizarre situation—in this instance by overplaying his role as patriot sleuth. He spent much of the following week speaking to his staff in code and running the water in his office basin to foil any hidden microphones. "Another habit," a newsman recalled, "was his tapping the mouthpiece of his telephone with a pencil. This was supposed to frustrate any bugs planted in his phone. Knowing Joe McCarthy, I concluded that this was not paranoia, but sheer childish delight in playing spy games."[26]

On March 30 Joe sent word to Ken Wherry that he was ready to document his charges. It was time to round up the troops.

CHAPTER TEN

The Lattimore Connection

EARLY IN 1950 SENATOR KEM received an "urgent letter" from a live-stock buyer in Kansas City. Fearful of a surprise attack by local Communists, the writer asked that "the Government issue firearms to responsible American men and women everywhere who apply for them —say a .38 or a .45 Colt's pistol." Lunatics and subversives could be weeded out, he suggested, by requiring a note from one's minister. "This is unusual, but not radical. . . . I honestly believe all America will thank me for this letter. Let us have prompt action before American morale is shattered by wanton wholesale massacre!"[1]

The writer was mistaken in one respect: His letter was not that unusual. Such homespun remedies had become commonplace. There were suggestions that America spray bugs on the East German potato crop, that Sears, Roebuck catalogues be dropped behind the Iron Curtain, that germs be transmitted to the enemy through Alaskan Eskimos. In Pennsylvania, the normally judicious governor, James Duff, echoed the growing demand that Communists be hanged. And a Gallup Poll showed most Americans expecting to be at war with Russia in the near future.[2]

The most bizarre display of anti-Red fervor occurred in little Mosinee, Wisconsin. On May Day, American Legionnaires disguised themselves as Russian soldiers and staged a mock takeover. The mayor was dragged from his home in nightclothes, and clergymen were herded into

a makeshift stockade near "Red Square." All businesses were nationalized, and local restaurants were forced to serve potato soup, dark bread,
and black coffee. The library was checked for objectionable books, firearms were confiscated, and only Young Communist Leaguers were allowed to eat candy. At dusk, after Mosinee was "liberated," a mass rally
took place amidst the burning of Communist literature and the sounds
of patriotic music.

What new insights had Mosinee gained from its day under "Soviet
rule"? Mainly that the food got worse. "We really learned about what 100
percent Communism would be like," claimed one resident. "The people
didn't like the soup." Said another: "I know some people who even drove
to [neighboring] Wausau to get something to eat. In Russia I guess you
wouldn't be able to get anything else anywhere." There was one unexpected casualty, the mayor. Overcome by the events, he suffered a heart
attack the next day.[3]

At the same time, state and local governments competed to see who
could crack down hardest on the Red Menace. Indiana forced professional wrestlers to sign a loyalty oath. Ohio declared Communists ineli-
gible for unemployment benefits. Pennsylvania barred them from all
state programs with one exception: Blind Communists would be cared
for. In Nebraska each school district was directed to inspect textbooks
for foreign ideas and to set aside a few hours each week for the singing
of patriotic songs. Tennessee ordered the death penalty for those seeking
to overthrow the *state* government, while Mississippi went after the local
Communist Party—and its single member. "This lone conspirator must
be kept busy indeed," one cynic teased, "as he fulfills the duties of . . .
chairman of his party, its rank-and-file membership, and the foreign-
directed forces that menace the state."[4]

More than 150 municipalities took similar action. Birmingham, Alabama, ordered all Communists to leave town. Jacksonville, Florida,
made it a crime to communicate with a present or former Red. When
the city council of McKeesport, Pennsylvania, discussed a similar proposal, two Communists appeared to lobby against its passage. One was
jailed for disorderly conduct, the other run out of town. Said the mayor:
"We are going to treat Communists in McKeesport just as Americans
would be treated in Moscow if they violated the Russian laws." In New
Rochelle, New York, an ordinance designed to register Communists
netted one perplexed citizen. He came to police headquarters thinking it
applied to commuters.[5]

The spring primaries showed that anti-Communist rhetoric could pay
big dividends at the ballot box. In California, Richard Nixon won the
GOP senatorial primary by ignoring the meager competition and Red-
baiting Harry Truman. "The Commies really don't like it when I smash
into him," Nixon told the Chicago *Tribune*. ". . . But the more the Com-

mies yell, the surer I am that I'm . . . bringing the Red danger . . . to the attention of the voters." Wherever he spoke, his wife Pat worked the crowd, handing out thimbles inscribed, "Safeguard the American Home." In North Carolina, Senator Frank Graham, a liberal Democrat, was beaten in a vicious campaign that stressed his humane views on race and his alleged membership in eighteen Communist fronts. And Iowa's Republican voters renominated Bourke Hickenlooper by a lopsided four-to-one margin. His support of McCarthy was seen as a tremendous asset.[6]

Nothing quite matched Florida's Democratic primary, where Senator Claude Pepper was upended by George Smathers in the year's biggest mudbath. Like Frank Graham, Pepper held more moderate views on race and the Russians than did his constituents. Realizing this, Smathers spread rumors about "Red" Pepper's "friendship" with Joseph Stalin. "He likes Joe," the challenger would say, "and Joe likes him." Campaigning one day in the Florida Panhandle, Smathers implied that his opponent was a left-wing degenerate. Did people know, he asked, that Pepper's daughter had gone to New York City to become a "thespian"? Or that Pepper himself practiced "celibacy" before marriage? Such tactics frightened and disgusted the incumbent, who compared Smathers to "that poison-purveying, headline-hunting Republican senator from Wisconsin, Joseph McCarthy."[7]

This comparison was revealing. It showed, inadvertently perhaps, how quickly people associated McCarthy with the hatred and the tension that gripped America. In three short months he had emerged as the nation's dominant Cold War politician—the new yardstick by which citizens measured patriotic or scurrilous behavior. Not since Franklin Roosevelt had a public figure been as clearly identified with the country's mood, or held as responsible for its excesses. The more Americans worried about the Russians, atomic war, loyalty oaths, or spies in government, the more they thought about Joe McCarthy. And the less certain they seemed about their own future.

UNTIL 1950 HARRY TRUMAN had rarely spoken, written, or thought much about McCarthy. He had had no reason to. Democratic presidents do not generally concern themselves with obscure Republican senators. Yet there was one incident involving McCarthy that must have infuriated the President. It occurred in the summer of 1949, during a Senate investigation of five-percenters (influence peddlers) who worked in and around the capital.

McCarthy, a subcommittee member, had been tough on Administration witnesses, particularly Harry Vaughan, the President's close friend and adviser. That was bad enough, but the senator went further by dragging Mrs. Truman into the fray. Noting that her name had appeared on a lobbyist's gift list—she had been given a "deep freeze"—he asked that the country judge this indiscretion with mercy and understanding. "She is in an embarrassing position," he purred, "but definitely not because of anything she has done, but for the—want of a better word—activities of her husband's military aide, so I would like to make it very clear, in my opinion . . . there is nothing on the record that indicates anything, as I say, even remotely improper on the part of the President's wife."[8]

Senator Hoey thanked his colleague for the "very proper" statement and tried to move on. But McCarthy hadn't finished.

> I think we all know from the picture here that the President's wife took this gift as she, perhaps, would take a gift of a 20-pound cheese or a turkey or something like that. . . . I am *sure* she did not know anything at all of the attempts to smuggle—the smuggling activities, for example, on the part of an employee of this perfume company. . . . In fact, I think she is one of the finest things about the White House. That is one of the few times that Harry used good judgment when he picked Bess.[9]

The President had a temper, a bad one. He could be loud and tactless when responding to criticism. Yet he ignored McCarthy's remarks, in public at least, and he tried to ignore his later charges as well. In a letter to Vice President Barkley, Truman recounted an old fable to describe the senator's behavior. Long ago there had been a mad dog that went around biting people. To deter him, his master had fastened a clog around the dog's neck. Even though the clog was a badge of dishonor, the dog foolishly viewed it as a positive symbol. The moral, Truman concluded, was that some men "often mistake notoriety for fame, and would rather be remarked for their vices and follies than not be noticed at all."[10]

Before long, though, McCarthy had worked his way under the President's skin. The ill-mannered attacks upon Dean Acheson were bad enough. Then came the Lattimore charge, that for ten years the State Department had pampered, rewarded, and mapped strategy with someone whose FBI dossier read "Joe Stalin's top agent." Truman was furious. He felt that America's foreign policy and its image abroad were gravely threatened. His patience had evaporated.

The President did not know quite how to deal with the charges. He wanted them stopped, but he feared that a White House statement would only exaggerate their importance. After much soul-searching, he decided on a more personal approach. He would contact some of his old Senate pals in the Republican Party. Perhaps they could help him out.

First on the list was Styles Bridges, a man who listed William Loeb, Chiang Kai-shek, and Francisco Franco among his closest friends and admirers. Truman had always liked Bridges while despising his politics. The two men had socialized throughout their years in the Senate. By exploiting this friendship, the President hoped to rally a prominent right-winger to his side. What could be more satisfying, he must have felt, than using Styles Bridges to muzzle Joe McCarthy?

On March 26 the President wrote a "Dear Styles" letter that pleaded for an end to the "indefensible attacks upon Mr. Acheson." It was typical Harry Truman: direct, abrasive, emotional. One can only imagine Bridges's expression when he read: "What you and other McCarthy supporters are proposing to do is not only unpatriotic, but is also a most dangerous procedure, likely to cause a situation in which young Americans may lose their lives by the thousands." Still, the letter ended on a warm note: "I am appealing to you as your old-time friend . . . and if you desire a discussion of [this] with me personally, I will be glad to go into every detail with you." [11]

The letter reached Bridges the evening of March 27, only hours after he had delivered a Senate harangue about high treason in Washington. Sensing that Truman would view this attack as a *response* to his letter, Bridges sent him an immediate clarification. But the President was in no mood to be appeased. At a press conference on March 30, he finally vented his frustration:

REPORTER: Do you think Senator McCarthy can show that any disloyalty exists in the State Department?

THE PRESIDENT: I think that the greatest asset the Kremlin has is Senator McCarthy.

REPORTER: Would you care to elaborate on that?

THE PRESIDENT: I don't think it needs any elaboration. . . .

REPORTER: Brother, will that hit page one tomorrow!

.   .   .

REPORTER: Mr. President, would you like to name any others besides Senator McCarthy who have participated in this attempt to sabotage our foreign policy?

THE PRESIDENT: Senator Wherry.

REPORTER: Yes, sir?

THE PRESIDENT: Senator Bridges.

REPORTER: Yes, sir?

THE PRESIDENT: That's about as far as I care to go.

REPORTER: Okay, sir. [12]

What little remained of bipartisanship went down the drain with these remarks. It was one thing for a Democratic President to complain of GOP partisanship, intransigence, or stupidity. It was quite another for him to label three of its Senators as saboteurs and Kremlin assets. Bob Taft spoke for many Republicans when he accused Truman of "libeling . . . a fighting Marine who risked his life to preserve the liberties of the United States." (When the President was asked at his next press conference whether he had, indeed, libeled McCarthy, he smiled as he said, "Do you think that is possible?") With the Lattimore confrontation only days away, the lines dividing the two parties were etched with bitterness and wounded pride. It was hard to imagine that things could get worse.[13]

AT 2 P.M. ON THURSDAY, MARCH 30, a Senate guard brought idle reporters to attention with the shout, "McCarthy's up." In the public gallery, spectators scurried madly for space, filling every seat and lining the back wall shoulder to shoulder. The Senate floor was already bustling with curious members, some of whom crossed the Republican aisle to watch attendants unload a dolly crammed with photostats. At 2:06, the chamber was called to order, the invocation read, and Wisconsin's junior senator recognized. Gulping cough medicine to ease a sore throat and bicarbonate of soda to calm an angry stomach, Joe began his case against Owen Lattimore. When he sat down again, he looked like a subway commuter in an August heat wave: hair rumpled and damp with sweat, necktie yanked askew, legs swollen and unsteady. The Senate clock read 6:18.[14]

In the previous weeks McCarthy had brazenly magnified Lattimore's danger to the nation. Starting out as a "bad security risk," the professor had been transformed into the "top Russian spy." By March 30 the absurdity of this escalation was apparent to all, and Joe wisely backtracked to safety. "I fear in the case of Lattimore," he told his colleagues, "I have perhaps placed too much stress on the question of whether or not he has been an espionage agent." Pausing slightly, McCarthy rushed forward with new evidence of treachery. He promised to produce two ex-Communists who knew Lattimore as a Party member with close contacts in Moscow.

The speech was almost identical to the ones he would deliver in the coming years. He began, as always, by stressing the dirty, thankless, and downright frightening nature of his task. "In discussing this matter with some of my friends . . . they pointed out to me . . . that the road has been strewn with the political corpses of those who dared to attempt an exposure of the type of individuals I intend to discuss today." But Joe was a scrapper, doing battle for 140 million God-fearing Americans. He would not let them down. "Many . . . people have expressed a deep concern for fear I may quit this fight. I want to assure them now that, in the words of John Paul Jones, 'I have just begun to fight.' "

Typically, the speech bulged with pompous jargon and historical minutiae. Why McCarthy did this is hard to say. It may have been an attempt to compensate for his educational deficiencies; it may have been his idea of a joke. But he always looked silly, like someone grappling with words that were strangely beyond him. "Lamaism is a form of Buddhism believed chiefly by peoples of Tibet and Mongolia, and is a mixture of Buddhism and shamanistic practices," he said during the Lattimore speech. And later: "Of the important living Hutuktus, the following are the most prominent: Changchia Hutuktu, Galdan Siretu Hutuktu, Minchur Hutuktu, Chilung Hutuktu, Namuka Hutuktu, Achia Hutuktu, Lakuo Hutuktu, Tsahantarkhan Hutuktu."

The speech also provided a textbook example of how to overstate one's case. Words like "fantastic," "unheard of," "sensational," "unbelievable," and "incredible" jumped from the pages. His charges against Lattimore were "made only after the most deep and painstakingly thorough study." The State Department had in its midst a "small but dominant percentage of disloyal, twisted, and, in some cases, perverted thinkers who were rendering futile the Herculean efforts of the vast majority of loyal Americans." At one point McCarthy convulsed the press box by stating, "I believe you can ask almost any school child who the architect of our far eastern policy is, and he will say, 'Owen Lattimore.' "

When the senator spoke, angry flareups and interruptions were expected—even encouraged. During the Lattimore speech, he precipitated one by quoting from a "classified letter" while refusing to place the entire letter into the *Record*. Charlie Tobey thought this absurd:

MR. TOBEY: Is it the Senator's intention to place the entire letter into the *Record?*

MR. MCCARTHY: No, it is not.

MR. TOBEY: I suggest that this be done. The quotation from it is taken out of context.

MR. MCCARTHY: I shall refuse the Senator's request at this time. The letter is marked "secret," and it is my present intention not to put any secret documents into the *Record.* . . .

MR. TOBEY: Mr. President, will the Senator yield further?

MR. MCCARTHY: I yield.

MR. TOBEY: If the letter is marked "secret," I suppose that applies in toto. If the Senator is reading excerpts from the letter, is he not violating his own principle when the whole letter is marked "secret"?

MR. McCarthy: This will become abundantly clear as I proceed.

When Senator Lehman objected further, McCarthy invited him over to his desk for a look at the document.

MR. McCarthy: . . . Does the Senator care to step over? (Laughter)

MR. Lehman: I am delighted to.

(Mr. Lehman thereupon crossed the Chamber and approached Mr. McCarthy's desk.)

MR. Lehman: May I see the letter?

MR. McCarthy: The Senator may step to my desk and read the letter.

MR. Lehman: I should like to see it. The Senator invited me to come over to read the letter. I am here to read the letter. Will the Senator from Wisconsin let me see the letter?

MR. McCarthy: Does the Senator wish to come close enough to come here and see it?

MR. Lehman: I think I would like to read it in my own way.

MR. McCarthy: Will the Senator come here and see it?

MR. Lehman: I would like to read it in my own way.

MR. McCarthy: Will the Senator sit down?

MR. Lehman: May I say, Mr. President—

MR. McCarthy: I do not yield any further at this time. *

The two men stood face to face for a few uneasy moments before Joe snatched up the document and mumbled a nasty retort. (Newsmen positioned above them said it was, "Go back to your seat, old man.") As Lehman withdrew, Stewart Alsop turned to his wife and whispered, "There goes the end of the republic!" [15]

---

* McCarthy had good reason for not showing the letter to Lehman. For, in its entirety, it proved the opposite of what he had been saying. Joe charged that during World War II, Lattimore had tried to rid the Office of War Information of all Chinese loyal to Chiang Kai-shek. The letter, from Lattimore to Joseph Barnes, said no such thing. It was a careful analysis of Chinese pressure groups, and it even contained a warning against the hiring of pro-Communist Chinese workers: "While we need to avoid recruiting any Chinese Communists we must be careful not to be frightened out of hiring people who have been loosely accused of being Communists."

What truly seemed at an end was McCarthy's hour in the sun. Despite some gallery applause, his speech was not well received in Congress or in the press. The Democrats viewed it as a rehash of already discredited charges. They were hopeful that Tydings would demolish them when the hearings resumed. And few Republicans were satisfied, although most refrained from saying so in public. Worse still was the response of the Luce publications, *Time* and *Life*, which had long supported GOP attacks upon the China Service. *Life* warned its readers "not to join the McCarthy lynching bee." *Time* noted that the senator "had promised to stand or fall on his case against Owen Lattimore, and he clearly had little left to stand on." [16]

The next day, Senator Wherry asked his colleagues to hold their questions. Sick and exhausted, Joe had gone to the Bethesda Naval Hospital to get his sinuses drained. But he would be back tomorrow, Wherry promised, fit as ever and ready for business. Tom Connally groaned in disappointment, having hoped, no doubt, for a slower recovery. And Wherry probably agreed. "Oh, Mac has gone out on a limb and made a fool of himself," he was quoted as saying, " and we have to back him up now." [17]

OWEN LATTIMORE FIRST LEARNED of the charges against him while on a U.N. mission in Kabul, Afghanistan. The Associated Press wired him that "McCarthy says off record you top Russian espionage agent in United States and that his whole case rests on you." Lattimore's response minced no words:

> McCARTHY'S OFF RECORD RANTINGS PURE MOONSHINE STOP DELIGHTED HIS WHOLE CASE RESTS ON ME AS THIS MEANS HE WILL FALL FLAT ON HIS FACE STOP EXACTLY WHAT HE SAID ON RECORD UNKNOWN HERE SO CANNOT REPLY IN DETAIL BUT WILL BE HOME IN A FEW DAYS AND WILL CONTACT YOU THEN STOP.[18]

Lattimore's appearance before the Tydings Committee drew the largest hearing room crowd since Wendell Willkie had pleaded for aid to Britain a decade before. The professor, a smartly dressed little man with thick glasses and a scraggly mustache, was accompanied by his Washington attorney, Abe Fortas. Seated directly across from them, no more than fifteen feet away, was Joe McCarthy. The two adversaries seemed to glare at one another, although Lattimore claimed that Joe refused to look him in the eye. At Tydings's signal, the witness began reading his prepared statement. An accomplished lecturer, he probably knew the forty-two pages by heart, for he barely glanced at them.[19]

Like Jessup and Kenyon, Lattimore played the game of innocence by association. He reeled off his anti-Communist credentials, including a letter of commendation from Chiang Kai-shek, whom he admittedly despised. At the same time, he insisted that he was a private citizen, whose influence upon the government was minimal: "The fact is that . . . I am the least consulted man of all those who have a public reputation in this country as specialists on the Far East."

Lattimore then treated his audience to a seminar on Sino-American relations. He did not deny that the United States had acted poorly in China. He just felt that the blame was being fixed on the wrong people. It was silly, he observed, to hold the State Department responsible for the fall of Chiang Kai-shek. That was nothing but mindless scapegoating. Chiang had lost because his regime was brutal, corrupt, and hopelessly incompetent. The real tragedy, Lattimore contended, was that America had supported him so well for so long.

What about the future? Lattimore had a few suggestions. It was time to admit that Chiang could not be resurrected, and to go on from there. America's best course was to encourage the growth of Chinese nationalism—even Communist nationalism—in order to woo Mao Tse-tung away from the Soviet orbit. "Now, gentlemen" he lectured sternly, "my analysis of this may be partly or wholly wrong. But if anybody says it is disloyal or un-American, he is a fool or a knave."

In retrospect, these views on China seem remarkably perceptive. But they were lost that day in the torrent of invective that Lattimore hurled at his accuser. To loud applause, he denounced McCarthy for "instituting a reign of terror among officials and employees of the United States Government." The senator, he charged, was "the dupe of a bitter and implacable and fanatical group of people who will not tolerate any discussion of China which is not based upon absolute, total, and complete support of the Nationalist Government in Formosa." Joe sat calmly through the attack, smiling indulgently and letting his eyes drift up toward the ceiling. But he did not return for the afternoon session—a sign, some thought, that the professor had knocked the fight out of him. At day's end, Majority Counsel Ed Morgan smiled at Lattimore and said, "You and Senator McCarthy are now even."

Most observers disagreed. They saw Joe as the big loser. By first overstating his case and then retreating to safer ground, he seemed unsure of his own evidence. And Lattimore had proved to be a tough adversary, someone more than willing to slug it out in public. The blood had begun to flow, but most of it was on Joe's face. One reporter noted that "a majority of Senate Republicans are clearly, if silently, exasperated and alarmed. They are deeply disturbed over the injury to the country's prestige . . . and they are certain that, politically, McCarthy's blast is going to do more harm by its backfire than it is on the target."[20]

Yet Joe was not discouraged. He had, after all, become a national figure, attracting great media attention. Congressional mail was heavy and generally favorable. Invitations to address patriotic groups poured into his office. On March 19 he appeared on NBC's "Meet the Press." And when things looked worst, he revealed that Tydings had subpoenaed his first ex-Communist witness. By week's end, McCarthy promised, Owen Lattimore would be exposed for the fraud he was.

THE WITNESS WAS LOUIS BUDENZ, a man whose strange personal odyssey had taken him from Catholicism to Marxism and back—the so-called Moscow-to-Rome express. Born and raised a Catholic, Budenz had drifted into radical politics at an early age. Joining the Communist Party in 1935, he rose quickly to become managing editor of the *Daily Worker*. Although never a member of the Politburo, which directed the Party, he had attended some of its meetings in Chicago and New York. In 1945 Budenz came under the influence of Bishop Fulton J. Sheen, who prodded him to rejoin the church. Budenz was suspicious, but a simple request from Sheen—"Let us talk of the Blessed Virgin"—began his amazing conversion. "Immediately," Budenz wrote, "I was conscious of the senselessness and sinfulness of my life as I then lived it. The peace that flows from Mary, and which had been mine in the early days, flashed back to me with an overwhelming vividness." [21]

After the conversion took hold, Budenz turned on his former comrades with a vengeance. He spent much of his free time (about 3,000 hours, he estimated) explaining the Party's inner workings to the FBI; he helped to identify Alger Hiss as a Red; he was the government's star witness in the trial of eleven high-ranking Communist leaders. Budenz would later admit to grossing about $70,000 from his activities as an ex-Communist, with a small chunk coming directly from McCarthy's office. But in 1950, at least, he had the respect—and the ear—of many prominent Americans, including J. Edgar Hoover. He was not a witness to be taken lightly. [22]

Budenz saw his new role as indispensable to a nation involved in a life-and-death struggle with Communism. He felt that former Reds had a *duty* to inform, to share their expertise with the "proper authorities." Of course, not everyone trusted his memory—or his credentials. Historian Bernard DeVoto spoke for many anti-Communist liberals when he interpreted the Budenz message this way: "Understand, I am right now *because* I was wrong then. *Only* the ex-Communist can understand Communism. Trust me to lead you aright *because* I tried to lead you astray. My intelligence has been vindicated *in that* it made an all-out commitment to error." [23]

How did McCarthy find Budenz? There are conflicting accounts, but it seems likely that Representative Charles Kersten, an old Wisconsin

crony, acted as the liaison. As Kersten remembers, Joe kept badgering
his friends for information about Lattimore. Kersten pleaded ignorance,
but he promised to phone Budenz, whom he had met at an earlier
congressional probe. Their conversation was dramatic. "Of course I
know Lattimore," said Budenz. "He was a member of the Party assigned
to Far Eastern matters." Kersten hurried back to McCarthy with the
news. "Joe was extremely happy to find out about that," he recalled. "He
kind of danced in the office there, saying, 'Gee, this is wonderful.' "[24]*

The Senate hearing room was jammed for Budenz's appearance, sur-
passing, everyone agreed, the newly established Lattimore record. About
700 people had been shoehorned into a space designed for 300. There
were politicians, State Department officers, columnists, newsreel cam-
eramen, a row of black-suited Catholic priests, and hundreds of spectators who had waited in line for much of the night. Robert Morris, the
minority counsel, arrived to find that no chair had been provided for
him. So, to spite Tydings, he found an abandoned box and drew it up
beside Lodge and Hickenlooper, where he knew he'd be safe. McCarthy
was already inside, joking with some hometown friends who had flown
in for the occasion. Was he nervous? "Well, I drove over to the Capitol
with him that morning," said one. "Along the way we passed some kids
who were playing ball in the street. The ball rolled in front of the car and
Joe got out and began tossing it around with them. I remember thinking,
'God, for a guy whose ass is on the line, he's awfully loose.' But Joe was
always that way."[25]

After first listing his credentials, Budenz spoke of a "Communist cell"
that had infiltrated the Institute of Pacific Relations. Its members, he
said, included Philip Jaffe and Professor Owen Lattimore. Excitement
swept the room. While Tydings gaveled for quiet, the three wire-service
men jumped up and bulled their way to the corridor phones. McCarthy's
surprise witness had done as promised: He had called Lattimore a
Red.[26]

How did Budenz know this? Secret "onionskin documents" had
crossed his desk identifying Lattimore as "X" or "XL." Party disciplinar-
ian Jack Stachel had advised him "to consider Owen Lattimore . . . a
Communist." Party boss Earl Browder had privately "commended Mr.
Lattimore's zeal." Budenz did not agree that the professor was a Russian
spy. "To my knowledge, [McCarthy's] statement is not technically accurate," he said. Lattimore's main task was to recruit and direct writers

---

* Others who claim to have introduced Budenz to McCarthy include Robert Morris,
Alfred Kohlberg, and Congressman Walter Judd. In fact, Budenz was friendly with all three
men. Of Kohlberg, he recalled, "We went to lunch together at least once a week, and
oftener if something interesting was doing." Before testifying, Budenz skimmed Kohlberg's
voluminous files on the China "sell-out." Interview with Robert Morris; Joseph Keeley, *The
China Lobby Man*, 1969, p. 270.

"in representing the Chinese Communists as agrarian reformers." It was an important job, Budenz claimed, and Lattimore was good at it.

Virtually all of Budenz's testimony was based on hearsay, what he claimed to have been told by Party officials. "This point was so obvious," wrote Herbert Packer, an expert on congressional witnesses, "that one wonders why Budenz did not disarm criticism by bringing it up himself. But he did not, and it was pried out of him with telling effect." Budenz suggested, for example, that Earl Browder be subpoenaed for corroboration, but then added that Browder would probably lie through his teeth. He spoke of the need to view the onionskin documents but produced no copies, because "we had strict instructions to tear them up in small pieces and destroy them through the toilet." In short, Budenz had no hard evidence. He was asking the committee to judge him by reputation alone.

The Democrats naturally refused. Led by Ed Morgan, they pressed Budenz to the wall. Wasn't it true, asked Morgan, that Lattimore's *Solution in Asia* had been condemned by the *Daily Worker?* Yes, Budenz replied, but the Party often protected its members by criticizing them, "that is to say, that is, to damn them with faint praise—rather, to praise them with faint damns, is the way I want to put it." And hadn't Lattimore publicly opposed the Soviet invasion of Finland? True enough, said Budenz, but Party members were sometimes given "exemptions" in order to disguise their real purpose. The explanation was novel. Owen Lattimore was displaying his allegiance to Russia each time he chose to attack her. A new technique had been unveiled, guilt by *dis*association.

The grilling continued. In his 3,000 hours with the FBI, the Democrats wondered, had he ever mentioned Lattimore's name? The answer was no; Budenz hadn't gotten around to him yet. But did he not tell a State Department officer in 1947 that he knew nothing about Lattimore's Party membership? Budenz wasn't sure, "but if I did, it was in a telephone conversation, and I am very evasive on the telephone." And wasn't it true that his latest book on Communist subversion made no mention of Lattimore? Yes, Budenz said lamely, but "in another book which I am writing Mr. Lattimore is very prominent."

Senator Green then asked Budenz whether he was really familiar with Lattimore's written work. "How much of his published writings, I won't limit it to books, have you read?"

MR. BUDENZ: Very few indeed.

SENATOR GREEN: How many?

MR. BUDENZ: Well, that I cannot say, offhand.

SENATOR GREEN: Have you read one book?

MR. BUDENZ: I have read hurriedly *Situation in Asia.*

SENATOR GREEN: Just looked it through?

MR. BUDENZ: Yes, sir.

To extricate himself, Budenz offered to "analyze" Lattimore's work and submit his findings to the committee. He never did.

The most damaging questions concerned a flurry of recent meetings with McCarthy's allies—Kersten, Kohlberg, and Robert Morris.

SENATOR GREEN: In that connection have you discussed the Lattimore case with [Kohlberg]?

MR. BUDENZ: Not to any great extent, no.

SENATOR GREEN: You have discussed it with him?

MR. BUDENZ: To some extent; yes.

· · ·

SENATOR GREEN: Who was with you and Mr. Kersten when you had
your discussion?

MR. BUDENZ: Mr. Kersten?

SENATOR GREEN: Yes.

MR. BUDENZ: Well, the only persons I know, on one occasion Mr.
Morris was at my house with Mr. Kersten.

SENATOR GREEN: You three?

MR. BUDENZ: Yes, sir.

SENATOR GREEN: When was that?

MR. BUDENZ: Well, that was in the last couple of days—the last
couple of days. . . .

In fact, Budenz was quite friendly with Kohlberg, Matthews, Morris, and the whole New York crowd. As Morris remembered, "I spent a couple of days with Budenz at his home in Westchester, helping him prepare his case. On one of those evenings, Ed Morgan came to the door with the subpoena. I didn't want to be seen in the house. It would have looked bad, like I was coaching Budenz, which I wasn't. I hid in another room until Morgan had gone. It was pretty odd. Here was the Republican counsel hiding in the bedroom while the Democratic counsel was in the living room with a subpoena."[27]

The most remarkable thing about Budenz's testimony was the favorable response it elicited. People seemed to believe him. He had been right about Hiss and other Communists. Why not Lattimore? *Time* did a complete flip-flop, claiming that Budenz's story "could not be lightly dismissed. Owen Lattimore had not been proved a Communist," it conceded, "but he had not proved that he was not one." Columnist Arthur Krock wrote that "many fair-minded persons" were now changing their minds about McCarthy. Among them was Senator Flanders, who said of the latest development, "I find it disturbing."[28]

More than any single event, the Budenz appearance was responsible for keeping Joe in business. Until that point, he had been waging a struggle with outdated weaponry that often exploded in his hands. True, his charges seemed vaguely plausible, but they lacked the slightest hint of proof. Then along came Budenz, a leading ex-Communist informer. Not only did he testify for McCarthy, he supported the pivotal contention that Lattimore was part of a Far Eastern conspiracy. Budenz had become McCarthy's Whittaker Chambers—the veteran crusader who arrives to rescue a courageous but outgunned young patriot.

"What is surprising, and indeed not a little alarming," wrote one historian, "is how little convincing so many people needed" about Lattimore. Neither Budenz nor McCarthy could prove that he was a Russian spy. Budenz, in fact, denied that he was. And neither could demonstrate how much influence, if any, Lattimore had upon America's Far Eastern policy. They could only allege that he was a Communist, a charge that was vigorously denied and never substantiated. But China had fallen and *someone* would take the blame. In this highly charged atmosphere, more people were willing to believe the accusers than the accused. And there the matter rested.[29]

———

THE HEARINGS DRAGGED ON FOR SIX MORE WEEKS, like a novel whose climax had come too early. They would never again match the drama of the Lattimore–Budenz showdown. On May 3 McCarthy produced his second ex-Communist witness, the ubiquitous Freda Utley. A brilliant, unstable woman, she had studied in England, married a Russian, and moved to Moscow, where she met and befriended Owen Lattimore, then the editor of *Pacific Affairs*. In 1936 her husband, Arcadi, was arrested by Stalin's police and never heard from again. In 1938 she traveled to China as a war correspondent for a London magazine. Though no longer a Marxist, she described the Communist movement there in lyrical terms: "Its aim has become social and political reform along capitalist and democratic lines. The Chinese Communists have become radicals in the English 19th century meaning of the word."

Utley soon reversed herself, claiming temporary political insanity. In the 1940s, recovering slowly, she flirted with the Nazis before coming to America and joining the Matthews-Kohlberg-Sokolsky crowd in New

York. Her new writings—in Kohlberg's *Plain Talk* and other pro-Chiang journals—portrayed the Generalissimo as a beleagured saint, undercut and finally overthrown by "the IPR-State Department pro-Chinese Communist axis" of Philip Jessup, John Service, Owen Lattimore, Dean Acheson, and Dean Rusk. But Lattimore was the real villain, the man who defended the Moscow Trials that had banished her husband to the Gulag Archipelago. "I knew that Lattimore was as aware as I that hundreds of thousands of people had been arrested and sentenced to slave labor in Russia without trial," she wrote many years later. "When I saw clearly that he had become an apologist for Stalin's tyranny, I broke off relations with him and his wife."

Utley did not call Lattimore a Communist or a spy. "To suggest that his great talents have been utilized in espionage," she told the Tydings committee, "seems . . . as absurd as to suggest that Mr. Gromyko or Mr. Molotov employ their leisure hours . . . in snatching documents." Lattimore's talents, she added, were those of the propagandist. "Soviet Russia, in all of his writings, is always sinned against and is always represented . . . as standing like a beacon of hope for the peoples of Asia. . . . Russia is never in the wrong."[30]

Utley came well prepared. She had read most of Lattimore's writings (which was more than could be said for McCarthy or the members of the Tydings committee). But when she tried to demonstrate her knowledge of these writings, the Democrats closed their ears. "We want facts, f-a-c-t-s," Tydings shouted. "We are getting very few of them. We are getting mostly opinion."*

Abe Fortas countered by unveiling *his* ex-Communist witness, the well-traveled Bella Dodd. Describing Budenz as an oddball, she poked fun at his onionskin story. "Whatever errors we made in the Communist Party," Dodd sneered, "we did not fall into the habit of taking our methods from dime detective novels." The committee then heard from Earl Browder, who said that Lattimore had never been a Communist. But no one was about to believe him anyway.[31]

These appearances were followed by a curious episode involving John J. Huber, the disappearing witness. Huber, a friend of J. B. Matthews, had a fine story to tell—or so he said. While working "under cover" for the FBI, he had seen Owen Lattimore in the presence of known Communists. Huber was quickly subpoenaed, and McCarthy even journeyed to New York to provide him with a personal escort. Huber checked into

---

* This, of course, was in marked contrast to the committee's treatment of Owen Lattimore, who was allowed—indeed, encouraged—to say whatever he wanted. The following year, Utley devoted an entire chapter to Lattimore's writings in her best-selling book *The China Story*. She concluded: "He may not have been the 'architect' of our disastrous China policy . . . but there can be no reasonable doubt that the Far Eastern policy advocated, and to a large degree followed, by the Administration, was inspired by Lattimore and his disciples, protégés, and friends." (p. 214).

a Washington hotel, went over his testimony at McCarthy's office, and appeared quite confident. Then he vanished.

The next day, after missing his scheduled appearance, Huber telephoned the Associated Press. He said he had "blacked out" and found himself back in New York City. He couldn't remember anything else. Robert Morris had a different explanation. Huber, it seemed, was told that he would testify in executive session. "When he got down here and saw all the klieg lights, he was very much disturbed, and said he had an emotional upset; and I believe him, because the guy is very excitable."

There were others who felt that the disappearing act was triggered by Huber's fear of prison, not klieg lights. False testimony is no laughing matter. Tydings threatened for a time to haul Huber back to Washington but relented after getting word that he was "on the verge of a mental collapse." Huber later wound up on the McCarthy payroll.[32]

The committee then reopened the *Amerasia* case, a sordid affair that had been "thoroughly investigated" (the Democratic account) or "completely whitewashed" (the Republican account) several years before. Nothing new was uncovered. The Democrats were not interested in prying too deeply, and the Republicans, led by McCarthy, produced a series of witnesses who turned the inquiry into a circus.

The star performer was Frank Brooks Bielaski, the OSS agent who had led the raid against *Amerasia*. By any standard, Bielaski came from a security-conscious family. His brother had been J. Edgar Hoover's predecessor at the (later-named) FBI and a great believer in the use of vigilante action against dissidents. His sister, Ruth Shipley, had ruled the State Department's passport division for almost three decades. A devotee of the "better safe than sorry" approach to free expression, she felt that those who criticized the government (from the left, of course) should not be allowed to leave the country.[33]

Bielaski's own credentials were hardly reassuring. A detective by trade, he was under investigation in Pennsylvania for supposedly using prostitutes to entrap local politicians. And Rhode Island had caught him tapping the state attorney general's phone. Still, he had been at the scene of the crime, he professed to hate Communists, and he liked to testify about *Amerasia*. For McCarthy, this was not a bad combination.[34]

Bielaski had been well coached for his appearance. After some preliminary remarks, he recalled something new about the raid: While in the *Amerasia* office, he had come across a stolen document stamped "A bomb." The Democrats jumped all over him. Had any of the other agents at the raid seen the document? No, Bielaski admitted, they had not. What about the FBI? Had their men seen it? No.[35]

What happened next was bizarre even by McCarthy's standards. Someone in the committee room noticed that the Washington *Star*'s early edition had already summarized Bielaski's testimony. And here sat

Bielaski, who had not yet finished giving it. McCarthy solved the riddle by admitting that he had leaked the testimony a few hours before. His plan, of course, was to have the newspapers print Bielaski's charges before Bielaski himself was discredited. It worked to perfection. The headlines were sensational. And the truth, when it emerged, went almost unnoticed.

THE TYDINGS INVESTIGATION had always hinged on a single frustrating question: Who should produce the evidence, McCarthy or the committee? McCarthy claimed that his job was to come forward with charges of State Department misconduct—nothing more. He would supply leads and an occasional witness, but it was up to Tydings and his colleagues to get the proof. "I don't answer accusations," Joe told Wayne Morse. "I make them."

Tydings disagreed. He felt that his committee had been formed to *judge* the evidence brought by McCarthy, not to dig it up for him. Facts would be carefully checked, but the accuser had to present them first. "Lay the evidence before us and sustain it," Tydings liked to say. "Otherwise it's just a lot of hocus-pocus."[36]

The stalemate had worked to Joe's advantage. It allowed him to make wild allegations; it put pressure on Truman to open the loyalty files (where the "proof" supposedly resided); and it denied Tydings his anticipated first-round knockout. Before long, the hearings had degenerated into an angry brawl, with senators battling witnesses, and sometimes each other. It was the very atmosphere in which McCarthy thrived.

Tydings finally capitulated. He wrote a personal letter to the President asking that his committee be given the loyalty files of those attacked by McCarthy. Without them, he predicted, the State Department would remain under a cloud of suspicion. Truman responded with a qualified yes. The files would be brought to the White House, where committee members could inspect them at their leisure. They were not to take notes, however, or to discuss their contents with anyone else. The process could begin at once.[37]

Truman's decision had been difficult. He believed that closed files were essential to State Department morale. And he knew that any disclosure would weaken all future claims of executive privilege. But the political pressures were simply too great. The public seemed to endorse McCarthy's charge that the President was withholding evidence of treason. If State Department employees were loyal and honest, people wondered, why not release their complete files?

On May 10 the committee members began their daily forays to the White House. But the job of sifting through the files proved more tedious than expected. It took Tydings two days to complete thirteen dossiers.

Within a week the senators were bored with the task. Lodge and Green left for Europe to look into State Department security at foreign installations; Hickenlooper returned to Iowa for his primary campaign. And McCarthy added to the mess by charging that the files had been "thoroughly raped." He had no evidence of this, only the comforting knowledge that Truman could never prove otherwise. After all, the files *had* been under Democratic lock and key for eighteen years.

By this time Tydings's confidence had begun to waver. During a strategy meeting with Ed Morgan he expressed his dismay at the Administration's lukewarm support. The next day he begged his Democratic colleagues "to go after McCarthy." Tydings had a plan: Each senator would attack Joe on a different issue—his changing numbers game, his unreliable witnesses, his frightening image abroad. No politician, he told them, could withstand such collective abuse.

It wasn't like the proud Tydings to plead for support. But he had no choice; events were out of control. Only weeks before, he had referred to Joe as "this boy" and predicted his early demise. Now, with McCarthy stronger than ever, the chairman had become a frantic recruiter, urging fresh but reluctant troops into battle. It was more than a little pathetic.

A handful of Democrats answered the call. Pennsylvania's Francis Meyers accused Joe of "a deliberate and malicious" attempt to undermine the nation's foreign policy. Connecticut's William Benton called him a propagandist "of the Soviet type. McCarthy doesn't argue, he doesn't answer, he doesn't reason," Benton noted angrily. "He hits and runs." The most vicious attack, however, came from an unexpected source: New Mexico's mild-mannered Dennis Chavez. It was his speech that showed how edgy the Democrats had become.[38]

A devout Roman Catholic, Chavez savaged the reputation of co-religionist Louis Budenz. He revealed that the informer had had three children out of wedlock and that he had been arrested twenty-one times before joining the Communist Party. "I believe in clemency to sinners," Chavez went on, "but with repentance should go humility, not hypocrisy. My ancestors brought the Cross to this hemisphere. Louis Budenz has been using the Cross as a club."[39]

McCarthy's response was typical enough. He called Benton an idiot and a subversive. He charged that Chavez had been "duped" by unnamed Red propagandists. He said that Tydings was an Administration lackey, dutifully conducting "Operation Whitewash." And he vowed that nothing would deter him from exposing the "egg-sucking phony liberals" and the "Communists and queers" who inhabited the State Department. Nothing at all.[40]

CHAPTER ELEVEN

Declaration of Conscience

When 1950 began Joe McCarthy was an obscure, forgettable, and somewhat frightened young senator. The national press ignored him. Politicians sought neither his backing nor his advice. He could walk the streets of any city, save Appleton, without causing a stir. It is doubtful whether one American in a hundred knew or cared who he was. At forty-one his future seemed uncertain. He was up for reelection in 1952, and most observers expected him to lose.

Five months later he was a towering national figure. His face adorned the covers of *Newsweek* and *Time*. *The Nation* and *The New Republic* devoted almost unlimited space to his charges. The major newspapers rarely took him off their front pages. A new word had been coined to describe his antics, "McCarthyism." Several people—Owen Lattimore, columnist Max Lerner, and cartoonist Herbert Block—took credit for it, although Joe told everybody that the *Daily Worker* was responsible.

In May the first opinion polls on McCarthy were published. The results bore out what most analysts had been saying: His support was widespread. Both the Minnesota and Gallup polls showed about 40 percent of their samples agreeing that Joe's charges were "a good thing for the country" (28 percent felt they "did harm" or were untrue; 16 percent had no opinion; and another 16 percent hadn't heard of them). Guy Gabrielson, the GOP national chairman, was naturally elated. "The people wholeheartedly agree with McCarthy," he said with some exaggeration. "I don't think the average person is close enough to know or care about the methods employed by the senator. Certainly, his objectives have received great support in the country generally."[1]

Joe's celebrity status was apparent in many little ways. He was now the "must" speaker that every group desired, from the National Press Club to the Wisconsin Retail Furniture Dealers. And his fee quickly doubled to $1,000. He could no longer go out in public without drawing scores of curious onlookers. In one incident, an Irish cabbie verbally assaulted him on a busy street. "You oughta keep still until you can prove what you've been saying," he told McCarthy. "You've done yourself and . . . the government a lot of harm." But this was exceptional. Most people wanted only to shake his hand or to offer words of encouragement. Shouts of "Let 'em have it, Joe" followed him everywhere.[2]

He was rarely alone in those frantic early days. His office was filled with aides, tipsters, and newsmen, all vying for his ear. He spent hours on the phone milking his sources. Often, late at night, he would call Appleton to find out what the "real" people were thinking. His friend Van Susteren recalled: "Some secretary would get on first and say, 'I have a collect call from Mr. Dean Acheson in Washington. Will you accept the charges?' Then Joe would come on and we'd laugh and talk about how things looked for him. He really loved all that commotion."[3]

The Senate Post Office began carting mail to his office in burlap sacks. Other congressmen reported an increase in their volume, due largely, they said, to the Tydings investigation. The letters were strongly pro-McCarthy, offering support to his allies and stern rebukes to his critics. "If you aren't too busy," a St. Louis attorney wrote Senator Kem, "please take a moment to tell Joe McCarthy that the plain people of America are grateful to him." A New Bedford, Massachusetts, newspaper editor was less gracious to Margaret Chase Smith: "Apparently you give no thought to the all-important fact that it is Senator McCarthy who . . . is responsible for the attention this Communist issue, which you describe as most grave, is now receiving in Congress and the country." Edgar Leslie, the songwriter, sent along an official ballad, "Fall in Line with Joe McCarthy" (sung to the tune of "Glory, Glory, Hallelujah"), which, mercifully, remained unpublished:

> This is a land of freedom and when the Communists appear
> They represent a menace we must recognize and fear.
> So get behind the movement of the modern Paul Revere.
> His truth is marching on.
>
> Chorus:
>
> *Fall in line with Joe McCarthy*
> *Fall in line with Joe McCarthy*

Fall in line with Joe McCarthy
His truth is marching on.

The battle must be fought until the victory's complete
And you can help to bring about the Communist defeat
By following the footsteps of the man who won't retreat.
His truth is marching on.

Let no misguided patriots appease the Communist
With powder-puff diplomacy and not the iron fist.
You never score a knockout with a slap upon the wrist.
His truth is marching on.[4]

Many of the letters to McCarthy contained checks or cash. Often, when speaking at a convention or appearing on radio, he'd complain about the great expense involved in running down all the new leads. "It's sort of breaking me," he'd say. "Investigators don't work for peanuts. Right now, I've got four and a half investigators, that is, four working full time, one half time. . . . They average $25 or $30 a day plus their expenses."

The result was a deluge of money. W. A. Schaeffer, president of the Schaeffer Pen Company, sent a check for $1,000. So did Sewell Avery of Montgomery Ward. Some supporters, like Tom Coleman, raised money from friends and employees. Coleman sent Joe four checks in six weeks: May 17, 1950—$500; June 12—$1,500; June 23—$475; June 29—$750.

Most of the donations were small and in cash. One aide estimated that McCarthy took in as much as $1,000 a day during the early 1950s. Often the donors received certificates making them "honorary card-carrying anti-Communists." But the public never knew how much money was collected or exactly how it was spent.* By 1951, however, the senator had paid off his Appleton bank loan as well as the $14,000 he had borrowed from Frank J. Sensenbrenner, the powerful Wisconsin Republican who ran Kimberly-Clark.[5]

His name reappeared on the society page, often as Washington's "most eligible bachelor." He was usually seen in the company of Jean Kerr, his attractive assistant; Martha Roundtree of "Meet the Press"; and Bazy Miller of the McCormick publishing family. In June the Washington Gridiron Club honored him at its annual celebrity roast. When everyone was seated, he burst into the Statler ballroom carrying a ma-

---

* During interviews with the author, the newsmen who followed McCarthy had some interesting recollections about the handling of these donations. Willard Edwards claimed that Joe sometimes stuffed the money into his pocket or used it to play the soybean futures market. And Robert Fleming recalled that some of the letters addressed to "Congressman McCarthy" would up in Eugene McCarthy's office. According to Fleming, Eugene McCarthy notified the senator, who replied, "We've got so much of it here, you just keep it." So the congressman sent what came in to a Minnesota college for its scholarship fund.

chine gun, a rifle, a revolver, and a sling shot. As the audience drew back
in mock horror, he discarded his weaponry in favor of a tiny baby's
diaper. "I'll never let that go," he deadpanned. "That's my cloak of immunity." On cue from the band, he performed a quick rendition of the
latest Bert Williams spoof:

> Somebody lied,
> Somebody lied, dear, dear;
> Some say there is no evidence,
> While others say it's clear.
> Somebody lied, as plain as plain
>   can be;
> Somebody's lied as sure's you're
>   born—
> Somebody falsified to me.[6]

The applause was thunderous. Many of the guests had never seen
the human, fun-loving side of McCarthy. There were very impressed.

So were the folks in Wisconsin. After the Wheeling speech, Joe's
standing back home increased dramatically. People seemed proud that a
local boy was leading the fight against the Communists, the perverts, the
smug Eastern types who "ran" the government. Sure he played rough,
but the stakes were high and the enemy was elusive. He was doing what
had to be done, and he wouldn't let up until the job was completed.
"Joe's a hero up our way," a Republican leader exulted. "We haven't had
such a fighter since Old Bob LaFollette." Said another: "As soon as they
jumped on Joe, I said, 'Oh, oh, they got the wrong guy.' He's like a
stubborn bulldog; he'll never give up."[7]

In April Wisconsin's GOP Strategy Committee endorsed McCarthy's
crusade. "Our party is finally on the attack and should stay there," it
remarked. "And best of all, we may get rid of many Communist sympathizers and queers who now control policy [in Washington]." Tom Coleman reduced the issue to political terms. "The Republican job," he
explained, ". . . is to keep the people believing, as they should, that
through McCarthy this is a Republican exposé." To emphasize this
point, Joe was invited to keynote the GOP state convention in Milwaukee.[8]

No one could remember a more emotional welcome. When the senator first appeared at the Schroeder Hotel, it took him more than an hour
to walk across the lobby; he was besieged by well-wishers and autograph-
seekers. On the convention floor, the 2,500 delegates cheered wildly as a
resolution was read calling him "a great American." Political observers
were startled by this turnabout. "Joe has hit the ten strike," frowned
Milwaukee's Socialist Mayor, Frank Zeidler. "He's unbeatable now. He's
a Northern Huey Long."[9]

There was one ominous note, however. McCarthy's health had become a problem. For months he had been working under the most extreme pressures. Despite an occasional vacation in Arizona, he looked tired and drawn. He complained privately of the "terrific burden" he shouldered, telling a friend:

> I sometimes think that everyone with a story to tell is coming to me. . . . Senators, government workers, career people, the public, crackpots all shove information at me. Some senators who weren't friendly before . . . now come around regularly. I know how they figure. They think McCarthy's already bloody, so I'll pass this on to him, and if he makes something of it, fine, and if not, I'm not in a mess.[10]

Joe's stomach was constantly upset, the result of too much liquor and a diaphragmatic hernia that would soon require surgery. Senator Milton Young, who knew McCarthy well in those days, recalled that his colleague would often fill a water glass halfway with whisky and down it in a few slugs. The drink would then be followed with a bicarbonate of soda. "It was an odd combination," said Young, "and Joe's stomach was really aching him." On top of this, McCarthy's sinus problems made him prone to respiratory infections. After visiting the senator's office late in 1950, Robert Fleming noted: "During our conversation, while extremely genial, he was coughing heavily and often. He said it was the first day the cough had bothered him, but he also called in Ray Kiermas and asked him to go out to his car and 'get some of that Navy cough medicine for me.' He seemed more tired than I had seen him in several years." Joe's physical deterioration was well under way.[11]

———

AFTER FOUR MONTHS in the national spotlight, McCarthy had almost everybody talking about him. And taking sides. In the Senate his behavior was the main topic of conversation, dominating the working lunches and the weekly poker sessions. But not the public record. By June only twelve Democrats had spoken out against their colleague. They were the three Tydings Committee members; the most loyal Administration supporters, like Connally and Lucas; and a handful of Northern liberals, including Benton and Lehman. The others talked only in private—a posture that infuriated President Truman and no doubt encouraged Senator McCarthy.

Why such indifference? Fear played a role, fear of Joe's strongarm methods and his growing popularity. But it was not the only factor. The Senate's Democratic power bloc was Southern and conservative, composed of men who despised intellectuals like Owen Lattimore and who resented the snobbish manner of Dean Acheson. They were, in fact, as appalled by McCarthy's targets as by McCarthy himself. And, while sensitive to violations of Senate rules and courtesies, they were quite unwilling to fight fire with fire. Tussling with McCarthy, they believed, would mean a gutter brawl and an accompanying loss of stature.. "He who plays with a pup," mused one veteran Democrat, "gets licked in the face."[12]

Across the aisle sat fifteen more silent members, the GOP moderates. They were disturbed by Joe's behavior, thinking it boorish, self-serving, and narrowly political. Still, as good Republicans, they could not lightly dismiss his charges. What the moderates sought was a middle ground, a way to reprimand McCarthy without exonerating the Democrats. After all, he "would never have had any influence," Ralph Flanders commented, "had it not been for the fact that our late, departed saint, Franklin Delano Roosevelt, was soft as taffy on the subject of Communism."[13]

There were individual reasons as well. Charlie Tobey came from New Hamsphire, where the leading newspaper, the Manchester *Morning Union*, was rabidly pro-McCarthy. Flanders represented Vermont, where voters generally supported attacks upon the federal bureaucracy. Lodge and Leverett Saltonstall came from Massachusetts, which had a large Irish-Catholic population. "Attacking McCarthy was no easy matter," said Saltonstall. "He had a lot of support in Boston. No politician could ignore that."[14]

For months, the moderates had straddled the fence. The dilemma of satisfying party, conscience, and the national interest seemed to paralyze them. But in early June a voice was heard from the ranks. It belonged to Margaret Chase Smith of Maine, the Senate's only female member. And it spelled out the moderate position with exceptional clarity.

Smith was hardly a powerhouse in the upper chamber. A quiet, reserved woman, she sat on few important committees and was regarded with indifference by Senate leaders. But Smith did have a widespread reputation for patience and integrity. To raise her hackles, someone would have to step far out of line. In 1950 that someone was Joe McCarthy.

Smith had been introduced to Joe by her friend May Craig, the reporter who badgered politicians so mercilessly at press conferences. Thinking the world of McCarthy, Craig had hoped that he and Smith would become good friends. It hadn't happened. When the two sat on the same committee in 1949, Joe had offended his colleague by leaking secret information to the press. And he was forever peppering her with silly compliments, telling people that she was his "personal choice" for vice president in 1952. "I found him pleasant," Smith recalled, "but I was not as impressed with him as May obviously was."[15]

When McCarthy made his initial charges against the State Department, Smith believed he "was on to something disturbing and frightening." But the more she listened the less sense he seemed to make. At first, Smith stifled her doubts. As a "nonlawyer," she felt uncomfortable dealing with the allegations. By mid-May, however, she "began to wonder whether I was as stupid as I had thought." McCarthy's charges went nowhere; they added up to nothing. Perhaps he was perpetrating a hoax upon the Senate.

There were other disturbing signs. "Joe began to get publicity crazy," Smith remembered. "And the other senators were now afraid to speak their minds, to take issue with him. It got to the point where some of us refused to be seen with people he disapproved of. A wave of fear had struck Washington."[16]

Smith responded by drafting a short statement and quietly circulating it among her moderate colleagues. Six of them—Tobey, Aiken, Morse, Ives, Thye, and Hendrickson—agreed to act as cosponsors. As luck would have it, Smith bumped into McCarthy just minutes before she was to deliver her "Declaration of Conscience."

> "Margaret," he said, "you look very serious. Are you going to make a speech?"
> I said, "Yes, and you will not like it."
> He smiled. "Is it about me?"
> "Yes, but I'm not going to mention your name."
> Then he frowned. "Remember, Margaret, I control Wisconsin's twenty-seven convention votes."
> "For what?" I said.[17]

This was apparently Joe's way of telling Smith that he might not support her after all for the vice presidential nomination. Smith bristled and went on her way.

The speech was billed as an even-handed attack upon the Democrats for their "complacency to the threat of communism" and the Republicans for their "selfish political exploitation of fear, bigotry, ignorance, and intolerance." But no one had to guess who the real villain was. "Those of us who shout the loudest about Americanism," Smith noted, ". . . are all too frequently those who, by our own words and acts, ignore some of the basic principles of Americanism:

> The right to criticize;
> The right to hold unpopular beliefs;
> The right to protest;
> The right of independent thought."

Smith concluded:

> Freedom of speech is not what it used to be in America. It has been so abused by some that it has not been exercised by others. . . . I am not proud of the way we smear outsiders from the Floor of the Senate and hide behind the cloak of congressional immunity. . . . As an American, I want to see our

nation recapture the strength and unity it once had when we fought the enemy instead of ourselves.

When she had finished, her colleagues crowded around to offer congratulations. H. Alexander Smith wanted his name added to the "Declaration." Bob Hendrickson called the speech a "clarion warning." Millard Tydings claimed that a new word had been coined, "stateswomanship." In the ensuing hubbub, few people noticed that McCarthy, who sat just behind Smith, had slipped quietly from the chamber.[18]

Politically speaking, the Declaration had no real impact. For one thing, its focus was too narrow. While attacking Joe's excesses, it did not doubt his sincerity or dispute his claim that the government was riddled with subversives. For another, its sponsors were essentially a leaderless band. Unlike the conservatives, they lacked a Bob Taft or a Styles Bridges to press their case. There was no one to take charge, map strategy, or attempt further recruiting. Strangely isolated from one another, the moderates could not easily combat the advances of McCarthy's powerful allies. Margaret Chase Smith, for example, remembers being approached for "chats" by Styles Bridges and William Jenner within days of her speech:

> Styles and I spoke for almost three hours. I respected him and listened carefully to what he said. He told me that Joe's charges were serious and that China *had* fallen as a result of State Department treachery. I think all of us who signed the "Declaration" got this sort of visit. Styles didn't convince me but we remained friends. This was not the case with Mrs. Bridges, who really admired McCarthy. She was very cold to me after the speech, and she would remain so throughout my years in Washington.[19]

The moderates soon drifted apart. Irving Ives startled his colleagues by publicly applauding Joe's attacks. "I've had occasion to be *slightly critical* of you in the past," he told McCarthy, "but I feel very strongly that all subversives must be weeded out of the government. I offer my full cooperation." H. Alexander Smith followed suit, telling other moderates that he would "try to convert McCarthy rather than get him reprimanded publicly." A few days later, Charles Tobey wrote an angry constituent: "I think you are laboring under a misapprehension. I have not disavowed Senator McCarthy. Many senators feel that his objectives are good, and I share that feeling." Margaret Chase Smith was deeply offended. She had seen her cosponsors jump off the bandwagon one by one, until only Wayne Morse remained at her side.[20]

On June 27 news came that Korea was at war. Most Americans were puzzled. They had been expecting trouble from the Russians, probably somewhere in Europe. But Korea? Few people were aware of its location,

much less its politics. All anyone knew was that a pro-Communist dictator from the North had attacked an anti-Communist dictator from the
South. And America was somehow mixed up with the latter.

Korea had been arbitrarily divided by Russian and American troops
at the end of World War II. The idea was to have Russia supervise the
North and America the South, until a unifying election could be held.
The problem was that Stalin had canceled the election by refusing to
allow U.N. observers above the dividing line at the 38th parallel. A stalemate thus developed, with Kim Il Sung, the pro-Soviet despot, and Syng-
man Rhee, the pro-American despot, making nasty threats about
"liberating" each other's land. The only difference was that Kim Il Sung
had a tough, well-supplied army. He could back up his saber-rattling
with real force. Rhee's troops were pitiful by comparison. Their primary
function, in fact, was to protect the corrupt dictator from his own constituents.[21]

The North Korean attack put great pressure on Harry Truman. His
Administration had always treated the Rhee government with a mixture
of indifference and contempt. In 1949 the President had removed American combat troops from Korea; in 1950 Dean Acheson had omitted that
country from the so-called Asian Defense Perimeter, implying that it was
not vital to the free world's security.* Yet here was a classic case of
aggression. To ignore it, Truman felt, was to encourage it elsewhere.
What, exactly, would containment mean if the Communists were allowed to overpower a neighbor without fear of retaliation?

There were political considerations as well. On the heels of the China
debacle, the Hiss case, and the rise of McCarthy, a tough stand in Korea
was essential. If Truman backed down, he would only reinforce the
Republican charge that he was soft on Communism. By standing firm,
however, he could defuse that charge once and for all. "McCarthyism
will have a hollow sound," glowed *The Nation*, "when applied to the
government that stood up to the Russians."[22]

The Administration moved swiftly. America's U.N. Ambassador,
Warren Austin, secured a resolution condemning North Korea and
promising "such assistance . . . as may be necessary to repel armed attack." (The Soviets, boycotting the Security Council to protest the
U.N.'s refusal to seat Red China, were unable to cast their paralyzing
veto.) In yet another reversal of policy, President Truman positioned the
Seventh Fleet between the Chinese mainland and the island of Formosa,
thereby ensuring the survival of Chiang Kai-shek. A week later, without

---

* Despite Republican claims to the contrary, Truman and Acheson were not alone in
holding these views. The Joint Chiefs of Staff had said much the same thing in 1947; so had
General MacArthur in 1949. And congressional Republicans had repeatedly undermined
the Administration's modest attempts to supply South Korea with economic and military
aid.

consulting Congress, he dispatched American ground troops to South Korea.[23]

For the moment, at least, Americans rallied around Harry Truman. Letters and telegrams of support poured into the White House. Writing from Washington, William S. White described the new sense of unity and purpose that gripped the city: "It has been a week of melancholy decisions, firmly made by President Truman and strongly backed by the Senate and the House of Representatives. It has been a week, also, of high motives, and even of a certain approach to majesty."[24]

This new atmosphere was hardly to McCarthy's advantage. He thrived on partisanship, recrimination, and mutual distrust. For now, the people wanted no more of that. It was time to close ranks behind the President, not attack him. It was time for Joe to hold his tongue.

Which he did. As a good judge of public opinion, McCarthy sensed the danger of remaining apart from the community as it prepared for war. And he knew that the press was too busy with battle stories to give him much ink. "My only forum is page one," Joe told a reporter. "I don't have that now, so I'll keep quiet."[25]

These feelings were reinforced by the harsh advice he received from his friends. Early in July Tom Coleman sent along an agonized letter from Wisconsin. "I have been trying to figure out what the future holds for your particular activity," he wrote, "and it is difficult for me to make up my mind. I am inclined to think, however, that contributions will cease to come in. The publicity, of course, must necessarily drop in view of war news and the mood of the people has certainly changed." It was imperative, Coleman warned, "to make a complete recast of the situation before making important moves." An impulsive statement or a half-baked charge would almost surely backfire with terrible consequences.[26]

Joe took the letter seriously. His reply was long and thoughtful, unlike the good-luck-and-thanks-for-writing forms he sent everyone else. He agreed that "the war situation makes it difficult to continue the anti-Communist fight effectively—at least temporarily." But he saw storm clouds gathering over the White House. "I am inclined to think," he went on, "that as the casualty lists mount and the attention of the people is focused on what actually has happened in the Far East, they can't help but realize there was something rotten in the State Department." This analysis was most perceptive. The war would not be a quick or an easy one; it would be drawn out and bloody, with many American casualties. And the longer it lasted, the more people would begin to ask themselves how Truman ever got mixed up in it. "I still think this is going to be the major issue this fall, Tom," the senator wrote prophetically.[27]

McCarthy's feelings were based largely on what he saw and heard around Washington. He knew, for example, that some Republicans were supporting the war with great reluctance. Robert Taft was one. He complained to a friend that "Truman's policy . . . constituted almost an open invitation to the Communists to move in with the assurance that no effective action would be taken against them. I believe that the Republicans should give every possible support to the conduct of the war, but should not hesitate to point out the weakness of the Administration's foreign policy which brought it about." Ken Wherry was another. After reading a Republican Party pamphlet, "Background on Korea," he told the author: "The foreword ought to be strengthened. The Truman Administration stands convicted of betraying the United States."[28]

McCarthy was optimistic about his future. He knew that the Republicans still valued his political clout, and he sensed how quickly the nation's mood would change if the war went badly or if doubts arose about Truman's will to win it. Time was on his side, Joe believed. He did not intend to remain bottled up much longer.

WITHIN DAYS OF THE NORTH KOREAN INVASION, the Tydings Committee began drafting its final report. There was some grumbling from Lodge and Hickenlooper, who claimed that more work remained to be done. But the Democrats overruled them. As Edward Morgan remembered, Tydings was "sick of the pressure on him, and the Republicans passed the word that 'we'll keep you on this till November and you won't have time to campaign.' " A report was promised by mid-July.[29]

The Democrats hoped to win the support of Senator Lodge. Privately, they appealed to his sense of fair play, his disdain for name-calling and reckless charges. As a bonus, Tydings threw in a free trip to Europe, where Lodge could "investigate" State Department security overseas. But Lodge refused to sign the report. He complained that the hearings had been superficial, that the Democrats had ignored the larger issues— and the spirit of Resolution 231—by placing the burden of proof on Senator McCarthy. According to Lodge, the Democrats had shown more interest in discrediting Joe than in investigating the security practices of the State Department.*[30]

The report thus became a partisan document, supported only by Tydings, Green, and McMahon. And its language was embarrassingly blunt. It charged that McCarthy had perpetrated a "fraud and a hoax . . . on the Senate," that he had "stooped to a new low in his cavalier disregard of the facts." His accusations, it said, "represent perhaps the

---

* Lodge had a point, of course, though he was speaking out of both sides of his mouth. Despite his poor attendance record, he said at the end of the hearings: "In all the years I have been here, I have never been on a committee . . . where a more sincere effort was made . . . where the members put in more time and worked harder." Put simply, Lodge was not about to stand out as the only Republican senator to criticize McCarthy *by name.*

most nefarious campaign of half-truths and untruths in the history of this republic." The report even took a swipe at Lodge and Hickenlooper, citing their flagrant absenteeism and their failure to read the files.[31]

From there, the Democrats proceeded to exonerate each and every one of McCarthy's targets. Owen Lattimore: "In no instance has it been shown that he knowingly associated with Communists." Philip Jessup: "The facts fail completely to establish that he has 'an unusual affinity for Communist causes' or is a 'dupe' of anyone." Dorothy Kenyon: "The number of admitted affiliations suggests a high degree of naivete and perhaps gullibility, but the evidence fails to establish that she is a Communist or otherwise disloyal." Even the *Amerasia* case was dismissed as a minor indiscretion.[32]

The report went to the Foreign Relations Committee, where its contents were scrutinized in an angry session. The Republicans demanded major changes. The Democrats wouldn't budge. After hours of wrangling, a decision was made to "receive" the report and to "transmit" it to the Senate floor without comment. Why hadn't more been accomplished, reporters asked Tom Connally as he left the committee room. "We wanted to go home by Christmas," was his sheepish reply.[33]

On the morning of July 20, just hours before the scheduled Senate debate, the Democrats caucused in a side room of the Capitol. They listened for thirty minutes as Tydings poured out his heart, pleading for a united front against McCarthy. "I've stuck out my neck for you," he told them, "and now you've got to get me off the hook." The speech worked wonders, for the Democrats came away angry and determined. One reporter at the scene was startled by their vehemence. They were "positively growling for revenge," he observed.[34]

What followed was the meanest Senate debate in recent memory. Those who witnessed it still have difficulty believing what transpired. "Looking back over a quarter century of covering the Senate," wrote *The New Republic*'s Washington staff, "we honestly think the scene was the most spectacular we ever saw." Some called it "Millard Tydings's Revenge."[35]

There was the usual preliminary sparring. The Republicans tried to kill the report, noting that it had not been "accepted" by the Foreign Relations Committee. They were overruled. Wherry moved to send the report back to committee. He was overruled. Each time a Republican rose to speak, the Democrats would start talking rudely among themselves. "How can we get the Reds out of Korea if we cannot get them out of Washington?" Jenner yelled across the aisle.[36]

Only minutes into the debate, Wherry tried to get Edward Morgan thrown off the Senate floor. When this failed, he took matters into his own hands by cornering the committee lawyer near the back door. Their brief exchange was loud enough to grab everyone's attention:

WHERRY: Did you write this report?

MORGAN: I have no apologies to make. I helped prepare it.

WHERRY: You dirty son of a bitch.[37]

At this point, the Republican senator threw a haymaker that glanced off Morgan's shoulder. Tom Connally rushed in to separate them, and the incident was quickly ended. Morgan, a large and athletic man, had never lost his composure. "I could have punched his lights out," he said later.

The clamor receded as Millard Tydings took the floor. This was the main event, the speech people had been waiting to hear. The chairman did not disappoint them. For the past three months, he began, he had "taken punishment from a colleague of mine who used every epithet and every form of opprobrium and calumny to blackguard me. . . . I have not returned the favor because I did not want to sink to that kind of level, even off the Senate floor." But the time had come to set the record straight.

McCarthy was a charlatan, Tydings claimed, a man who knew nothing about the Communist menace. His idiotic charges were the sort of thing one would expect from the town dunce. But he was also a United States senator, and people were more likely to believe him than someone "on the corner of 9th and G streets who is carrying on a casual conversation." McCarthy was exploiting his office, using it as a platform to deceive the citizenry. When people heard him, they assumed he was "the voice of the republic . . . the voice of the government." This had to be stopped.

The chairman was well prepared. He had notes and charts, clippings and photostats; but his strangest prop was a record player that sat precariously on the edge of his desk. It was there, Tydings explained, to clear up one of the riddles surrounding McCarthy's charges. McCarthy insisted that he *had not* used the figure 205 at Wheeling; almost everyone who heard him insisted that he *had*. Well, the proof was right here. "I am not asking the senators to take my word but to hear the senator's voice," Tydings said. The controversial Wheeling speech had finally been found.

Or had it? When Ken Wherry objected to the playing of the record, Tydings backed off quickly—much too quickly. "I withdraw the request," he sneered. "I will play it off the Senate floor in due time—but admission will be by card only." In fact, Tydings could not have played the record. It didn't exist. He was bluffing. And Wherry, who should have known better, had fallen prey to a shell game.

What Tydings did possess was a record of McCarthy's radio interview from Salt Lake City, where Joe had used the figure 57, not 205. Wasn't he taking an awfully big gamble? Not really, said Edward Morgan. Tydings had considered all the angles. "He was sure they wouldn't let him play it." [38]

Tydings now seemed in control, mixing bombast with logic as he strolled about the chamber. Suddenly, though, he made a beeline for Jenner, who had recklessly impugned his patriotism a few days before. Thrusting his face down to Jenner's, Tydings vented months of pent-up frustration. "You know, I have been in some pretty tough places in my boyhood—on battlefields where real men were killed," he said, referring to his days as a machine gunner in World War I. "Perhaps the senator does not know that. When it is suggested that I would protect Communist spies in the country that I love, I find . . . no, I cannot say here what I want to say." Tydings's voice broke, and he struggled to compose himself. Bill Jenner was the real traitor, he fumed. It was he who had voted against the Marshall Plan and NATO. It was he who had encouraged Soviet aggression. It was he who had followed "the same thing that Stalin is saying, that the *Daily Worker* is saying."

Tydings walked back to his desk. He was exhausted and soaked with perspiration. His performance had lasted for more than two hours. Before sitting down, though, he directed one more blast at the Republicans. "You will find out who has been whitewashing—with mud and slime, with filth, with the dregs of publicity at the expense of the people's love for their country. I ask the Senate: What are you going to do about it? I leave it up to your conscience."

What the Senate did was to accept the Tydings Report on a straight party vote. No minds had been changed, in or out of the chamber. Partisanship prevailed everywhere. The pro-Administration Baltimore *Sun* said that McCarthy "had been shown up for what he is—a conscienceless, unprincipled man." *The Nation* called on the Senate to begin immediate censure proceedings, while Harold Ickes demanded Joe's expulsion from that body. McCarthyism, he wrote with typical self-control, is "a putrescent and scabrous object that is odious and loathsome, and not to be touched except with sterilized fire tongs." [39]

The pro-McCarthy forces responded in kind. The New York *Journal–American* called the Tydings Report "the most disgracefully partisan document ever to emanate from the Congress of the United States. As a public paper prepared in parlous times, it verges on DISLOYALTY." And the Chicago *Tribune* went after each Democratic committee member in shotgun style. Millard Tydings? What could one expect of a man whose father-in-law, Joseph Davies, was "a Russophile and a pro-Soviet propagandist"? Brien McMahon? "An old hand at sweeping New Deal dirt under the rug." Theodore Green? "Chiefly distinguished as the one-time little Hitler of his tiny New England state." Americans now had "a simple criterion for determining Communist influence in this country," the *Tribune* suggested. "It will be evidenced fully by counting up those who support the Tydings Report."[40]

———

TOM COLEMAN HAD BEEN WRONG. The Korean War had not stifled McCarthy, it had given him new momentum.

After a brief lull, the senator was back in action, fueled by a bloodbath that grew increasingly difficult to explain. Fighting Communism was all well and good. The people supported that. But many could not understand why little Korea was being defended while a giant like China had been allowed to slip away. How did the State Department justify such logic? And what, exactly, was the extent of America's commitment to South Korea? Was it limited in scope or did it signal the start of an endless war with the "yellow hordes" of Asia? No one seemed quite sure.

Worse still was the fear that Korea would escalate into atomic war. Ever since Hiroshima, Americans had been taught to depend on nuclear superiority, to assume that the technology involved was uniquely their own. When the Russians matched it, the people felt betrayed. Someone must have given these secrets away. Certainly the Soviets could not have developed such a weapon by themselves. On July 18, as Millard Tydings was releasing his final report, FBI agents arrested a New York engineer named Julius Rosenberg. A month later his wife Ethel and his friend Morton Sobell joined him in prison. All were charged with transmitting atomic secrets to Russia.

The reaction was frightening. Although the Soviets hadn't the ability to deliver such a weapon, Administration officials prepared for the worst. Air raid drills became the order of the day, with "simulated" Russian bombings in large metropolitan centers. The sheriff of Kansas City inspected the surrounding quarries and found they could accommodate 840,000 people—or bodies. New York's Sherry-Netherland Hotel placed Geiger counters in its best suites. For the first time, the clamor for a preventive atomic strike against Russia gained *responsible* adherents. "It would win for us a proud and popular title," argued Navy Secretary Francis Matthews. "We would become the first aggressors for peace." Senator John McClellan thought likewise. Since war with Stalin was inevitable, why not fire the first shot?[41]

While the public's response to Korea would never match the excessive displays of 1917 or 1941, it was disturbing nonetheless. For decades the menace of Bolshevism had been drummed into American heads by the government, the schools, the churches, and the media. Surely the threat seemed real enough. The Communists had worked their way into the government; they were gaining in Europe and in Asia; they possessed the atomic bomb. Now they were killing American boys.

Such factors eroded the public's slim tolerance for left-wing activity.

In Brooklyn a judge sentenced five people to jail for scrawling "PEACE" on a wall in Prospect Park. While not labeling them Communists, he did say that "when you see a bird that has the characteristics of a duck and associates with ducks, then it is reasonable to assume it is a duck." Forty "peace arrests" were made in Philadelphia, where the court advised the defendants to "go back to Russia." One Hollywood studio shelved a proposed movie on Hiawatha for fear it would "aid the enemy." "It was Hiawatha's efforts as peacemaker among warring Indian tribes . . . that gave Monogram Studios particular concern," wrote the New York *Times.* "These [efforts], it was decided, might cause the picture to be regarded as a message for peace and therefore helpful to the present Communist designs." [42]

Had Hiawatha been around in 1950, he might have been seriously harassed under the new Internal Security Act. Passed in September, it reflected a war mentality that equated dissent with treason. The law required the federal registration of ill-defined "Communist-action" groups and their members (who were then denied passports and the right to work in defense-related industries). It made political belief, not action, a standard for admission to, and deportation from, America. And it provided for concentration camps to detain subversives "in time of national emergency." Not since the bleakest days of World War I had American civil liberties been as seriously compromised. [43]

Truman vetoed it. His stand took great courage. It would have been easy to give in, to sign something that the public clearly wanted. But the bill made no sense to him. While admitting that "Communist types" were "noisy and troublesome," he did not believe in weakening everyone's rights in order to punish them. If anything, he added, the bill would *aid* the Communist cause "by discrediting as hypocrisy the efforts of the United States on behalf of freedom." [44]

The House overrode him at once. In a bizarre scene, Speaker Sam Rayburn had to plead for quiet in order to have the veto message read aloud. Angry members chanting "Vote! Vote!" didn't want to hear it. Things were no better in the Senate, where "Wild Bill" Langer, the man who had recently suggested that foreign aid money be diverted to his pet project, a national urinalysis fund, tried to filibuster against the bill. He collapsed after five hours and had to be taken away on a stretcher. Virtually everyone deserted the President. "As I look back on it I am ashamed of my vote on the Internal Security Act," wrote William Benton. "I do have some excuses and alibis, though in retrospect they are not good ones." [45]

Senator McCarthy had nothing to do with the writing or passage of the bill. It was the brainchild of Nevada's Pat McCarran, a right-wing Democrat, and conservative Republicans like Karl Mundt. These men were insiders, traditional politicians who understood the legislative process and used it to full advantage. McCarthy was different. Reckless, uncompromising, bored with detail, he was ill-suited for lawmaking. But he and McCarran did have something in common. They were both producers and products of the ugly climate that gripped America in 1950. And they both knew how to exploit that climate for their own political ends.

———

AS ELECTION DAY 1950 APPROACHED, the Democratic mood was understandably grim. Rarely had a majority party come to the polls with so much explaining to do. Charges of corruption involving the President's closest friends had rocked the White House staff. And Truman did nothing. Placing personal loyalty above good common sense, he refused to acknowledge the wrongdoing of his cronies, even after several went to jail. The Republicans happily exploited this inaction. Truman, they reasoned, was marching in step with the ghosts of Ulysses S. Grant and Warren G. Harding.[46]

Then, in rapid succession, came news of the Russian A-bomb test, the fall of China, the Hiss conviction, the Fuchs arrest, and the North Korean invasion. These events destroyed Truman's credibility. How could anyone talk of containment when millions upon millions of people had been lost to the Communists? And how well were subversives being monitored when top-secret information was routinely passed to the enemy? A complete housecleaning seemed in order.

There was also a mystery element to the campaign—what one analyst called "the McCarthy factor." Not up for reelection himself, Joe was eager to help those who were. By October he had 2,000 requests for speaking engagements, more than every other senator combined. One GOP leader summed up his popularity this way: The Democrats were the majority party. Despite all of their problems, they still had the country "bought." So the Republicans had to play dirty, to go for the jugular. "Only by 'mucking' can we win," he smiled, "and only a mucker can muck."[47]

GOP strategists were banking heavily on McCarthy. He was their new political alchemist, the man who would turn fear and distrust into Republican votes. "The issue," said one, "is fairly simple. It comes down to this: Are we going to try to win an election or aren't we?" Another explained: "The public may agree with the intellectuals that McCarthy has never proved a single one of his charges. But I'm sure the public is still saying, 'There must be something to this.' I think it all adds up to a frustration and a feeling of insecurity." The voters were not logical, the man admitted, just mad as hell. And that was fine with the Republicans.[48]

Although he campaigned in fifteen states, Joe's primary interest was Maryland, where Millard Tydings was up for reelection. Tydings was one of the few men in politics whom McCarthy genuinely disliked. He was prissy and condescending. And he had treated Joe like dirt, like some barbarian who had entered the Senate through a back door. His final report, which used the words "fraud," "hoax," "untruth," "half-truth," "deceived," "misled," and "big lie," was meant to drum McCarthy out of Washington. It hadn't, of course, but it still hurt him deeply. "Joe was so preoccupied with Tydings," a friend recalled, "that he'd sit by the hour figuring ways to get revenge."[49]

Tydings's Republican opponent was John Marshall Butler, a little-known Baltimore attorney. Doubtful about his chances, Butler welcomed McCarthy's support. Before long, Joe's staff had taken over the campaign—and the fund-raising. Money arrived from Alfred Kohlberg, oilman Clint Murchison, and the McCormick newspaper chain. "McCarthy asked me for some help against Tydings," Murchison noted. "I was glad to do it. Tydings was part and parcel of an Administration that was entirely too friendly to Communism. So I sent up $10,000—not so very much."[50]

Not so very much by Murchison's standards, but enough to bankroll what one Senate committee called "a despicable 'back street' type of campaign." It was that and more. Barging into Maryland, Joe accused Tydings of "protecting Communists for political reasons." He said that Acheson was "the procurer of pinks and punks in the State Department" and that the Democrats should be renamed the "Commiecrats." Just before Election Day, his staff produced a campaign tabloid, "From the Record," that accused Tydings of every conceivable misdeed. In it was the famous "composite picture," which fused two separate photographs —one of Tydings gazing pensively, the other of Earl Browder stroking his chin—into one showing the men in friendly conversation. The caption read:

> Communist Earl Browder, shown at left, in the composite picture, was a star witness at the Tydings Committee hearings, and was cajoled into saying Owen Lattimore and others accused of disloyalty were not Communists. Tydings (right) answered "Oh, thank you, sir." Browder testified in the best interests of those accused, naturally.[51]

Technically, the caption explained the photo since the phrase "composite picture" did appear—albeit unobtrusively. And one could even argue that a "real event" was portrayed. When Browder testified that spring, Tydings had used the phrase "Thank you, sir." * What was wrong

---

* Throughout Browder's testimony, Tydings remained strangely silent. The bulk of the questioning was done by McMahon and Hickenlooper. At the very end, however, Tydings asked Browder whether two State Department employees, John Carter Vincent and John Stewart Service, were known to him as Communists. Browder at first refused to answer, saying that he would not be reduced "to the status of a Budenz." Tydings politely asked him to reconsider, and Browder did so. "I would say that regarding the two names you mentioned, to the best of my knowledge and belief, they never had any direct or indirect connections with the Communist Party." Tydings replied, "Thank you, sir." See Tydings Subcommittee Hearings, p. 706.

with the photo was its deceptive intent. The reader had no idea that the two men had never met before, or that Browder was a most belligerent witness. What the reader saw was ol' Millard chewing the fat with his good buddy Earl, the Communist.

When Tydings lost by more than 40,000 votes, no one bothered to look beyond the obvious conclusion. "The thing that chiefly beat him," *Time* observed, "was the charge that he had whitewashed the McCarthy investigation." There is some truth to this. Had Tydings not chaired that committee, he *might* have been reelected. But it was no sure thing. By Election Day the Korean War had begun to go badly. Reports of high American casualties were compounded by rumors that China might intervene. This was bad news for all Democrats, and particularly for Tydings, who chaired the Armed Services Committee. He was closely linked with the military reverses.[52]

There were problems in Maryland too. Black voters were annoyed by Tydings's opposition to the Fair Employment Practices Committee. The labor unions viewed him as a political dinosaur. His home state, normally a Democratic bastion, had experienced a spectacular rise in Republican strength since 1940. And he was running on a ticket headed by the first Maryland governor to sign a sales tax bill, a most unlucky break. Tydings's defeat was caused by many factors, but the press saw only one: McCarthy. It had turned Joe into a giant-killer, enhancing both his power and his prestige.[53]

McCarthy tried to take some credit—indeed, the lion's share—for the campaign's other big surprise, the defeat of Scott Lucas by Everett McKinley Dirksen. A decided underdog, Dirksen made up ground with an exhausting two-year effort that logged 250,000 miles. His strategy was to push the conservative line—Communism, Acheson, and inflation—in the hope of wooing enough "downstate" votes to offset Chicago's fabled Democratic machine. In this effort, McCarthy was a helpful addition. He spoke about a half-dozen times in Illinois, telling audiences that a vote for Dirksen was a "prayer for America." The crowds he drew were large and enthusiastic.[54]

What is generally ignored, though, is that Communism was not the big issue in the Illinois race. Corruption was. And it revolved around the presence of one Daniel "Tubbo" Gilbert, a Chicago cop who was running for Cook County sheriff on the Democratic ticket. A penurious fellow, Gilbert had just been cited for squirreling away $300,000 on a $9,000 salary. The disclosure was troublesome. What made it fatal was the man's refusal to step aside. Before long, his candidacy had crippled the Chicago machine and splattered mud over the whole Democratic slate. According to one source, Lucas "never got out from under Tubbo's shadow."[55]

McCarthy's role in the other Senate races was minimal. In Connecticut, William Benton and Brien McMahon were reelected despite his active opposition. In Missouri, Senator Forrest Donnell was overwhelmed despite his active support. Moderate Republicans like Aiken and Tobey suffered no ill effects from their reluctance to embrace McCarthy, both winning easily. And conservatives like Taft and Nixon discouraged Joe from campaigning in their states. They were in no mood for the controversy he would generate or the credit he would undoubtedly take for their hard-earned victories.

Nixon's defeat of Congresswoman Helen Gahagan Douglas showed that "McCarthyism" was not the exclusive property of Joe McCarthy. From Nixon's perspective, Douglas was too good to be true. A former Hollywood actress, a New Deal liberal, a strict civil libertarian, she had opposed the Internal Security Act and the continued funding of HUAC. Like many Democrats, she believed that the real threat to America's security came from the political right, not from the left. And she said so in public.

Nixon began by calling her "an ex-movie actress with ultra-radical leanings and artificial glamour." Since Hollywood symbolized laziness and divorce, he portrayed himself as the frugal, hard-working family man. "Possessed of great vigor and youthful enthusiasm," said one campaign blurb,

> Congressman Nixon takes a sixteen-hour day in stride and still has time for his family, who are very close to his heart. Mrs. Nixon has great difficulty persuading little Tricia—now at the mature age of four—that she shouldn't hop out of bed in the wee hours to share a sandwich and a glass of milk with Daddy, just home from the office. And Daddy isn't much help on that score. He says a half hour with one of his little girls is worth three hours of sleep. [56]

But Nixon spent most of the campaign pushing the "Pink Lady" theme—that Douglas had "consciously fought to prevent the exposure and control of Communists in this country." Her victory, Nixon told the voters, would be a signal to Joe Stalin that his influence in America was on the rise. ("EVERY COMMUNIST WHO GOES TO THE POLLS WILL VOTE AGAINST NIXON AND FOR MRS. DOUGLAS. WHICH WAY WILL YOU VOTE?") In the campaign's final days, California was blitzed by penny postcards reading: "Vote for our Helen for Senator. We are With Her 100%." They were sent by Nixon volunteers, who signed them, "Communist League of Negro Women." [57]

All in all, the 1950 campaign proved to be a mixed blessing for the Republicans. While they had picked up five Senate and twenty-eight House seats, their gains were smaller than in any midterm election since 1934. And the Democrats remained firmly in control of Congress. Given Truman's low public standing, most analysts were surprised that the GOP hadn't done better.

McCarthy's role is more difficult to assess. On the one hand, he *had* helped to popularize the best issue the Republicans had—Communist influence in government. He had made big headlines, named some important names, and generally put the Democrats on the defensive. On the other hand, after China, Korea, and the Rosenbergs, the Communist issue was self-propelled—and McCarthy fed off it more than it fed off him. Clearly, his involvement in the various races was exaggerated by the media. William S. White, for example, claimed that Joe "contributed a heavy part, if not the decisive part" to the defeats of Tydings and Lucas. Drew Pearson saw him as the pivotal figure in the entire campaign. Before long, an aura of political invincibility had enveloped McCarthy. "You couldn't imagine the change in his stature when he returned to Washington," recalled William Fulbright. "The Republicans looked upon him as the new messiah. The Democrats were just scared to death. He was the same old McCarthy, as odious as ever. But, oh my, how things had changed."[58]

CHAPTER TWELVE

The Fourth Estate

Monday, December 13, 1950, was Drew Pearson's fifty-third birthday. To celebrate the occasion his wife, Luvie, took him to a party at Washington's plush Sulgrave Club. Pearson was in good spirits, totally unaware that the festivities had been arranged by Mrs. Louise Ansberry, who, in the columnist's words, "was noted for having a lot of punks at her dinner parties." Among the invited guests was Joe McCarthy.[1]

The two men were not exactly strangers. According to Jack Anderson, McCarthy had once been Pearson's best contact in the Republican Party. "When Joe first came to Washington," Anderson explained, "he tried very hard to please the press. He would do things for Drew and me that were incredible, that no congressman had ever done for us. If I needed to find out something about Senator Taft, Joe would call up Taft and let me listen in on the extension in his outer office. Taft never knew I was on the phone. This sort of thing was Joe's way of being friendly. I felt a little funny about being part of it. But I was a reporter who took what he would give."[2]

Pearson had soured on McCarthy after the Wheeling speech. As a close friend and supporter of Dean Acheson, he was disgusted by the senator's vicious attacks on State Department personnel. At the same time, he began receiving derogatory material about Joe from Wisconsin —compliments of Bill Evjue and the Madison *Capital–Times*. In 1950 alone Pearson had attacked McCarthy in fifty-eight of his nationally syndicated columns. He rehashed the senator's income tax troubles, his "quickie" divorces, and his obnoxious behavior during the Malmedy probe. He broke the Lustron payoff story and even uncovered a "sexual pervert" who worked in Joe's office.

McCarthy was itching to get even. When he ran into Pearson at the Gridiron Club dinner, he smiled, put out his hand, and said, "Someday I'm going to break your leg, Drew, but for the time being I just wanted to say hello." Pearson was concerned enough to note the incident in his diary. "I am more and more convinced that there is a screw loose somewhere," he concluded. By December McCarthy had publicly sworn revenge. He told people he wasn't sure "whether to kill Pearson or just to maim him."[3]

Joe got the chance to decide when Mrs. Ansberry mischievously seated him at the Pearsons' table. Between shots of bourbon, he told Luvie about a speech he would soon deliver. It was a blockbuster, he warned, which would end Drew's career and "cause a divorce in the family." Luvie said nothing, but her husband quipped, "Joe, how is your income tax case coming along? . . . How long are they going to let you stay out of jail?" With that, Pearson remembered, McCarthy jumped up, "put his thumb and index finger behind the nerves at the back of my neck, gouged me there as hard as he could . . . and said, 'You come out. We will settle this.' " Congressman Charles Bennett, a polio victim, tried to separate the two but fell on his face. As Joe bent over to pick him up, Pearson walked away. Smaller and much older than McCarthy, the columnist did not want to fight. He was, in fact, a pacifist.

Joe finally cornered Pearson in the coat room. "Well, Drew," he sneered, "a pleasant evening, wasn't it?" Pearson said nothing. As he reached into his pocket for the coat check, McCarthy wheeled around and kneed him twice in the groin—an instinctive move, the senator explained later, to protect him from assassins. As Pearson doubled over, Joe floored him with an open-handed slap. At that point Richard Nixon burst onto the scene yelling, "Let a Quaker stop this fight." He grabbed McCarthy's arm and tried to pull him from the room. It wasn't easy. "I won't turn my back on that son-of-a-bitch," Joe exploded. "He's got to go first." After Pearson had left, Nixon escorted McCarthy outside and spent the next half-hour trying to locate his colleague's automobile. Joe was too drunk to remember where he had parked it.[4]

The Washington papers provided a blow-by-blow account of the brawl. McCarthy admitted slapping Pearson, but he took the Fifth about the groin kicks. Pearson seemed intent on deflating Joe's punching power. It was, he sniffed, "about as effective as his senatorial behavior." Nixon polished his image even as he declined comment, saying that "such foolishness should not be bandied about in times like these." Privately, though, he claimed that he had never seen anyone slapped as hard. "If I hadn't pulled McCarthy away, he might have killed Pearson," Nixon told a friend.[5]

A few days later Joe made his celebrated Senate attack upon the columnist. The gallery was packed with reporters, some of whom suspected that McCarthy had beaten Pearson to ensure a good press turnout. He began—as he so often did—by talking of the dangers involved, of how a colleague had just warned him: "McCarthy, don't do it. . . . You will be merely inundated by the slime and the smear and he will go on every day polluting otherwise fine newspapers and poisoning the airwaves." But Joe would not back off. What happened to him was not important, he said. Exposing Drew Pearson was![6]

This self-serving introduction was typical McCarthy bluster. Everyone knew that Pearson had more powerful enemies than he could count, that he had been called almost every name in the book. Franklin Roosevelt had questioned his morality; Harry Truman had traduced his ancestry; and scores of others, from Douglas MacArthur to Walter Reuther, had impugned his integrity. Doing battle with the columnist, it seemed, was a sure way to *enhance* one's popularity. When word of the Sulgrave fight got out, more than twenty senators phoned Joe's office to congratulate him. Utah's Arthur Watkins put his arm around McCarthy in the Capitol elevator and exclaimed: "Joe, I've heard conflicting accounts of where you hit Pearson. I hope both are true."[7]

McCarthy's oration was predictably mean. Speaking with full immunity, he accused the columnist of protecting "subversive elements" in Washington. Heads shook all over the Senate. Even Pearson's critics regarded him as a tough anti-Communist, a man whose loyalty to America was beyond question. Yet McCarthy persisted. Pearson was not only a "degenerate liar," he was also a "sugar-coated voice of Russia." It was time for the people to rise up and still "this Moscow-directed character assassin."[8]

How might this be done? Joe had a plan. Every loyal American should threaten Pearson's radio sponsor, the Adam Hat Company, with an economic boycott if it did not withdraw from his show at once. Looking up toward the gallery, he declared that "anyone who buys an Adam Hat, any store that stocks an Adam Hat . . . is unknowingly and innocently contributing at least something to the cause of international Communism." His speech completed, he plunked a gray fedora on his head and walked out into the brisk winter air. It was an Adam hat, size seven and three-eighths, which the columnist had once given him as a gift.[9]

Almost immediately, Adam Hat announced the termination of its $5,000-a-week contract with Pearson. Company president Charles Molesworth insisted that McCarthy had played no role in this decision. It had been made long before, he explained, and it was based on the need to substitute television for radio advertising. Of course, few people believed him. The very timing of the announcement said it all: Joe had bullied the firm into submission.

In fact, Molesworth was telling the truth. Adam Hat and Pearson *had* agreed to part company before the Sulgrave incident. It is possible, however, that Joe got wind of the decision in advance. Styles Bridges told one newsman that he had overheard McCarthy and Senator Byrd discussing it a couple of days *before* Joe belted the columnist. If that was true, then McCarthy may have staged the fisticuffs and his Senate diatribe in order to take full credit for the cancellation. It could have been his way of telling the press corps: "Think twice before you take me on. You could wind up like Drew Pearson."[10]

Bizarre though it was, the Pearson–McCarthy donnybrook raised some serious questions. Was it a meaningless tiff between two volatile personalities, or was the senator engaged in a campaign to silence his journalistic critics? If his object was intimidation, how successful was he? And how responsible was the press in covering his early charges? Was it being unfair to him? Fair? Perhaps too fair? How, exactly, did it respond to McCarthy and his antics?

———

WHEN JOE BEGAN HIS ATTACKS upon the State Department, he quickly won the support of America's right-wing press. That included the Hearst and McCormick chains; commentators like Walter Winchell, George Sokolsky, Westbrook Pegler, and H. V. Kaltenborn; and a host of less influential Republican dailies. According to Willard Edwards of the Chicago *Tribune*, McCarthy "just fitted into what we had been saying long before." As a result, "we gave him complete support. We never criticized him in any way. We just went all the way with him editorially—one of the very few newspapers that did."[11]

Lined up against McCarthy was a more formidable contingent, including the major news magazines and every one of the nation's "ten best" dailies.* They were generally moderate in outlook, supportive of bipartisanship, and unwilling to believe that the government was riddled with Communists. This posed a serious problem. How could the senator get his message across when those who packaged the news were hostile to him? One way was intimidation.

Joe was never subtle or secretive about the methods he employed. After Marvin Arrowsmith of the Associated Press wrote several uncomplimentary pieces, he was invited to the Senate Office Building for a

———

* The New York *Times,* Washington *Post, Christian Science Monitor,* St. Louis *Post–Dispatch,* Baltimore *Sun,* Chicago *Daily News,* New York *Herald–Tribune,* Milwaukee *Journal,* Kansas City *Star,* and Louisville *Courier–Journal.*

High school graduation picture of Joe McCarthy, 1930, Manawa, Wisconsin.
Wisconsin Historical Society

Evenings deep in the South Pacific jungles found McCarthy holding court for pilots returning from bombing raids. He often opened the sessions with: "All right, what kind of hell did you give the Japs today?" *Wisconsin Historical Society*

Pictured in full fighting gear, "Tail-gunner Joe" sent photos like this one to folks back home to promote his daredevil image. *Wisconsin Historical Society*

McCarthy casts his ballot in the Wisconsin Republican Primary, a race in which he rode to victory over his opponent, Robert M. LaFollette, Jr. *AP/Wide World Photos*

In a surprise move after two days as senator-elect in Washington, McCarthy called the press conference pictured here, at which he demanded that John L. Lewis and the 400,000 striking coal miners in his union be drafted into the Army, and court-martialed if they failed to produce coal. *AP/Wide World Photos*

Owen Lattimore (lower left), the professor of Far Eastern studies who was accused by McCarthy of being a top Russian spy, leaving hearing room on April 20, 1950. *AP/ Wide World Photos*

Jean Kerr, then Joe McCarthy's assistant and bride-to-be, in 1953. *AP/Wide World Photos*

Facing page, top   Millard Tydings faces McCarthy at a March 8, 1950, Senate foreign relations subcommittee hearing bearing on Joe's charges that a Communist spy ring was operating in the State Department. *AP/Wide World Photos*

Facing page, bottom   In the standing-room-only Senate Caucus room, McCarthy (seated at far right middle foreground, with head down) testifies that the State Department is riddled with Communists. Senators at table facing him are (left to right): Bourke Hickenlooper, Millard Tydings, Theodore Green, Brien McMahon, and Tom Connally. *AP/Wide World Photos*

At an April 27, 1954, hearing, McCarthy examines a photo of Pvt. Schine in the company of Secretary Stevens and Col. Bradley. Looking on are Senator Jackson (left) and Francis Carr (center) of McCarthy's staff. The Army charged that a photo of Stevens and Schine displayed on April 26 was a "doctored" version of this picture. McCarthy called the charge "completely false." *AP/Wide World Photos*

David Schine (left) and Roy Cohn (right) with McCarthy at the Army-McCarthy hearings. Schine received sixteen passes during a period when his buddies got three. *Wisconsin Historical Society*

McCarthy and his aides—Roy Cohn (left) and Francis Carr (right)—enjoy a good laugh as the April 30, 1954, Senate Investigations subcommittee session gets underway. *AP/Wide World Photos*

Seated left to right at the Army-McCarthy hearings are Robert Stevens, Robert Young, Roy Cohn, and Joe McCarthy. Stevens' over-the-shoulder conversation is with John Adams. *AP/Wide World Photos*

Just prior to the start of the May 27 Senate subcommittee hearing, Joseph N. Welch, special counsel to the Army, exchanges pleasantries with McCarthy in the Senate Caucus room. *AP/Wide World Photos*

Facing page, top Finger on lips, a pensive McCarthy listens to the testimony of Army Secretary Robert Stevens. At his left is Roy Cohn; on his right are Francis Carr and Senators Henry Jackson, Stuart Symington, and John McClellan. *AP/Wide World Photos*

Facing page, bottom Karl Mundt (left), the unwilling chairman of the investigating committee, talks to McCarthy after end of April 23 morning session. Roy Cohn is between them. *AP/Wide World Photos*

Jean Kerr McCarthy holds a handkerchief to her face as she leaves the Capitol on May 6, 1957, after a Senate Chamber funeral service for her husband. *AP/Wide World Photos*

Facing page   Pain from an injured arm increases his look of weariness as the burden of McCarthy's one-man campaign against Communism begins to show on his face. *Copyright © UPI. All rights reserved. Distributed by Valeo IP*

A long line of mourners outside St. Mary Catholic Church,
Appleton, Wisconsin, waiting to pass the bier of Senator
McCarthy, May 6, 1957. More than 17,000 viewed the body.
The Post-Crescent, Appleton, Wisconsin

The grave of Joseph R. McCarthy at
St. Mary's Cemetery in Appleton,
Wisconsin. *The Post-Crescent*,
Appleton, Wisconsin

chat. "I know you've got six kids, Marv, and I don't want to kick about your work," McCarthy told him, "so I hope there is no further reason to do so." When Arrowsmith remained uncooperative, Joe sent a letter to hundreds of newspapers complaining about the AP's biased coverage. That got results. Arrowsmith's next story was positive, centering on the coast-to-coast support shown in the senator's mail. "He used to call regularly," said one reporter of McCarthy. ". . . He'd kid me about my sources, or some minor point that I had made that he said was wrong. . . . He just wanted me to know he was watching."[12]

Phil Potter, the Baltimore *Sun*'s veteran correspondent, was given sterner treatment. Within weeks of his first anti-McCarthy story, he discovered that investigators from Joe's office had come to Baltimore seeking dirt from his past. "He also threatened to subpoena me three or four times," Potter remembered. "He never did . . . but it was all kinds of silly little threats." Potter stood firm, however, because his editors, who despised McCarthy, gave him active encouragement.[13]

Any newsperson who persisted in criticizing the senator could expect to be labeled a Communist dupe, a degenerate, or both. Elmer Davis, the erudite broadcaster, was scolded for telling stories that "might well have emanated from Moscow itself." Richard Strout of the *Christian Science Monitor* was admonished for "shaking the hand of Rob Hall of the Communist *Daily Worker*." The Alsop brothers were accused of writing articles that were "almost 100 percent in line with the official instructions issued to all Communists and fellow travelers." McCarthy's favorite ploy, however, was to compare hostile newspapers with the *Daily Worker*. By 1951 this category included the New York *Post*, New York *Times*, Milwaukee *Journal*, St. Louis *Post–Dispatch*, Madison *Capital–Times*, Denver *Post*, and *Christian Science Monitor*. For good measure, he added *The Nation*, *The New Republic*, *Time*, *Life*, and *Newsweek*.[14]

Joe often displayed real ingenuity in striking back at his critics. While headlining a banquet in Milwaukee, he spotted a young writer, Ronald May, who had just co-authored a biography critical of him. Discarding his prepared text, McCarthy complained of being harassed by Communist spies. Why, one of them was now in the audience, he said, sitting right down in front. "He aroused such feeling against this 'spy,'" May wrote later, "that the audience soon resembled a mob. Then he named myself, and dared me to stand up. I stood up, and pandemonium broke loose." May tried to escape, but his path was blocked by one of Joe's bodyguards. Retreating slowly, he was jostled and verbally abused by the angry diners. Outside he was set upon by curious reporters, who listened to his tale with knowing smiles. As a final indignity, the Hearst-owned Milwaukee *Sentinel* captioned the fracas: "McCarthy Points Finger at Snooper: Charges He Is Seeking Smear Material."[15]

Of all the press battles, none quite matched his running feud with the Milwaukee *Journal*, Wisconsin's largest newspaper.* Never warm to McCarthy, the *Journal* had turned downright hostile after the Wheeling speech. It called him a liar and a bully. It employed a staffer, Bob Fleming, to dog his tracks. And it caused a stir by publicly questioning his sanity. "We wonder if the senator's friends shouldn't persuade him to see a psychiatrist," the *Journal* remarked during the 1950 campaign.[16]

Joe responded by lambasting the *Journal* as he traveled across Wisconsin. "Hey, there's Bob Fleming of the Milwaukee *Daily Worker*," he would tell the jeering crowds. "Hell of a guy. He's quoted a lot in *Pravda*, you know." This stuff never bothered Fleming. He viewed it as a ritualistic gesture, akin to Harry Truman's jibes at the Chicago *Tribune*. Yet McCarthy never let up. He once told Fleming—off the record—that he knew of two *Journal* editorial writers who had contributed to the Alger Hiss Defense Fund. Fleming was skeptical, but he had to check out the story on the slim chance that it might be true. After an exhaustive search, he discovered that it wasn't. Joe was just having some fun—and reminding the *Journal* that there were easier targets around to attack.

He also called for an economic boycott of the newspaper. "Keep in mind," he lectured state business groups, "that when you send checks over to the *Journal* . . . you are contributing to bringing the Communist Party line into the homes of Wisconsin." The boycott never got off the ground—a fact that bothered McCarthy not at all. He had a different end in mind, and he gladly told Robert Fleming what it was when they met for a drink at the Schroeder Hotel. "I don't have any idea that I can break the *Journal*. Off the record, I don't know that I can cut its profits at all. . . . But if you show a newspaper as unfriendly and having a reason for being antagonistic, you can take the sting out of what it says about you. I think I can convince a lot of people that they can't believe what they read in the *Journal*."[17]

McCarthy's strategy was simple. He portrayed the differences between the critic and himself as ideological (pro-Communist versus anti-Communist); he attempted to maximize the critic's discomfort; and he never backed away from a fight. It didn't matter if the critic was a liberal or a conservative, a Democrat or a Republican, a powerhouse or a nonentity. *Anyone* who attacked Joe McCarthy could expect some trouble. When the Syracuse *Post–Standard* ran an inaccurate story, Joe sued for

---

* The possible exception, of course, was Joe's decade-long battle with the Madison *Capital–Times*. He had muddied the paper in the Cedric Parker case, and, according to editor Miles McMillin, he kept the *Capital–Times* from acquiring a Madison television station by threatening the Federal Communications Commission with a full-scale investigation. See Mary Jane Ferguson, "McCarthy vs. Pearson: Criticism or Intimidation," unpublished master's thesis, University of Wisconsin, 1969, p. 20; Jean Deaver, "A Study of Senator Joseph R. McCarthy and 'McCarthyism' as Influences upon the News Media . . . ," unpublished doctoral dissertation, University of Texas, 1969, pp. 150–56.

libel and won a small out-of-court settlement. When Hank Greenspun, editor of the Las Vegas *Sun*, wrote that McCarthy might be assassinated by "some poor innocent slob whose reputation and life he has destroyed," Joe had him indicted for "tending to incite murder." (Greenspun was acquitted.) When the Sheboygan *Press* condemned his unruly behavior, Joe used his next appearance in that city to lash out at the newspaper's "pro-Communist sympathies." His audience, a group of Sheboygan schoolchildren, seemed bewildered by it all.[18]

In this brass-knuckle world, it was hardly surprising that McCarthy's most impressive victory should come at the expense of *Time–Life*'s Henry Luce, a dependable Republican ally. Luce was a ferocious anti-Communist who took a back seat to no one in his fear and loathing of the Red Menace. Yet he could not bear the senator. He saw him as a political opportunist whose scatter-gun methods were discrediting "responsible" anti-Communists like Richard Nixon. Late in 1951, after convincing himself that McCarthy was slipping, Luce mobilized his forces for battle. On October 22 Joe made *Time*'s cover as "Demagogue McCarthy," the fellow with "no regard for fair play, no scruple for exact truth." Rarely, if ever, had a Red-hunting Republican been treated so harshly by a Luce publication.

McCarthy was furious. The story somehow penetrated his thick skin and aroused in him a hatred for *Time–Life* that never quite disappeared. He fired off an angry note to Luce, demanding that several "deliberately misrepresented" statements be corrected. When the publisher refused, McCarthy wrote him again: "As you, of course, know, I am preparing material on *Time* to furnish to all of your advertisers so that they may be fully aware of the type of publication they are supporting." Franked letters were then mailed to the large corporations, asking them not to do business with a "pro-Communist" magazine. Luce quickly retreated. His publications "withdrew to a safe distance," wrote one Luce biographer. They "played the McCarthy issue very cautiously as the weeks went on, avoiding any suggestion that Joe might be dangerous, now and then slapping his wrist or patting his back." In the fall of 1952 *Life* apologized for not attacking McCarthy sooner—"it seems that every week we had something more important to talk about"—and grudgingly crossed the Rubicon. "McCarthyism," it stated, "is a venial sin, which every one of us needs to fight against in himself. Communism is, in our time, The Great Sin Against Humanity. We need to fight against that—together and unitedly."[19]

THERE WERE MANY JOURNALISTS who believed that the intimidation factor was overplayed, that it did not really explain why McCarthy, and no one else in Congress, ruled America's front pages for almost five years. To their thinking, the senator was a publicity genius, a man who understood how the press worked and was able to exploit its weaknesses. No one was better, they said, at timing releases for the newspapers, at keeping old stories alive and new ones flowing, or at stealing someone else's thunder.[20]

Early in 1950 a reporter wrote that he had "never seen the press quite so frustrated. It's as if you lacked the words to describe what's going on." He was referring to McCarthy's stranglehold on a system known as "straight" or "objective" journalism—a system that requires the reporter to present the facts, not to interpret them. When a politician makes a controversial statement, the public, in a free society, must be able to read it without being told that it is filled with errors, or that the politician is not to be trusted. These judgments must rest with the reader—and no one else.[21]

Quite often, then, the reporter becomes a conveyor belt for material he knows to be false. He is helpless because the system inhibits him from imparting *his* version of the truth. In McCarthy's case this objective approach was particularly frustrating. "My own impression was that Joe was a demagogue," a newsman remarked. "But what could I do? I had to report—and quote—McCarthy. How do you say in the middle of your story, 'This is a lie'? The press is supposedly neutral. You write what the man says."[22]

Most newspapers compound the problem by reporting almost *anything* a United States senator cares to do or say—a policy that Elmer Davis once called "the Honorable John P. Hoozis" syndrome. It doesn't matter if the senator is lying or just plain ignorant. On the contrary, the more outrageous his statement, the more likely it is to wind up on page one. Knowing this, the ambitious reporter seeks out those who provide sensational, though not necessarily accurate, information. In the 1950s there was no better or quicker or more sensationally inaccurate source than Joe McCarthy. He attracted reporters like flies.[23]

When, for example, McCarthy called Owen Lattimore a Russian spy, the press, like McCarthy himself, had no idea whether the accusation was valid. All it knew was that a high public official had made it—and that alone was news. The charge merited a banner headline—"McCarthy Names Lattimore as Top Russian Spy"—because it was controversial and came from the mouth of an important person. Lattimore's denial got a much smaller headline. It was less controversial, and it came from the mouth of an obscure professor. "If Lattimore had said McCarthy was telling the truth," a journalist explained, "that would have had a bigger headline rating and consequently a bigger headline."[24]

Joe's critics were well aware that he was playing them for suckers. They simply did not know what to do about it. There were all kinds of suggestions, the simplest being to ignore him or, at the least, to downplay his newsworthiness. One feisty paper, the Manhattan (Kansas) *Mercury–Chronicle*, decided to take all McCarthy stories off page one and to run them on page three. But its experiment unleashed a storm of protest. "Banishing McCarthy to the inside of the paper," the Louisville *Courier–Journal* admonished, "suspends the one rule on which a newspaper can be run. That is the pure act of news judgment." Walter Lippmann added his reluctant support. "McCarthy's charges . . . are news which cannot be suppressed or ignored," he wrote. "They come from a United States senator and a politician . . . in good standing at the headquarters of the Republican Party. When he makes such attacks against the State Department . . . it is news which has to be published."[25]

Lippmann was right, of course. To ignore McCarthy was to deny political reality. He was not talking about fishing rights in Louisiana or the price of cheese in Wisconsin. He was raising—and redefining—the most spectacular issue of his day. A Senate committee had been formed to investigate his charges; the President of the United States had spoken out against him; powerful Republicans had rushed to his defense. Like it or not, he was the hottest item in Washington, a man whose antics had to be reported. But how? Could his charges be printed without damaging the reputations of innocent men and women? And who was responsible for checking their accuracy? Was it possible, in short, to cover McCarthy without legitimizing his distortions and outright lies?

The press never found a way. Perhaps there was none. The senator remained on the front pages until the public tired of him and a majority of his colleagues mustered the courage to condemn his behavior. Still, many newspapers did what they could, within the confines of objectivity, to present the "facts" as they saw them. They used the editorial, the cartoon, and the syndicated column; a few relied on "investigative" stories, which rattled the skeletons in Joe's copious political closet. Yet these efforts were generally unproductive. Even a casual reader must have wondered why a man so thoroughly savaged in the editorials was given unlimited front-page coverage. If McCarthy was a fraud, why report his every charge with such straight-faced solemnity?

That question seemed to paralyze the press. After running a string of McCarthy allegations that later proved groundless, the New York *Times* admitted that it had inadvertently misled the public. But was there a choice? "It is difficult, if not impossible, to ignore charges by Senator McCarthy just because they are usually proved exaggerated or false," the *Times* wrote apologetically. "The remedy lies with the reader." Richard Rovere quipped that this was "rather like saying . . . if a restaurant serves poisoned food, it is up to the diner to refuse it." But he still felt that the *Times* was "essentially right." The press had no business telling the public which "facts" were really "facts," and which were not. When that happened, it had far exceeded its role in a free society.[26]

A handful of newspapers rejected this contention. The Denver *Post*, for one, simply refused to print Joe's charges as "straight" news. Its publisher demanded that "news stories and headlines about Senator McCarthy be presented in such a manner that the reading public will be able to measure . . . the true meaning of the stories." This allowed the reporter to show how and where and when Joe was misleading the public. Thus, the editorial page was brought to the front page, and the reporter's interpretation of the facts was given precedence over McCarthy's. The Milwaukee *Journal* took similar precautions. "We thought objectivity involved telling the reader that last week Joe said there were 59 Communists but that he couldn't scare up a single one, so that today when he says that there are 137, maybe you'd better wonder about the 137 too," said its executive editor. Before long, the *Journal* was inserting parenthetical corrections into its McCarthy stories, pointing out faulty statistics and inaccurate quotations.[27]

Most publishers, though, saw this remedy as worse than the disease. And the Washington press corps dismissed it as unworkable. The average newsman was too busy meeting deadlines to keep accurate tabs on the senator. George Reedy, who worked for United Press, insists that McCarthy was a master at exploiting the reporter's time problems. All newspapers have a similar rhythm, he explained. "Things have to be done at a certain time. And Joe somewhat instinctively picked up the absolutely vital course of the cycle. He knew that every wire service man had to have a lead by eleven o'clock. There just wasn't any question about it; you had to have a lead." So he would hold a press conference at ten o'clock, make a stupendous charge, and back it up with a mass of documents that could not humanly be analzyed in the next hour. Most reporters, desperate for their lead, would write up the charge without really checking it out. They got their story and Joe got his publicity.[28]

Even newsmen who were not slaves to the morning deadline seemed bewildered by the sheer volume of McCarthy's output. Every day brought a torrent of fresh charges, photostats, press releases, memos, interviews, and speeches. Elmer Davis complained that his desk was overflowing with the senator's material, "but when he says something that stirs a vague recollection that he once said something very different, I seldom have time to run through it. I can't afford to hire a full-time specialist to keep up with what McCarthy has said."[29]

That point was well taken. Covering Joe McCarthy could be a thankless and frustrating task. Yet the fact remained that most reporters *liked* the duty, that before long a strange and mutually supportive bond had emerged between subject and author. With few exceptions—Drew Pearson and the Alsops in particular—the press was quite fond of McCarthy. Its members knew he was a fountain of sordid misinformation. ("I don't think that Joe could have found a Communist on May Day in Union

Square in 1928," mused Reedy, "and frankly I don't think Joe gave a damn.") But they loved to kibbitz with him, swap stories, have a few drinks, or play some cards. "He was really an ingratiating Irishman," said one of his sternest critics. "I liked him, and he seemed to like me." Another commented: "You knew very well that he was a bum—still, you liked this kind of bum."[30]

Much of this fondness was due to Joe's accessibility. Unlike some public officials, who hid behind their aides, he did his own press work. Reporters knew that his door was always open. They could show up at any hour, day or night, and get right through to him. Bob Fleming remembers that McCarthy even developed a series of hand signals to communicate with newsmen who followed him around the banquet circuit. If he came over to the press table, slapped someone on the back, and said, "Glad to see you, talk with you later," it meant, "Don't eat too much because we'll go out for supper later and shoot the breeze." If, after dinner, he clasped his hands over his head like a boxer, it meant, "Give me a few minutes and come up and tell me I've got a phone call from Washington; I've spent enough time shaking hands with the people here; let's get out of this." The reporters would then go back to his hotel room for an evening of good talk and good liquor. "He would always prefer, I think, to argue with [us]," Fleming recalled, "than to sit with a group of people who might be less interesting to him at the time."[31]

This did not mean that the reporters who followed McCarthy wrote favorably about his activities. They rarely praised him, condemned him when they could, and repeatedly warned their editors about the perils of dealing objectively with a demagogue. At the same time, however, they viewed Joe as a "dream story," a guy who put those lucky enough to cover him on page one, where every reporter feels he belongs. The press flocked to McCarthy because he was bizarre, unpredictable, entertaining, and always newsworthy. "It got to the point that the big newsgathering agencies—Associated Press, International Press, the New York *Times* and the other big outfits—would send men with him wherever he went," Senator Watkins recalled. "Right on the plane with him, a permanent squad, they went with him all the time. Well, he always tried to see that they got their stories. He was one of the boys, and he knew it was a two-way street." One critic diagnosed this odd relationship as phobophilia: The press, he claimed, was in love with its enemy.[32]

Needless to say, the press did not create Joe McCarthy. He was the product of other forces: the Cold War, the long-simmering Republican–Democratic feud in Washington, the failure of his own colleagues to deal with artfully disruptive behavior. Nor, for that matter, was it less successful than other institutions in finding ways to control him. The press was baffled by McCarthy. And utterly fascinated. Like everyone else, it recognized the paradox of giving serious attention to someone so manipulative and devoid of truth. But it saw no alternative. Unable to ignore McCarthy, the press became his captive, offering its services until the political process finally rose up to silence him. Wallace Carroll of the New York *Times* phrased the dilemma well: "I am sure that if a scholarly study were made of the part played by American newspapers in the rise of Senator McCarthy, it would show that the senator understood the deadly virtues of the American press much more clearly than we do ourselves." [33]

CHAPTER THIRTEEN

"An Infamy So Black . . ."

THERE WAS A BRIEF PERIOD in the autumn of 1950 when the nation's mood seemed to brighten and people told themselves that things were getting better. The McCarran Act had just been passed, ending weeks of bitter wrangling. And the news from Korea was finally good. After two months of backward movement, the U.N. forces under General MacArthur had outflanked the enemy with a brilliant amphibious landing at Inchon. By October they had recaptured Seoul and crossed the 38th parallel in pursuit of the routed North Korean Army. As Americans listened in amazement, MacArthur spoke of having his men "home before Christmas." The war was no longer in doubt—or so it seemed.

There were a few ominous signs, however. It was clear that the President and the general did not see eye to eye on foreign policy. Truman's first concern was Europe; MacArthur's was Asia. "Europe is a dying system," the general liked to say. "The lands touching the Pacific with their billions of inhabitants will determine the course of history for the next ten thousand years!" Predictably, MacArthur viewed Korea as part of the larger struggle to liberate Asia from Communism. He even spoke of rearming Chiang Kai-shek for an invasion of the Chinese mainland. Such views were anathema to Harry Truman, as the general well knew. Yet he refused to hold his tongue.[1]

Far more distressing was MacArthur's indifference to the possibility that Red China might enter the war. As his forces drove north toward Manchuria they had captured scores of Chinese Communist "volunteers." In early November the New York *Times* reported that "Chinese Communist hordes, attacking on horse and on foot to the sound of bugle calls, cut up Americans and South Koreans at Unsan today in an Indian-style massacre." Then the Chinese broke off contact and slipped into the heavily camouflaged hills near the Yalu River. MacArthur disregarded them. As a self-proclaimed expert on the Oriental mind, he could not imagine that they would confront a Western army led by the world's greatest general. He had no idea that several hundred thousand Red Chinese soldiers were already in North Korea, waiting quietly in ambush.[2]

They struck on November 26, pushing the startled Westerners back toward the 38th parallel. The retreat—MacArthur called it a "planned withdrawal"—was so rapid that serious thought was given to a Dunkirk-style evacuation of the entire U.N. command. On December 3 Mac-Arthur cabled Washington. "Unless some positive and immediate action is taken . . . our destruction can reasonably be contemplated." His pessimism was short-lived. In the following weeks the outmanned U.S. Eighth Army hacked its way through mountain blizzards and a wall of Chinese infantry to form a defense line just south of the 38th parallel. ("The enemy is in front of us, behind us, to the left of us, and to the right of us," said Marine Colonel "Chesty" Puller in the campaign's most spirited pep talk. "They won't escape *this* time.") Although disaster had been averted, the nation was shocked by the turn of events. *Time* called the reversal "the worst the United States has ever suffered." while the New York *Herald–Tribune* labeled it "a colossal blunder," demonstrating that MacArthur "can no longer be accepted as the final authority on military matters."[3]

By March 1951 the Red offensive had been stalled. U.N. forces again took Seoul and pushed ahead to the 38th parallel, where the two sides faced each other in a bloody standoff. As expected, MacArthur called for an escalation of the war. Killing Chinese soldiers was not enough, he argued, for replacements could always be found. It was time to destroy China's *ability* to wage war. The general recommended a naval blockade of China's coast, a massive air bombardment of its industry, and the "unleashing" of Chiang for a mainland invasion. Anything less, he said, would betray the brave soldiers who were fighting and dying in a senseless stalemate.[4]

This plea for a no-holds-barred response was understandable. Mac-Arthur, like most Americans, believed firmly in the concepts of total victory and unconditional surrender. Talk of limited war disgusted him; he spoke instead of America's omnipotence, of its capacity to defeat North Korea, China, and anyone else who might enter the fray. Mac-

Arthur's message was painfully clear. The lands surrendered to the Communists by weak-kneed civilians like Truman and Acheson could easily be recaptured by the full exercise of American military power. It was that simple.

The President saw things differently. Any attempt to widen the war, he realized, would dismay the other U.N. participants. England would surely pull out, thereby increasing America's military burden. And an attack inside China—by Chiang or MacArthur—could bring Russia into the conflict. It might send troops to the Asian front or put pressure on Western Europe, where America's strength was already sapped by the Korean call-up. Russia's involvement also posed the threat of nuclear war, with atomic bombs raining down on populated areas. As General Omar Bradley noted, MacArthur's strategy was the very antithesis of the one proposed by the President, the State Department, and the Joint Chiefs of Staff. "So long as we regarded the Soviet Union as the main antagonist and Western Europe as the main prize," he said, "it would involve us in the wrong war, at the wrong place, at the wrong time, and with the wrong enemy."[5]

Despite repeated warnings from the President, MacArthur kept up his public drumfire for an expanded Asian war. He was encouraged, no doubt, by the pro-Chiang bloc in Congress, which expressed growing outrage at America's "no-win" policy. Truman's limited approach, Robert Taft fumed, was "like a football game in which our team, when it reaches the 50-yard line, is always instructed to kick. Our team can never score." Styles Bridges demanded an immediate mainland invasion by Chiang Kai-shek. "If we can exploit this situation at once by supporting a second front," he said, "China can be rewon for the free world." And Joe McCarthy took the Senate floor to pummel his favorite target. "With half a million Communists in Korea . . . killing American men, Acheson says, 'Now let's be calm . . . let's do nothing. . . .' It is like advising a man whose . . . family is being killed . . . not to take hasty action for fear he might alienate the affection of the murderers."[6]

The final blowup came in April, when Joseph Martin, the House minority leader, released a letter that MacArthur had sent him from the battlefield. In it the general bemoaned Truman's refusal to "follow the conventional pattern of meeting force with maximum counterforce, as we have never failed to do in the past." And he ended with the oft-quoted, "There is no substitute for victory." Furious at such insubordination, the President called reporters to the White House, where they were handed a simple mimeographed announcement. "With deep regret," it read, "I have concluded that General . . . Douglas MacArthur is unable to give his wholehearted support to the policies of the United States Government. . . . I have, therefore, relieved General MacArthur of his commands."[7]

THE GENERAL'S PLANE TOUCHED DOWN at the San Francisco airport on April 17, 1951. He returned home, after fifteen years and two Asian wars, as a genuine folk hero, a man who symbolized old military values in a world complicated by the horror of atomic war. San Franciscans were so overcome with emotion that they almost trampled him to death. In New York more than seven million people lined his parade route—twice the record crowd that had greeted General Eisenhower's return from Europe in 1945. His appearance before a joint session of Congress touched off a thunderous standing ovation. "We saw a great hunk of God in the flesh, and we heard the voice of God," cried Dewey Short. Herbert Hoover was more reserved, comparing MacArthur to "a reincarnation of St. Paul." When the general failed to show up on time for a press conference, a reporter wondered whether there had been some trouble unnailing him from the cross.[8]

The adulation showered on MacArthur was matched only by the abuse directed at the man who fired him. Harry Truman's old standard —"If you can't stand the heat, stay out of the kitchen"—was never more strenuously tested than in the weeks following the general's dismissal. Cities from Worcester, Massachusetts, to San Gabriel, California, burned the President in effigy. The Los Angeles City Council adjourned "in sorrowful contemplation of the political assassination" of Douglas MacArthur. Letters and wires flooded into the White House running twenty to one against the firing. It was the same on Capitol Hill, where angry representatives placed some of their telegrams into the *Congressional Record:* "IMPEACH THE IMBECILE; WE WISH TO PROTEST THE LATEST OUTRAGE ON THE PART OF THE PIG IN THE WHITE HOUSE"; "IMPEACH THE B WHO CALLS HIMSELF PRESIDENT"; and "IMPEACH THE RED HERRING FROM THE PRESIDENTIAL CHAIR."[9]

Many politicians had similar ideas. Taft, Martin, and Wherry held a powwow at which "the question of possible impeachment was discussed." William Jenner, a devoted conspiracy buff, charged that America "today is in the hands of a secret inner coterie . . . directed by agents of the Soviet Union." The most intemperate remarks, however, came from Milwaukee, where Senator McCarthy was addressing six hundred furniture dealers at the Schroeder Hotel. Before the speech he warmed up by telling reporters, "The son of a bitch should be impeached." Later, he hinted that the President had been drunk when he fired MacArthur. "Truman is surrounded by the Jessups, the Achesons, the old Hiss crowd," he said. "Most of the tragic things are done at 1:30 and 2 o'clock in the morning when they've had time to get the President cheerful." Specific as always, Joe even disclosed what Truman had been drinking: bourbon and benedictine.[10]

These remarks were hardly surprising. McCarthy had a long history of turning backroom gossip into front page news. But this time he had gone too far. Despite Truman's low standing, *most* Americans did not want to hear their President called a drunkard and a son of a bitch. It demeaned the office as well as the man. According to Urban Van Susteren, who was with Joe at the Schroeder, the scurrilous presidential reference was made while McCarthy, surrounded by six or seven reporters, was shaving in the bathroom. "I'm not sure that Joe expected to be quoted," he recalled. "He didn't tell reporters that he was going off the record, which was stupid, but he was just talking man to man. When I heard the remark and looked at the startled faces in the bathroom, I knew there'd be hell to pay." [11]

The senator did not apologize. "In all the years I knew him," Van Susteren continued, "he never said 'I'm sorry.' He might act sorry or try to make amends in other ways. But he could never utter those words." Instead, McCarthy tried to "clarify" his remarks. When asked if he had, indeed, called Truman a "son of a bitch," he hemmed and hawed, saying only that he was "quoted as using one of the President's pet names"—a clever reminder that barroom language was also quite common in the White House. What about the "bourbon and benedictine" reference? Here Joe put on his most concerned face. "I do not think the President is a *heavy* drinker," he explained. "What I was pointing out was that it was a great mistake for the President, even after one or two cocktails, at midnight, under the influence of the old Yalta crowd, to sign orders and write letters." Put simply, why trust an unsteady insomniac who fears the cold light of day? [12]

This clarification only made things worse. It was heavy-handed, and it again obscured Joe's real message. The original speech was meant as an attack upon Truman's henchmen, particularly Dean Acheson; yet it came out as a tactless diatribe against Truman himself. Realizing this at last, McCarthy set out to clarify his clarification. In his next public appearance, he graciously absolved the President of any wrongdoing in the MacArthur affair. Mr. Truman was "essentially just as loyal as the average American," Joe assured a friendly gathering in Cudahy, Wisconsin. Unfortunately, he was "President in name only" because "the Acheson group has almost hypnotic powers over him." Without specifically saying so, McCarthy admitted that he had been hasty in calling for Truman's removal. "We must impeach Acheson, the heart of the octopus," he now insisted. That would free the President to govern in the best interests of all patriotic Americans. [13]

By laying the blame on Acheson, Joe moved back to safer ground. Like his right-wing allies, he had discovered that the office of Secretary of State is particularly vulnerable to attack. For one thing, the Secretary has no constituency to defend or to reelect him. On the contrary, he holds an office of which many people are inherently suspicious. They tend to view it as a privileged sanctuary for Waspish Ivy League smooth-ies. And no secretary, as McCarthy well knew, fitted this caricature better than Mr. Acheson—the arrogant, Yale-educated, English-tailored "Red Dean of Fashion." [14]

For these reasons alone, Acheson had few friends in Congress. Then came the fall of China, the unfortunate Hiss remark, the frustrating Korean stalemate, and the MacArthur dismissal. By the spring of 1951 perhaps half of the Senate—including Democrats James Eastland and Pat McCarran—was calling for his head. But no one had the audacity to portray him in quite the same light that McCarthy did. On May 24 Joe took the Senate floor to demand the Secretary's impeachment. His re-marks were devoid of the usual shenanigans. He made no new charges, declassified no secret documents, added no public official to his ever-growing list of subversives. His desk top was curiously bare, and his voice betrayed uncharacteristic anger. On this day he talked about Bob Smith, an obscure G.I. who had just come home from Korea. Like so many soldiers, Smith had not returned in one piece.

"I suggest that . . . when Bob Smith can walk, when he gets his arti-ficial limbs," McCarthy roared at his Democratic colleagues,

> he first walk over to the State Department and call upon the Secretary if he is still there. . . . He should say to Acheson: "You and your lace handkerchief crowd have never had to fight in the cold, so you cannot know its bitterness."
>
> He should say to him, "You never felt the shock of bullets, so you cannot know their pain."
>
> He should say to him, "Dean, thousands of American boys have faced those twin killers [Red China and North Korea] because you and your crim-son crowd betrayed us."
>
> He should say, "Mr. Acheson, if you want at long last to perform one service for the American people you should not only resign from the State Department but you should remove yourself from this country and go to the nation for which you have been struggling and fighting so long." [15]

It is ironic that Acheson and McCarthy, who had attended the same hearings and functions since 1947, were perfect strangers. Their paths had never crossed, not even by accident. Yet within days of this ha-rangue, the two came face to face in a Senate elevator. As Acheson remembers, his bodyguard, "a pleasant but stupid former football player, ran ahead to hold the elevator for me. As I entered, McCarthy was already there. 'Hello, Mr. Secretary,' he said, and stuck out his hand. Instinctively I took it, simultaneously recognizing his much-cartooned, black-jowled face." They rode together in silence for a few seconds be-fore Acheson got off. Later, when asked what had transpired, McCarthy quipped, "Neither of us turned his back on the other." The next day's Washington *Post* had a picture of the two standing together as the ele-vator door opened. Joe was smiling broadly; the Secretary, who rarely lost his composure, appeared to be sucking on an invisible lemon. [16]

THE SCENE WAS FAMILIAR ENOUGH. On the afternoon of June 14, 1951, McCarthy popped out of his Senate office, lugging an overstuffed brief-case and a paper bag filled with sandwiches. His destination was the Senate floor, where, by his own modest assessment, he was set to unravel "a conspiracy so immense and an infamy so black as to dwarf any pre-vious venture in the history of man." Truman and Acheson were in-cluded, of course; no conspiracy was quite whole without them. But the central figure was someone else, someone less tarnished and even more spectacular. Never one for secrets, Joe had already offered up his name: George Catlett Marshall.

The June 14 attack has been described as the most daring and sedi-tious of McCarthy's career. Marshall, after all, was a man of enormous stature; unlike Owen Lattimore, his accomplishments *were* known to the average schoolboy. As General of the Army, he had coordinated the famous Normandy invasion; as Secretary of State, he had initiated the European Recovery Program, or Marshall Plan. Harry Truman called him "the greatest living American." Dean Acheson said that his physical presence "compelled respect." A leading journalist saw in Marshall "the very image of the strong, noble, gentle Southern man of arms who could be no more dishonored by enemies and critics, if he had any, than the great progenitor of the tradition . . . Robert E. Lee." [17]

Such adulation, however, was less than universal. The general had some angry detractors, who viewed him as a weak-kneed, pro-Soviet apologist. "George Marshall was the willing instrument of the tragic policy which held that Russia was an ally to be trusted, that Joe [Stalin] was 'good old Joe,'" wrote Walter Trohan of the Chicago *Tribune*. "[He] was the willing instrument of the Hisses and the Achesons, the Latti-mores and the Jessups, the misguided men who let American boys die to make Eurasia safe for Communism." While conceding that Marshall was "a devoted old warrior—patriotic and loyal," Trohan complained that "whenever the American people have depended on him in the clutch, he has come up with advice or decisions which have led to disaster." [18]

In 1950 eleven Republican senators went on record against Marshall's confirmation as Secretary of Defense. Jenner, for one, savaged the gen-eral as "a living lie" and "a front man for traitors." McCarthy also got in some body blows, calling him "a pathetic thing . . . completely unfit to hold office." But these were isolated thrusts, overshadowed by America's early military success in Korea. It was not until later, when the war had turned sour, that Marshall would find himself under bitter and sustained political attack. [19]

The situation was further aggravated by Marshall's competitive rela-tionship with Douglas MacArthur, the GOP's favorite soldier. Hardly a day would pass without some columnist or politician making a comparison between them. (During one Senate session, Bill Benton had angered Herman Welker by reminding him that Marshall had been a great college football player, while MacArthur hadn't even gone out for the team.) In fact, the generals *were* polar opposites in style and personality. MacArthur was the dashing field commander—arrogant, flamboyant, and egomaniacal. Marshall was the proper staff officer—quiet, efficient, and self-effacing. For these and other reasons, the two men did not get along well. Marshall was particularly offended by MacArthur's vanity and sometimes had trouble containing his feelings. At one wartime meeting, when MacArthur used the phrase, "My staff tells me—," Marshall cut him off, saying, "General, you don't have a staff; you have a court."[20]

It was also no secret that Marshall had been instrumental in MacArthur's dismissal. He had recommended this action to the President, and he said so in public. Retaliation came swiftly. The Republican Policy Committee issued an angry manifesto charging the "Truman–Acheson–Marshall triumvirate" with a "super-Munich" in Asia. Among some MacArthur supporters, the feeling was, "O.K., you bastards, you've gotten our general; now we're going to get yours."[21]

Clearly, then, McCarthy's attack upon Marshall was but one more skirmish in a much larger war. What turned it into a major event was the combination of the MacArthur firing and the senator's genius for publicity. Had Jenner given this speech, or Welker, or Mundt, there would have been no great outcry. The press would probably have ignored it, as it had previous attacks upon Marshall by lesser politicians. But Joe was different. Only weeks before he had called Truman a son of a bitch. Then he had demeaned Acheson as a Kremlin lackey and urged him to seek asylum in Russia. Now, with great fanfare, he was about to place Marshall at the hub of the blackest conspiracy in the history of mankind. The Washington reporters, like Pavlov's dogs, were trained to respond. They sent the message to every corner of the land.

There was, however, an ironic twist to the McCarthy attack. While the senator had little respect for Marshall, he had even less for MacArthur, the presumptive beneficiary of these remarks. A Marine officer who had been stationed at Bougainville during World War II claimed that McCarthy "hated MacArthur's guts." In bull sessions "Joe led the griping against the way the general seemed to hog the credit for things the Marines . . . deserved recognition for." During the 1948 presidential campaign, when the Hearst press had backed MacArthur as Wisconsin's favorite son, McCarthy had worked to undermine the general's chances. As a Harold Stassen supporter, he wrote a public letter which questioned MacArthur's claim to Wisconsin residence, highlighted his divorce, and hinted that he was too old for the job. It read, in part:

Dear Folks:

General MacArthur has been a great General. But he is now ready for retirement. He would be 72 years old before a term as President ended. Twice before we have had Presidents who became physically weakened during their term of office and both times it had very sad results for our country. . . .

The General was born in Little Rock, Arkansas, on January 26, 1880, and not in Wisconsin. . . . Neither his first nor his second marriage, nor his divorce, took place in Wisconsin. He was first married in Florida to Mrs. Walter Brooks of Baltimore, who now lives in Washington, D.C. After she divorced him in Reno, Nevada, he was remarried in New York City. Neither wife ever resided in Wisconsin. . . .

By 1951 Joe had changed his tune. "The Communists," he said, "have been leading the smear attack on General MacArthur." [22]

Just before McCarthy's address, the Democratic senators caucused to hammer out a strategy of rebuttal. Hubert Humphrey spoke first. Comparing McCarthy to Hitler, he called for a mass walkout the moment Joe took the floor. Lyndon Johnson favored a more direct confrontation, suggesting that the Democrats choose a powerful Southerner to defend Marshall's reputation. "Anyone else who tried it would be branded a Communist by McCarthy," he explained. While neatly fitting his own description, Johnson recommended Harry Byrd, from Marshall's native Virginia. Brien McMahon demurred. Debating McCarthy was futile, he cautioned, since it was impossible "to pin him down to the facts of the issue." In the end the Democrats agreed to ignore the speech, to boycott it entirely. [23]

The Senate chamber had an odd look on the afternoon of June 14. The galleries were full, but the floor was almost empty. When Ken Wherry suggested a quorum call, McCarthy told him to forget it. "I have informed many senators," he said, eyeing the rows of empty desks, "that in view of the fact that this speech is approximately 60,000 words, I do not expect them to sit and listen to it as I deliver it." Then Joe turned to the disagreeable task at hand. "I realize full well," he began, "how unpopular it is to lay hands on the laurels of a man who has been built into a great hero. I very much dislike it, but I feel that it must be done if we are to intelligently make the proper decisions in the issues of life and death before us." [24]

The thrust of McCarthy's attack was that George Marshall had made suggestions and decisions which aided the Communist drive for world domination. In this sense, it paralleled the contentions of Trohan and other right-wingers. But there was one crucial addition: the motive. While claiming not to know "whether General Marshall was aware that he was implementing the will of Stalin," McCarthy *assumed* that the answer was self-evident. "If Marshall was merely stupid," he said at one point, "the laws of probability would dictate that part of his decisions would serve America's interests." And later, "I do not think that this monstrous perversion of sound and understandable national policy was accidental." Without putting it in so many words, he had called the general a traitor to his country.

What had Marshall done? According to McCarthy, he had marched "side by side" with Stalin in war and peace. He had been party to the "sellout" of China. And he had "stood at Roosevelt's elbow at Yalta" when Poland was delivered to the Reds.

As McCarthy droned on that afternoon, it became apparent that he was reading from an alien document, one that he himself barely understood. At one point, he saluted his staff for working "18, 19, and 20 hours a day" over the various drafts. But it seems unlikely that Jean Kerr or Don Surine or Ray Kiermas, a poorly educated meat-locker salesman, were quite capable of writing, "Since Marshall resumed his place as mayor of the palace last September, with Acheson as captain of the palace guard and that weak, fitful, bad-tempered and usable Merovingian in their custody, the outlines of the defeat they meditate have grown plainer." And even Joe seemed to smirk as he quoted "a wise and axiomatic utterance . . . by the great Swedish chancellor Oxenstiern, to his son departing on the tour of Europe: He said, 'Go forth my son and see with what folly the affairs of mankind are governed.' "

Who wrote the speech? McCarthy never let on, insisting, often vehemently, that the wording was largely his own. Richard Rovere attributed it to "a member of the Georgetown School [of revisionist historians] or someone heavily influenced by it." But Joe's good friend Robert Morris claims that the speech was part of a larger manuscript written by Forrest Davis, a well-known and well-connected journalist who had worked for Robert Taft, Styles Bridges, and Alfred Kohlberg, among others. Davis had a reputation as "a fierce anti-Communist"; he had attacked Marshall before it became a fashionable right-wing sport. There is no way of knowing whether he wrote the 60,000 words. But he certainly had the ability and the temperament to have done so.[*][25]

It is safe to say that few people ever read the speech, although it was later published in book form as *America's Retreat from Victory*. Almost everyone learned of its contents through the press, which again show-

* Forrest Davis, author of *The Red China Lobby* and eleven other books, had enjoyed a rather remarkable career as a journalist. He had covered the Scopes "Monkey" trial and was a companion of Clarence Darrow and William Jennings Bryan. He was in the Chicago police cruiser with Leopold and Loeb when they confessed to the murder of Bobby Franks. On the night of the Lindbergh kidnapping, he was, quite by accident, having dinner at the home of Charles Lindbergh's in-laws, the Morrows. His reporting of the tragedy won him national acclaim. When the Dionne quintuplets were born in Callender, Ontario, Davis was there. In what capacity? he was asked. "Well, certainly not as the distraught, bewitched, bewildered father," he replied. See Earl T. Barnes, "Forrest Davis," *Biography News*, September–October, 1975, pp. 973–75; also John Chamberlain, "Forrest Davis, RIP," *National Review*, May 22, 1962, p. 357.

ered McCarthy with banner headlines and angry editorials. The New York *Herald–Tribune* labeled his performance "an offense against good taste and good sense." The Raleigh *News and Observer* called it "vicious and inexcusable." After receiving a copy of the speech from McCarthy's office, the Youngstown *Vindicator* complained: "His secretary hadn't put enough stamps on it, and our mail clerk had to pay 25 cents postage due. It wasn't worth it. It was a Stink Bomb." *Collier's* thought it "incredible that any American who is both sane and honest can believe that George Marshall or Dean Acheson is a traitorous hireling of the Kremlin." It then suggested that Republicans treat McCarthy like any misbehaving child: "Why not spank him?" [26]

The moderates seemed quite ready to supply the paddle. Wayne Morse and James Duff were openly critical. Leverett Saltonstall, who later called the speech "sickening, simply disgusting," rushed to Marshall's defense. Margaret Chase Smith made her feelings known by reintroducing the Declaration of Conscience. "What I said then is even more applicable today," she fumed, "particularly in view of the statements made in the past few days." [27]

No one cared to dispute her, not even Wherry and Jenner, who must have relished the sight of mud on George Marshall's uniform. Like most conservatives, they held off until the dust had settled and the damage could be assessed. But one fact was plain enough: The biggest *potential* loser, with the exception of McCarthy, was Robert Taft, the GOP's leading presidential contender.

Ever since Wheeling, Taft had walked a fine line on the McCarthy issue. One journalist described it as "the same carefully studied attitude of public indifference and private approval that a nineteenth-century gentleman might have displayed towards the village Jezebel." Until the Marshall speech, his position was politically defensible. After all, many liberals were disturbed by *Amerasia* and the Lattimore case. But George Marshall? The charge seemed preposterous, the work of charlatans or malicious fools. And the pressure now mounted for Taft to say so, to finally strike out against his rambunctious colleague. "The time has come," wrote one angry columnist, "when Taft, as Republican leader, must repudiate the notion that a man like Marshall, who has devoted his life to his country, can be a traitor." Even *Life* agreed. "The cumulative debasement of U.S. politics has gone far enough," it said. Taft must "renounce" McCarthy. [28]

In private, Taft dismissed Joe's latest charge as "bunk." "I thought if McCarthy was going into this fight," he complained, "he ought to be carefully prepared and get some experts to help him. He agreed in principle but never did much about it." Yet Taft did not make such feelings public until October 1951—just as the *Life* editorial appeared. "I don't think one who overstates his case helps his own case," he said in reply to a newsman's question. "There are certain points on which I wouldn't agree with McCarthy. His extreme attack against General Marshall is one of the things on which I cannot agree." No one was more startled by this turnabout than McCarthy. When informed of Taft's remark, he told reporters, "I will not believe it until I get his word that he said it." [29]

Taft soon had second thoughts, however, as supporters of McCarthy flooded his office with mail. The volume was such that he was forced to draft a form letter explaining his position. Yes, he said, he sometimes disagreed with McCarthy; but this was not unusual because "I often disagree with other Republican senators." Yes, "broadly speaking, I approve of Senator McCarthy's program"; but "as for Senator McCarthy's charges, some of them are justified and others perhaps not." By the end of the letter, it was impossible to say exactly where Taft stood. Which was precisely his intention. [30]

Taft's ambivalence reflected the general Republican attitude toward McCarthy. No one was quite sure whether he would remain a Republican asset; and few GOP senators were anxious to work with him. In 1951, for example, Senators Welker and Jenner recommended Joe's appointment to the Republican Policy Committee. When no member volunteered to step down, Wherry asked that the body be enlarged by one. But Chairman Eugene Millikin, a rock-ribbed conservative, objected on the grounds that the appointment would be seen as an endorsement of the Marshall speech. Angry and embarrassed, Joe vowed to continue his lonely battle against Communism. But one magazine phrased his dilemma well: "Is McCarthy Slipping?" [31]

CHAPTER FOURTEEN

"Slimy Creatures"

B<small>Y THE AUTUMN OF</small> 1951 McCarthy seemed more vulnerable to attack than at any time in the preceding eighteen months. No one seriously thought him finished, and few doubted his recuperative powers. But the signs of wear and tear were apparent, particularly to his critics. The Gallup Poll showed a significant, though temporary, drop in the senator's popularity. Drew Pearson had just sued him for $250,000 in damages, claiming "unprovoked physical assault" at the Sulgrave Club. William Benton, a freshman Democrat, was preparing a resolution to expel him from the Senate. And Harry Truman had decided to make "McCarthyism" a major campaign issue in 1952.

Joe responded, as he always did, with a flurry of new charges and diversions. He laughed at Pearson, called Benton an "odd mental midget," released the names of twenty-six "pro-Communist" State Department employees, and took part in a number of well-publicized cloak-and-dagger operations. McCarthy, said *Time*, seemed "busier than a terrier in a cow barn. Wherever there was news, there was Joe." [1]

The cloak-and-dagger work was particularly bizarre. It involved far-flung attempts—in Switzerland, Cuba, and New York City—to smoke out "some important subversives." The initial operation, a cooperative effort, was directed against Anna Rosenberg, the first woman to receive the Medal of Freedom, America's highest civilian award. During the

Korean War Mrs. Rosenberg had been asked by Defense Secretary George Marshall to direct the mobilization program. She agreed. In November 1950 the Senate Armed Services Committee recommended her confirmation as Assistant Secretary of Defense. The vote was unanimous.[2]

Unfortunately for Rosenberg, a group of right-wing bigots appeared in Washington to work against her appointment. The ring-leaders included Gerald L. K. Smith ("Is Communism Jewish?"); "Reverend" Wesley Swift ("All Jews must be destroyed"); and Benjamin Freedman ("The Zionist pressure seems to kill off all my attempts to engage in business"). These men saw Rosenberg as the worst of all possible choices. She was foreign-born, liberal-minded, and Jewish.

Freedman, an "excommunicated Jew," had already obtained data from HUAC files showing that a woman named Anna Rosenberg from New York City had belonged to the Communist John Reed Club in the 1930s. Since there were at least forty-six Anna Rosenbergs living in the New York City area, the information seemed a bit speculative. But Freedman produced an ex-Communist witness who claimed to have *seen* the nominee at a John Reed Club meeting. His name was Ralph DeSola. He knew J. B. Matthews. He had worked for Alfred Kohlberg. It all seemed oddly familiar.[3]

Smith and "Reverend" Swift began making the rounds of sympathetic congressmen, including Mississippi's John Rankin, a notorious anti-Semite. After listening to their pitch, Rankin rushed to the floor of the House and said of Rosenberg, "Mr. Speaker, while our boys are dying by the thousands in foreign fields, I submit it is no time to put any questionable character, especially a foreign-born character, in a position of this importance."[4]

Swift met with McCarthy and seemed to impress him. The senator asked Ken Wherry to block the Rosenberg nomination temporarily, and he sent his top investigator, Don Surine, to confirm the story with Freedman. Surine arrived at Freedman's house in the middle of the night with a letter of introduction from Gerald L. K. Smith that began, "Congratulations on the terrific job you are doing in helping to keep the Zionist Jew Anna M. Rosenberg from becoming dictator of the Pentagon." Surine then went to see DeSola, listened to his story, and returned to Washington.[5]

The Armed Services Committee moved quickly to reopen the confirmation hearings. As expected, DeSola and Freedman were the primary witnesses. They arrived together from New York (Freedman playing the chaperon) and made a quick stop before going over to testify.

> MR. FREEDMAN: . . . When Mr. DeSola and I came on the train together we went to Senator McCarthy's office where he was told to go, I think.

SENATOR RUSSELL: Told by whom?

MR. FREEDMAN: I don't know, but he said, "Come on. I am going over to Senator McCarthy's office"—and there I heard the name Surine.

DeSola's testimony was predictable. He said that he had met Mrs. Rosenberg at a John Reed Club meeting and that a friend had once told him she was a Communist. Rosenberg denied it all. "He is a liar," she told the committee. "I would like to lay my hands on that man. It is inhuman what he has done to me in the past few days." Senator Russell then called DeSola back into the hearing room for a face-to-face confrontation reminiscent of the Hiss-Chambers affair. "Yes," said DeSola, "that is Mrs. Anna Rosenberg."[6]

He was right. That certainly was Mrs. Anna Rosenberg. But, as the FBI soon disclosed, she was not the same person who had once belonged to the John Reed Club. *That* Anna Rosenberg was now living quietly in California. Before long the committee discovered what McCarthy and Surine must have already known: DeSola was a pathological liar. He gave the committee the names of people who would "corroborate" his story, but each of them repudiated it. As his ex-wife testified, "He is a truthful person with some limitations. I think he believes what he says: I think sometimes there might be a far-fetched something behind it. It is an awfully difficult thing to explain."[7]

McCarthy moved to cut his losses. He not only dropped his opposition to Rosenberg, he turned right around and voted for her confirmation. Unlike Gerald L. K. Smith or Wesley Swift, he harbored no ill feelings toward the woman. She was just a pawn in a larger struggle, someone to be used against Marshall and then discarded. In this case the pawn escaped with much of her reputation intact; others would be less fortunate.*

An even stranger episode involved McCarthy's attempt to discredit John Carter Vincent, the American Minister to Switzerland. Vincent, a well-known China hand, had once headed the State Department's Far Eastern Division. He had opposed massive aid to Chiang Kai-shek, arguing, among other things, that such assistance "would lead inevitably to [U.S.] intervention in China's civil war." As a result, Styles Bridges

---

* On the heels of the Malmedy investigation, the Rosenberg episode raised serious questions about McCarthy's feelings toward Jews. However, what emerged in both cases was not anti-Semitism—as William Evjue, Drew Pearson, and numerous others alleged—but rather the reckless desire to win at all costs. Unlike so many anti-Communist figures—Martin Dies, Charles Coughlin, and John Rankin come quickly to mind—Joe never engaged in anti-Semitic diatribes or made the loaded connection between Jews and left-wing radicalism. Despite the unrelenting hostility of organized Jewry to his crusade, McCarthy still praised the state of Israel, condemned the Soviet persecution of Jews, and argued for retention of the Voice of America's Hebrew language desk. When asked why, he replied, "I have many friends who are Jewish." Among the more prominent were Roy Cohn, George Sokolsky, Alfred Kohlberg, and Steve Miller, his campaign manager in 1952.

had strongly opposed Vincent's promotion to the rank of career minister. Vincent was confirmed by the Senate, but only after assurances were given that he would not be assigned to an important post in Europe or the Far East. He was shipped to Geneva and all but forgotten until McCarthy resurrected him in 1950.[8]

Vincent was Case Number 2 of the 81 "security risks" that Joe had presented to the Senate in 1950. ("If we can get rid of [him] we will have done something to break the back of the espionage ring within the State Department.") His life quickly became a security nightmare. The FBI began a full field investigation, and Robert Morris accused him, falsely, of being a Communist. In 1951 Morris and McCarthy hooked up with a weird character named Charles Davis—an ex-Communist, then living in Europe, who had been dishonorably discharged from the Navy as a homosexual. After receiving $200 from Joe's office, Mr. Davis sent Vincent a telegram suggesting that they meet to discuss "a matter of interest to us both." He signed it "Emile Stamfli"—the name of a prominent Swiss Communist. His plan (apparently concocted without Joe's knowledge) was to entrap the minister, to show that he had communicated with a Red. But Vincent turned over the telegram to Swiss authorities, who tracked down Davis and arrested him on a charge of political espionage.

McCarthy denied any connection with Davis until the Swiss authorities produced a letter he had written to the troubled young man. That seemed to jog his memory. Yes, he did recall Mr. Davis, but only as "one of the many thousands of people who write to me offering to sell information." Davis, understandably upset, said he "never dreamed the senator would turn his back on me." From prison, he even wrote a letter of apology to Vincent for the trouble he had caused.[9]

Combined with the Marshall speech, these episodes should have gone a long way toward discrediting McCarthy. In fact, they barely bruised him. There was criticism, of course, but Joe dismissed it as the work of bleeding-heart liberals who did not understand how devious the enemy could be. Certainly some mistakes would be made, but they were unavoidable mistakes, caused by the unique conditions of battle. In the fight against Communism, Joe liked to say, there were no rules.

Millions of Americans seemed to agree with him. For better or worse, they saw McCarthy as the nation's most active and aggressive opponent of Communism. And they were less interested in platitudes about free speech and fair play than they were in seeing subversives thrown out of government. As the American Legion noted, "McCarthy's blunderbuss, loaded with rock-salt, birdshot, and nuts and bolts . . . is almost bound to bring down several important Reds and spies even though a few comparatively innocent people may get some rock-salt in their hides." To catch an Alger Hiss, it seemed, one had to smear an occasional Anna Rosenberg.[10]

McCarthy played heavily upon his theme. Fighting Communism was a rough business, he declared, requiring more than "sugared phrases in a British accent." To win, America needed men who were unafraid, who took risks, who could deliver an occasional knee to the groin. Said Tail-Gunner Joe: "I will have to blame some of the roughness in fighting the enemy to my training in the Marine Corps. We weren't taught to wear lace panties and fight with lace hankies."

McCarthy became a master at turning the debate over means and ends to his own advantage. Speaking before the Midwest Council of Young Republicans, he remarked, "There are those who honestly say, 'Oh, we think that you are on the right track, McCarthy, and we like the results you are getting, but we don't like your methods.' Ladies and gentlemen, take my word for it. . . . Either I have to do a brass-knuckle job or suffer the same defeat that a vast number of well-meaning men have suffered over the past years." And his favorite anecdote, which he repeated hundreds of times, went like this:

> When I was a small boy on the farm, mother raised chickens. . . . We lived fairly close to the woods, and weasels, snakes and skunks would steal the baby chicks from beneath the mother and kill them. One of the jobs which my brothers and I had was to dig out and destroy those killers. It was not a pleasant job and sometimes we did not smell too good when the job was finished. But the skunks were dead and the chickens were alive.
>
> A much more dangerous and smellier breed of skunk is now being dug out of Washington. And to those of you who do not like rough tactics—any farm boy can tell you that there is no dainty way of clubbing the fangs off a rattler or killing a skunk.[11]

For some of McCarthy's critics the debate over means and ends was irrelevant, because the senator had never exposed a real subversive. It was time to stop quibbling over his methods, they argued, and to start looking at his record. Had he proved his case against Jessup or Kenyon, or even Lattimore? In fact, he hadn't come close. His talent, said one observer, was "to raise questions, unsupported by data, which, in a time of suspicion, were taken by many people as answers."[12]

In 1951 McCarthy got a break. A conservative Senate body began to raise the very same questions. That body was known as the Internal Security Subcommittee, and it was headed by Pat McCarran, one of the Senate's legendary obstructionists. McCarran, a Nevada Democrat, was also chairman of the parent Judiciary Committee, to which 40 percent of the Senate's bills and most of the federal patronage jobs were referred. He had enormous influence, and he wielded it to sidetrack virtually everything that the Administration proposed. He was against aid to education, labor unions, and federal health insurance. He hated the U.N., calling it "a haven for spies and Communists." He despised immigrants —"undesirables from abroad," he called them—and did what he could to slam America's "golden door" in their faces. When the chairmanship of the Subcommittee on Civil Rights became vacant, he filled it with his friend James Eastland, the Senate's leading segregationist. Why, McCarran was asked, did he not join the Republican Party? Because, he responded, "I can do more good by staying in the Democratic Party and watching the lunatic fringe—the Roosevelt crowd."[13]

McCarran was a fanatical anti-Communist who believed that only a handful of world leaders were alert to the Red Menace—Franco, Chiang, and the Pope, in particular. On the home front, he saw Communists everywhere. During an interview with *U.S. News*, he was asked:

> Q.: Has this infiltration gone on in all walks of life? For example, do you think there's been infiltration in the press?
>
> A.: Oh, yes.
>
> Q.: How about the churches?
>
> A.: Yes, all kinds of churches.
>
> Q.: How about educational institutions?
>
> A.: Yes, if you mean faculties.
>
> Q.: How about labor unions?
>
> A.: Oh, yes.
>
> Q.: What about nationality groups?
>
> A.: There are nationality groups in which there are Communists. As a matter of fact, the Communists make special efforts to influence and use foreign language groups in this country.[14]

After Wheeling, McCarthy had made a determined effort to win McCarran's favor. He praised him widely, passed along "hot tips," and even sat in on some of the Internal Security hearings. If the chairman was flattered, he hid it well, telling friends that Joe was "a bit irresponsible" and "a publicity hound." Still, he was impressed by the damage McCarthy had done to the Administration—and more than willing to help him do more.[15]

In July 1951 McCarran and two other subcommittee members, James Eastland and Homer Ferguson, set out to investigate the Institute of Pacific Relations. All three were anti-Administration conservatives who accepted the McCarthy–Kohlberg line about the fall of China. Like so many congressional committees, this one had a prearranged objective: to show that pro-Communists in America were responsible for Chiang's demise. Not surprisingly, McCarran chose Robert Morris to be his chief counsel.

Several of the main figures in the McCarran hearings had been active in the Tydings investigation, although their roles were completely reversed. Morris was one. Where Tydings had barely tolerated his presence, McCarran gave him free rein and watched with pleasure as he skillfully tore into hostile witnesses. Louis Budenz was another. Where Tydings had pressed him at every turn, McCarran sat back and encouraged his questionable allegations. Owen Lattimore was a third. Where Tydings had treated him with fawning respect, McCarran bristled at his aggressive behavior and subjected him to twelve days of withering cross-examination.[16]

The committee's *Final Report* was both predictable and disturbing. It concluded that China had been "lost" by the State Department; in particular, "Owen Lattimore and John Carter Vincent were influential in bringing about a change in United States policy . . . favorable to the Chinese Communists." While not specifically calling Lattimore a Red, the *Report* came very, very close, noting, "Owen Lattimore was, from some time beginning in the 1930's, a conscious, articulate instrument of the Soviet conspiracy."

Predictably, the liberal press dismissed these findings as "extravagant nonsense." In a perceptive editorial, the Washington *Post* challenged the thesis that

> . . . China was a sort of political dependency of the United States to be retained or given away to Moscow by a single administrative decision taken in Washington. It was not. China was—and still is—a vast continental land, diverse and disunited, peopled by some half a billion human beings—most of them living at a level of bare subsistence, immemorially exploited by landlords and harassed by warlords, in the throes of revolutionary pressures and counter-pressures that have been felt the world over. The United States has never at any time been in a position to exercise more than a minor influence on China's destiny. China was lost by the Chinese.[17]

The bodies began to fall. John S. Service was fired by Acheson in December; "Good, good, good," McCarthy exclaimed. In the following months, other China hands—Vincent, Davies, and Clubb—were bullied into retirement. Then Owen Lattimore was indicted for perjury by a grand jury in Washington, D.C. The case dragged on for three years before the charges were dismissed. Shortly thereafter, Lattimore left America to take a teaching job at Leeds University in England. He was sixty-three years old.[18]

━━━━━

SOON THERE WAS ANOTHER BODY. In 1951 the President nominated Philip Jessup as a delegate to the fall session of the U.N. General Assembly. On the surface, it all seemed quite routine. Jessup had been confirmed by the Senate on five previous occasions, three times for a U.N. post. But that was before 1950, when McCarthy had publicly questioned the diplomat's loyalty. This confirmation was hardly routine; it shaped up as a donnybrook.

Was Truman looking for trouble? The answer was yes and no. He admired Jessup and thought him well-qualified for the post. But he also wanted a showdown with McCarthy. The Marshall speech had energized him, shattering his belief that the senator was a momentary though disgusting nuisance. Remarked one presidential aide, "the 'be quiet and he will go away' approach was tried and it did not work." [19]

Truman responded with a series of oblique attacks, which did not mention McCarthy by name. He accused the Republicans of employing Hitler-like "big lie" tactics. He warned that American civil liberties could be destroyed as easily from the "right" as from the "left." And he condemned the "hate-mongers and character assassins" who made people "so hysterical that no one will stand up to them for fear of being called a Communist." On September 3, in the midst of these attacks, the President sent Philip Jessup's name to the Senate for confirmation. [20]

Many Democrats were against the move. House Speaker Sam Rayburn and majority leader Ernest McFarland * begged the President to reconsider. They feared that the nomination would reopen old wounds and cause a tremendous floor fight. Tom Connally minced no words. "I do not care for Mr. Jessup," he told a newsman. Yet Truman held firm. He had anticipated a floor fight, and perhaps a heavy vote against Jessup. But he was certain of victory. [21]

The nomination was sent to a Foreign Relations subcommittee that included three Democrats, John Sparkman, J. William Fulbright, and Guy Gillette, and two Republicans, Owen Brewster and H. Alexander Smith. Sparkman and Fulbright were strong Administration supporters, sure to vote for confirmation. Brewster, a McCarthyite, was sure to vote no. That left Gillette and Smith, two moderate and very timid senators, holding the balance of power.

McCarthy was the leadoff witness. He explained his presence as a patriotic and nonpartisan gesture. "Men of little minds are still trying to make this a political issue," he cautioned. Fulbright began to smile: "You would not do anything like that, would you?" Certainly not, Joe replied. But he quickly gave the game away:

> I intend to bring this story to the American people, from the Atlantic to the Pacific, from New Orleans to St. Paul, because it . . . is the only way we can get a housecleaning . . . of the administrative branch of the Democratic Party. . . . It should probably be labeled as the Commiecrat Party, seeing that you brought up the question of politics, Senator. [22]

* McFarland, an Arizona Democrat, had replaced Scott Lucas as majority leader when Lucas was defeated for reelection in 1950.

McCarthy's case was familiar. It was the same one he had presented to the Tydings committee the year before. He claimed that Jessup had "an affinity for Communist causes," as shown by his alleged membership in six Red fronts. But Joe knew almost nothing about these fronts and even less about Jessup's role in them. He was counting on his quick wits and bully-boy reputation to pull him through.

Fulbright led the opposition. This alone was significant, for he had paid scant attention to McCarthy in the past. What turned him around was the series of increasingly irrational assaults upon State Department officials. Unlike most Southern Democrats, Fulbright admired Jessup and saw his GOP critics as political opportunists. "Jessup was a fine man and a fine diplomat," Fulbright said later. "I was determined to see that the nation was not deprived of his services."[23]

Fulbright did what he could. When McCarthy raised his shopworn charge that Jessup had been among the sponsors of a dinner held by the American–Russian Institute, this exchange ensued:

SENATOR FULBRIGHT: What is the extent of his affiliation with this institute? This seems to be a dinner that was being given.

SENATOR MCCARTHY: The extent of his affiliation, Senator, I do not know. Philip Jessup and I aren't on a "Dear Phil, Dear Joe" basis. . . .

SENATOR FULBRIGHT: How are we to understand there was any affiliation other than this dinner? Apparently there are many people on this list of sponsors.

SENATOR MCCARTHY: Senator, I am giving you the evidence. You can evaluate it.

SENATOR FULBRIGHT: I haven't seen any evidence yet.

SENATOR MCCARTHY: Just a minute; just a minute. I am telling you that we are giving you information to show that he sponsored a dinner put on by a Communist-front organization.

SENATOR FULBRIGHT: . . . There has to be something in each of these cases, it seems to me—active participation in the organizations that were subversive. The fact that there were a number of zeros doesn't make it amount to one if you put them all together. There has to be some substance to each one of your pieces of evidence.

SENATOR MCCARTHY: If the Senator considers it as zero that a man belongs to one Communist front, then I am wasting my time presenting to him any evidence.

SENATOR FULBRIGHT: Are you going to answer my question? I am asking the questions.

SENATOR MCCARTHY: I am going to.

SENATOR FULBRIGHT: You are arguing.

A bit later, Fulbright and Sparkman battled with McCarthy over another piece of "evidence."

SENATOR SPARKMAN: Now wait a minute. Let me ask you a few more questions about the American Law Students' Association. First, what was Mr. Jessup's position with this organization?

SENATOR MCCARTHY: He was on the faculty advisory board.

SENATOR SPARKMAN: There were quite a number on that board, were there not? . . . I notice the dean of the School of Law of Northwestern University, five members of the faculty of New York University, three members of St. John's University, three members of Columbia University, two members of Brooklyn Law School, and two members from Yale Law School.

SENATOR MCCARTHY: I call your attention to the one that is from Yale, Prof. Abe Fortas, Owen Lattimore's lawyer—Fortas of many fronts.

SENATOR FULBRIGHT: Is he a Communist?

SENATOR MCCARTHY: Oh, Senator, I don't know that he pays dues or not. I haven't any idea. I haven't been attending their meetings.

Fulbright would not be deterred. He wanted the "details" about Jessup's affiliation with these groups. McCarthy was evasive.

SENATOR FULBRIGHT: . . . I asked you only a simple question. Do you have even one detail of your own indicating the nature of the affiliation? If you do not, all right. If you do, I don't want to hear another long speech.

SENATOR MCCARTHY: The answer is "yes."

SENATOR FULBRIGHT: Can you give one detail?

SENATOR MCCARTHY: The answer is "yes."

SENATOR FULBRIGHT: What is it?

McCarthy exploded. "I don't have all this. I can't carry all this stuff in my mind. It is impossible. I am dealing with too many of these slimy creatures to keep all the details of each in my mind."

The outburst was shocking. Even McCarthy realized that he had gone too far. He tried to correct himself. "I should say 'creations,'" he explained. "I am talking about Communist fronts; I am referring to the

Communist fronts and not to the particular individuals." Sparkman looked sternly ahead. "Is there anything further?" he asked.

McCarthy had little to add. He had come off badly, and he knew it. His remarks had been careless and poorly focused. Jessup's "problem" was his role in the China controversy, not his peripheral involvement with a few Red fronts. The senator should have known better; after all, the "problem" was one he had helped to create.

Remarkably, the panel voted against Jessup's confirmation. The tally was three to two, with Gillette and Smith joining Brewster in the majority. Gillette's logic was ingenious. He praised Jessup and condemned the attacks upon him as distorted and unfair. However, since these attacks had undermined public confidence in the diplomat, his confirmation would be a mistake. *The New Republic* summed up the explanation this way, "Not Guilty—You're Fired."[24]

Smith also took the opportunity to praise Jessup as "one of the most honorable men I know." But he said he felt that the nomination lacked public support, that it was "too controversial." Years later, Smith tacked on a perplexing afterthought. It was true, he said, that McCarthy had never proved any of his charges, but equally true that "he had discovered a group of pro-Chinese Communists and anti-Chiang agitators. And this group was setting the pattern for our Far Eastern policy, which Acheson and Jessup had been following."[25]

Had the White House been stubborn, it could have pressed for a full Senate vote on the nomination. But it declined after learning that ten Democrats were firmly opposed and five more were leaning that way. To avoid a humiliating defeat, Truman waited for Congress to adjourn before giving Jessup a recess appointment.[26]

The press accurately portrayed the episode as a triumph for McCarthy. He had carved another notch in his gun, and he had done it largely by reputation, by convincing two shaky colleagues that a vote against Jessup was the safe and easy way out. Joe was understandably pleased. He called the verdict "a great day for America" and predicted even greater days to come. Yet, as always, there was trouble around the corner.

CHAPTER FIFTEEN

Tydings's Revenge

Tʜᴇ ᴏᴘᴇɴɪɴɢ Sᴇɴᴀᴛᴇ ꜱᴇꜱꜱɪᴏɴ ᴏꜰ 1951 had been marked by an odd parliamentary maneuver. One of the new members, John Marshall Butler, was seated "without prejudice"—a device that left the Senate free to reject him on a simple majority vote. The reason was obvious: Butler, with McCarthy's generous help, had just defeated Millard Tydings in a vicious political campaign. When Tydings lodged a formal complaint, the Democrats had backed it. Still in the majority, they were content to let Butler dangle until the issue was settled to their satisfaction.

There were several reasons for this Democratic concern. One was the desire to pacify Tydings, a good party man. Another was revenge, using Butler to settle the score with McCarthy. But the main reason, analysts agreed, was "fear that what happened to Mr. Tydings, with all his standing in the Senate, could happen to any man in the Senate."[1]

During a secret Democratic caucus, New Mexico's Clinton Anderson gave an emotional talk about the meaning of the Maryland campaign. He began by waving a copy of the Tydings–Browder "photo" in front of his colleagues. "All you boys will be under this sort of attack if you don't do something about it," he warned. "Now I have seen a picture of a very wonderful member of the United States Senate who had visited Bikini and had gone bathing in the surf, very scantily attired. It would be a simple process to take his outstretched hand and place the hand of a woman in his, against the backdrop of a South Sea isle. That is what this type of campaigning is coming to."[2]

On February 3, 1951, the Subcommittee on Privileges and Elections of the Committee on Rules voted unanimously to investigate the Maryland campaign. The task was so controversial that four of the five subcommittee members were empaneled, instead of the usual two. They included Democrats Mike Monroney and Thomas Hennings and Republicans Robert Hendrickson and Margaret Chase Smith. The fifth member, who chose not to participate, was Chairman Guy Gillette. He said that the panel needed "political balance," but insiders confided that "he began to sweat bullets within four city blocks of McCarthy."[3]

Given the subject at hand, charges of personal prejudice were sure to surface. And this panel was especially vulnerable, because several of its members were on record against McCarthy's behavior. Hendrickson, for example, had signed the Declaration of Conscience, while Tom Hennings had called McCarthyism the refuge of "those who have little regard for democracy or its processes." And, of course, there was Margaret Chase Smith.[4]

She and McCarthy had been going at one another since the Declaration of Conscience was issued in June 1950. Joe had first tried ridicule, calling Smith and her cosigners "Snow White and the Seven Dwarfs." Six months later, as the ranking Republican on Expenditures in the Executive Departments, he had bumped her from the investigations subcommittee. According to Smith, "McCarthy waited until the last minute to send notice that he was eliminating me. . . . He did it by having a member of his staff deliver to my office, after 6 P.M., . . . a copy of a memo which he had prepared for all Republican members. The door to my office was locked. McCarthy's staff member put the letter under the door."[5]

At the next meeting of the Expenditures Committee, Joe said that his act was neither spiteful nor unfriendly. He had replaced Smith with Richard Nixon because she lacked proper investigative experience. When Smith tried to defend herself McCarthy rudely interrupted. "Joe," she fumed, "you keep quiet for a minute. I haven't said anything while you were talking—now I am going to have my say and you keep quiet!"[6]

Smith then appealed to John McClellan, the committee chairman. Could he not overrule such an arbitrary maneuver? McClellan, a Democrat, said that his hands were tied; he had to abide by the wishes of the ranking Republican. When McCarthy refused to budge, Smith left the room in disgust. It was a slight she would not soon forget.

Throughout the spring of 1951, the Subcommittee on Privileges and Elections held extensive public hearings on the Maryland campaign. The star witnesses were McCarthy's staff members—Kerr, Kiermas, and Surine. McCarthy did not appear, although he was invited to do so. As expected, the hearings reinforced the common belief that there had been two campaigns in Maryland: a "dignified 'front street' campaign," conducted by Butler; and a "despicable 'back street' type of campaign," conducted by "outsiders" like McCarthy. The most important questions, pertaining to Butler's knowledge and encouragement of this outside help, were never fully explored.[7]

Still, the hearings uncovered some useful information. Butler's campaign, it turned out, was financed by the likes of Alfred Kohlberg, oilman Clint Murchison, and Senator Owen Brewster. The Butler "postcard blitz" was organized by Robert E. Lee, the government loyalty investigator. Most of the campaign research was done by Jean Kerr. And the Tydings–Browder "photo" was produced in the offices of the Washington Times–Herald, a newspaper run by McCarthy's friend "Bazy" Miller. These were some of the back street outsiders.

It took the subcommittee almost four months to write a final report. Monroney, said one columnist, was "not the prosecutor type." And the cautious Hendrickson was afraid to antagonize McCarthy. This left Smith and Hennings to do most of the work; but they were hindered by petty jealousies and the absence of a committee counsel. Tensions were such that all four members regularly threatened to resign.[8]

In the end, the subcommittee exonerated Butler and recommended no punishment for McCarthy. But it did portray the latter's behavior as dishonest and malicious. When the Final Report reached the Rules Committee, Joe moved to suppress it. He was voted down, nine to three, with only Jenner and Wherry coming to his defense.

Even Wherry had some doubts. While supporting McCarthy in public, he told Smith in private that she had done "a whale of a job"—a compliment that Smith repeated on the Senate floor. A few days later, when Wherry tried to pacify Joe at a Rules Committee session, the two got into a heated argument. Said McCarthy, "I don't need your protection and I don't want it. I can take care of myself."[9]

On August 20 McCarthy took the Senate floor to present his "individual views" on the Maryland campaign. They were "individual views" because no one else would endorse them. Of course, McCarthy had his own explanation. He was going it alone to protect his many friends from "the left-wing smear and character assassination which is the tried and proven method of discouraging people . . . from effectively fighting Communists at home."[10]

Joe spent the next two hours defending everything he had done in Maryland. The Tydings–Browder picture? Well, "composite photographs in general are improper," but this one "did not misrepresent the attitude of the former Senator from Maryland towards the notorious Communist leader." It was, in fact, a learning tool, designed to educate people about the "Tydings whitewash."

He then took a swipe at Smith and Hendrickson, citing the Declaration of Conscience as evidence of their prejudice against him. "One of the most vigorous attacks . . . upon my exposure of Communists," he remarked, "was made by the Senator from Maine . . . in which the Senator from New Jersey joined." Since the two were "honest, loyal Americans," their failure to disqualify themselves was surely the result of "a lack of judicial or legal training." Hendrickson, a lawyer, took mild exception to this statement, and Joe admitted his error. "I was not aware of that fact," he said, "and I beg the senator's pardon."

When McCarthy had finished, Smith responded by placing her Declaration of Conscience into the *Record* for the third time. "Opposition to Communism," she declared, "is surely not the exclusive possession of Senator McCarthy. Nor does differing with him on tactics automatically make one a Communist." Even Hendrickson rose to defend the *Final Report*. "Probably I made some errors in approving some of the words and phrases," he said with an eye toward McCarthy. "However, I cannot recall, in my long public service, any act of a public nature which I performed with a clearer conscience."

———

EARLY IN AUGUST THE *Final Report* was sent to the printers, with advance copies going to members of the Rules Committee. William Benton took his copy home to Southport, Connecticut, where he spent a weekend perusing its contents. The report did not really shock him; he already thought the worst of McCarthy. What *disturbed* him was the likelihood of Senate inaction. The report was controversial and poorly timed, coming in the heat of summer, when everyone seemed "tired, snappish, and in no mood for any extra stress." Benton was worried. He sensed that only drastic action could keep the report from being filed and forgotten.

William Burnett Benton was known as a master publicist. During the 1920s he and his friend Chester Bowles had formed Benton and Bowles, which quickly became the world's largest single-office advertising agency. B and B's success was based on the use of radio as a mass marketing device. It invented the soap opera ("Young Doctor Malone," "Portia Faces Life") and pioneered consumer research surveys, one of which established Benton as "the world's greatest authority on the sanitary napkin." A tireless wheeler-dealer, Benton also gained control of Muzak and the *Encyclopaedia Britannica*, two enterprises that thrived under his watchful eye.[11]

He left the business world in 1936 to become vice president and chief public relations officer at the University of Chicago. Then it was on to Washington for a stint as Assistant Secretary of State in charge of the State Department's overseas information programs. When Raymond Baldwin retired from the Senate, Chester Bowles, then Governor of

Connecticut, chose Benton to fill the slot. In 1950 the voters elected Benton to serve out the remaining two years of Baldwin's term. He won by 1,100 votes.

Benton had almost no influence in the Senate. His colleagues viewed him as an "ad man" among attorneys—too impatient, exuberant, and opinionated for his own good. As a liberal and a defender of Dean Acheson, he had offended many conservative Democrats. As a harsh critic of McCarthy, he had focused attention on a "problem" that most senators wanted to ignore. One of them, half in jest, quipped that the Benton–McCarthy feud had the makings of "an ideal double murder." [12]

Yet Benton was not without his assets. He was competitive, he understood the media, and he had plenty of courage. A close friend would later tell him: "You were the only person in the Senate in an ideal position to go after McCarthy. You had little political background in elective office, and thus there weren't too many grounds on which McCarthy could launch an attack on you. You had the money with which to hire lawyers to defend yourself. And you weren't afraid of defeat because you had plenty of activities beckoning to you if you lost your Senate seat." [13]

Benton also liked a good fight. After reading the *Final Report*, he conferred with his top aide, John Howe, who urged him to call for McCarthy's resignation. "I realize in retrospect that this wasn't too bright," Howe recalled. "You don't strike at the king without killing him." Yet Benton thought the proposal too timid. "I am going to ask for McCarthy's resignation, all right. But that's not all I'm going to do. I'm going to introduce a resolution in the Senate calling for McCarthy's expulsion." [14]

The next day Benton rose to address the Senate. He began with a reference to the West Point cheating scandal, which had just decimated Army's football team. Calling the athletes "victims of a vicious system, not its perpetrators," he urged that football be abolished at the service academies. Several Republicans rose in protest, but Benton refused to yield. He would speak first about "the corruption which strikes very close to home, far closer than West Point or even Annapolis." [15]

This corruption, he said, involved a United States senator, not a college athlete. The senator was charged with subverting the electoral process, as shown in the *Final Report*, and it was now imperative that "the Committee on Rules . . . be authorized and directed to . . . determine whether or not it should initiate action with a view toward the expulsion . . . of Joseph R. McCarthy." Since the process would take some time, Benton suggested that his colleague resign at once.

There was virtually no debate. Not one senator came to Benton's aid, and only Herman Welker demanded time for rebuttal. He was given three minutes, which put him in something of a quandary. He wanted to defend McCarthy, but he was in a lather over Benton's remarks about football. Putting first things first, Welker used his three minutes as most everyone knew he would. "I am not in favor of this long-haired type of education," he raged. "I am for vigorous intercollegiate athletics. I am not for the glee club type of athletics, or the military ball type of athletics. I like hard, fine-blocking football." Then, close to tears, he said, "I love the American athlete. I feel he is the very essence of nearly everything that is good, real, and wholesome in American youth. . . . As a product of competitive athletics, I shudder to think what America would do without intercollegiate football." [16]

Benton hadn't bothered to clear his resolution with the Rules Committee or the Democratic caucus. He simply dumped it into the lap of the Senate and hoped for the best. Initially his colleagues were horrified. Ralph Flanders, one of Benton's few Senate friends, felt that the resolution focused attention on McCarthy at the very time he was "rapidly fading from the public scene." Margaret Chase Smith thought it a tactical disaster. "I felt Benton should have proposed censure, which would require only a simple majority and would have been possible, whereas expulsion required a two-thirds vote." One elderly senator told a newsman that Benton had made "a great mistake." Why? Because he left the impression that the Senate was helpless to maintain high standards among its members. "That such an impression is very close to the truth had not occurred to him," the newsman remarked. [17]

William Fulbright captured the Senate's true mood when he called the resolution "a very drastic step" which could set a "dangerous precedent." Put simply, senators do not like to investigate each other. From 1871 until 1947, the old Committee on Privileges and Elections had heard only eight expulsion and three censure cases; and in no instance had it voted to expel a member from the Senate. Benton's resolution had frightening overtones. "It could be viewed by every senator as a potential attack upon any other senator." [18]

The resolution seemed certain to lose. It was tactically unsound, it bucked tradition, and it had partisan overtones. In addition, it pitted a political novice against a rough-and-tumble operator, capable of doing real damage to his critics. According to Joseph Harsch of the *Christian Science Monitor*, McCarthy "seems to thrive on abuse. Anyone who has tangled with him has regretted it in the end. . . . This might look like David and Goliath, except that this David doesn't have a slingshot, or any other visible weapon. . . . The odds are 99 to 1 on the slugger from Wisconsin." [19]

Not surprisingly, Guy Gillette told the press that his Subcommittee on Privileges and Elections had no plans to consider the resolution. It was a dead issue and would have remained one had not McCarthy barged in to play the role of undertaker. First he called Benton "the hero of every crook and Communist in and out of government." Then he insulted Smith and Hendrickson during the presentation of his "individual views" on the Maryland campaign. A week later, in Savannah, Georgia, he charged that several unnamed senators had "known Communists on their staffs." This allegation upset the Southern Democrats, who did not like to be threatened on their home turf, particularly by a Northern Republican.[20]

By September the resolution was gaining ground. While the Gillette committee had not yet decided whether to hear Benton in public session, it was certainly more receptive than before. What finally decided the issue was two rash acts by McCarthy, designed to intimidate the committee members further.

On September 17 Joe fired off a letter to Gillette, which began, "I understand that your subcommittee is planning to start hearings . . . on the question of whether your subcommittee should recommend that McCarthy be expelled from the Senate for having exposed Communists in government." This was disturbing because the subcommittee had not formally voted on the matter. Even more disturbing was the letter's second paragraph, in which McCarthy demanded the right to cross-examine all witnesses "who appear to ask for my expulsion." He wrote, "If your subcommittee attempts to deny me this right, I think it might be well to have the full committee meet prior to the date set for your hearings to pass upon this question. For that reason, it is urgent that you inform me immediately what your position is on the matter."[21]

The very next day McCarthy sent a "Dear Tom" letter to Senator Hennings (despite the personal touch, it had been released to the press several hours before it got to Hennings):

> The official publication of the Communist Party, the *Daily Worker*, on Monday August 6 . . . carried a story to the effect that John Raeburn Green, a senior member of the law firm of Green, Hennings, Henry & Evans, is now counsel for John Gates, a Communist editor of the *Daily Worker*, who was recently convicted of plotting to overthrow the Government of the United States.
>
> I, of course, have no way of knowing whether you receive a percentage of the general income in your office which would put you on the payroll of the *Daily Worker*, nor do I know what, if any, fee your senior partner is collecting from the Communist Party for this work. The *Daily Worker* indicates that it is a labor of love. . . .
>
> This raises the very important question of whether you should disqualify yourself as a member of the committee which, upon Benton's request, is about to hold hearings to determine whether McCarthy should be expelled from the Senate for exposing Communists in Government.[22]

Hennings received the letter at the Washington airport as he was boarding a flight to New York. Enraged by its contents, he penned a quick note to McCarthy: "I propose to discuss you in the Senate on Friday. I hope that you will have time to be there even if it requires your temporary absence from inventing smears and lies about others."[23]

Hennings's speech drew a fine crowd, although McCarthy was among the absentees. He had "pressing business" elsewhere. The speech was largely a defense of John Raeburn Green, a man who had taken on an unpopular assignment, without fee, because of his commitment to civil liberties. As Hennings noted, the American Bar Association had just praised Green for exemplifying "what is pure and noble in our profession." Yet a reckless politician had seen fit to drag his good name through the mud.

"It is perfectly obvious," Hennings said, ". . . that the suggestions contained in this letter are a thinly veiled attempt—and not the first one —to discredit the work of the subcommittee and invalidate its findings by devious means and irrelevant attacks upon its members." He vowed not to resign.[24]

From McCarthy's standpoint, the Hennings letter made good sense. It was part of a larger strategy to scare off his potential jurors. Almost everyone else saw the letter as a mistake. Hennings was bright and charming, a favorite of the Southern Democrats who already mourned the loss of Millard Tydings. One of them said, "McCarthy will never be got by the Bentons. He will never be got, here, by the State Department. But a while back, in June, he made a big mistake by attacking Marshall. He made a mistake down in Georgia the other day by asserting that some senators have Communists on their payrolls. But he made the biggest mistake of all now in taking on Tom Hennings. Tom is one of us."[25]

———

ON SEPTEMBER 24 THE GILLETTE COMMITTEE voted to take up the Benton resolution and to deny McCarthy's request to cross-examine the "hostile" witnesses. No member was about to repeat the mistake of Raymond Baldwin, who had given Joe free rein in the Malmedy probe—and lived to regret it. McCarthy could attend the public sessions and testify when called. But that was all.[26]

The hearings began four days later, with Benton as the leadoff witness. He produced a scathing critique of Joe's behavior, from the Malmedy affair to the Marshall attack, from the Lustron deal to the Tydings campaign. One of Benton's lawyers called it the "most libelous" statement he had ever read. At one point, Benton warned the committee that it was dealing "with a senator thought to be of unsound mind." He meant McCarthy, of course, but to some analysts the remark had an odd double meaning.[27]

Gillette asked McCarthy to respond. He declined.

Frankly, Guy, I have not and do not intend to even read, much less answer Benton's smear attack. I am sure you realize that the Benton type of material can be found in the *Daily Worker* almost any day of the week.[28]

Before long it was hard to tell who was being investigated—McCarthy or the subcommittee members. Joe's staff was already in the field gathering information, spreading rumors, and making life miserable for Hennings, Gillette, and the others. "Rumors are flying around here more than usual," an aide wrote to Benton. "I don't know if you've heard this one, but Hennings is supposed to be messed up with his staff. The Missouri members have left him, and at least one of the higher staff members is supposed to be linked with Communists." The rumor had been started by McCarthy.[29]

One day, Monroney took Benton aside and asked him whether he assumed that his phone was tapped. Did he also assume that people entered his office at night to open his mail and to photograph his files? Benton replied that he had never thought in those terms. "Bill," said Monroney, "I assume this is true in my case as a member of the Gillette Committee. I therefore think you would be wise to assume that it is all the more true in your case—since you are McCarthy's chief target."

Benton took the advice to heart. He put private telephones in his New York and Washington hotel suites to bypass the public switchboard. And he told his chauffeur to be on the lookout for suspicious characters. This new vigilance led Benton to discover that some of his mail had been opened before delivery and that his income tax returns from 1947 through 1951 had fallen into McCarthy's hands. He was flabbergasted. "There couldn't be a better example anywhere," he fumed, "to illustrate why experienced politicians don't get mixed up with fellows like McCarthy."[30]

The Democrats were hardly innocent bystanders. They slapped a mail cover on McCarthy, Kerr, and Surine, directing the Post Office to provide Hennings with the names and addresses of everyone who corresponded with them. Hennings denied responsibility, saying that a zealous staffer had "rubber-stamped" his signature. But Democrat Carl Hayden, the Rules Committee chairman, defended the cover as a standard and proper investigative technique.[31]

For a time, the Democrats tried to pin down rumors of Joe's "homosexual activity." A Benton staffer noted:

Today we received a letter from a purported Army lieutenant claiming that he had been picked up in the Wardman Park by McCarthy, gone with him to McCarthy's home, and while the lieutenant was half-drunk, McCarthy committed sodomy. He offered to testify and said he knew other officers whom

McCarthy had picked up. He claims McCarthy promised him a transfer and never got it. This all sounds very doubtful, but since I don't want to miss any tricks . . . I decided to take it down to Senator Hayden who was also doubtful about it, but who promised to run it down and let us know.[32]

Doubtful or not, Benton passed on the information to Millard Tydings and Drew Pearson, McCarthy's two worst enemies. Pearson wanted Jack Anderson to begin an investigation, but Benton told him that the Justice Department was working on the matter. On January 16, 1952, Pearson noted in his diary: "This is the third report on McCarthy's homosexual activity and the most definite of all."[33]

Hope turned to disappointment when the letter was found to be a fraud. "I heard from Benton and Tydings that the FBI's interview with the young lieutenant . . . flopped," Pearson wrote on January 21. "He denied writing the letter, claimed it was planted by another homo who was jealous."[34]

Caught in the crossfire was the amiable Guy Gillette. Loyal to his party, yet fearful of McCarthy, he wanted to conduct the hearings without offending either side. When that proved impossible, he tried to slow the process down, to keep it from getting out of hand. According to one newsman, he "proceeded to move with the determined deliberation of a sick cow."[35]

Much of Gillette's discomfort was due to McCarthy, who mixed threats with flattery in an attempt to snap the chairman's fragile backbone. After snubbing numerous invitations to testify, he told Gillette that "a horde of investigators, hired by your committee," had been sent out "to smear McCarthy," adding: "If one of the Administration's lackeys were chairman of this committee, I would not waste the time or energy to write and point out the committee's complete dishonesty, but from you, Guy, the Senate and the country expect honest adherence to the rules of the Senate."[36]

Gillette replied immediately, noting that his committee had a small staff and a very limited budget. "Your information," he said, ". . . is, of course, erroneous." McCarthy then increased the pressure by demanding the names, salaries, and employment backgrounds of all committee staffers. When Gillette supplied just the names and salaries, Joe wrote him again. "Why, Senator, do you refuse to give me the employment background of these individuals? . . . Your failure to give this information highlights the fact that your subcommittee is . . . concerned with dishonestly spending the taxpayers' money . . . as an arm of the Democratic National Committee." McCarthy even dropped his references to "Guy" and "Dear Guy"—an omission that did little to ameliorate Gillette's shaky condition.[37]

On at least one occasion, Joe took Gillette aside and warned him not to take his job too seriously. After the chat, Gillette came over to Benton and said, "McCarthy just threatened me. He says that if I continue to press the investigation of your charges, he's going into Iowa and campaign against me and defeat me." Determined not to be the next Millard Tydings, Gillette eventually resigned the chairmanship "in the best interests" of all concerned—mainly himself.[38]

The subcommittee was further disrupted by a shakeup of the parent Rules Committee. Wherry died in December, leaving one vacancy. Then McCarthy left to take a spot on the Appropriations Committee. The Republicans quickly filled their places with Welker and Everett Dirksen, two rabid McCarthyites. On the surface these changes seemed to retain the existing political balance: Welker and Dirksen were replenishing Joe's strength, not adding to it. The difference, however, was that the new members were freshmen, and freshmen were traditionally given duty on the Subcommittee on Privileges and Elections.

No one was certain whether the present Republican members Smith and Hendrickson would stay put or move on to other assignments. Both had expressed an interest in leaving. The subcommittee was a thankless job, made worse by McCarthy's persistent attacks upon the members. If they quit, however, the Benton resolution was finished—and Joe was home free.

Hendrickson was seen as the weak link. Having battled with McCarthy over the *Maryland Report*, he did not relish the prospect of a rematch. There was now a vacancy on the safe Library of Congress Subcommittee, and he seemed anxious to fill it.

He would have, too, had not Joe come up to him in the Senate cloakroom and said, "You're doing the right thing by resigning, Bob. It's the only thing to do with your prejudice." This silly remark not only offended Hendrickson, it made him realize how cowardly his resignation would look. He wrote to his brother, "I do not feel that I can run out in the 'midst of a trial' so to speak, despite Joe McCarthy's wishes to the contrary."[39]

Ironically, it was Smith who capitulated. She decided to leave Privileges and Elections to fill Wherry's vacancy on the Rules Subcommittee. According to Smith, her new assignment was a step up, a real promotion. "It literally ran the full committee," she enthused. In fact, the Rules Subcommittee was a do-nothing body which hadn't even met in the previous year.[40]

Why had Smith resigned? Some Democrats thought she had been "talked off" Privileges and Elections by Taft and Bridges. That is possible, but a more likely explanation is that she was tired of fighting the lonely battle against McCarthy. After issuing her Declaration of Conscience, she had been deserted by all but one of her co-sponsors. After signing and defending the *Maryland Report*, she had been privately commended and publicly criticized by the GOP floor leader. The better part of her Senate career had been spent in combat with McCarthy. She probably needed a rest.

Smith's vacancy was filled by Herman Welker, a switch that Mike Monroney termed "catastrophic." To some observers, it was akin to taking the counsel for the defense and putting him on the jury. In addition, the 1952 elections were almost at hand. This meant a slowdown of Senate business, particularly the more controversial items. For the moment, McCarthy's Washington troubles had abated. Now he had to face the voters in Wisconsin.[41]

CHAPTER SIXTEEN

Ike

On March 29, 1952, Harry Truman announced that he would not seek reelection. Many Democratic leaders were relieved. They knew that Truman could not possibly win. A combination of factors—McCarthy, Korea, and corruption—had stripped him of his popularity. Just two weeks before, in the New Hampshire presidential primary, he had been trounced by Senator Estes Kefauver. It was time for him to step aside.

At first Kefauver had the inside track. A decent, thoughtful man, he was best known for his televised investigation of organized crime, an investigation that had infuriated the party bosses—Truman included—by linking prominent gangsters to the Democratic city machines. Kefauver soon fell by the wayside, a victim, many believed, of his own naive integrity.

There were other active candidates, but each had an insurmountable handicap. Vice President Alben Barkley was seventy-two years old. Senator Richard Russell came from the Deep South. And W. Averell Harriman was too closely linked with the Administration's controversial foreign policy.[1]

Among the inactive candidates—those who didn't seek the nomination but would modestly accept it—was Adlai Stevenson, the governor of Illinois. Stevenson was eloquent and well-regarded; he had won office in 1948 by a record margin of 572,000 votes. As governor, he had established himself as a pragmatic reformer, one who worked nicely with the legislature and the Cook County Democratic machine. He had the support of Truman, the party leaders, and organized labor. After three convention ballots, the Democrats chose Stevenson to head the national ticket. Senator John Sparkman, a moderate Southerner, was given the vice presidential nomination.

Stevenson had his handicaps. His status as a divorced man was unsettling. Some believed he would alienate the Catholic vote, which was crucial to Democratic hopes. In addition, he had known Alger Hiss and had given testimony in the Hiss perjury trial that read in part:

Q.: Have you known other persons who have known Mr. Alger Hiss?

A.: Yes.

Q.: From the speech of those persons, can you state what the reputation of Alger Hiss is for integrity, loyalty, and veracity?

A.: Yes.

Q.: Specify whether his reputation for integrity is good or bad.

A.: Good.

Q.: Specify whether his reputation for loyalty is good or bad.

A.: Good.

Q.: Specify whether his reputation for veracity is good or bad.

A.: Good.

As governor, Stevenson had offended right-wing elements by his veto of the Broyles bill, which required public employees to take a loyalty oath and made it a felony to belong to any subversive group. At the same time, however, his veto message had won him the admiration of many writers and academics who were militantly opposed to Communism but fearful of the McCarrans and the McCarthys. "The whole notion of loyalty inquisitions," it said, "is a national characteristic of the police state, not of democracy. . . . The history of Soviet Russia is a modern example of this ancient practice. . . . I must, in good conscience, protest against any unnecessary suppression of our rights as free men. . . . We must not burn down the house to kill the rats."[2]

The veto was indicative of the liberal anti-Communist approach. Stevenson was concerned about the Soviet threat and put off by those who defended Stalin. But domestically he saw the real threat coming from the right, from men like McCarthy who had undermined confidence in government, trampled on First Amendment freedoms, and diverted attention from the nation's true priorities. One Stevenson aide, commenting on the Broyles bill, said that "it simply violated the governor's instincts—and moreover he thought it was a lot of bullshit—the state had a lot more important things to do, and why bother with this."[3]

THE BATTLE FOR THE REPUBLICAN PRESIDENTIAL NOMINATION was, in many ways, a battle for control of the Republican Party. It pitted the "moderate" Eastern wing of Dewey, Lodge, Saltonstall, Flanders, Brownell, and the New York *Herald–Tribune* against the "conservative" Midwestern wing of Taft, Jenner, Dirksen, Bricker, McCarthy, and the Chicago *Tribune.* The Eastern wing was more sympathetic to New Deal domestic reforms. In foreign affairs, it supported the U.N., the Marshall Plan, and NATO. Like the Truman Administration, it saw the defense of Europe as the key to America's long-range security interests.

The Midwestern wing was opposed to big government, heavy federal spending, and powerful labor unions. It viewed the New Deal as an alien assault upon free enterprise, led by intellectuals and greedy urban politicians. In foreign affairs, it opposed the Administration's expanding global commitments, particularly in Western Europe. America had only limited resources, the conservatives argued. Why waste them on people who seemed unwilling to defend themselves?[4]

By 1952 the conservatives were clearly the more powerful faction. They outnumbered the moderates two to one in Congress and controlled the Republican National Committee. With few exceptions, they were united behind a single presidential candidate, Robert A. Taft. His chances for the nomination seemed very good indeed.

Taft was far more flexible than the Brickers and the Jenners. He had backed the Administration on key issues like housing, education, and, initially, Korea. His weakness was his passion for the White House. He had tried and failed before, and he sensed that 1952 would be his last, best chance. If he had to embrace the forces of reaction to win, he would embrace them.

Following the MacArthur dismissal, Taft radically altered his outlook on Korea. He described the war as "needless and expensive," adding that Truman lacked the skill to avoid it and the guts "to win it by every means at our command." A few weeks later Taft accused Acheson of abandoning Chiang Kai-shek and relishing a Communist victory in China. "For what reason?" a newsman asked. "Because in the State Department," Taft replied, "there's been a strong Communist sympathy, as far as the Chinese Communists are concerned."[5]

Early in 1952 Taft made a strong pitch for McCarthy's endorsement. Despite his moral reservations, he saw his colleague as an asset, someone who could appeal to the party's right wing as well as to working-class Democrats. Soon Taft was stumping Wisconsin, telling the crowds that

"Senator McCarthy has dramatized the fight to exclude Communists from the State Department. I think he did a great job in undertaking that goal."[6]

Privately, Taft persuaded McCarthy's friends to intervene in his behalf. "I have talked over the matter at length with Tom Coleman," he wrote Herbert Hoover, "and he feels that he can bring McCarthy around." But this proved more difficult than expected. McCarthy said that he would endorse Taft's candidacy only if Taft endorsed his *entire* crusade, including the Marshall attack. When Taft wisely refused, Joe withheld his support. He never did like compromises.*[7]

────────

IN THE FALL OF 1951 Henry Cabot Lodge journeyed to Paris to confer with Dwight D. Eisenhower, the Supreme Allied Commander in Europe. Lodge told him that all was not well at home. The Republican Party had been captured by irresponsible reactionaries who spoke of scuttling the programs designed to fortify Western Europe against Soviet expansion. Only one man had the strength and the popularity to beat back the right-wing challenge, General Eisenhower himself. Lodge fairly begged him to seek the GOP presidential nomination.[8]

It is widely believed that Eisenhower could have won the nomination of either party in 1952. A Gallup Poll showed him leading Truman 40 percent to 20 percent among Democrats, and Taft 30 percent to 22 percent among Republicans. An Elmo Roper survey had him ahead of Taft even in Cincinnati, the senator's home city. In 1945 Truman had tried to coax the general into the Democratic fold, telling him, "There is nothing that you may want that I won't try to help you get. That definitely and specifically includes the presidency in 1948." According to one columnist, Truman made the same offer in 1952, and Ike again turned him down, explaining that the Administration's programs were too liberal for him. He felt more comfortable with the Republicans.[9]

Like Adlai Stevenson, Eisenhower played the role of reluctant candidate. Even after his name was placed on the New Hampshire ballot, he would not commit himself to the presidential race. Still, despite a vigorous Taft challenge, he outpolled the senator 50 percent to 38 percent and captured all of the state's fourteen convention delegates. Ike was on his way.

The New Hampshire primary was important in several respects. First,

* Coleman, who served as Taft's floor manager during the 1952 Republican convention, was clearly annoyed by Joe's "Christ-like complex." He wrote Taft that McCarthy was "way up in the clouds . . . but you may be sure he feels that he has the upper hand. I cannot feel that any sense of loyalty to us or to anyone else at all has any part in the picture." See John Ricks, "Mr. Integrity and McCarthyism," unpublished doctoral dissertation, University of North Carolina, 1974, p. 127.

it demonstrated that Taft was far more popular with GOP officials than he was with rank-and-file voters. For a minority party, which hadn't seen the inside of the White House in twenty years, this was something to consider. Second, the tactics employed by certain right-wing elements marked the beginning of an ugly campaign year, one of the worst on record. In New Hampshire, a photograph was distributed showing Ike in friendly conversation with Marshal Georgy A. Zhukov. It was captioned: "Zhukov, Communist general, decorates drinking companion Eisenhower, at Frankfort, Germany." Stories also circulated that Mamie Eisenhower was an alcoholic, that the general was seriously ill, that he was Jewish, and that he had been baptized by the Pope.[10]

Taft's best chance for victory lay with the many party regulars who saw Ike as a carpetbagger and a "fake Republican." To no one's surprise, they packed the Platform Committee with conservatives, chose Douglas MacArthur as the convention's keynote speaker, and asked Herbert Hoover, Joe McCarthy, and Joe Martin to give the other major addresses. The moderates fumed at such tactics but were powerless to stop them. The party machinery was not in their hands.

On the first night the convention heard MacArthur assail the free world's "headlong retreat from victory." On the second, Herbert Hoover warned against wasteful efforts to rearm Western Europe. Then it was McCarthy's turn. Walter Hallanan, the convention chairman, gaveled the hall to order. "When they tell you Joe McCarthy has smeared the names of innocent men," he yelled, "ask them to name just one. . . . We will not turn our backs at any time on that fighting Irish Marine, the honorable Joe McCarthy." The band struck up "The Halls of Montezuma." A Wisconsin delegate grabbed the state standard and led a snake dance down the aisle. Herring-shaped placards appeared, painted red, bearing the names "Hiss," "Acheson," and "Lattimore." Herman Welker jumped to his feet and started swearing at the Eisenhower people. His behavior "scared my wife to death," a moderate senator recalled. "She started to cry."[11]

The speech itself was anticlimactic. Joe blasted Jessup and Acheson, warned of their "abysmal stupidity and treason," and promised never to fight Communism "with a perfumed silk handkerchief." The one dramatic moment came when he spoke of Robert Vogeler, an American businessman who had just been released after spending eighteen months in a Hungarian jail. "Bob Vogeler is in this hall," he shouted. Quickly, the spotlight moved to a flag-draped box where Vogeler and his wife were seated. The delegates stood and cheered.

Joe played a minor convention role. He signed autographs, gave interviews, sat in on a few platform sessions, but refused to endorse a presidential candidate. His only partisan gesture was made privately, in a letter to Tom Coleman, the Taft floor manager. "I have a good friend here in Washington," he wrote, "a young lawyer by the name of John Sirica. He has been close to politics and politicians for quite some time and knows a number of the delegates who will be in Chicago. He perhaps will know of some Eisenhower delegates who may be on the fence, and, for that reason, may be of some help. I have asked him to get in touch with you." [12]

In the end, the Eisenhower forces won the presidential nomination and chose Richard Nixon to run for vice president. Some conservatives were displeased by both selections; they wanted Taft somewhere on the ticket and possibly Everett Dirksen too. But they were encouraged by Nixon's promise to campaign hard against "treason in high places." The Republican strategy, said Karl Mundt, would still be "K_1C_2—Korea, Communism, Corruption." [13]

━━━━━━━

IN WISCONSIN MCCARTHY'S CAMPAIGN for reelection had become the political story of 1952. Not since the days of Fighting Bob LaFollette had a public figure inspired such loyalty and such hatred among his constituents. Voter registration was way up; so was campaign spending. Heavy press coverage abounded: "Can McCarthy Win Again?" "The Team Against McCarthy," "The Chances of McCarthy's Defeat," "Is This the Man to Beat McCarthy?" Only the presidential race attracted more national attention. [14]

The senator's reelection chances seemed good but not certain. On the positive side, he had strong organizational support, a huge campaign chest, and a name that almost everyone recognized. On the negative side, he was a classic one-issue candidate. In the words of a friend, Joe had not accepted the fact that "there are agricultural and labor and tax and military issues before the government and the Congress." This was disconcerting. [15]

So, too, was his health. In June he entered the Bethesda Naval Hospital for an operation on his sinuses. (The operation was unsuccessful. His sinus problem remained, and migraine headaches appeared shortly thereafter.) In July he underwent major surgery to repair a hernia in the large muscle separating the chest and abdominal cavities. (The operation required the removal of a rib.) Even worse, he had started to display what one companion called "the classic signs of bottle disease." Joe had always been a drinker in Washington, but a drinker under control. Now, as the pressures and demands upon him increased, he seemed to be crossing that line with disturbing regularity. He began to drink early in the day and to carry a bottle in his briefcase. He developed a slight tremor of the hands and the head. At parties and small gatherings, he could often be found in the kitchen or the basement drinking by himself. When his stomach rebelled, he would wash down the whisky with huge handfuls of antacid. On one occasion a reporter saw him take out a quarter-pound stick of butter and swallow half of it in one bite.

"What the hell are you doing?" the reporter asked.

"Oh, this helps me hold my liquor better," Joe replied.[16]

There were political problems as well. While McCarthy was close with party boss Tom Coleman, he got on poorly with several of the GOP's top officeholders. Alexander Wiley, Wisconsin's senior senator, was quietly distressed by his "name-calling." (Joe had called Wiley "a bag of fetid air.") Wisconsin Secretary of State Fred Zimmermann, a ten-term incumbent, was publicly critical. Asked in 1951 why he didn't attend one of the senator's local rallies, he snapped, "I don't want to go any-where where McCarthy is." Governor Walter Kohler showed the same attitude. "At one time," an aide remarked, "Kohler believed that Mc-Carthy would prove to be either a great American or one of the worst scoundrels in national politics. . . . Today I'd say the governor does not think McCarthy is a great American."[17]

For a while Kohler flirted with the idea of opposing Joe in the Repub-lican primary. There were many who thought he would win. He was rich, well bred, and popular. His moderate stand on domestic issues appealed to a wide range of voters. Public opinion samplings actually gave Kohler a slight edge over McCarthy. A survey of farmers showed him leading 37 percent to 32 percent, with 31 percent undecided. In a poll of fifty Wisconsin newspaper editors, twenty-nine thought Kohler the stronger candidate.[18]

But Kohler soon changed his mind, deciding instead to seek reelec-tion as governor. His public explanation was that he did not want to split the Republican Party. This made sense, but there were many who be-lieved that Kohler was afraid of Joe, that he did not want to campaign against someone who might spread ugly rumors, bring up his divorce, muddy his fine reputation. And he was not at all sure he could win under the best of circumstances. He had stumped with McCarthy in 1950, and he was amazed by the size of crowds and the depth of their feelings. Years later Kohler said, "I've seen tears come to people's eyes and people kiss Joe's hand when he was campaigning. He was that much of an emotional mover. Too bad, but that's the way it was. I mean, no politi-cian should ever evoke that kind of response, I don't believe."[19]

With Kohler out of the race, McCarthy's only real challenger was a north country attorney named Len Schmitt. Schmitt never posed a se-rious threat, although the liberal press tried to pretend otherwise. It played up his assets—vigorous campaigner, good war record, German background—and overlooked his liabilities, which were substantial. He had no organization, little money, and a poor track record in statewide elections. Kohler had trounced him two years before in the gubernatorial primary.[20]

Schmitt made the mistake of playing to McCarthy's strength: the Communists-in-government issue. He ignored the senator's domestic record in favor of attacks upon his shortcomings as a Red-hunter. McCarthy, he charged, had done "absolutely nothing to chase Communists out of the government."[21]

He got nowhere. While driving around Wisconsin in a sound truck, he noticed that the crowds were restive and sullen; they stared at him "like dumb animals." Joe hardly bothered to campaign. In the middle of the primary campaign he entered the hospital for his abdominal operation and spent the following six weeks in Appleton, resting and showing off his scar to the neighborhood children.[22]

McCarthy's campaign staff played upon the obvious themes. Its flyers and direct mailings portrayed the senator as the virile "skunk-hunter," the scrapper, the brawler, the bare-knuckled fighter, the guy the Reds feared most. One press release stated:

> Senator Joe McCarthy fights like a real American. He fights like a truck driver who faces wind and snow and slippery roads night after night. He fights like a man who goes down into the mines where there's been a cave-in to rescue those he can. . . . These are the kind of fighters we most highly respect for these are the fighters who made America mighty. . . . We never want to see him lounging on the end of his spine, talking about "beauty" and smelling a rose, as if the odor of the world was a bit too much for him.[23]

This theme had extraordinary appeal. In interview after interview, people would say, "Joe deals with Commies via the fist; he's a slugger," or, "you've got to kick and maybe kick hard. Joe's fighting a barroom brawl against a crowd that sure has messed things up for this country." A study of constituent mail revealed the same sentiments. "Frankly, this Communist issue has me scared," the president of a Kansas bank wrote to Senator Frank Carlson. "They're a tough lot and it takes someone with the fortitude McCarthy has to stay in there and battle it out." Another letter said, "We need an all-out cleanup of Communism, rough and tumble as that may be. We have no confidence in shrinking violets who will shadow-box with the Reds." *[24]

The McCarthy people also claimed that a vote for their man was a vote against Communism—and vice versa. For example, a "Dear

---

* Dr. Karl Menninger, director of the famed psychiatric clinic, was disturbed by the "sadistic nature" of McCarthy's pitch, which he compared to that employed by Mike Hammer, the savage Mickey Spillane detective who stuck ice-picks into the eyes of his Communist adversaries. "I killed more people tonight than I have fingers on my hands," said Hammer in *One Lonely Night*. "I shot them in cold blood and enjoyed every minute of it. . . . They were Commies, Lee. They were Red sons-of-bitches who should have died long ago." As Menninger wrote to Senator Carlson, "Many people delight in the vulgarity, irresponsibility, and, to my mind, viciousness of Senator McCarthy. Twenty-four million copies of these vicious Mickey Spillane books have been snapped up by *someone*." See Dr. Karl Menninger to Senator Frank Carlson, November 10, 1954, *Senator Frank Carlson Papers*, Kansas State Historical Society.

Friend" letter from the McCarthy Club warned that the senator's defeat would be "a signal to all the world that the Communists and their followers are still in control and will remain so for many years." There was no middle ground. The choice, it seemed, was between Joe McCarthy and Alger Hiss. One campaign flyer asked, "WHICH SIDE OF THIS FIGHT ARE YOU ON?"[25]

Given the alternatives, most everyone lined up behind the hometown skunk-hunter. A New York reporter who journeyed to Wisconsin was amazed at the way the voters perceived the GOP contest. "Yes," a farmer told him, "I guess almost everybody in this part of the country is for McCarthy. He's against Communism—and we're against Communism." Said another, "I don't care what Joe has or hasn't done, he's against Communism." A young woman in Milwaukee put it this way: "I don't like McCarthy and don't think I'd ordinarily vote for him, but if he's beaten it would look like it's a victory for Communism."[26]

On September 9, primary day, the voters turned out in droves. Balloting was so heavy that most cities kept the polls open long after the announced closing time. Almost a million votes were tallied—a figure 300,000 higher than the old primary record, established in 1940. McCarthy was the reason, of course. He polled 515,000 votes, substantially more than the combined total of the other senatorial candidates, two Democrats and five Republicans. He won easily in blue-collar West Allis and in plush Whitefish Bay, in Polish Catholic South Milwaukee, and in the rural Protestant towns. Len Schmitt was devastated. "I think," he said, "that Wisconsin people are voting against Stalin."[27]

McCarthy still had to face a Democrat in the November election. But no one expected much trouble. His primary victory had been so resounding, so complete, that the notion of his political invincibility began to resurface. One local Democrat wrote to Arthur Schlesinger, Jr.: "The people are against Communism. They are afraid of Communism. They see the vast gains Communism has made since 1945. They feel frustrated because the whole situation seems completely beyond them. McCarthy offers a simple 'cops and robbers' explanation that they can understand." A headline in the Milwaukee *Sentinel* said it well: "Joe Landslide Shows Faith in War on Reds."[28]

According to friends, McCarthy was overwhelmed by his victory. Tom Korb remembers driving him to the Milwaukee airport that night. "He was damned near tears. He kept telling us that he was unworthy of this appreciation. You know, all his life he wanted so much for people to like him, and when it finally happened it was almost too much for him."[29]

THE PRIMARY RESULTS disheartened the Eisenhower camp. It was common knowledge that the general despised McCarthy. He was aware of the senator's flip-flop on NATO* and especially critical of his attacks upon government personnel. As president of Columbia University Eisenhower had condemned "name-calling" as a "behind-the-Iron-Curtain trick." In 1950 he had rushed to the aid of Philip Jessup, writing, "No one who has known you for a moment questions the depth or sincerity of your devotion to the principles of Americanism." What most infuriated him, of course, was the attack upon George Marshall, his close friend and mentor.[30]

After winning the presidential nomination, Eisenhower tried to defend Marshall without criticizing McCarthy by name. He suspected, with good reason, that direct criticism would alienate the party's right wing and greatly jeopardize his own chances for election. At a press conference in Denver he declared that he would support all duly nominated Republican candidates. He added, however, that he would not give "blanket support to anyone . . . who holds views that would violate my conception of what is decent, right, just, and fair." In what seemed an obvious example, the general said he had "no patience with anyone who can find in Marshall's record of service for his country anything to criticize."[31]

These remarks were widely praised. The Republican moderates saw them as an obvious, though indirect, attack upon McCarthy; the conservatives read them as an endorsement of *all* GOP candidates. Perhaps the most interesting response came from Marshall himself. He sent Eisenhower a news story which professed that Marshall was "deeply touched" that his "boy" Ike had defended him against McCarthy. In a one-sentence cover letter, the proud Marshall wrote: "Dear Eisenhower: I am concerned to have you know that I made no such comment as indicated in the attached clipping."[32]

On September 9 the general faced one of his most unpleasant campaign chores. He was scheduled to stump Indiana with Bill Jenner, the man who had called Marshall "a front man for traitors." When Ike's plane landed, Jenner was at the gate to greet him. The two men shook hands and climbed into a convertible for the ride through downtown Indianapolis. Then it was on to a GOP luncheon, where Jenner spoke

* In 1949 McCarthy had written, "The North Atlantic Defense Pact is part of an attempt to strengthen the non-Communist world. . . . I believe that it is necessary in view of the continual forward movement of Communism since the war." In 1951, after his crusade began, he condemned "the present dangerous planning for a phony defense of Europe built around a closed corporation of European Pact nations."

Although Ike and McCarthy would not meet until the GOP convention in 1952, they had exchanged letters in 1951, after Drew Pearson reported that Joe was about to "smear" the general. Wrote McCarthy, "The thought occurs to me that you may not be aware of how degenerate a liar Pearson is, and therefore may have put some stock in this statement. . . . I want to assure you that there is not even any remote basis for Pearson's statement." Senator Joe McCarthy to General Dwight Eisenhower, March 22, 1951, *Dwight Eisenhower, Pre-Presidential Papers*, Eisenhower Library.

and Eisenhower politely applauded. As Murray Kempton observed, "The luncheon was ended, and Eisenhower walked off the platform, stopping for a minute to catch his breath and raising his right hand to lean on a friendly shoulder. He reached for Bill Jenner's shoulder, then saw who it was, and let his hand drop. Let it be said for Dwight Eisenhower that he did the thing he did not utterly without shame." [33]

That evening the general spoke to an overflow crowd at the Butler University Field House. While careful not to mention Jenner by name, he did ask the cheering Hoosiers "to support the ticket from top to bottom." As the speech ended, Jenner rushed forward and grabbed him in a near embrace. Ike flushed. "Charlie, get me out of here!" he whispered to Representative Halleck, and the two men walked briskly off the stage. Later the general told an aide, "I felt dirty from the touch of the man." [34]

When the McCarthy camp pressed for equal time Eisenhower balked, asking his staff to omit Wisconsin from the campaign itinerary. The request was ignored by the Republican National Committee, which scheduled whistle stops in Green Bay, Appleton, and Neenah and a major address in Milwaukee. The general relented. He would go to Wisconsin, he said, but he would speak his mind there. The Jenner fiasco would not be repeated.

Before departing, Eisenhower conferred with his speechwriter Emmet Hughes. "Listen," he said, "couldn't we make this an occasion for me to pay a personal tribute to Marshall—right in McCarthy's back yard?" Hughes was eager to oblige. He wrote a draft of the Milwaukee speech which included these words:

> Let me be specific. I know that charges of disloyalty have, in the past, been leveled against General George C. Marshall. I have been privileged for thirty-five years to know General Marshall personally. I know him, as a man and as a soldier, to be dedicated with singular selflessness and the profoundest patriotism to the service of America. And this episode is a sobering lesson in the way freedom must *not* defend itself. [35]

The paragraph provoked an angry battle aboard the Eisenhower train as it rolled through the Midwest toward Wisconsin. Some advisers supported the general; others felt he had picked a needless and dangerous fight with McCarthy. Tom Coleman joined the train in Michigan to argue the latter point; so did Arthur Summerfield, the Republican National Chairman. When the train reached Peoria, it was met by Kohler and McCarthy, who had flown down from Madison in a strong gesture of unity. That evening Joe was ushered into Eisenhower's room for the first of several meetings.

What happened next is unclear. Only one specific account is available, that of an Eisenhower aide who claims to have been present at the first meeting. According to his recollection, McCarthy asked that the

Marshall reference be dropped, and the general, "in red hot anger," told him off. Afterward neither man would give any details, although McCarthy did say that he would be aboard the train as it crossed into Wisconsin. This alone was news. "For your information," a Democratic "spy" cabled the White House, "Senator McCarthy joined the Ike train at Peoria last night. He will introduce Ike at Appleton and will accompany him to Milwaukee. . . . Looks like a complete embrace is in the works."[36]

The two men met again next morning as the train sped north toward Green Bay. Governor Sherman Adams of New Hampshire sat in. He recalls the brief conversation:

EISENHOWER: I'm going to say that I disagree with you.

McCARTHY: If you say that, you'll be booed.

EISENHOWER: I've been booed before, and being booed doesn't bother me.[37]

The general spoke to huge crowds from the back of the train. In Green Bay he called for the usual "top to bottom" endorsement, and Joe began to smile. But then he spoke of his "differences" with the senator's "methods" and Joe's smile turned to head-shaking disapproval. In Appleton the general wisely said nothing about "differences" and "methods." His main worry was that McCarthy would sneak up from behind and give him a Jenner-like bear hug. He told Kohler to stand between them at all times.[38]

The train left Appleton and headed south toward Milwaukee. On the way Kohler met with Sherman Adams and told him that Ike's next speech, the big one, would cause "some real problems" in Wisconsin. It was wholly gratuitous—like calling on the Pope and "telling him what a fine person Martin Luther was." Adams fully agreed. He took Kohler to the general's compartment, where the three men talked over the situation. Eisenhower turned to Adams. "Are you suggesting that the reference to George Marshall be dropped?" Adams nodded yes. "Well, drop it," Ike said. "I handled that subject pretty thoroughly in Denver two weeks ago, and there's no real reason to repeat it tonight."[39]

The general's Milwaukee address dealt with Communist subversion in government. Without the Marshall paragraph for balance, it sounded like an endorsement of McCarthy's crusade. The audience was ecstatic, cheering wildly when Eisenhower reached out to shake the senator's hand. According to Bob Fleming, this was an odd moment indeed. Not wanting to get too close, the general leaned over from a distance of several feet, like a man retrieving his wallet from a pond. Then he quickly turned away.[40]

It was impossible to hide what had happened. The press knew of the Eisenhower–McCarthy meetings, and it had seen the original text with the Marshall reference intact. What the press did not know, however, was that the general had stood up to McCarthy, that the real pressure had come from his own advisers, the "pros," the men who knew what was "best" for the party. Don't defend Marshall here, they told him; defend him elsewhere—which he did in Newark and Baltimore. Harold Stassen said later, "It is easy to judge harshly . . . not knowing the pressures that go on inside that insane campaign train. You are trapped there. You don't have a chance to get out in the clean air and think things through. You have to decide fast. Time is always running out on you. And when all of them around you gang up, to insist you do this or that, it is just impossible to fight back."[41]

Eisenhower suffered not politically but personally. The whole episode degraded him; he said later that he had regretted his decision very much. Among other things, it embarrassed some of his supporters, it called his courage into question, and it ended all hope of a cordial relationship with the outgoing President. As one of Truman's close friends recalled, "Eisenhower's failure to defend Marshall and his embrace with Jenner and McCarthy caused the real cooling. . . . I think this made President Truman as mad as anything that I know of *ever*. And I think the more he thought of that the madder he got and the less he thought of General Eisenhower."[42]

———

AFTER THE SEPTEMBER PRIMARY, McCarthy felt well enough to campaign for other Republicans who wanted his help. Many did. In all, he spoke in thirteen states, stumping for incumbents like Kem, Jenner, and Malone, for newcomers like Frank Barrett, Charles Potter, and Barry Goldwater. His speeches held fairly close to form. His guy was "a patriot" or "a great American"; the other guy was "a bleeding heart" or "a dupe." For some reason, though, things never went as smoothly as in 1950. The weather was worse, making travel more difficult. In Seattle a television station canceled his speech for fear of a libel suit. In Wyoming his appearance at a picnic was followed by an outbreak of food poisoning.[43]

Real trouble occurred in Las Vegas when McCarthy came to endorse his friend "Molly" Malone. After paying tribute to Malone and to Pat McCarran, he decided to do them a favor by attacking their foremost critic, the Las Vegas *Sun*. He called it "the local *Daily Worker*" and charged, erroneously, that its editor, Hank Greenspun, was an Army deserter and an "ex-Communist." Apparently Joe meant to say "ex-convict." Greenspun had once been convicted of running guns to Israel.

McCarthy did not know that the quick-tempered Greenspun was in the audience. But he soon found out, as a burly figure came rumbling toward the stage, yelling and waving his arms. Fearing the worst, Joe leaped over the footlights and bolted out a side door. This left the microphone free for Greenspun, who spent the next half hour listing the senator's political and physical deficiencies.[44]

McCarthy's primary concern was Connecticut, where two Senate seats—one of them Bill Benton's—were up for grabs. He was disappointed when neither Prescott Bush nor William Purtell, the GOP candidates, asked for his support. But the state organization did, thinking that he would appeal to the large Catholic population.

Joe spent several days in Connecticut, delighting the crowds with his "skunk-and-chicken" story and charging that Benton was worth a hundred million dollars to the Kremlin. According to Prescott Bush, McCarthy's very presence at a rally was enough to start a riot. He describes their first meeting at Memorial Hall in Bridgeport. "Well, we got down there, and the place is packed, with standing room only. I never saw such a wild bunch of monkeys in any meeting I've ever attended. I went out on the stage with my knees shaking." When it came time to speak, Bush mumbled a few lines about his admiration for McCarthy's objectives, but not his methods. He recalls:

> With that, the roof went off with hisses and catcalls and "Throw him out." They booed and screamed at me. And Joe McCarthy got up, from across the stage, and he walked over and shook hands with me. I was taken aback by this very friendly gesture, in view of all the booing going on. And he said, "Pres"—he'd never seen me before—"Pres, I want you to have dinner with me after the show's over."[45]

Later that evening the two men dined at a local café, where Joe soothed his companion's ego and offered him a rather large campaign gift. Bush politely refused, but he couldn't help thinking how different McCarthy seemed in person. Despite his better judgment, he had come to *like* the man.

McCarthy played an interesting role in the Massachusetts senatorial contest between Henry Cabot Lodge and John Fitzgerald Kennedy. Ironically, he did so *in absentia*, without ever setting foot in the commonwealth.

Massachusetts was undeniably pro-McCarthy, a truth best explained by its large Catholic population. While religion has often been exaggerated as a factor in determining support for the senator, it was vital in the Bay State, which had a long history of "closed-in Catholicism." The Catholic community—largely Irish and working-class—had been led for generations by extremely conservative church leaders and by politicians who were constantly feuding with the privileged sanctuaries of "liberal" Protestantism. To many Bostonians, McCarthy's attacks upon Harvard, lace-handkerchief Brahmins, and the *Christian Science Monitor* were reminiscent of Mayor James Michael Curley's. Both men "slyly broke the rules and winked roguishly while doing it—but all for a good cause."[46]

By 1952 not one prominent Massachusetts Democrat had spoken out against McCarthy. It was simply too dangerous. "Attacking him in this state," said the Boston *Post,* "is regarded as a certain method for committing political suicide." So John McCormack stayed comfortably neutral, as did Thomas "Tip" O'Neill, who told one college audience, "If you invited me here because you thought I would attack McCarthy or criticize the way he treats that kind of scum, you've got the wrong man." On the eve of his swing through Massachusetts, Adlai Stevenson received this note from Sargent Shriver: "Things to avoid—it would not be wise . . . to attack Joe McCarthy now. He is very popular up here and with people of both parties."[47]

Congressman John Kennedy was in a particularly sensitive position. His constituents were solid for McCarthy, and his father was too. Joseph Kennedy did not hide his feelings. He praised the senator, invited him to Cape Cod for visits, and introduced him to influential Catholic leaders. At times, his enthusiasm was a little unsettling. Roy Cohn remembers entering McCarthy's Senate office in the midst of a long, advice-filled phone call from Boston. The senator was slumped down in his chair, toying with a pencil, uttering an occasional "sure, Joe," "I see," "that's a good point." After a while he scribbled a note and passed it across his desk to Cohn. "Remind me to check the size of his campaign contribution. I'm not sure it's worth it"

As the congressman from Jim Curley's district, young Kennedy had taken a predictably tough stand on the Communist issue. He had blamed Acheson for the fall of China; he had applauded Nixon's Senate victory over Helen Douglas; and he had warmly endorsed the McCarran act. In addition, he had criticized McCarthy only once, and the criticism was directed at the senator's stand on economic matters. A Kennedy aide admitted, "That's like being against Khrushchev because of his farm program."[48]

Yet, unlike his constituents, Kennedy was not enthusiastic about the Wisconsin senator. McCarthy was too crude for him, too much like the rough-and-tumble ward bosses from the Curley days. Kennedy's image was that of the cultured Irish Brahmin, the fellow who had made it into the establishment, who could appeal to Irish Catholic voters without alienating their traditional enemies. For John Kennedy, embracing Joe McCarthy was a step in the wrong direction.

During the 1952 campaign a few of Kennedy's liberal advisers pressed him to speak out against the senator. Gardner "Pat" Jackson even prepared a statement which cited the Declaration of Conscience and condemned "the twin evils of McCarthyism and Communism." Kennedy was cautious; he would sign the statement, he said, only if Representative John McCormack (the unofficial "Bishop of Boston") would do likewise. Surprisingly, McCormack agreed.

Jackson then took the statement over to Kennedy's Beacon Hill apartment. He started to read it aloud, he recalled, reaching line three before Joe Kennedy rushed over and let loose with a barrage of obscenities. "I can't estimate how long he poured it on me," Jackson said. "It was just a stream of stuff—always referring to 'you and your sheeny friends.' " The senior Kennedy swore that "this statement will never be published." It wasn't.[49]

For most of Kennedy's advisers, the key factor in 1952 was keeping McCarthy neutral. If he came into Massachusetts at all it would be to stump reluctantly for Lodge, the Republican candidate. According to several accounts, Joe Kennedy foreclosed this possibility by contacting McCarthy through a mutual friend, columnist Westbrook Pegler. Kennedy reminded the senator of the family's past generosity and then asked him to stay out of the race. McCarthy agreed.[50]

Pegler, a none-too-reliable source, insisted that this incident actually occurred. The Kennedy family denied it saying that its generosity toward McCarthy had no strings attached. Six years later, in a personal note to Pegler, John Kennedy wrote:

> [Y]ou are incorrect in stating that my father "diligently sought" assistance from the late Senator McCarthy during my campaign for the Senate in 1952. . . . My father at no time asked Senator McCarthy for any assistance, nor did he authorize anyone else to do so; nor was any such assistance rendered or received. On the contrary, my opponent Senator Lodge decided, after some deliberation, not to invite Senator McCarthy to come into the state, for fear that it might cost him more votes than it would gain him. Whether Senator McCarthy would have accepted such an invitation, had it been offered, is, of course, not known to any of us.[51]

It is impossible to determine whether the Pegler incident was fictitious or real. But John Kennedy was correct on one point: The man most responsible for keeping McCarthy out of Massachusetts was not Joe Kennedy; it was Henry Cabot Lodge. "I had a standing offer from McCarthy to campaign for me," Lodge said later. "He made it first during the Tydings hearings—probably to sway me—and he made it again in 1952. After thinking it over I decided to tell him no. I felt that his endorsement was problematical in the Catholic areas, which were pretty solid for Kennedy, and that it would really hurt me with some of my own supporters."

But Lodge did make an unusual last-minute request of McCarthy. "I asked him whether he would come into Massachusetts and campaign against Kennedy *without* mentioning me in any way. He told me that he couldn't do this. He would endorse me but he would say nothing against the son of Joe Kennedy. I told McCarthy 'thanks but no thanks.' So he never did come into Massachusetts."[52]

MANY OBSERVERS viewed the Eisenhower–Stevenson contest as one of the dirtiest on record. "This has been an ugly campaign," wrote Walter Lippmann, "not quite so foul it seems as the campaign of 1928, but in the perspective of the times we live in, much too ugly." The Republicans, led by Nixon, Jenner, and McCarthy, hammered away at Stevenson's "softness" on Communism. Nixon, speaking in Indiana, condemned the nominee as "an appeaser," a man with "a PhD from Dean Acheson's cowardly college of Communist containment." "Somebody had to testify for Alger Hiss," he told the crowds, "but you don't have to elect him President of the United States." Jenner, too, was in good form, warning his Hoosier friends that "if Adlai gets into the White House, Alger gets out of the jail house." And the two-fisted McCarthy pleaded for a chance to manhandle Ike's "cowardly" opponent. "If you'll give me a slippery elm club and put me aboard Adlai Stevenson's campaign train," he boasted, "I could use it on some of his advisers and I might be able to make a good American out of him."[53]

Such attacks nudged Stevenson to the right. He applauded the Smith Act prosecutions, endorsed the Truman loyalty program, and agreed that Communist teachers should be fired. At the same time, however, he spoke proudly of his Broyles bill veto and boldly lectured the American Legion about the dangers posed by "phony patriots," "ill-informed censors," and "self-appointed thought police." "Most of us favor free enterprise for business," he told the Legionnaires. "Let us also favor free enterprise for the mind."[54]

Stevenson's high-minded campaign did not keep other Democrats from hurling their mudballs. The National Committee, for example, circulated a twenty-year-old photograph of Eisenhower and MacArthur routing the Bonus Army from Washington. (The caption had them "discussing battle tactics.") John Sparkman, the vice presidential nominee, took note of Ike's presidency at Columbia University, a place, he said, which had spawned "more Communists . . . than any other school in the United States." And perhaps it was no accident that the Justice Department used the campaign months of September and October to indict eighteen Communist leaders, deport eight of them, and arraign Earl Browder on a perjury charge.[55]

The campaign's most celebrated low blow was landed by McCarthy. On October 27 he made a nationwide television address from the Palmer House in Chicago. This was not a formal speech, Joe said solemnly. "Tonight I'm a lawyer, giving you the facts on the evidence in the case of Stevenson versus Stevenson."[56]

The address had that familiar McCarthy ring. He spoke of his "unpleasant task," of "facts which cannot be answered." He employed the usual phrases: "incredibly fantastic," "retreat from victory," "I hold in my hand—" He used the standard gimmicks: "It hasn't been used until tonight. Let me read you just one paragraph. . . . I have much, much more of the documentation here."

The "documentation" was meant to show that Stevenson had surrounded himself with notorious left-wing advisers. McCarthy named James Wechsler, an admitted former Communist, but somehow overlooked Wechsler's later record as a hard-nosed *anti*-Communist. He condemned Arthur Schlesinger, Jr., for once having written, "I happen to believe that . . . Communists should be allowed to teach in universities," but conveniently ignored the additional words, "so long as they do not disqualify themselves by intellectual distortions in the classroom." He claimed, falsely, that the *Daily Worker* was backing Stevenson. He twice made the ugly slip, "Alger—I mean Adlai." And so it went.

The Eisenhower camp was embarrassed by the speech and thankful that only a portion of it had been televised.* One disappointed sponsor called the evening "a waste of time as well as money." *Newsday* thought it "the biggest television bust since Dagmar." Said Elmer Davis, "When I heard the applause for McCarthy last night an echo of memory seemed to give it an undertone—Sieg Heil, Sieg Heil, Sieg Heil." Adlai Stevenson chose to ignore the attack. Already exhausted, he had neither the time nor the energy to respond. But his biographer wrote that "it was the worst night of the campaign. For the first time, Stevenson seemed physically beaten; he questioned whether he could go on."[57]

JOE DIDN'T SPEND MUCH TIME in Wisconsin. It hardly seemed necessary. He had already trounced Schmitt and made his peace with Eisenhower. He had strong newspaper support and a full campaign chest. Contributions poured in from Wisconsin-based corporations: Cutler–Hammer, Kimberly–Clark, Allis–Chalmers, Harnischfeger, and the Milwaukee breweries. Out-of-state donors included Clint Murchison, H. L. Hunt, and the Hollywood Committee for the Re-election of Joe McCarthy, manned by Dick Powell, John Wayne, Louis B. Mayer, Ray Milland, and Adolphe Menjou. The McCarthy Club had so much money, in fact, that it contributed to the campaigns of other Republicans in the state.

Opposing McCarthy was Democrat Tom Fairchild, the Federal attor-

* The GOP had nothing to do with the speech, although National Chairman Arthur Summerfield had already attacked Stevenson's advisers as "ultra-left-wingers." The speech was bankrolled by a group of Midwestern businessmen, led by Robert E. Wood of Sears, Roebuck. Typically, Joe rambled on for forty minutes after the cameras clicked off.

ney from western Wisconsin. The two men could not have been more different. Fairchild was dry, aloof, and meticulous. In politics he was regarded as a liberal, a man who supported the Fair Deal's social welfare programs. A student of the 1952 campaign described him this way: "Even his gestures on the speaking platform were restrained. His waving from an open car was jerky and cautious, as if he feared that bystanders really did not want him to wave at them. He inspired respect but little enthusiasm."[58]

Fairchild had a simple strategy: to direct attention away from the anti-Communist issue through sustained attacks upon McCarthy's day-to-day failings as a legislator. He reasoned, correctly, that Schmitt had gone wrong by confronting Joe at his strongest point. But how would the voters react when they learned that McCarthy had neglected their bread-and-butter interests; that he had voted against public housing, public power, and hikes in the minimum wage; that he had voted for higher gas and oil prices and tax cuts for the wealthy?

Fairchild had the backing of the Milwaukee *Journal*, the Madison *Capital-Times*, and other urban dailies. He received substantial sums from the Lib-Lab lobby; CIO-PAC, Americans for Democratic Action, and the National Committee for an Effective Congress. But his strongest support came from the Wisconsin labor movement, which spent countless hours and approximately $100,000 on the senatorial campaign. The state CIO circulated a pamphlet, "Smear Incorporated: The Record of Joe McCarthy's One Man Mob Operation," which focused on the senator's income tax troubles, his dealings with lobbyists, and his censure by the Wisconsin Supreme Court. The state AFL followed with "Case of the People vs. Slippery Joe McCarthy," which highlighted his votes against federal aid to education and social security. The message was crude—"Do you hate the old folks, just as you apparently hate the youngsters, Joe?"—but it came through loud and clear. McCarthy had no interest in the "little people," the farmers and the workers; he was an opportunist, a "water boy" for big business; he had no program for the betterment of Wisconsin.[59]

The election results were surprising. Although the Republicans swept Wisconsin, Joe badly trailed the ticket (see table).

WISCONSIN REPUBLICAN VOTE
NOVEMBER 1952

Secretary of State (Zimmermann)	1,039,000	66%
Governor (Kohler)	1,009,000	64
Lieut. Governor (Smith)	995,000	64
Treasurer (Smith)	992,000	64
President (Eisenhower)	980,000	61
U.S. Senator (McCarthy)	870,000	54

A closer look showed that McCarthy ran behind the state Republican average in most of the counties. His best showing was in the very rural areas, in the towns and villages surrounding Appleton, and in the non-urban counties with Catholic populations. Had Wisconsin not been over-whelmingly Republican, and had Eisenhower not headed the ticket, McCarthy would have been beaten.

Why did he do so badly? There were several reasons. His failure to campaign hard was one (although he campaigned less in the primary and did better). The decision by Wisconsin Democrats to work almost exclu-sively for his defeat was another. But the key reason was his poor showing in the large cities—Milwaukee, Madison, Kenosha, Racine, and Sheboy-gan—where the unions were active, the newspapers were hostile, and the Democratic Party was strong. In Milwaukee, for example, Fairchild overwhelmed McCarthy. He won 63 percent of the vote and a whopping 75 percent in the blue-collar Polish-Catholic wards. The Stevenson vote was far less impressive: 51 percent (city) and 63 percent (blue-collar wards).

The voting patterns of rural and urban Catholics were also revealing. Both groups were disturbed by Soviet expansion in Europe, and both expressed strong support for McCarthy's Red-hunting crusade. But the urban Catholics had stronger ties to labor unions and to the New Deal Democratic reforms. They knew where McCarthy stood on price con-trols, public housing, Taft–Hartley, tax cuts, social security, and the like. They had come to view him as a reactionary, a tool of special interests, a man whose domestic shortcomings outweighed his value as a militant anti-Communist. In the end, they voted accordingly.

JOE'S INFLUENCE OUTSIDE WISCONSIN was apparently nil. Several of his closest supporters—James Kem, Harry Cain, and Zales Ecton—were trounced; several others—Barry Goldwater, Bill Jenner, and "Molly" Malone—were swept in on Eisenhower's coattails. In Massachusetts, John Kennedy was probably aided by McCarthy's neutral stance; he won a narrow victory over Henry Cabot Lodge. In Connecticut Bill Benton was defeated, but he managed to outpoll Stevenson in the Catholic areas and in the state as a whole. Analyst Louis Bean has written:

> It will probably surprise most people to learn that in all states where Mc-Carthy pinpointed his charges against Democratic senatorial candidates the Democratic candidates ran ahead of the general ticket. . . . In the 15 north-ern states in which he did not campaign, the Democratic senatorial candi-dates received about the same percentage of the votes, on the average, as did the presidential candidate.[60]

Still, the press viewed the election results as something of a McCarthy victory. *Newsweek* spoke of the "political scalps dangling from his belt."

William S. White saw "a political landscape . . . littered with the wreck-age of anti-McCarthy careers." Despite all of the statistics and the polls, Joe remained in the Senate. Tydings, Lucas, and Benton were gone. For many, this was all that mattered.

CHAPTER SEVENTEEN

Gearing for Battle

IN MANY WAYS 1952 had been a difficult year for McCarthy, despite his reelection to the Senate. On a personal level, his health and stamina could no longer be taken for granted. He had undergone two operations, and his drinking had become a serious (though not yet a public) problem. Politically, he had suffered the double embarrassment of running behind his ticket and riding the coattails of a man who quietly despised him. In Washington, meanwhile, the Gillette investigation had been reopened after several frustrating delays. This was disturbing, for it meant that Joe's election victory could be nullified by his expulsion from the Senate.

To sidetrack the original investigation, McCarthy had launched a series of attacks upon the committee members—Gillette, Hennings, Hendrickson, and Smith. Those attacks had been partially successful. They had shaken Gillette and probably forced Smith's departure from the committee. At the same time they had angered Hennings and Hendrickson and probably stiffened their resistance. When the hearings reopened, Joe wisely switched targets. He went after William Benton, the man who had started his problems. By discrediting him, he hoped to discredit the Benton resolution as well.

In March 1952 McCarthy called Benton a coward and dared him to make his "slanderous charges" away from the Senate, where he could be sued in court. Benton responded, on the Senate floor, by agreeing "to

unequivocally waive any immunity which I may enjoy." Coyly Joe wrote
him. "Not being a lawyer, you may not be aware of the fact that immunity is not waived by merely so stating on the Senate floor. . . . I would
appreciate your notifying me as to what time would be convenient for
our attorneys to meet and draft the documents necessary for your signature in order to legally waive your immunity." Benton took the bait.
"Your suggestion that I pay a lawyer and sign some papers is a grandstand
gesture," he replied. "If you want my signature to attest to my statement
on the floor, you have it in this letter." [1]

Joe then sued him for $2 million. His purpose was not to win the case;
he knew he didn't have a chance. It was rather to reverse the roles, to
make himself the accuser and Benton the accused. Before long, Benton
realized his mistake. "I am now on trial," he told an aide, "with *him* as
the prosecuting attorney." [2]

In July McCarthy made his first and only appearance before the
Gillette Committee. He came not to answer Benton's charges but to
make new charges against Benton. He presented the committee with
twenty-four exhibits, artfully numbered from 1 to 62. They were meant
to show that Benton had been responsible for the purchase and display
of "lewd art works" while serving as Assistant Secretary of State; that he
had protected known Communists in the State Department; and that his
Encyclopaedia Britannica had been printed in England to avoid the
union wage scales in America. The committee members, except for
Welker, were appalled by this charade, but they sat through it for fear of
appearing pro-Benton. "We gave McCarthy his inning," one of them
said later. [3]

On September 9, Wisconsin primary day, Welker called the committee "a political vehicle for the Democratic Party" and resigned. This
move, followed by McCarthy's primary triumph, persuaded Guy Gillette
to step aside. ("I realize, of course, that I will be attacked severely for
alleged 'running out on responsibilities' " he told Carl Hayden, the Rules
Committee chairman.) Then Mike Monroney departed for a vacation in
Europe, leaving Hennings and Hendrickson to finish the investigation,
which once again seemed hopelessly stalled. [4]

But Hayden stood firm. He accepted Welker's resignation, bumped
Monroney, and personally took his place. The streamlined Hayden–
Hennings–Hendrickson Committee invited the principals to make their
final appearances. Benton showed up; McCarthy did not. "I thought
perhaps the election might have taught you that your boss and mine—
the American people—do not approve of treason and incompetence,"
Joe responded by public letter. The committee then adjourned to write
its final report. [5]

It was no easy task. The two Democrats, Hayden and Hennings, were
determined to expose McCarthy, yet fearful of losing Hendrickson's sig-

nature in the process. Without it, their report would be seen as a partisan document, reminiscent of the Tydings fiasco. In addition, the report had to be completed before January 3, when the Republicans took control of Congress, or it would surely be ignored.

Hayden pushed for an early report. Hendrickson was cautious. And Hennings, a fine legislator when sober, spent much of this period in an alcoholic fog. After missing several committee meetings, he was located in New York and rushed back to Washington by Drew Pearson, who noted in his diary: "December 23: Tom has not sobered up yet. Hayden has postponed any meeting until next Monday, December 28. They lost one whole valuable week in getting the McCarthy report out to the public."[6]

Hennings made the December 28 meetings, but Hendrickson stayed away. He remained in New Jersey, nervously conferring by phone with McCarthy and several Republican leaders. He finally told Hayden that he would sign the report on one condition: It must not be released until 4 P.M. January 2—too late for the Democrats to move against McCarthy. Hayden reluctantly agreed.[7]

The *Final Report* was a confusing document. It began with a long and somewhat understated explanation of the troubles the committee had encountered. "The record of what took place," it said, "leaves the inescapable conclusion that Senator McCarthy deliberately set out to thwart any investigation of him by obscuring the real issue and the responsibility of the committee. . . . Senator McCarthy's methods, his contempt for [our] efforts . . . and his refusal to cooperate in any way, were effective up to a point, but did not resolve the issue."[8]

The report said nothing about the Wheeling speech, the Marshall attack, or McCarthy's many charges against government officials. It concentrated instead upon McCarthy's finances, posing the obvious questions and inviting the logical conclusions. What had happened, it asked, to the money sent along by private citizens to aid McCarthy in his fight against Communism? How much of this money was diverted to other purposes, like speculation in railroad stock and soybean futures? Was it coincidental that McCarthy's personal savings increased dramatically during the early 1950s? Had McCarthy acted properly when he accepted a $20,000 note from a "person vitally interested in sugar legislation"? Or when he received a $10,000 author's fee from Lustron while serving as vice chairman of a joint committee on housing?

The report ended oddly. It claimed that a resolution of the McCarthy case was vital to the Senate's integrity, but it made no recommendations. "The issue raised is one for the entire Senate," it said, adding that "the committee's files, of course, will be available to the Department of Justice and the Bureau of Internal Revenue for any action deemed appropriate by such agencies."

At the last moment Carl Hayden thought of asking McCarthy to "stand aside" at the swearing-in ceremony. Some of his Democratic colleagues assented, but others did not. McCarthy had just been reelected, and there was a real aversion to overruling the will of the voters. Furthermore, Bob Taft made it clear that any challenge to McCarthy's seat would be countered by a Republican move against Dennis Chavez, who had won a disputed victory in New Mexico. On January 3 McCarthy answered to his name, walked briskly down the aisle, slapped Hayden on the back, and took his oath of office. "There was not one objection," Drew Pearson wrote bitterly. "The press rose in the gallery and looked forward expectantly, but not one senator had the courage to raise his voice. . . . It was the most cowardly exhibition I have seen in Washington since I came here twenty-seven years ago."[9]

McCarthy could not resist a few parting shots. He called Hayden a "Truman lackey," portrayed Hendrickson as a "living miracle . . . the only man in the world who has lived so long with neither brains nor guts," and dropped his $2,000,000 libel suit, explaining that he couldn't find a single person who believed Benton's charges. Anyway, he purred, it was time to get on with the more important business of running the Reds out of Washington.[10]

Although McCarthy claimed victory over his critics, he had won no more than a temporary reprieve. The Benton Resolution was not dead. It would live on and ultimately provide the basis for McCarthy's censure. The problem, Benton admitted, was that his charges were a bit premature. They had come "two years before the timing was right."[11]

———

WHEN THE REPUBLICANS RETURNED TO CONGRESS in 1953, a mad scramble ensued over the control and direction of the Communist issue. No one doubted that the federal bureaucracy was about to be vacuumed clean. The only question was by whom. Would the State Department be probed by John Foster Dulles, the new Secretary, or by Joe McCarthy? What role would HUAC play? Would its business conflict with, or duplicate, the work of Senate committees? What about the new Administration? Would it try to head off the Congress by taking drastic measures of its own?

Almost everyone wanted a piece of the action. In the House 185 of the 221 Republicans applied for duty on HUAC, where Chairman Harold Velde, a zealous ex-FBI agent, promised to hunt down the Reds like wild muskrats. "They are foreign to our nation and to our God," he warned. "In the world of humanity they are aliens." Velde's chief concern, however, was Communist influence in the schools and the churches, not in the government. For this the Administration was thankful. It never really saw Velde as a menace—just an "excruciating embarrassment."[12]

In the Senate the first rights should logically have gone to McCarthy. His name, after all, was synonymous with hard-nosed anti-Communism. He had done more to popularize and to politicize the issue than anyone else. Yet he was passed over by the Republican leadership in favor of his friend Bill Jenner, who was quickly installed as chairman of the powerful Internal Security Subcommittee. Jenner, it seemed, was more amenable to party discipline. He could be trusted "to pummel the Democrats without embarrassing the Republicans as well." McCarthy was a poor team player—erratic and very difficult to control. There was some doubt as to whether he understood, or really cared, that a new Administration was in power. Cautiously, the leadership gave him "secondary rights" in the field.[13]

As expected, McCarthy assumed the chairmanship of the relatively unimportant Committee on Government Operations.* This pleased Robert Taft, the new majority leader, who boasted that "We've got Joe where he can't do any harm." But McCarthy knew better. He knew that Government Operations had a Permanent Subcommittee on Investigations with the stated, though little-used, authority to scrutinize "government activities at all levels." It lacked only an aggressive chairman, willing to lay claim to what was rightfully his.[14]

During the early 1950s the subcommittee had been chaired by Senator Clyde Hoey, a mild-mannered Democrat from North Carolina. Under Hoey's leadership, the subcommittee had investigated such bland subjects as the disposal of surplus property at a Missouri arsenal, the sale of a government-owned aluminum plant in California, and the reorganization of the Bureau of Customs. McCarthy, the ranking Republican, had attended fewer than 20 percent of the public hearings. He had obviously had more important things on his mind.†

As the new chairman, McCarthy did not immediately publicize his Red-hunting plans. He knew that many senators were wary of him, and he wanted to increase his chances for a hefty budget appropriation. Since Government Operations normally investigated waste and corruption, he began by tracking down "allegations" that the Army had helped Harry Truman move out of the White House. Angrily Truman responded: "Every President is moved out of the White House at the expense of the

---

* The Committee on Government Operations was the old Committee on Expenditures in the Executive Departments.

† Only once did McCarthy get into the flow of action. During a public hearing on the sale of government-owned tankers, he pummeled a witness for supposedly having engaged in trade with Red China. "You are either . . . the greatest dope or dupe of all time . . . or you are directly responsible for making a vast amount of money soaked in American blood," Joe told him. The witness was understandably upset. "Why don't you ask questions the way Senator Hoey does? Be a gentleman," he pleaded. Later the witness said of McCarthy, "He is like a terrier. He likes to shake the animal." See U.S. Congress, Senate, Permanent Subcommittee on Investigations of the Committee on Government Operations, *Sale of Government-owned Tanker Vessels,* 1952, pp. 521, 547.

government. It was done for Mr. Hoover. It was done for Roosevelt, and it was done for me. McCarthy had better get his facts straight . . . or he'll get his ass in a sling." [15]

The Republicans must have chuckled at Truman's discomfort. In January they recommended a large budget increase for Government Operations, hoping, no doubt, to steer McCarthy from the spectacular to the mundane. But a feeling lingered that all was not well. Senator Hoey quickly resigned from the Permanent Investigations Subcommittee. Having worked with Joe in the past, he did "not wish to be responsible for what might develop." Elmer Davis put it this way: "Jenner is not very bright and Velde is so inept that the friends of freedom may reasonably regard him as our secret weapon. McCarthy, on the other hand, is very smart." He would not easily be deposed. [16]

Davis was right. By February McCarthy was back in his old playground, armed with a $200,000 budget and the power to hold hearings, call witnesses, issue subpoenas, threaten contempt citations, and publish final reports. As expected, he made himself chairman of the subcommittee and filled the other Republican seats with his loyal supporters—Karl Mundt, Everett Dirksen, and Charles Potter.* "No one can push me out of anything," he boasted. "I am not retiring from the field of exposing Communists." [17]

Like most chairmen, McCarthy took a hand in the recruitment and hiring of his subcommittee staff. For the post of research director he chose Howard Rushmore, a burly ex-Communist and former movie critic for the *Daily Worker*. After leaving the Party in 1940, Rushmore had joined the Hearst-owned New York *Journal–American* as a feature writer specializing in attacks upon his former comrades. There he met the likes of George Sokolsky, Westbrook Pegler, and the ubiquitous J. B. Matthews, who supposedly introduced him to McCarthy. One cynic described Rushmore as "a rather classic instance of a journalist whose solitary claim to distinction lies in having had the foresight to be a Communist." Pegler called him "one of the most effective enemies of treason in American journalsim." [18]

The job of chief counsel proved harder to fill. The New York crowd —Sokolsky, Matthews, Bob Morris, Dick Berlin, and Walter Winchell— suggested a local prosecutor named Roy Cohn; Joseph Kennedy recommended his son Bob. Since both candidates were young and extraordi-

---

* Mundt and Dirksen were McCarthy's good friends. They could be counted on to give him a free hand as chairman. Potter, a legless war hero, had established some impressive Red-hunting credentials as a member of HUAC. He was already known as a "junior McCarthy." Two of the investigation subcommittee's Democrats, Henry Jackson and Stuart Symington, had just won big victories over pro-McCarthy incumbents, Harry Cain and James Kem, respectively. They would not face reelection until 1958. The third Democrat, John McClellan, was a powerful Southern conservative. For the first half of 1953, the Democrats would offer virtually no resistance to McCarthy.

narily ambitious, McCarthy feared the the selection of one would almost certainly offend the other. So he telephoned Bob Morris and offered him the job. "I told Joe that I couldn't take it," Morris recalled. "I had already committed myself to Senator Jenner. But I told him that Roy had more experience and would make a more effective counsel. I then suggested that Kennedy be hired in some other capacity. Joe thanked me and said that that was exactly what he was going to do."[19]

At a press conference McCarthy announced that Roy Cohn would be his chief counsel while Robert Kennedy would become assistant to the general counsel, Francis Flanagan. "Senator," a reporter asked, "you stated that Mr. Cohn is becoming chief counsel . . . and that Mr. Flanagan is to remain on as general counsel. Who is superior to whom? What does each title mean?" McCarthy didn't know. He hadn't bothered to define anyone's jurisdiction. Said Cohn, "I had my first hint of the chaos that was to prevail."[20]

ROY MARCUS COHN WAS THE ONLY SON of Albert Cohn, a New York State judge with good connections in the Democratic Party. As a boy he received the best private education that Manhattan could offer. When a nervous condition forced his departure from the Community School for gifted students, he attended the Fieldston Lower School and then Horace Mann. After skipping his senior year, he went on to Columbia College and Columbia Law School, completing both before his twentieth birthday. He was admitted to the bar at twenty-one and immediately sworn in as an Assistant U.S. Attorney.[21]

His first cases were routine, ranging from stamp and currency violations to traffic in hard drugs. Yet he made a name for himself by bombarding newsmen with reports of the "biggest," "most sensational," "worldwide" vice operations in the history of organized crime. Before long he had moved into the glamorous internal security field and become the star pupil of Matthews, Sokolsky, and Morris. His career took off. He played a prominent role in the New York trial of eleven Communist leaders, in the Remington case, and in the prosecution of Julius and Ethel Rosenberg. A celebrity at twenty-three, Cohn spent his evenings at the plush Stork Club, where, according to Winchell, he "kept Sammy-Glicking from table to table, greeting friends of his family and people he knew—lawyers, judges, politicians, *et al.*"[22]

At twenty-four he went to Washington to become special assistant to Attorney General James McGranery, As *Time* reported,

His first day on the job was memorable because: (1) he was ceremoniously sworn in right in the Attorney General's private office (actually no new oath of office was necessary); (2) after one department press release announced his coming but neglected to mention his title, a second was issued to correct the oversight; (3) three Department of Justice juniors were evicted from their office so it could become Roy's private office; (4) he demanded a private cable address (denied) and a private telephone line to his old office in New York (also denied).[23]

In Washington, Cohn ran into some trouble. He prepared the ill-fated Lattimore perjury indictment and then alienated his superiors by charging that they had sidetracked his efforts to rid the U.N. staff of American Communists. The dispute grew so ugly that a congressional committee looked into the matter, exonerated the Attorney General, and noted that "Cohn, who testified before the committee, left . . . the impression that he is an extremely bright young man aggressive in the performance of his duties and probably not free from the pressures of personal ambition."[24]

Cohn left another impression as well: the impression of a Jew who was frightened and embarrassed by the conspicuous radicalism of some of his coreligionists. He seemed obsessed by the need to prove that Jews were not inherently disloyal, that they too were devoted and patriotic Americans. He wrote about the "boys of Jewish faith who died fighting for freedom in Korea." He praised the "staunch Americanism of such Jews as" Bernard Baruch, Hyman Rickover, George Sokolsky, and Alfred Kohlberg. He bemoaned the "mishandling of this Communist issue by some Jewish organizations." A close friend said of Cohn, "He feels that every American has got to take up the fight against the Reds. He also feels keenly that Americans of the Jewish faith have an added obligation. Roy has often explained to me that, more than any other minority, the Jew should be grateful for the advantages America has given him." *[25]

Cohn joined the subcommittee at twenty-five, making him the youngest chief counsel in Washington. He quickly replaced Don Surine as McCarthy's right-hand man and even assumed some of the chairman's routine duties. At the FBI, his friend Roy Nichols complained to Clyde Tolson, the associate director:

> The attached letter from Roy Cohn requests name checks. . . . I have told Cohn on two specific occasions that any requests along these lines should come in the form of a letter from the Chairman of the Committee to the Director. As we all know, Cohn is given to being impetuous and I do not think we should be handling matters like this on Cohn's representation until after definite liaison is established.[26]

* Ironically, Cohn's religious background was instrumental in landing him the job on the subcommittee. The reason was simple: McCarthy believed that he needed Jewish staffers to offset the publicity triggered by the Malmedy probe, the attack on Anna Rosenberg, and the public endorsements by professional Jew-baiters like Joseph Kamp, Upton Close, and Gerald L. K. Smith. McCarthy told his friend John Sirica—who also claimed to have been offered the job of chief counsel—that the selection of Cohn "might convince people I am not anti-Semitic." See John Sirica, *To Set the Record Straight*, 1979, pp. 37–38.

Actually, McCarthy encouraged this sort of behavior. He trusted Cohn and marveled at his talents. On one occasion, when Urban Van Susteren berated Cohn as "a rude s.o.b." and a political liability, McCarthy said, "Van, you're getting sucked in by the press. You don't know Roy. He's a brilliant fellow. He works his butt off and he's loyal to me. I don't think I could make it without him."[27]

Within a month, the principal staff positions had been filled. Howard Rushmore had become the research director, Roy Cohn the chief counsel, Don Surine the assistant counsel, Francis Flanagan the general counsel, and Robert Kennedy the assistant to Flanagan. The senator's personal staff remained largely unchanged, with Ray Kiermas and Jean Kerr in command, and the comical Otis Gomillion, a Milwaukee detective, doubling as bodyguard and executive assistant. Had McCarthy stopped there he would have done himself a favor. Instead, to satisfy Cohn, he created a new subcommittee post, chief consultant (unpaid), and filled it with Cohn's best friend, G. David Schine.[28]

Schine, a strikingly handsome man of twenty-five, had come to the subcommittee via Harvard College, the Vaughan Monroe orchestra, and the Schine Hotel Corporation, which his father owned and young Dave nominally ran as president and general manager. At Harvard he was best remembered for his running battles with the university administration— he allegedly demanded a single room and the right to keep his personal secretary there after hours—and his spendthrift ways. "Wealth of course is not out of place here," said the *Harvard Crimson*, "but Schine, certainly one of the richest men in his class, made it so. He lived in a style which went out here with the era of the Gold Coast: an exquisitely furnished room, a valet, a big black convertible equipped with a two-way phone–radio and a fabulous electric phonograph." For recreation, Schine collected rare cigars, played cymbals in the college band, wrote popular songs, and dated Hollywood starlets. A natty dresser, he leaned toward monogramed silk shirts, blue serge suits, gold and platinum tie clasps, and imported English shoes. One source claimed that Dave had "a plentiful assortment of lotions, creams, and skin applications. . . . The atmosphere in his dressing room is fully rounded out with a tinted photograph of himself, the business administrator, in color. This self-adulation is evident to many people now. The Greeks had a word for it."[29]

Schine's anti-Communist credentials were not altogether convincing. They rested on a six-page pamphlet he had written ("Definition of Communism"), which was offered as a "public service" by the Schine hotels. For all its brevity, the pamphlet managed to get Lenin's first name wrong, to misdate the Russian Revolution, the five-year plans, and the formation of the Communist Party; to confuse Kerensky with Prince Lvov; and to butcher Marx's theory of revolution. It did get tough with the Reds, however, accusing them of "stealing words, such as freedom, security, and equality from the Bible, and other good covenants to confuse issues, and deceive the mind into ensnarement." [30]

Whereas Cohn and Schine were both young, single, and Jewish, they were also a study in contrasts. Cohn was short, dark, intense, and abrasive; Schine was tall, fair, frivolous, and complacent. According to some observers, it was Schine who held the upper hand. "In the Cohn–Schine team," said one, "Schine seems to have the dominant influence, even though Cohn clearly outranks him in everything intellectual. He seems to be fond of humiliating Cohn in front of strangers, quick in putting him into his place. He is most outspoken in his criticism of Cohn's mannerisms and acts generally as if Cohn were his inferior." If that was true, the relationship must have puzzled McCarthy. "Joe often told us that he had little use for Dave Schine," remarked a Washington reporter. "He kept him on, I think, out of loyalty to Roy. I guess he figured that one more guy around the office wasn't going to kill him. Of course, *this* guy just about did." [31]

━━━━━━

McCARTHY'S FORMAL STAFF, numbering perhaps twenty-five, could well be compared to the exposed tip of an iceberg. Hidden from public view were hundreds of government workers who, for reasons ranging from misguided patriotism to personal grudge-settling, kept the senator well stocked with rumors, classified documents, and ideas for new investigations. Some were high-ranking officials; others were file clerks; still others remained anonymous even to McCarthy himself. They came from all of the major branches and departments of government—the FBI, the Army, the State Department, the Post Office, the Internal Revenue Service, the Civil Service Commission, and the Government Printing Office, to name a few. They were known as the "Loyal American Underground." [32]

Joe was understandably close-mouthed about his sources. Although he often sent along the material he received to the FBI, he took steps to protect the donor's anonymity. In a memorandum dated February 7, 1953, the Bureau's assistant director advised his staff: "Surine says we are authorized to use this material any way we see fit. . . . He also says we should use good judgment. . . . For example, if a writer asked the Senator to keep confidential the source of the information, we likewise should keep confidential the source and should it become necessary to interview the original complainant, we should not divulge that Senator McCarthy's office has furnished us the information." [33]

The information that Joe received was sometimes petty and sometimes quite remarkable. During the Voice of America hearings, internal VOA memos routinely reached his office before they got to the addressee. During the Army–McCarthy hearings the senator frequently asked the Army to produce confidential reports, giving the exact dates and demonstrating a precise knowledge of their contents. On one occasion, after General Telford Taylor spoke out against congressional inquisitions, Joe charged that Taylor's career file had a "flag" attached, indicating an unresolved security question. His charge was verified by Philip Young, chairman of the Civil Service Commission, who said, "McCarthy had photostats of the record. We don't know how he gets these things, but he does get them." * [34]

Much of what he got came directly from the FBI, which had a habit of leaking information to favored politicians. Not only was Joe friendly with J. Edgar Hoover, but several of his aides had either worked for the Bureau or built up good contacts there. Roy Cohn, for example, was very close with Lou Nichols, the assistant director. One source said that Cohn knew

> . . . all about FBI lists of suspect Communists and has a fantastic memory for the names and backgrounds of practically all the important ex-Communists in the country. My friend has frequently been with Cohn when he picks up the phone, calls the FBI and demands to know the whereabouts of some ex-Communist or suspect Communist. Within a half hour or so the Bureau will call him back and give him the name of the special agent who is riding herd on the particular individual and Cohn will shortly thereafter get a call from the agent.

Despite his repeated denials, Cohn also had access to confidential FBI reports. One agent revealed that his colleagues "put in long hours poring over Bureau security files, abstracting them for Roy Cohn." And Ruth Watt, chief clerk of the Government Operations Committee, recalled that "we had a lot of FBI reports because we could get them, you see." Watt added that "Roy and J. Edgar Hoover knew each other pretty well, so it was not too difficult to get these things." [35]

The same could be said for McCarthy, of course. He and Hoover often went to the track together or dined at Harvey's Restaurant in Washington. When they corresponded, their letters were filled with effusive compliments. "No one need erect a monument to you," Joe told "Edgar" in 1952. "You have built your own monument in the form of the FBI— for the FBI is J. Edgar Hoover and I think we can rest assured that it will always be." "Any success the FBI has had," Hoover replied, "is due in no small measure to the wholehearted support and cooperation we have always received from such fine friends as you." [36]

Hoover was sometimes distressed by McCarthy's irresponsibility. He cautioned his friend against using dramatic lists with specific numbers

---

* Joe probably got the photostats from the FBI. Early in 1954 he wrote Hoover: "I would appreciate any information you can give me on General Telford Taylor." See Senator Joe McCarthy to J. Edgar Hoover, January 26, 1954, *Papers of the FBI*, Washington, D.C.

attached, such as fifty-seven card-carrying Communists or eighty-one
security risks. But he believed that Joe was serious and sincere and that
he was performing a valuable public service. "Hoover knew that Joe
wasn't the best guy in the world to be doing this job. We all did," said
Bob Morris. "But his attitude was, 'Thank God somebody's doing it.'
They were fighting the same enemy, you know."[37]

EVER SINCE WHEELING, the critics of McCarthy had been waiting for
someone to come along and cut him down to size. The list of those who
had tried and failed—Truman, Tydings, Lucas, Hayden, Benton—was
impressive but narrowly partisan. Occasionally a moderate Republican
voice would be raised, but with little real effect. The frustrating truth
was that the men with the power to blunt McCarthy—Bob Taft, perhaps,
or J. Edgar Hoover—were not inclined to do so. They generally viewed
him as a political asset, a patriot, or sometimes both.

As expected, the Eisenhower landslide added an element of uncertainty to the McCarthy crusade. From 1950 until 1952 the senator had
been a potent force in Republican politics, hammering away at the competence and the loyalty of those who formulated the nation's foreign
policy. This was fine as long as the Democrats were in power. But, as
Earl Latham has written, the 1952 election results drastically altered
McCarthy's standing within his own party:

> The frustrations of twenty years had been eased. Although it had seemed
> desirable and even necessary for the more aggressive and less liberal Repub-
> licans, when they were out on the sidewalks looking in, to throw rocks at the
> house they hoped to occupy, they were now inside and had an interest in
> keeping the property intact. But McCarthy was inside also and, although he
> was no longer throwing rocks, he was breaking up the furniture.[38]

From the very outset, McCarthy had made it clear that he would not
be pushed out of the limelight by Eisenhower or anyone else. His great
strength—and ultimate weakness—was his outrageous independence.
He did not really care who occupied the White House. His only boss, he
said, was the American people. They had demanded the roughest possible fight against Communism, and he intended to oblige them. He
would welcome Eisenhower's support, but he would not scrape for it, or
pull his punches, or sit quietly as the President tried to put his new house
in order. The fight against disloyalty would continue.

Some observers predicted a "tough" White House response to Mc-
Carthy. There were rumors that Eisenhower would undercut him by
appointing a panel of distinguished citizens to "seriously study" the internal security problem. There were knowing smiles when he gave
George Marshall a place of honor at his inauguration and then spoke of

his desire to shoulder the "primary responsibility for dealing with the disloyal and the dangerous" in the federal bureaucracy. The word was out: Ike would soon "chop McCarthy down to size."[39]

It didn't happen. Despite the urgings of some of his closest friends and advisers, the President refused to meet the challenge head-on. He had already decided that he would do nothing to provoke a showdown. "I had made up my mind how I was going to handle McCarthy," he said later. "This was to ignore him. . . . I would give him no satisfaction. I'd never defend anything. I don't care what he called me, or mentioned, or put in the papers. I'd just ignore him."[40]

This position may not have been daring, but it did make good political sense. The Senate balance in 1953 was 48–47 in favor of the Republicans. That made every vote crucial and thereby enhanced the leverage of party recalcitrants. Eisenhower felt, with good reason, that an open clash with McCarthy would cost him dearly. On the one hand, he would lose the support of perhaps a dozen Senate reactionaries—"namely those," he said, "who are trying to use the McCarthy issue to strengthen the indefensible position they hold in the realm of political philosophy." * On the other, he would surely jeopardize relations between the executive and legislative branches of government. Many senators were already disturbed by the growing power of the presidency. Whatever their feelings about McCarthy, they might interpret a White House attack upon him as an attack upon the Senate itself and dutifully rally to his side.[41]

There were other reasons as well. Eisenhower was known as a harmonizer, a man who could get diverse factions to work toward a common goal. He had helped reconcile British–American differences during World War II and had earned high marks as the NATO commander a few years later. Leadership, he explained, meant patience and conciliation, not "hitting people over the head." After assuming the presidency he told a friend, "I have developed a practice which, so far as I know, I have never violated. That practice is to avoid public mention of any name *unless it can be done with favorable intent and connotation.* . . . This is not namby-pamby. It is certainly not Pollyanna-ish. It is just sheer common sense. A leader's job is to get others to go along with him in the promotion of something. To do this he needs their good will." Then, turning to the problem of McCarthy, he said, "I would not have you believe that I have acquiesced in, or by any means approve, the methods he uses. . . . I despise them. . . . But I am quite sure that the people who want me to stand up and publicly label McCarthy with derogatory titles are mistaken."[42]

---

* According to the White House, the "reactionaries" were John Bricker, Barry Goldwater, Bourke Hickenlooper, Karl Mundt, Styles Bridges, Herman Welker, William Jenner, "Molly" Malone, Everett Dirksen, Andrew Schoeppel, Harry Dworshak, and Pat McCarran.

They were mistaken, he felt, because they did not understand why McCarthy had come as far as he had. Privately, Eisenhower blamed Harry Truman for the senator's rise to prominence. He thought Truman's public attacks had kept McCarthy in the limelight and even raised him to the level of an opposing Secretary of State. "This particular individual wants, above all else, publicity," Eisenhower said of McCarthy. "Nothing would probably please him more than the publicity that would be generated by public repudiation by the President." By ignoring him, Eisenhower hoped to minimize his visibility while riveting attention upon the "truly important" matters of state. "We have side shows and freaks," he wrote a friend, "where we ought to be in the main tent with our attention on the chariot race. This is serious."[43]

Eisenhower's closest aides have acknowledged that political considerations played a large role in the failure to confront McCarthy. But they insist that at least one other factor was involved. According to Arthur Larson, the President had "a profound—almost exaggerated—respect for the dignity of his office." This led him to avoid men like McCarthy, who loved to brawl in public and splatter mud on their critics. Time and time again, when prodded by friends and advisers to "crack down" on the senator, Eisenhower would protest: "I just will not—I *refuse*—to get into the gutter with that guy."[44]

Nevertheless, the President did not discourage his subordinates from dealing with McCarthy on a regular basis. He knew that Richard Nixon and Jerry Persons were meeting privately with the senator, lauding his Red-hunting efforts and urging him to work with fellow Republicans in the Administration. This seemed to make good sense, because the ultimate goal was to co-opt McCarthy, to swallow him up by making him part of the team. On one occasion, Eisenhower did lose his temper with Persons, telling him, "Jerry, I don't understand how you can come into this office altogether clean after shaking hands with that fellow." But Persons silenced the President by responding, "Maybe I'd feel that way, too, if I were . . . trying to get something for myself. But if it's to get him to do something *you* want, I'll shake hands with him as often as I have to."[45]

THIS GUARDED APPROACH to the "McCarthy problem"—what Emmet Hughes called "silent, passive resistance"—was quickly adopted by other Administration officials. They could see that Eisenhower wanted to avoid a confrontation and that he might not back them if one developed. This generally spelled appeasement, for even the boldest officials were unwilling to challenge McCarthy on their own. He was dangerous under the best of circumstances; under anything less he would surely overwhelm them.[46]

No one knew this better than John Foster Dulles, the incoming Secretary of State. At first glance, Dulles seemed impregnable to threats and pressures from the right. He was a man of stature—solid, solemn, God-fearing, and thoroughly Republican. Yet the appearance was deceiving. Dulles had long been at odds with the McCarthyites on a variety of issues, ranging from his contempt for Chiang Kai-shek to his enthusiasm for NATO and foreign aid. In addition, he had an old and familiar skeleton rattling in his closet. After World War II, Dulles had served as a trustee for the Carnegie Endowment for International Peace. In that role he had strongly defended the president of the Endowment—a man named Alger Hiss. "I am confident that there is no reason to doubt Mr. Hiss' complete loyalty to our American institutions," Dulles had written. "I have been thrown into intimate contact with him at San Francisco, London, and Washington . . . and have seen him actually at work in meeting alien efforts." [47]

The Hiss episode would plague Dulles throughout his career. Like so many others—Acheson, Jessup, Stevenson—he could never quite erase it from his past. In 1952, for example, Richard Nixon wrote him privately:

Dear Foster:
I just received a letter from one of my constituents which had the following interesting comment: "I heard the other day that Mr. Dulles feels that within five years Alger Hiss will be vindicated." I assume that this is just another of those wild stories that gets around but thought it would be well to call it to your attention.

Later, when Nixon was chosen as Eisenhower's running mate, Dulles replied:

Dear Dick:
It occurred to me that the Hiss case . . . may come up in the course of the campaign and that you may be asked questions . . . about my relationship to Hiss. . . . I have prepared the enclosed statement so that you will have the facts in mind. . . . It is significant that, by the time it came to try Hiss, I was a witness for the Prosecution and Adlai Stevenson was a witness for the Defense. [48]

As Secretary of State, Dulles once called in a subordinate who had come under sustained attack from the McCarthyites. Dulles knew that the charges were spurious, told the man so, and then asked him to resign. "Don't you know that I went through this kind of thing?" he said, referring to the Hiss case. "You can't pacify these people. There's no reasoning with these people." Recalling the incident years later, the subordinate remarked, "I never saw a man as scared of this situation as he was." [49]

Shortly before Dulles took office, McCarthy sent along a personal note that contained a good bit more than his best wishes. In a few well-crafted paragraphs, the senator took most of the credit for Eisenhower's victory, spoke of his deep interest in foreign affairs, and then added, "As you know, I have carefully documented cases against a sizable number of those whom I consider bad for America. I would be glad to sit down and go over the matter with you whenever you can spare the time."[50]

Dulles replied at once, asking for "the documented cases to which you refer" but ignoring the offer for a face-to-face meeting. This seemed to upset McCarthy. While forwarding some material to Dulles,* he again expressed his desire "to go into this matter with you or your security officer at any time." Dulles did not respond. He simply scrawled "File— No Answer" across the top of McCarthy's letter.[51]

In the following weeks, however, Dulles tried to placate the McCarthyites by taking a tough public stand on loyalty and security matters. He knew that his department was suspect in the eyes of Congress, and he was determined to avoid the rancor of the Acheson years. If this meant feeding an occasional body to the sharks, Dulles was more than willing to supply it. His position, a newsman recalled, was that if someone "got into trouble . . . on the Hill, he was liable to throw him to the McCarthyites—which, in a way, he did, I think. He was saying, 'Well, this may be too bad about these people, but I am not going to waste a whole lot of political capital on them.' "[52]

The department that Dulles inherited already had a serious morale problem. Years of constant attacks by the McCarthys and the McCarrans had taken their toll. Under Dulles things quickly got worse. At his swearing-in ceremony, he demanded "positive loyalty" from his subordinates, a term that implied that a loyalty problem did, in fact, exist. A few days later he hired a belligerent superpatriot named R. W. Scott McLeod to head the department's newly created Bureau of Security and Consular Affairs. The Dulles strategy, it seemed, was to get the McCarthyites to stop banging on the windows by inviting them in through the front door.

Almost everyone assumed that McLeod, an ex-FBI agent, had been foisted upon Dulles by Senator McCarthy. In fact, the appointment was a joint effort, sponsored by Bridges and McCarran as well. Dulles acquiesced because he assumed, quite correctly, that McLeod was popular with the Red-hunters. "Fine appointment," said McCarthy, "excellent man."[53]

Scott McLeod knew what was expected of him. "Congress wants heads to roll and I let 'em roll," he said. "Blood in the streets and all that." But McLeod was more than a yes man; he was a true believer. He never doubted that the department was filled with longhairs and homosexuals, and he was determined to get rid of them. One of McLeod's friends described him this way:

---

* McCarthy's letter had an "enclosure attached" at the bottom. Unfortunately, the enclosure was not put into the Dulles Papers.

He was a bulldog. He had tenacity. . . . But he lived in an essentially simple world that didn't involve a lot of philosophical concepts. . . . He loved conspiracies. He was deeply suspicious of the things in the State Department that he didn't understand, particularly the intellectuals. He knew shortly from his own records and investigations . . . what he had suspected viscerally—there was a part of the Foreign Service that had been infiltrated by fairies, which made him suspicious. Because, as I say, Scotty had the essentially simple approach to a fairy that you will find in a cop who has never had the benefit of, let us say, courses in abnormal psychology at Yale. . . . Scotty had a very black and white kind of approach—and this wasn't white.[54]

As Dulles conveniently looked the other way, the energetic McLeod took over the divisions of security, personnel, passports, and visas.* His primary function, however, was to investigate the backgrounds of the department's 11,000 employees. Under a new Eisenhower directive, federal workers in "sensitive positions"—a term that applied to all State Department personnel—could be discharged as "security risks" for reasons other than disloyalty. These reasons included "sexual perversion," "immoral or notoriously disgraceful conduct," or the suspicion that "the individual may be subjected to coercion, influence, or pressure which may cause him to act contrary to the best interests of national security." The directive had a dual purpose. It allowed the government to dismiss those who posed "security problems" but were in no way disloyal, like alcoholics, gossips, or homosexuals. And it supposedly protected those "security risks" from the stigma of disloyalty.

McLeod and his hand-picked investigators went right to work. They checked out everyone, from top to bottom, with methods that reminded some of the Gestapo and others of the sleazy hotel detective. Diplomats found "steam marks" on their personal correspondence. An embassy official in Jordan discovered that his letters from home were routinely opened and news clippings about McCarthy removed. Employees were forced to take lie detector tests. Telephones were tapped. The interrogations were ludicrous and degrading. (A Foreign Service officer stationed in Europe during World War II was asked, "So you were working to get Finland and Russia to agree? Hm. Let's see, who was President then?") After completing a two-month study of McLeod's security program for *Collier's*, a reporter concluded that "a shocking proportion of State Department employees are completely fed up. Their morale is shot. . . . Hundreds of workers are disillusioned with government service, dismayed at the trend toward conformity, discouraged and often downright disgusted with the practices employed in the name of security.

* When a reporter told Dulles that no State Department officer had ever controlled security *and* personnel, the secretary was genuinely surprised, asking, "Is that bad?" See especially William Hale, " 'Big Brother' in Foggy Bottom," *The Reporter*, August 17, 1954, pp. 10–16.

Worst of all, the handling of foreign affairs in the field has—in the opinion of some of our foremost diplomats and former diplomats—been greatly damaged." [55]

Although figures were hard to come by, the reporter estimated that in the first seven months of McLeod's regime, 193 "security risks" had been terminated—of whom one was a suspected, but unproved, subversive. McLeod did not deal in specifics. "I don't think the people are concerned with any breakdown," he said. "They don't care if they were drunks, perverts, or Communists—they just want us to get rid of them." Ironically, those cleared by the system were often afraid to seek employment elsewhere. "Suppose I apply for a job in private industry," an employee explained. "Resigned from the State Department? Why, they'd say, he must be a Commie, or at least a sexual deviate." [56]

The McLeod appointment was one of the worst blunders that Dulles would make as Secretary. He had done it primarily to appease the McCarthyites, to get them to take the heat off his department. As one analyst noted, Dulles was willing to "cave in on the sides in order to salvage the core—retaining executive control over the affairs of the Department and regaining congressional and public confidence in the Foreign Service." He felt that the main tasks at hand—the Korean peace settlement, the preservation of NATO, and the extension of foreign aid —could well be subverted by the McCarthyites, and he hoped to avoid this by rewarding them in other ways. Scott McLeod was the ultimate reward. [57]

The problem, of course, was that once McLeod was appointed, Dulles found it impossible to fire or even to discipline him without offending his supporters. The Secretary was boxed in, and he knew it. In December 1953—by which time McLeod had alienated the entire White House staff and most of the Senate—Dulles penned this pathetic little note:

Dear Scotty:
As 1953 comes to an end I want to thank you for your good service during the past year. Your task has been a hard one and I know you have done your best to handle it. I feel you have made a very real contribution.

Joe McCarthy could not have said it better. [58]

CHAPTER EIGHTEEN

Voices Within the Voice

IN THE SPRING OF 1793 the House of Representatives set up a special committee to investigate the stunning defeat of General Arthur St. Clair's army by Indian tribes on the Ohio frontier. The committee's vindication of St. Clair was a milestone of sorts, marking the first exercise of the congressional power to probe. Since that time the history of legislative investigations has become in large part the history of American politics. Congressional committees have scrutinized everything from the Seminole War to the debacle at Pearl Harbor, from the treason of General James Wilkinson to the activities of Alger Hiss. As Chief Justice Earl Warren observed in *Watkins* v. *United States:*

> The power of Congress to conduct investigations . . . is very broad. It encompasses inquiries concerning the administration of existing laws as well as proposed or possibly needed statutes. It includes surveys of the defects in our social, economic, or political system for the purpose of enabling the Congress to remedy them. It comprehends probes into departments of the federal government to expose corruption, inefficiency, and waste.[1]

In the 1950s the power to probe and the power of Senator McCarthy were virtually synonymous in the public mind. As chairman of the Subcommittee on Investigations, he presided over a series of spectacular hearings, many of which were televised nationwide. Along the way his behavior raised fundamental questions about the investigatory process. For example: What constitutional protections were available to witnesses who appeared at these hearings? What were the limits of the "informing function"—that is, the committee's right to instruct people about wrong-doing in their government? What could be done to stop leaks of confidential information by committee members and their staffs? And what restrictions, if any, should be placed on the media's coverage of congressional investigations? [2]

These questions were debated endlessly in the McCarthy era. And why not? They affected the lives of countless Americans, the relationship between the Executive and Legislative branches of government, and the day-to-day operation of numerous federal agencies and departments, including the Voice of America, the United States Army, and the CIA.

THE VOICE OF AMERICA, part of a sprawling State Department operation known as the International Information Agency (IIA), had been created by executive order in 1942 and dramatically upgraded during the early Cold War years. Its star had soared after President Truman called for a "Campaign of Truth" against Communist propaganda and junketing congressmen returned with firsthand accounts of the "aggressive psychological warfare" being employed to "discredit us and drive us out of Europe." By 1950 the Voice stood third in size among the world's communication networks, behind Radio Moscow and the BBC. Its 75 transmitting stations, spread over four continents, reached an estimated 300 million people in 46 languages and dialects. [3]

For a time this impressive growth had overshadowed a host of problems relating to output and personnel. The Voice was big but mediocre, and the reasons were clear. Unlike Radio Moscow and the BBC, it had to compete for talent with thriving commercial networks in the United States. Yet, as a government agency, it could not pay competitive salaries or discharge someone when someone better was available for the job. Thus, with few exceptions, the Voice attracted people who could not find employment anywhere else. Its writers, technicians, and broadcasters were often second-rate. [4]

This problem was compounded by disputes over the "mission" of the VOA. Most of the administrators were sympathetic to the BBC approach, which served British policy without slanting the news or blanketing the airwaves with political propaganda. But the key foreign language desks were manned by East European exiles who believed in the "hard sell," or Radio Moscow approach. They were determined to stir up *resistance* to Communism, and their outlook had strong popular appeal. As a result, the Voice abandoned its original mission—"honest news reporting"—over the objections of much of its staff. "Congress expected us to 'make propaganda,' and we made it," said one VOA official. "Anything more subtle than a bludgeon was considered 'soft on Communism.'"[5]

These disputes were bitter, disruptive, and devastating to morale. At the Voice headquarters in Manhattan, a group calling itself the American Underground, organized by a Rumanian exile named Paul Deac, began forwarding information about "subversive" employees to Senator McCarthy and his friends in the press—Howard Rushmore, Ralph de Toledano, and George Sokolsky, among others. The senator was busy but interested. He wrote a friend in 1950 that he had just hired the "former head of General Clay's Intelligence Staff" to collect material "on three of the top people in the Voice of America in Germany." While this sounded like typical McCarthy bluster, his staff did forward a packet of VOA documents to de Toledano a few weeks later. Attached was this warning: "They are secret . . . and we would not desire that you publish any . . . of the detailed facts until you have cleared it with Senator McCarthy or Jean Kerr."[6]

In the following months, rumors about "Communist trouble" at the VOA appeared regularly in the columns of Rushmore and Sokolsky. But nothing came of them until the Republicans regained control of Congress in 1953, determined to root out the Communism and corruption they'd been railing against for years. In short order a House committee (Appropriations) and a Senate committee (Foreign Relations) announced plans to investigate the overseas information program, which included a network of libraries and cultural centers as well as the VOA. Publicly the House chairman spoke about checking budgets and cutting costs. Privately he told IIA officials: "Your agency is full of Communists, left-wingers, New Dealers, radicals, and pinkos, and the best thing you can do is to take the funds you have on hand, liquidate it, and go back [home]."[7]

The news quickly got worse. On February 12 George Sokolsky informed John Foster Dulles that McCarthy planned to launch an investigation of his own. According to a summary of their telephone conversation, "Mr. Sokolsky said that the probe . . . would focus on VOA material. The interpretation is that they are still pro-left and that this will come out in the hearings."

Dulles replied that he knew very little about the VOA, having been in office for less than a month. He added, with considerable anxiety, that he welcomed the investigation as long as McCarthy did not "unfairly try to blame him for things he has had nothing to do with." Sokolsky told

Dulles not to worry. "He just wanted him to know these things and that he will be protected." * 8

This was exactly what Dulles wanted to hear. He was so anxious to cooperate that he instructed Donald Lourie, his Under Secretary for Administration, to forward the IIA's "political guidance material" to McCarthy's office at once. Lourie opposed the move, arguing that the material contained "sensitive data" on foreign policy aims. But Dulles replied that politics came first, the politics of survival. "We must not be put in a position of defending the past mistakes of others," he said. "The campaign brought out all these things and the people apparently wanted a change . . . or they would have continued the old Administration in power." Dulles ended the conversation with a warning: "Don't take an arbitrary position on the sanctity of all of this stuff. . . . It will turn the Republicans in Congress against us."9

Lourie sent the material to Cohn and Schine, who were supervising the investigation from a pair of luxurious command posts in Washington and New York. Accustomed to the best of everything, they had set up shop—for themselves, not the staff—in a government building near Capitol Hill. "All their operation was out of there. . . ," Ruth Watt recalled. "Roy apparently corralled expensive furniture from everywhere and had quite a plush apartment as well as a bar, I understand." †

In New York the two men used Dave Schine's apartment at the Waldorf Towers. Working closely with Howard Rushmore, the subcommittee's new research director, they interviewed a hundred witnesses in less than a week. At the Voice offices on 57th Street, the words "going to the Waldorf" took on new meaning as subpoenas fluttered about like confetti. A visitor to the Schine apartment observed: "Coats and hats were piled high on the Recamier chairs and settees. Witnesses, friendly, reserved, or reticent, lined the walls of the enormous living room, sitting uneasily on the Louis XV armchairs, pretending to read magazines, and gazing abstractedly at the many photos of the Schine family scattered about the room." Paul Deac played the role of receptionist, greeting

---

* From the day he took office in 1953, Dulles had his phone calls monitored by a secretary, who then summarized them for the files. This practice, apparently done without the knowledge of the other party, was not uncommon in Washington, as we shall see. The summaries of the Dulles phone calls can be found at the Seeley Mudd Library, Princeton University.

† Watt, a strong McCarthy supporter, was chief clerk of the Subcommittee on Investigations. In her lengthy oral history, she described Cohn and Schine as pampered, self-important adolescents who worked overtime to win petty privileges for themselves. She recalled that Schine once wrote a letter to the Rules Committee saying "it would be desirous if Dave Schine could go in the Senators' baths . . . and he signed Joe McCarthy's name on it." (The Rules Committee said no.) She also recalled that Schine would phone his friends and relatives, nationwide, before every televised hearing, remind them to watch, and then stick Cohn with the bill. See *Ruth Watt Oral History*, Senate Historical Office, Washington, D.C.

friends and sorting out witnesses. He waved at Fernand Auberjonois, head of the French Desk, and said, "We're certainly packing them in tonight."[10]

_____

THE HEARINGS BEGAN ON FEBRUARY 16, 1953, at a courthouse in downtown New York. The scene was impressive yet familiar: reporters milling about, technicians testing cameras and klieg lights, and spectators fighting for space. Cohn and Schine were there, along with Rushmore, Sokolsky, and the subcommittee members. The new chairman started things, a bit nervously, by calling his first witness to the stand. He did not bother with a statement of purpose—or a word about the subject under investigation.

The hearings were in two parts, although only Cohn and McCarthy seemed to know this at the time. Part one concerned the VOA's decision to locate powerful transmitters—Baker East and Baker West—in North Carolina and Washington state. The decision, based on studies by the Army Signal Corps and the Research Electronics Laboratory at MIT, had been bitterly opposed by several Voice engineers, including Louis McKesson, the first witness, who argued that the sites were too close to areas of magnetic storms. In 1952 McKesson had quit his job in disgust. "I was very dissatisfied with the engineering," he said, ". . . and found that I was unable to correct some of the things . . . which were going on."[11]

McKesson claimed that the Voice could save about $18,000,000 by moving the transmitters to Florida and California, where the atmospheric conditions were ideal. He spoke convincingly about dipoles and geomagnetic fields; McCarthy responded with prepared questions about auroral absorption belts and the high cost of the rhombic antenna. Finally the chairman said: "Let me ask you this, Mr. McKesson. As well as the question of waste, what other significance do you find in the location of Baker East and Baker West?"

The witness stumbled, missing his cue. McCarthy tried again.

THE CHAIRMAN: Let us put it this way: Let us assume we have a good Voice of America, a voice that is really the voice of America. Assume I do not want that to reach Communist territory. Would not the best way to sabotage that voice be to place your transmitters within that magnetic storm area, so that you would have this tremendous interference?

MR. MCKESSON: I would agree with you a hundred percent, sir.

And later:

THE CHAIRMAN: In other words, you feel that mere incompetence could not explain away all this waste?

MR. McKESSON: That is right.

THE CHAIRMAN: . . . you think if a man is merely stupid he cannot be consistently mistaken. . . . He has to make a right decision once in a while?

MR. McKESSON: That is right.

As the hearings wore on, McCarthy questioned the competence or the loyalty of almost everyone who supported the original Baker locations. At one point, for example, he belittled the VOA's chief engineer by reading his freshman college grades into the record: Mechanical Drawing, C; Chemistry, D; Calculus, F. At another point he described MIT as "a department store" filled with "newcomers in the radio signals field." At no point, however, did the chairman invite these people to testify at the hearings. Indeed, when Senator Mundt raised the issue, Roy Cohn replied that it was irrelevant because Dr. Jerome Wiesner, head of the Research Electronics Laboratory, had already reversed his position on Baker West.

MR. COHN: We talked to him, three of us on the line, for over 1 hour. Dr. Wiesner stated . . . his conclusion that Baker West, from a standpoint of efficiency and reliability, should be moved South and away from Seattle, and that he would just as soon not come down and testify as that would be his conclusion.[12]

Wiesner told a different story, however. Interviewed by journalist Frederick Woltman, a onetime McCarthy supporter, he said: "Virtually all of the engineers still favor Seattle. I told Cohn. . . . We had a long, heated discussion in which he tried to get me to agree that the Seattle site was inferior. I refused . . ."
Wiesner added: ". . . at the end of our final discussion, Cohn said, 'I don't intend to subpoena you but you are free to come down and make any statement you want to.' He did not ask me to come. Since I had no idea he was going to misrepresent me, I thought I had no need of coming."[13]
On February 17 the State Department suspended work on the Baker projects for "the time being." There followed, in rapid succession, the sacking of chief engineer George Herrick, the "resignation" of IIA Administrator Wilson Compton, and the announcement that the Baker projects had been halted for good. Privately there was talk about liquidating the entire VOA—with Dulles himself taking the lead. But he apparently backed down after receiving a confidential memo from presi-

dential assistant C. D. Jackson, a specialist in Cold War strategy. "Dear Foster," it began,

> I think it would be a bad idea on two counts.
>
> 1. It would almost inevitably be interpreted as evidence of panic on the part of the Administration, particularly on the part of the Secretary of State, as a result of Senator McCarthy's vigorous attacks.
>
> 2. The repercussions outside the United States would be tremendous and almost entirely unfavorable. Our friends would have their confidence shaken in any U.S. Government information program, and our enemies would have gloating material that would last them for months.[14]

In the end the Battle of the Bakers cost some men their jobs and one man his life. On March 6 a young engineer threw himself under a speeding truck in Cambridge, Massachusetts. His name was Raymond Kaplan, and he had been the liaison between the Research Electronics Laboratory and the VOA.

Kaplan had been interviewed at the Waldorf a few weeks before. McCarthy acknowledged this fact, describing Kaplan—now dead—as a cooperative fellow who "had expressed the desire to appear and testify" in public. "Mr. Kaplan had no fear of this committee whatsoever," the chairman said, adding that sinister forces, not suicide, had probably done him in.

The coroner disagreed. He ruled the death a suicide and released the handwritten note that Kaplan had left for his wife and child. It read, in part: "I have not done anything in my job which I did not think was in the best interests of this country. . . . When the dogs are set on you, everything you have done since the beginning of time is suspect. . . . I love you and David beyond life itself. You are innocent victims of unfortunate circumstances . . . I can say no more now."[15]

In the second week of the hearings, McCarthy moved from "the sabotage of key transmitting stations" to the "Communist infiltration of key departments," including the French Desk, the Hebrew Language Section, and the Programs Allocations Board. In this phase—the vital phase—he relied heavily upon Deac and Rushmore for the rumors, the allegations, and, most of all, the witnesses who were willing to spew them in public.

Their stories were trivial, their grudges very real. For example: Dr. Nancy Lenkeith, a script writer in the French Section, had apparently been fired for (1) refusing to join a Marxist commune, (2) writing a favorable book review of *Witness* by Whittaker Chambers, and (3) defending the good name of Abraham Lincoln to her superiors.

> MR. COHN: What did [your producer] say to you about the idea of doing a Lincoln's Day broadcast?

DR. LENKEITH: Well, he said: "That damn Lincoln! Why do we have to talk about him again? We talk about him all the time, and he bores the French." [16]

On closer inspection, however, it became apparent that Dr. Lenkeith had serious psychological problems. Her testimony was almost incoherent as she described her troubles at the VOA—and other places before that. "I taught at Queens College for two years," she began. "I ran into difficulties there, because I . . . find it difficult to teach undergraduates, sophomores. . . . I am bilingual; trilingual, in fact. . . . And I am also not particularly interested in a high-geared business career. And, you know, the State Department, the Voice of America—I am not interested in achieving a high salary. If I were a young man—"

McCarthy did what he could. He begged the witness to stop rambling and to concentrate on his questions. When this failed, he turned to Roy Cohn and said, "Mr. Counsel, you have interviewed her several times, and you may be able to get the facts." When Cohn could do nothing, McCarthy tried again.

THE CHAIRMAN: Is there any doubt in your mind today that you were fired because you favorably reviewed Chambers's book?

DR. LENKEITH: Well, it is not such a simple—it is difficult for me to state. The fact is this. To my knowledge—and I am not sure of this—

THE CHAIRMAN: I am going to ask you a very simple question. Do you think you were fired because you favorably reviewed Chambers's book?

DR. LENKEITH: I think, Senator, that I was fired because of the reasons that made me review that book, and that was just the last—

THE CHAIRMAN: And the reason that made you review it is that you were anti-Communist; is that right?

DR. LENKEITH: Yes.

That was good enough for McCarthy. "You may step down," he said. "Thank you very much."

———

ANOTHER EXAMPLE : Dr. John Cocutz of the Rumanian Section suggested that Roger Lyons, the Director of Religious Programming, did not believe in God. "I am just quoting Mr. Kretzmann," * said Mr. Cocutz. "Mr. Kretzmann told me that he had told somebody else also that Mr. Lyons was an atheist."

* Mr. Edwin Kretzmann was the chief policy adviser of the Voice of America.

Called to the witness stand, Mr. Lyons declared that, yes, he did believe in God, but, no, he did not attend church on a regular basis.

THE CHAIRMAN: Did you write a thesis for Columbia University?

MR. LYONS: I did.

THE CHAIRMAN: What was the subject?

MR. LYONS: Toward a Clearer Criterion of Moral Value.

THE CHAIRMAN: . . . Did you express an opinion in that whether you believed in a Divine Being?

MR. LYONS: I did not.[17]

The other subcommittee members did not object to this line of questioning. On the contrary, they welcomed the chance to humiliate a suspected atheist on national TV. Senator McClellan demanded *proof* that Lyons believed in God, while Senator Jackson asked him what "fraternal organizations" be belonged to. Finally the witness said: "It seems to me that the statement of Mr. Cocutz was made second- or third-hand, and there was no attempt to verify it. I think that there is something wrong with committee procedure." This irritated the members, and Senator Jackson rushed to McCarthy's defense. "Do you not think the committee has been pretty fair?" he wondered. "You were . . . notified immediately and had a chance to be heard today."

MR. LYONS: But the charge was released to the press.

SENATOR JACKSON: You are here before the press now to answer it, and this is a pretty serious charge . . .

MR. LYONS: I would suggest that the committee could have heard this testimony in private, and have attempted to check it with the party that told it, and also have come to me and asked me.

SENATOR JACKSON: Even if it had been heard in executive session it would have to come out in public because it is your word against Mr. Cocutz's and Mr. Kretzmann's; is that not right?

The answer was no. It was wrong—terribly wrong—as the senators discovered when Edwin Kretzmann took the stand. Holding his temper in check, but barely, Mr. Kretzmann said: "I was asked at one time by a superior . . . about Roger Lyons's specific religious adherence. My answer was that that was not a pertinent question for him to ask; and laughingly I added, 'For all I know, he may be an atheist.' "

Somehow, Kretzmann went on, "the story in Mr. Cocutz's mind . . . has been transferred into something quite different. . . . Roger Lyons is a man of profound religious beliefs, and he has done a magnificent job in stepping up the religious output of the Voice."[18]

That should have ended the matter, but McCarthy wouldn't quit. As the members sat in silence, he swore in a Voice staffer who recalled that Lyons had been a "very confused" atheist in 1945, and then a Voice producer who claimed that Lyons had opposed some "key words" in a "Back to God" documentary starring Richard Nixon, a rabbi, and a Negro clergyman. "I am a Roman Catholic," the producer declared, "and to my perhaps myopic view, I do not think he was very religious." [19]

At last Senator Symington interrupted. It had dawned on him—a bit late—that the previous witness had said: "*I was going with Mr. Lyons in 1945 and I don't believe that he believed in God then.*" Symington recalled the witness to the stand. "You are not in the position of a jilted lady or anything like that?" he asked. "Oh, no. My gosh, no . . . ," the woman replied. "I am not disgruntled; no." [20]

Bang went the gavel. "We will adjourn until 10:30 tomorrow morning," the chairman said, and that, quite literally, was that. He never mentioned Roger Lyons again.

———

A THIRD EXAMPLE: In public testimony a Voice official roasted his superiors for suspending Hebrew language broadcasts at a time when anti-Semitism in Communist countries was on the rise. He charged that America had lost a "splendid opportunity" to stir up anti-Soviet feelings in Israel, and McCarthy took it from there.

THE CHAIRMAN: . . . you feel that the reason why the Hebrew language desk was being discontinued was because it was doing a good job of combating Communism?

MR. DOOHER: Again, sir, I don't want to go into the thinking of the people who gave the directive, but the result was the same.

THE CHAIRMAN: Let us put it this way: If I had been in a position of power, if I were an ardent member of the Communist Party, would I have not taken the same action that was taken to discontinue the Hebrew Language desk . . . ?

MR. DOOHER: I believe so, sir.

THE CHAIRMAN: So that while you do not want to delve into the minds of the individuals . . . you feel that the action would have been the same had they been representing Joe Stalin?

MR. DOOHER: That is correct, sir. [21]

The directive had been signed by Reed Harris, deputy administrator of the IIA. Harris had spent nineteen years in government service. His record was impeccable, and he welcomed the chance to testify in public. He assumed, erroneously, that the members wanted to know more about the Hebrew Language desk—its high cost, its small audience, and its replacement by more effective propaganda tools inside the State of Israel.

Harris got a chance to testify, but only about himself. He discovered, to his astonishment, that the subject would not be Israel, or even the IIA. The subject would be Reed Harris—his youth, his college years, his thoughts in 1932. Said McCarthy: "We are going to go into your background a bit today. I want to make it clear that I don't think anyone on this committee thinks because a man may have made some mistakes 20 years ago he . . . may not be an outstanding American at this time. But we must start with the record and bring it down to date and find out whether there has been any change of heart." [22]

And so it began, three brutal days of testimony based on what Harris had done or not done, written or not written, at Columbia University two decades before. As millions watched on television, he admitted that, yes, he had been suspended for protesting the dismissal of a Marxist professor; and, yes, he had written a book (*King Football*) which attacked marriage, conformity, college sport, the American Legion, and the DAR. It was a sad, sometimes pathetic scene, reminiscent of a sinner near death. "I declare that I have changed my mind," he said. "I believe in the institution of marriage; I have three fine children at home. . . . I have two close friends right now who are commanders of American Legion posts. . . . I wrote that book in 3 weeks, sir. . . . It is part of the thing that I regret. It goes back 21 years, I repeat; 21 years ago."

The chairman was not impressed. He kept quoting the book, passage by passage, as if it were a current bestseller. And he rattled the witness —and slowly wore him down—by challenging his assertion that the Reed Harris of 1932 and the Reed Harris of 1953 were *probably* different men. Did McCarthy have any evidence? No, none at all. Did Harris? Only if one believed his "liberal" friends and a system that McCarthy had been attacking for years.

> THE CHAIRMAN: Mr. Harris, you repeat over and over that you have been cleared by the Civil Service Commission to do this job. Now, I am not comparing you to him, but understand that . . . Alger Hiss was also cleared.
>
> MR. HARRIS: Mr. Chairman, that is really a fantastic thing to do. . . . Why do you mention a man who has nothing to do with this case today?
>
> THE CHAIRMAN: We are concerned beyond the clearances given by the Acheson regime. They have cleared some very unusual people . . . and I am not impressed by the fact that the Acheson regime cleared you for this top job.

Although McCarthy hardly needed his support, Senator Mundt rushed in to remind the viewers that "many Civil Service Commission clearances wind up in the federal penitentiary because they are Communists." The statement was true—if one substituted "several" for "many"—but the implication was cruel. Even worse, when Harris protested, he seemed only to reinforce his image as a complainer, a hostile witness, a man with something to hide. The chairman was probably telling the truth when he said: "We have been getting a great flood of mail from the television audience, and almost down to the last letter they . . . have marveled at the patience we have had with you."

Reed Harris left the government a few weeks later. His resignation was "voluntary." No one forced him out, or comforted him, or helped him in any way. To be sure, his boss sent him a note of regret—but only after conferring with two State Department officials who privately praised Harris to the skies. "Frankly I hate to see you go," IIA chief Robert Johnson wrote. "Since coming on this new assignment of mine, I have learned to depend upon you and respect you for the fine contribution you have made to the Information Program."[23]

THE INVESTIGATION ENDED IN LATE MARCH, without warning or explanation. It simply ended—a casualty of poor planning, exhausted possibilities, and private complaints by some of McCarthy's close friends and advisers. According to inside accounts,

> Alexander Barmine became very disturbed at the way the investigation was injuring . . . some of the really strong anti-Soviet elements inside the Voice. Barmine went to see Robert Morris . . . and together they phoned McCarthy, who told them to meet him at the Stork Club that evening at Walter Winchell's table. When the two arrived there, they found Joe . . . with Winchell and Cohn and Schine. They presented their case against C&S tactics and something of a row followed. Winchell tended to agree with the B&M case and in his column the next day . . . stated that Joe was out to cure the Voice, not to kill it. Joe himself took the same line, in almost the same words, in a statement to the press.[*][24]

* Barmine, 53, was a former Soviet diplomat and intelligence agent, who fled to the West in 1937. At first he told the FBI that he could not identify any Soviet agents working in the United States. In later years, however, he claimed that Alger Hiss and Owen Lattimore had been mentioned to him in long ago conversations with General Berzin, General Krivitsky, and others in the Soviet intelligence network. Robert Morris introduced Barmine to McCarthy in 1950, and some people—including Lattimore—believed that Barmine played an important behind-the-scenes role in the Tydings investigation. By 1953 Barmine had become the chief of the Russian Branch of the VOA. He testified at the public hearings, but rarely to the chairman's advantage. At one point he said: "I think . . . the American press is rather unfair to the Voice. Because the Voice of America is doing a rather effective job." At another point Senator Mundt asked him about Roger Lyons, the religious director, hoping to hear the worst. "We work in perfect cooperation," Barmine replied, "and I have no difficulties or disagreements whatsoever." See *Voice of America Hearings*, pp. 480, 487; also Allen Weinstein, *Perjury*, 1978, p. 351; interview with Robert Morris; interview with Owen Lattimore.

This did not mean that McCarthy had lost interest in the IIA. All he had done, it turned out, was to abandon an unpromising target, the Voice of America, in favor of a promising one, the Overseas Library Program. Armed with the IIA's political guidance material, he proceeded to investigate the way in which controversial books were allowed to reach the library shelves.

The background was simple enough. For years the IIA had been using books by Communist authors—books that were nonpolitical in nature or that "accurately portrayed" the American scene. The policy directives were clear on this point. They followed the recommendations of a blue-ribbon advisory commission comprising the presidents of three publishing houses—Macmillan, Thomas Y. Crowell, and Harper and Brothers—and the director of libraries for Harvard University. The commission had called for a book selection process "based on content without regard to authorship," adding that "it would be deplorable if books expressing views critical of the political and economic situation in this country . . . were eliminated from the program and the books selected were only representative of the views of the Department of State. . . ."[25]

The rule of thumb, then, was to include "controversial" books while excluding blatantly pro-Communist or anti-American propaganda. This was a difficult process under the best of circumstances. It relied on judgments that were necessarily subjective; and, in the case of the overseas libraries, it had to be enforced at hundreds of different locations. As a result some of the books that reached the shelves *did* offend any reasonable standard of merit or truth. A good example was *African Journey* by Eslanda C. D. Robeson, the wife of Paul Robeson, written in 1945:

> And the one hopeful light on the horizon—the exciting and encouraging conditions in Soviet Russia, where for the first time in history our race problem has been squarely faced and solved; where . . . the fine words of the poets, philosophers and well-meaning politicians have been made a living reality; where . . . men and women and children of all races, colors and creeds walk the streets and work out their lives in dignity, safety and comradeship.[26]

Still, the number of pro-Communist books in these libraries did not appear to be very large. Senator McCarthy put the figure at 30,000—out of 2,000,000 total volumes—but that included *all* books by "Communists," "pro-Communists," "former Communists," and "anti-anti-Communists," including *The Maltese Falcon* by Dashiel Hammett and the children's stories of Helen Goldfrank. In 1953 a House committee reported that only thirty-nine books by eight authors could be described as definitely supporting the Communist cause.[27]

McCarthy's interest in the overseas libraries had been heightened by the political guidance material he received from the Secretary of State. He knew that Dulles had ordered changes in the book selection policy because he (McCarthy) had seen the classified document (P.O.5) that set down the new criteria. It read, in part: "Materials produced by a person whose ideology or views are questionable or controversial will *not* be used unless—the material is *substantially better than other material available for the . . . support of a specific IIA objective.*"

This new order was issued on February 5, 1953. On February 18 McCarthy "declassified" it at the VOA hearings and demanded the removal of all books by "controversial" authors. The result was familiar; the Administration canceled P.O.5 and came up with P.O.6. "In order to avoid all misunderstanding," said Carl McArdle, the Assistant Secretary for Public Affairs, "no material by any controversial persons, Communists, fellow travelers, etc., will be used by the IIA." McArdle did not define what he meant by a controversial person, much less an et cetera.[28]

Anger, panic, and confusion swept the IIA. Books were removed from library shelves, and a few dozen were burned by workers who could find no place to store them. Included in the purge were the works of Vera Michaels, head of the Foreign Policy Association; Walter White, president of the NAACP; and Foster Rhea Dulles, the well-known diplomatic historian. ("Why," the Secretary of State wondered aloud, "is my cousin on the list?") In London, Ambassador Winthrop Aldrich hesitated before including Stalin's name in his annual Pilgrims Day address. His caution made sense. A few days before VOA chief Alfred Morton had wired Washington that, directive or no directive, he intended "to use the words and works of Communists, fellow travelers, et cetera to expose them and to make them eat their words . . ." In response, State Department officials had wired back a warning and then *suspended* Morton after learning that both cables had been intercepted by a McCarthy informer and sent to the senator's office. Typically, Morton was "fired" on page one of the New York *Times*—and reinstated on page thirteen the following day. "The reinstatement did not mean much," a colleague recalled. "Morton had lost heart and interest, and the control of his agency."[29]

The press blamed Dulles for the fiasco, and this was only fair. But its primary assumption, that Dulles had capitulated in order to steer McCarthy away from the overseas libraries, was certainly false. The Secretary did *not* oppose a public investigation by McCarthy. In fact, he welcomed one so long as it focused on "past mistakes" and left the new Administration alone. This was good politics, of course; but politics did not tell the whole story. If anything, it obscured the fact that Dulles and McCarthy held very similar opinions on this issue. Like the senator, Dulles believed that overseas libraries were there to "sell" America, not to run her down. He viewed them as vessels of propaganda, remarking privately that "American libraries are one thing, and overseas libraries are a different breed of cat." Why, then, would anybody want to place controversial books on the shelves?[30]

THE PUBLIC HEARINGS WERE PRECEDED by one of the great media events of 1953—the whirlwind tour of Cohn and Schine through the overseas libraries in Europe. It began in Paris on April 4, ended in London on April 21, and included stops in Berlin, Frankfurt, Munich, Bonn, Vienna, Belgrade, Athens, and Rome. In truth, the journey was about as pointless and superficial as any one of a hundred such junkets by congressmen and their staffs. What made it different was the press coverage, the dozens of reporters and photographers who followed the pair from city to city, pouncing on everything they said and did. "We soon realized," Cohn wrote later, "that [the trip] was a colossal mistake. . . . David Schine and I unwittingly handed Joe McCarthy's enemies a perfect opportunity to spread the tale that a couple of young, inexperienced clowns were hustling about Europe, ordering State Department officials around, burning books, creating chaos wherever they went, and disrupting foreign relations."[31]

Cohn was correct. The trip was a colossal mistake. The European newspapers were hostile and often unfair. They wanted to report the worst, and the young travelers rudely obliged them at every turn. In Vienna, Cohn and Schine visited the U.S. Information Library and the Soviet Union's House of Culture, searching for books that both sides found acceptable. They found several—the works of Mark Twain, for example—and dutifully wrote them down. In Munich, they loudly demanded separate hotel rooms, explaining none too subtly that "we don't work for the State Department." In Paris, they railed against economic extravagance and wound up personifying it—apparently at government expense. An American official recalled that, despite receiving $2,000 in counterpart funds, the pair went on a huge buying spree, charged everything to the American Embassy, and then ran out on their hotel bill.[32]

The Embassy paid the bills, but it couldn't repair the damage done in other areas. At the time, a diplomat recalled, the United States had been making "considerable headway" in persuading the French to remove Communists from sensitive positions in their government. The trip "just made anti-Communists look ridiculous," he added, "and we couldn't get the French to do anything further about it." This may have accounted for the private anguish expressed by General Lauris Norstad, the new NATO commander. Asked by a friend if the Cohn–Schine visit had been all *that* bad, the general muttered, "It was so bad it can't possibly be exaggerated. It was awful."[33]

THE "PURPOSE" OF THE PUBLIC HEARINGS was to determine the extent of Communist influence in the overseas libraries. The method was to parade two sets of witnesses before the television cameras: the ex-Communist informers who appeared regularly at such proceedings, and the "Communists, fellow travelers, et cetera" whose books were currently on the shelves. There were only fifteen sessions, though McCarthy spread them over three and a half months, from April to the middle of July.

The ex-Communists included Louis Budenz, Freda Utley, and Harvey Matusow, a young McCarthy aide who had previously named names for a living. Matusow had appeared before grand juries, deportation boards, and numerous congressional committees. He had testified at the second Smith Act trial (where he met Roy Cohn, the assistant U.S. attorney); and at the IPR hearings (where he linked Owen Lattimore to the Communist Party). Matusow would later retract much of his testimony, claiming he had perjured himself with the blessings of Cohn and McCarthy, among others. Understandably, his recantation impressed liberal columnists more than the nation as a whole. Most people had trouble believing a man who had lied so often in the past.[34]

At the hearings Budenz supplied the committee with a list of seventy-five Communist authors he had known from his days as managing editor of the *Daily Worker*. Matusow added the names of Philip Foner and Herbert Aptheker, two party-line historians. And Utley offered her impressions of the U.S. libraries in Germany, which she had visited a few weeks before. "The bookshelves are loaded up with what you might call anti-anti-Communist material," she said, adding that her personal favorites—*Seeds of Treason* by Ralph de Toledano and *Brain Washing in Red China* by Edward Hunter—were nowhere to be found.*

There followed the second set of witnesses—the "controversial" authors themselves. Many were members of the Communist Party; others were fellow travelers or longtime apologists for the Stalin regime. The problem, however, was that all of them were private citizens, not government workers, and none of them knew how or why his books had landed on the library shelves. They were subpoenaed—instead of the bureaucrats who implemented policy—because they were natural villains, ideally suited to the chairman's immediate needs.

---

* Two points should be made about the testimony of these ex-Communists. First, unlike the Tydings investigation, the Democratic members treated Budenz with fawning respect. They encouraged him to say whatever he wanted about religion, politics, and the state of the world; and they agreed with it all. Symington asked the most obsequious questions—"Because of your experience in the field, and if it is out of order please don't answer it, but I was just wondering what you thought about . . ."—but McClellan was not far behind.

Second, Utley had gone to Germany to write an article for *The Freeman*, an extreme right-wing publication, about book selection in the overseas libraries. There she met Cohn and Schine, she recalled, and "they managed to mix up the lists I had given them of books in Amerika Haus libraries, presenting my compilation of anti-Communist books . . . as pro-Communist books!" Utley went on to describe Cohn and Schine as "unscrupulous careerists" and "badly behaved ignoramuses." See Freda Utley, *Odyssey of a Liberal*, 1970, p. 279.

The exchanges were often acrimonious, often quite bizarre. Earl Browder refused to offer any information—even the title of his book.

THE CHAIRMAN: I do not think that you can incriminate yourself by reading that.

MR. BROWDER: In a committee headed by Senator McCarthy, it is very difficult to tell how one can incriminate himself.[35]

Another witness began: "My name is William Marx Mandell. And to save you the trouble . . . I would like to make it clear that I am a Jew."

MR. COHN: So am I, and I don't see that that is an issue here.

MR. MANDELL: Well, a Jew who works for McCarthy is thought of very ill by most of the Jewish people in the country.

McCarthy broke in. "I think the Jewish people are a great race of people," he said. "I do not think you represent them. . . . Each race has its renegades." Mandell looked directly at Cohn and replied: "It certainly does."[36]

Most of the witnesses took the Fifth Amendment on all questions relating to political affiliations and beliefs. There were some exceptions, however. Harvey O'Connor objected on First Amendment grounds, saying, "my writings, my book, and my political beliefs are of no legitimate concern to this committee," while Eslanda C. D. Robeson claimed "the Fifteenth Amendment as a Negro."

THE CHAIRMAN: The Fifteenth Amendment? That deals solely with your right to vote. You will be given no less consideration because of your race. . . . You can only refuse to answer if you feel that an honest, truthful answer might tend to incriminate you.[37]

Mrs. Robeson stuck with the Fifteenth. McCarthy was puzzled but polite. "I am not going to order you to answer," he replied. "I just want you to know that you are getting special attention today. . . . I do not propose to argue with a lady." *

Was chivalry alive and well in Washington? Consider the case of Miss Gene Weltfish, a professor at Columbia University, an officer in several pro-Communist organizations, and the author of three books in the field of anthropology. In the midst of her interrogation, Senator McClellan of Arkansas broke in with a question: "Do you [McCarthy] have some quotations from her books that might be entered into the record at this time?" The chairman had been waiting for this. He was wickedly well

---

* McCarthy always warned the witnesses that they could be cited for contempt if they based their refusal to answer a question on any grounds other than self-incrimination. He suspended this rule for Mrs. Robeson, but O'Connor was cited, convicted, fined $500, and sentenced to a year in jail. The sentence was suspended.

prepared. "Just opening at random," he replied, "I find something on page 18 of the book entitled *The Races of Mankind* which should interest my Southern colleague to some extent. It shows the intelligence tests of the Southern whites: Arkansas, 41.55; Northern Negroes, Ohio, 49.50"[38]

McClellan was furious. He accused the witness of hiding behind the Fifth Amendment and concealing the truth about her past. A few days later Columbia announced that Miss Weltfish's contract would be terminated at the end of the school year. It denied, of course, that its decision had been motivated by political considerations.

OF THE THIRTY-THREE WITNESSES who testified at the hearings, one stood out clearly from the rest—James Wechsler, editor of the New York *Post*, a liberal Democratic newspaper known for its hostility to Senator McCarthy and his friends. Wechsler had been a member of the Young Communist League during his college days in New York City, a fact he didn't try to hide. He had joined the League at nineteen, quit at twenty-two, and written extensively about the experience. In the 1940s he had battled to eliminate Communist influence in the American Veterans Committee, the American Newspaper Guild, and the newspaper *PM*, from which he eventually resigned. He was the author of four books— *Revolt on the Campus*, *War: Our Heritage*, *War Propaganda and the United States*, and *Labor Baron*, a biography of John L. Lewis. All of these books appeared on the master list for the overseas libraries, and two of them—*Revolt on the Campus*, and *War: Our Heritage*—had been written while Wechsler was a member of the Young Communist League.[39]

McCarthy knew little and cared less about these books. He did care about the New York *Post*, however:

THE CHAIRMAN: Have you ever, in your editorial columns, over the last 2 years, praised the FBI?

MR. WECHSLER: Well, sir, I would have to go back and read our editorials. . . . I did not understand that I was being called down here for a discussion of *Post* editorial policy. . . .

THE CHAIRMAN: Do you think Bill Jenner is doing a good job?

MR. WECHSLER: I believe that in the battle of ideas we can compete effectively any day of the week with the Communists without resorting to methods which I regard as imitative of theirs. I see by your expression that you feel as if you have heard this before, so I will not pursue the point.

THE CHAIRMAN: I have. I have read it in the *Daily Worker* and in the New York *Post*.

The grilling lasted for an hour and a half. Cohn and McCarthy were relentless; the other members did not intervene. Near the end the chairman said to Wechsler, "You have not been intimidated, have you?"

MR. WECHSLER: I am fully aware that this is a proceeding designed to smear the New York *Post*. I recognize that, Senator. We are both grown up. But this is a free country, and I am going to keep fighting.

Roy Cohn let out a yawn. The chairman smiled and rephrased his question. "Do you feel you have been abused?

MR. WECHSLER: Why, of course I have been abused. The suggestion that my break with Communism is not authentic is the greatest affront you can recite anywhere. . . .

THE CHAIRMAN: I feel that you have not broken with Communist ideals. I feel that you are serving them very, very actively. . . . I have no knowledge whether you have a card in the Party.

MR. WECHSLER: I appreciate that concession. I should like to say that . . . the only way I could in your view prove my devotion to America and the validity of my break with Communism would be to come out in support of Senator McCarthy. This I do not plan to do.

There was another way to prove one's devotion, however. One could do what Budenz, Utley, Rushmore, and Matusow had done; one could name names. This was the acid test for ex-Communists, the *true sign* of their break with the past. In the words of Mr. Budenz, "No ex-Communist can be accepted as having left the Communist conspiracy unless he proves by his deeds that he has done so. And what does that mean? That he cooperates fully with the FBI; that he cooperates with congressional committees. . . ."

SENATOR McCLELLAN: In other words, you would not accept repentance . . . without actions that conform to opposition?

MR. BUDENZ: Most decidedly not.[40]

The issue arose when McCarthy asked Wechsler if anyone working at the *Post* "is or was a member of the Communist Party." Though Wechsler could not rely on the Fifth Amendment, he might have said, at some risk to himself, that he would not answer questions that were clearly beyond the scope of the authorized investigation.* Instead he

---

* In *Rogers* v. *United States* (340 U.S. 367, 1951), the Supreme Court ruled that a witness who testified freely about himself could no longer refuse, on Fifth Amendment grounds, to testify about someone else. This was the so-called waiver doctrine: "If the witness . . . elects to waive the privilege . . . he is not permitted to stop, but must go on and make a full disclosure."

replied: "I am going to answer that question because I believe that it is a citizen's responsibility to testify before a Senate committee whether he likes the committee or not."

Wechsler named several writers, all of whom had left the Party, admitted their membership, and become "vigorous, emphatic anti-Communists." But this was only the beginning. Five minutes later McCarthy asked for the names "of any of those who were with you in the Young Communist League." And Wechsler responded: "Sure. Do you want a long list? A short list? How do you want this?"

THE CHAIRMAN: I think all of those that you can think of.

Wechsler named five names ("the major characters") but McCarthy wanted more. He told the witness to prepare a list "under oath of *all* the Young Communist Leaguers you knew as such," adding, "That is an order."

MR. WECHSLER: I would just like to say . . . that I am here as a responsive but not a friendly witness.

The following day, accompanied by a New York *Post* attorney, Wechsler submitted his list after urging the subcommittee members to exclude it from the public record. He spoke movingly about his past mistakes and his present responsibilities, saying,

Many of those on the list were young people who joined the League out of deeply idealistic motivations. . . . I know that some of them have repudiated Communism . . . and it is highly probable that numerous others with whom I have had utterly no contact in the past fifteen years or more have similarly changed their views and allegiances.

The majority agreed with Wechsler's position, and McCarthy went along. The list was never published.*

———

BY THE TIME THE HEARINGS ENDED IN JULY, the IIA was in ruins. Morale was so bad that Robert Johnson, the *new* director, and Martin Merson, his assistant, resigned in disgust. No one on the subcommittee or inside the Administration had lifted a finger in their defense. The subcommit-

* In considering the harm that public disclosure could do to innocent people, the senators were clearly swayed by the news of Raymond Kaplan's suicide. Symington said, for example, "Based on some of the things the committee has been criticized for, like the death of some man out of Boston, I would not be for releasing the names."
It is also likely that the list contained no "new" or interesting names—nothing worth leaking to the press. Wechsler later claimed that, to his knowledge, only one person had suffered any consequences at all—a businessman who ran into a problem with his visa. See *State Department Information Program—Information Centers*, pp. 295–96; Victor Navasky, *Naming Names*, 1980, p. 63.

tee members were too busy showing McCarthy—and the TV cameras—that they, too, could be tough on the Reds. And the Administration? Senator Hennings summed it up best:

> The confusion generated in the last five months by some eleven directives issued to those in charge . . . should now be dispelled. It is unfortunate that the State Department in this period departed from its sound and well-considered policy and undertook to readjust its program to meet each vicissitude of Congressional investigations.[41]

From McCarthy's perspective the hearings had been a tremendous success. He had received enormous publicity and no resistance at all. He seemed completely in charge and more serious than before. Those who followed him sensed an important change in his behavior. The jauntiness and the self-mockery were gone. There were no more winks at newsmen who questioned his charges. Now, like the true believer, he lectured them about Communists in the colleges, the defense plants, and the VOA. "You don't understand," he told columnist Jack Anderson. "This is the real thing, the *real thing.*"[42]

CHAPTER NINETEEN

Of Diplomats
and Greek Ships

DURING THE EARLY MONTHS OF 1953 Senator McCarthy could usually be found in his Capitol Hill office or in the Government Operations Committee hearing room, which doubled as the site for his numerous press conferences. He visited the Senate chamber only to vote or deliver an occasional speech about the dangers of international Communism. He took almost no interest in pending legislation. He avoided mundane subjects like taxation, federal spending, labor relations, and farm price supports. His attendance at other committee meetings was so sporadic that Styles Bridges, the Appropriations chairman, thought seriously about replacing him with a responsible freshman senator. Only once did a piece of "regular" Senate business attract McCarthy's attention for any length of time. This occurred in March, during the Voice of America hearings, when the President nominated a new American Ambassador to the Soviet Union. His name was Charles E. "Chip" Bohlen.

Under normal circumstances a nomination of this sort is rather dull stuff. The White House submits a name; the Foreign Relations Committee holds a quick hearing; the full Senate praises the choice and votes its overwhelming approval. What made this nomination unique, however, was the precarious state of Soviet–American relations and the controversial background of the nominee. In 1952 the previous Ambassador, George F. Kennan, had been declared *persona non grata* by Moscow for a statement he made comparing his wartime internment in Nazi Germany with present conditions in the Soviet Union. When Harry Truman stubbornly refused to name a replacement, America went without an ambassador for more than seven months, a period that included the death of Stalin and a radical shakeup of Kremlin personnel. Eisenhower aimed to fill the vacancy as quickly as possible.[1]

Chip Bohlen, the President's personal choice, was the kind of fellow Joe McCarthy loved to hate. Rich and cultured, born into a family of leisure, he had attended the best private schools, including Harvard College, before entering the Foreign Service in 1929. An acknowledged "Russian expert," he had served two tours of duty in Moscow, the second as America's vice consul. He spoke Russian fluently, knew most of the Kremlin leaders, and had the reported ability "to match them drink for drink in the vodka bouts which are an inevitable part of diplomacy there." In the late 1940s, as Minister to France, he had struck up a friendship with Eisenhower, who was then based at NATO headquarters in Paris. It was no secret that the new President admired Chip Bohlen and thought him ideally suited for the vacant Moscow post.[2]

John Foster Dulles thought otherwise. He did not question Bohlen's obvious talents; what disturbed him was Bohlen's close relationship with the Roosevelt and Truman administrations. As the author of the Republican foreign policy plank in 1952, Dulles had promised, among other things, "to repudiate all commitments contained in secret understandings, such as those of Yalta that aid Communist enslavements." Now, in deference to Eisenhower, he would have to embrace a man who had been a presidential adviser at Yalta and the only witness to Roosevelt's private talks with Stalin. This was sure to infuriate the McCarthyites, as Dulles well knew. He had already told friends of his desire to "exile" Bohlen, to send him to "some pleasant country" like Guatemala or Tanganyika.[3]

On the eve of the confirmation hearings, Dulles and Bohlen met privately to work out a common strategy. Dulles spoke first, suggesting that Bohlen downplay his role at Yalta by portraying himself as an interpreter, nothing more. Bohlen refused, saying he would not play the "village idiot" before a congressional committee. Dulles changed the subject. Was there anything in Bohlen's past, he inquired, that might prove particularly embarrassing to the Administration? "I of course gave the requisite assurances," Bohlen recalled, "at which Dulles said: "I'm glad to hear this. I couldn't stand another Alger Hiss.' " As the meeting broke up, Dulles noted that an arrangement had been made for the two men to ride to Capitol Hill in different cars. This way, he explained, they would not have to be photographed together.[4]

The next day, while perusing Bohlen's career file, Dulles noticed that the diplomat had never undergone a security check. As a matter of routine he phoned Attorney General Brownell, who ordered J. Edgar Hoover to begin a full field investigation. Since Bohlen had worked in the Foreign Service, the FBI focused almost instinctively upon his sexual preferences. On March 5 Drew Pearson wrote in his diary, "The FBI came to see me regarding Chip Bohlen. . . . I was amazed when they asked me whether he was a homo and then quoted me as once having said he was. I disabused them as far as any statements by me were concerned." In Europe, meanwhile, Scott McLeod's investigators combed the various embassies, interviewing maids, butlers, and chauffeurs, and demanding to be told the worst about Bohlen. "The result," said one columnist, "was to start the wildest and most damaging rumors among the puzzled Europeans, who are pardonably confused by the methods of our new American gestapo." * [5]

When Bohlen testified before the Foreign Relations Committee, word of his growing "security problems" had not yet reached the Senate. The questioning, therefore, centered largely on Yalta. Some Republicans pressed hard, hoping to force the admission that Roosevelt and his advisers had signed away China and most of Eastern Europe to the Communists. Bohlen stood firm. The Yalta accords were perfectly honorable, he said. It was Stalin's violation of them that had caused the trouble.

SENATOR FERGUSON: Well, wouldn't you say that the agreement . . . is now the basis of the situation in Europe?

MR. BOHLEN: No sir; I would not.

SENATOR FERGUSON: Both East and West?

MR. BOHLEN: I would not. . . .

SENATOR FERGUSON: You don't say then that these agreements are the cause of this enslavement?

MR. BOHLEN: I don't sir. I say it is the violation of them. [6]

McCarthy responded at once, calling the nomination a "tremendous mistake" and joining with several other Republicans to suggest that it be withdrawn. Fortunately for the White House, Bob Taft was not among them. While conceding privately that Bohlen was a poor choice, Taft

---

* McLeod's investigators were particularly interested in Bohlen's brother-in-law, Charles Thayer, the Consul-General in Munich. According to Bohlen they discovered, quite by accident, that Thayer had once had an affair with a Russian woman. According to other sources the evidence against Thayer consisted of "anonymous letters" claiming that Thayer was "a homosexual . . . and easy prey for Communist blackmail." In any event, the material was passed on to McCarthy, who threatened to subpoena Thayer before the Subcommittee on Investigations. Rather than submit to a public hearing on his morals, Thayer resigned from the Foreign Service. See Charles E. Bohlen, *Witness to History*, 1973; also, "Memo #2, Munich, March 8, 1953," in *Papers of The Reporter Magazine*, Boston University Library.

said he felt duty-bound as majority leader to support the President. Anyway, he explained, "our Russian ambassador can't do anything. All he can do is observe and report. He will not influence policy materially."[7]

Dulles took a more positive approach when he testified before the Foreign Relations Committee on March 18. His description of the nominee was hardly effusive, but it did serve to neutralize some of the hostility that had been building in Congress. The Yalta issue? Dulles got around it by condemning the accords while skillfully portraying Bohlen as a blameless interpreter. The security issue? Dulles temporarily defused it by giving his personal evaluation of the FBI's Summary Report, written by J. Edgar Hoover himself. "There is no derogatory material," Dulles said, "which questions the loyalty of Mr. Bohlen to the United States, or which suggests that he is not a good security risk." The committee members were impressed. They voted unanimously (15–0) to recommend Bohlen's appointment.[8]

In his remarks to the committee Dulles omitted one vital piece of information. He did not say that Scott McLeod had also seen the Summary Report and come to a far different conclusion about its contents. This omission was understandable, for Dulles did not want to admit that he had overruled the judgment of his own security officer on such a controversial matter. Incredibly, Dulles assumed that McLeod would keep the matter to himself. Predictably, McLeod told anyone willing to listen, including Joe McCarthy. Before long the story was front page news.

Dulles was furious. He thought of firing McLeod, thought some more, then called a press conference to smooth over their differences.

Q.: In the Bohlen case could you say whether your security officer agreed with your evaluation?

A.: The security officer made no attempt at evaluation. That was left to the Secretary. Mr. McLeod called the Secretary's attention to certain parts of the FBI report. But there was no difference of opinion.

Q.: Mr. McLeod did not suggest to you that Bohlen not be approved?

A.: No. . . .

Q.: Can you throw any light on this alleged dispute between yourself and McLeod? Is there any basis for it?

A.: No basis whatsoever.[9]

This hairsplitting performance was too much for McCarthy. He felt sure that Dulles was lying, and he intended to prove it by forcing McLeod to testify before the Subcommittee on Investigations. His plan went awry, however, when the witness suddenly disappeared. The White House, guessing correctly, had assigned someone to guard McLeod around the clock, keeping him "secure" from any public place where a subpoena might be served. The game went on for several days, until McCarthy gave up in disgust.[10]

The Senate began debating the nomination on March 23. Only four members were absent, two on official business, and the galleries were jammed with demonstrative spectators. For the most part, the floor battle pitted Republican against Republican. The Democrats, except for Pat McCarran, stayed quietly in the background. Their strategy was to vote for Bohlen en masse but to say little for fear of turning the uncommitted Republicans against him. At one point Herman Welker peered over at Lyndon Johnson, the minority leader, and asked if he was "getting any hilarity out of the debate on this side of the aisle?" Johnson said no, "the Senator from Texas is sad in this hour."[11]

The debate itself was long, angry, sometimes eloquent, sometimes quite personal. McCarthy got things started by attacking the Administration's credibility. He did not come right out and call anyone a liar; he simply suggested that Bohlen take a polygraph test—"I have a great respect for it. I have used it in my court in Wisconsin a great number of times"—and that Dulles return to Capitol Hill to testify *under oath* about the Summary Report. "This matter is completely up in the air," Joe added. "At least half the senators on this floor are convinced that [McLeod] turned down Mr. Bohlen on security grounds."

Ralph Flanders interrupted to lecture his colleague about the virtues of party loyalty. "It has seemed to me, in my confused and muddled brain, that we have on trial a Republican Secretary of State, and, by inference, a Republican President," Flanders said. "I should like to suggest that the Republican junior senator from Wisconsin give this Administration a chance and put the responsibility on it." The galleries broke into applause.

Joe responded deftly, noting that he would never allow partisan considerations to overrule his conscience. "I do not think this is the proper attitude for a senator to take," he replied. "I do not care whether a president is a Democrat or a Republican, when he has made a bad nomination I intend to oppose it on the floor of the Senate or elsewhere." The applause was so loud that Richard Nixon, the presiding officer, had to warn against "any further demonstrations on the part of the occupants of the galleries."

Bob Taft took the floor. Described as "red with anger," he lashed out at McCarthy, calling his polygraph scheme idiotic and defending, with great emotion, the integrity of John Foster Dulles. "So far as I am concerned, Mr. Dulles' statement not under oath is just as good as Mr. Dulles' statement under oath," he said acidly. McCarthy did not respond.

At this point, considerably calmer, Taft stepped back into the role of majority leader and offered a compromise proposal. It was clear, he said, that the rumors surrounding the Summary Report had clouded the entire nomination process. These rumors could be dispelled, however, if Mr. Dulles would allow two senators, one from each party, to view the report for themselves. The Senate quickly endorsed the proposal, as did Dulles, Hoover, and the White House. The next day two Senate representatives—Taft and Sparkman—went over to the State Department and spent several hours reading through the report. Upon returning to the Senate, Taft had this to say:

> We read the entire summary of the F.B.I. file on Mr. Bohlen. . . . I thought we should see the raw files. I called and talked to Mr. Hoover about it. He assured me . . . that everything of any importance which may adversely reflect on Mr. Bohlen was fully set forth in the summary and that there is nothing of importance that was not in the summary. . . .
>
> There was no suggestion anywhere by anyone reflecting on the loyalty of Mr. Bohlen in any way, or any association by him with communism or support of communism or even tolerance of communism. . . .
>
> So I myself came to the conclusion that Mr. Bohlen was a completely good security risk in every respect, and I am glad so to report to the Senate of the United States.*

This statement turned the confirmation battle into a rout. The final tally was 74–13, with almost every holdout explaining his vote as a protest against Yalta, not against Bohlen's character or the President's judgment. Everett Dirksen said: "I know 'Chip' Bohlen. He is a very charming and affable person. . . . I am confident he is able. . . . But 'Chip' Bohlen was at Yalta. . . . In the language of Missouri, the tail has to go with the hide. I reject Yalta, so I reject Yalta men."

McCarthy was far less conciliatory. He spoke for more than an hour, casting his net in all directions. He chided Taft for calling the Moscow post "unimportant" when Dulles himself had described it as "one of the most important assignments that we have." He criticized Dulles for sug-

---

* Actually, Taft had misled his Senate colleagues and seriously distorted the truth. For one thing, his "spontaneous" compromise proposal had already been worked out in a series of private meetings with Dulles, Hoover, Brownell—and Eisenhower himself. From the outset, Taft and Sparkman had demanded access to the complete FBI file on Bohlen, not just the Summary Report. Brownell and Hoover had objected—Brownell for political reasons (he did not want a Democratic senator involved in the process), and both men for practical reasons ("it would . . . create a precedent that would be hard to overlook.") At Taft's insistence the matter was taken to President Eisenhower, who ruled that "it was all right to have a member of each side *look at the file*." Naturally, this ruling upset Hoover and Brownell. They complained that other Senate committees would now demand equal access to the raw FBI files. The problem was solved, however, when Taft and Sparkman discreetly informed the Senate that they had seen a complete summary of the FBI files, not the files themselves. See "Telephone Conversation with J. Edgar Hoover and Attorney General Brownell," March 24, 1953; "Telephone Conversation with Senator Wiley," March 24, 1953, both in *John Foster Dulles Papers*, Princeton University Library.

gesting that Bohlen was "only an interpreter" at Yalta when the facts clearly showed otherwise. He made much of the friendship between Bohlen and Averell Harriman, portraying the latter, to most everyone's astonishment, as "a guy whose admiration for everything Russian is unrivaled outside the confines of the Communist Party." At one point he was reproached by Senator Knowland, a political ally, for quoting the statements of men who "categorically denied" ever making them.

McCarthy played his trump card about halfway through the speech. It was an affidavit from one Igor Bogolepov, a former Kremlin official who freelanced in Washington as a professional anti-Communist. According to the affidavit, the Soviet secret police had labeled Bohlen "a friendly person . . . a possible source of information." This charge made little impact, however, because Mr. Bogolepov was well known on Capitol Hill as something of a screwball. Once employed by the Soviet Foreign Service, he had gone over to the Nazis during World War II, found them difficult to deal with, then defected to the West. "It was not that the Nazis were too bad," he told a Senate committee in 1950. "But I didn't know the Germans were so silly as they were." [12]

At the end, McCarthy spoke of the qualities that were needed to stop the Soviet onslaught—qualities, he said, that Bohlen so obviously lacked. "In these grim days when we battle for survival—when we fight for life itself—we can ill afford ambassadors who retreat before the enemy. . . . This nation cannot afford to place in a position of power a man who is either so blind that he cannot recognize the enemy or who for reasons of expedience or cowardice fails to measure up to his job." The galleries did not applaud.

As expected, the news media wrote up the Bohlen affair as a personal triumph for Dwight Eisenhower. It applauded his firm defense of the nominee, a defense, said *Newsweek*, that reaffirmed "the right of the Chief Executive to choose his own envoys to foreign nations." What was overlooked, however, was the extraordinarily narrow approach the President had taken. It was true that he had stood by his friend Chip Bohlen; it was also true that he had said nothing about the victimization of so many others in the Foreign Service. No one knew this better than Bohlen, who visited the White House after his confirmation to speak directly to this issue. According to Bohlen, the President listened attentively, asked some questions, admitted that the McLeod appointment was a mistake, but said "that more harm would be done by trying to change it now." Bohlen left with the grim feeling that things were not about to improve. [13]

Like the President, the Secretary of State emerged from the Bohlen affair with his reputation enhanced. The press lauded Dulles for coolness under fire and for standing up to the McCarthyites. It had no inkling of the private Dulles, the man who asked Bohlen to shade his testimony before Congress and then astonished two White House aides by "pondering the possible desirability of withdrawing Bohlen's name." Nor was this the worst of it. Following the confirmation vote, Dulles pleaded with Bohlen not to leave for Moscow a few weeks ahead of his family, as the diplomat had planned, explaining that such an arrangement would embarrass the Administration by again raising the issue of Bohlen's "immoral behavior." Bohlen was stunned. He later told a friend that it took every ounce of his patience to keep from smashing Dulles in the face.[14]

The Bohlen affair was seen in most quarters as a serious defeat for Joe McCarthy. *Newsweek* read the lopsided confirmation vote as a sign of his "reduced influence." *The Nation* called his clashes with Knowland and Taft "a serious mistake . . . isolating him on the fringe of his own party." Even the New York *Daily News*, a pro-McCarthy sheet, conceded that its hero was temporarily "off the beam." McCarthy disagreed, of course, and his logic was interesting. He had known all along, he said, that he could not prevent Bohlen's confirmation. On the contrary, he had played the game expecting to lose but hoping to raise serious questions about the Administration's commitment to anti-Communism. This he thought he had done—by publicizing the disagreement between Dulles and McLeod and by highlighting the President's failure to carry out the Republican campaign plank on Yalta. Buoyant as ever, McCarthy told one reporter that the *real* battle had only just begun. "You wait," he said, "we're gunna get Dulles' head." *[15]

ON THE MORNING OF MARCH 28, just two days after the Bohlen vote, Senator McCarthy left his private office, accompanied by Robert Kennedy, and walked briskly to the Government Operations Committee hearing room, where a special news conference had been scheduled for 11:30. By 11:00 the room was filled with reporters. They had come with high hopes, sensing that McCarthy would try to "blanket" the Bohlen affair with something spectacular. It was Saturday, after all, and the Sunday headline, a McCarthy trademark, was still up for grabs.

McCarthy did not disappoint them. For the past several weeks, he said, his staff had been studying ways to control Western trade with the Soviet-bloc nations. Already there was big news to report. "As a result of negotiations undertaken by representatives of this subcommittee," the

---

* After the confirmation vote Senator Taft went to the White House and told the President, "No more Bohlens." Eisenhower supposedly agreed. A few days later, the Alsops contend, the White House "hastened to spread the happy word on Capitol Hill that Senator McCarthy and his ilk would thereafter enjoy a virtual veto on all presidential appointments." See James Patterson, *Mr. Republican; A Biography of Robert A. Taft*, 1972, p. 596; Joseph and Stewart Alsop, "Matter of Fact," Washington *Post*, July 5, 1953.

Greek owners of 242 merchant ships had agreed to stop trading with Red China, North Korea, and other Communist countries. "They cannot be commended too highly," Joe said of the shipowners. "With this single agreement they are removing approximately 2,750,000 deadweight tons, which is more tonnage than all the Communist countries, including the U.S.S.R., own themselves." [16]

The news was dramatic, to say the least. By even attempting to negotiate this deal, McCarthy had usurped a vital State Department function; by negotiating it successfully, he had done what the State Department had been unwilling or unable to do for three years—namely curtail Red China's ability to wage war in Korea.

The shipping controversy dated back to the 1940s, when America began dismantling its huge wartime tanker fleet. To save money and speed the delivery of Marshall Plan aid, the U.S. Maritime Commission had turned over a hundred Liberty Ships to the Greek government and sold hundreds more to American-owned companies. In many cases, however, these ships were resold, illegally, to foreign nationals, including Stavros Niarchos and Aristotle Onassis. Before long the wartime tanker fleet had become a vital cog in the flourishing trade between Western Europe and the Communist world. *

Once the Korean War began, America put pressure on its allies to blacklist Red China. Greece went along; the United Kingdom did not. Although its soldiers were fighting and dying in Korea, it insisted on the right to export "nonstrategic" items—cotton, chemicals, fertilizer—to the enemy. In addition, Britain encouraged Greek shipowners to fly the British flag on their vessels, thus increasing the tonnage available to the China trade. The State Department held back, fearing that a conflict with Britain might force its withdrawal from Korea. Its policy, under Acheson and Dulles, was to bar—insofar as possible—the shipment of "strategic" items to China while keeping the shipment of "nonstrategic" items at an acceptable level. [17]

McCarthy saw the makings of a splendid investigation. America was at war, yet its old tankers were being used to supply the enemy. Where did Dulles stand on this? Did he know, or care, that the Pentagon was strongly opposed to *all* Western trade with Red China? And what about the British? Would they be allowed to line their pockets at the expense of the U.N. troops in Korea, 95 percent of whom were American? These questions seemed so logical that even McCarthy's strongest critics wished him well. "He's absolutely right," said a bemused Drew Pearson. "He should proceed vigorously." [18]

---

* Under the Ship Sales Act of 1946 only American-controlled companies were allowed to buy T-2 tankers. The Greek owners often got around this law by forming Panamanian corporations and placing relatives with American citizenship in nominal control. See Rodney Carlisle, *Sovereignty for Sale*, 1981, pp. 145–46.

McCarthy turned over the investigation to Robert Kennedy, mainly because Cohn and Schine were busy dismantling the VOA. Working from the records of the Maritime Commission and the Lloyds of London shipping index, Kennedy gleaned some interesting statistics. Since 1950 non-Communist trade with Red China had reached the $2-billion mark. It was carried on largely by the British and by Greek nationals who sailed America's surplus tankers under the British flag. In one instance a Greek freighter carrying "fertilizer" had blown up at sea, leading to speculation that munitions were on board; in two cases British vessels had been spotted ferrying Communist troops and weapons along the Chinese coast. It was obvious, Kennedy concluded, that "strategic" as well as "nonstrategic" items were pouring into China from the West.

McCarthy moved quickly. After scheduling public hearings on the subject, he contacted several of the big Greek shippers, told them of Kennedy's findings, and asked for their promise to stop trading with the Communists. The shippers wisely agreed. They knew how McCarthy operated. They could picture him at the hearings, playing up their "blood trade" with the enemy, questioning their title to the old tankers, jeopardizing their contracts with American firms. Put simply, he had them over a barrel.

News of the shipping deal took Washington by storm. With one quick thrust, McCarthy had angered the British, embarrassed Secretary Dulles, and emerged as the grand protector of the boys in Korea. The Administration was, by various accounts, stunned, shocked, confused, and quietly furious. According to one report, the news "caused more flushed and angry faces, a greater gnashing of teeth and a longer and louder chorus of sturdy Anglo-Saxon expletives in the Department of State, the White House, and the Mutual Security Agency, than there had ever been provoked by the steady flow of goods from our 'free world' allies to the enemy."[19]

The public hearings opened on March 30, with Harold Stassen, the new Mutual Security Administrator, testifying first. McCarthy expected no trouble. He was sure that Stassen and other Administration witnesses would have no choice but to support the Greek shipping deal. He had even invited several television crews to come in and broadcast their words of praise. But Stassen, an old friend of McCarthy's, refused to go along. Instead of lauding the chairman, he portrayed him as a dangerous meddler whose private deals had seriously "undermined our enforcement that we are trying to carry on."[20]

McCarthy struck back hard. He demanded to know what had come over the witness. Hadn't Stassen privately encouraged the shipping deal? Hadn't he told the subcommittee in closed-door meetings that it was a step in the right direction?

MR. STASSEN: No, Senator, I did not say that to you . . .

THE CHAIRMAN: Didn't your aide testify that Mr. Flanagan and Mr. Kennedy were correct [in estimating] that 35 percent of the shipping with Red China would be eliminated by this agreement?

MR. STASSEN: He did not say that, Senator. He said that was incorrect. You have just restated it the other way.[21]

What really angered McCarthy was Stassen's observation that the shipping deal had been harmful to America's war effort. On this point Stassen refused to budge, despite extreme pressure from the Chair.

THE CHAIRMAN: If you feel that the removal of 242 ships is aiding the Communists in Korea and China . . . we should go to the Greek shipowners and ask them to put their ships back in the trade. . . . I get the impression from what you said here it is good to have ships removed from that trade if the State Department does it, but bad if the committee succeeds in having them removed. That startles me.[22]

Stassen's feisty performance took almost everyone by surprise. The President had repeatedly warned his subordinates to mind their manners on Capitol Hill; Dulles had done the same. And McCarthy had been doing business with Stassen for years. "I, of course, knew Joe very well from the very early days in Wisconsin," Stassen said later. "In 1948, in fact, along with Governor Kohler and others, he'd been a member of my presidential delegation out there." After Wheeling, Stassen had returned the favor by publicly supporting some of McCarthy's charges and by dismissing Haldore Hanson from his post in the Mutual Security Administration.*

According to Stassen, the friendship ended early in 1953, when the Republicans came to power. Acting alone, he recalls, he met with McCarthy and urged him to be quiescent, to give the new Administration a chance. Joe promised that he would, but the Bohlen affair and the shipping deal convinced Stassen that the senator was hopelessly out of control. "You see, by this time," he said, "I had reached the conclusion that you could not compromise with this kind of action; that is, that when you were not able to persuade him to come within normal bounds of action . . . you could not yield to it."[23]

The Administration obviously felt otherwise. Fearing a major party squabble, Vice President Nixon arranged a meeting between Dulles and McCarthy to iron out their differences over the trade question. On

---

* Stassen was particularly helpful to McCarthy in the Philip Jessup case. See U.S. Senate, Subcommittee of the Committee on Foreign Relations, *Nomination of Philip C. Jessup to Be United States Representative to the Sixth General Assembly of the United Nations*, 1951. For Hanson, see below, pp. 127–28.

April 1 the senator was invited to join the Secretary at his customary deskside luncheon in the State Department. The meeting, which lasted almost ninety minutes, was described by both men as cordial and constructive. Afterward a joint statement was issued. It said that foreign relations were "in the exclusive jurisdiction of the Chief Executive" but added that McCarthy's activity "was in the national interest." [24]

The senator then returned to his office, where a mob of reporters had already assembled. "Girls," he yelled to his secretaries, "I'm going into my room. If you hear any news about Stassen jumping out of a tall building, let me know at once." A newsman interrupted to ask what Dulles had served for lunch. "It was very pleasant," Joe replied, "Stassen-meat." [25]

For Harold Stassen the worst was yet to come. On April 2 the President told a news conference that his Mutual Security Administrator had probably meant to say "infringed" rather than "undermined" when he testified before McCarthy's committee. A reporter asked, "Mr. President . . . are you unhappy with what Mr. Stassen said the other day, or with what Senator McCarthy—" but Eisenhower cut him off. "I am not the slightest bit unhappy," he replied. "I think that I know what we are trying to do. I think, by and large, we are developing and getting better cooperation with the Senate and the House every day. The mere fact that some little incident arises is not going to disturb me. I have been scared by experts, in war and peace, and I am not frightened by this." [26]

Stassen got the message. The next day, in a humiliating reversal, he admitted that his choice of words had certainly been poor and said that McCarthy's attitude had now taken a "constructive turn." Stassen-meat, indeed!

At the hearings, meanwhile, the Administration continued to waver on the issue of Western trade with Red China. The Defense Department obviously wanted it stopped; the State Department apparently did not. This disagreement led Stuart Symington to suggest "that the chairman write a letter to the President and ask him what is the policy of the American Government." Said McCarthy, "I think that is an excellent suggestion, and the chair will write that letter this afternoon." [27]

The letter was drafted and hand-delivered to the White House by Robert Kennedy. While respectful in tone, it posed some very embarrassing questions.

> On March 28, 1953, Secretary of Defense Wilson advised this subcommittee that it was the position of the Department of Defense that the shipment of goods or the provision of any services to the Communist Chinese contributes to their economic and military potential. Mr. Leddy, acting Deputy Assistant Secretary of State for economic affairs, today informed the subcommittee that the Department of State does not agree with this position. The subcommittee would appreciate being advised as to which view reflects the position

of this Government. . . . We have been informed by the Department of Defense and the State Department that it would constitute a breach of security to identify the amounts and kinds of these strategic materials which are being shipped into China by our allies. Is it the policy of our Government to withhold from the public information concerning the amounts and kinds of goods which we believe to be strategic which are being shipped to Red China by our allies?[28]

The letter seemed almost impossible to answer. Eisenhower couldn't release this material without offending the British; and he couldn't refuse to release it without offending most of the Senate, which saw McCarthy's request as perfectly legitimate. According to Sherman Adams, "it was Nixon who finally got us out of it. He called McCarthy and pointed out to him that his Democratic fellow Senators, Symington and McClellan, had gotten him to embarrass the Republican Administration and that if he insisted on a reply from Eisenhower only the Democrats would benefit from it." McCarthy trusted Nixon and admired his political savvy. Fearing a Democratic trap, he asked the Vice President to intercept the letter before it reached the Oval Office. Nixon was happy to oblige. Once again he had avoided a showdown by playing what Marquis Childs called "his familiar role of mother's busy little helper."[29]

The subcommittee filed its interim report with the Senate on July 1. Written by Kennedy and Flanagan, it described—and condemned—the flourishing Western trade with Red China but avoided anything resembling a conspiracy theory. The report was so well researched, so judicious in tone, that most columnists had trouble linking it to McCarthy. Drew Pearson applauded it, grudgingly, as did Marquis Childs. Arthur Krock thought it "an example of congressional investigation at its highest level." Doris Fleeson called it McCarthy's "rara-avis—a documented and sober story." The chairman had good reason to gloat, of course. This was the first time that a document bearing his name had gotten such warm and widespread public support. It would be the last time as well.[30]

———

BY THE MIDDLE OF 1953 the so-called McCarthy problem had become a regular topic of conversation at the White House. Some staffers admitted spending as much time on it as they did on the tax problem, the budget problem, or the farm problem. They carefully considered its effect upon congressional relations, Republican politics, and government morale. And they worried more and more about its global implications, particularly its impact on America's image abroad. They realized, to their dismay, that McCarthy had become an international celebrity. Foreign newspapers gave him the type of coverage they normally reserved for American presidents or movie stars. The Cohn–Schine junket, the Bohlen affair, the Greek shipping deal, the book burnings—all were front page news in many parts of the world.

Americans who lived and traveled abroad were amazed by the mixture of curiosity and hostility that McCarthy seemed to generate. During a junket to Australia and New Zealand, Ralph Flanders found himself deluged with questions about his Wisconsin colleague. "I discovered then for the first time," he wrote, "that there was a strong impression abroad that McCarthy was something like a new Hitler, and that the United States might be following the Nazi path." Walter Reuther, back from a six-week tour of the Continent, said he had met "not one person who wasn't willing to admit privately that Joe McCarthy has done more to strengthen the Communist movement than any other one person in history." Both Winthrop Aldrich, the Ambassador to England, and C. Douglas Dillon, the Ambassador to France, sent cables home warning of the senator's negative impact on American prestige. From Paris, author Rebecca West wrote a friend: "I have been here a week and a situation that depresses me profoundly is driving me into the Seine with a brick around my neck. YOU CANNOT BELIEVE THE EFFECT OF McCARTHY ON THE FRENCH POPULACE. They do not see why Eisenhower does not take him by the scruff of the neck and throw him into the Potomac."[31]

The European perception of McCarthy was understandable, if somewhat exaggerated. By 1953 the senator had become a convenient symbol of the new America, the belligerent free world colossus, arrogant, inflexible, dominated by congressional extremists. Many Europeans believed that McCarthy had taken over in Washington, that Dulles and Eisenhower had been pushed aside and rendered powerless. As one American noted after completing a tour of Austria, Germany, and Switzerland, "I was shaken when I found myself obliged to answer arguments implying that the threat of war was greater from us than Russia. I soon discovered that this was a widely shared view."[32]

Harry Bullis, the board chairman of General Mills, sent much the same message to "President Ike" in Washington. Writing with genuine alarm, he warned that McCarthy had seriously weakened the Administration and undermined its credibility abroad. "In the opinion of many of us who are your loyal friends," he added, "it is a fallacy to assume that McCarthy will kill himself. This can only be accomplished by too much liquor and women. It is our belief that McCarthy should be stopped soon."[33]

Eisenhower responded with a "personal and confidential" letter, dated May 18, 1953, which listed many of the standard reasons for steering clear of McCarthy. ("I continue to believe that I cannot afford to name names. . . . Nothing would probably please him more than to get the publicity that would be generated by public repudiation by the President.") At the same time, however, the letter was charged with emotion. It called McCarthy's behavior "a sorry mess," which left decent men "hanging their heads in shame." And it hinted at future action against the senator if his behavior did not improve. "I do not mean that there is no possibility that I shall ever change my mind. . . . I merely mean that *as of this moment*, I consider that the wisest course of action is to continue to pursue a steady, positive foreign policy . . . and in all other areas where McCarthy seems to take such a specific and personal interest."[34]

Slowly but surely the President was moving toward the very showdown he had hoped to avoid.

CHAPTER TWENTY

Friends and Enemies

LATE IN 1953 *Look* magazine carried an interesting and generally accurate piece about "The Ring Around McCarthy." The main characters —"a heady mixture of rich men, beautiful women, and smart advisors" —included Jean Fraser Kerr; Roy Cohn; Bazy McCormick; George Sokolsky; Mr. and Mrs. William R. Hearst, Jr.; Clint Murchison and H. L. Hunt, the Texas oilmen; V. K. Wellington Koo; and Mrs. Alice Longworth, the sharp-tongued daughter of Teddy Roosevelt. At their first meeting, the story goes, Mrs. Longworth took offense at McCarthy's informal manner. "The trash man can call me Alice," she said, "and so can the clerk in the store and the policeman on the beat, but *you* may not call me Alice." Their friendship blossomed slowly.[1]

While Joe still preferred life's simpler pleasures—a good card game, a day at the track, a thick steak in the Grill Room of the Carroll Arms Hotel—he was obviously impressed by the people he met at Bazy McCormick's Maryland horse farm or the New York apartment of Richard Berlin, a well-placed Hearst executive. At one New York party, a guest recalled, McCarthy got into "a spirited discussion concerning Communists in government and the policy of our country with reference to England and other nations. He handled himself very well until the hours passed and he became slightly inebriated." By that time, however, he had picked up a couple of interesting supporters. "The Duke and Duchess of Windsor enjoyed, in fact contributed to the lively discussion," the guest noted, "and much to my edification they agreed with McCarthy."[2]

In Washington the gossip columnists perceived a major change in his life. His roving days were over. Still a bachelor, he had settled on one companion, the elegant Jean Fraser Kerr, a graduate of Northwestern University, class of 1948. He met her accidentally when she dropped by his office to visit a friend. Buzzing his secretary, he said, "Whoever that girl is, hire her!" She joined his staff a few months later.[3]

Kerr proved indispensable to McCarthy. She cleaned up his language, enlarged his wardrobe, and tried, with some success, to order his chaotic life-style. At the office she wrote press releases, did political research, and lined up potential supporters. Politicians actively sought her advice, asking Joe to "see what Jeannie thinks about this." A Washington reporter wrote: "Jeannie is the woman behind McCarthy. . . . She is no secretary or mere home critic. She is hand-in-hand with him on political policy."[4]

Above all, she was devoted to her boss and not the least bit squeamish about the methods employed to further his cause. (It was she who coordinated, and later defended, the assault upon Millard Tydings in 1950.) A Northwestern professor remembered Kerr as "an activist, a right-wing agitator" during her college days, while Ruth Watt, a close friend, described her as "a smart girl and a little hungry for publicity, too." One of the best descriptions of Kerr and McCarthy was offered by a Harvard professor who met them prior to a committee hearing on Communism in the colleges. Over dinner an argument ensued about the merits of academic freedom. Joe's remarks, the man recalled, "were extremely bright, often brilliant as far as the immediate argument was concerned. . . . But he had no long-range purpose; he was inconsistent." Kerr, on the other hand, "had no verve to her conversation. . . . But she, more than he, kept her mind on the long-range objective . . . and would see how the overall argument was going. I had the feeling that she would do far more than he to direct his ultimate objectives."[5]

———

AMONG THE SENATOR'S NEWER and more generous friends were Clint Murchison, Hugh Roy Cullen, and H. L. Hunt, the Texas oil barons. They were men of great wealth, recently acquired, who felt themselves and their empires threatened by hostile forces in Moscow, Washington, and New York. Said one oilman: "We all made money fast. We were interested in nothing else. Then this Communist business burst upon us. Were we going to lose what we had gained?"

When Texas oilmen spoke of "this Communist business" they meant a good bit more than Soviet expansion in Europe or the loyalty problem at home. They were also talking about the parallel growth of big government and domestic reform. H. L. Hunt, for example, defined anti-Communism in terms of free enterprise, racial segregation, the open shop, and Christian fundamentalism. ("It isn't that Hunt is to the right of McKinley," a friend reported. "He thinks that Communism began in this country when the government took over the distribution of mail.") Murchison's list of those "trying to ruin the American system" included the ADA, the CIO, and most of the intellectual community. A Dallas newsman put it this way: "The word Communist, at least in the Texas usage, has come to mean practically anybody the rest of us don't like—a regrettable perversion of the old-fashioned son-of-a-bitch."[6]

The pro-McCarthy sentiments of these oilmen were not difficult to understand. They applauded the senator's attacks upon the New and Fair Deals, and they identified with his self-made, rough-and-tumble image. He was, they believed, the political equivalent of a Texas tycoon —combative and opportunistic, yet God-fearing and patriotic. Hugh Roy Cullen called him "the greatest man in America."[7]

Before long, McCarthy had become something of a "third senator" to the state of Texas. He visited there frequently, keynoting the San Jacinto Day exercises in Houston and a huge Republican fund-raiser in Dallas. He vacationed at Murchison's palatial hunting lodge in Mexico and lunched at the exclusive Petroleum Club in Fort Worth. By coincidence, perhaps, he voted with the oil interests on every piece of legislation of that era, including the 27.5 percent depletion allowance, the Tidelands Oil bill (which provided for state rather than federal control of submerged oil lands on the continental shelf), and the Kerr–Thomas Gas bill (which exempted the sale of natural gas from Federal Power Commission rate regulation). When he married Jean Kerr in the fall of 1953, a group of Texans surprised the couple with a brand new Cadillac.[8]

This generosity took other forms as well. Murchison sent along $10,000 for the battle against Tydings in 1950 and $15,000 more to help defeat Benton in 1952. (Murchison claimed to have turned down Joe's request for a producing oil well.) Hugh Roy Cullen contributed $5,000— the legal limit—to the senator's reelection campaign, while H. B. Keck, president of Superior Oil, chipped in $2,500 and the use of a company plane. H. L. Hunt, the founder of "Facts-Forum," an ultra-conservative radio and television program with hundreds of local outlets, used McCarthy as a featured speaker and distributed copies of *McCarthyism: The Fight for America* to interested listeners. In 1953 Hunt added Jean Kerr and Robert E. Lee to the "Facts-Forum" payroll. "I like McCarthy," Hunt told the Washington *Post*. "His idea of getting the Reds out of the government—well, I think that's wonderful."[9]

It should be noted, however, that the sentiments of these Texas oilmen were quite apart from those of the larger business community. To equate them is a serious mistake.* The Gallup Poll, for example, showed anti-McCarthy feeling to be consistently highest among business and professional people. A straw vote taken at New York City's exclusive Links Club in June 1953 had three-quarters of the members expressing disapproval of McCarthy and predicting his early demise. *Fortune* magazine got much the same result six months later. Its survey of 253 top executives showed a clear majority opposing the senator and most of the rest "displaying unmistakable signs of boredom and impatience" with his crusade.[10]

The reasons for this opposition are not altogether clear. Some analysts, like Seymour M. Lipset, have stressed the education factor:

> The relationship between less education and support for McCarthy is consistent with what is known about the effect of education in general: higher education often makes for greater tolerance, greater regard for due process, and increased tolerance of ambiguity.
>
> The findings from the surveys with respect to occupation are what might be anticipated. . . . Nonmanual occupations that require the highest education—that is, professional and executive or managerial positions—were the most anti-McCarthy.

Others have taken the psychological approach. Businessmen were *afraid* of McCarthy. They viewed him as a rabble-rouser, a threat to the established order. His followers were irrational, status-anxious, disdainful of privilege, and jealous of those above them. His main targets were not really Communists; they were the well-dressed, well-educated managers of modern society. "In the scapegoat theory in which McCarthy thrives, the professional man is a prime target. For him, as well as for the man in a large corporation, the upsurge of a mass movement represents an implicit threat."[11]

The business community explained its opposition in simpler terms. Harry Bullis felt that McCarthy had lowered America's standing in the world. So did board chairman Philip Reed (General Electric), Paul Hoffman (Studebaker), Roger Strauss (American Smelting and Refining), and Henry Ford II. "He's hurting us abroad," Strauss complained. "I know our European friends exaggerate his importance and I've tried to tell

---

* Aside from the Texas oilmen, McCarthy enjoyed his greatest popularity in the Midwest, where business leaders were more suspicious of Eisenhower, more isolationist in outlook, and more sympathetic to Joe's assaults upon the symbols and products of Eastern breeding and prestige. When the senator appeared before the Executives' Club of Chicago in December 1953, he easily outdrew the year's previous speakers—Attorney General Brownell, General Van Fleet (just back from Korea), and Arthur Godfrey (who had the advantage of a Ladies' Day audience). Joe received a standing ovation from the crowd of 2,500. His Chicago supporters included Robert R. McCormick, publisher of the Chicago *Tribune;* Robert E. Wood, board chairman of Sears Roebuck; John McCaffery, president of International Harvester; and Earl Muzzy, president of Quaker Oats.

them so. But they've seen right-wing demagogues come into power on their own continent and it's hard to convince them the situation is different." Strauss continued, "Equally important, McCarthy's hurting the Administration. Brownell's tough and intelligent—I've known him for years and Dulles even longer. What I can't understand is why McCarthy has to keep up his haranguing, instead of letting the new Administration clean house." [12]

Here, perhaps, was the heart of the matter. Many corporation executives were "moderate" Republicans. Some had supported McCarthy's early charges. At the time they seemed plausible and politically important. But that time had passed. A new Administration had come to power, a friendly administration that had promised to root out subversives in government. Despite all this, Joe kept on attacking. He seemed oblivious to the switch. As a result many businessmen turned openly hostile. They portrayed him, in one interview after another, as a punch-drunk brawler who didn't know when to quit. "His usefulness is over. . . . He ought to be toned down. . . . Ike's doing fine. I hate to see McCarthy embarrass him." A New England merchant summed it up well: "McCarthy has served his purpose. It's too bad he can't seem to taper off." [13]

━━━━━

IN 1954 THE REVEREND ROBERT MCCRACKEN, pastor of the Riverside Church in New York City, delivered a blistering sermon on the evils of McCarthyism. His thesis was simple: To understand McCarthy one had to understand his church—a church that had "never disavowed the Inquisition, that makes a policy of censorship, that insists on conformity." McCarthyism and Catholicism were virtually synonymous. Both were narrow-minded and repressive. Both threatened traditional American liberties. [14]

This view was not that unusual. It was widely shared by the liberal Protestant clergy and by liberals in general. The 1950s were years of great religious tension in America. The Catholic population was booming; it far outnumbered any other single denomination. For some, the implications were ominous. More Catholics meant more Catholic power. More Catholic power meant more pressure for federal aid to parochial schools, more campaigns to censor objectionable books and movies, and more votes for politicians like Joe McCarthy. The signs were everywhere. Cardinal Spellman had praised the senator on numerous occasions. So had the Catholic War Veterans, the Holy Name Society of New York, the Ancient Order of Hibernians, and many powerful Catholic newspapers. The Brooklyn *Tablet* said, "Every American is burdened with the obligation of saving his country before it is too late. Write your support of Senator McCarthy NOW!" [15]

What many overlooked, however, was the limited nature of this support. It came, by and large, from old-line conservatives, those who had traditionally opposed social reform and interfaith cooperation. They were a powerful element in the Catholic community, but they were not the only element. There was a large and articulate group of anti-McCarthyites led by Bishop Sheil of Chicago, the Association of Catholic Trade Unionists, and the men and women who wrote for *Commonweal* and *America*. More significantly, there were dozens of Catholic leaders, perhaps a majority, who feared the personal or religious consequences of a donnybrook over McCarthy and chose to say nothing at all.[16]

What about the Catholic masses? According to public opinion polls, they *were* more pro-McCarthy than other Americans. The difference was generally about eight percentage points—a significant but hardly a startling disparity. In addition, the percentage of Catholics who registered strong approval for McCarthy, never rose above 21, while the percentage who registered strong disapproval ranged from 14 to 25. The clear majority was somewhere in between—holding mildly positive or negative opinions, or no opinion at all. As Father Donald Crosby has noted, the Catholic debate over McCarthy was "predominantly an affair of elites—of conservative editors, politicians, educators, business leaders, and leading clergymen—all ranged against liberals drawn largely from the same ranks. Only in New York and Boston did the Catholic masses actively support his campaign, and even in those cities a conservative elite pushed the McCarthy bandwagon fully as much as the masses followed it."[17]

To his credit, the senator rarely linked himself or his crusade to the Catholic Church. The common portrait of him dashing from one Communion breakfast to the next is outrageously false. "If anything," wrote John Cogley, a Catholic opponent, "he seemed to shy away from too-close identification with his own Church." At the same time, however, McCarthy *assumed* that Catholics were naturally sympathetic to his goals. This left him baffled and hurt by the criticism he received in the Catholic press. In 1952 he wrote the editor of *America*:

> I realize that your magazine has been extremely critical of my fight to expose Communists in government. Obviously that is your right. I am sure you will agree with me, however, that while you owe no duty to me to correct the vicious smear job which you have attempted to do on me, you do owe a heavy duty to the vast number of good Catholic people who assume that at least in a Jesuit operated magazine they can read the truth.[18]

This public letter was followed by a private one, which mixed angry criticism with a plea for support against the common enemy—atheistic Communism. (Calling himself "an ardent Catholic," McCarthy noted that his "very religious mother" had taught him "a deep and abiding respect for the priesthood.") The letter did no good. *America* continued its attacks, and McCarthy responded with public attacks of his own. Before long the dispute had become so acrimonious that the Vatican stepped in to end it. "If we look for the deeper reasons for this sad state of affairs," wrote John Baptist Janssens, Father General of the Jesuits in Rome, "we find it in the failure of the Editor of *America* to follow the precepts which my predecessor has so clearly enunciated: 'Merely political or secular matters should not be a concern of our periodical. Bitter disputes among Catholics are to be avoided even more assiduously.' Knowing these words . . . let the Father Provincial see to it that the Editor withdraws himself from the dispute immediately." [19]

America obeyed the order without protest. Its editor resigned the next year, claiming personal considerations and a desire to see new blood at the top. According to Father Crosby, "*America* said nothing more about McCarthy until his death in 1957, when it noted the senator's demise almost in passing." [20]

━━━━━━

ON THE FRINGE OF "The Ring Around McCarthy," out beyond the Cohns and Sokolskys, stood a small group of conservative intellectuals who admired the senator and gave him their articulate public support. The group was oddly mixed, containing ex-New Dealers, Ivy League patricians, and cranky former Marxists—all sharing a set of common assumptions. They believed that the nation was in great peril, that its traditional values and its global influence were rapidly declining. The problem, they felt, was one of leadership. For the past two decades America had been mismanaged by political hacks and left-wing softies who spent wildly, discouraged free enterprise, incited class conflict, babied the Soviets, and did virtually nothing to weed out and punish subversive elements at home.

These intellectuals were obsessed by matters relating to loyalty and security in government. Dismissing coexistence with Communism as morally unthinkable, they saw the West engaged in a fight to the finish —a fight in which a few well-placed traitors could play *the* decisive role. Unfortunately, the people in power did not recognize this fact. Their loyalty–security programs were ill conceived and poorly enforced; they protected the civil liberties of government workers at the expense of the national interest. "The new consequences of treason," wrote William F. Buckley and L. Brent Bozell, "will not allow us to settle for a security program based on the idea—in itself venerable—that ten suspected traitors working in the State Department should not be molested lest one of them should prove to be loyal. . . . *Justice*, we are saying, *is not the major objective here*." [21]

Some conservatives applied this standard to the legal system as well.

They were furious at the courts for allowing "known subversives" to go unpunished. The six men arrested in the *Amerasia* affair had escaped on a legal technicality; so had Judith Coplon and Owen Lattimore. Obviously, then, the standard mechanisms for dealing with subversion were ineffective. "That," said Max Eastman, the one-time disciple of Trotsky,

> is why "red baiting"—in the sense of reasoned, documented exposure of Communist and pro-Communist infiltration of government departments and private agencies of information and communication—is absolutely necessary. . . . We are not dealing with honest fanatics of a new idea, willing to give testimony for their faith straightforwardly, regardless of the cost. We are dealing with conspirators who try to sneak in their Moscow-inspired propaganda by stealth and double talk, who run for shelter to the Fifth Amendment when they are not only permitted but invited and urged by Congressional committees to state what they believe.[22]

This was where Joe McCarthy came in. Over the opposition of two Presidents and a bloodthirsty press, he had fought for loyalty–security standards tough enough to protect the country from well-camouflaged subversives. In the process he had managed to uncover a good many of them, thereby demonstrating the incredible laxity of existing security systems. Better still, he had taught the American people to see Communism for what it was—a political–military conspiracy—and to reject its claim as a legitimate reform movement, free to compete in the market place of ideas. "I myself," wrote Eastman, "after struggling for years to get this fact recognized . . . give McCarthy the major credit for implanting it in the mind of the whole nation."[23]

This did not mean that conservative intellectuals were blind to the senator's faults. Ever since Wheeling, McCarthy and his methods had been hotly debated in *The Freeman, Human Events* and other right-wing journals. Some contributors, like the flamboyant John T. Flynn, saw little to criticize. "There is no mystery about Joe McCarthy," said Flynn. "He just doesn't like Communists. . . . What is so peculiar about this point of view that it should call for an explanation?" Others, like Eastman, Buckley, and William Schlamm, freely acknowledged the senator's excesses but thought them minor in comparison with those of his liberal critics, who defended known traitors and rushed blindly to the defense of each and every one of McCarthy's targets. In Schlamm's words, the choice was really between "a young, not at all subtle, entirely self-made Midwestern politician" who sometimes made mistakes, and a bunch of "certified gentlemen" whose "atrocious misjudgments . . . have dropped ('Oops, sorry!') half of the world into irrevocable perdition."[24]

There were, however, a few conservative intellectuals who disliked and distrusted McCarthy but refused to say so in public. Foremost among them was Whittaker Chambers, the most prominent, and believable, ex-Communist witness of that era. Chambers viewed McCarthy as a living, breathing disaster—crude, self-seeking and often dishonest. He "is a bore," Chambers told a friend,

> for the same reason that Rocky Marciano . . . is a bore to people who are not exclusively interested in fist throwing. The senator is not, like Truman, a swift jabber who does his dirty work with a glee that is infectiously impish; nor, like F. D. Roosevelt, an artful and experienced ringmaster whose techniques may be studied again and again and again. . . . The senator . . . is a heavy-handed slugger who telegraphs his fouls in advance. What is worse, he had to learn from consequences or counselors that he has fouled. I know he thinks this is a superior technique that the rest of us are too far behind to appreciate.[25]

What worried Chambers were the likely consequences of such behavior. In a letter to William Buckley, he portrayed the senator as an enormously self-destructive man, quite capable of dragging down those who rallied to his side. "None of us are his enemies," Chambers explained.

> . . . But, all of us, to one degree or another, have slowly come to question his judgment and to fear acutely that his flair for the sensational, his inaccuracies and distortions, his tendency to sacrifice the greater objective for the momentary effect, will lead him and us into trouble. In fact, it is no exaggeration to say that we live in terror that Senator McCarthy will one day make some irreparable blunder which will play directly into the hands of our common enemy and discredit the whole anti-Communist effort for a long while to come.

The letter was written early in 1954—at the height of McCarthy's popularity. The Army–McCarthy hearings were just around the corner.[26]

———

DURING THE 1950S THE FRIENDS AND SUPPORTERS of McCarthy complained bitterly about the "double standard" employed by his liberal critics. In particular, they charged that the righteous people who condemned his name-calling were the same people who called him a Nazi, a jackal, and a thug; that the people who yelled loudest at his "dirty" tactics were the same people who spread rumors of his alleged homosexuality and hired spies to infiltrate his office and dredge up material about the personal habits of his aides. Needless to say, the liberal press ignored these shameful and frequently illegal acts; they were too busy portraying the senator as an enemy of democratic institutions and free society.

There is a good bit of truth to this contention. McCarthy's critics could be hypocritical and cruel. Many viewed him as the new Hitler, a man to be stopped quickly and at all costs.* The means were often

---

* For a devastating critique of this comparison, see Will Herberg, "McCarthy and Hitler: A Delusive Parallel," *The New Republic*, August 23, 1954, pp. 13–15. According to Herberg, the comparison "had begun to acquire the status of an article of faith in most liberal circles."

irrelevant; they treated him the same way that he might treat a Communist—as someone immune from the traditional forms of exposure and punishment, someone to be pursued relentlessly, beyond the boundaries imposed by fair play and sometimes by the law itself. *Commonweal* called it "McCarthyism against McCarthy."

This double standard was invoked in several ways. Among liberal journalists, it was common knowledge that the Justice Department had investigated McCarthy's sex life, tapped his office phone, and given the results to his political opponents. Somehow, these stories were allowed to die. The press showed little interest in pursuing them.

Other stories, however, were tracked down with remarkable diligence. The readers of Drew Pearson's column learned that one McCarthy staffer had been arrested during a homosexual encounter; that another had been discharged from the FBI for "fraternizing" with a prostitute; that a third had a history of mental illness. Jack Anderson looked into charges that McCarthy, as a judge in Appleton, had received $80,000 from Ralph Capone, Al's brother, to prevent the revocation of a hotel lease, and that McCarthy had frequented the Gateway resort, a hangout for organized crime figures in Wisconsin. (The charges led nowhere; they were never published.) Bob Fleming checked out rumors that Joe's staff had kicked back part of their salaries to him. In Fleming's personal files there is this additional notation: "Joe had quite a stable of girls . . . and he [an unnamed source] feels that the hotel registries in Baltimore and New York would make some interesting reading." [27]

Some newsmen searched for evidence of homosexuality. Drew Pearson had collected a file on the subject, filled with dubious affidavits from men who claimed to have had sexual relations with McCarthy. Pearson said nothing in print, preferring the cocktail grapevine instead. The rumors did not reach the newspapers until late in 1952, when Hank Greenspun published them in the Las Vegas *Sun*. According to one source, Greenspun had visited Pearson's office after his run-in with McCarthy and obtained access to the homosexual file. Returning to Nevada, Greenspun did just what Pearson expected him to do. He called the senator a homosexual. "Joe McCarthy is a bachelor of 43 years," Greenspun told his readers. "He seldom dates girls and if he does he laughingly describes it as window dressing. It is common talk among homosexuals in Milwaukee who rendezvous at the White Horse Inn that Senator Joe McCarthy has often engaged in homosexual activities. The persons in Nevada who listened to McCarthy's radio talk thought he had the queerest laugh. He has. He is." [28]

By 1953 these rumors were freely discussed on Capitol Hill. Newsmen and even senators joked about "the boys" in McCarthy's office. When a man in New York sent along his thoughts on McCarthy to the ADA, an official replied, "I was particularly interested in your response to his vulnerability as a crackpot. As you probably know, he is generally considered a homosexual in Washington." Joe never mentioned these rumors, at least not in public. Privately, however, he fretted about them and did what he could to lessen their impact. In June, *Capital–Times* editor William Evjue told Drew Pearson that the homosexual issue was causing McCarthy great pain. Evjue said that Herman Edelsberg, director of the Anti-Defamation League, had recently confirmed this after meeting with the senator:

> Edelsberg said that McCarthy opened up the discussion of the thing that was troubling him. . . . It was the homo story that was printed by . . . Hank Greenspun. . . . McCarthy asked Edelsberg if he thought it would be advisable to start a criminal libel suit against Greenspun. . . . Edelsberg pointed out that McCarthy would be compelled to take the witness stand and to refute the charges made in the affidavit of the young man, which was the basis for Greenspun's story. Edelsberg said that it was evident that McCarthy feels that the story is doing him great damage and that further damage to his reputation would be brought about in a libel suit where he would be subject to cross-examination.

Evjue concluded, "There are facts that I am sure you will want to have."[29]

The list goes on. In 1953 *The Reporter* magazine put together an entire issue on McCarthy and his staff. The lead piece, a crisp attack on Cohn and Schine, was written by Richard Rovere but researched by an army of legmen whose methods rivaled those of Scott McLeod. A Harvard student was hired to find out what he could about Schine's college days in Cambridge. He found quite a lot, although editor Philip Horton pressed him "to get more details on the business activities that Schine conducted from his Adams House room." A second researcher, working on the private lives of Cohn and Schine in Washington, was told by Horton to "look into the bellhop angle that I mentioned to you. I have always heard, up until the other day, that the two boys lived and worked out of the Mayflower." Even more remarkable was the advice Horton gave to an aide as she left to inspect transcripts of the Voice of America hearings, which had not yet been published. "I assume the only way we can help Dick [Rovere] on this," he wrote, "is for you . . . to pick a few questions and answers, with Cohn doing the questioning, which will serve Dick's purpose and which he could quote. . . . You understand, of course, that it's not a question of big chunks but of carefully selected details." *[30]

The most bizarre attempt to discredit McCarthy involved a superb

---

* To his credit, Richard Rovere ignored most of the material that was collected. His article was perceptive, meanly argued, and very amusing. See "The Adventures of Cohn and Schine," *The Reporter*, July 21, 1953, pp. 9–16; also, Cohn–Schine File, *Papers of The Reporter Magazine*, Boston University Library.

con artist named Paul Hughes and a host of collaborators, including Joseph Rauh, chairman of the ADA; Clayton Fritchie, deputy chairman of the Democratic National Committee; and Philip Graham, publisher of the Washington *Post*. Sometime in 1953 Paul Hughes arrived in Washington and applied for a job on McCarthy's staff. During his interview with Frank Carr and Don Surine, he told a fantastic story about security leaks at a U.S. air base in Saudi Arabia, where he had recently been stationed. The men listened with interest. They checked out the story, learned it was untrue, and sent Hughes on his way. McCarthy had no dealings with him.[31]

A few weeks later Hughes turned up at Clayton Fritchie's office, posing as a disillusioned McCarthy staffer. He beguiled Fritchie with stories about the senator's "illegal" activities and promised to supply the corroborating evidence—for a price. Fritchie jumped at the prospect. He advanced Hughes $2,300, took on the alias "Ewing"—Hughes chose "Junius" for himself—and sat back to await the sensational disclosures from McCarthy's files.

Paul Hughes decided to expand his operation. He went to see Joseph Rauh, again posing as a McCarthy staffer and again promising to reveal the senator's darkest secrets. This time, however, he added a new twist, telling Rauh that the job was too big for one man to handle. Hughes suggested an accomplice, his old friend Bill Decker, and Rauh agreed to pay the "expenses" of both men. By year's end Rauh had funneled $8,500 to Hughes and Decker, although Decker did not, in fact, exist. Hughes had simply made him up.

Rauh and Fritchie soon got what they wanted—a ninety-four-page report filled with "memos" and "documents" from McCarthy's files. The evidence was spectacular. There were notes of a secret White House meeting at which Eisenhower had joined McCarthy to plot Red-hunting strategy. There was a list of McCarthy "spies" on liberal newspapers (including the New York *Post*'s cooking editor). There was a report claiming that Joe kept an arsenal of machine guns, rifles, Lugers and grenades in the basement of the Senate. There was secret testimony from executive sessions of the Investigations Subcommittee.

MR. COHN: We don't expect you to produce evidence. That's our problem.

MR. KROLICK: I understand, but anything I say is just my opinion.

MR. COHN: Opinion by you, unsubstantiated or not, will allow the Committee to make accusations. After all, you may be right.

There was also a problem: Hughes had invented the whole report. Like Bill Decker, it was a figment of his imagination.[32]

Rauh did not know this, of course. The evidence *seemed* plausible, for it confirmed his worst suspicions about Cohn and McCarthy. He sent the report to his friend Philip Graham at the Washington *Post*. Graham was astonished. The report, if true, would end McCarthy's career and probably send him to jail. This was the story of a lifetime, with the *Post* in on the ground floor. Graham passed on the report to his editors, who met with Hughes and found him credible. They allegedly promised him financial aid in return for the exclusive rights to his story. Hughes agreed.

There were some comical moments. In the summer of 1954 Hughes told his collaborators that someone in McCarthy's office would soon arrive in New York to purchase classified documents from a State Department official. This was what everyone had been waiting for—the chance to catch McCarthy in an illegal act. Graham rushed over to the Justice Department, conferred with Attorney General Herbert Brownell, and promised to call him as soon as further details became available. The next day, however, Hughes reported that the meeting was off. Weaving a remarkable story, he explained that Brownell had probably alerted J. Edgar Hoover, who had likely tipped off McCarthy. "It was incredible," said Thomas Bolan, a U.S. attorney who worked on the Hughes case. "For the next few weeks, the boys at the *Post* went around cursing Brownell as an untruthworthy idiot. Hughes could get them to believe anything. He was like the Pied Piper."[33]

Despite this setback the *Post* prepared a series of twelve articles based on the Hughes report. Only then, with everything written and ready to go, did it make a routine check of the "facts" that were verifiable. Not surprisingly, the reporter assigned to this task could not locate any of the people who had furnished Bill Decker with affidavits. He told his superiors, who called Hughes and asked him to produce Bill Decker at once. When Hughes procrastinated, the series was killed and its contents were physically destroyed.

Rauh, Graham, and Fritchie seemed quite anxious to forget the whole episode. Hughes had other ideas. He now approached the Justice Department with "proof" that his former associates had once bribed a government witness to recant his previous testimony. This was serious stuff, so serious that a grand jury looked into the charge before indicting Hughes for perjury. Because Rauh and Fritchie had no choice but to testify against him, the plot against McCarthy unraveled like a ball of dirty twine.

On the witness stand Rauh portrayed himself as a victim of circumstances. His only motive, he said, was patriotism: "to expose America's leading assaulter of civil rights—Senator McCarthy." The judge seemed puzzled. Did not the witness consider it wrong to hire an employee to spy on his employer?

> MR. RAUH: It still seems to me that any serious effort to expose an illegal action is justified. I'd take the same action today.

JUDGE DAWSON: In other words, you believe that the end justifies the means.

MR. RAUH: No sir, that is a foul totalitarian tactic and I reject it.[34]

The *Post* explained its role in a single editorial:

> The staff members who interviewed Hughes on his McCarthy story behaved as careful reporters ought to behave in checking allegations against public officials. Much time was spent on this story. The time it takes to prove a story false is as well spent as the time it takes to prove a story true. Newspapers ought to be credulous in listening to charges and skeptical before printing them. This sort of credulity in the past produced the Teapot Dome story. Investigations by this newspaper led to the reform of the Washington Police Department and helped launch the Kefauver inquiry into organized crime. By the same token, the Hughes story is not the only story that our skepticism has kept out of print. Both qualities—credulity and skepticism—will, we trust, continue to be found in our staff.[35]

There was no mention that the *Post* had prepared a dozen articles *before* checking the facts. Or that it was quite content to bury the episode after learning what really happened.

For whatever reasons, the Hughes affair has been virtually ignored by students of the McCarthy era. Following the trial, Richard Rovere informed the *National Review* that he "most certainly intend[ed] to write" about the Hughes case. His biography of McCarthy, published in 1960, makes no mention of it. Nor, for that matter, do the more recent works by Lately Thomas, Fred J. Cook, Edwin Bayley, and Thomas C. Reeves. There was cause for hope when David Halberstam published *The Powers That Be,* a first-rate study of *Time,* CBS, the Washington *Post,* and the Los Angeles *Times.* Halberstam covers the relationship between the *Post* and McCarthy in great detail, giving the former a good bit of credit for humbling the latter. There is, regrettably, not one word about the remarkable case of Paul H. Hughes.[36]

CHAPTER TWENTY-ONE

A Discouraging Summer

During his years in the Senate McCarthy had lived by his own set of rules. His trademark was his arrogance. He was the guy who thumbed his nose at tradition, who baffled, infuriated, terrorized, and sometimes amused his colleagues, but who rarely won their esteem. Party loyalty did not affect him. He browbeat his elders and mocked the spirit of senatorial courtesy, the vital lubricant that allows a hundred competitive personalities to function as a civilized unit. At first this sort of behavior had worked against McCarthy. He had been stripped of his major committees in 1949 and branded as a troublemaker. But that was before Wheeling—before he captured the press, imprisoned a President, and "masterminded" the defeats of Lucas, Tydings, and Benton. By 1953 his behavior was as arrogant as ever, and far more difficult to control. He had just been reelected to a six-year term; he chaired a Senate committee and two subcommittees; he had friends in the FBI and informants in every branch of government. His position seemed relatively secure, his capacity for mischief almost unlimited.

There were some danger signs, however. For one thing, his attacks upon the new Administration had begun to alarm his Republican colleagues. For another, his assaults upon fellow members had begun to include some powerful Southerners who might otherwise have ignored him. In 1953, for example, he turned an appropriations hearing on the

State Department's Scholar-Exchange Program into a nasty donny-brook, involving most of the participants. He started by firing angry questions at William Fulbright. Were there Communist students in the program? Communist teachers? Communist books? When Fulbright objected, Joe grabbed an ashtray, banged it loudly on the table, and demanded "some answers."

SENATOR ELLENDER: Is Senator McCarthy the Chairman of the Committee?

SENATOR McCARTHY: The Chairman gave me the right to ask questions. If you object to the questions, I will be glad to hear from you.

SENATOR FULBRIGHT: Mr. Chairman, I do not know what the procedure in this Committee is. I would be perfectly willing to answer questions from all the members except the Senator from Wisconsin who I am clear is determined to destroy my testimony. I will answer his questions after I am through. . . .

SENATOR McCARTHY: May I say this to the Chair, that he allow the witness to do that with the understanding that I have to go to the Senate floor for a short period of time. . . . I do not want the witness to disappear while I am gone. He is reluctant to answer questions.

SENATOR FERGUSON: Mr. McCarthy.

SENATOR McCARTHY: May I finish?

SENATOR FERGUSON: There is no justification for saying the witness might disappear.

And, moments later:

SENATOR McCARTHY: You should not be afraid to answer these questions.

SENATOR FULBRIGHT: I am not afraid but I do not see the relevance. . . .

SENATOR McCARTHY: I have not asked for a speech. If you quit making speeches and answer my questions, we will get along better.

SENATOR McCLELLAN: He has a right to answer in his own way.

SENATOR McCARTHY: He has a duty to answer.

SENATOR McCLELLAN: I do not think we should tell a Senator that he cannot answer a question in his own way.

SENATOR McCARTHY: He has a duty to answer.

SENATOR MCCLELLAN: He has the privilege of answering your questions in his own way and I insist upon it, Mr. Chairman.

SENATOR FERGUSON: He may.

Before departing, Joe called the program "the half-bright," but said that no offense was intended.[1]

Even more disturbing were the methods he employed to get back at his Senate critics. Everything was fair game, it seemed, including their personal lives and their family problems. Just before his death in 1953 Charles Tobey told Sherman Adams, an old New Hampshire friend, that McCarthy "had enlisted the aid of enemies in our state to see if they could get anything on me for his personal use." Shortly thereafter, unfavorable stories about Tobey's son began appearing in the New Hampshire papers. Clifford Case received much the same treatment—or so he suspected. During his campaign for the Senate he had criticized McCarthy's behavior and promised to work for his removal as chairman of the Subcommittee on Investigations. In response, the Newark *Star– Ledger*, a pro-McCarthy paper, broke the story that Case's sister was a mental patient and a former member of the Communist Party. "The story was true," Case said later. "I don't know how they found out about it and I never asked McCarthy if he was directly involved. Let's just say it came from his people."[2]

This sort of behavior was particularly galling to the Senate's Republican leaders. In the majority at last, they were finding their gains threatened by a junior member whose antics were splitting the party and soiling its public image. McCarthy would not listen to reason. Only Taft and Nixon seemed able to reach him, and Taft was now too sick to try. He would soon die of cancer. Homer Ferguson had several talks with Joe, but his words were ignored. "I would go to see him," he recalled, "and Styles Bridges would go with me sometimes, and we'd say, 'Joe, talk this thing over . . .' And you know, he'd get up in the middle of a sentence and walk out and call a press conference." Bill Jenner tried his luck, but he was no more successful. "I talked to him . . . the other day," Jenner told a colleague, "and he assured me that he wouldn't make any more speeches for a while. Thirty minutes later, while I was having lunch in the Senate restaurant, I heard someone saying, 'McCarthy's up.' How can you keep a fellow like that quiet?"[3]

The answer, a formal Senate condemnation, was only a year or so away.

FROM THE MOMENT HE ASSUMED HIS CHAIRMANSHIP in 1953, McCarthy had been plagued by staff problems, largely of his own making. Haphazard by nature, he hired haphazardly, filling key positions with friends,

friends of friends, oddballs, and sycophants. In general, his staffers were loyal, hard-working, sloppy, ill-tempered, indiscreet, and powerfully jealous of one another. They would play an active role in his downfall.

Howard Rushmore left first, in the spring of 1953. There were rumors that he had been hired to lead the subcommittee's assault on unfriendly journalists, then fired when the press got wind of it prematurely. In truth, he was a victim of the staff's internecine warfare. Volatile and eccentric, he "resigned" following a series of run-ins with Cohn and Schine, whom he described as "bumbling publicity-seekers." His replacement, Karl Baarslag, the author of "How to Spot a Communist" and other right-wing tracts, was hardly an improvement. He had just quit his job as director of antisubversive activities for the American Legion, claiming, oddly, that the group was soft on Communism.[4]

Rushmore's dismissal was followed by the resignations of Francis Flanagan and Robert Kennedy. Flanagan, a Democratic holdover, was anxious to leave. Kennedy had mixed feelings. While retaining both a personal fondness and a professional respect for McCarthy, he despised Cohn and blamed him for the chairman's troubles. Most of the investigations, he complained, "were instituted on the basis of some preconceived notion by the chief counsel or his staff members and not on the basis of any information that had been developed. . . . I thought Senator McCarthy made a mistake in allowing the Committee to operate in such a fashion, told him so and resigned."[5]

On June 22, 1953, McCarthy announced that J. B. Matthews would replace Flanagan as the staff director of the subcommittee. In some ways the appointment made good sense. "Doc" Matthews was the spiritual leader of the Far Right in America. He had tutored Martin Dies and the Hearsts. He had set up the HUAC filing system. His writings—"Reds in the White House" and "Reds in Our Colleges"—had been quoted, and challenged, before numerous congressional committees. Howard Rushmore called him "the best informed man on the subject of Communism in the United States."[6]

Matthews had been feeding documents to McCarthy for years. During the Tydings investigation he had gone to Washington on "six to eight" different occasions to help prepare the cases against Jessup and Kenyon. Afterward Joe had presented him with a desk set inscribed, "To a star-spangled American, from one of his pupils and admirers." Early in 1953, when a few hundred well-wishers honored Matthews at the Waldorf-Astoria, McCarthy had given the featured address. Several of Matthews's Jewish friends were there, including toastmaster George Sokolsky, Alfred Kohlberg, and Roy Cohn. They were seated across the room from Harry Jung, publisher of *American Gentile*; Joseph Kamp, chairman of the pro-fascist Constitutional Education League; and Merwin K. Hart, executive director of American Action, a group that applauded Hitler, Franco, and white supremacy.[7]

The Matthews appointment came as a complete surprise to the other subcommittee members. They had not been consulted, despite previous complaints about the chairman's exclusive handling of personnel matters. The Democrats grumbled a bit, but they would have gone along had not Matthews's latest article, "Reds and Our Churches," appeared in the July issue of *American Mercury,* an extreme right-wing publication. It began: "The largest single group supporting the Communist apparatus in the United States is composed of Protestant clergymen."[8]

With Matthews already in the news, his charge was picked up by the wire services and given nationwide coverage. The response was dramatic; protests poured in to Congress from the Presbyterian Church, the United Lutheran Church, the National Council of Churches, and scores of Protestant clergymen. Said one Baptist leader: "It may be that some are 'pinkish.' But I don't know a single one in the Southern Baptist Convention with a pinkish tint, and I know them pretty well."[9]

In the Senate, meanwhile, the pressure to jettison Doc Matthews began to mount. Powerful Southerners, like Burnet Maybank and John Stennis, rushed in to defend the clergy. Virginia's Harry Flood Byrd described Matthews as "a cheap demagogue," a term he normally reserved for civil rights leaders. Michigan's Charles Potter urged him to resign after conferring with the Episcopal Bishop of Detroit. McClellan and Fulbright did likewise after sampling their constituent mail. As Doris Fleeson explained, "McCarthy cuts no ice in Arkansas, but the Methodists and the Baptists do." * [10]

On July 7 the subcommittee met to decide Matthews's future. Four members—McClellan, Symington, Jackson, and Potter—demanded his immediate removal. Everett Dirksen did not attend. Karl Mundt, a notorious fence-straddler, said nothing and left early. Standing alone, the Chairman seemed to waver. He defended his right to hire and fire staffers, then adjourned the meeting before a vote could be taken.

McCarthy knew that the game was over. What he needed was a way out, a way to dump Matthews without losing too much face. As usual, Richard Nixon supplied it. According to several sources, Nixon arranged a meeting of the subcommittee Republicans and worked out a compro-

---

* In his article Matthews wrote, "It hardly needs to be said that the vast majority of American Protestant clergymen are loyal to the free institutions of this country, as well as loyal to their solemn trust as ministers of the Gospel." He also wrote, "Clergymen outnumber professors two-to-one in supporting the Communist-front apparatus of the Kremlin conspiracy." He put the number of disloyal clergymen at about seven thousand. When asked how he arrived at this figure, he said, "Out of my own files. I have about a quarter-million cards listing affiliations with Communist and Communist-front organizations."

According to Roy Cohn, McCarthy was as shocked as everyone else by Matthews's allegation. McCarthy told the press that he hadn't known of the article, adding, "As a free-lance writer, Matthews wrote many articles. I have not read them and don't intend to. I do not set myself up as a censor." See J. B. Matthews, "Reds and Our Churches," *American Mercury*, July 1953, pp. 3–13, Roy Cohn, *McCarthy*, 1968, p. 59; New York *Times*, July 8 and 9, 1953.

mise in which they affirmed McCarthy's *exclusive* right to hire and fire staffers and McCarthy promised to get himself a new staff director. Doc Matthews was finished.[11]

Unbeknownst to McCarthy, the Vice-President was working behind the scenes to doublecross him. This meeting, it seemed, was part of a larger plan to force Matthews's removal while giving the White House full credit for having arranged it. On July 9—the day of the meeting—a presidential aide wrote in his diary:

> I talked with the head of the National Conference of Christians and Jews, a very intimate friend of mine. We discussed the question of sending a telegram to the White House castigating the retention of Matthews by Senator Mc-Carthy. . . . I told him that by all means we would like the telegram to be signed by three prelates, a Catholic, Jew and Protestant. I sought out Emmet Hughes . . . and discovered we were working towards the same purpose. He had been in touch with Bill Rogers, Deputy Attorney General, and they had pulled Dick Nixon into the situation.[12]

Nixon's role was crucial. He was to meet with the subcommittee Republicans, arrange for Matthews's removal, then block the news of that removal until the telegram arrived and the President could reply with a blistering public attack upon Matthews. This would make it appear that McCarthy had knuckled under, that he had fired his friend *in response* to the President's statement.

The telegram reached the White House a little behind schedule. As the reply was being drafted. Bill Rogers called Hughes from the Capitol to report that the meeting had just broken up. Hughes pleaded for time. He asked Rogers to stall McCarthy, to keep him away from the press for ten or fifteen minutes more, until the President's statement had safely reached the news ticker. This Rogers did, with a big assist from Nixon. Afterward he told Hughes:

> McCarthy wandered into Dick's office just as I put down the phone from talking with you. . . . Dick and I kept on and on asking him all kinds of thoughtful questions. . . . He even looked puzzled at our sudden interest. As he was rambling on, of course, your message got to the press, which he had no way of knowing. So as he headed for the door finally, he said with a big grin, "Gotta rush now—I want to be sure I get the news of dumping Matthews to Fulton Lewis in time for him to break it on his broadcast."[13]

It was too late, of course. By the time Joe got his news out, the President's statement had already arrived. Addressed to the Conference of Christians and Jews, it lauded America's clergymen and condemned "generalized and irresponsible attacks" upon them. McCarthy was trapped. He claimed to know nothing about the President's statement, which was true; and he insisted that it had no bearing on Matthews's removal, which also was true. But no one seemed to believe him.

McCarthy suffered yet another setback when the subcommittee Democrats challenged the compromise that had given him the exclusive right to hire and fire staffers. During an angry session on July 10, McClellan, Jackson, and Symington stormed out of the hearing room and vowed to stay away until the chairman ended his "domineering one-man rule." At first Joe refused to budge. "I will accept their resignations," he told the press. "If they don't want to take part in uncovering the graft and corruption of the old Truman–Acheson Administration they are, of course, entitled to refuse." By week's end, however, he had begun to retreat. "I sincerely hope," he wrote the Democrats, "that you will not permit such differences of opinion among us on details on housekeeping to cause you not to continue the service which you have been rendering the country. . . . The work should and must go on. It is very important to America."[14]

The Democrats did not return. (They would continue their boycott for the rest of the year.) This was remarkable. Nothing like it had ever occurred in the Senate. "Officially, publicly, and studiedly," wrote William S. White in the New York *Times*, "to boycott one's fellow senator is about as grave a step as can be imagined. To lose face in the club that is the Senate is, sometimes, actually to lose all."[15]

━━━━━

WITH THE DEPARTURE OF J. B. MATTHEWS, McCarthy added two former FBI agents to the payroll—Frank Carr as staff director and Jim Juliana as chief investigator. Carr, a quiet, moon-faced man, had supervised the Bureau's "Red Squad" in New York City; Juliana, a six-year veteran, had been his assistant. McCarthy described Carr as "the most outstanding man I have ever seen with the most outstanding record"—an accolade he normally reserved for Roy Cohn. With these newcomers on board, every major staff position—chief counsel (Cohn), assistant counsel (Surine), staff director (Carr), and chief investigator (Juliana)—was filled by a former FBI agent or a man with superb contacts inside the Bureau.

Still, the Matthews affair had been more than an embarrassment to McCarthy. It had hurt him in the Senate and tarnished the myth of invincibility so vital to his fortunes. According to the Gallup Poll, his favorable rating had dropped a few points while his unfavorable rating had climbed from 30 to 42 percent. He seemed more vulnerable and less menacing than before.

His critics began to press him hard. Mike Monroney took the Senate floor in July to read his "pan mail" from McCarthy's supporters—"You are a murderer and a traitor. Read this, fall dead"—and to belittle Cohn and Schine as "Keystone Kops." When Joe called the remark "a flagrant example of anti-Semitism," Herbert Lehman rushed to Monroney's defense. "I—a Jew, sensitive to any religious bias—have been strongly critical of the behavior of these young men," he said, "and have pointed out that they have been doing our country and the cause of anti-Communism great harm both home and abroad." The last word came from B'nai B'rith, which expressed "shock" at McCarthy's charge and described Monroney as "a first-class human being."[16]

The news from Wisconsin was not much better. For the first time a fair number of Joe's allies had begun to criticize his behavior and to question his value as a legislator. A close friend admitted, "He has given less than ordinary congressional service to the state that he represents. . . . If his sedition-in-government issue ever subsides—as it must under a government of his own party—he will have a thinner record than most to show to the people of his own constituency."[17]

In July McCarthy committed a serious blunder at home. To the astonishment of his friends in Appleton, he assaulted the character of Nathan Pusey, a popular native son, after learning that Pusey had resigned as president of Lawrence College in Appleton to accept the same post at Harvard University. The two men had never gotten along; Pusey, in fact, had opposed the senator's reelection in 1952. Now, to even the score, McCarthy told reporters that Appleton was fortunate to be rid of the phony, snobbish, and unpatriotic Mr. Pusey. "I don't think Pusey is or has been a member of the Communist Party," he added, "but he is a rabid anti-anti-Communist." *[18]

McCarthy had no idea that his remarks would offend the people of Appleton. He assumed that his opinion of Pusey was the generally accepted one in town. When a local businessman wrote him to say he had "let down so many old friends," Joe responded by telegram: "Curious to know which old friends are being let down by the exposure of bigoted, intolerant, mudslinging enemy of mine." He soon found out. In a blistering editorial, the Appleton *Post–Crescent* wrote: "By stating 'I do not think Dr. Pusey is or has been a member of the Communist Party,' McCarthy has used a gutter-type approach. He could have referred as correctly to Pope or President. It is an insult not only to Dr. Pusey, but to all who know him and are proud to call him friend."[19]

Although McCarthy did not apologize for his remarks, he did try to smooth things over when he next returned to Appleton. "He placed a call to the *Post–Crescent* from my house," Urban Van Susteren recalled. "He spoke with the editor, John Riedl, an old friend of his. I remember he started off with, 'Hello, John, this is Joe McCarthy. I hear you're looking for a new editorial writer and I'd like to apply for the job.' Well,

---

* Pusey was also a sponsor of *The McCarthy Record*, a campaign pamphlet documenting the senator's many misstatements and tangled financial transactions. Joe knew this, of course; what he didn't know was that Pusey had told friends that McCarthy carried a copy of *Mein Kampf* on his person, often quoting his favorite sections in the barber shops and boarding houses around Appleton. See, for example, Dean Acheson, *Present at the Creation*, 1969, p. 370.

Reidl liked Joe and forgave him. I personally thought Pusey was a spine-less bastard, but a lot of people saw him as a local fellow who made good, just like McCarthy. They were mad as hell."[20]

IN THE SUMMER OF 1953 a Washington reporter observed that McCarthy had adopted the motto of the French revolutionary Danton: "Audacity, more audacity, always audacity." This observation came in the wake of the Matthews episode, when the senator, counterpunching as usual, threw out a flurry of new charges. He alleged, falsely, that several State Department officials had "shaken down" a Latin American government for $150,000. He hinted, erroneously, that Lavrenty Beria, Stalin's for-mer aide, had fled Russia and might soon testify before his committee. On July 9 he attacked the CIA and said he would begin an investigation of its lax security problems. That was big news indeed.

Many viewed the probe as little more than a smokescreen, a way of diverting attention from his recent failures. This was true enough, al-though McCarthy had been collecting information about the CIA for quite some time. The "leads" came from FBI officials who feared the growth of a rival intelligence unit; congressional conservatives who dis-trusted the "Ivy League crowd" at the CIA; and disgruntled employees, past and present, who spoke of rampant homosexuality and Red-thinking in the ranks. In 1952 Walter "Beetle" Smith, the outgoing director, tes-tified that Communist agents had probably infiltrated the CIA—a fun-damental assumption, no doubt, but a public relations mistake. Furthermore, the Agency *had* become a refuge for liberals and foreign policy "free-thinkers" in government. Its "covert action" included large subsidies to the non-Communist left in Europe and elsewhere—the sort of thing the State Department might have administered had the political climate been different at home. As one CIA officer explained: "In the early 1950s . . . the idea that Congress would have approved many of our projects was about as likely as the John Birch Society's approving Medicare."[21]

By 1953 the CIA's inspector general, Lyman Kirkpatrick, had been dubbed the "McCarthy Case Officer." It was Kirkpatrick's job to oversee the security program and to keep the "McCarthy Underground" from penetrating the Agency staff. "Within the CIA," he recalled, "we had cases where individuals would be contacted by telephone and told it was known that they drank too much, or were having an 'affair,' and that the caller would make no issue of this if they would come around and tell everything that they knew about the Agency." In order to halt this pen-etration, Director Allen Dulles, John Foster's brother, told a gathering of 600 CIA officers that he would stand by them in time of trouble—and fire anyone who called on McCarthy without seeing him first.[22]

In 1953 the CIA man in trouble was William P. Bundy, an assistant to one of the deputy directors. Well bred, the product of Groton and Yale, he had come to Washington as a corporation lawyer and entered government service at the request of Allen Dulles himself. "There was a tendency in Bill Bundy, when challenged," a journalist wrote, "to rely even more on his background, to seem even more the snob." He was, in this respect, a good bit like Dean Acheson, his father-in-law. [23]

In a personal letter to Allen Dulles, McCarthy laid out the charges against Bundy:

1. That he contributed $400 to pay for the defense of Alger Hiss
2. That he was active in at least one organization which had been officially named as a front doing the work of the Communist Party

"If the facts are true," he concluded, "then I am sure you will agree that Mr. Bundy should not be holding a top job in the CIA." [24]

The facts were true, though not very meaningful. In the summer of 1940 Bundy had joined the United Public Workers Union, attended one meeting, and quit shortly thereafter. At the time of his membership— which McCarthy described as "active"—the union had not been officially listed as a Communist front. That came six years later. As for the other charge, Bundy had donated $400 to the Alger Hiss Defense Fund before joining the CIA. He had done so because he admired Alger's brother, Donald, a former law partner, and because he wanted Alger to have the best defense that money could buy. "We had some knowledge of the Sacco–Vanzetti Case in my family," Bundy said later, "and I thought it important that Hiss had a good lawyer the first time around." [25]

These charges were well known at the CIA. Bundy had told a department loyalty board about them, and the board had accepted his explanation. The problem was that the charges were also known at the FBI. "And I am as sure as anything," Bundy said, "that J. Edgar Hoover walked the file over to McCarthy's office the moment he got it. That's how charming a fellow he was." [26]

A good guess, indeed. In 1953 the Bureau had composed and forwarded a background report on Harvey Bundy and his children McGeorge, William, and Katherine—all of whom had been checked previously by the FBI upon entering government service. On July 9 Roy Cohn called the CIA to demand Bundy's immediate appearance before the subcommittee. "I'm calling you first," he told Walter Pforzheimer, the legislative counsel. "The son-of-a-bitch has contributed to the Alger Hiss Defense Fund. . . . Get him up here." [27]

Allen Dulles was alarmed. He knew how McCarthy operated, how one case led to another and suddenly the whole fort was under attack. It had happened to his brother at the State Department, and it seemed to be happening again. On July 10 Dulles met with the Republican members of the subcommittee. He told them that Bundy had been checked and double-checked as to loyalty, and that he would not be permitted to testify. Joe replied that he would *force* Bundy to testify, that the CIA was neither sacrosanct nor immune from investigation. After the meeting Allen called John Foster at the State Department. He described "the bout" as "something of a draw," adding that McCarthy "was in an ugly mood having been slapped down pretty hard yesterday" in the Matthews affair.[28]

Dulles then approached Richard Nixon, who took it from there. Over lunch with the subcommittee members, the Vice President portrayed the CIA as a unique entity—not sacrosanct, perhaps, but beyond the scope of a well-publicized investigation. "I enlisted their support," Nixon recalled, "and McCarthy with obvious reluctance agreed to drop his investigation of Bundy and the CIA.*[29]

There followed the inevitable statement to the press. This one lauded the cooperation and restraint of the parties, adding that McCarthy would "forgo" the subpoena and turn over his information to Allen Dulles, who would evaluate it and take whatever action he deemed necessary. (Dulles, of course, had already evaluated the information and deemed it worthless.) Afterward Joe described the agreement as "neither a victory nor a defeat," but the press knew better. McCarthy's explanation, said one newsman, "reads like the Nazi communiques of World War II that talked of advances to the rear." Said another: "Senator Joseph R. McCarthy has just suffered his first total, unmitigated, unqualified defeat."[30]

Actually, the episode did not end here. In the following weeks Joe peppered Dulles with requests for more information about the Bundy case—and Dulles politely said no. On August 3 McCarthy sent his final letter (written, ominously, on the stationery of the Senate Appropriations Committee):

> Your insistence that Congress is not entitled to obtain information about improper conduct on the part of your top officers is extremely revealing. . . . I think it is unnecessary for me to call attention to the tremendous damage you thereby do this organization. That the matter cannot and will not rest here is, of course, obvious.[31]

---

* Besides enlisting their support, Nixon also twisted their arms. He told them that Allen Dulles had the firm backing of President Eisenhower and the National Security Counsel. Ironically, Dulles's position was widely praised in the media, especially among the liberal newspapers which would heavily criticize "CIA secrecy" in the 1970s. Of the prominent columnists, only Walter Lippmann and Hanson Baldwin questioned the Dulles position. "Secrecy," Lippmann wrote, "is not a criterion for immunity. . . . The argument that the CIA is something apart, that it is so secret that it differs in kind from the State Department or for that matter . . . the Department of Agriculture, is untenable." Washington *Post,* July 21, 1953.

Lippmann's column upset Allen Dulles, and Dulles told him so in a four-page, single-spaced personal letter. The CIA *was* something apart, Dulles contended. "The mere disclosure that a particular person is working for us may destroy an entire operation. This has already happened to us in connection with other congressional investigations. . . . When I get back and you return to Washington, we can talk this over." Allen Dulles to Walter Lippmann, August 7, 1953, *Allen Dulles Papers,* Princeton University.

This time Dulles did not bother to reply. He took the letter for what it was—an angry parting shot—and filed it away.

———

IN AUGUST McCARTHY BEGAN AN INVESTIGATION of security leaks at the Government Printing Office, a huge operation that serviced the needs of Congress and the executive agencies. With the Democratic members still on strike and Mundt and Potter out of town, only Everett Dirksen remained to lend a hand. McCarthy noted that Dirksen had canceled some "important engagements" to participate in the inquiry and that he himself had canceled a junket to Ireland. This was serious business, he said. It demanded their immediate attention.

The GPO's security problems were already well known to the FBI. In the 1940s the Bureau had compiled an impressive dossier on one Edward Rothschild, a GPO bookbinder, who was named by several sources as a Communist and a possible espionage agent for the Soviet Union. Rothschild, it seemed, had freely handled "secret" and "top secret" documents from the Departments of State and Defense and had once been accused of pilfering a secret code of the Merchant Marine. Remarkably, the GPO's loyalty board had cleared him on four separate occasions without ever questioning his accusers. It had relied on Rothschild's repeated denials, nothing more. In 1953 the FBI leaked the Rothschild file to McCarthy, who promised to get it the attention it deserved. He did just that, calling the situation "fantastic," "unbelievable beyond words," and possibly "worse than the Hiss case." He even hinted that the secrets of the atomic and hydrogen bombs had been compromised, but he backed off when the Atomic Energy Commission said that its classified documents were not printed at the GPO.[32]

McCarthy had a field day at the public hearings, which opened on August 17. He called a series of witnesses, who identified Mr. and Mrs. Rothschild as Communists, and then the Rothschilds, who took the Fifth Amendment on virtually every question. "Your refusal to answer is telling the world that you have been selling secrets and you have been engaged in espionage," the chairman snapped. Next came the GPO officials who had cleared Rothschild at the loyalty hearings. Said McCarthy, "The FBI reports showed that the Rothschilds were Communists. They showed that he was stealing papers. . . . Why was he working in the Government Printing Office until yesterday? Man, you had the FBI report! What more did you need?"[33]

A surprise witness then appeared, an elderly printer named Carl Lundmark. "Do you operate a horserace betting parlor within the GPO?" he was asked. "Under the Fifth Amendment," Lundmark replied, "I decline to answer that question on the ground the answer may tend to incriminate me." As the spectators laughed and applauded, the chairman said that his investigators had uncovered a major gambling ring at the GPO. This was serious, he went on, for gambling could easily subject a government worker to blackmail. Outside the hearing room, Lundmark told a reporter, "I'm in a bad spot. My son owns some race horses. When I went to the track I sometimes took some bets for the boys. That's why it was done." [34]

When the hearings ended, the GPO announced that it was returning to "a wartime security status." Rothschild and Lundmark were quickly suspended; the loyalty board was fired en masse. At the White House the situation was analyzed and dismissed as hopeless. As one aide confided in his diary:

> August 24, 1953. . . . I did a little checking up on the GPO. . . . It was a mess and after talking the matter over with the vice-president, we both concluded that the smartest thing to do was to stay away from it as most of the damage was done and not much could be done to rectify the situation, except to pull the White House into it. This, of course, was the last thing in the world that I wanted to do. [35]

In general, the press accounts of the hearings were straightforward and favorable to McCarthy. While noting his exaggerations, they applauded him for exposing a major security problem and for respecting the rights of the witnesses he had called. There were, however, a few nagging questions, which related primarily to the behavior of the main witness, Edward Rothschild. It was known that Rothschild had testified freely at an earlier closed-door session of the subcommittee. Why, then, did he turn around and take the Fifth Amendment at the public hearings? It didn't make sense.

Years later, Rothschild's attorney offered a startling explanation for his client's change of heart. The attorney, Stanley B. Frosh, now a Maryland judge, described the events this way: "That August I got a call from Edward Rothschild. I had never met him before. He told me about his trouble and asked me if I would accompany him to a closed-door hearing of the subcommittee. I said I would. When we got to the hearing room, Cohn and Schine and McCarthy and some others were already there. There were no spectators. I remember that Cohn came up to me and said, 'Take my advice and get out of this. You're only going to get hurt. We've got your client dead to rights.' "

Frosh continued: "For the next half hour or so, McCarthy and Cohn asked Rothschild all sorts of questions about his past. Rothschild answered without hesitation. He denied that he was a Communist. When the hearing broke up, there was a big crowd outside, many, many reporters. I heard McCarthy tell them that he knew of two top Communists who had access to secret documents from the Atomic Energy Commission. I remember thinking, 'God, he can't mean the Rothschilds, can he?'

"The next day Rothschild was subpoenaed to appear at the public hearings. I then called McCarthy's office and asked to see the transcript of Rothschild's previous testimony. They said it wasn't ready yet but they'd let me see it before Rothschild testified again. I finally got a call which told me to come to a small basement office in the Capitol that very afternoon. When I arrived, one of McCarthy's boys told me to read the transcript there; I could not take it from the room. Well, the transcript was *very different* from the way Rothschild had testified. In the transcript, Rothschild admitted knowing people and meeting people who, I assume, were Communists. But he had never admitted these things at the closed-door hearing. The transcript had been altered.

"I knew then that Rothschild had been set up. If he testified at the public hearing that he didn't know these Communists, he could be accused of perjury because his earlier testimony would show that he *had* admitted knowing them. It would be our word against that of everybody else who was in the room. I immediately called Charles E. Ford, a prominent Washington attorney who had represented other witnesses before congressional committees. Ford agreed to come along with Rothschild and me to the public hearing. When we got there, I tried to make a statement but McCarthy told me, in effect, to sit down and shut up. We then advised Rothschild to take the Fifth Amendment on all questions. It was the only way we could protect him from perjury.

"Of course Rothschild was suspended from his job. But he was never prosecuted, which I found odd given the serious charges against him. He went to work as a counterman at a delicatessen in Bethesda, Maryland. To this day, I have no idea whether he was a Communist. He told me he wasn't, but I don't really know." [36]

———

THE AUTUMN BROUGHT SOME HAPPY NEWS. On September 23, Joe married Jeannie Kerr, his longtime aide, at St. Matthew's Cathedral in Washington. After the ceremony the groom, attired in striped pants and a morning coat, worked his way through a crowd of 2,500 well-wishers, helped his bride into a limousine, and sped off to a reception at the plush Washington Club on DuPont Circle. The guest list of one thousand contained many old friends from Outagamie County and some of the biggest names in America. Eisenhower sent his regrets, saying that he had to entertain the president of Panama. But the Administration was well represented by Vice President and Mrs. Richard Nixon, Sherman Adams, Attorney General Herbert Brownell, Postmaster General Arthur Summerfield, and, to most everyone's surprise, Allen Dulles and Harold Stassen. Other guests included Jack Dempsey; Joe Kennedy and his children John, Pat, and Robert; Senators Barry Goldwater, Bourke Hicken-looper, Theodore Green, Karl Mundt, and Irving Ives; Roy Cohn, G. David Schine, and Louis Budenz. "It was a beautiful ceremony," Nixon said. "The bride was lovely. But then I've never seen a bride who wasn't." [37]

The wedding—like everything else involving McCarthy—generated a good deal of controversy. The press wondered about the guest list. Why had so many Administration officials been invited? Was McCarthy trying to patch up his differences with the White House? (He was, for the moment.) And why had Bill Jenner stayed away? Was he angry at Joe for invading his territory in the Senate? (He was very angry.) Many liberals were disturbed because Pope Pius XII had sent a cablegram imparting his "paternal apostolic blessing" to the couple. Was this a routine gesture or did it imply indirect Vatican approval of McCarthy's political activities? (It was a routine gesture.) And what of the marriage itself? Had the senator timed it to offset his declining political fortunes? Or to squelch rumors of homosexuality that had begun to surface? The speculation was endless.

After spending their wedding night in Washington, the McCarthys left for a three-week honeymoon at Spanish Key in the British West Indies. The only communication there was by radio. Joe gave the call number to Roy Cohn and instructed him to use it only in an emergency. A week later, Cohn radioed Spanish Key and told of sensational developments in a new probe of the Army Signal Corps at Fort Monmouth, New Jersey. The McCarthys caught the next plane home.

CHAPTER TWENTY-TWO

The Monmouth Hearings

FORT MONMOUTH, NEW JERSEY, an hour's drive south from Manhattan, was the main research center for the U.S. Army Signal Corps. Its laboratories—on the base and in the surrounding communities of Red Bank and Belmar—employed some of the best scientists and engineers in America. Their projects included the development of new power sources, guided missile controls, and ground radar systems. One observer described Fort Monmouth as "more vital" to America's security than the Los Alamos atomic testing grounds. "In the latter," he explained, "weapons are developed to attack the enemy. In the former are developed those instruments of defense calculated to protect us from the enemy's weapons."[1]

The concern over security and possible espionage at Monmouth did not begin with Joe McCarthy. Ever since World War II, the Army and the FBI had been investigating reports of a major spy ring on the premises. Julius Rosenberg had been a Signal Corps employee from 1940 until his suspension in 1945; he had visited the base on numerous occasions. So had Joel Barr and Alfred Salant, two likely Soviet agents who fled the country in the late 1940s. And Morton Sobell, tried and convicted with Rosenberg for conspiracy to commit espionage, had been employed as an electronics engineer by the Reeves Instrument Company, which did classified work for the Signal Corps.

In 1951 the FBI forwarded the names of thirty-five possible "security risks" to Army Intelligence in Washington. The following year a group of Monmouth security officers complained openly about "Communist talk" and "espionage" at the fort. Though the Chicago *Tribune* made much of these allegations, the congressional Red-hunters did not. For the moment they accepted the Army's statement that "a thorough investigation" had uncovered "no evidence of subversive activities in the Signal Corps."[2]

In 1953 President Eisenhower issued Executive Order 10450, which called for the reinvestigation of federal workers who had "derogatory information" in their files. By August the thirty-five Monmouth "security cases" were all under review. Most of them involved civilian workers who had been suspended and cleared by the Army in previous years.

The order reopened some old and ugly wounds at Monmouth. For years the base had been a refuge for Jewish engineers who faced severe discrimination in private industry. Most came from the New York metropolitan area. Many had attended City College, a hotbed of left-wing political activity. Some had joined the Young Communist League; others had gone to a meeting or two without joining; still others had friends or relatives who participated in radical causes. Conversely, the Monmouth area was rural and conservative, with a history of religious intolerance. There had been numerous cross-burnings in the 1920s, pro-Hitler rallies in the 1930s, and hate mail campaigns in the 1950s. Many Jews believed that anti-Semitism was rampant at Fort Monmouth, particularly within the security staff and its grapevine of civilian informers. A civilian engineer complained: "If, say, one William Kunnigan, white, Protestant, is reported through the informer system on five counts, he may escape without punishment of any sort. But let Abraham Garfinkel be reported on the same five counts, he would be immediately picked up and would receive a letter of interrogation asking him to answer the charges made against him."[*][3]

The role played by anti-Semitism in the security process is difficult to evaluate. Some Jews at Monmouth were cleared for top secret work. Yet Jewish workers, who comprised less than 30 percent of the civilian workforce, were involved in more than 90 percent of the suspensions and dismissals. The Pentagon did its best to downplay these statistics. In response to numerous queries by the Anti-Defamation League, it issued

---

* The number of similar complaints was staggering. One Jewish worker charged that the Monmouth security force was run by "crackpots and anti-Semites." Another said, "Finally it happened! A Catholic at Fort Monmouth was threatened with suspension as a security risk and forced to resign." A third said, "There is a large amount of religious and national prejudice among all faiths. . . . The prejudices are intensified, I believe, by the obvious anti-Semitic slant of the loyalty–security program." See the various letters and affidavits in the "McCarthy–Fort Monmouth File," *Paul Tillett Papers*, Princeton University.

a statement saying it was "unable to establish that religious bias had a bearing upon the activities of . . . personnel responsible for initiating or processing of security cases." No details were released.[4]

THROUGHOUT THE SUMMER OF 1953, McCarthy's office had been receiving a steady flow of information about security problems at Fort Monmouth and other military bases. The information had come from a variety of sources, including the FBI, the right-wing press, and the Loyal American Underground. In general, it portrayed the Army's security system as a pathetic entity, mired in red tape and dominated by screening boards that were hopelessly incompetent. According to some reports a potential security risk had a better chance of being promoted than he did of being discharged.*

When Congress reconvened in the fall, McCarthy was eager, if somewhat ill prepared, to investigate these reports. His first hearing, on September 8, was a modest affair, highlighting the subversive activities of three civilian workers, the most controversial of whom "had access to invoices and requisitions which would indicate where food was being shipped at various Army bases." Despite his thin material, or perhaps because of it, the chairman worked up a terrific head of steam. He was "shocked beyond words" by the Army's failure to discharge these workers. It was "the most unusual, the most unbelievable, the most unexplainable situation" he had ever come across.[5]

While otherwise pointless, the hearing did offer an accurate preview of the treatment that awaited Army personnel who would testify at future sessions. In this instance, the unfortunate witness was General Miles Reber, chief of the Pentagon's legislative liaison office. Reber had information that McCarthy wanted—specifically, the names of those who had voted to clear the three civilian employees. Reber politely refused to divulge these names, citing the Truman directive of 1948: "No information shall be supplied as to any specific steps or . . . actions taken in processing individuals under loyalty or security programs."

---

* Taken together, the Malmedy probe, the Marshall speech, and the Monmouth investigation have led some historians to speculate about McCarthy's "irrational hatred" of the U.S. Army. See, for example, Fawn Brodie's chapter on McCarthy in *Richard Nixon: The Shaping of His Character*, 1981. What is overlooked, of course, are the *political* motives behind these assaults. McCarthy's role in Malmedy was supported by many German–Americans in Wisconsin and by newspapers like the Appleton *Post–Crescent*, the Green Bay *Press–Gazette*, and the Chicago *Tribune*. His attack upon Marshall undoubtedly *enhanced* his standing among the more reactionary elements in the Republican Party. And the investigation of the Army Signal Corps was begun by Roy Cohn and other staffers who had personal motives of their own. McCarthy's interest in the probe came later. It was fueled by a number of factors: the immediate (and generally favorable) reaction of the media, the obvious anxiety expressed by Administration officials, and the senator's blind devotion to Cohn and the subcommittee staff.

THE CHAIRMAN: Do you think we should or should not have the names of those who clear Communists?

GENERAL REBER: . . . may I say, as sincerely and honestly as I possibly can, that the Department of the Army . . . is doing everything in its power to eliminate any possibility of Communist infiltration into the Army. . . .

THE CHAIRMAN: I might say . . . your general statement that you are doing everything you can to remove Communists does not mean too much. I read those statements by Dean Acheson. . . . I personally went out and promised the people from coast to coast that if they would vote to get rid of the Achesons, there would be a new day down here. There would be no longer the old cover-up. That no matter how much it hurt, we would expose those responsible for Communism and treason. We have a test of that now whether we are going to continue following the order which you read, which is a Truman order, or not.[6]

Two weeks later the chairman held a quick one-man session on the subject of "Communist infiltration in the Army." He presented no suspects this time, only an Army training book used by the intelligence division "to develop an understanding of the Soviet people . . . in case of war." McCarthy did not like the book; neither did Louis Budenz or Igor Bogolepov, the "expert" witnesses he called to evaluate its contents.

THE CHAIRMAN: Do I understand that it is your testimony that you found the same material in this Army intelligence document, practically word for word, that you find in the Soviet bible, if you call it that, *The Problems of Leninism?*

MR. BOGOLEPOV: That is right.

. . .

THE CHAIRMAN: . . . Would you say that any military man or anyone who read that document put out under the approval of our military, would get a completely false picture of Communism?

MR. BUDENZ: Yes, sir. He would get the picture that would be desired by the Communist conspiracy. . . .

McCarthy also questioned General Richard Partridge, chief of Army Intelligence, and Samuel McKee, his civilian consultant. Both men defended the book, although neither one seemed to know much about it.

THE CHAIRMAN: . . . Do you know that this book quotes verbatim from Joe Stalin, without attributing it to him, as the stamp of approval of the United States Army? Are you aware of that?

GEN. PARTRIDGE: I don't know that it quotes from Joe Stalin or not.

THE CHAIRMAN: Don't you think you are incompetent to testify before you know that?

GEN. PARTRIDGE: No, sir.

· · ·

THE CHAIRMAN: . . . Do you think this should be withdrawn or continued in use?

MR. MCKEE: I do not think it should be withdrawn, sir.

THE CHAIRMAN: I sincerely hope you are withdrawn because you are certainly incompetent to hold a job in intelligence.*[7]

Behind the scenes, however, the McCarthy forces were working on a much larger project: "Subversion and Espionage in the Signal Corps." At first glance the material did not appear to be especially fresh or impressive; it was, in fact, the same stuff the Chicago *Tribune* had been peddling for years. Why, then, this burst of interest in 1953? The reason is simple: Roy Cohn knew that the Army was reviewing the Monmouth security cases under Executive Order 10450. Indeed, the major item of review—the 1951 FBI list—was sitting on his desk.

How it got there is a matter of dispute. Willard Edwards recalled that it came directly from the FBI. Roy Cohn told a different story. In 1953 an Army Intelligence officer

> . . . made a telephone call . . . to our subcommittee and asked if he could meet with the Senator. A secret meeting was arranged, at which he told McCarthy he was "disgusted" and "alarmed" because nothing was being done about a memorandum the FBI had sent to the Army. . . . He handed it over to the senator, who turned it over to the investigative staff.

In early October the Chicago *Tribune* broke the "new" Monmouth story on page one. Written by Willard Edwards, it began: "Two of the

---

* What disturbed McCarthy, Budenz, and Bogolepov was the fact that in places the book portrayed the Soviet citizenry as generally supportive of the Communist regime. "The people are extremely patriotic," it said at one point, "and tend to approve of the present government because it has made Russia a world power and was able to defeat the Germans." However, a more objective reader could hardly have overlooked the fact that the book was strongly anti-Communist in tone. When speaking of the Soviet worker, it said, "He has no voice in determining his place of work, working conditions or wages. His only advantage over the convict is that he can live with his family and can spend his limited income as he sees fit. He has no redress against a harsh authoritarian government. He is forbidden to raise his voice in criticism. . . . His voting rights are a travesty on the ideas and purpose of democracy. . . . He is the helpless prisoner of a slave state." And it concluded: "In the event of a general war, it will become the mission of the free people of the west to overcome the menace of Communism and to convert the victimized people of the U.S.S.R. and other Communist nations." A copy of the book is found in the appendix of the hearing. See "Psychological and Cultural Traits of Soviet Siberia," pp. 44–77.

nation's top scientists engaged in the development of America's radar secrets against enemy attack have been suspended by the Army as security risks." Edwards added that others were under investigation and that Army Secretary Robert T. Stevens was cooperating with McCarthy in a full-scale probe of the Monmouth installation.

On October 10 Roy Cohn sent the dramatic SOS that ended McCarthy's honeymoon at Spanish Key. Two days later the chairman flew to New York City to begin a series of hearings on the "extremely dangerous espionage" his staff had uncovered at the radar laboratories. Cohn, Schine, and Carr were already in town, lining up witnesses and even holding a press conference to offer their unanimous opinion that they had nothing to say. The hearings were scheduled at the Federal Courthouse in Foley Square—the same courthouse in which Julius and Ethel Rosenberg had been tried, convicted, and sentenced to death for passing atomic secrets to the Russians.[8]

The hearings lasted for several weeks. After each session, McCarthy would emerge from the guarded chamber to give the press its daily headline. On October 14 he charged that America's top radar secrets had been stolen by enemy agents ("PAPERS MICROFILMED, SENT TO EAST GERMANY"). The next day he spoke of a "Rosenberg Spy Ring" at Monmouth and warned that it "may still be in operation" ("EXECUTED SPY BARED AS HEAD OF RADAR RING"). On October 17 he claimed that a vital witness had cracked under Roy Cohn's potent cross-examination and agreed "to tell the truth." The press caught a glimpse of the fellow as he left the hearing room to seek medical attention. He was shaking with fright ("RADAR WITNESS BREAKS DOWN: WILL TELL ALL ABOUT SPY RING").[9]

Witnesses came and went by the dozen. Some were Monmouth employees; others were not. Some had known Julius Rosenberg; others had not. Some took the Fifth Amendment; others did not. The picture seemed dangerous yet terribly confused. And each day brought a staggering rush of new information. On October 20 McCarthy announced that his top investigator, James Juliana, had gone to West Germany to interrogate a Communist defector who knew all about the radar secrets developed at Monmouth. Soon this story was overshadowed by news that Cohn and Schine had arrived at the federal prison in Lewisburg, Pennsylvania, to interview David Greenglass, the brother of Ethel Rosenberg.* They returned with a statement that supposedly "removed any lingering doubts that Russian agents stole America's radar secrets from the Signal Corps."[10]

McCarthy left New York on October 24 for a quick speaking tour of

* Greenglass had admitted his guilt in the "atomic conspiracy." He testified for the government against his sister and his brother-in-law. He was sentenced to fifteen years in prison.

the Midwest. Before departing, he promised that open hearings—"show-down sessions," he called them—would begin sometime in November. Most everyone thought this a good idea. As Drew Pearson noted, "Joe McCarthy will almost drop dead when he reads this, but in my opinion he is absolutely right in probing the leaks of Signal Corps radar secrets at Fort Monmouth. Furthermore, he is absolutely right in saying that the leaks go back about ten years. Actually, they go back even further."[11]

———

ARMY SECRETARY ROBERT TEN BROECK STEVENS was less enthusiastic about McCarthy's future plans. He, too, had been disturbed by the security problems he found at Monmouth. But he felt that things were now under control: The problems had been identified and the proper measures had been taken to rectify them. To his thinking, a public investigation would be disastrous. It would panic the country without uncovering anything that the Army did not already know.

There were personal reasons as well. Stevens had arrived in Washington only months before, with orders to streamline the Army, to cut costs without cutting fire power or fighting morale. The job had not been easy. He had clashed with Congress over charges of an ammunition shortage in Korea. And he had alienated many career officers, who resented his attempts to satisfy a budget-conscious Administration at their expense. By the time he came up against McCarthy, Bob Stevens was already in trouble. Showdown sessions were exactly what he hoped to avoid.

Stevens was often described as a cheerful, unspectacular man who believed in team play and loyalty to his superiors. Born to wealth, schooled at Andover and Yale, he had joined the family textile business after returning from military service in World War I. Under his leadership the already prosperous J. P. Stevens Company had emerged as one of the giants in its field, with annual sales of $300 million by 1950. At his confirmation hearing Stevens had raised some eyebrows by initially refusing to divest himself of his stock in the firm, despite its long and lucrative relationship with the Army. "I am steeped in sentiment and tradition with respect to the company that bears my father's name," he told the Armed Services Committee. He capitulated, reluctantly, after the Senate brushed aside his promise to dissociate himself from all decisions affecting the Stevens concern. In the words of one charitable observer, "The troubles of Robert T. Stevens . . . are a symbol of a problem that has dogged the Eisenhower Administration from its beginning—the problem of the well-meaning businessman who suddenly must cope with the political hazards of Washington."[12]

Stevens first learned of McCarthy's intentions on Labor Day, 1953, while vacationing at his 10,000-acre cattle ranch near Great Falls, Montana. He read in the local paper that the Subcommittee on Investigations had uncovered a "disturbing situation" within the Army's civilian work force. Immediately he wired McCarthy: "Am returning to Washington. . . . Will call your office to offer my services in trying to assist you to correct anything that may be wrong." Stevens met with McCarthy on September 8 and promised him his full cooperation. Three weeks later, with Cohn and Carr at his side, the Secretary phoned General Kirke B. Lawton, the Monmouth commandant, and told him to provide the sub-committee with everything it needed, including access to the personnel files. That same day he announced the suspension of five civilian workers at Fort Monmouth.[13]

Stevens flew to New York City on October 13 to attend the closed hearings as McCarthy's guest. "The Army is cooperating in every way," he declared. Then it was off to lunch with McCarthy at the swank Merchants Club, followed by dinner with Cohn and Schine at the Waldorf Astoria. The next morning Stevens returned to the hearings in the Schine limousine. Four more suspensions were announced.

A week later Stevens accompanied the senator and his staff on a guided tour of Fort Monmouth. While McCarthy wandered freely, some trouble erupted when Cohn was denied access to a secret laboratory. According to the officer who restrained him, Cohn shouted, "This is war! We will really investigate the Army now!" But Stevens and McCarthy got on well. They talked about teamwork and they promised to "clean up any situation which needs cleaning up." Twelve more suspensions were announced.[14]

To this point the press had been remarkably helpful to McCarthy, listing his charges in flashy front-page stories that began, "Senator McCarthy said today . . ." It was the old megaphone effect—he says it, you print it—compounded by the widespread belief that McCarthy was onto something real, something *worth* reporting, at long last. There were some skeptics, however. One newsman tracked down the "eminent East German scientist" who had "seen" America's top radar secrets. The man turned out to be thirty years old and working on a military post exchange in West Germany. His story had been checked—and dismissed—by Army Intelligence nine months before. Then a newspaper in Asbury Park, New Jersey, identified the witness who had "cracked" under questioning and "agreed to tell all about espionage rings." The witness, Carl Greenblum, a research engineer, described himself as a very nervous man. Furthermore, his mother had died just two days before his interrogation at Foley Square. "It's true that I broke down and they took me to another room and brought in a doctor and a nurse," he said. "A few minutes later I sent word that I wanted to go back and tell my story from the beginning. That may have been interpreted to mean that I had been lying, previously, but that certainly was not the case." Greenblum insisted that he knew nothing about espionage at Fort Monmouth.

On November 9 the Washington *Post* broke a dramatic story about McCarthy's handling of the probe. "For over a month," it began,

> this vital Army Signal Corps Center has been the target of sensational accusations, implications, and innuendoes which portray it as a hotbed of Communism and espionage. . . . Nothing that can be independently ascertained from information available here or in Washington indicates that there is any known evidence to support such a conclusion.

The story was researched and written by Murray Marder, the *Post*'s "McCarthy man." Marder had friends at the Pentagon. He had spoken with intelligence officers and the lawyers representing the suspended employees. He had learned that nobody at Monmouth stood accused of espionage or attempted espionage. The charges—compiled by Army investigators and the FBI—related to past associations and personal beliefs. One man supposedly favored the "leftist views" of Max Lerner, a columnist for the New York *Post*. Another had attended several meetings of the Young Communist League while a student at City College. A third had been employed at a summer camp "which is reported to have been a Communist-created organization." In addition, said Marder, "it is generally unknown, or overlooked, that the Russians had official representatives actually in Fort Monmouth, handling classified documents during World War II when Russia was an ally. Classified communications equipment was being given to the Russians under Lend Lease; they did not have to steal it."[15]

At a press conference on November 13, Stevens was barraged with questions about the Marder story. The conclusions were essentially correct, he said. The Army had been "unable to find anything resembling current espionage at Fort Monmouth." Three days later the Secretary got an unscheduled visit from Roy Cohn and Frank Carr. They told him, Stevens said later, "that Senator McCarthy was very mad and felt I had double-crossed him." Stevens tried to patch things up. He called the senator and arranged to meet him for lunch. Afterward he told the press, "When I stated . . . the Army had no proof of current espionage, I want to make it unmistakably clear that I was speaking of the Army investigation only, and not of the inquiry of the Permanent Investigations Subcommittee, of which Senator McCarthy is chairman." Then he said, "There was espionage . . . at Fort Monmouth in the late stages of the war and in later years. Whether it was cut off in 1949, 1950, or 1951 is difficult to determine."[16]

———

ON THE EVE OF THE PUBLIC HEARINGS, Joe and Jean moved into an eight-room row house on Third Street, N.E., a short distance from the Capitol. It had been purchased by Jean's mother, who lived in one half and rented the other half to the McCarthys. Those who visited the couple—even months later—were amazed by the noise and the clutter, the people who wandered in and out, the constantly ringing telephone, the hundreds of unopened wedding gifts stacked in boxes on the floor. Joe had bought himself a Doberman pinscher, which obviously fitted his image; and he proudly displayed a ten-foot poster of Jesse James in his study—"Wanted Dead or Alive!"

The public hearings—"Army Signal Corps: Subversion and Espionage"—opened on November 24 and continued, in fits and starts, for the next several weeks. As usual, McCarthy had promised more than he could deliver. He had absolutely no proof of current espionage at Monmouth—a fact that became increasingly obvious as the hearings wore on. Most of the witnesses were former employees of the Signal Corps or related private concerns who had quit their jobs shortly after World War II. In general their testimony was hostile, evasive, or both. Virtually all of them took the Fifth Amendment when asked about their involvement in the so-called Rosenberg spy ring.

As chairman, and the only senator in attendance, McCarthy assumed the multiple roles of prosecutor, judge, and jury. His behavior was often outrageous. He and Cohn would pepper witnesses with questions like, "What have you got against this country?" and "Who do you think was at fault in starting the Korean War?" A witness who refused to discuss his political beliefs was asked, "Do you feel that if Rosenberg was properly executed, you deserve the same fate?" On one occasion McCarthy opened a session by stating, "Today we have a number of witnesses who will testify positively as to Mr. Hyman's Communist activities. We told Mr. Hyman to be here so that he could deny that testimony if he feels it is untrue. His attorney advises me that he is parking his Cadillac now."[17]

From a legal standpoint there was little the chairman could do to punish these witnesses. Their reluctant testimony was protected by the Fifth Amendment. They had committed no crimes, at least none that the committee could uncover. And they no longer worked for the Army or for companies that did classified work for the government. What McCarthy could do, however, was to highlight their "subversive activities" and then urge the community at large to deal with them accordingly. This informal sanction—known as "prescriptive publicity"—had been employed with telling effect in the past, particularly by the House Un-American Activities Committee.[18]

McCarthy relied heavily upon this tactic. He used it in almost all cases where the witness invoked his constitutional privilege against self-incrimination.

THE CHAIRMAN: . . . Just one more question before you leave: Is this cooperative of which you are manager tax-exempt?

MR. STOLBERG: I answered that in executive session.

THE CHAIRMAN: Answer it now.

MR. STOLBERG: Yes, it is tax-exempt. . . .

THE CHAIRMAN: Does the membership of the co-op know that you are a functionary of the Communist Party?

MR. STOLBERG: I decline to answer that Mr. Chairman, for the reasons I have stated before. . . .

THE CHAIRMAN: You may step down.

· · ·

THE CHAIRMAN: You belong to what bar association?

MR. PERCOFF: I belong to the Bronx Bar Association. . . .

THE CHAIRMAN: . . . Who is president of the Bronx Bar Association?

MR. PERCOFF: I don't know.

THE CHAIRMAN: Frank, I wonder if you would have the Bronx Bar Association notified of this testimony. . . . You may step down.[19]

Several of the witnesses worked for the New York City Board of Education, which had threatened to fire any teacher who invoked the Fifth Amendment before a Congressional committee. In these cases McCarthy played the role of gleeful executioner.

THE CHAIRMAN: Mrs. Wolman, the New York Board of Education has apparently decided to summarily dismiss anyone who refused to state whether or not they are Communists on the ground that their answer might tend to incriminate them. Harvard, for example, takes the opposite position. I just wonder whether you think the New York Board of Education or Harvard's rule is the better insofar as members of the Communist Party are concerned?

MRS. WOLMAN: I have no opinion on it.

THE CHAIRMAN: You have no opinion on that at all?

MRS. WOLMAN: No.

THE CHAIRMAN: You may step down.

· · ·

THE CHAIRMAN: Well, if the Board of Education follows the rule which they have laid down, and I am sure they will, I think they should be complimented for it, you might apply for a job over at

Harvard. It seems to be a privileged sanctuary for Fifth Amendment cases. The president of Harvard has announced that he will not discharge Fifth Amendment cases.

MISS BERKE: Are these remarks necessary?

THE CHAIRMAN: Assuming you lose your job in the New York school system.[20]

Diana Wolman and Sylvia Berke were fired a few weeks later.

Only a handful of the suspended Monmouth workers were asked to testify at the open hearings. Most came willingly to deny allegations that they had ever been Communists or members of an espionage ring. While McCarthy could not prove otherwise, he did raise some interesting questions about the way their dossiers had been evaluated by the Army Screening Board in Washington. One case—that of Aaron H. Coleman, a section chief—was particularly revealing.

Coleman had worked at Monmouth for fifteen years. He had been a key figure in the research and development of America's radar defense system. His superiors had praised his "outstanding record of achievement." He had received a top security clearance as late as 1951, although his Army file bulged with "derogatory information." Coleman had known Julius Rosenberg in college. They had attended a Communist meeting together. In 1946 Coleman had been officially reprimanded after a search of his home had turned up classified Army documents. The following year Morton Sobell had listed him as an employment reference, known to the applicant for approximately twelve years.

Coleman had been interviewed by Army investigators and the FBI on numerous occasions. He had an explanation for everything. Yes, he had attended a Communist meeting with Rosenberg. But the experience had turned him into a forceful anti-Communist and he had never socialized with Rosenberg again. Yes, he had known Morton Sobell, but only peripherally. He had no inkling of Sobell's Communist leanings and no idea why Sobell had used him as a reference. Yes, he had violated security procedures by removing classified documents from the Fort. But he had done so for the best of reasons—to work overtime on a project of great importance to the Army. His reprimand had contained the opinion that "the motives which led to your having had classified documents in your possession were highly praiseworthy."[21]

McCarthy was unimpressed. He had seen the FBI report and he had seen the Monmouth personnel files, compliments of Robert T. Stevens. Both sources had painted a bleak picture of Aaron Coleman. They disclosed a long association with known Communists and a remarkably cavalier attitude in the handling of classified documents.

Cohn and McCarthy had a field day with this material. They produced one witness—probably an FBI source—who identified Coleman as a member of the Young Communist League.

MR. COHN: And where did you belong to the Young Communist League?

MR. SUSSMAN: From 1935 to 1938 at City College. . . .

MR. COHN: Did you know Aaron Coleman?

MR. SUSSMAN: Yes, sir, I did. . . .

MR. COHN: Was he a member of the Young Communist League?

MR. SUSSMAN: He was.

And they produced testimony from the Rosenberg spy trial in which Rosenberg himself admitted to later contact with Aaron Coleman.

Q.: And can you give us the names of some other classmates with whom you had either social or business relations after your graduation?

A.: Well, there were people who were in my squad in the electrical engineering courses—Mr. Aaron Coleman, who, subsequent to graduation, I met at Fort Monmouth when I was assigned there.[22]

Even more damaging was the testimony of Andrew J. Reid, the chief security officer at Fort Monmouth. With Cohn leading him on, he vividly described the incident that had led to Coleman's reprimand in 1946.

MR. REID: I called Mr. Coleman into the office and I asked him for an explanation . . . and if he had any documents in his home.

MR. COHN: That is very important. You say you asked him whether or not he had any other documents, any other classified documents in his home, is that correct?

MR. REID: Yes, sir.

MR. COHN: What did Mr. Coleman tell you when you asked him that question?

MR. REID: Well, I specifically asked him the same question three times, and the first time he denied having any documents in his home.

MR. COHN: The first time you asked him that question, he flatly denied having any of these documents?

MR. REID: Yes, sir. . . .

MR. COHN: Did the statement later turn out to be untrue?

Mr. REID: The second time I asked him he said maybe, and the third time I asked Mr. Coleman he said, "Yes."[23]

Coleman followed Reid to the witness stand. He was questioned roughly, skillfully, by Roy Cohn. He denied that he had been a member of the Young Communist League or that he had ever met with Rosenberg at Fort Monmouth.

Mr. COHN: Did you know Mr. Sussman was a Communist?

Mr. COLEMAN: Yes, sir; Rosenberg told me. . . .

Mr. COHN: Who else did Rosenberg tell you was a Communist?

Mr. COLEMAN: He didn't tell me of anybody else.

Mr. COHN: You were a casual acquaintance of Rosenberg and you didn't know him socially and he was lying when he said he knew you down at Fort Monmouth; but nevertheless he took you to a secret meeting of the Young Communist League . . . and he confided in you as to the name of at least one other person who was a Communist with him; is that right? Is that a fact?[24]

Coleman began to wilt. He conferred with his lawyer. He asked Cohn to slow down. He said that the meeting he had attended with Rosenberg was not "secret" at all.

Mr. COHN: Was it an open meeting? Was it advertised?

Mr. COLEMAN: It was not advertised.

Mr. COHN: Were you introduced to other people at the meeting?

Mr. COLEMAN: No, sir.

Mr. COHN: Were names given?

Mr. COLEMAN: No.

By this time, Coleman was in full retreat. His memory deserted him entirely.

THE CHAIRMAN: Did you ever live with Mr. Sachs?

Mr. COLEMAN: I believe he shared our apartment in 1943 for a month or two. I am not sure of the exact length of time.

THE CHAIRMAN: Did you know Sachs was a Communist at that time?

Mr. COLEMAN: . . . I did not think he was a member of the Communist Party. I thought he might be sympathetic.

THE CHAIRMAN: At that time, did you have secret documents in your home?

MR. COLEMAN: I don't recollect. . . .

THE CHAIRMAN: But you might have?

MR. COLEMAN: I might have.

The Coleman case was tailor-made for McCarthy. It seemed like a perfect example of bad judgment (or worse!) at the top of the security ladder. Aaron Coleman had been thoroughly investigated. He had been suspended by a regional board but reinstated by the screening board in Washington. So had thirty-three others at Monmouth. As the chairman told Andrew Reid, "I think the files indicate that you and the FBI have done a good job; the fault is not at your level, it is at the level of those who refuse to recognize the material that you dig up."

At this point McCarthy repeated the demand that would lock him into a collision course with the Army. In a brief but angry exchange with Army Counsel John Adams, he demanded the names of those who had voted to reinstate Aaron Coleman.

MR. ADAMS: We can give you the names of the members of the screening board . . . and the dates on which they have served. We may not, under existing policy, give you the names of the members of the board who sat on particular panels which considered any particular case. So we will be restricted by that limitation.

THE CHAIRMAN: We will have to call all of the members of the board and put them under oath. . . . I think it is ridiculous beyond words to follow the old Truman order to the effect a congressional committee cannot get the names of a board who cleared men with clear-cut Communist connections, and I am not referring to the Coleman case, but to the situation in general.[25]

Adams said he'd take up the matter with Secretary Stevens. He promised quick action, one way or the other.

CHAPTER TWENTY-THREE

White House Blues

As THE MONMOUTH HEARINGS BEGAN, the word around Washington was that Joe McCarthy had seen his better days. His recent embarrassments—the J. B. Matthews affair, the subcommittee walkout, the CIA probe—had led many to conclude that he was "in trouble," perhaps "at the end of his string." In addition, the global tensions that had fueled his crusade now appeared to be easing. Stalin was dead and the new Kremlin leaders were speaking openly of détente with the West. "At the present time," said Prime Minister Georgi Malenkov, "there is no disputed or unresolved question that cannot be settled peacefully. . . . This includes our relations with all states, including the United States of America." Four months later, on July 27, an armistice was signed that officially ended the fighting in Korea.[1]

As it turned out, these factors did not work to McCarthy's disadvantage. In the short run they helped to revive him and to spur him along. Embarrassing or not, the walkout by subcommittee Democrats removed the main obstacle in his drive for uncontested one-man rule. He could now pick his targets and run his hearings with no interference at all. (Would strong military supporters like Symington and McClellan have tolerated the browbeating of Army generals or the closed-door shenanigans at Foley Square?) Furthermore, the partial relaxation of East–West tensions served to widen the rift between the White House and the

Republican right, which demanded more pressure, not less, in America's future dealings with the Russians and the Communist Chinese. Before long McCarthy and his allies were charging that Eisenhower had purposely misled them, that the "new" foreign policy was not much different from the old.

What disturbed the McCarthyites was the obvious gap between Republican rhetoric and the Administration's performance. In 1952 the GOP had pledged to repudiate the Yalta accords and to work for the liberation of "captive peoples" under Communist rule. Eisenhower had supported these pledges, and Dulles had written them into the party platform. The motive was strictly political: to pacify the conservatives and to coax "ethnic voters" into the Republican fold. Once in office, however, the President had backed away from these pledges. In March he had selected Chip Bohlen (a "Yalta man") for the Moscow post and strongly opposed Republican attempts to declare the Yalta accords "null and void and of no binding force whatsoever." In June, as German workers battled Soviet tanks in the streets of East Berlin, he had remained conspicuously silent about the liberation of captive peoples. This infuriated the Republican right, which felt that *some* response was in order. The rebellion was crushed in a matter of days.

The Korean armistice only made things worse. It was, at best, a carbon copy of what the Democrats had been seeking—and the Republicans had been attacking—for the past three years. It ended the war, but it left the Communists in control of the same territory they had occupied when the fighting began. There would be no "victory" in Korea. The country would remain divided; the aggressors would go unpunished. Some Republicans viewed the armistice as a sellout, engineered by U.N. "allies" who had done little of the fighting and raked in huge profits on the side. The lesson seemed clear enough: Collective action did not work. America should set its own goals and be prepared to go it alone. "We must give notice," said an angry Bill Jenner, "that the ceasefire agreement was the end of an era, the last tribute to appeasement. We are done with the illusions of the forties." [2]

On July 31 Robert Taft died of cancer at sixty-four. As majority leader, he had been invaluable to the new Administration. He had given his loyal support to programs and appointments that personally displeased him. He had been the strongest link—some said the only link—between East and Midwest in the Republican party. While no one could hope to fill his shoes, the selection of William Knowland as the new majority leader was particularly distressing. An irritable, suspicious man, Knowland seemed to judge America's foreign policy by the effect it had upon his hero, Chiang Kai-shek. He had opposed the Korean armistice and recently brought Dulles to tears by heckling him at a hearing on foreign aid. Like Taft, Bill Knowland had encouraged McCarthy's attacks in the past; unlike Taft, he made little effort to discourage them once the Republicans took control in 1953. The difference would become painfully obvious as the months wore on.

———

THE WHITE HOUSE HAD LITTLE TO SAY about the Monmouth hearings. It responded indirectly at best, ignoring McCarthy while citing the Administration's deep concern over security matters and the good results it had achieved. On October 22 Eisenhower announced that 1,456 people had been removed from the government under the beefed-up Republican loyalty program. He spoke of "1,456 subversives," but this was hardly the case. Many were alcoholics, blabbermouths, and malingerers. Some had resigned to take other government jobs. Very few were dismissed for reasons pertaining to disloyalty.[3]

The White House kept on plugging. In November it encouraged Herbert Brownell, the Attorney General, to release some damaging information about security lapses during the Truman years. Brownell had free access to the FBI files. He had learned, among other things, that Truman once ignored an FBI report on the subversive activities of Harry Dexter White, a prominent government official. Brownell wanted to make this information public. He conferred with Sherman Adams, who sent him directly to the President. According to Adams, Brownell said that "the disclosure was justified political criticism and that it would take away some of the glamour of the McCarthy stage play." The President agreed.[4]

Brownell dropped his bombshell a few days later in a luncheon address to the Executive Club of Chicago. "I can now announce for the first time in public," he said, "that White's spying activities for the Soviet Government were reported in detail by the FBI to the White House by means of a report delivered to President Truman. . . . In the face of this information, and incredible though it may seem, President Truman subsequently nominated White, who was then Assistant Secretary of the Treasury, for an even more important position as executive director for the United States in the International Monetary Fund."[5]

The reaction was volcanic. Eleanor Roosevelt and Adlai Stevenson rushed to Truman's defense. So did Marquis Childs, the Alsops, and most of the Washington press corps. Drew Pearson heard the "drums of fascism beating louder." Walter Lippmann said, "I have always thought highly of Mr. Brownell. But what he did was a truly terrible thing to do." HUAC's Harold Velde thought otherwise. He subpoenaed Truman to appear before his committee—a move that Francis Walter, the ranking Democrat, called "the most incredible, insulting, un-American thing I've encountered in my twenty-one years in Congress." Truman rejected the subpoena, citing the separation of powers. The next morning, surrounded by reporters, he went for his morning walk in the brisk November air. "You're fouling me up," a photographer protested. "My office told me to get a picture of you looking glum and all you've done is smile." "You're not going to get a picture of me looking glum," Truman replied. "You can tell them I said they should go to hell."[6]

There were few smiles at the White House. On November 11 President Eisenhower faced a press grilling that shook him to the core.

> QUESTION: Do you think the Administration's action in virtually putting a label of traitor on a former President is likely to damage our foreign relations?

> THE PRESIDENT: I reject [that] I would not answer the question.

> QUESTION: What did you understand was the purpose of bringing information from the files of the FBI before a luncheon group . . . ?

> THE PRESIDENT: You can get direct evidence on that . . . You can go directly to the Attorney General.

> QUESTION: Mr. President, I think this case is at best a pretty squalid one. . . .

> THE PRESIDENT: Look, all of you are trying to get my personal opinion about certain things. I am not either a judge nor am I an accomplished lawyer. . . . The Attorney General is here to answer it himself. Let him answer it.

> QUESTION: He has refused to answer the questions, you see. [Laughter][7]

On November 16 Harry Truman gave a nationally televised explanation of his role in the H. D. White affair. He spoke from a small studio in Kansas City, flanked by an American flag and wearing an American Legion pin in the lapel of his suit. His talk was short and simple: Yes, he had seen the FBI report on White. It had contained serious allegations but no hard facts. And it had reached his desk too late to stop the nomination. Furthermore, once confirmed by the Senate, White could not be fired without undermining the FBI's secret probe of Communists in the government. J. Edgar Hoover understood this. He had given the White House his full support.

In closing, Truman leveled some accusations of his own. "It is now evident," he declared, "that the present Administration has fully embraced, for political advantage, McCarthyism. I am not referring to the Senator from Wisconsin. He is only important in that his name has taken on a dictionary meaning of the word. It is the corruption of truth, the abandonment of the due process of law. It is the use of the big lie and the unfounded accusation against any citizen in the name of Americanism or security. It is the rise to power of the demagogue who lives on untruth; it is the spreading of fear and the destruction of faith in every level of our society."[8]

Truman's rebuttal set off a chain reaction of its own. The following day J. Edgar Hoover publicly debunked the notion that White had been kept on to help the FBI trap more Communists. In fact, he told the Jenner Committee, "I felt it was unwise for White to serve." James Reston praised the FBI director for "a brilliant and extraordinary performance." But others saw it as nothing more than petty revenge. "Hoover has been waiting a long time for this moment," Drew Pearson wrote in his diary. "He hated Truman and almost everyone around him."[*][9]

Then McCarthy joined the fracas, claiming that Truman had smeared him and demanding free radio and television time to defend his good name. The networks were surprised. They had expected the Administration to make this demand, but no one had stepped forward. Meanwhile the senator threatened to ask the Federal Communications Commission to review the license of any station that failed to carry *his* rebuttal. The networks quickly went along. They set aside a free half hour—worth about $300,000—on the evening of November 24.

McCarthy delivered his speech from a television studio in New York. "Last Monday night," he began, "a former President of the United States made a completely untruthful attack upon me. Tonight I shall spend little time on Harry Truman. He is no more important than any other defeated politician."

What followed was one of the more remarkable perorations of McCarthy's career. After dismissing Truman in a few choice sentences, he turned his guns on the new Republican Administration. It was "infinitely better" than the old one, he admitted. But it was not good enough. After nine months in office, the Eisenhower–Dulles team had failed to reverse the "whining, whimpering appeasement" that characterized America's foreign policy.

> How free are we when American aviators fighting under the American flag at this moment . . . are being brainwashed, starved or murdered behind an Iron

---

* Hoover's version was later supported by James Byrnes, Truman's Secretary of State. In the end serious doubts were raised about the accuracy of Truman's explanation. But the Eisenhower camp failed to pursue the White affair for obvious reasons. First, rather than pushing McCarthy off center stage, it seemed to vindicate his charges about Reds in the government. Second, it infuriated the Democrats at a time when their votes in Congress were vital to the success of Eisenhower's foreign and domestic programs. In 1953 thirty-eight of forty-two Senate roll calls were won by the Administration because of strong Democratic support. As Walter Lippmann noted, Brownell's extreme partisanship had seriously threatened the President's bipartisan constituency. See Lippmann, "A Review of the Brownell–Truman–McCarthy Episode," Louisville *Times*, December 22, 1953.

or Bamboo curtain? How brave are we—how brave are we when we do not use all the power of this nation to rescue those airmen and the 900 other military men who have been unaccounted for for months?

. . . The Republican Party did not create the situation, I admit. We inherited it. But we are responsible for the proper handling of the situation as of tonight. Now what are we going to do about it? Are we going to continue to send perfumed notes, following the style of the Truman–Acheson regime?

. . . We can deal a death blow to the war-making power of Communist China. We can, without firing a shot, force the Communists to open their filthy Communist dungeons and release every American. We can blockade the coast of China without using a single ship, a single sailor or a single gun.

. . . We can handle this by saying to our allies; If you continue to ship to Red China, while they are imprisoning and torturing American men, you will not get one cent of American money.

If we do that, my good friends, this trading in blood-money will cease. No doubt about that.

He ended with a quote from Abraham Lincoln: "If this nation is to be destroyed, it will be destroyed from within, if it is not destroyed from within, it will live for all time to come." [10]

———

THE CHALLENGE could hardly have been more direct. A Republican senator had lambasted a Republican Administration. He had accused the Western allies of aiding and abetting the torture of American POWs. He had blasted the Secretary of State for responding to this outrage with a series of perfumed notes. And he had delivered the speech only two weeks before the Bermuda Summit, the first meeting of Western heads of state (Eisenhower, Churchill, and Laniel of France) since the President took office.

Yet, as McCarthy well knew, the speech would not be easy to rebut. For all the hyperbole, it had raised some legitimate questions: Why hadn't the Administration done more to stop "free world" trade with the enemy? Why did it continue to subsidize the major offenders? In Congress other prominent Republicans, including Knowland and House Speaker Martin, were asking the very same questions. And public opinion polls showed strong support for the "get tough" approach. As Stewart Alsop observed, "The China trade issue is tailor-made for McCarthy. It has the necessary anti-Communist overtones. . . . It also has some real factual basis, plus a simple emotional appeal which he can exploit to the top of his bent." [11]

At first the White House said nothing. Ike was safely out of town on a golfing vacation in Georgia. His only comment was that he had played eighteen tough holes and gone to bed before McCarthy started speaking. His aides proved equally elusive, although one published report described them as "hopping mad"—which, in fact, they were. On November 25 C. D. Jackson sent this confidential note to Sherman Adams:

> Listening to Senator McCarthy last night was an exceptionally horrible experience. . . . Obviously the President cannot get down in the same gutter—but neither can he avoid a question, if not several questions, at the next press conference. . . .
> Is there no way of having some Republican senator pick up the McCarthy challenge and do something right away? If every egghead in the country can rise to a fever pitch when Brownell talks about Truman, can't a single Republican senator work up some temperature when McCarthy refers to Eisenhower as he did?[12]

Jackson decided to force the issue. He visited with John Foster Dulles on Sunday, November 29, hoping to win his approval for a hard-hitting response to McCarthy. Dulles was sympathetic. He wanted very much to retaliate, he said, but this would require presidential support, which might be difficult to obtain. To Jackson's astonishment, he claimed that Eisenhower still hadn't read the speech, and neither had Brownell. Jackson recorded the visit in his diary: "Foster profoundly perturbed about McCarthy business because it messes up his affairs. He is worried about presidential leadership. . . . This place is really falling apart."[13]

The following day, at a White House staff meeting, Jackson called for a declaration of war against McCarthy. He reviewed the situation carefully, noting that "the Three Little Monkeys act was not working and would not work," that "appeasing McCarthy in order to save his 7 votes for this year's legislative program was poor tactics, poor strategy and poor arithmetic." Jackson suggested that the President cancel his Wednesday press conference and face up to McCarthy in a nationally televised address. "Big rhubarb," he noted. "Finally agreed to have press conference. The men have really separated out from the boys."[14]

Dulles arrived at the White House a few hours later. He had come to show the President a statement he'd written which defended the Administration's handling of the China trade issue. The President liked the statement. It seemed forceful yet indirect. It challenged McCarthy's allegations without mentioning McCarthy by name. He told Dulles to go ahead and release it. He promised to back him "to the hilt."[15]

Dulles did more than release the statement. He called in the press and read it aloud, his voice crackling with emotion. In recent days, he said, the Administration had been attacked for sending perfumed notes to its allies, "instead of using threats and intimidation to compel them to do our bidding." These attacks were malicious and absurd. Our allies were not our satellites; they were our good friends and sovereign equals. They stood by America in NATO and Korea. They provided an early warning system, without which "the great industrial centers of Detroit,

Cleveland, Chicago and Milwaukee would be sitting ducks for atomic bombs." America depended upon these nations every bit as much as these nations depended upon America. When disagreements arose, they would be handled in an atmosphere of friendship and mutual respect. The Administration fully rejected the "domineering methods" proposed by its critics. They were undemocratic and unjust. They would only divide the free world in its moment of ultimate peril. * 16

McCarthy's critics were naturally elated. Hubert Humphrey commended Dulles for his statesmanship. John Sherman Cooper praised his eloquence in "reaffirming the moral and just foundations of our foreign policy." Stewart Alsop applauded his decency and his courage. "John Foster Dulles," he wrote, "is apparently a much braver man than many people have thought." McCarthy himself appeared typically unruffled by the Secretary's riposte. He grabbed a reporter's copy, looked it over, and asked no one in particular, "Do you think he could have been referring to me?" 17

At the White House, meanwhile, the staff could not agree upon the proper wording for the President's statement to the press. As a result, two drafts were prepared—one, by James Hagerty, endorsed the Dulles remarks; the other, by C. D. Jackson, struck directly at McCarthy. The staff then assembled in the Oval Office. The President's mood was grim. He read the Jackson draft quickly, with obvious irritation. He flipped it back across his desk, uttering the oft-quoted "I will not get in the gutter with that guy." He was about to accept the Hagerty draft, word for word, when Jackson cut in to urge a tougher response. The President must lead his party, he argued, or the McCarthyites surely would. According to Jackson, "the needling and the goosing began to take effect." Ike reread the Hagerty text, adding sentences and whole paragraphs as he went along. The staff closed ranks behind him. When the meeting ended, "the group almost cheered." 18

Eisenhower read the statement at his press conference the next day. He named no names, but he really didn't have to. He promised to "protect the rights of loyal Americans." He condemned the "impatient coercion of other free nations." And he put the GOP on notice that "fear of Communists' actively undermining our government" would not be an issue in the 1954 elections. "Long before that," the President explained, "this Administration will have made such progress in rooting them out . . . that this can no longer be considered a serious menace." 19

---

* The Dulles statement was eloquent but also inaccurate. When dealing with issues he deemed *important*, the Secretary was quite willing to threaten the European allies. Several weeks later he warned the French and British that America might begin an "agonizing reappraisal" of its commitment in Europe if the Administration's proposal for an integrated European army (with West German participation) was rejected. On this point see Townsend Hoopes, *The Devil and John Foster Dulles*, 1973, pp. 162–67, 189–90.

C. D. Jackson was happy with the way things turned out. By standing firm, he thought, he had persuaded the President to exert some influence in Republican Party affairs. But Jackson still had his doubts. He wrote in his diary that evening: "Problem now is, having zippered the toga of Republican leadership on the President's shoulders, how to keep that zipper shut." [20]

———

ON DECEMBER 3 McCarthy announced plans for a press conference of his own. No one seemed surprised. The senator did not normally let personal or political criticism roll lightly off his back. In this case, moreover, he had a lot to lose. He was deeply committed to the China trade issue and he resented (and obviously feared) the boast that domestic subversion would be all but eradicated by 1954. As usual, the press speculated freely about what McCarthy might say. The consensus was that he'd renew the challenge, selectively, by ignoring the President and ripping into Dulles, who was far more vulnerable to attack. As one columnist put it, "Dulles is in for a rough time from the man who considers a baseball bat a suitable instrument for teaching his peculiar brand of Americanism." [21]

The following day McCarthy was visited by Len Hall, the Republican national chairman, and by Arthur Summerfield, the Postmaster General. Both men liked Joe; both viewed him as a party asset. They had come, separately, after hearing rumors that he would use his press conference to highlight Dulles's tenure at the Carnegie Endowment (the Hiss connection) and to link Dulles's former law partner, Arthur Dean, to the Institute for Pacific Relations (the Lattimore connection). They learned, to their dismay, that the rumors were true.

Summerfield preached moderation. Hall talked tough. According to one account, "It was always Len and Joe. However, Len told Joe that if he went ahead with his blast, he, Hall, and every Republican leader would issue statements against him." McCarthy was impressed. He was close with Summerfield, and he knew Hall as a careful, placid man who did not normally threaten people to get his point across. He agreed to rewrite the statement and to show it to Hall before releasing it. Hall thought this a very good idea. [22]

The new statement was remarkably tame. It lauded "the honesty and sincerity" of Foster Dulles. It debunked the notion "that I am challenging President Eisenhower's party leadership." But it gave no ground on the crucial issue—America's failure to stop the "blood-trade" with Red China. "I have such deep convictions on this subject," it said, "that I shall continue to discuss the matter at every opportunity and I urge Secretary Dulles to reappraise our whole policy in this regard."

McCarthy then released the statement—twice. He handed out copies to the press, and he read a copy aloud for the newsreel and television cameras. The press release was identical to the one Len Hall had seen. The newsreel and television copy contained an additional paragraph, which McCarthy had written only minutes before. It was the final paragraph, and it said, "I think President Eisenhower is an honorable man. I think he will follow the will of the American people as that will is made known to him. Therefore, I strongly urge each and every American who feels as I do about this blood-trade with a mortal enemy to write or wire the President and let him know how they feel, so he will be properly guided on the matter."[23]

There was little that the White House could say in return. The appeal was deferential and polite; it contained no extreme phrases or silly threats. And it was democratic in tone. It asked the people to advise their President, and it asked the President to consider their advice. McCarthy knew that this was an alien concept in the making of foreign policy—but one that the White House could not easily challenge in public.

On December 5 Assistant Press Secretary Murray Snyder announced that 4,300 telegrams had reached the White House and that an equal number were awaiting delivery at the Western Union office in Washington. So far, he admitted, they were running two-to-one in McCarthy's favor. The next day McCarthy disputed these figures. He had heard from his own "sources" at Western Union that 8,500 telegrams were already at the White House and that 6,000 more were on the way. Calling Snyder's count a "grievous mistake," he suggested that the "real figure" be sent along to Eisenhower and Dulles at the Bermuda Summit. Snyder was furious. "I'm sure," he replied, "that the President has much more important matters to concern him."[24]

McCarthy won the battle of the telegrams by a lopsided margin. About 50,000 wires and letters were finally received, with the vast majority supporting his call for a crackdown on the China trade. The total was quite impressive, despite White House attempts to prove otherwise. It didn't compare with the big telegram campaigns of the past—by Townsendites and Coughlinites, opponents of Taft–Hartley and supporters of General MacArthur—but it was the second largest the Eisenhower White House had seen, right behind the well-organized campaign to "Save the Rosenbergs" in the spring of 1953. McCarthy took his victory in stride. He was careful not to claim too much or to personalize the results in any way. "This is not a popularity contest," he explained. "If it were, Eisenhower would win it 20–1." Of his own plans, he said modestly, "I have no intention of ever running for president—no desire to run . . . I hope the people of Wisconsin will keep me in the Senate. I happen to like it here."

CHAPTER TWENTY-FOUR

Who Promoted Peress?

W<small>HEN</small> E<small>ISENHOWER</small> <small>TOOK OFFICE IN</small> 1953, he had already decided to steer clear of McCarthy. He had expected some early trouble, but he felt sure that public opinion and Republican pressure would soon force the senator into line. Meanwhile, he hoped to avoid a donnybrook that would divide the GOP and demean the presidential office. On April 1 he wrote in his diary:

> McCarthy's actions create trouble on the Hill with members of the Party; they irritate, frustrate, and infuriate members of the Executive Department. I really believe that nothing will be so effective in combating this particular brand of troublemaking as to ignore him. This he cannot stand.[1]

The President had hoped to neutralize McCarthy by taking control of the internal security issue, by demonstrating that the Executive branch could sort out the "dangerous" and "disloyal" without congressional assistance. In February he revealed that his top appointees had been investigated by the FBI at their own request. In April he issued Executive Order 10450, a loyalty–security directive that broadened the grounds for dismissal from the federal service. Where the Truman program had focused on "loyalty risks," those with "subversive" associations and beliefs, the new program focused on "security risks," a term that encompassed everything from disloyalty to incompetent judgment to

355

"criminal, infamous, dishonest, immoral, or notoriously disgraceful behavior." In October the President amended the order to include the
automatic dismissal of federal workers who took the Fifth Amendment
before a congressional committee. In November he allowed the Attorney
General to "out-McCarthy McCarthy" in the case of Harry Dexter
White. A few weeks later, on the eve of the Bermuda Summit, he told
C. L. Sulzberger that he would ask England and France to join America
in a pact that outlawed the Communist Party. According to Sulzberger,
the President said "he detested the methods of McCarthyism, but nevertheless it certainly was necessary to fight Communism and fight it hard."[2]

There was one problem, however. This vigilance did little to defuse
McCarthy, who carried on as though Truman and Acheson were still
minding the store. In 1953 his subcommittee had conducted seventeen
public or semipublic hearings, including ten that focused on *current*
espionage and subversion in the government.* It had survived a rocky
start, gathering force with its probes of the China trade, the Government
Printing Office, and the Army Signal Corps. By year's end McCarthy
seemed more powerful, more popular, more belligerently independent
than ever. In December the Gallup Poll asked, "What is your opinion of
Senator Joseph McCarthy—is it favorable or unfavorable?" The results
—50 percent favorable, 29 percent unfavorable, 21 percent no opinion
—showed how far the senator had come. The favorable response was up
18 percent from the summer, more than 30 percent from the early
spring. In addition the polls suggested that McCarthy had seriously undermined public confidence in the Administration's war on domestic
subversion. In November, for example, the Gallup Poll asked, "Would
you like to see President Eisenhower take a stronger stand on any problem? If yes, what one in particular?" Of the 65 percent who answered
yes, the most frequent response was "getting rid of Communists in the
government." It ranked above "more aid to farmers," "preventing World
War III," "formulating a clear-cut U.S. foreign policy," "lowering taxes,"
and "cutting down on government spending." At the bottom of the list:
"taking a firm stand on McCarthyism."[3]

The President's dilemma was clear. He wanted to maintain his Olympian detachment, yet he could no longer assume that McCarthy would
self-destruct or that others would somehow force him into line. The
public seemed to support the senator. So did many Republican leaders,

* In contrast, William Jenner's Internal Security Subcommittee conducted one hearing
on subversion in government, a hearing that focused largely on the administrations of
Truman and FDR. It held eleven hearings in all, with topics that ranged from "Subversive
Influences in the Educational Process" to "Communist Underground Printing Facilities" to
"Communism in Labor Unions." Harold Velde's House Un-American Activities Committee
conducted twenty-four hearings in 1953, but not one touched on subversion in government.
Under Velde's inept leadership, HUAC became a traveling carnival, investigating "Com-
munist activities" in cities like Chicago, Philadelphia, Baltimore, and Albany, New York.
One hearing was on the "Soviet Schedule for War," with the war supposedly set for 1955.
See, U.S. Senate, *Internal Security Manual*, 1955.

including Len Hall, the national chairman; Arthur Summerfield, the previous chairman; and Richard Simson, who headed the Congressional Campaign Committee. When Simson boasted that "we've got one thing the Democrats haven't got," a newsman asked him if he meant Ike's great popularity. "No," Simson replied, "I mean McCarthy."[4]

In the Senate, too, his prospects seemed brighter. He had a committee chairmanship, a hefty budget, and a network of sympathizers and spies in the various Executive departments. Furthermore, he had the support of powerful Republicans like Knowland, Bridges, Dirksen, and Jenner, who considered him a useful ally in their attempts to reverse the dramatic growth of presidential power since FDR, particularly in foreign affairs. In 1953 they had clashed with Eisenhower over the Korean truce, the Yalta accords, and foreign aid. In 1954, with the help of Southern Democrats, they would come within a single vote of passing the revised Bricker Amendment, a measure that required Senate approval for *all* international agreements. During the final debate, Jenner would claim:

> The perversion of the treaty power and the misuse of executive agreements have meshed us into a system which rests on Soviet Russia's ideas of human rights, of full employment, of compulsory labor, of government management of the press. . . . The line of division today is between real Democrats and real Republicans, in defense of the Constitution, and the secret revolutionists and those they have brainwashed in their ruthless pursuit of power.[5]

On the other hand, the President's natural Senate allies, the Republican moderates, were reluctant to criticize McCarthy in public. Some were simply afraid of him—of his rough-and-tumble tactics and his popularity among their own constituents. Others, who personally despised him, felt uneasy about saying or doing anything that might encourage "outside forces"—the White House, the courts, the press—to question the legitimate investigative powers of Congress. Still others were wary of the sort of confrontation that would pit them against members of their own party. As Ralph Flanders quipped in 1953, "I shall leave to the Democrats the problem of making a case for the expulsion of a Republican senator."[6]

Naturally, the President expected something more from the moderates. In private he cursed them for not having the "guts" to challenge McCarthy on the Senate floor. "Boy," he'd tell his aides, "we really need a few good hatchet men on *our* side up there."[7]

―――

As the months went by, the President faced mounting pressure to rethink his position, to consider a different approach, a direct, forceful, public showdown with McCarthy. This pressure was largely external; it came from outside the Administration, from Eisenhower's friends, relatives, and supporters—his brother Milton and his boyhood pal "Swede"

Hazlett; board chairmen Philip Reed (General Electric), Harry Bullis (General Mills), and Paul Hoffman (Studebaker); publishers William Robinson (New York *Herald–Tribune*) and Palmer Hoyt (Denver *Post*). Their message was simple: McCarthy had diverted attention from pressing domestic problems. He had demoralized the Foreign Service. He had made America look ridiculous in the eyes of the world. He had to be stopped, and Dwight Eisenhower was the man, perhaps the only man, who could stop him.

After returning from a tour of Europe, Philip Reed urged the President to "take issue with McCarthy and make it stick."

> People in high and low places see in him a potential Hitler, seeking the presidency of the United States. . . . That he could get away with what he already has in America has made some of them wonder whether our concept of democratic government and the rights of individuals is really different from that of the Communists and Fascists. . . . All this adds up to the fact that the stature of your administration . . . is momentarily, at least, impaired in the countries I visited. . . . The impression of abject appeasement should be corrected, not only for general consumption but because I have never seen the morale of the State Department people, both at home and abroad, so shattered.

Paul Hoffman was equally blunt, writing that "the sooner the people of our country understand that it is Dwight D. Eisenhower, and not Senator McCarthy, who is 'calling the tune,' the sooner the attention of the country will be directed toward the really serious business which confronts us." He added, "McCarthyism has passed far beyond being merely a nuisance and has now become a deadly menace."[8]

Meanwhile the Washington columnists were picking the President apart. Almost unanimously opposed to McCarthy, they had spent much of 1953 predicting a White House crackdown and relishing the obvious result. But Ike had refused to play his part. He kept avoiding his duty, despite numerous provocations from the other side. By 1954 these columnists were speculating that he was either afraid of the senator or oblivious to the dangers that he posed to the nation's well-being. As Walter Lippmann wrote, "McCarthy's influence has grown as the President has appeased him. . . . His power will cease to grow and will diminish . . . when he is resisted, and it has been shown to our people that those to whom we look for leadership and to preserve our institutions are not afraid of him."*[9]

---

* Other columnists who held this view included Drew Pearson, Ernest Lindley, the Alsop brothers, Roscoe Drummond, James Reston, Doris Fleeson, and Marquis Childs.
   The President was obviously irritated by their criticism. He wrote one publisher: "No one has been more insistent and vociferous in urging me to challenge McCarthy than the people who built him up, namely writers, editors, and publishers. They have shown some of the earmarks of acting from a guilty conscience—after all, McCarthy and McCarthyism existed a long time before I came to Washington." See Dwight Eisenhower to William Robinson, March 12, 1954, *Eisenhower Presidential Papers*, Eisenhower Library.

Eisenhower still rejected this "advice," thinking it pointless and polit-ically naive. His own reading of history had taught him that presidents made heroes of scoundrels, and fools of themselves, by confronting their enemies in public. Roosevelt had made this mistake with Huey Long, he believed, and Truman had made it with McCarthy. The problem, he wrote George N. Craig, the Republican governor of Indiana, "is one to which I have devoted many hours of thoughtful consideration. . . . I think that were I to stand up in public and label McCarthy with deroga-tory titles, I would make a serious error. I still feel that such an attempt would advertise him still more. It would make the presidency look ridic-ulous . . . and make the citizens of our country very unhappy indeed." [10]

Nevertheless, the President's hatred of McCarthy triggered frequent explosions behind closed doors. In private, friends observed, "he would go up in an utter blaze over him." His face would redden as he con-demned the senator's headline-grabbing, his coarse familiarity, his shot-gun attacks on Marshall, Bohlen, and the European allies. He specu-lated, at different times, that McCarthy was crazy, that he wanted to be president, that Texas oil money kept him afloat, that the Kremlin had sent him to divide the nation and disrupt its foreign affairs. Arthur Lar-son claimed that Ike's "loathing and contempt" for McCarthy had "to be seen to be believed." Larson recalled a White House meeting where someone described a new type of federal insurance, which he termed a "sudden death policy." Eisenhower broke his bored silence by remarking, "I know one fellow I'd like to take the policy out for." [11]

―――――――

IN DECEMBER the Administration made numerous appeals to McCarthy, numerous attempts to bring him into line. They included everything from flattery to bribery and everyone from Brownell to Nixon to Eisen-hower himself. On December 18 McCarthy was invited to lunch at the White House. The President was there, as were Jenner, Velde, and Brownell. The purpose was to acquaint the men with the Administra-tion's "new offensive" against domestic subversion. Brownell did most of the talking. He spoke about legislation to outlaw the Communist Party and to legalize wiretap evidence in cases involving espionage. Under serious consideration, he added, was a proposal to strip U.S. citizenship from native-born and naturalized Communists.* Jenner and Velde were

* Also in December the government suspended the Q (top security) clearance of J. Robert Oppenheimer, the so-called father of the atomic bomb. Under the wording of Executive Order 10450, Oppenheimer *was* a security risk—despite his unquestioned loyalty to the United States. He had been a fellow traveler in the 1930s. His brother and sister-in-law were Communists. His wife had been married previously to a Communist. Yet Oppen-heimer had been checked and rechecked by the FBI, cleared and recleared by the Atomic Energy Commission. As Eisenhower wrote in his diary: "The overall conclusion has always been that there is no evidence that implies disloyalty on the part of Dr. Oppenheimer. However, this does not mean that he might not be a security risk."

impressed, but McCarthy viewed the meeting as a clear sign of presidential weakness. "Ike's really leaning," he bragged to friends. "Now he's asking my advice." [12]

In his book *McCarthy*, Roy Cohn listed other White House attempts to conciliate the senator. Among them, he said, was a secret meeting between his boss and I. Jack Martin, a White House staffer with superb contacts on Capitol Hill. According to Cohn, Martin offered the following compromise: end the public hearings on the Signal Corps; return to closed sessions; send the transcripts to the President, who will study them and take whatever action he deems appropriate. McCarthy said no. He was, we are told, "amazed at Martin's suggestion because it violated one of the fundamental principles upon which this government rests . . . the system of checks and balances devised by the Fathers of this Republic." [13]

The meeting probably took place, although McCarthy's concern for "the system of checks and balances" is a bit harder to believe. In December the White House *was* trying to end the Monmouth probe. Over Christmas, in fact, McCarthy was invited to Key Biscayne, Florida, where Nixon and Rogers "double-teamed him about the dangers of pushing the Army investigation too hard." According to several sources, Nixon advised Joe to drop his exclusive reliance upon the Communist issue and branch out into other fields. He even offered to help him by providing inside information about fraud and mismanagement during the Truman years. [14]

Under normal circumstances McCarthy would have laughed at such advice, despite his respect for Nixon and Rogers. In this case, however, the timing was perfect. In a few weeks the Senate would be voting new appropriations for its various committees. And there was some grumbling about Joe's treatment of witnesses and his one-man investigations. Even his allies were disturbed by his frequent claim-jumping, his invasion of territory that belonged to other Senate bodies, such as Armed Services and Internal Security. Pat McCarran complained that McCarthy had "stepped into a field where he was not intended to function at all." And Bill Jenner said, "I think it was a mistake for him to concentrate so much in the field of subversion and I don't think he'll do it this year." [15]

McCarthy got the message. While promising no let-up in his war

---

McCarthy's role in this case was minimal, although the Administration pursued it with an eye in his direction. He had learned of Oppenheimer's security problems in the spring of 1953. He met with "top Administration officials" (probably Richard Nixon and William Rogers) who persuaded him to lay off, promising that the case "would not be neglected." On December 2 Defense Secretary Charles Wilson telephoned the President. The transcript reads: "Wilson asked DDE if he had seen J. Edgar Hoover report on Dr. Oppenheimer. DDE has not. . . . AEC Chairman Lewis Strauss told Wilson, last night, that McCarthy knows about it and might pull it on us. DDE not worried about McCarthy, but does think it should be brought to attention of Brownell." The next day Eisenhower ordered that "a blank wall" be placed between the scientist and "all access to our government operations . . . whether sensitive . . . or otherwise."

against subversion, he spoke about a new and wider role for the Subcommittee on Investigations. He told reporters of his plans to review fifty income tax compromise cases that the Truman Administration had settled at "ridiculously low figures." He expressed interest in a probe of laws relating to tax-free foundations. He vowed to go to Alaska to check out reports of fraud and mismanagement—just as soon as the weather there improved. Of course, he added, these investigations would require more funding and manpower than the committee currently had at its disposal. He said he would need ten more staffers and a budget of perhaps $350,000, almost double the previous appropriation.[16]

The major stumbling block, as McCarthy well knew, was the continued absence of the subcommittee Democrats—Symington, Jackson, and McClellan. Their boycott made additional funding unlikely, for it dramatized the chairman's refusal to obey the rules of the Senate. By January both sides seemed willing to compromise, although the Democrats clearly held the upper hand. "I will lean over backward and do anything within reason that they ask for," McCarthy purred. "I've got an open mind on this thing." What the Democrats asked for—and got—was a minority counsel and a clerk, a voice in planning the subcommittee agenda, and a promise from McCarthy to relinquish his exclusive control over the hiring of subcommittee personnel. The Democrats returned on January 25. They appointed Robert Kennedy as the new minority counsel.[17]

On February 2 the Senate approved McCarthy's formal request for $218,000. (The original figure of $350,000 was an obvious bluff, designed to make the final figure look more reasonable.) The vote was 85–1, Fulbright being the lone dissenter. The Democrats went along because they saw no alternative. Their continued opposition in the face of these concessions would have angered many Republicans and allowed McCarthy to pose as a martyr. "I have nothing to say," Lyndon Johnson remarked, "except that he is a Republican problem."[18]

Some observers saw the makings of a "new" McCarthy. "There is a considerable amount of evidence," wrote W. H. Lawrence of the New York *Times*, "that during the next year he will not pay as much attention to investigating Communism and subversion. . . . This does not mean, of course, that he will abandon the Communist hunt entirely. It means that he will place greater emphasis upon graft, corruption, inefficiency and incompetence . . . in the field of government operations." There were others, however, who placed the "new" McCarthy in the same category with the Tooth Fairy and Peter Pan. "It's too good to be true," said the Washington *Post*. "No bear leaves a honey pot while it's full of honey."[19]

━━━━━

THE 19TH OF JANUARY, 1954, was a painfully slow newsday in Washington. The White House had little to report, Congress even less. The *Post* ran front page stories about a $200 robbery and the weather, which was sunny and cold. In the right-hand corner was the photo of a little boy who had choked to death on a frankfurter.

Robert Stevens was out of town that day touring military installations in Korea. McCarthy was on Capitol Hill warning the Republican Caucus about "farm problems" in the Midwest. And Frank Carr was on the telephone informing Army Counsel John Adams about the senator's desire to interrogate members of the Army Loyalty and Security Appeals Board in a closed session later that week.

Carr told Adams that the board members would be questioned about several matters, including graft and corruption. This was an obvious ploy, but a perfectly legitimate one. The Truman directive of 1948, still in force, prevented Executive officials from testifying about loyalty and security matters. It said nothing about graft and corruption. Yet once McCarthy got the board members before his committee, he could do anything he wanted. He could ask them why they voted to reinstate Aaron Coleman or what role the Communist Party had played in their decision. If the members refused to answer such questions—and they surely would refuse—the headlines would be spectacular.

Adams was alarmed. He and McCarthy had discussed the matter before. He thought they had reached an understanding that "it would not become an issue." With Stevens in Korea, Adams conferred with H. Struve Hensel, counsel for the Department of Defense, who advised him to sit tight and ignore the request. When McCarthy responded with a threat to subpoena the entire Loyalty Board, Hensel sent Adams to see William Rogers at the Department of Justice.[20]

Rogers, thirty-nine, was a man of enormous charm and political skill. He seemed to get along with everyone. "I don't know anyone else," said a Justice Department veteran, "who ever got J. Edward Hoover to come to his home and sing songs around the piano." His close friends included Richard Nixon, who leaned heavily on Rogers during the celebrated Checkers affair, and Joe McCarthy, who met Rogers in the 1940s and promptly hired away his secretary. Her name was Jeannie Kerr.[21]

By 1953 Rogers was known as "Eisenhower's number one executive in charge of Joe McCarthy problems." His job, quite simply, was to preach restraint and party loyalty to a man who believed in neither. It was Rogers who first urged Joe to cooperate with the White House and who helped force the resignation of J. B. Matthews. On one occasion Rogers's teenage daughter complained that McCarthy was disrupting the Rogers household. "That man," she remarked, "comes to our house and spends hours with Daddy."[22]

Rogers quickly arranged a meeting to consider McCarthy's latest challenge. It was held in Brownell's office on the morning of January 21, and it included several of the President's closest advisers—Rogers, Brownell, Sherman Adams, Gerald Morgan, and Henry Cabot Lodge. After considering the legal and political implications of the threatened subpoenas, the men listened in amazement as John Adams described his relationship with McCarthy and the subcommittee staff. Adams claimed that Roy Cohn in particular was putting tremendous pressure on the Army in order to obtain preferential treatment for G. David Schine, who had been inducted the previous November. According to Adams, the Monmouth hearings and the threatened subpoenas were part of this pressure. The story was so bizarre (and potentially damaging to McCarthy) that Adams was urged to prepare a detailed chronological account for the other subcommitte members and perhaps a few friendly journalists as well. Adams promised to do just that.[23]

THE FIRST PART OF THE ADAMS STORY—preferential treatment for Schine —was not exactly new. Drew Pearson had been writing about it since the summer of 1953. In July Pearson had publicly questioned the patriotism of McCarthy's staff—asking simply (and rhetorically) how men like Cohn and Schine had managed to avoid the draft while thousands of their peers were fighting and dying in Korea. Having obtained the draft records of both men, Pearson dutifully supplied the answers. Cohn had arranged for himself a safe commission in the inactive reserves while Schine had wangled a series of questionable deferments, including treatment for a slipped disc and a schizoid personality. "Schine is delighted to discuss his career," said Pearson, "except when you get near the touchy question of military service. Then he becomes just as evasive as a McCarthy witness."[24]

At first the story fell flat. It seemed rather petty, like so many of the mortar rounds that Pearson kept lobbing at McCarthy. But Pearson would not quit. He was so persistent, so typically obnoxious, that Schine's California draft board decided to reopen the case. It reclassified Schine 1A and drafted him in the fall of 1953.

Pearson kept the pressure on. In November he accused McCarthy of pulling "backstage wires" in a futile attempt to keep his "millionaire playboy consultant" out of the draft. In December he revealed that Cohn had been pressuring the brass at Fort Dix, New Jersey, to make life easier for Private Schine, and that Schine had already been excused from kitchen police, guard duty, and "other disagreeable chores." Pearson added that General Cornelius Ryan, the base commander, had complained to Secretary Stevens, who told him, "General, this is one you've got to handle yourself."[25]

Pearson did not know that these developments were somehow related to the Monmouth probe. He viewed the Schine affair as a separate story, but he was virtually alone in grasping the impact it would have upon the American people. "He was convinced," wrote Jack Anderson, his friend and associate, "that at last McCarthy had been caught in the one offense that is indefensible in a society that runs on egalitarian rhetoric—the use of political pull to excuse a millionaire's boy from peeling the potatoes that other mothers' sons had to peel."[26]

ON JANUARY 22 Adams went to Capitol Hill to confer with Dirksen and Mundt, the subcommittee Republicans who knew McCarthy best. His purpose was to enlist their aid in killing the threatened subpoenas. He saw Mundt first and gave him a detailed account of the Schine affair. He told Mundt, a friend and fellow South Dakotan, that in his opinion the subpoenas were a form of blackmail to obtain preferential treatment for Schine. Mundt was shocked by the charge but typically unwilling to pursue it. He said, "Well, John, I want to tell you my position right now. I believe in the subpoena power of Congress, and exercising it every chance we get."[27]

Adams saw Dirksen a few hours later. He told him the same story, but this time he got results.* Dirksen tracked down McCarthy (who was speaking in Illinois) and got him to delay the subpoenas. The next day Joe met privately with the subcommittee Republicans—Dirksen, Potter, and Mundt. The session began at 2 o'clock and continued for most of the afternoon. Dirksen spoke first, recalling the Adams visit and the charges that Adams had raised. "If what was revealed to me . . . is correct," he said, "I think Roy Cohn ought to be fired forthwith and I think every member of the committee will bear me out." McCarthy responded by offering a different, though equally disturbing, version of the Schine affair. He claimed that Adams had been "needling" Cohn for months in an attempt to end the Monmouth probe. This needling, he said, had begun with promises of preferential treatment for Schine. When these promises were rightly ignored, Adams had threatened to leak a phony report about Cohn's attempts to "blackmail" the Army. In short, said McCarthy, Private Schine was a hostage in the larger struggle between the devious Mr. Adams and the virtuous Mr. Cohn.[28]

The senators were puzzled by the conflicting stories. They agreed that Cohn and Adams would have to be heard. As the meeting broke up, McCarthy was handed the following letter:

---

* When Adams visited Dirksen, he brought along White House adviser Gerald Morgan, who knew Dirksen well. Morgan's presence was extremely helpful in getting Dirksen to intervene. See U.S. Senate, Subcommittee on Investigations of the Committee on Government Operations, *Army–McCarthy Hearings*, 1954, p. 1177.

I wish to confirm the position which has earlier been given to you informally . . . that the Department of the Army will not reveal the names of persons who sat on particular panels and that the Department will not permit such persons, including those whose names are already known to the Committee, to testify before Congressional Committees concerning proceedings of the loyalty–security hearings of their particular boards. . . .

The letter was signed "John Slezak, Acting Secretary of the Army." *

———

FOR THE MOMENT, at least, the Army appeared to have the upper hand. The Monmouth probe was now in limbo, the result of a direct constitutional challenge and a nasty battle over the exploits of Roy Cohn and his favorite recruit. Even McCarthy had his doubts about keeping the hearings alive. In public he accused the Army of "stonewalling" him; in private he seemed rather relieved. He knew that he had reached the point of diminishing returns, that he could not hope to make good on his earlier charges about *current* espionage at the base. Better to end the hearings—and to complain loudly that the Army had left him no alternative.

But McCarthy was far from discouraged. He had been probing the Army for several months now, checking hundreds of tips and rumors that poured into his office. He had accumulated other promising cases, including one that seemed to pinpoint the remarkable carelessness—or worse!—in the Army's security system. It was the case of Irving Peress.

Peress, thirty-six, was a dentist who lived and practiced in the Borough of Queens, New York. His parents were Russian-born Jews. He had attended City College with Rosenberg and Sobell. He had been drafted during World War II but deferred for medical reasons (a hernia). In 1951 he had registered with Selective Service, as required by the Doctor Draft Act. The following year he completed D.D. Form 390, which contained the statement:

I am not now and I have not been a member of any foreign or domestic organization, association, movement, group, or combination of persons advocating a subversive policy or seeking to alter the form of the Government of the United States by unconstitutional means.

On October 15, 1952, he became Captain Irving Peress, United States Army Reserves.[29]

In November Peress completed D.D. Form 398, the Army Loyalty Certificate. He now claimed "federal constitutional privilege" on all questions relating to membership in subversive organizations. In January

* Slezak was "Acting Secretary" because Robert Stevens was still in the Far East. Stevens had not been informed about the crisis. The Slezak letter was almost certainly written by John Adams.

1953 he was called to active duty and shipped to Fort Lewis, Washington, for further assignment to the Far East Command. At Fort Lewis, however, he applied for emergency leave, claiming that his wife and daughter were ill and undergoing medical treatment in New York. According to Army files,

> . . . the Red Cross dispatched a strong telegram to the commanding officer, Fort Lewis, recommending immediate cancellation of his overseas orders and a reassignment within the United States. . . . Peress further requested a reassignment for compassionate reasons. This was also approved solely because of the Red Cross statements and he was reassigned to Camp Kilmer [New Jersey] on 16 March 1953.

In New York, meanwhile, First Army Intelligence had run a check on Peress and reported "sufficient evidence of subversive and disloyal tendencies to warrant his removal." Following numerous delays, the Peress file was forwarded to Fort Lewis on April 24, 1953. By that time, however, Peress had returned to the jurisdiction of the intelligence unit that had just mailed his papers to the West Coast. The file reached Camp Kilmer in June—three and a half months after the Army had recommended the Captain's removal. Even worse, the G-2 at Kilmer did not notify the base commander; instead he placed Peress under the "personal surveillance" of another dentist at the camp.

On June 15 the Peress file was forwarded to First Army Headquarters in New York. Three weeks passed before anyone bothered to read it. According to Army regulations, a loyalty suspect had to complete a detailed interrogatory before final action could be taken against him. Peress did not receive the form until August 25, 1953. He furnished his name, address, date of birth, and the names of his parents; he wrote "federal constitutional privilege" in response to all remaining questions. The interrogatory was routed back to Army Intelligence through the Surgeon General's Office. It reached its destination on September 10, 1953.

Peress seemed remarkably unconcerned about the Army's interest in his past. On September 9 he applied for a promotion under the amended Doctor Draft Act, citing his considerable professional experience. His request was shipped to First Army Headquarters—along with a memo from Colonel Brown, the G-2 at Kilmer, recommending that "the application for promotion be *disapproved* at this time." But here came the worst blunder of all: The processing officers either overlooked or ignored the security information in the file. They judged Peress solely on his professional qualifications, and they recommended his promotion.

At this point a new player came on the scene: Ralph W. Zwicker, the commanding general at Camp Kilmer. A native of Wisconsin and a West Point graduate, Zwicker had served with the infantry in World War II. His decorations included the Silver Star, the Legion of Merit with cluster, the Bronze Star with two clusters, and the British Distinguished

Service Order. In an address to the National War College in 1947, General Eisenhower said that if Zwicker's regiment had not held the vital "north shoulder" during the Battle of the Bulge, allied resistance would likely have crumbled. He recommended a presidential citation for Zwicker and his men.

Zwicker had assumed the Kilmer command in July 1953, four months after his promotion to brigadier general. He had not been briefed on the Peress case until October. Outraged, he sent a note to W. A. Burress, the commanding general of First Army in New York. "The retention of Captain Peress," he wrote, "is clearly not consistent with the interests of national security. It is requested that immediate steps be taken to effect his relief from active duty. Two days later, on October 23, Peress was promoted to major.

The comedy continued. On November 3 General Burress made a routine visit to Camp Kilmer. When Zwicker asked him about the Peress case, Burress said he had never heard of it. He phoned his office in New York. The transcript read:

> General Burress called General Murphy from Camp Kilmer and stated that General Zwicker wrote a letter to us on October 21, Subject: Elimination of Security Risk—Captain Irving Peress . . . General Murphy declared that it should have rung a bell. The implications are obvious—if the Senator who has been investigating at Fort Monmouth finds out that the Army is promoting that type of fellow. He directed General Murphy to get on it right away.

What Burress feared, of course, was the possibility that McCarthy would learn of the case before the Army had time to cover its tracks. On November 6 Burress sent a memo to the Pentagon: "I have taken the liberty of writing . . . about this case, believing that you should know about it in view of its obvious implications. It seems to me . . . that Peress should be separated from the Army as soon as possible."

The Burress memo spurred things along. On November 18 the Army Personnel Board met to decide the matter. Three options were considered:

1. Court-martial
2. Appearance before a board of officers to show cause why suspect should not be eliminated from the Service
3. Discharge under the Involuntary Release Program

The first option was rejected because Peress "had done nothing during his military service which was an offense against military law." * The second was rejected because such proceedings were "time-consuming"

---

* If Peress was, in fact, a member of the Communist Party—and the Army had strong evidence that he was—then he had committed a federal offense by swearing falsely to the first of the loyalty forms, D.D. 390. The Army later admitted that Peress should have been court-martialed for this offense. On this point, see Lionel Lokos, *Who Promoted Peress?*, 1956, pp. 98–99.

and "expensive." The third option was perfect, for it allowed the Army to drop Peress without fanfare or messy public records. As it turned out, however, the board members did not realize that the Involuntary Release Program could result in an honorable discharge for the major. In fact, by failing to consider this point, the members left the erroneous impression that they wanted Peress to receive one.

The Board's "ruling" was supported by the Surgeon General, the Adjutant General, and the Secretary of the Army. General Burress got the word on January 18, 1954—two months later:

> It is desired that Major Irving Peress be relieved from active duty and honorably discharged from the Army at the earliest practical date, depending on the officer's desire, but in any event no later than 90 days from the date of the receipt of this letter.

Peress was notified at once. He chose March 31, 1954, as the date for his honorable discharge.

━━━━━━

COHN AND MCCARTHY learned of the Peress affair in December 1953. They were tipped off, Cohn wrote later, by a general "convinced that the Army was planning to cover up the entire scandalous situation." * This may be correct, although information about "problems" at Camp Kilmer and other Army bases had been flowing into McCarthy's office for most of 1953. A typical example was this letter from an enlisted man:

> . . . I am in possession of information which you, my favorite senator, might perhaps like to have. It contains certain details relative to Camp Kilmer, N.J. . . .
>
> Is it possible for me to furnish this data without being implicated in military channels by name? Am sure you, as good American, would certainly be interested in obtaining such data in order to eventually eliminate what all good Americans would look upon with shame.[30]

On January 4 Cohn telephoned John Adams and told him that the committee had learned about a "Communist officer" at Camp Kilmer. Adams, who was then unfamiliar with the case, promised to check it out. He called back a few days later, telling Cohn, "the doctor [sic] that you spoke about, we know about him. The Army is on top of it and he is being put out of the Army."

The case remained in limbo until January 22, when George Anastos, a committee aide, called General Zwicker to ask about "the major under investigation." According to Anastos, the general was remarkably cooperative. He identified Peress by name and volunteered confidential infor-

---

* In a later interview, Cohn told the author that the mysterious general was Zwicker himself, still furious over the Army's handling of the case.

mation from his security file. He described Peress as a Communist Party organizer, adding that Mrs. Peress had held Communist meetings in her home as late as 1952. Zwicker had a different recollection. He admitted identifying Peress as the suspect, but he denied leaking security information to Anastos or anyone else.

On January 27 Frank Carr phoned Adams to demand the appearance of Major Peress on Saturday morning, January 30, at the Federal Courthouse in Foley Square. Carr was angry. "This is the fellow that you told us was being put out of the Army," he said. "He hasn't been put out of the Army and we want him now." Adams did not object. He called Zwicker who notified Peress, who promised to appear. Then the major changed his mind. On Saturday morning he told Zwicker that he would not testify after all. Zwicker hit the roof. He said, "Now, Major Peress, you give me the answer again. I assure you that disciplinary action will be taken if it is not the correct one." Peress gave the correct answer. He left for New York City a few minutes later.[31]

Peress arrived with his lawyer at 10:30 that morning. He was wearing civilian clothes, as Zwicker had ordered. McCarthy was the only senator in attendance. Cohn and Carr were at his side. The hearing was closed to all visitors, including the press.[32]

Cohn got things started. He was careful and polite. "By the way," he began, "any time you want to you can consult with counsel. He can talk to you or nudge you and you can do likewise." Then McCarthy cut in.

> THE CHAIRMAN: Did anyone in the Army ever ask you whether you were a member of the Communist Party or a Communist Party organizer?

> MAJOR PERESS: I decline to answer that question under the protection of the fifth amendment on the ground that it might tend to incriminate me.

The questions came in flurries: "Is your wife a member of the Communist Party?" "Have you attempted to recruit soldiers into the Communist Party in the last week?" "Do you think Communists should be commissioned in our military?" While McCarthy did not attempt to deny Peress his constitutional rights, he made it clear—as he always did—that the exercise of these rights was proof enough that the witness was guilty. He did not say that Peress might be a Communist or that the evidence pointed in that direction. He *called* Peress a Communist and hinted that other Communists had conspired to cancel his traveling orders to the Far East.

> THE CHAIRMAN: I am curious to know how Communists can get their orders changed so easily. The average man would be sent to Yokahama. You can suddenly have your orders changed and kept in

this country. You told the Army that your wife and daughter were sick. If the sickness would be embarrassing to discuss, we will not ask about it, otherwise I want to know about it.

Peress did not want to discuss the matter. It was personal, he said.

THE CHAIRMAN: Mister, I don't know whether the reason is sufficient. . . . I want to find out how you stopped at the point of embarkation; who stopped you when they knew you were a Communist; whether another Communist did it for you, and I am going to order you to tell us what the alleged illness was.

MAJOR PERESS: The reason is simply that my wife and daughter were undergoing psychiatric treatment. . . .

THE CHAIRMAN: In other words, there was no physical illness . . . is that correct?

MAJOR PERESS: I don't know if you feel there is a difference between physical and mental illness—if there is a different validity of illnesses. As I said, they were under psychiatric treatment.

As the hearing ended, McCarthy asked Peress about his resignation date from the Army.

MAJOR PERESS: It is no later than the 31st of March, but I can move it up if I so desire.

THE CHAIRMAN: You are being given an honorable discharge?

MAJOR PERESS: I haven't been given—

THE CHAIRMAN: So far as you know, you are being allowed to resign with no reflection on your record?

MAJOR PERESS: There was no discussion of that.

"O.K.," said McCarthy, "you may step down." The hearing adjourned at 11:30 A.M.

———

PERESS WAS BADLY SHAKEN by the proceedings. He met with Zwicker on Monday morning, February 1, to request his immediate discharge from the Army. Zwicker was elated. He phoned the request to General Murphy at First Army Headquarters. Murphy told him to discharge Peress the following day.

McCarthy was unaware of the change. On Monday he sent Robert Stevens a long letter about the Peress affair. While personal in tone ("Dear Bob"), a copy reached the news wire before the original reached Stevens's office. The letter contained several "suggestions":

1. Court-martial Peress for conduct unbecoming an officer
2. Determine who promoted Peress and who canceled his orders to the Far East
3. Court-martial the parties responsible[33]

The letter reached the Pentagon by special messenger at 4:30 that afternoon. It was opened by an aide to Stevens—the Secretary was still in Korea—and routed to John Adams, who read it with obvious dismay. At 5:10 Adams took the letter to General Walter L. Weible, Deputy Chief of Staff for Operations. He told Weible that the Army should ignore it, that McCarthy had produced no evidence to warrant a reconsideration of the case. Weible went along—though mainly out of ignorance. He had no idea that an *honorable* discharge had been granted. And Adams was not about to tell him the truth.

Peress was honorably discharged at 2 o'clock the following afternoon. His commission in the Army Reserve was "irrevocably terminated." He assumed that his troubles were over. He could hardly have imagined that the circumstances surrounding his promotion and discharge were about to trigger one of the most remarkable confrontations in the history of American politics.

CHAPTER TWENTY-FIVE

The Chicken Luncheon

THE CASE OF IRVING PERESS has almost always been described as a trivial affair, involving a pink dentist who managed to parlay some unanswered loyalty forms into a nice promotion and an honorable discharge from the Army. That was the view of Robert Stevens, the Alsops, and the editorial writers of the time. It is also the view of the historians and journalists who have come along since. The case, said Richard Rovere, was comically insignificant. "It mattered not at all, except to the paymaster, what rank was held by this obscure jawsmith . . . but McCarthy claimed that in Peress's promotion he had found 'the key to the deliberate Communist infiltration of our Armed Forces.' "[1]

It wasn't quite that simple. For one thing McCarthy did not argue that Peress himself posed a danger to America's security, that he planned to drill healthy teeth in the name of Lenin and Marx. He argued, instead, that the Army lacked (1) a clear and consistent policy on the handling of security cases and (2) the ability to track them at any level of the Pentagon's swollen bureaucracy. Five officers had been involved in the induction of Peress, six in the promotion process, and thirteen more in the honorable discharge. "There were so many divisions of labor," wrote one critic in a long forgotten book, "that it would have taken a divining rod to affix any individual responsibility."[2]

Furthermore, McCarthy had investigated other "Fifth Amendment" cases in early 1954, although the press seemed not to notice. In one case, a private who refused to answer questions about his Communist affiliations had been discharged under "honorable conditions." In another case, a private who quit the Communist Party as a teenager had been given a general—or less than honorable—discharge after only fifteen months in the Army.

THE CHAIRMAN: Had you refused to sign the loyalty oath?

MR. RUBINSTEIN: No sir. I requested to sign it but I couldn't. . . . The oath was whether you have *ever* belonged to any of these organizations. . . . It would have constituted a falsification.

McCarthy was perplexed. Three individuals—including Dr. Peress—had been handled in three different ways. If the Army *had* a policy, it seemed to be one of hanging the innocent and wrist-slapping the guilty. The chairman turned to John Adams, who was sitting at his right: "Why didn't this young man receive an honorable discharge? He seems to be completely frank and honest and is willing to talk to the committee." Adams could only shrug his shoulders. He didn't really know.

―――――

IN THE FOLLOWING WEEKS, McCarthy pursued the Peress matter to the exclusion of everything else. Furious at the circumstances surrounding the honorable discharge, he ordered the dentist to return for public questioning on Thursday, February 18, despite the fact that he was no longer in the Army. Meanwhile, Jim Juliana discussed the case with General Zwicker, who seemed perfectly willing to cooperate. Not surprisingly, the general was asked to testify as well.

On Thursday morning the Foley Square courthouse was jammed with witnesses, staff members, spectators, and reporters—although, once again, McCarthy was the only senator in attendance. The hearing began an hour late—at 11:30—because Joe was not feeling well. The night before he and Jeannie had been involved in a nasty traffic accident near the Waldorf Astoria; the taxi in which they were riding had been rammed by a drunk driver. The impact had knocked Joe unconscious and left Jeannie with terrible pains in her legs.

Peress took the stand, more defiant than before. He spent most of his time claiming his constitutional privilege and quoting passages from the Bible. "I highly recommend to you, senator, and your counsel," he said, "Book 7 of the Psalms, which reads: 'His mischief shall return upon his head and his violence shall come down upon his pate.' "[3]

McCarthy brushed it all aside. He wanted Peress there as a visible symbol of the Communist problem, not as an informational source. In fact, his real words were directed at John Adams, who was sitting in the crowd: "I am going to ask you to give us the names of every officer . . . who had anything to do with this man's promotion . . . and honorable discharge. I will not take any double-talk on this, John. . . . I will want to know within twenty-four hours."

The moment the session ended, Joe rushed to the hospital to visit his wife. He spent almost an hour there, learning the bad news that Jeannie had broken her ankle. Returning to the courthouse, he chatted briefly with General Zwicker in a small office set aside for the subcommittee staff. (The conversation was friendly, Zwicker recalled, and the Peress case was not discussed.) Moments later, however, McCarthy was introduced to a spectator who had been seated directly behind the general at the morning session. The spectator claimed that Zwicker had been privately disrespectful, calling Joe an "SOB" and muttering, "You see, I told you this was what we'd get." (Zwicker would testify, months later, that "I've searched my memory . . . and have no recollection of having made any such remarks.")[4]

In any event, Joe was in a very bad mood. He had not slept the night before. He had a large, painful lump on his head. He had chaired a tough morning session, skipped lunch, rushed to the hospital and discovered that his wife would be on crutches for the next several months. He was tired, bruised, worried, hungry—and quite ready to explode.

The subcommittee met in closed session that afternoon because the scheduled witnesses—General Zwicker and Colonel Brown, the G-2 at Kilmer—were expected to discuss the Peress matter in intimate detail. Colonel Brown testified first, with Zwicker, John Adams, and Captain William Woodward, a medical officer, seated nearby. Zwicker had already told reporters that he had a touch of the flu, thus explaining Woodward's presence in the room. But Woodward wrote privately that the general had been experiencing "some vague chest pains" in recent days and "I was told by the committee that . . . they would be as brief as possible."[5]

As the questioning began, John Adams leaned over to whisper something to Colonel Brown. Joe responded by ordering Adams to take the stand. Adams refused. "All right," the chairman thundered, "there is a new rule in effect. Nobody can be in the committee room excepting the witness." With that, Zwicker, Woodward, and Adams were escorted to the corridor outside.

Colonel Brown's testimony was never made public. According to Zwicker, "it lasted for quite some time and I could tell by talking to him that he had had quite an experience." Then Zwicker and Woodward were called into the room, but Adams was told to wait outside. This left the general without benefit of counsel—a circumstance he did not bother to challenge. In a sworn statement two weeks later, he claimed that "at no time during the hearing in question did Senator McCarthy offer me counsel," and "at no time . . . did I ask for or ever intimate a desire for counsel." In short, the matter never came up.*

Cohn began by asking Zwicker to summarize the steps the Army had taken to get rid of Major Peress. "That is a toughie," the general replied. "I may say that if I were in a position to do so, I would be perfectly glad to give the committee any information they desired." McCarthy did not like the answer. He had expected more cooperation, especially with Adams out of the room.

> THE CHAIRMAN: Well, you know that somebody has kept Peress on, knowing he was a Communist, do you not?
>
> GENERAL ZWICKER: No, sir.
>
> THE CHAIRMAN: You know that somebody has kept him on knowing that he has refused to tell whether he was a Communist, do you not?
>
> GENERAL ZWICKER: I am afraid that would come under the category of the Executive Order, Mr. Chairman.[6]

At this point, with no one to guide him, the witness made a crucial mistake. Rather than standing his ground—citing the Executive Order and saying no more—he began to spar with McCarthy.

> THE CHAIRMAN: The day the honorable discharge was signed for Peress, were you aware of the fact that he had appeared before our committee?
>
> GENERAL ZWICKER: I was.
>
> THE CHAIRMAN: And that he refused to answer certain questions?
>
> GENERAL ZWICKER: No, sir, not specifically on answering any questions. I knew that he had appeared before your committee.

This was absurd. Zwicker knew everything there was to know about the appearance of Major Peress. And by saying otherwise, he was literally inviting McCarthy to batter him in search of the truth.

---

* At first Zwicker alleged that McCarthy *had* denied him counsel. See Zwicker's "Memorandum for the Record," February 19, 1954, and his first affidavit, February 20, 1954, both on file at the Eisenhower Library, and both stamped "confidential" by the Army. This claim was later amended in Zwicker's affidavit of March 6, 1954, quoted above. Upon taking the stand, Zwicker even announced that "there is no need for a medical officer to be here." He seemed genuinely embarrassed by the presence of Captain Woodward. Under the circumstances, Roy Cohn's reply was ironic indeed: "A man who is his own lawyer has a fool for a client, and it is the same thing for a man who tries to be his own doctor." See Permanent Subcommittee on Investigations of the Committee on Government Operations, *Communist Infiltration of the Army*, 1954, p. 145.

THE CHAIRMAN: Didn't you read the news?

GENERAL ZWICKER: I read the news releases.

THE CHAIRMAN: And the news releases were to the effect that he had refused to tell whether he was a Communist. . . . It was all in the wire stories, was it not?

Slowly, painfully, the general gave ground. Yes, he admitted, he did recall that Peress had taken the Fifth Amendment that day. However, he wasn't "too certain" about the questions that Peress had refused to answer. "General," McCarthy shot back, "let's try and be truthful. I am going to keep you here as long as you keep hedging and hawing."

GENERAL ZWICKER: I am not hedging.

THE CHAIRMAN: Or hawing.

GENERAL ZWICKER: I am not hawing, and I don't like to have anyone impugn my honesty, which you just about did.

THE CHAIRMAN: Either your honesty or your intelligence; I can't help impugning one or the other. . . .

As the sparring continued, the general found himself in the uncomfortable and utterly unnecessary position of defending the very blunders that he himself had uncovered and quietly tried to correct. Finally, the chairman asked: "Do you think, general, that anyone who is responsible for giving an honorable discharge to a man who has been named under oath as a member of the Communist conspiracy should himself be removed from the military?"

Zwicker was trapped. He could not answer "yes" without appearing to support the removal of his direct superiors. And he could not answer "no" without appearing to cover up serious wrongdoing on their part.

GENERAL ZWICKER: Well, that is pretty hypothetical.

THE CHAIRMAN: It is pretty real, general, and you are going to answer it.

GENERAL ZWICKER: Repeat it.

(The question was reread by the reporter.)

GENERAL ZWICKER: That is not a question for me to decide, Senator.

THE CHAIRMAN: You are ordered to answer it, general. You are an employee of the people. . . . I want to know how you feel about getting rid of Communists.

GENERAL ZWICKER: I am all for it.

THE CHAIRMAN: All right. You will answer that question, unless you take the Fifth Amendment. I do not care how long we stay here, you are going to answer it.

GENERAL ZWICKER: Do you mean how I feel toward Communists?

THE CHAIRMAN: I mean exactly what I asked you, general, nothing else. And anyone with the brains of a five-year-old child can understand that question. The reporter will read it to you as often as you need to hear it . . .

GENERAL ZWICKER: Start it over, please.

(The question was reread by the reporter.)

GENERAL ZWICKER: I do not think he should be removed from the military.

McCarthy simply exploded. His face flushed as he spat out the words that would plague him for the rest of his life:

> Then, general, you should be removed from any command. Any man who has been given the honor of being promoted to general and who says "I will protect another general who protects Communists' is not fit to wear that uniform, general. I think it is a tremendous disgrace to the Army to have this sort of thing given to the public. I intend to give it to them. I have a duty to do that. I intend to report to the press exactly what you said. So you know that. You will be back here, general.

That evening Joe met with several friends and staffers to review the events of the day. Much calmer now, he seemed embarrassed by his loss of control and worried that it might shift the public's attention from the Peress case to the abuse of a decorated Army general. "I guess I treated Zwicker pretty rough," he said, adding that never in his years as a lawyer, a judge, and a senator had he come across a more irritating witness.

———

GENERAL ZWICKER SPENT THAT EVENING at his Camp Kilmer office, drafting a three-page account of his run-in with McCarthy. This done, he called W. T. Burress, the First Army commander, and threatened to resign. "I don't have to take this," Zwicker declared. "I'm going to quit." Burress urged him to calm down and do nothing he would later regret. Then Burress phoned the Pentagon and repeated the story to General Matthew B. Ridgway, the Army Chief of Staff.[7]

Ridgway was a large, mute, ill-tempered man, known for his toughness and his courage under fire. As commander of the 82d Airborne in World War II, he had directed the largest paratroop assaults in U.S. history, often jumping with his men. As commander of the Eighth Army in Korea, he had led the counteroffensive that recaptured Seoul and

drove the Red Chinese back across the 38th parallel. His trademark—
like MacArthur's braided cap and Patton's ivory-handled pistols—was a
string of live grenades dangling precariously from his chest.

The news from General Burress was more than Ridgway could bear.
It came at a time when the Army's morale, sapped by sweeping budget
cuts and the failure to "win" in Korea, was dangerously low. And it
marked the senator's fourth attack upon an Army general in two years,
the third since Ridgway assumed his duties in the spring of 1953. "We're
like men with our hands tied behind our back," he muttered. "Mc-
Carthy's only choice is whether to kick us in the groin or kick us in the
face."[8]

On Friday afternoon, February 19, Ridgway went to Robert Stevens
with a copy of the Zwicker memo, which had arrived a few hours before.
"I was berated by Senator McCarthy," it said, ". . . told that I was a
disgrace to the uniform . . . that I was either stupid or deliberately trying
to protect Communist conspirators." While Zwicker did not repeat his
threat to resign, he did offer some sharply worded advice:

> I feel strongly that if at the highest levels in the Department of the Army,
> and our government, prompt steps are not taken to protect other officers . . .
> from being subjected to the kind of treatment to which I was subjected that
> the Army will lose materially in the loyal support of its officer corps.[9]

Ridgway warned that the incident was too dangerous to ignore; the
Army could not allow its best officers to be roughed up like common
criminals. He reminded Stevens of their duty to protect the men in
uniform, and Stevens replied that he would do what had to be done.
"This," he said, "is the end of the line."

━━━━━

STEVENS WAS SERIOUS. He phoned Joe the next morning, determined to
"set things straight." Their conversation—monitored secretly by Pentagon stenographers—began with tough talk on both ends of the line.

> MR. STEVENS: . . . I am going to try to prevent my officers from going
> before your committee until you and I have an understanding as
> to the abuse they are going to get.

> SENATOR McCARTHY: . . . Just go ahead and try it, Robert. I am
> going to kick the brains out of anyone who protects Communists.
> . . . I will guarantee you that you will live to regret it.

But Stevens stood firm. He said that he would not allow Zwicker to
testify again—subpoena or no subpoena.

> SENATOR McCARTHY: Would you consider yourself subpoenaed for
> 10 o'clock Thursday morning?

MR. STEVENS: I will take that under advisement.

SENATOR MCCARTHY: . . . I am telling the press that you have been told to appear. If you decide not to, we will take steps from there on. I am all through with this covering up of Communists. I am sorry that Bob Stevens is the one that is doing it, too.

With that, McCarthy slammed down the phone.[10]

Stevens had done his duty as he saw it. He had stood by his men. But the more he thought about the phone call, the more anxious he became. He knew that he had acted on impulse, without waiting for the official transcript of the hearing and without considering the legal and political implications of his threat to withhold witnesses from a congressional committee. Furthermore, he did not know whether the Administration would do for him what it had failed to do for Harold Stassen, Robert Johnson, and countless others. Above all, he did not want to face McCarthy alone.

Stevens called the other subcommittee members, seeking their protection and advice. His phone log read like a fever chart: Dirksen at 9:50, McClellan at 9:55, Potter at 9:59, Symington at 10:05 and 10:25, Mundt at 11:30. (Jackson was out of town.) McCarthy just "raked me over," "beat my brains out," and "batted me pretty good," he told them. "I'm a coddler of Reds, you see."[11]

The Republican members did not rush to Stevens's defense. Senator Dirksen, one of Joe's few friends on the Hill, was formal and aloof, while Senator Mundt, who posed as everyone's friend, was (in Stevens's wonderful description) "highly distressed . . . but noncommittal." That left Senator Potter, a good-natured, inconspicuous man, who seemed increasingly anti-McCarthy yet well aware of his status as the group's junior Republican member. He promised "to contact Ev and Karl . . . and see what we can do."[12]

Stevens had more luck with Stuart Symington and John McClellan, which was understandable enough. As Democrats, they did not have to worry about the effects of a Stevens–McCarthy donnybrook upon the Administration or the GOP. And *these* Democrats were especially sensitive to the issues at hand. Both men were strong, almost reverent military supporters, and both had suffered the kind of hardship and pain that McCarthy's hand-picked assistants seemed so determined to avoid.*

McClellan's advice was simple. After gently reminding Stevens that no one had the power to subpoena by telephone, he urged him to announce his *willingness* to testify before a formal subpoena could be delivered. That way, the chairman could not portray Stevens as a reluctant witness, a man with something to hide.

* See below, pp. 407–408.

MR. STEVENS: I think that has got a lot of merit.

SENATOR McCLELLAN: Just beat him to the punch.[13]

Symington had other ideas. Departing that day on a junket to France, he wanted Stevens to postpone the showdown until he returned to Washington in early March. His advice, therefore, was to counterpunch and not to lead. "I wouldn't go until I am here," he said. "This boy [McCarthy] gets awfully rough. . . . He might be sick, you know. . . . We can throw blocks in this thing."[14]

Stevens felt trapped. He did not want a showdown with McCarthy, yet he saw no way out unless the chairman called off the hearings himself. "I'm not looking forward to going up there," he replied. "On the other hand, Stu, I can't create the impression in the mind of the public that I'm afraid of this guy."

Symington did not press the point. He promised Stevens his support, urged him to stay tough ("I don't mean silly tough; I mean firm."), and gave him this parting advice: "If you are going to play with McCarthy, you have to forget about these Marquis of Queensberry rules."

On Sunday morning Stevens went out and beat McCarthy to the punch. After breaking the news of the Zwicker incident in a solemn and sometimes misleading statement to the press, he ordered the general not to appear before the subcommittee on Thursday morning, February 25. "I am unwilling for him to run the risk of further abuse," Stevens declared. "The prestige and morale of our Armed Forces are too important to the security of the nation to have them weakened by unfair attacks on our officer corps." Then, following McClellan's advice, the Secretary expressed his willingness to testify in Zwicker's place. "Thus far, I have not received a formal notification to appear," he said, shading the truth a bit. "I consider it not only a duty but a privilege to be available to the committees of Congress whenever they may want me."[15]

THE PRESIDENT WAS IN PALM SPRINGS, golfing with Ben Hogan, putting superbly, and shooting in the low eighties, one of his best rounds in years. He learned of the Zwicker incident on Sunday evening, and he had every reason to explode. This was no diplomat or college professor who had been humiliated; this was a friend, a fellow officer, a man who had served him gallantly in World War II. But the President did not explode. He did what he usually did. He told James Hagerty that he intended to "remain aloof," and Hagerty so informed the press.

Other Republican leaders did not have this luxury. They were disturbed by the Zwicker incident and horrified by Steven's response. They viewed his attempt to protect his officers by ordering them not to testify as an abuse of executive power, an affront to the Senate, and a tacit admission that the Army had something to hide. Fearing the worst—a televised brawl between an overmatched Republican department head and a bully boy Republican crusader—they hoped to convince both sides that the only winner in this fray would be the Democratic Party.

On Monday, Washington's birthday, Karl Mundt and Robert Stevens were honored by the Freedom Foundation at Valley Forge. Traveling together, they discussed the Zwicker incident and the showdown with McCarthy, now just seventy-two hours away. Mundt told Stevens that he had no chance to win. For one thing, he explained, the chairman would control the flow of the hearing. As a result, he would hammer at the Peress case, item by item, showing the Army in the worst possible light. By the time another senator got a chance to ask about the Zwicker incident, the session would be over, the cameras clicked off.[16]

Mundt also warned about the dangers of withholding witnesses from a committee of Congress. This, he said, was the worst blunder of all. It would trigger a constitutional crisis and force the Senate to unite behind its most controversial member. "It is a most unfortunate issue," Mundt declared. "Joe's worst enemies would support him in this one. I think he will lick you hopelessly."[17]

Stevens either missed the point or chose to ignore it. He saw only one issue, the morale of his men. And that issue made compromise impossible unless McCarthy apologized to General Zwicker and promised to treat future Army witnesses with courtesy and respect. "I've got to do something," he kept repeating. "I've got to do something to restore Army morale."

At Valley Forge that afternoon Stevens earned a standing ovation—and the temporary nickname "Fighting Bob"—by vowing to protect the "loyal men and women in our Army." By chance, McCarthy was in nearby Philadelphia, accepting a good citizenship award from the local branch of the Sons of the American Revolution. In his hand was a copy of the Zwicker transcript, which he quoted at length. "As I look it over," he told the large, friendly crowd, "I was too temperate in what I said. If I were doing it today, I would be much stronger in my language."[18]

That evening McCarthy announced that the subcommittee would meet in special session the following day. And he turned up the dial a notch by promising to expose another "Red link" to the Army. "This is primarily for Steven's benefit," he said between giggles and winks at the press. "It should be known to him before he testifies under oath. I don't want him to be in the embarrassing position of not having the full picture."

———

THE NEW "RED LINK" was identified as Annie Lee Moss, a black mother of four who had worked at the Pentagon since World War II. Starting as a custard cook, she had been promoted to the position of communications clerk at a salary of $3,335 a year. McCarthy claimed that her job description placed her "in the Army's code room . . . handling the encoding and decoding of confidential and top secret messages." The Army described her as a "relay machine operator" who handled secret messages only in scrambled and unreadable form. It insisted that she had no access to the codes or to the cryptograph room where the messages were deciphered.

The charges against her were difficult to assess. They rested entirely on the word of one Mary Stalcup Markward, a beautician-turned-FBI-informer who had infiltrated the Communist Party and become its membership director for Washington, D.C. A strong, apparently convincing witness, Mrs. Markward had testified at the Smith Act trials and at numerous congressional hearings. In fact, she had "named" Mrs. Moss at a closed HUAC session on February 22, 1954—the very day that McCarthy announced his own interest in the case. This coincidence was too much for some HUAC members, who angrily accused the senator of stealing *their* unfinished business. While Joe denied the theft, he did commend the House Committee for doing "some excellent research in this same case." [19]

Markward testified before the subcommittee on Tuesday morning, February 23—her second congressional appearance in as many days. The hearing was open, and what stood out clearly was the presence of five subcommittee members instead of the usual one or two. This was understandable, for the Democrats had just ended their boycott and the Republicans were under increasing pressure to keep the chairman in line. Their failure to attend the Zwicker hearing had been duly noted and roundly condemned in the press. They could not afford to stay away now.

McCarthy introduced the witness as "a full-fledged FBI agent . . . and not an informer." * He asked her, "Was Annie Lee Moss a member of the Communist Party?"

MRS. MARKWARD: She was.

THE CHAIRMAN: . . . There is no doubt in your mind?

MRS. MARKWARD: Absolutely not. [20]

The Democrats had their doubts, however. They did not question the integrity of the witnesses, but they did want proof that Annie Lee Moss, the Communist, was the *same* Annie Lee Moss who worked at the Pentagon.

---

* Mrs. Markward was not an FBI agent. She later testified that she had received only "expense money" from the Bureau. If so, she lived well. The FBI paid her more than $24,000 for her information. See, New York *Times*, January 10, 1958.

SENATOR McCLELLAN: . . . Did you know her personally . . . or was it a name to you as a member of the Communist Party?

MRS. MARKWARD: I don't specifically recall that I do know her as a person. I don't recall that I don't know her as a person, either. . . .

SENATOR JACKSON: Did you ever have information that she attended a meeting or was active in the Communist Party?

MRS. MARKWARD: . . . I cannot specifically say she did any particular act on any particular date, no.

As the noon hour approached, McCarthy announced that Annie Lee Moss would testify the following day. Then, by reflex, it seemed, he began to testify for her. "I believe she will deny membership in the Party. . . . She will not claim it is misidentity. She will not claim that she is reformed." In short order he added the verdict as well: "There is no question that this woman, Annie Lee Moss, who is handling the encoding, decoding, the routing of classified work, has been an active member of the Communist Party."

———

THAT WAS TUESDAY MORNING. On Tuesday afternoon Richard Nixon invited representatives from the Army (Robert Stevens, John Adams), the White House (Jack Martin, Jerry Persons), and the Senate (Everett Dirksen, William Knowland) to his hideaway office on Capitol Hill. Because Stevens had come seeking tactical advice, the group listened with polite amusement as he outlined his plan to "go in [Thursday morning] and finesse the Peress case . . . and then move on the Zwicker incident and talk about how badly McCarthy had behaved." When the Secretary finished, he got much the same lecture that Mundt had given him the day before: it was McCarthy as chairman, not Stevens as witness, who would control the hearing. Put simply, "Joe will tear you to pieces."[21]

At this point, Nixon recalled, the group "agreed that Dirksen should try to arrange a luncheon meeting with Stevens and McCarthy for the next day." They urged Stevens to be reasonable, to promise McCarthy his full cooperation in return for McCarthy's promise to treat Army witnesses more respectfully in the future. Stevens "agreed" because he really had no choice—not after the Vice President and the majority leader had made their feelings known. Anyway, he assumed that he had nothing to lose. If the meeting worked out, all well and good. If it didn't, he would be no worse off than before.[22]

Stevens returned to the Pentagon in good spirits. But that evening, to be safe, he prepared the statement he would deliver to the subcommittee if a deal could not be made. The wording was significant, for it demonstrated that the Secretary's faith in his own position had by no means disappeared. "I am not here to defend Peress. . . . Captain Peress is not the issue here," he wrote, stubbornly. "The issue is the treatment given a distinguished combat soldier who followed official Army orders. I am here to defend that man."

━━━━━

ON WEDNESDAY MORNING the subcommittee met in open session to hear the testimony of Annie Lee Moss. The scene was truly pathetic as the witness, shivering visibly through a battered overcoat, walked slowly to the stand. Her attorney, George F. C. Hayes, a black man, insisted that she was too sick to testify, and the chairman quickly agreed. "I do not want a woman . . . in ill health . . . indicted for perjury," he said. "She does not look well to me."[23]

Hayes objected to these remarks. He was unwilling to concede that Mrs. Moss was a perjurer—or even a potentially uncooperative witness. On the contrary, he said, his client had just "appeared before another congressional committee on this same subject and answered spontaneously and, I believe, sir, truthfully." In that case, the chairman shot back, "it is very important that she return here at the very earliest date. Her testimony, I understand, before the House Committee was to the effect that she had been in close contact with a top member of the Communist Party and purchased the *Daily Worker* from him." Calmly Hayes replied, "That is not correct, sir."

Getting nowhere, McCarthy tried a different approach. He asked Hayes to place the interests of his country above the interests of his "Communist" client. "You appear to be an honest, intelligent lawyer," the chairman declared. ". . . You are not the typical type of Communist lawyer that appears before this committee. . . . I suggest that you advise this woman to come in here and tell the truth."*

But Hayes rejected the compliment and bristled at the advice. In fact, he proceeded to lecture McCarthy about his shortcomings as chairman —just like the "typical type of Communist lawyers" who had appeared in the past. "It is disturbing," he said, "to come before a committee that begins by telling me that 'We have already condemned your client and we have all the evidence . . .' It does not seem that is a proper approach."

This time McCarthy held his temper in check. For one thing, he could not turn on this "honest, intelligent lawyer" without looking rather ridiculous. And he did not want another Zwicker incident, not with reporters and other subcommittee members in the room.

---

* When Henry Jackson objected to these words, McCarthy replied, "I made the statement because I know something about the background of this lawyer." The chairman never did say what he knew—or liked—about Mr. Hayes. In fact, Hayes had represented several prominent black radicals, including Paul Robeson.

THE CHAIRMAN: You may step down.

MR. HAYES: Yes, sir.

SENATOR JACKSON: Did you have any further statements in connection with your client?

MR. HAYES: I simply wanted to say that it seems to me—

THE CHAIRMAN: You may step down.

When the session ended, Mundt and McCarthy went directly to Room P-54, the office of the Senate's Republican campaign committee chairman, Everett McKinley Dirksen. Robert Stevens arrived a few minutes later, looking shaken and confused. The luncheon meeting was supposed to be "super-secret," yet the Secretary had emerged from the back stairway to find a mob of reporters and photographers surrounding the office door. And once inside he discovered that Senator Potter, his most likely ally among the Republican members, would not be there to help him out.* One reporter likened the scene to a goldfish entering a tank of barracuda.[24]

Over a luncheon table that included fried chicken, salad, and coffee, the senators went at Stevens like a police interrogation team, with Mundt and Dirksen playing the friendly cops and McCarthy playing himself. First Joe would rage at Stevens—only to have Mundt remind him that he was no longer dealing with Dean Acheson and the Democrats. Then he would get up and threaten to leave—he apparently made three such attempts—only to have Dirksen coax him back with soothing appeals to "party unity." Before long, Joe had "cooled off," the tension had eased, and Mundt, puffing a dollar cigar, had typed out the words "Memorandum of Understanding, February 24."[25]

Two hours and five paragraphs later the door opened and the press crowded inside. Stevens and McCarthy were seated together on a green leather couch, the Secretary frozen in place, staring blankly ahead. A reporter described him as a man "in shock . . . wearing a blue suit, silver hair, and a red face." Then the TV lights clicked on and Mundt read the Memorandum aloud. "There is complete agreement," he said, "that the Secretary of the Army will . . . complete the investigation . . . of the Peress case as rapidly as possible. He will give the subcommittee the names of everyone involved in the promotion and honorable discharge of Peress, and such individuals will be available to appear before the

---

* Many press reports claimed that Potter had attended the luncheon meeting. This error was due to the fact that he came to the picture-taking session after the meeting broke up. Several weeks later, in a phone conversation, Stevens told Potter, "if it had been possible for you to attend that luncheon meeting, things would not have turned out as they did." See *Army–McCarthy Hearings*, p. 2137.

subcommittee." Of course, Mundt agreed, the Secretary's own appearance, set for Thursday morning, had been indefinitely postponed.[26]

The Memorandum could hardly be called a compromise, although Mundt gamely insisted that it was. On paper, at least, the Army had come away with nothing—neither the admission that its officers had been mistreated in the past nor the written assurance that they would be well treated in the future. When asked about these startling omissions, the Secretary refused comment and hurried from the room. But McCarthy stayed behind to joke with the press—"Anybody want a commission? I can fix it up!"—and to gloat over his victory. He was quoted as saying that Stevens could not have surrendered more if he crawled on his hands and knees.

When Stevens returned to the Pentagon, however, he announced that the meeting had gone well, that he had got what he went for—*private assurances* of fair treatment in the future. Was this possible? Was there more to the meeting than the Memorandum of Understanding? McCarthy said no, while Mundt and Dirksen said nothing at all. This left Richard Nixon, who spoke with several of the participants as the meeting broke up. According to his *Memoirs*, published in 1978, "there *was* an understanding, not mentioned in the agreement itself, that McCarthy would treat these witnesses respectfully."[27]

But these words are suspect, for on February 26, 1954—just two days after the meeting—Nixon said precisely the opposite in a "private interview" with columnist Arthur Krock, one of the Administration's most articulate supporters. According to the notes of that interview,

> Nixon was utterly dumbfounded when he saw the Memorandum of Understanding to which Stevens agreed. He thinks Stevens was in such an emotional state that he didn't know what he had agreed to. *In proof of this Stevens did not recall . . . that any assurances had been given him of good treatment for Army witnesses.*[28]

That night, after reading the news reports of his "surrender," Robert Stevens broke down and cried. He was sobbing as he phoned Nixon and Hagerty to say that he had "lost standing" and decided to resign. Both men argued against it, although both were dismayed by his embarrassingly inept behavior under fire. "I told him to cool off overnight," Hagerty wrote in his diary. ". . . He walked right into a bear trap and now I'll have to work like hell to get him out of it. What a job!"[29]

Hagerty was right, of course. The reaction was furious, with everyone agreeing that Stevens had eaten more than fried chicken the previous afternoon. By most accounts, the Secretary had either "caved in" or "retreated" or "collapsed." By some accounts he had done even worse. The Richmond *News–Leader* accused him of reviving the myth that "McCarthy bestrides this nation like a Colossus, while petty men walk about under his huge legs." The Detroit *Free Press* set down February 24, 1954, beside July 21, 1861—the date of the first Battle of Bull Run. The *Times* of London went back farther still: "Senator McCarthy this afternoon achieved what General Burgoyne and General Cornwallis never achieved—the surrender of the American Army." [30]

The President also took his lumps, especially from those who had condemned his public silence on McCarthy in the past. The Alsop brothers compared Washington after the "chicken luncheon" to Berlin after the Reichstag fire—with Stevens cast as the dull-witted arsonist, Eisenhower as the aging Hindenburg, and Hitler played by "you know who." The St. Louis *Post–Dispatch* claimed that control "of our national defense has passed, in part at least, from the White House to the unscrupulous hands of Senator McCarthy." The Washington *Post* said much the same thing, although its publisher, Philip Graham, went a step further by urging the White House to dump Stevens, defend Zwicker, and denounce McCarthy in one fell swoop. "Excuse what must seem . . . rank effrontry," he wrote Sherman Adams. "But do believe me that if you do not *now* break specifically with this monster you will become his pawns." [31]

━━━━━━━

EISENHOWER HAD RETURNED TO WASHINGTON on Tuesday afternoon, February 23, feeling rested and relaxed. He had been told nothing about the plans for the luncheon meeting because his aides assumed that he didn't want to know. As a result the President had learned the details at the same time, and in much the same way, as almost everyone else—by reading the front page of his newspaper. "You can imagine my astonishment," he told his friend Lucius Clay. ". . . The press says I came back to tell Stevens to go. . . . Nothing could be further from the truth. . . . Not a single soul queried me about this thing." [32]

The President did not fault his aides, who were merely respecting his oft-stated desire to remain above the fray. What disturbed him was the end result, the way the meeting had turned out. He was amazed that Mundt and Dirksen would propose such a compromise and equally amazed that a representative of the Army would agree to sign it. He wondered how anyone, even the slow-thinking Stevens, could have gone ahead with a "top secret" meeting after spotting a hundred reporters camped outside the door. "At that point, if not before," the President fumed, "he should have returned to his office." [33]

The luncheon meeting was a pivotal event. The more the President thought about it, the angrier he became. He was not about to battle McCarthy in public; that would always be out of the question. But he was ready, at long last, to assume the decision-making responsibilities that had so divided his staff. From this point forward there would be no more appeasement of McCarthy. The policy, instead, would be one of firm but quiet resistance, intended to isolate and embarrass the senator without resorting to fits of public displeasure.

Step one involved the Memorandum of Understanding, which had to be revised. After conferring with his aides, the President summoned Everett Dirksen to the Oval Office. He did not threaten or berate the senator; he simply told him that the White House was drafting a new agreement to be issued *that day* in the name of Robert Stevens and the subcommittee Republicans. "I want you to help me with this," the President said, and Dirksen promised to try.

The senator then walked to the East Wing of the White House, where the draft was being prepared. According to Hagerty, the session went well. Dirksen promised to support a new statement saying that the committee had "complete confidence in Stevens" and that "Army officers, if called, would be treated with proper respect." In the conversation that followed, Dirksen also agreed that Roy Cohn would have to be fired. This was very important, for the White House had come to view Cohn as the driving force behind the committee's attacks on the Army. That afternoon, in fact, Richard Nixon had told Arthur Krock—off the record —about a new arrangement "to correct the problems that brought on the fight with Stevens." He added, almost gleefully, that "the Army has a file two inches thick of Cohn's interventions in behalf of David Schine. This will ruin Cohn, and McCarthy knows he had better get rid of Cohn fast if he can beat the Army to it."[34]

But the agreement never came off. When Dirksen returned to Capitol Hill, he did not bring up Cohn's name at all. He simply showed the statement to his colleagues and asked for their thoughts. Mundt was cautious, as always, and McCarthy refused to sign. He fumed at the inference that Army officers had been mistreated in the past. When word reached the White House, Eisenhower decided to go it alone. He told his staffers to prepare a face-saving statement for Stevens to issue that evening. And then, to relieve his anger, he went out and hit golf balls on the frozen South Lawn.

Stevens read the statement to reporters in Hagerty's East Wing office. He claimed that General Zwicker had been severely mistreated (which was true); that Zwicker had been deprived of counsel (which was questionable); and that promises of better treatment had been made at the luncheon meeting (which was probably untrue). "I shall never accede to the abuse of Army personnel under any circumstances," he said bravely. "I shall never accede to them being browbeaten or humiliated."

The moment he finished, Hagerty leaned over and told him to say no more. "Stick to your statement," he whispered. When a reporter asked Stevens if he intended to remain on the job, Hagerty grabbed the microphone himself. "I'll answer that one," he said. "The answer is—of course." But what about the Secretary? Does he have anything to add? Stevens stood there beaming. Yes, indeed, he replied. "We certainly have a Commander-in-Chief. He stepped right up to the plate and hit a home run." [35]

———

IN NEW YORK CITY THAT EVENING a group of youths bombarded the Peress home with rocks and debris. Peress did not seem surprised. He blamed the incident on "fascist hoodlums" who were harassing his family with obscene phone calls and anti-Semitic remarks. "Since my appearance before the committee," he said, "I have been accorded the treatment typical of innocent victims hounded and abused by Senator McCarthy." [36]

CHAPTER TWENTY-SIX

"The Fault, Dear Brutus"

SHORTLY AFTER THE CHICKEN LUNCHEON, a Republican leader was heard to remark: "We had Munich last week. Now the only question is whether we'll have guts enough to guarantee Poland." The remark may have been apocryphal. It appeared in the column of Joseph and Stewart Alsop, who were forever quoting unnamed sources about the historical similarities between the Germany of Adolph Hitler and the America of Joe McCarthy. But the question still made sense, for many Republicans *were* wondering about guts and guarantees—about the consequences of further appeasement, on the one hand, and meaningful resistance, on the other. Either way, it seemed, the Grand Old Party was certain to lose a large measure of support.[1]

By early March the first signs of Republican resistance had begun to appear. On Capitol Hill, for example, GOP leaders were considering the merits of "fair play" guidelines for the various investigating groups (including an end to one-man hearings and hastily scheduled out-of-town probes). At the White House C. D. Jackson was writing McCarthy that, no, the overseas libraries did not need autographed copies of *McCarthyism: The Fight for America*, or *The Story of George Catlett Marshall*. At Foggy Bottom John Foster Dulles was announcing the formation of a blue-ribbon committee to recommend ways of strengthening the diplomatic service, now low in numbers and shaky in morale.

Dulles even speeded the process by stripping Scott McLeod of his powers with respect to personnel. "Dear Scottie" was on his way out.[2]

And the President? In public he was backing Robert Stevens with strong statements of support. In private he was considering the larger question of how to protect his "people" in the future. On March 2 he phoned William Rogers and said: "Suppose I make up my mind that McCarthy is abusing someone in a Department. What is constitutional for me to do in this regard?" (Rogers promised an answer as quickly as possible.) A few days later Ike composed a "personal and confidential" memorandum on the treatment of government personnel. "Fairness, justice, and decency must characterize all the procedures," he wrote. "We cannot defeat Communism by destroying Americanism. . . . No threat from *any* source should lead us to forsake these principles."[3]

On March 3 the President was scheduled to hold his first news conference since the Zwicker incident. Aides described him as "ripping mad" at McCarthy—a familiar phrase, but one that set off intense excitement in the press. It also alerted the senator, who announced that he would hold a news conference of his own. Perhaps the big showdown had finally arrived.

The President's news conference was attended by 238 reporters, the largest crowd in years. Ike looked more nervous than usual. He read from a prepared statement, calling it "my complete and full expression of one incident of recent weeks," a polite but firm signal that he did not intend to answer any questions on the subject.

The President made four simple points that day. First, he admitted that the Peress case had been handled badly. "The Army is correcting its procedures," he said, "and I am completely confident that Secretary Stevens will be successful in this effort." Second, he praised the courage and patriotism of General Zwicker, "who was decorated for gallantry in the field." Third, he reminded Congress that cooperation was a two-way street, that members of the Executive branch must be accorded "the same respect and courtesy that I require they show the members of the Legislative branch." Fourth, he placed the "primary responsibility" for fair and honorable treatment on the shoulders of the Republican members of Congress. "They are the majority party," he said, "They control the committees."

Ike did not mention McCarthy by name. He never intended to, though he did say at the end:

I regard it as unfortunate when we are diverted from grave problems—one of which is vigilance against any kind of internal subversion—through disregard of the standards of fair play recognized by the American people. . . . And that is my last word on any subject even closely related to that particular matter.[4]

The reporters were stunned. They had expected a much bigger story, a slashing presidential attack on McCarthy. They kept looking around, asking the same question: What was the lead? As the conference broke up, Joe Alsop's voice filled the room: "Why, the yellow son of a bitch!"[5]

On hand that day was Willard Edwards of the Chicago *Tribune*. Edwards was worried. He knew that McCarthy's rebuttal was far too strong for what Eisenhower had *actually* said. So he ran to Pennsylvania Avenue, grabbed a taxi, and sped to the Senate Office Building, where he found Joe at his desk, skimming a copy of the President's remarks. Edwards begged him to soften his rebuttal, but there wasn't enough time. McCarthy grabbed a pencil, crossed out a word here, a sentence there, and rushed off to meet the press.

The rebuttal was as belligerent and insulting as Edwards had feared. It tore into Zwicker: "If a stupid, arrogant, or witless man in a position of power appears before our committee and is found aiding the Communist Party, he will be exposed." It patronized Dwight Eisenhower: "Apparently, the President and I *now* agree on the necessity of getting rid of Communists." And, as usual, it promised no let-up in the war against the Reds: "I shall spend my time in action—in the continued exposure of those who are dedicated to the Communist enslavement of the world." At the end a reporter snapped, "Pretty conciliatory statement, Joe." And McCarthy replied: "You should have seen it before I changed it."[6]

The changes were minor, of course. McCarthy had dropped one sentence and modified another.* The only important revision came later —when Joe learned that Republican leaders were furious at his portrayal of Eisenhower as a Johnny-come-lately to the anti-Communist cause. After talking to Edwards, he sent this note to the press gallery: "It has come to my attention that the word 'now' in this sentence is being given a false interpretation never intended and completely unjustified. For that reason . . . the word 'now' should be stricken from the sentence to avoid any possible misinterpretation."

Any possible misinterpretation? The chances were slim, indeed. McCarthy had done to Eisenhower what the pundits had expected Eisenhower to do to McCarthy. He had slapped the President's face and thrown down the glove. He had assaulted him in public and done, by most accounts, a brutally effective job. "The senator's statement," wrote James Reston, no friend of McCarthy's, "was a perfect illustration of his mastery of mass communication techniques. He knows the importance

---

* According to Edwards, who saw the original draft, the omitted sentence read: "Too much wind has been blowing from high places in defense of this Fifth Amendment Communist [Peress]." The other sentence read: "If a stupid, arrogant, or witless man in a position of power is found aiding the Communist Party, he will be exposed." But Joe added the phrase "appears before our committee" after the word "power" to emphasize that he was referring to General Zwicker, not President Eisenhower.

of timing and of violence and of brevity in a political fight. . . . As a result, the McCarthy image and McCarthy melody lingered on the TV screens tonight, long after the President had gone to bed."[7]

This time, however, the image and the melody may not have done Joe much good. If the pundits were impressed, others, more important to the senator's future, were not. "Before the day was over," Willard Edwards recalled, "McCarthy had received telephone calls from at least one Cabinet member sympathetic to him and others highly placed in government. . . . They were through with him, they said; he had gone too far." Edwards considered this the turning point, the most crucial blunder of his friend's political career. He called it "the day McCarthy died."[8]

EDWARDS WAS RIGHT IN ONE RESPECT: McCarthy had gone too far. He had picked the fight that Republican leaders feared most; and, in doing so, he had raised serious questions about his future value to the GOP. For the first time, really, the Nixons and the Halls understood what Walter Lippmann meant when he spoke of "the unappeasable aggressor." And worse, what Arthur Krock meant when he spoke of the inevitable Republican choice: Eisenhower or McCarthy.

A few days later Adlai Stevenson delivered a slashing attack on the President's failure to condemn McCarthy, the first by a prominent Democrat since the Harry Dexter White episode almost six months before. Speaking on national television, he portrayed the GOP ("half Eisenhower, half McCarthy") as a party that would tolerate anything in its quest for harmony and political advantage. As expected the senator asked the networks for a free half-hour to answer this "vicious attack on me personally." This time, however, the request was challenged by Len Hall, who demanded—and received—the right of rebuttal for *one* Republican spokesman approved by the party itself. Joe was furious. He threatened the networks: "They will grant me time or learn what the law is—I guarantee that." But the bluster ended when Robert E. Lee, the new FCC commissioner, told the press: "McCarthy's my friend, but in this case I'd have to say, 'Look pal, it seems like a square deal to me.' "[9]

Quietly, the White House had taken charge. It was Eisenhower who ordered Len Hall to demand free time from the networks. "Get busy right away," he said. "This is a good job for you." Furthermore, the White House had pressured Lee to come out publicly against McCarthy's demand for equal time. The commissioner issued his statement only hours after conferring with Sherman Adams, who told him exactly what the President wanted done.[10]

At a White House meeting on March 8 Eisenhower chose Richard Nixon to deliver the televised rebuttal. Nixon was perfect, he explained, because McCarthy could not possibly accuse him of being soft on Communism. Nixon could bring up the Hiss case; he could defend the Administration's record; and he could talk about *real* leadership—how the "great" Presidents (Washington and Lincoln) had also suffered personal abuse without responding in kind. Ike seemed more cheerful and confident than before. He concluded that McCarthy was a pest—"a pimple on the road to progress."[11]

Nixon spent five full days on the speech, writing dozens of outlines and drafts. He geared it to the "large middle ground of public opinion," the people who believed that McCarthy was right, that one could not be fair *and* successful in fighting the enemies of America. Nixon included a "personal reference" to the Hiss case—a reminder, he said, that "I have fought the Communists all my political life and I am proud to say they've fought me . . . too." Then to the business at hand: "Why all this hullabaloo about being fair when you're dealing with a gang of traitors and rats?"

> When you go out and shoot rats, you have to shoot straight because when you shoot wildly, it not only means that the rats may get away more easily . . . but you might hit someone else who is trying to shoot rats, too. So we have to be fair—for two very good reasons: one, because it is right; and two, because it is the most effective way of doing the job.

The problem, he said, was that some of the rat-shooters had gone too far. They had wounded innocent people, embarrassed their natural allies, and diverted attention from the successful Republican programs to deal with Communism at home and abroad. Nixon did not mention McCarthy, but his meaning was clear: "Men who have in the past done effective work exposing Communists in this country have, by reckless talk and questionable methods, made themselves the issue rather than the cause they believe in so deeply."

In closing Nixon spoke of leadership, the good, clean, American brand that Dwight Eisenhower had brought to the job. Unlike Harry Truman, the new President did not engage in "personal vituperation and vulgar name-calling." The new President led by example. He was "a great expert," a "great military leader," a "great man" with the "greatest possible program" for this "great and good country." Nixon added: "I have never seen him mean. I have never seen him rash. . . . I have never seen him panicked. . . . I think we are lucky to have this man as President of the United States."[12]

The radio and television audience, estimated at ten million, included the President, who liked what he heard, and the senator, who did not. Addressing a smaller crowd that night—the annual dinner of the Manitowoc, Wisconsin, Junior Chamber of Commerce—McCarthy promised to stay with the methods that had worked for him in the past. "Some people have told me that I shouldn't get so rough," he said, without naming names himself. "I don't care how high or low they are. . . . As long as I am in the United States Senate . . . I don't intend to treat traitors like gentlemen." [13]

ON MARCH 9 THE SENATOR WAS JOLTED by two more public attacks—one a television documentary seen by millions, the other a Senate speech heard by a handful at best. Both came from new critics, men from the center, which added to their impact. And both did enormous damage to McCarthy, although the Senate speech, delivered by Ralph E. Flanders, a seventy-three-year-old Republican from Vermont, got far less attention at the time.

When newsmen described Senator Flanders, they used words like "solid," "sensible," and "fair." Until the day he took on McCarthy, however, the word "invisible" probably described him best. Flanders sat on no major committees. He introduced no important legislation. On the major issues of the day, his views were largely unknown. The press called him everything from "a conservative of impeccable credentials" to "a quiet . . . and soundly liberal man." Flanders did not care to label himself, although "moderate" and "independent" were the words he sometimes used. "I am no good at talking with lifelong Republicans," he wrote Sherman Adams in the midst of the 1952 campaign. "We don't see eye to eye, and I stir no enthusiasm." [14]

Flanders was an engineer by profession, a self-made and deeply religious man. He had come to the Senate in 1946, the same year as McCarthy, whom he quietly despised. The two men had clashed on several occasions—over sugar decontrol and the public housing bill—with Flanders recalling that Joe did not lose many contests "in which deviousness and complexity were factors." As a result Flanders had mixed feelings about his colleague's assault on the State Department in 1950. He honestly believed that the Democrats had been "soft" on Communism, that Truman and Acheson had sold Chiang Kai-shek down the river, "and the State Department . . . had kept him there." At the same time he admitted that "no more than 5 or 10 percent" of McCarthy's accusations could be sustained by the evidence that McCarthy himself had presented. "He is reckless," Flanders wrote a friend, but "he has drawn attention to a serious problem. I don't know just how to apply moral standards to activities of this sort." [15]

Then came the Republican landslide of 1952—a victory that solved the "problem" but failed to silence the senator from Wisconsin. Flanders grew impatient. He worried about two things in particular: the way McCarthy distorted America's image abroad and the way he riveted public attention on the "small details" of Communist activity at home. According to Flanders, at least, the McCarthy investigations had "blinded the eyes and muffled the ears to the alarming worldwide advance of Communist power which, if not checked, would shortly turn our country into a surrounded and besieged citadel—its citizens no longer free, but doomed to travel and trade in a Communist world on terms set by our Communist masters."[16]

Flanders had no reason to fear McCarthy. He had been overwhelmingly reelected in 1952, running well ahead of the Eisenhower vote, and he had already decided to retire at the end of his term, when he would be seventy-eight years old. Furthermore, while Flanders understood the general reluctance to face up to McCarthy, he sensed—correctly, it turned out—that his colleague was more vulnerable than the Republican leadership cared to believe. "I may be wrong," he wrote on February 15, 1954, "but it is my conviction that the man . . . does not cut as much mustard as he used to."[17]

When Flanders addressed the Senate on the afternoon of March 9, his colleagues had no idea that he intended to talk about McCarthy. The floor was quiet, the galleries almost empty. "Mr. President," he began, "this brief talk is in the nature of advice to the junior Senator from Wisconsin. I had hoped that he would be present. I don't feel constrained to put off the talk in his absence."

Flanders did not talk about civil liberties or innocent victims or the best way to shoot rats. His weapon was his humor—the folksy, homespun variety that one associated with the front porches and general stores of rural Vermont.

> In January of last year the Republican family moved into quarters which had been occupied by another family for twenty long years. The outgoing family did not clean up before it left. . . .
> Into these dirty premises the junior Senator from Wisconsin charged with all the energy and enthusiasm of a natural-born housekeeper. He found dirt under the rug. . . . He found cobwebs and spiders in the cellarway. All the dirt he found, and displayed, and the clean-up he personally superintended.
> Of course it was not done quietly. . . . The neighbors across the yard were apprised of each newly discovered deposit of grime. . . . Much in his long life has the junior Senator from Vermont seen or heard, but . . . nothing to match the dust and racket of this particular housecleaning. Perhaps these extremes are necessary if a one-man party is to be kept in the headlines and in the limelight.

The image of the housewife—mopping, dusting, chattering away—drew chuckles from both sides of the aisle. Flanders went on. He urged McCarthy to take off his apron and have a look around:

> Whole countries are now being taken over by the Communists. Others . . . are undergoing relentless infiltration. . . . In very truth, the world seems to

be mobilizing for the great battle of Armageddon. Now is a crisis in the agelong warfare between God and the Devil for the souls of men.

And what role had McCarthy played in the battle?

He dons his war paint. He goes into his war dance. He emits war whoops. He goes forth to battle and proudly returns with the scalp of a pink dentist.

For Ralph Flanders, this speech was only the beginning. He would attack McCarthy again and again in the coming weeks, antagonizing some of his Republican colleagues and stiffening the backbones of a good many more. On this day, however, he received a letter of congratulations that made the fight seem worthwhile. It came from President Eisenhower and it said: "I was very much interested in reading the comments you made in the Senate today. I think America needs to hear more Republican voices like yours."[18]

━━━━━

ON THAT DAY —March 9, 1954—the New York *Times* carried a small advertisement on the radio and television page: "Tonight at 10:30, SEE IT NOW, a report on Senator Joseph R. McCarthy over Channel 2. Fred W. Friendly and Edward R. Murrow, co-producers." The advertisement did not contain the CBS logo—the open eye. Murrow and Friendly had placed the ad—and paid for it—themselves.

If Ed Murrow was not the most popular newscaster in America, he was certainly the most secure. His wartime broadcasts and his ability to spot new talent—including Eric Severeid, William Shirer, and Howard K. Smith—had made CBS News the leader in its field. By 1954 Murrow's credits included a nightly radio newscast and two weekly television shows —"See It Now," a news documentary devoted to the "hard" issues of the day, and "Person to Person," a popular though frequently uncomfortable "visit" to the homes of celebrities like Roy Campanella or Marilyn Monroe. Critics sometimes referred to the programs as Higher Murrow and Lower Murrow, a description that Murrow himself did not really dispute. When asked why a serious newsman would host the televised equivalent of *House Beautiful*, Murrow replied that to do the show he wanted to do, he had to do the show he didn't want to do.[19]

In the fall of 1953 "See It Now" had presented "The Case Against Milo Radulovich," an Air Force Reserve officer who was labeled a security risk on the basis of hearsay information about the reading habits and political beliefs of his relatives. Murrow saw the case as a classic example of guilt by association. "It cannot be blamed upon Malenkov, or Mao Tse-tung or even our allies." he said. "It seems to us—that is, to Fred Friendly and myself—that it is a subject that should be argued about endlessly." A month later "See It Now" broadcast "An Argument in Indianapolis," a story about the American Legion's unsuccessful campaign to prevent the American Civil Liberties Union from organizing a chapter in that city. Murrow was a generous (though anonymous) contributor to the ACLU. He ended the show simply: "Indianapolis is still there, and the controversy is everywhere. Good night—and good luck."[20]

At about this time a "See It Now" reporter named Joseph Wershba was approached by Don Surine of McCarthy's staff. "Hey, Joe," said Surine, "what would you say if I told you that Murrow was on the Soviet payroll in 1934?"

Surine handed Wershba the "evidence": a photostat of a nineteen-year-old newspaper story about a group of American students and educators who were planning to attend a seminar at Moscow University. Under the Hearst headline, "American Professors Trained by Soviet, Teach in U.S. Schools," the story listed Edward R. Murrow, an assistant director of the Institute on International Education, as one of the seminar's many sponsors.

Surine made no threats in the conversation. He simply implied that Murrow would be wise to watch his step. "Mind you, Joe," he added. "I'm not saying that Murrow is a Commie himself. But he's one of those goddam anti-anti-Communists, and they're just as dangerous. And let's face it. If it walks like a duck, talks like a duck, and acts like a duck, then, goddamit, it *is* a duck."[21]

When Murrow learned what had happened, he ordered his staff to gather all the available film clips on McCarthy. The incident angered and embarrassed Murrow. He hated the senator, yet he had done almost nothing to oppose him. When friends asked why, he had complained about the built-in restrictions of his medium—the sponsors, the nervous network executives, the FCC. By this time, however, he no longer believed these excuses himself. He knew that he had to act, and quickly. The signs of resistance were everywhere; the center was moving; and the possibility existed that McCarthy might strike first, making any subsequent broadcast by Murrow seem less a matter of conscience than a blatant act of revenge. On March 2, 1954, he announced that the next "See It Now" program would deal with the climate of "unreasoning fear" in America.

The broadcast was carried in prime time in thirty-six cities. "Good evening," said Murrow in his familiar grave-yard voice. "Tonight 'See It Now' devotes its entire half-hour to a report on Senator Joseph R. McCarthy, told mainly in his own words and pictures." Murrow looked grim. He said that he would read directly from his script "because a report on Senator McCarthy is by definition controversial" and "we want to say exactly what we mean to say." He offered the senator free time to reply.

Murrow had gone through fifteen thousand feet of film. The clips he chose were chillingly effective. One showed McCarthy as chairman, terrorizing Reed Harris of the VOA. Another showed McCarthy as campaigner, chuckling at his "Alger—I mean Adlai" remark. Still others showed him patronizing the President, giggling uncontrollably, belching, and picking his nose. "It is necessary to investigate before legislating," Murrow intoned. "But the line between investigating and persecuting is a very fine one, and the junior Senator from Wisconsin has stepped over it repeatedly. His primary achievement has been in confusing the public mind between the internal and external threat of Communism."

Murrow concluded the broadcast with a call to arms:

This is no time for men who oppose Senator McCarthy's methods to keep silent—or for those who approve. . . . We proclaim ourselves, as indeed we are, the defenders of freedom—what's left of it—but we cannot defend freedom abroad by deserting it at home. The actions of the junior Senator from Wisconsin have caused alarm and dismay amongst our allies abroad and given considerable comfort to our enemies. And whose fault is that? Not really his. He didn't create this situation of fear. He merely exploited it, and rather successfully. Cassius was right: "The fault, dear Brutus, is not in our stars but in ourselves." Good night—and good luck.[22]

The reaction was quick and dramatic, with CBS—the official counter —claiming records all around. Dozens of operators were hired to take the 15,000 calls, which ran about ten-to-one for Murrow nationwide. The 22,000 letters and telegrams were placed in huge, equal-sized cartons—eighteen marked "favorable" and four "unfavorable." The letters were sampled by one enterprising reporter, who described their contents this way: "The pro-Murrow letters . . . were well-expressed, neatly written or typewritten, and signed. . . . The anti-Murrow letters . . . were scrawled and abusive. . . . They described Murrow in such familiar terms as a 'bleeding-heart pinko,' a 'pet of the *Daily Worker*,' a 'dupe of the Kremlin,' a 'Jewish bootlicker,' and a 'first-class skunk.' "*

The media reaction was no less intense. *Variety* called Murrow "a national hero," while the New York *Times* announced that broadcasting had "recaptured its soul." In response the senator's outnumbered supporters accused "Mr. Egghead R. Murrow" of "portsided political pitching" and other "slimy techniques." Said newscaster Fulton Lewis, Jr.: "I have long been sick in the stomach of the sanctimonious, self-righteous pretext that Mr. Murrow is objective, and such rot. . . . Mr. Murrow is, and always has been, heavily slanted on the left side."

* See "The People vs. McCarthy," *The Reporter*, April 27, 1954, pp. 25–28. The reporter who looked at the letters was Marya Mannes, a vehement critic of McCarthy. Whether this affected her sampling technique is not known. However, a careful study of the constituent mail of Senator Flanders showed much the same thing. Those who supported McCarthy were more abusive and less articulate than those who opposed him. See below, pp. 486–87.

There were two unexpected critics of the broadcast: John Cogley of *Commonweal* and Gilbert Seldes of the *Saturday Review*. Both men were longtime opponents of McCarthy, yet both men thought that Murrow had been unfair, that his program had been an "attack" and not a "report." Cogley reasoned that a different broadcaster, using different words and different clips, could have easily made McCarthy into a saint—mature, reasonable, well-intentioned, and devoted to his cause. Seldes went a step further. He claimed that Murrow had made a serious mistake by portraying a shrewd and dangerously manipulative man as a giggling buffoon. "I got the impression that the giant Murrow had been fighting a pygmy," he wrote. "Intellectually, this may be right; politically, I remain as frightened as if I had seen a ghost—the ghost of Hitler to be specific." [23]

Seldes did not have the last word, however. His editors, apparently dismayed by *any* criticism of the broadcast, placed a rare footnote at the bottom of the page: "We have the greatest respect for our Radio and TV columnist, who is entitled to his opinions, but it is only fair to say that this particular column has caused considerable discussion and debate among the staff." Such were the perils, it seemed, of appearing "soft" on McCarthy in the liberal journals of the time.

━━━━━

THESE WERE THE PUBLIC EVENTS of early March: the angry speeches, the televised attacks, the swelling chorus of anti-McCarthy voices. In private, another drama was unfolding—a drama that would dwarf all others in a matter of days.

This one had begun on January 21, when John Adams told several Administration officials about the "Cohn–Schine thing"—the persistent campaign by Roy Cohn to win preferential treatment for David Schine. These officials had "advised" Adams to prepare a report on the subject; they had also informed the President, who approved a plan to force Cohn's removal from the Committee. By March the so-called Adams Chronology had reached the Oval Office. "It's a pip," Hagerty wrote in his diary. "Shows constant pressure by Cohn to get Schine a soft Army job, with Joe in and out of threats. Really bad report that could break this thing wide open."

On March 9—fateful March 9—the trump card was played. Defense Secretary Charles Wilson invited McCarthy to lunch at the Pentagon and told him about the report. It was devastating, he said, and the Army intended to release it unless Cohn resigned at once. But McCarthy never blinked. The Army could go to hell, he replied. Roy Cohn would stay where he was.

When the luncheon broke up, Wilson called Senator Potter, a longtime friend, and asked for his help. He wanted Potter to write a letter to the Defense Department requesting a copy of the report. This way a Republican committee member could go to McCarthy, evidence in hand, and press for Roy Cohn's resignation. Potter agreed. He sent the letter by messenger that afternoon. Thirty minutes later the report was sitting on his desk.[24]

After skimming the contents, Potter went directly to McCarthy's fourth-floor office. He handed Joe the report and said, "Cohn has to go. We've got to get rid of him." But McCarthy wouldn't budge. "It's *blackmail*, Potter. . . . It's a *fraud*," he shouted. "If I get rid of Roy it would be the greatest victory the Communists have scored up to now. He's indispensable."

That evening Potter called Secretary Wilson at his home. "It's no go, Charlie," he said. "He refused to fire Cohn. He says the Army is blackmailing him."

The answer, Potter recalled, was "lucid and profane."[25]

━━━━━

THE DAM BURST ON MARCH 11 —a day on which the McCarthy saga generated more news than the Washington *Post* could handle, despite a banner headline, a lead editorial, a dozen articles, a Herblock cartoon, and pictures of Cohn, Schine, McCarthy, and Annie Lee Moss. It began in the morning, when Mrs. Moss offered her long-awaited testimony before a standing-room-only crowd and a camera crew from "See It Now." Bundled up in an overcoat and a pair of frayed white gloves, she did not have the look of a menacing security risk, although the Army had suspended her a few days before. Speaking in whispers, she told the subcommittee that she was not a Communist. In fact, she had never heard of Communism until 1948, "and I asked them what was that." Senator McCarthy, feigning boredom, excused himself and headed for the door. "I have a rather important appointment," he said, "which I have to work on right now." This was a mistake, a bad mistake, for it left Roy Cohn all by himself, facing both the television cameras and a group of senators who were determined to cut him down to size.[26]

Cohn took over the interrogation. "Isn't it a fact," he said, "that you regularly received the *Daily Worker* . . . through Rob Hall . . . one of the leading Communists in the District of Columbia?" Mrs. Moss replied that a "colored man" had dropped off some copies at her house, and he could have been the same Rob Hall who had worked for her union in 1940. "I didn't read them," she added, "because I don't read any newspaper very much."

At this point a reporter informed Robert Kennedy, the minority counsel, that the Communist Rob Hall was a white man. Senator Jackson said, "Mr. Kennedy has something."

MR. KENNEDY: When you spoke about the union organizer, you spoke about Rob Hall and I think we all felt that he was a colored gentleman?

MR. COHN: I was not talking about a union organizer, Bob. I was talking about a Communist organizer . . .

MR. KENNEDY: Evidently it was a different Rob Hall.

MR. COHN: I don't know that it was. Our information is that it was the same Rob Hall.

SENATOR McCLELLAN: If one is black and the other is white, there is a difference.

MR. COHN: I think that might be something we should look into and get some information on.

MR. KENNEDY: I think so, too.

Now the Democrats took over, raising the possibility of mistaken identity—there were three A. L. Mosses in the Washington phone book —and railing against "rumor and hearsay and innuendo." Symington asked Mrs. Moss to read her suspension order out loud; she stumbled over the three-and-four-syllable words. McClellan seemed close to tears. "Did you read that the best you could?" he asked. "Yes, sir, I did," she answered.

Then Symington asked her whether she had heard of Karl Marx. "Who is that?" she replied—and laughter swept the room.

SENATOR SYMINGTON: Do you think you are a good American?

MRS. MOSS: Yes.

SENATOR SYMINGTON: Would you ever do anything to hurt your country?

MRS. MOSS: No, sir.

. . .

SENATOR SYMINGTON: Do you need work?

MRS. MOSS: Sure I do.

SENATOR SYMINGTON: If you don't get work soon, what are you going to do?

MRS. MOSS: I am going down to the welfare.

It was a vivid, human scene, and Symington responded with the cavalier recklessness of a man who had virtue—and the entire audience

—on his side. "I may be sticking my neck out," he said, "but I think you are telling the truth. If you are not taken back in your Army job, come around and see me. I am going to see that you get a job." The hearing ended with thunderous applause.

The Moss case was a disaster for Cohn and McCarthy. It appeared to be a repeat of the Anna Rosenberg affair, a cruel and careless assault upon an apparently innocent victim. And it was seen by millions the following week, compliments of Ed Murrow and "See It Now." As the television critic John Crosby wrote: "The American people fought a revolution to defend, among other things, the right of Annie Lee Moss to earn a living, and Senator McCarthy now decided she had no such right." *

On this remarkable news day, however, the Moss case was overshadowed by a bigger event that afternoon—the release of the Adams Chronology. On orders from the White House, a copy was delivered to each member of the subcommittee. Then the press was alerted, and editors across the country held up the morning edition while their correspondents banged out the story.

The news caught many senators by surprise. Among them was William Knowland, who called the White House and threatened to resign as majority leader. "I did not see the report," he fumed. "I read it in the *Post* this morning. . . . I don't think you can operate a team this way." At first the President played dumb. He had heard *something* about a report on "a man named Cohn," but he didn't know "a damned thing about it." As Knowland raged on, however, the President took some responsibility for his role in the project. "This," he said, "is the first intimation I have had that you have not been cut in. . . . There has been a blunder and I am sorry." [27]

The report was a bombshell. It accused McCarthy and Frank Carr, his staff director, of joining with Cohn to demand preferential treatment for G. David Schine. The report listed forty-four counts of improper pressure over a period of eight months, from July 1953 to February 1954.

---

* One point was clear, however: this was *not* a case of mistaken identity. According to Mrs. Markward, the Communist Annie Lee Moss had lived at 72 R Street, S.W. In her own testimony, Mrs. Moss said, "We didn't get this Communist paper until after we had moved to Southwest, at 72 R Street"—a statement the Democrats (and many students of the Moss case) completely overlooked. Roy Cohn would later claim that his information was correct, that Annie Lee Moss, the Communist, and Annie Lee Moss, the Pentagon clerk, were one and the same person. In fact he had proved no such thing. His information showed that Annie Lee Moss of 72 R Street had appeared on a Communist membership list. The list *may* have been accurate, although the ones compiled by FBI informers like Mrs. Markward were often wildly inflated. Of course, this hardly excused the performance of the Army's security branch, which had known of Mrs. Markward's allegations for several years and never bothered to pursue them. In 1955 the Army rehired Mrs. Moss and transferred her to a "nonsensitive" position in the Finance and Accounts Office. At that time Secretary of Defense Wilson admitted that her file contained "certain derogatory information" prior to 1946.

Prior to Schine's induction, it began, Roy Cohn had orchestrated a campaign to get him a direct commission in the Army, then in the Navy, and finally in the Air Force. When these efforts failed, Cohn launched a new campaign to get him assigned to the New York area. He even suggested that Schine study "evidence of pro-Communist leanings in West Point textbooks." Again, the Army said no.

In November Schine began his basic training at Fort Dix, New Jersey. According to the report, Cohn bombarded the Army with requests for weekend and evening passes so that Schine could return to New York for "committee work." This presented a problem; passes were not normally granted during the first four weeks of basic training. But Robert Stevens bent the rules because he did not want to appear "uncooperative" at a time when Fort Monmouth was under investigation. There followed a flood of leaves and passes—for evenings, weekends, Thanksgiving, Christmas, and New Year's Eve. Before long the commandant at Fort Dix complained that Schine was rarely around. He asked for permission to terminate the midweek passes, and Adams told him to go right ahead. But this made Roy Cohn angry.

> Mr. Cohn, using extremely vituperative language, told Mr. Adams that the Army had again "double-crossed" Mr. Cohn, Private Schine, and Senator McCarthy.
> The first double-cross, according to Mr. Cohn, was when the Army had not given a commission to Schine after promising him one; the second double-cross . . . was that the Army had not assigned Private Schine immediately to New York; and another was that the Army cancelled Private Schine's availability during week nights.[28]

The report went on and on, listing the phone calls, the meetings, the threats, and the demands. Cohn was clearly the instigator, vowing (at various times) to "wreck the Army" and to show it "in the worst possible light." McCarthy, on the other hand, was pictured as playing two roles at once. In private conversations with Adams and Stevens, he referred to Schine as "a nuisance" and "a pest." In Cohn's presence, however, he supported the demands for preferential treatment, including a New York assignment for Schine.

Actually, the report could have been worse. The original version, seen by the Alsop brothers and other anti-McCarthy journalists, had been longer and blunter and studded with Roy Cohn's obscenities. The Alsops were disappointed by the omissions; they called the report a "story half told." But that story, sanitized or not, would wound Joe McCarthy as nothing had ever wounded him before.

CHAPTER TWENTY-SEVEN

Setting the Ground Rules

THE ADAMS CHRONOLOGY was the last link in a chain of events that had begun with the Monmouth investigation in October 1953. That investigation had included threats to subpoena the members of the Army's Loyalty–Security Board. These threats had led to the (still secret) meeting of January 21, where Adams was "advised" to fight the subpoenas and to compile a report on Cohn and Schine. That meeting had effectively derailed the Monmouth investigation, but McCarthy, undaunted, had come up with Irving Peress. The Peress case had led to the Zwicker incident; the Zwicker incident had led to the Chicken Luncheon; and the Chicken Luncheon had convinced President Eisenhower that McCarthy could not be mollified or appeased. Two weeks later the Adams Chronology had been released to the press.

A counterattack was inevitable. As McCarthy often said, "I don't answer charges; I make them." And the following day he struck back hard, accusing the Army of blackmail and bribery in its dealings with the chairman and the subcommittee staff. As evidence he produced a file of eleven neatly typed memoranda, dating from October 2, 1953, to March 11, 1954—the very day of the Army's blast. The reaction was one of astonishment mixed with suspicion. No one, not even the subcommittee members, had been aware of their existence.[1]

The first three memos discussed the alleged attempts by Stevens and

Adams to halt the Monmouth investigation. ("Stevens said he wished we could get onto the Air Force and Navy . . . instead of continuing with the Army hearings. . . . Adams said he had gotten specific information about an Air Force Base where there were a large number of homosexuals.") The fourth memo, from Cohn to McCarthy, brought Private Schine into the fray. ("I'm getting fed up with the way the Army is trying to use Dave as a hostage to pressure us to stop our hearings.") The ninth memo, from Cohn to McCarthy, addressed the personal motives of Mr. Adams. ("He said this was the last chance for me to arrange that law partnership in New York which he wanted. . . . He said he had turned down a job in industry at $17,555, and needed a guarantee of $25,000 from a law firm.") The tenth memo, from Frank Carr to the files, supported the charge that Adams was "blackmailing" Cohn. ("He is baiting Roy pretty much lately on the hostage situation. They get pretty heated before Roy buys the lunch, but it's going to lead to trouble.")

Stevens sputtered that the charges were "utterly untrue." Adams called them "fantastic and false." But there they were, out in the open, and they could hardly be ignored. "Someone is lying," said the alert Senator Potter, "and we've got to find out who it is." [2]

▬▬▬▬

On the morning of March 16 the subcommittee met to discuss the charges and countercharges behind closed doors. An investigation was inevitable, the members realized. The big questions were: Who should conduct it? What ground rules and procedures should be employed? The maneuvering was intense. Karl Mundt suggested that another committee —perhaps Armed Services—handle the probe. Everett Dirksen favored a quick, private hearing, followed by the resignations of John Adams and Roy Cohn.* But the majority—the three Democrats and Potter—refused to go along. "This is our baby, and our linen," they argued, "and we have got to wash it in public." [3]

The next question concerned McCarthy himself. He had agreed to step down as chairman during the inquiry, but he demanded the right to remain on the subcommittee, where he could cross-examine witnesses, vote on matters of procedure, and determine the verdict as well. The Democrats objected to this, while the Republicans wavered for days. Meanwhile the President stepped in, telling reporters that "a party to a

---

* Dirksen's position was held by McCarthy's strongest supporters in the Senate. All of them saw what Joe chose to ignore—that Cohn had become an enormous burden to his cause. On March 25, for example, Hagerty wrote in his diary: "Went to lunch in the Senate. . . . When I walked in there were Joe McCarthy, Welker, Mundt, Malone, Hickenlooper, Butler. . . . McCarthy, Mundt, and Malone left after lunch. . . . Then Welker and Hickenlooper started in—proposed both Cohn and Adams resign and case be dropped." Hagerty said nothing. He knew that there was no turning back—that the President wanted a quick hearing, but also a public one, with McCarthy taking the stand in full view of the nation.

dispute, directly or indirectly, does not sit in judgment on his case." Privately he added, "I've made up my mind you can't do business with Joe and to hell with any attempt to compromise. . . ."[4]

But compromise won the day, despite some Presidential arm-twisting behind the scenes. First, McCarthy agreed to step down as a member, but not before appointing Idaho's Henry Dworshak, a dependable ally, to sit in his place. Second, he won the right of cross-examination—a right that was granted to the Army as well. These were major concessions, not unlike the ones that allowed him to dominate the Malmedy hearings a few years before. In the words of historian Robert Griffith, "Conflict is the spring which drives the play, and conflict, thanks to McCarthy's insistence on the right of cross-examination, was built into the very structure of the hearings."[5]

WHEN MCCARTHY STEPPED DOWN from the subcommittee, the chairmanship passed to the ranking Republican member, Karl Mundt. This was ironic, for no one wanted it less, or feared it more, than this cheerful, roly-poly man from Humboldt, South Dakota. Karl Mundt had built a career on getting along with people, avoiding controversial issues, and attacking the safest of targets. Now, on the eve of his reelection race, he'd be presiding over a televised fight among Republicans, with both sides looking for scapegoats—and for blood.

On balance, Mundt's sympathies were with McCarthy. He may not have been Joe's loudest booster on the committee, but he was his closest friend. The two men had vacationed together, played the stock market together, and joined the same committees by choice. In addition, their wives were constant companions, and Mary Mundt, an ambitious and politically astute woman, made no secret of her enthusiasm for the McCarthy crusade.[6]

What about the other members? Where did they stand? Under normal conditions, McCarthy could count on strong support from Everett Dirksen, his mellifluous admirer, and Henry Dworshak, who was handpicked for the job. The other Republican, Charles Potter, was a question mark. He had embraced McCarthy in the 1952 campaign but kept his distance ever since. That left the Democratic members, fresh from their triumph in the Annie Lee Moss affair. They were likely to cause trouble, although their leader, John McClellan, had rarely criticized Joe in the past.

Still, the members would not be investigating McCarthy *per se*, but rather the tangle of charges and countercharges involving Roy Cohn, Army officials, and preferential treatment for Schine. This meant, in all likelihood, that their feelings about duty, honor, and sacrifice would play a very important role. All of them, except Mundt, had served in one or the other of the two World Wars. Symington had enlisted in the Army at seventeen; his two sons had also enlisted at seventeen, one in the Army, the other in the Marine Corps. Five of his cousins had been killed in World War II and Korea. Potter, a recipient of the Purple Heart with two clusters and a Silver Star, had lost both legs to German shrapnel at Colmar. He considered Schine a slacker—"a youngster who wants a joyride in peacetime"—and he told McCarthy so in private. McClellan, a veteran of World War I, had buried two of his three sons in the early days of World War II. One of them had written home from North Africa, saying he was ill but insisting that a senator's boy be treated like anyone else. He died of spinal meningitis a few weeks later.[7]

———

AS CHAIRMAN, it was Mundt's responsibility to find the special counsel, the man to lead the probe. (Obviously, Roy Cohn could not investigate Roy Cohn.) But this would not be easy. The job offered high risks and low pay. It demanded objectivity. And it required the combined skills of the prosecutor and the public defender—in short, a talented, tough-minded attorney who had never uttered a public word about any of the principals in the dispute.

Early on, Mundt told reporters that "the job would seek the man, and not the man the job." But the days passed and the seeking got nowhere. After two weeks and numerous dead ends, the committee settled on Samuel P. Sears, a Republican lawyer from Massachusetts. His main qualification was his willingness—indeed, his eagerness—to take on the job.

The selection was due to a combination of factors: a desire to fill the job with someone—anyone—after so many rejections; a strong lobbying effort by Sears himself; and some hasty investigative work by Robert Kennedy, the minority counsel.* It turned out that Sears had approached both Massachusetts senators—John Kennedy and Leverett Saltonstall—and told them of his interest in the job. The senators had relayed the information to Mundt, who asked Robert Kennedy to check "the objectivity, impartiality, and competency of Mr. Sears." But Kennedy was pressed for time. Instead of checking carefully, he phoned a

_____

* Mundt's first choice had been William Rogers, but Rogers turned him down. Mundt had no idea that Rogers was working secretly on the Army's side; still, it was an odd choice given Rogers's past associations with virtually all of the principals. Mundt also considered Robert Morris, but even McCarthy objected on grounds that Morris was his close friend. See Minutes of the Executive Session of the Subcommittee on Investigations, March 16, 1954, in *Army–McCarthy Hearings*, 1954, pp. 1–26.

Mundt then approached William Jameson, head of the American Bar Association, without success. After that he called Chief Justice Earl Warren to see if he would "lend a district judge," but Warren demurred as well. See Presidential Phone Calls, *Whitman File*, March 18, 1954, Eisenhower Library.

few Massachusetts congressmen, who described Sears as a competent attorney—and something of a publicity hound. On April 1 the subcommittee approved him for the job. A few hours later the Boston papers reported that Sears had raised money for McCarthy in 1952 and spoken of his "great job" in driving "the pinks and commies out of the government."

Incredibly, Mundt did not see this as proper grounds for disqualification. In a private letter to the other members, he wrote: "I cannot for the life of me see how a statement made two years ago about the general proposition of getting Communists out of the government is pertinent to the current controversy." But his colleagues had heard enough. "He's got to go," said McClellan, and he did, a few days later.[8]

The search ended the following week with the selection of Ray Howard Jenkins, a flamboyant, leather-lunged attorney from Knoxville, Tennessee. Recommended by Everett Dirksen, a family friend, he came with impeccable credentials. His criminal practice—defending the *very* guilty, he liked to say—was the largest in the state. His politics were middle-of-the-road Republican. He had attended the 1952 convention as a Taft delegate and emerged as an enthusiastic supporter of General Eisenhower. Best of all, he claimed to have no opinion of Senator McCarthy, and the press could not prove him a liar. In the words of a disappointed journalist, his record was one "of unbroken silence on the sharpest domestic issue of the day."[9]

According to the ground rules Robert Stevens and the Army were to have separate counsel, with the right to cross-examine all witnesses. Since objectivity was not at issue here, the press expected *this* attorney to be a Washington insider, a man of stature and influence on Capitol Hill. At a news conference on April 3 the Army announced that Joseph Nye Welch, a trial lawyer from Boston, had accepted the job. The reporters on hand that day sounded a bit like Annie Lee Moss. They kept asking, "Who is that?"

Welch, sixty-three, was a tall, graceful man with the courtly manners of a Charles Dickens hero. This was deceptive, however, for his background was strikingly similar to that of the other Joe—the slugger from Grand Chute. Like McCarthy, he had come from a large farm family in the Midwest, attended a country school, worked at numerous jobs, and gone to the local college (Grinnell) with the blessings of his father, a former seaman, and his mother, an indentured servant from the British Isles. "When he prepared to leave for Harvard Law School," a friend recalled, "his father went to a hiding place and took out a few dollars he had saved over many months. As Joe later told a television audience, 'He gave me all a father could—all he had.' "

Welch had joined the prestigious Boston law firm of Hale and Dorr following service in World War I. He had become a full partner and head of the trial department in 1929. A superb courtroom lawyer, his style—unlike Ray Jenkins's—was subtle, self-effacing, and sly. He had been recommended for the Army job by Thomas Dewey and Herbert Brownell (although he told reporters that he did not know how or why he was chosen). Asked about his stand on "McCarthyism," he said, "I am a registered Republican and a trial lawyer. I am just for facts."

His friends knew better. They knew that he worried about "McCarthyism," about its hold on the people and politics of Massachusetts. They knew that he quietly defended "radicals" without pay because he could not forget Sacco-Vanzetti, a case in which his best friends had participated. Before his death he composed a long memo that compared the case to the Red-hunting excesses of the 1950s.

> I had concluded that Sacco and Vanzetti had not had a fair trial, and I had grave doubts about their guilt. There were many men in Massachusetts who said in substance, and loudly, "I no longer care about guilt or innocence. I have less interest in whether or not they had a fair trial. . . . Their death is politically desirable. Let's not be squeamish."

He added that "to a degree, these men turned out to be right. Sacco and Vanzetti have not had the impact on history that they thought they would have. They have not been elevated to sainthood. . . . The crime that led to their deaths was committed thirty-nine years ago. Come to think of it, it is perhaps a little odd that I should dictate so many words about it." [10]

———

ALMOST SIX WEEKS ELAPSED between the release of the Adams Chronology and the start of the Army hearings on April 22. McCarthy spent much of that time on the road, preaching to large and friendly crowds. At a St. Patrick's Day dinner in Chicago, he told 1,200 well-lubricated supporters that he intended to play rough with the Reds and rougher still with those who protected them. "St. Patrick drove the snakes out of Ireland," he roared, "and the snakes didn't like his methods either." From there he went to Milwaukee ("I'm fighting for America now."); Oklahoma City ("I didn't start this fight, but I guarantee you that I'll finish it."); Houston ("Luckily . . . there were no 'Fifth Amendment Texans' at the Alamo."); and east to New York City, where 6,000 members of the Police Department's Holy Name Society heard him assault the "Pentagon politicians" who gave honorable discharges to Communists while letting American POWs rot in Red Chinese jails. The audience went wild; it cheered and whistled and rose to its feet when Cardinal Spellman walked up and shook hands with the speaker. The press called it a spontaneous tribute to a hero. McCarthy called it the greatest reception of his life. [11]

But these were the true believers. The polls told a different story: Joe was slipping. His favorable rating had dropped dramatically—the result, said pollsters, of the Zwicker affair, the Murrow broadcast, and the report on Private Schine. In Wisconsin, moreover, a movement was under way to "recall" McCarthy, to make him stand for reelection at once, only two years into his term. Launched by a small-town Republican newspaper editor named Leroy Gore, the movement showed great early strength. Petitions were printed, distributed by volunteers, and signed by thousands of voters. The words "Joe Must Go" were plastered on cars, barns, billboards, and traffic signs. At first the senator pretended not to notice. "You can make headlines every day of the week," he groused, "if you want to call McCarthy an SOB." [12]

But the recall was a serious matter. It went deeper than the Zwicker incident or the fight with other Republican leaders. It reflected, as nothing before, a growing unhappiness with McCarthy the legislator, the man who represented Wisconsin's interests in the Senate. When times were prosperous, there had been little criticism of his one-issue approach. But 1954 was a bad year in Dairyland—the worst since the Great Depression. Surpluses piled up, prices fell, and the Department of Agriculture announced plans to lower the dairy price support from 90 to 75 percent. Across Wisconsin, farmers gathered to protest the cut. In February a group of them traveled to Washington to see their elected officials. According to one account,

> . . . a leader of the delegation complained that McCarthy was too preoccupied with chasing Communists and that his secretary "didn't seem to know anything had happened to farm prices." On 3 March all the state's Republicans in Washington, except McCarthy, met to plan their strategy. On 9 March Governor Kohler discussed the problem with the same group, but McCarthy sent only an aide to represent him. [13]

This angered the farm leaders, who had strongly supported Joe in the past. One of them wrote James Green, executive secretary of the Wisconsin Farm Bureau Federation: "By and large what McCarthy has been doing regarding Communists is all for the good. I do believe, however, that he is grossly uninformed about agriculture." And Green replied: "Senator McCarthy confers with no one on farm issues except his cheese broker. . . . I have given up all hopes. I firmly believe that only a psychiatrist has any chance of talking this confused man out of his chaotic dilemma." [14]

In April and May McCarthy returned to Wisconsin almost every weekend, trying to mend the fences he had ignored for so long. (He now urged that dairy prices be supported at 100 percent—a ploy that stunned the farm leaders, who were ready to compromise at 82½ percent.) The recall gathered steam; charges of fraud and harassment flew back and forth. Hate mail, much of it anti-Semitic in tone, poured into Gore's

Sauk City office. Volunteers were threatened. A Door for Gore Club was organized, with the intention of driving him from the town. By May 15, however, some 300,000 voters had signed the recall petitions. The filing date was June 6, and the goal of 400,000 signatures was clearly in sight.*

THIS WAS NOT THE WORST OF IT. There were signs—serious signs—that Joe was coming apart inside. Friends noticed with real alarm that he seemed to be preparing himself for Armageddon. He told Mundt in late night conversations that he intended to win his fight or die in the attempt. He plastered the walls of his office with inspirational mottoes. His favorite read:

> Oh God, don't let me weaken.
> Help me to continue on.
> When I go down,
> let me go down like an oak tree
> felled by a woodsman's ax.[15]

He worried, too, about the many threats on his life. In the past he had brushed them aside. Now he bought a gun and carried it everywhere. One night in March Len Hall went to McCarthy's home for a private talk. He was startled to see Joe at the door, pistol in hand, expecting the worst.†

The signs of physical damage were also apparent. In 1950 a friend wrote: "I have seen him rush from place to place, make a speech here and a deal there, slap backs, tell jokes—to what would seem to be the point of total exhaustion. Then he would lie down on a hotel room floor for an hour or two and arise genuinely refreshed to start on his rounds again." His schedule was still frenetic, but the pace was punishing him now. He was tired and tense, unable to sleep or to relax with his friends. He was drinking so heavily that Urban Van Susteren, among others,

---

* To be successful, recall petitions had to be signed within a sixty-day period by at least 25 percent of the voters who had cast ballots in the previous gubernatorial election. In the end the recall drive failed narrowly. It was hampered by time constraints, poor organization, inadequate funding, Republican harassment, and serious questions about its constitutionality. See David Thelen and Esther Thelen, "Joe Must Go: The Movement to Recall Senator Joseph McCarthy, *Wisconsin Magazine of History*, Spring 1966, pp. 185–209; also Michael O'Brien, *McCarthy and McCarthyism in Wisconsin*, 1980, pp. 161–65.

† His fear of assassination may have been heightened by the actions of Puerto Rican terrorists who shot up the House of Representatives on March 3, 1954, seriously wounding several congressmen. A week later, Joe received a note from J. Edgar Hoover saying that an informant had told FBI agents that "Nick" (a Puerto Rican serving time in the Atlanta Penitentiary for attempting to kill President Truman) "said you were to be killed in Washington by an individual posing as a Western Union messenger who would appear at your hotel room. [Informant] reported that if this plan fails an individual is to go to your room dressed in a bell boy's uniform and kill you." See J. Edgar Hoover to Senator Joseph R. McCarthy, March 12, 1954, *FBI Papers*, Washington, D.C.

feared a breakdown at any moment. His weight fluctuated wildly, with swings of 15 to 20 pounds in a matter of weeks. He was in and out of Bethesda Naval Hospital with sinus problems, leg problems, stomach problems, and "simple fatigue." He was forty-four years old and a prisoner to his cause.[16]

ON APRIL 13 Joe Welch filed his Bill of Particulars with the subcommittee. "The Department of the Army," it began, "alleges that Senator Joseph R. McCarthy . . . and Chief Counsel Roy M. Cohn, as well as other members of the staff, sought by improper means to obtain preferential treatment for one Pvt. G. David Schine, United States Army." The document differed from the Adams Chronology in two respects: first, it linked the Schine affair *directly* to the Monmouth investigation; second, it highlighted the role played by Senator McCarthy, making him almost a full partner in the maneuvers on behalf of Schine. For example:

Charge #13. On or about November 17, 1953, Senator McCarthy, Mr. Cohn, and Mr. Carr made known to Secretary Stevens the importance attached by them to Private Schine's military assignment and there by innuendo and inference indicated that their plans for continuing further investigation of the military installation at Fort Monmouth, N.J., were related to the importance attached by them to Private Schine's military assignment.

Charge #18. On or about December 10, 1953, Senator McCarthy and Mr. Carr sought to obtain a special assignment for Private Schine in New York City for the purpose of studying textbooks at West Point.

Charge #28. On or about January 22, 1954, Senator McCarthy requested Mr. Adams to obtain a special assignment for Private Schine in New York and suggested that Mr. Cohn would continue to harass the Army unless this demand was acceded to.[17]

Senator McCarthy filed his Bill of Particulars a week later. It, too, included the original charges—those contained in the eleven memoranda—and some new ones as well.

Charge #24. On or about October 13, 1953, Mr. Adams suggested that the subcommittee "go after" the Navy and Air Force and drop its probe of Communist infiltration in the Army.

Charge #30. On or about December 16, 1953, Mr. Adams again urged that the subcommittee begin to investigate security risks in the Air Force, and offered specific information in return for certain information desired from us in forestalling further investigation of his department.

> Charge #37. On or about January 22, 1954, Mr. Adams made to the chairman and Mrs. McCarthy the threat that unless the investigation of the loyalty setup were halted, he would cause to be issued a report on Mr. Cohn, casting events in such a light as to attempt to embarrass the committee and its staff. . . . When the chairman told Mr. Adams he would expose the old team which had great responsibility for Communist infiltration, Mr. Adams replied, "I am part of the old team, and the people you are threatening are friends of mine."[18]

But McCarthy did not stop here. His mudballs flew in all directions. He claimed, for example, that the Adams Chronology had "given greater aid and comfort to Communists and security risks than any single obstacle ever designed." He charged that Joe Welch had chosen a Communist attorney to work on the Army's defense.* He said that Stevens and Adams were "Pentagon civilians" who had no right to speak for the millions of "loyal Americans" in the Armed Forces. And, in the biggest surprise of all, he extended his charges to include H. Struve Hensel, counsel for the Department of Defense.

Where did Struve Hensel fit in? He was the man who had "received" the Chronology from Adams and signed the covering letter that transmitted it to members of the subcommittee. In his Bill of Particulars, McCarthy claimed that "Mr. Adams apparently acted with the influence and guidance of H. Struve Hensel . . . who was himself under investigation by the subcommittee for misconduct and possible law violation. Hensel had, and has, every motivation to act as he did in attempting to discredit the subcommittee." This was an outrageous assertion, for the charges against Hensel were ten years old and absolutely irrelevant to the issues at hand. Furthermore, Hensel had not come "under investigation by the subcommittee" until the moment his name appeared on the covering letter.

The charges involved "war profiteering"—the fact that Hensel, as a naval procurement officer, had been associated with a ship's supply firm that sold food to the Navy during World War II. Hensel had been investigated and cleared by the Internal Revenue Service, and later by the Department of Defense. How McCarthy found out is both a mystery and a tribute to his remarkable sources within the government. In his Bill of Particulars he displayed a detailed knowledge of Hensel's tax returns. Hensel would later tell friends that the senator learned about the

---

* The attorney in question was Fred Fisher from Hale and Dorr. See below, pp. 457–64.

most confidential decisions in his office almost as soon as they were made.*

These charges were more than a smoke screen. They were meant to intimidate, to show the Army what lay ahead. McCarthy had already referred to the imminent hearings as "this television show of Adams versus Cohn." But he didn't believe it. He knew that *he* would be the man on trial, and he intended to fight as he had always fought—with knees and elbows flying, no holds barred.

---

* Hensel's remark can be found in Fred Fisher, "Joseph N. Welch," unpublished manuscript in the author's possession. Drew Pearson claimed that the information was supplied to McCarthy by his friend T. Coleman Andrews, the IRS Commissioner. According-ing to several accounts, two McCarthy staffers—Jim Juliana and Don Surine—tracked down Hensel's business partner in the ships' supply firm by posing as New York City detectives who were investigating a hit-and-run accident. See "Matter of Fact," Washington *Post*, April 23, 1954; "Washington Merry-Go-Round," Washington *Post*, June 24, 1954.

CHAPTER TWENTY-EIGHT

The Hearings Begin

In THEORY, at least, the Army–McCarthy hearings were supposed to focus on two distinct questions: Did the senator and members of the subcommittee staff exert improper pressure on the Army in an attempt to win preferential treatment for G. David Schine? Did Army officials use blackmail and bribery in order to derail the Monmouth investigation and related probes by the subcommittee? In reality, the stakes were much higher, the issues more complex. They ranged from the integrity of the Armed Forces to the moral responsibilities of federal workers, from the separation of powers to the future of Senator McCarthy. And they pitted Republican against Republican, the President against the Congress, and the subcommittee members against their chairman—and themselves.

If these issues were murky and dimly understood, the drama was very real indeed. Millions of Americans listened and watched on radio and TV. During week one, surveys revealed, about two-thirds of the households with television sets were tuned in to the hearings.* Department stores reported a jump in TV sales and a drop in the overall volume of

---

* After the first week of the hearings, NBC and CBS dropped their daytime coverage in favor of nightly excerpts, beginning at 11:15. They claimed that this was due to a drop in interest, although the loss of advertising revenue from canceled shows certainly played a role. The weaker networks—Dumont and ABC—held to their live coverage and picked up many new viewers. Following a storm of protest, NBC restored its live coverage as well.

daytime shopping, as people stayed home to follow the action. The news coverage was unprecedented; the hearings overshadowed events of far greater importance, including *Brown* v. *Board of Education* and the fall of Dien Bien Phu. The New York *Times* carried a dozen pages of testimony a day. *Time* and *Newsweek* lost interest in "national affairs" that did not include McCarthy. So did Drew Pearson, Arthur Krock, the Alsops, Doris Fleeson, and the cartoonist Herblock, who featured McCarthy eight times as often as his nearest competitor, the President of the United States. Walter Lippmann disparaged the hearings as "our national obsession"—and then dissected them in column after column. From California he wrote: "About affairs which are centered in Washington and govern the nation . . . only McCarthyism is much on people's minds."[1]

———

AT 7 O'CLOCK ON THE MORNING of April 22 the first spectators had already gathered in the rotunda of the Senate. At 10:00 the lucky ones were searched and herded into the Senate Caucus Room, where the choice seats were reserved for "distinguished visitors" such as Perle Mesta, Alice Roosevelt Longworth, Jean McCarthy, and Mary Mundt. At 10:20 the principals arrived: Cohn, Carr, and McCarthy, flanked by bodyguards who watched for would-be assassins; Stevens, Adams, and Hensel, surrounded by unsmiling generals who took up most of the front row. Finally the committee members filed in and positioned themselves around a coffin-shaped table. One journalist likened the scene to a theater in the round. "Relatives surrounded the senators. Spectators crowded the witnesses. Reporters fought grimly to defend little plots of table on which they scribbled." Joe Welch took one look through the doorway and recoiled in horror. "Don't worry," said a capital patrolman. "In three days there won't be twenty people here."[2]

At precisely 10:30 Karl Mundt put down his pipe, banged an ashtray on the table, and called the hearing to order. It was customary for the chairman to read a brief statement about the purposes and procedures of the inquiry. And this he did, explaining the groundrules, summarizing the charges, and pleading for fairness and cooperation all around. It was a fine statement—solemn yet hopeful. "Our counsel, Mr. Jenkins," he said, "will now call the first witness."[3]

McCarthy cut in. "A point of order, Mr. Chairman. May I raise a point of order?" Before Mundt could reply, Joe was off and running. He claimed that Stevens and Adams had no right to file their charges as "the Department of the Army." They did not speak for the Army—or the loyal American soldier. They were "Pentagon politicians" who spoke only for themselves.

A more forceful chairman would have objected. After all, these "Pentagon politicians" were the very symbol of civilian control over the military; they included the Secretary of the Army, who was appointed by the President of the United States. But Karl Mundt said nothing, and his silence encouraged McCarthy to make his point again and again. "I maintain it is a disgrace," he said, "and a reflection upon the millions of outstanding young men in the Army to let a few civilians who are trying to hold up an investigation of Communists, label themselves as the Department of the Army. I do think—"

SENATOR MUNDT: The chair will hold that the point of order should not be raised at this time.

SENATOR MCCARTHY: May I finish?

And he did, adding that "there is no contest between McCarthy and the Army. All that Senator McCarthy has been trying to do is expose the Communists who have infiltrated there, a very small percent."[4]

At last the witness took the stand. He was Miles Reber, commanding general, Western Area Command, of the United States Army in Europe. He had flown in from Germany the previous day. He recorded his name and rank before Joe interrupted: "I wonder if you could identify counsel for Mr. Reber who is sitting beside him." The man sitting beside Reber was H. Struve Hensel, who bristled at this petty attempt to embarrass him. "I am not counsel for *General* Reber," he fumed. "Senator McCarthy knows this well and so does everyone else here."[5]

MR. JENKINS: You are Mr. Hensel?

MR. HENSEL: That is correct.

Under direct examination, General Reber reviewed his persistent efforts to secure a commission for David Schine. In the summer of 1953, as the Army's chief of legislative liaison, he had been approached by Senator McCarthy and Mr. Cohn. Both men had recommended Schine for a commission, he recalled, and both had emphasized "the necessity for speed . . . because the status of Mr. Schine under the Selective Service Act was about to change." A few days later Schine had called his office, saying he wanted "to come to the Pentagon that afternoon and hold up his hand."[6]

MR. JENKINS: What is the significance of the statement "hold up his hand?"

GENERAL REBER: To me the significance . . . meant to be sworn in as a Reserve officer that afternoon.

Reber told Schine that it wasn't quite that simple. There were forms to fill out, exams to take, but he'd see what he could do. In the following weeks, he said, he contacted the Adjutant General, the Transportation Corps, the Office of Psychological Warfare, the Navy, and the Air Force —all to no avail. Meanwhile, the pressure mounted.

> GENERAL REBER: During this period . . . I received numerous phone calls from Mr. Cohn urging speed in the case, and urging a favorable result as soon as possible.

> MR. JENKINS: How many telephone calls would you estimate you received, General?

> GENERAL REBER: I could only make an estimate. . . . But I received consistently throughout that period possibly an average of two telephone calls a day.

Reber was careful with his words. His answers were crisp, factual, direct. When asked whether other members of Congress had requested commissions for their constituents, he replied: "Yes, a sizable number." When asked whether McCarthy had used intimidation or "improper means," he replied in the negative. When asked the same question about Cohn, he said there had been "persistent pressure" but no threats or warnings "or anything like that."

Throughout Reber's testimony Army counsel Joseph Welch had offered no comments, no objections, no points of order. Finally, his turn came, and he asked three simple questions.

> MR. WELCH: . . . were you acutely aware of Mr. Cohn's position as counsel for this committee in the course of your conversations with him?

> GENERAL REBER: I was, Mr. Welch.

> MR. WELCH: Did that position . . . increase or diminish the interest with which you pursued the problem?

> GENERAL REBER: . . . I feel that it increased the interest.

> MR. WELCH: . . . Disregarding the word "improper" influence, do you recall any instance comparable to this in which you were put under greater pressure?

> GENERAL REBER: To the best of my recollection, I recall no instance under which I was put under greater pressure.

McCarthy followed Welch. He asked, "Is Sam Reber your brother?" "Yes, sir," the general replied, and the crowd began to stir.

> SENATOR MCCARTHY: Do you know that . . . your brother, Mr. Sam Reber, repeatedly made attacks upon . . . Mr. Cohn and Mr.

Schine . . . who were sent to Europe by me to inspect the overseas libraries?

At once Ray Jenkins objected. The question was "wholly irrelevant," he said, and General Reber should not be allowed to answer it. But McCarthy replied that he had a duty—not simply a right—to "show motive" on the part of the witness. "If I cannot," he added, "then that is a violation of every law that I know of."

Mundt was not a lawyer. He turned to Jenkins, and Jenkins reversed himself, claiming that McCarthy could proceed with direct questions on the subject, not self-serving statements of fact. Joe thought the point "well taken." He turned to Reber and said, "You, of course, knew that your brother was the Acting Commissioner of Germany at that time?"

GENERAL REBER: I did, sir.

SENATOR MCCARTHY: And had you read the newspaper stories about the statements that your brother, Mr. Sam Reber, had made about Mr. Cohn and Mr. Schine?

GENERAL REBER: I do not, to the best of my ability, recall seeing any statements attributed to my brother in the newspapers about Mr. Cohn and Mr. Schine.

The hearing was recessed at 12:40. Welch and Reber drove back to the Pentagon. McCarthy walked to the Carroll Arms Hotel for drinks, lunch, and a quick meeting with his staff. The hearing reconvened at 2:30. Reber returned to the stand.

SENATOR MCCARTHY: May I say, I think we should apologize to the general of the Army to keep you here questioning you about the private in the Army who is still a private despite all the consideration he got.

Then it came, the rough stuff, the quick knee to the groin.

However, I would like to ask you this question: Are you aware of the fact that your brother was allowed to resign when charges that he was a bad security risk were made against him as a result of the investigations of this committee?

Jenkins objected, of course, but Joe brought up "motive" again, and Jenkins backed away. It was left to McClellan, the ranking Democrat, to remind the members that they were dealing with hearsay, that McCarthy's "facts" had not been established as facts. "Let us have a ruling on this [question]," he warned, "because we may be trying members of everybody's family before we get through."

But a ruling never came. The members—and counsels—spent the next hour deciding whether General Reber should be allowed to say a few words in his brother's defense. First Ray Jenkins said no: "General Reber, I think, is in error in stating that a serious attack has been made on his brother."

Henry Jackson blinked in astonishment: "The statement has been made in this room, and is apparent to millions of Americans that General Reber's brother was dismissed as a security risk."

Then Jenkins said yes: "I withdraw any objection I have interposed to it."

And General Reber was allowed to respond:

> I merely wanted to say, as I understand my brother's case, he retired, as he is entitled to by law, upon reaching the age of fifty. That is all I wanted to say. I know nothing about any security case involving him.

It hardly mattered that Reber was telling the truth about his brother. The damage was irreparable, the resistance almost nil. McCarthy left the room that day feeling very much in command. He walked through a large crowd of admirers, shaking hands, signing autographs, and joking with the children.

"What a nice hat," he told a mother in the group.

"I designed it myself," she giggled.

"Don't all women!" he said as his bodyguards whisked him away.

———

ROBERT STEVENS FOLLOWED REBER to the stand. Impeccably dressed, surrounded by generals and colonels, he began by reading a prepared statement to the committee. "It is my responsibility to speak for the Army," he said. "The Army is about a million and a half men and women . . . plus hundreds of thousands of loyal and faithful public servants—"

> SENATOR McCARTHY: Mr. Chairman, a point of order. Mr. Stevens is not speaking for the Army. He is speaking for Mr. Stevens. . . . I resent very much this attempt to connect the great American Army with this attempt to sabotage the efforts of this committee's investigation into Communism.[7]

Jenkins agreed with McCarthy, and so did Chairman Mundt. But Stevens repeated his claim before moving on to the "Schine story" and offering some statistics:

1. From mid-July of last year until March 1 of this year, David Schine was discussed between one branch or other of the Department of the Army and Senator McCarthy or members of his staff in more than 65 telephone calls.
2. During the same period, this matter was discussed at approxi-

mately 19 meetings between Army personnel and Senator Mc-
Carthy or members of his staff.

"The Schine case," he concluded, "is only an example of the wrong-
ful seeking of privilege, of the perversion of power. It has been a distrac-
tion that has kept many men from the performance of tasks far more
important to the welfare of this country than the convenience of a single
Army private."[8]

He then began his direct examination, designed to bring out his story
in his own words. And the story he told was one of pressure, relentless
pressure, on behalf of G. David Schine. He reviewed the attempts by
Roy Cohn to waive his friend's basic training requirement, to win him
an assignment in New York, and to get him leaves and passes for "committee work" still undone. He portrayed McCarthy as a nervous accomplice, fearful that Cohn was pushing too hard, yet unwilling to put
his foot down and risk the young man's displeasure.

> MR. STEVENS: Senator McCarthy said that one of the few things that
> he had trouble with Mr. Cohn about was David Schine. He said
> that "Roy thinks that Dave ought to be a general and operate from
> a penthouse at the Walford Astoria," or words to that effect.[9]

He also revealed the contents of a conversation he had with Schine
in October, 1953. "It was," said Stevens, "along the lines that I was doing
a good job in ferreting out Communists. . . . (Laughter) . . . That he
thought I could go a long way in the field. . . . (More laughter) . . . And
that he would like to help me . . . to become my assistant . . . instead of
being inducted into the Army."

———

THE DIRECT EXAMINATION WAS OVER. The cross-examination began. This
was the process that Ray Jenkins relished—the roughness of it, the excitement, the chance to freewheel, to get up and perform. At six feet,
three inches, the same height as Joe Welch, he seemed larger by far.
The New York *Times* called him "the sort of lawyer who completely
dominates a case and a court. . . . He reminds one of a boxer dog when
he sets his jaw. He laughs, cries, derides, always showing emotion." In
his thirty-four years of practice, Ray Jenkins had defended 600 murder
suspects without losing one to the electric chair. The secret, he said, was
to get the jury "so damned mad that they want to dig up the body and
kill the SOB all over again."[10]

Jenkins worked without notes. He clapped his hands to emphasize his
words. His questions came in bursts. He asked whether the Army had
been studying the situation at Fort Monmouth before McCarthy happened by. Yes, sir, Stevens replied. Had there been any suspensions?

Yes, six. And after the Monmouth hearings began? Twenty-nine more. Well, then, hadn't McCarthy "speeded up" the process? Hadn't he "enhanced national security" by forcing the Army's hand? Not really, Stevens shot back. The suspensions would have occurred anyway. The senator had simply exaggerated the danger and spread "a good deal of misinformation in the press."[11]

Well, where did Schine fit into this? What about the favors, the affability, the extraordinary indulgence?

> MR. JENKINS: . . . isn't it a fact that you were being especially nice and considerate and tender of this boy, Schine—

Stevens sputtered in protest.

> MR. JENKINS: wait, wait, wait, wait—in order to dissuade the senator from continuing his investigation?
>
> MR. STEVENS: Positively and completely not.
>
> MR. JENKINS: The treatment you accorded Schine then was just what you accorded every other private in the Army?
>
> MR. STEVENS: I certainly would treat privates in the Army, one and all of them, the same.

One and all of them, the same! Ray Jenkins shook his huge head in disbelief. Hadn't the Secretary been to dinner at Schine's Waldorf Towers apartment? Hadn't he traveled the streets of Manhattan in a Schine limousine? Hadn't he called Allen Dulles about a job for Schine at the CIA?

> MR. JENKINS: Was this not done for the purpose of mollifying or pacifying [Cohn and McCarthy] to get them to suspend the investigation at Fort Monmouth?
>
> MR. STEVENS: I say it certainly was not done for that purpose, Mr. Jenkins.
>
> MR. JENKINS: What purpose was it done for?
>
> MR. STEVENS: A friendly matter of convenience, when you get right down to it.

The questions kept coming. Had the Secretary ever asked to have his picture taken with Private Schine? Stevens wasn't sure. Had the two men ever been photographed alone? Stevens couldn't remember. He was photographed a lot.

Here was a big moment, a trap. Jenkins rose from his chair, holding a blown-up reproduction of the Secretary and the private standing shoulder to shoulder in front of a military plane.

MR. STEVENS: I unfortunately can recognize myself but I would not guarantee the soldier. . . . I do not know whether it is Schine or not . . .

Stevens was flustered. He looked again: "I think it probably is." And again: "I would say that this is a picture, undoubtedly, of David Schine, and a rather grim-looking . . . Secretary of the Army."

The problem, however, was that Stevens did not look grim at all. He looked rather comfortable, like a middle-aged father gazing proudly upon a uniformed son. This was important, for the picture had been snapped on November 17, 1953—a day on which Robert Stevens was reportedly furious at the McCarthy people for the demands they were making on Schine's behalf. Why, then, would the Secretary pose for the picture at this time? Why, indeed, unless he was still seeking the good will of McCarthy and his staff—unless he was still *volunteering* favors in a pathetic attempt to buy them off.

———

UNTIL THIS MOMENT the counsel for the Army had not been a factor at all. Unlike the free-wheeling Ray Jenkins, he seemed confused, even immobilized, by the anarchy of the proceedings: the cameras, the bright lights, the crowd noise, the whispering of attorneys to witnesses, the inattention of the judges—or were they the jurors?—and the endless repetition of testimony. It was "a strange experience," he recalled, "a shock to a lawyer used to the traditionally ordered interiors of court-rooms." [12]

On the third day, however, the counsel raised "a point of something" and started to speak. His point, he said, was that a "doctored" photograph —the one of Stevens and Schine—had been produced "in this court-room as if it were honest." Mundt cut in to say that this was a committee room, not a courtroom, and Joe Welch laughed at his mistake.

MR. WELCH: I charge that what was offered in evidence yesterday was an altered, shamefully cut down picture, so that somebody could say to Stevens, "Were you not photographed with David Schine," when in truth he was photographed in a group. . . . I would like to offer the picture that I have in my right hand as the original, undoctored, unaltered piece of evidence. [13]

The "real" photograph had a third individual, a Colonel Bradley, standing to the right of Private Schine. As Welch held it aloft, Senator McCarthy covered his microphone to exchange nervous whispers with his staff.

SENATOR McCARTHY: Mr. Chairman—a point of order. Mr. Welch . . . has testified that a picture is doctored. . . . He makes the completely false statement that this is a group picture, and it is not.

This was not a point of order, of course. This was testimony from a man who was not under oath. Ray Jenkins objected—and the battle was on.

SENATOR SYMINGTON: I would like to say that if this is not a point of order, it is out of order.

SENATOR McCARTHY: Oh, be quiet.

SENATOR SYMINGTON: I haven't the slightest intention of being quiet. Counsel is running this committee, and you are not running it.

By now the Democrats were demanding "the facts" about these pictures, and Ray Jenkins, the latest victim of the McCarthy School of Innovative Photography, was demanding them, too. As a result, Robert Stevens was excused from the witness stand, and the man with "the facts" was summoned in his place.

MR. JENKINS: I would like to call at this time, Mr. Roy Cohn.[14]

Ray Jenkins was embarrassed. He wanted it understood that Cohn had slipped him the photograph without mentioning the omission of Colonel Bradley or anyone else. But Roy Cohn was not Robert Stevens; he knew how to fight.

MR. JENKINS: Did you or did you not tell me that you had documentary evidence in the form of a photograph . . . ?

MR. COHN: Mr. Jenkins, I wonder if we could do it this way: Could I give my recollection as to exactly what I did do?

MR. JENKINS: I think that would be fine.

Cohn agreed that he had not told Jenkins about the omission. The reason, he said, was that he had not known about the omission himself. The photo had been cut down—quite innocently, he assumed—by someone on the subcommittee staff. More to the point—Cohn's point—the omission of Colonel Bradley was unimportant because it did not "materially alter" the meaning of the photograph. "The fact remains that Mr. Stevens and Mr. Schine are looking at each other and facing each other," Roy Cohn declared, "and that is that."

Welch sat quietly, his chin resting in his hand. When his turn came, he smiled at the young witness and said, "Mr. Cohn, I assume you would like it understood that although I sit at the same table, I am not your counsel." The witness replied, with inappropriate bravado, that "Roy

Cohn is here speaking for Roy Cohn, to give the facts. I have no counsel, and I feel the need of none, sir."

> MR. WELCH: In all modesty, sir, I am content that it should appear from *my end* that I am not your counsel.

The audience laughed, and the cross-examination began. Welch held up the photograph of Stevens, Schine, and Bradley. He asked, "Mr. Stevens is looking to his right, isn't he?"

> MR. COHN: Well, sir—

> MR. WELCH: Isn't he? You can answer that one easily.

Cohn could see what was coming. The smugness was gone, replaced by a kind of edginess and uncertainty that he hadn't shown before.

> MR. COHN: Mr. Welch . . . you asked me a question and then you say with the implication as though I can't answer it.

> MR. WELCH: Well, answer it. Mr. Stevens is looking to his right, isn't he?

> MR. COHN: Yes, I would say he probably is looking to his right . . .

> MR. WELCH: On Mr. Stevens's right there are two figures, is that correct?

> MR. COHN: Yes, that is correct . . .

Then perhaps Mr. Stevens was looking at Colonel Bradley, rather than at Private Schine. Perhaps that explained the "faint look of pleasure" on the colonel's face.

> MR. COHN: I would say that Colonel Bradley had a good steak dinner shortly afterward. Maybe he was anticipating it . . .

Welch never broke stride. "If Bradley is feeling good about a steak dinner," he riposted, "Schine must be considering a whole haunch of beef."

The crowd roared, the curtain fell, the players broke for lunch. On the way out McCarthy took Cohn by the arm and urged him to "run, don't walk" to the best lawyer he could find. "Roy," said the senator without a smile, "you were about the worst witness I ever heard in my life." [15]

THE MYSTERY OF THE "DOCTORED" PHOTOGRAPH, a curious matter and a trivial one, took up most of the week. Following Roy Cohn's testimony the other McCarthy staffers were examined and reexamined as if the fate of the Republic hung in the balance. Finally the faithful Jim Juliana stepped forward to take the responsibility, but not the blame.

> MR. JULIANA: It was not done to deceive anyone. . . . It was done because I had instructions to furnish Mr. Jenkins with a picture of Secretary Stevens and Mr. Schine.

> SENATOR MUNDT: . . . Are you quite sure that none of your associates had suggested to you that perhaps it might be a good trick to eliminate Colonel Bradley?

> MR. JULIANA: No one ever suggested any such thing to me.[16]

But Welch kept picking away, hoping to rattle the witness—or better, his friends down the row. Who had reproduced the photo? he asked. A pixie, perhaps?* The witness opened his mouth, but the voice came from the other end of the table.

> SENATOR MCCARTHY: Will counsel for my benefit define—I think he might be an expert on that—what a pixie is?

The remark was meant to do damage, and so was the reply.

> MR. WELCH: Yes, I should say, Mr. Senator, that a pixie is a close relative of a fairy.

The cameras focused on McCarthy as the room erupted in laughter. "As I said," the senator shot back, "I think you may be an authority on what a pixie is."

By day's end the matter of the cropped photo had been put to rest. Welch hadn't proved his charges of fraud and foul play, but that was beside the point. What he had done, with enormous skill, was to rekindle memories of the dishonest McCarthy—the guy who produced the "composite photo" of Millard Tydings and Earl Browder in 1950—and to create a smoke screen that diverted public attention from the real issues at hand. On November 17, 1953, Robert Stevens was supposed to be out of patience with McCarthy and his staff. Why, then, had he chauffered the senator and his counsel to Fort Dix in his Army plane? Why had he posed with the private at the airfield? And why, upon learning that Cohn and McCarthy were due in Boston that night, had he placed his C-47 at

---

* The actual reproduction had been done by Don Surine, the one man McCarthy wanted to keep off the stand. Surine was unpredictable, and he had left the FBI under questionable circumstances, a point that was sure to arise during his cross-examination. When Surine's name was brought into the picture, McCarthy carefully described him as "a messenger boy" who had carried the picture to the enlargement room and then brought it back to Juliana. During the recess, however, McCarthy used stronger tactics. He reportedly "grabbed Symington in the corridor and threatened that, if Surine were called, McCarthy would counter with a full-scale smear of Symington." Surine was not called. See *Army–McCarthy Hearings*, 1954, p. 548; Michael Straight, *Trial by Television*, 1954, p. 45.

their disposal? These questions—the important ones—were lost in the smoke.

McCarthy had been hurt in other ways as well. In attempting to protect his staff members, he had swung wildly at their interrogators, friend and foe alike. At one point, in a frightening rage, he called Ray Jenkins a braggart and a bully, and shouted that his conduct was "the most improper . . . I have ever seen." After retracting the remark, he informed Senator Dworshak that he, Joe McCarthy, had chosen him to sit on the committee, and that he, Joe McCarthy, was sorry about the choice. "May I say . . . there was a question of whether I should appoint . . . Senator Dworshak or Senator Butler. Senator Butler was not feeling well that day. I now wish he had been feeling well."

These outbursts were only the beginning. The attacks on his staffers would continue, and the senator would commit his most egregious blunders in their defense. His loyalty to his "boys" was so visceral, so complete, that he did not see—or care—how unpopular and politically ruinous they had become. In letter after letter McCarthy's own supporters complained about Cohn and Schine in particular—their draft records, their arrogance, their "Jewishness" and their wealth.* However, as Urban Van Susteren recalled, "there was no reasoning with Joe on this matter. These guys were part of the family—Roy, Surine, even Schine. You attacked them and you answered to Joe." [17]

"THERE WAS SOMETHING ABOUT THESE HEARINGS that seemed to affect the public like a habit-forming drug. Once you acquired the habit," Joseph Nye Welch recalled, "you put up with immense stretches of aridity because you believed that at any moment a rocket would take off from this dismal desert and you would be galvanized . . . able to sit back feeling somehow rewarded and fulfilled." Welch had fired the first rocket— the cropped photo charge—on the morning of April 27. The second blast —the reply—came exactly one week later. Launched by Senator McCarthy, it rose from the hearing room, circled the Departments of Justice and Defense, and landed, nose down, on the White House lawn. [18]

Robert Stevens was now in his ninth day of testimony, a prisoner in his chair, exhausted and fighting the flu. The questions that afternoon were about Communists at Fort Monmouth, and the questioners—

---

* A friend of Mundt's wrote McCarthy: "I'm hoping and praying that you will be successful. . . . But the mere fact that David Schine is wealthy and perhaps of Jewish extraction should not entitle him to any special consideration." A Protestant minister wrote Mundt: "the majority stands solidly behind Joe McCarthy, but they all wonder just who planted these two New York JEWS on his committee in the first place. . . . They seem to have caused all this mess, and it is a mess." See Paul Noren to Senator Joe McCarthy, May 4, 1954; Edward J. Smythe to Senator Karl Mundt, May 14, 1954; both in the *Karl Mundt Papers*, Dakota State College, Madison, South Dakota.

Cohn and McCarthy—were scoring at will. On and on it went—"I don't know . . . I can't recall . . . I have no recollection . . ."—until the senator drew a document from his briefcase and passed it to Frank Carr, his left-hand man.

"Shall I hit them with this one?"

"Oh, no," Carr replied, "put it back."[19]

Joe put it back, but only for a moment. The temptation was too strong. He opened his briefcase again.

> SENATOR McCARTHY: Mr. Secretary, I would like to give you a letter, one which was written incidentally before you took office but which was in the file, I understand, all during the time you are in office—I understand it is in the file today—from the FBI, pointing at the urgency in connection with certain cases at Fort Monmouth.[20]

In McCarthy's hand was a "carbon copy" of a letter purportedly written by J. Edgar Hoover to the Army on January 26, 1951. Stamped "personal and confidential," the letter contained a warning about subversive activities at Fort Monmouth and a list of thirty-four possible security risks. This was it, the smoking gun, the *written proof* that Army officials had ignored a "dangerous situation" at Monmouth until a determined Senate committee had forced them to act.*

Was the letter authentic? If so, where did it come from? The FBI? The Army files? As usual Ray Jenkins was too excited to care. He jumped at the letter as eagerly as he had jumped at the cut-down photo of Stevens and Schine. His words were virtually the same: "I hold now . . . on the assumption that no party of interest . . . would refer to a spurious manufactured document that Senator McCarthy's cross-examination of the Secretary with reference to this letter is wholly competent."

There were objections, of course.

> MR. WELCH: The mere fact that we have an impressive-looking purported copy of such a letter doesn't impress an old-time lawyer. I would like to have J. Edgar Hoover say that he wrote the letter and mailed it.

Welch added that the letter had not come from the Army files—he was certain of that.

> SENATOR McCARTHY: If Mr. Welch is going to say that there is not a copy of this in the Army files, he should be sworn, because that statement is untrue.

> MR. WELCH: I did not say that. I said that this purported copy did not come from the Army files, and you know that I am quite right, sir.

---

* For additional information on this document, see pp. 334–35.

And I have an absorbing curiosity to know how in the dickens you got hold of it.[21]

By this point the contents of the letter had been obscured by other matters, and the committee had no choice but to clear them up first. So Ray Jenkins promised to consult the FBI, Joe Welch promised to search the Army files, and Karl Mundt sighed a weary sigh, indeed. "We will stand in recess until 10:30 in the morning," he said, "but the Chair believes we may have to have both night sessions and Saturday sessions if we do not move more rapidly than we are now."

━━━━━━

THE FOLLOWING DAY ROBERT A. COLLIER, an assistant counsel, was called to the stand. Collier had just returned from a meeting with J. Edgar Hoover at the FBI. He said that Hoover had examined the letter and assured him that it had not come from the Bureau's files. The Director did say, however, that a fifteen-page memorandum had been sent to the Army on January 26, 1951—the same date as the letter in Collier's hand. While these documents were different in form, the witness added, "Mr. Hoover advised me . . . that the FBI memorandum and the two-and-one-quarter-page carbon copy contained information relating to the same subject, and that in some instances exact or identical language appear in both documents."[22]

Welch bore down hard. He wanted plain talk, honest talk, he said.

MR. WELCH: Let us have it straight from the shoulder. So far as you know, this is a carbon copy of precisely nothing.

MR. COLLIER: So far as I know, it is, yes, but that again is a conclusion.

MR. WELCH: . . . we can find no trace of an original, can we?

MR. COLLIER: Not yet.

MR. WELCH: Anywhere.

MR. COLLIER: No, sir.

Welch had done it again. He had shifted attention from the contents of this "perfect phony" to the question of "how in the dickens" McCarthy had obtained it. Reluctantly, Ray Jenkins called the Wisconsin senator to the stand. There was immediate confusion, a kind of musical chairs, as Cohn and Carr switched places with Welch and St. Clair in order to be near their boss. "No, no," McCarthy protested. "I don't want Mr. Welch examining my notes over there." Very well, Mundt replied. "Mr. Juliana, you sit at the counsel table . . . and safeguard the notes. . . . Mr. Welch, you sit on the other side. . . . Is everything all right now?"

McCarthy nodded; then he glared at Welch and said, "In other words, take a cold chair."[23]

Welch did, and the witness began. He said he had received the document from a young patriot in the Armed Forces, a man whose "duty" to his country was above any duty to any Truman Directive." The man, an intelligence officer, was "deeply disturbed" by the Army's failure to heed FBI warnings about Communist espionage in the Signal Corps. Needless to say, his name would not be revealed. That was Rule Number One, said McCarthy, and "there is no way on earth that any committee, any force, can get me to violate the confidence of the people who give me information from within the government."

But Welch played by other rules, including the U.S. Code, Title 18, Section 793, which makes it a crime to furnish classified information to persons not authorized to receive it. In his eyes the intelligence officer was a criminal who had placed his convictions above the law. And so, too, was the man who had protected these people and encouraged them to break the law.

> MR. WELCH: Senator McCarthy . . . the oath you took included a promise, a solemn promise by you to tell the truth, comma, the whole truth, comma, and nothing but the truth. Is that correct, sir?
>
> SENATOR McCARTHY: Mr. Welch, you are not the first individual that tried to get me to betray the confidence and give out the names of my informants. You will be no more successful than those who have tried in the past, period.

But Welch persisted. He aimed to humiliate the witness, to make him sound like the "Fifth Amendment Communists" he had been battering for years.

> MR. WELCH: Will you tell us where you were when you got the letter?
>
> SENATOR McCARTHY: No.
>
> MR. WELCH: How soon after you got it did you show it to anyone?
>
> SENATOR McCARTHY: I don't remember.
>
> MR. WELCH: To whom did you first show it?
>
> SENATOR McCARTHY: I don't recall.

Finally a hand reached out and pulled McCarthy from the fire.

> SENATOR DIRKSEN: May I raise a point of inquiry here. . . . Is it required of a witness consonant with his oath, that he reveal the source of a document when he had pledged himself to respect the

confidence and not reveal the name? . . . I think the advice of counsel ought to be taken on this matter. . . . I think we ought to dispose of it now.

Dirksen had nothing to fear, of course. He sat back and listened as his good friend from Tennessee rushed to the defense of his good friend from Wisconsin.

> MR. JENKINS: Mr. Chairman, it is elementary that the senator does not have to reveal the name of his informant. That is one of the most elementary principles engrafted in the law. Otherwise, law-enforcing officers would be so hamstrung and hampered as that they would never be able to ferret out crime. I unhesitatingly rule that Senator McCarthy does not have to reveal the name of his informant.

Ray Jenkins was right about one thing: he was dealing with an elementary principle of law. His mistake, however, was in applying that principle to the case at hand. Put simply, the senator was *not* a law-enforcing officer trying to ferret out crime. He was, instead, a fellow who frequently *assumed* the law enforcement powers of a branch of government to which he did not belong. Curiously, no one bothered to challenge the logic behind the ruling. That would come later, with telling effect.

When the session ended that day, Willard Edwards joined Cohn, Carr, and McCarthy for a drink in the senator's fourth-floor office. Everyone agreed that Joe had been truculent but fairly successful. He had protected his sources and encouraged potential informants. Then McCarthy asked, "By the way, where the hell *did* we get that letter?" The room rocked with laughter, Edwards recalled. "Nobody gave an answer and obviously none was expected."[24]

ON MAY 5, at the committee's request, Chairman Mundt asked Attorney General Brownell for "written advice" about the documents in question: the fifteen-page memo and two-and-one-quarter-page letter. Could the committee discuss these documents in public? Could it release their contents to the press? Brownell replied by letter the following day. He said that both documents contained confidential sources of information, unevaluated data, and the names of persons "against whom no derogatory material has been shown." Their publication, therefore, would not be in the "security interests" of the United States.[25]

The letter touched off an angry debate at the hearings. Senator McCarthy charged, with some justification, that the refusal to release these documents was a political move, designed to protect the Army from further embarrassment. If security were really the issue, Mr. Brownell could easily delete the sensitive portions, as he had done with other FBI documents in the past.

> SENATOR MCCARTHY: Mr. Brownell made a speech in Chicago some time ago. He named not the living spies that we are discussing here, who are poised with a razor over the jugular vein of this nation. . . . He named a very important dead spy (Harry Dexter White). I don't criticize him for that. I think this was information that the public . . . should have had long ago.[26]

As the hearings wore on, however, McCarthy's challenge grew bolder, his rhetoric more extreme. Before the Brownell letter he had simply promised to protect the confidentiality of his sources. After the letter he openly encouraged federal workers to break the law in order to "save the land." Mundt did not challenge these statements, but McClellan did. His exchanges with McCarthy were as important as any in the thirty-six days of the hearings.

> SENATOR MCCARTHY: I want to compliment the individuals who have placed their oath to defend the country against enemies—and certainly Communists are enemies—above any Presidential directive . . .

> SENATOR MCCLELLAN: I don't know of any oath that any man took for loyalty to his country that requires him to commit a crime.

> SENATOR MCCARTHY: As far as I am concerned I would like to notify those 2 million employees that I feel it is their *duty* to give us any information which they have.

> SENATOR MCCLELLAN: If this theory is followed . . . then you can have no security system in America. It will destroy it totally and irrevocably if all who have information give it out indiscriminately.* [27]

Nothing that McCarthy ever said or did—not even the Marshall attack—upset Dwight Eisenhower as much as this open appeal to the employees of the Executive branch. Pacing behind his desk, he told Hagerty: "This is nothing but a wholesale subversion of public service. McCarthy is making the same plea of loyalty to him that Hitler made to

---

* A fair number of senators supported McCarthy's position here, although their rhetoric was less extreme. In 1951 Karl Mundt wrote a friend: "In an era when the President refuses to cooperate with a congressional investigation by permitting congressional committees to see the personnel and security files, there is *no good and delicate way* in which an alert Congress can detect, expose, and eliminate the Communists." See Mundt to Rev. Daniel Poling, December 18, 1951, *Mundt Papers*.

the German people. . . . I think [it] is the most disloyal act we have ever had by anyone in the government of the United States."[28]

The following day Ike confronted this challenge in public. He released a statement, written by Hagerty, which read:

> The executive branch of the government has the sole and fundamental responsibility for the enforcement of our laws and presidential orders.
>
> That responsibility cannot be usurped by any individual who may seek to set himself above the laws of the land to override the orders of the President of the United States to federal employees of the executive branch of the government.[29]

CHAPTER TWENTY-NINE

Executive Privilege

ON THE EVE OF THE HEARINGS Karl Mundt had predicted that they'd be over in a week, or even less. He had notified the President, who seemed genuinely relieved. "Push," Ike told him, "and remember that there's honor and decency at stake."[1]

But Mundt had been wrong. He hadn't expected—or been able to control—the speeches, the outbursts, the points of order that flew back and forth. The first week had ended with Robert Stevens on the stand; the second week had ended like the first. At this rate the hearings would drag on for months—a rather frightening prospect for the Republican Party.

The pressure on Mundt was relentless. He had only to read his mail.

Dear Karl:
My personal view coincides with the views of the general run of Republicans who are engaged in fund raising. . . . The McCarthy–Stevens hearings are a disgraceful affair and the sooner they finish the better for the Party.
F.P. Heffelfinger
Chairman Republican
National Finance Committee

Dear Karl:
   . . . There will be a lot of Republicans who won't be voting in the forth-
coming election.

> George Stringfellow
> Senior Vice President
> Thomas Edison Inc.

My Dear Karl:
   The only way to stop is to stop!

> Alf M. Landon
> Topeka, Kansas[2]

Stopping should have been easy. The Republicans held four of the
seven seats on the committee, and a majority vote was all that was
needed. The problem, however, was that Mundt had promised to oppose
an early stoppage if *any* of the principals objected on grounds of justice
or equity. It was a noble promise—a promise he would honor and also
regret.

On the morning of May 11 Senator Dirksen offered a "compromise"
designed to shorten the hearings and to get them off TV. He proposed
(1) that the public sessions be limited to the testimony of Stevens and
McCarthy; (2) that all other witnesses be heard in executive session; and
(3) that McCarthy be authorized to resume his hearings "with respect to
any matters not related to the present controversy."[3]

The Republican members were enthusiastic. So was Senator Mc-
Carthy, who complained that the hearings had diverted his attention
from "the vast number of Communists working . . . with a razor, if you
please, poised over the jugular of this nation." But Robert Stevens was
not enthusiastic, not even lukewarm. "I don't want to be an obstruction-
ist," he said, "but I think we must get the facts from the witnesses who
can be seen . . . by those on television, just as I have done over these
days."

Mundt was appalled. He strongly supported the Dirksen Plan, yet his
vote—the deciding vote—was tied directly to Stevens's approval. In desperation, it seemed, he turned to the Secretary.

> SENATOR MUNDT: We find ourselves in a world where the cause of
> freedom is being challenged by tremendous forces. . . . The
> enemy has an atomic bomb. . . . It is terribly hard for the Chair to
> believe that this is the most important business to which we can
> devote ourselves. I hope and pray that during the noon hour men
> will search their souls and their consciences to determine whether
> there is not something more important than trying to protract these
> hearings.

After lunch the principals were polled, one by one. McCarthy agreed
to the proposal; Cohn agreed, and Carr did, too. But Robert Stevens was

missing; he had gone home with a fever and not returned. The chairman looked imploringly at Welch: Did his client oppose the Dirksen Plan?

MR. WELCH: I think I ought not to answer that without consultation. . . . I believe I could reach him by telephone if you would like me to.

SENATOR MUNDT: I would surely very much appreciate that, because if you are going to cast my proxy, both you and I want it to be cast intelligently.

So Welch walked to a pay phone in the corridor and put in a dime. Ten minutes later he returned with the news:

MR. WELCH: He said, "Well, primarily, it is up to the committee to decide . . . but I don't myself think it is fair and just and equitable that I should be stuck on the stand for fourteen days and that one or two of the parties . . . should never be there at all."

Nervously, Mundt asked for clarification. Was this a categorical no? Was Stevens objecting to this particular proposal?

MR. WELCH: I have another dime in my pocket if you want me to put it in the phone again.

SENATOR MUNDT: I wish you would do that, sir.

So Welch returned to the pay phone and placed his second call. This time the answer was direct:

MR. WELCH: He says, "I continue in my view that the proposed resolution will not result in fairness . . ."

SENATOR MUNDT: The Chair is certainly then prepared to vote.

The result was not surprising. McClellan, No. Dirksen, Aye. Jackson, No. Potter, Aye. Symington, No. Dworshak, Aye. Then Mundt spoke: "The Chair votes No. The motion fails."

━━━━━━

THE MOST PUZZLING ASPECT of this failure was the role played by Robert Stevens, a man who rarely resisted political pressure of any kind. By most accounts the Secretary had stood alone, defying senators, Pentagon officials, and the President himself. According to Michael Straight, "Secretary of Defense Wilson, Deputy Secretary Seaton, and other top leaders of Stevens's party had argued with him to give in." On May 14 Drew Pearson wrote in his diary: "I now learn that Eisenhower took the Secretary of the Army for a drive in Virginia with Nixon, and they poured it on him to agree to terminate the hearings. Stevens is showing more backbone than I ever thought he had. He refused."[4]

In fact, it didn't happen this way. Stevens did not stand alone. There was no pressure from Nixon or Wilson or Eisenhower. On the contrary, the President fully supported the Secretary's position. He wanted the hearings to continue, and he wanted them televised.* Why? Because he knew that the Army was losing and that a compromise would be viewed as a surrender. Furthermore, he figured that closed sessions would benefit McCarthy, who "would use his old trick of coming out . . . and telling reporters anything he wanted. He would have a forum and the Army would not."

Not everyone agreed with Eisenhower, of course. Some White House staffers, including Jerry Persons, the congressional liaison, were strongly in favor of the Dirksen plan. But the President, who found little to admire about Robert T. Stevens, said simply, "I think he did exactly right."[5]

———

THE NEXT SESSION BEGAN with a pep talk from Joe Welch. Yesterday's matter was done, he said; the committee had voted to plow the long, hard furrow. "So I say let's put on a kind of a grin of some sort and all smile at each other a little if we can and get on with the next witness."[6]

There were few smiles, however, as John Adams took the stand.

SENATOR MUNDT: You may be seated. Mr. Jenkins, you have unlimited time to examine the witness without interruption.

Prompted by Ray Jenkins, the witness began his remarkable story. A veteran of World War II, he had come to Washington as the secretary of Senator Chan Gurney, a South Dakota Republican. In the following years he had worked as chief clerk for the Senate Armed Services Committee, deputy counsel to the Department of Defense, and counselor to the Army, a position he assumed on October 1, 1953. His main function, he said, was to work as the Army's liaison with McCarthy and his staff. This meant being helpful and friendly, and he had tried to be both. As Adams explained it, only one factor had disrupted an otherwise splendid relationship between Roy Cohn and himself. That factor was the status of G. David Schine.[7]

In early October, Adams recalled, Senator McCarthy had first approached him about "the Schine problem."

MR. ADAMS: He made a remark to the effect that Schine was not much use to the committee . . . and that he hoped that nothing would happen to keep Schine from being drafted.

*On May 11, the day of the vote, Hagerty wrote in his diary: "Great pressure by Republicans to try to take hearings into executive session. . . . I think it would be terrible. Discussed it briefly with the President, and he agrees with me. He called Charlie Wilson and told him not to put any pressure at all on Stevens along these lines but to tell Stevens to 'do what you think is right'."

Adams added, however, that McCarthy had told him to say nothing of his attitude to Roy Cohn.

MR. JENKINS: Did he tell you why he did not want you to tell Mr. Cohn?

MR. ADAMS: No . . . but I asked for permission to tell Mr. Stevens . . . about his attitude concerning Schine, and he agreed that I could.

In November Private Schine began his basic training at Fort Dix, New Jersey. Cohn called Adams at once, asking that his friend be made available on weekends and evenings for the completion of his committee work. Adams was helpful, though somewhat perplexed. He had been told about Schine's marginal value to the committee, yet he did not want to cause a fuss. After all, he said, "I had found out already that Mr. Cohn had the capacity to control what happened to the committee . . . and I was not happy about having him angry at us."

On November 10 Adams phoned Cornelius Ryan, the commanding general at Fort Dix. He explained the need for special treatment, and the general replied that "he, of course, could arrange it." So Schine received passes for seventeen of the next thirty-one days. He missed guard duty, skipped KP, and left the drill field to place and accept scores of long distance calls. He became, in General Ryan's words, "a man apart"—a man who flaunted his privileges, who claimed, with apparent solemnity, that he'd come to Fort Dix to reorganize the U.S. Army along modern lines.

On December 8 General Ryan put a stop to the weekend passes. The general claimed that Schine had been bleary-eyed on the rifle range, that he'd "probably kill somebody if he kept this up." Nervously, Adams broke the news to Cohn.

MR. ADAMS: He considered this a double-cross, a Stevens double-cross, is the way he categorized it. . . . He was so persistent with reference to Schine . . . that I decided I would speak to Senator McCarthy about it.

So Adams went to McCarthy, who promised to straighten things out. But that afternoon, the counselor went on, "I received a telephone call from Mr. Cohn. He said he would teach me what it meant to go over his head. I said to him, 'Roy, is that a threat?' And he said, 'No, that is a promise.' "

On December 15 Drew Pearson broke the first of several stories about preferential treatment for Schine. Two days later, Adams continued, he ran into Senator McCarthy at the Monmouth hearings in New York. Joe was worried. He said that the "interference with officials at Fort Dix" was over; "it had ceased; he was not going to permit it any more." Adams replied that he was glad to get the information, "but it would be absolutely of no value . . . unless the senator stated it to Cohn in front of me."

That afternoon Adams lunched with Cohn and McCarthy at Gassner's Restaurant near Foley Square. His objective, he testified, was to get the senator on record—and Cohn off his back. "I said, 'Let's talk about Schine.' That started a chain of events, an experience similar to none I have ever had in my life."

According to Adams, "Mr. Cohn became extremely agitated . . . extremely abusive." He cursed the Army for its broken promises, and he cursed McCarthy for undermining the effort to get Schine an assignment in New York. "The abuse went in waves. . . . Everybody would eat a little . . . and then it would start in again. It just kept on."

Adams had a train to catch. He had already missed the 1:30 and the 2:30, and Cohn agreed to drive him to the station. On the ride uptown, "Cohn's anger erupted again. It was directed more toward Senator McCarthy . . . who turned to me on two or three occasions . . . and asked if I could not try to talk to Mr. Stevens and arrange an assignment in New York for Schine."

When the car reached 34th Street, Cohn flashed a badge at a traffic cop and attempted an illegal left turn. It didn't work; the cop said no and the car sped north, away from Penn Station. At 46th Street, Cohn slammed on the brakes and yelled, "Get there however you can." So, the witness recalled, "I climbed out of the car in the middle of a few lanes of traffic, ran across the street, and jumped into a cab to try to make the 3:30 train."

> MR. JENKINS: Senator Potter directs me to ask you whether you made the train. [Laughter]

Yes, Adams replied, "and Mr. Carr told me a few days later that I shouldn't feel badly . . . because I should have been there to see the way Senator McCarthy left the car a few blocks later."

In January Adams learned the worst news of all: Schine would soon be leaving Fort Dix for Camp Gordon, Georgia, and eventually, perhaps, a station overseas. The counselor phoned the news to Roy Cohn, who bombarded him with questions: How long would Schine be in Georgia? Could he live off the post? Could he get passes for his committee work? Who ran Camp Gordon, anyway? As always, Adams promised to find out. He spoke with a general at the Pentagon and the commandant at Camp Gordon. He also told Robert Stevens, who phoned a few more generals "to be sure that we were exactly accurate as to what was ahead for Private Schine."

Ray Jenkens was flabbergasted. "Did you and the Secretary have any time to attend to your other business outside of looking after the future of Schine?"

MR. ADAMS: I had never been in a situation like this before.

Finally Adams told Frank Carr what *was* ahead for Private Schine: five full months in Georgia. Carr relayed the news to Roy Cohn, who was vacationing at a Schine hotel near Miami. Cohn telephoned Adams "within the half hour."

> MR. ADAMS: It was obvious to me that he was very upset. I asked him if he intended to continue his vacation . . . and he said . . . "How can I, when this has happened?"
>
> That was on January 18. On the following morning, January 19, I received a telephone call from Mr. Carr requesting the appearance of certain members of the Army Loyalty and Security Appeals Board for questioning by the subcommittee.

To this point John Adams had been a very strong witness. He had made convincing claims about improper pressure on Schine's behalf; he had linked that pressure to the Monmouth investigation; and he had portrayed himself as the dutiful servant, quite willing to sacrifice his pride and self-respect. The irony, of course, was that he had sacrificed everything but the one item that would surely bring him peace: a New York assignment for Schine.

> SENATOR McCLELLAN: Why did you not agree, then, to appease by sending Schine up to New York? Why did you not agree to that?

> MR. ADAMS: I guess as good a reason as any is that we had 25,000 men killed in Korea who did not have the money or the influence to get themselves a New York assignment.

But Adams made one mistake. He talked too much. He offered information that nobody demanded.

> MR. ADAMS: On the following morning, January 21, I met in the Attorney General's office with Mr. Brownell, Deputy Attorney General Rogers, Presidential Assistant Sherman Adams . . . and U.N. Ambassador Henry Cabot Lodge.
>
> . . . I recounted the details of the loyalty board ultimatum, and at Mr. Rogers's request I described the problem we were having over Private Schine and how the two matters seemed to me to be related.
>
> . . . Governor Adams asked me if I had written a record of all the incidents with reference to Private Schine . . . and when I replied in the negative he stated he thought I should prepare one.

This was a startling admission, for it undermined the Army's claim that it had acted independently in its struggle with the subcommittee staff. Ironically, these words went virtually unnoticed that day. Jenkins pressed on with his examination, and the cameras caught McCarthy yawning as he perused a copy of the Washington *Star*. When the session ended, however, Welch latched on to the witness and led him past reporters at the door. "No comment," he said. "No comment at all."

WHILE JOHN ADAMS had committed an extraordinary blunder, his disclosure had not caught the White House entirely by surprise. For weeks the President had been considering ways to protect the confidentiality of all such meetings by constitutional means. On May 5, for example, he had asked Herbert Brownell to prepare an opinion on the limits of executive privilege. Could he prevent his advisers from testifying about their private discussions? If so, on what grounds? On May 7, before the opinion even arrived, the President had answered his questions in a spirited conversation with Henry Cabot Lodge. "I would be astonished," he said, "if any of my personal advisers would undertake to give testimony on intimate staff counsel and advice. The result would be to eliminate all such offices from the presidential staff. In turn, this would mean paralysis."[8]

On the morning of May 14 Adams was asked to testify about the meeting in Brownell's office. This time Welch objected, saying that the witness had been ordered to remain silent about "high level discussions" within the Executive department. The explanation satisfied no one. The committee members were angry, their questions hostile and sarcastic: Was this a "high level discussion" or simply an embarrassing one? Was the President claiming executive privilege? If so, for whom—for John Adams, who had *volunteered* this information to the committee, or for the other participants as well? And why in the world was Henry Cabot Lodge, the American Ambassador to the United Nations, involved in this matter? Was there some link between the U.N. and Schine?

Welch pleaded ignorance. He was only "a bearer of messages," he said, "a simple trial lawyer . . . and the world's leading amateur . . . in this field." He could not possibly answer these questions on his own. He needed time, and it was Friday, and perhaps the members would allow him the weekend to consult "with people wiser than Welch is." The members agreed—after telling the Bostonian exactly where they stood. "Insofar as I am concerned," said Senator McClellan, "unless something can be shown me, some law—and I do not know that an executive order will suffice in my case—I will ask . . . that all the participants testify . . . before this committee."[9]

Eisenhower could not allow this, of course. If his advisers testified, he ran the risk of further disclosures, far more embarrassing than the discussion of January 21. What if the committee learned that he had known about the Adams Chronology for months? Or that he had encouraged his subordinates to leak parts of it to the press? Or that he had approved a plan to use the Chronology to force Roy Cohn's resignation from the subcommittee? The result would be catastrophic. The whole focus of the hearings would change. The issue of White House complicity—and blackmail—would dominate everything else.

For the President this was clearly a case where constitutional principle coincided with political advantage. On Monday morning, May 17, he told a group of Republican congressional leaders that he intended to stand by the separation of powers, that "any man who testifies as to the advice he gave or got won't be working for me that night." These were powerful words, and Senator Knowland tested them by referring to the subpoena power of Congress. But Eisenhower held his ground. "Let me make one thing clear," he said. "Those people . . . who are my confidential advisers *are not going to be subpoenaed*. Their jobs are really a part of me, and they are not going up on the Hill." [10]

An hour later John Adams returned to the witness chair. In his hand was a letter from the President to the Secretary of Defense. Adams read it aloud, like a schoolboy with a note from home:

> . . . Because it is essential . . . that employees of the Executive Branch be in a position to be completely candid in advising with each other on official matters, and because it is not in the public interest that any of their conversations . . . concerning such advice be disclosed, you will instruct employees of your Department that . . . they are not to testify to any such conversations . . .*

The committee members were skeptical. They all saw the letter for what it was—a constitutional roadblock, designed to keep high Administration officials from implicating themselves in the controversy. Senator Jackson said, "I deeply respect the right of the President under the doctrine of separation of powers. . . . But I sincerely believe that there has been a bad abuse of that doctrine in this situation." Senators Mundt, Potter, Dirksen, and McClellan said much the same thing. Then McCarthy spoke, though only for a moment. His hands were trembling as he asked for a ten-minute recess "to determine what action I should take in view of this unprecedented, completely unusual, almost unbelievable situation we are confronted with this morning." [11]

He returned, ten minutes later, "at a loss to know what to do." The

* Attached to the letter was the memo from Brownell to Eisenhower about executive privilege, listing precedents from George Washington through Harry S. Truman. "Upon this firm principle," Brownell concluded, "our country's strength, liberty, and democratic form of government will continue to endure." See "Memorandum No. 20," *Army–McCarthy Hearings*, 1954, pp. 1269–75.

whole picture had changed, he said. Perhaps Adams and Stevens were not the real villains in this drama. Perhaps they were not responsible "for the smears that have held up the committee for weeks and weeks." Perhaps they were not responsible "for keeping all these Army officers down here and all the senators tied up while the whole world is going up in flames."

Was the President responsible? No, said McCarthy, "I don't think his judgment is that bad." The real culprits were the men who advised him —men like Rogers, Brownell, Sherman Adams, and Henry Cabot Lodge.

> SENATOR MCCARTHY: The Attorney General and his Deputy must pass upon questions of evidence. They must ultimately decide who is lying. . . . I think it is unheard of that you have an Attorney General and a Deputy Attorney General in on a smear like this. If they were not, they should be down here telling us they were not. The evidence is that they were. And they have been passing upon all the important questions.

These points were well taken. There *was* a conflict of interest here, and the testimony of Brownell and Rogers *was* essential to an understanding of the "whole picture." The problem, of course, was what to do next. The Republican members wanted a one-week suspension of the hearings "to develop a formula . . . to get the facts we want and the facts we need." The Democrats proposed a two-day recess "in a spirit of fairness." Anything more, they feared, would make it difficult, if not impossible, to get the hearings back on track.

This time, however, Chairman Mundt broke the tie in favor of his Republican colleagues. "We stand in recess," he said, "until 10 o'clock Monday morning." [12]

THE WEEK PASSED, the recess ended, and the impasse remained. President Eisenhower had refused to modify his directive despite the personal pleadings of Jenkins and Mundt. His logic was simple, his commitment complete: Congress had no right to compel testimony about counsel given inside the Executive branch. "If they want to make a test of this . . . I'll fight them tooth and nail," the President said. "It is a matter of principle with me and I will not permit it." [13]

The challenge did not materialize. There was grumbling from Congress but little support for a constitutional showdown with a popular and previously compliant Chief Executive. On Monday morning, May 24, the committee members listened wearily to the Pentagon's latest explanation, read aloud by Robert T. Stevens. "At no time," he said, "did the Army or I as its Secretary receive any orders from anyone in respect to the preparation or presentation of the Army's case . . . Actions taken by the Army prior or subsequent to the meeting of January 21 were independent actions, taken on the Army's own responsibility."[14]

The statement was technically correct. The Army had not been *ordered* to prepare the Chronology or to leak parts of it to the press. The Army had been *advised* by high-level officials who obviously wanted these things done. The difference was marginal, of course, but Stevens had nothing to fear. The presidential directive covered him like a suit of armor.

> SENATOR MCCARTHY: Do you think with some millions of American people listening to you, you want to, as the Secretary of the Army, say . . . that John Adams just had that meeting over there and then made all the decisions himself . . . ? Do you expect anyone with an ounce of brains to believe that?

> MR. STEVENS: Senator McCarthy, I have been over and over and over on this subject with you, and my contention is that Mr. Adams received certain suggestions, they were not orders, and I am sure that nobody that attended those meetings would say that they were orders, and he operated independently.[15]

McCarthy had lost the battle and he knew it. The recess had not been productive. The President had not backed down. He had successfully prevented his advisers from entering the committee room, where the tag-team tactics of Cohn, Jenkins, and McCarthy might well have turned the hearings into a rout. Reluctantly, the senators moved on to other witnesses and other events. A pivotal moment had passed.

CHAPTER THIRTY

The Eleven Memoranda

O<small>N THE MORNING OF</small> M<small>AY</small> 27 Roy Cohn was summoned to the witness stand. This was a milestone of sorts, for it marked the midpoint of the hearings. It had taken the Army almost twenty days to tell its story. It would take the other side a day or two less.

Roy Cohn had testified a month before. It had been a brief appearance about the cropped photo, and it had not gone well at all. Afterward his friends had urged him to get a lawyer, but Cohn had refused. He wanted to go it alone—to prepare his own case and to learn from his mistakes. "My own plan called for an objective appraisal of my initial appearance," he recalled. ". . . I made a long list . . . determined to work hard to change each debit into a credit."[1]

On the eve of his committee appearance Cohn had gone to McCarthy's home for a full-dress rehearsal. There to grill him were Frank Carr, Jim Juliana, Willard Edwards, and Joe McCarthy. The consensus that evening was that style, not substance, would determine the outcome, that what Cohn said was far less important than the manner in which he said it. As Edwards told the group: "Roy's greatest handicap is the general feeling that he's a cocky young bastard, and he should strive to remove that impression." Cohn looked at Edwards. "I *am* one," he shot back, "but I'll do the best I can." *

The change was truly remarkable. On May 27 a new Roy Cohn appeared on the stand—modest, respectful, patient, almost serene.

> MR. JENKINS: Mr. Cohn, you are quite alone there, sitting there yourself. You understand of course that you are entitled to counsel.
>
> MR. COHN: Yes, sir; I understand that.
>
> MR. JENKINS: You are not availing yourself of that privilege?
>
> MR. COHN: No, sir. I have served as counsel to the regular subcommittee and I hope I can give the facts here without the advice of counsel.[2]

Since this was the direct examination Ray Jenkins tried to put the witness at ease, to encourage him, and to bring out his story in a sympathetic way. "Mr. Cohn," he began, "tell us something of your background . . . and particularly your qualifications for the line of work in which you have been engaged since being with the McCarthy committee." This was a puffball, of course, and the new Cohn replied that he had successfully prosecuted some Communists and espionage agents, although the real credit belonged to the judges, the juries, the FBI, the other prosecutors—

> MR. JENKINS: We just want to know the facts. If you appear to be immodest, that is quite all right. . . . Go ahead and list the cases in which you have participated.

"The list of cases, Mr. Jenkins? Very well, sir." And out they poured, case after case, sir after sir. "The first of those cases, sir, was . . . the prosecution of the first-string leaders of the Communist Party. . . . After that, sir, I went into the prosecution of William W. Remington. After that, sir, I participated in the prosecution of the Rosenberg case. . . . After that, sir, I believe I presented . . . the evidence which resulted in the indictment of the second-string leaders—

> MR. JENKINS: Pardon the interruption, but one of the Senators whispers to me and suggests that I ask you the outcome of the Julius and Ethel Rosenberg case; and, for the benefit of those, especially

---

* Willard Edwards wrote a long memo about the evening in question. According to his account, Dave Schine arrived about 11:00 P.M., complaining that he was due back at Fort Myer in a few hours. He stopped Cohn in mid-sentence to ask someone—anyone—to call his colonel and get him an all-night pass. "Dave, for God's sake," Cohn exploded. "Do you realize that I'm going on trial before 20 million people tomorrow?" Schine looked confused. The irony of his request seemed to elude him entirely. He did not get his pass.

in the TV audience, who don't know, will you please state what the result was?

MR. COHN: Very final, sir. . . . They were executed as atom spies.*

A smile crossed Ray Jenkins's face. "I take it," he said, "you are not on the friendliest of terms with the Communist Party; is that right, Mr. Cohn?"

MR. COHN: I am not, sir.

MR. JENKINS: You have not been nominated as the editor of the *Daily Worker?*

MR. COHN: No, sir. I have been referred to in the *Daily Worker* very considerably, but I have not been nominated for any favorable offers.

Jenkins turned to the charges at hand—the charges that Cohn and McCarthy had lodged against the Army. One by one, he ran them down. Did Mr. Stevens and Mr. Adams attempt to discourage the investigation of spies, subversives, and security risks in the Army? "Yes, sir. Many times." Did they suggest that the Air Force and the Navy would make better targets than the Army? "Yes, sir, in so many words." Did Mr. Adams volunteer information about homosexuals in the Air Force?

MR. COHN: Yes, sir. . . . He said to me—You mark on this map the location of the Army place which you are going to investigate next, and I am going to mark down the location of an Air Force base where there are a large number of sex deviates which will make some good hearings for your committee.

MR. JENKINS: . . . Did you trade with him?

MR. COHN: No, sir.

What about David Schine? Did Adams refer to him as "the hostage?" Yes, sir, "he called him by that name . . . more frequently than he called him by the name of Schine." Did Adams threaten to ship the private overseas? Yes, sir.

MR. JENKINS: . . . if you persisted in investigating Fort Monmouth and in subpoenaing the members of the loyalty board, isn't that correct?

* The senator who whispered to Jenkins was McCarthy. He had already made it clear to Jenkins and to Cohn that he wanted these Red-hunting credentials to be highlighted, even at the expense of modesty. His theory, Willard Edwards recalled, was that "Roy would be telling the greatest spy story ever told in describing the preliminary history of his record as a criminal prosecutor in Communism cases. . . . It would all be familiar to us, he noted, but the TV audience would find it new and thrilling."

MR. COHN: I would say, sir, that is a sensible interpretation of what happened . . .

Finally, did John Adams threaten to release a phony report, the so-called Adams Chronology, in a last-ditch effort to end the Monmouth investigation? Yes, he did. "Mr. Adams said that I had to understand his position, that he had a job to do, that he would stop at nothing to see that the investigation was killed." Of course, Cohn added, "I told him that I could not understand . . . and that just about ended the conversation."

It was an exceptional performance, and when it ended that day Karl Mundt remarked that there had not been a single interruption, a single point of order. He smiled and said, "May that continue."

―――――――

THE NEXT DAY Ray Jenkins changed hats, and the cross-examination began. His voice was louder now, his manner sarcastic and gruff. Stacked beside him were the bound blue volumes covering four full weeks of testimony. He reached for one, pulled out a marker, and said, "Mr. Cohn, how many times did you call General Reber about a commission for your friend?"

MR. COHN: . . . three times, four times, something like that.

MR. JENKINS: He says that on occasions you called him two or three times a day.

MR. COHN: . . . I don't think the total number was more than four or five.

MR. JENKINS: It could have been more?

MR. COHN: It could have been more.[3]

This was the pattern. The counsel would fire his questions, and the witness would answer them, earnestly and politely, without uttering a firm yes or no. There were very few exceptions.

Did Mr. Cohn argue with John Adams about weekend passes for Schine? "No, sir. I did have a discussion." But Adams testified that obscene and vituperative language had been used. What about it? "Well, sir . . . I have talked to practically all of my friends about that, and the consensus of opinion is that if anything I use a good deal less of cuss words than most people do." Would you say, then, that John Adams testified falsely about this discussion? "Sir . . . I am loath to characterize what somebody else says as false."

Jenkins turned next to Cohn's relationship with Schine. "You have been," he said, "warm, personal friends, have you not?" Cohn resisted the trap. "He is one of my many good friends, yes sir." Jenkins tried again. "Mr. Cohn, you and this boy David Schine, as a matter of fact, now, were almost constant companions, as good, warm personal friends, weren't you?" Cohn resisted again. "I am pleased to say, sir, the truth is that . . . he is one of my many good friends. I have a lot of good friends, and I like them and respect them all."

Would the witness concede that his extraordinary efforts to get Schine the commission, the leaves, and the New York assignment were motivated to *some degree* by personal considerations?

> MR. COHN: Sir . . . what I did was done only with relation to committee work and without any regard to the fact that Dave Schine or anyone else on the staff might be a personal friend of mine.

Here Jenkins posed the obvious questions. What, exactly, did Schine do for the committee? What made him so valuable? Nervously, Cohn replied that Schine had been active in the Voice of America investigation and "related matters."

> MR. JENKINS: Of course, you had a file on Dave Schine's work with respect to the Voice of America, didn't you?

> MR. COHN: To a limited extent, sir.

> MR. JENKINS: Were your files on the other cases to a limited extent?

> MR. COHN: Very probably, sir.

Ray Jenkins slowly scratched his head. "Mr. Cohn, do you mean to tell us that Dave Schine in carrying on his work with respect to the Voice of America did not, after his conference or interview with each witness, make a memorandum for the file?"

> MR. COHN: No, sir. . . . that is why it became necessary on a number of occasions for us to communicate with him and get information or clarification or advice from him on certain occasions.

Well, then, where *did* Schine keep this information?

> MR. COHN: A good deal of it, sir, was information which he had in his mind.

In his mind? Hundreds of interviews in his mind?

> MR. JENKINS: Can you give the committee any explanation of why you conducted your investigations in that manner?

Yes, sir, Cohn replied. The committee had a very small staff. The people did a good job, a wonderful job, but there weren't enough stenographers to go around. "I am sure the blame is mine," he said, adding matter-of-factly that "Mr. Carr keeps the files as best he can, I think, according to an FBI technique, which I think is good. It is somewhat difficult to understand."

Although Jenkins did not press further that day, the questions he raised about Dave Schine's qualifications were too important and embarrassing simply to disappear. They would surface again and again in the coming weeks, with devastating consequences for the image of the new Roy Cohn.

ON JUNE 1 the action shifted from the hearing room to the Senate chamber, where Ralph E. Flanders delivered one of the meanest attacks on a fellow member in years. Likening McCarthy to Hitler and Dennis the Menace, among others, he accused him of setting party against party, religion against religion, neighbor against neighbor, and parent against child. "Were the junior Senator from Wisconsin in the pay of the Communists," he said, "he could not have done a better job for them."[4]

This was the tame part. The bulk of the speech dealt with "the mysterious personal relationship" of Roy Cohn and G. David Schine. "It is natural that Cohn should wish to retain the services of an able collaborator, but he seems to have an almost passionate anxiety to retain him. Why?" And what about McCarthy? "Does the assistant have some hold on him, too? Can it be that our Dennis, so effective in making trouble for his elders, has at last gotten into trouble himself? Does the committee plan to investigate the real issues at stake?"

Flanders had struck a nerve and he knew it. His mail increased dramatically. He received thousands of letters that week, some angry, some threatening, some filled with hate. An example:

> To Senator Flanders
> The Renegade Industrialist
> Who Votes like an ADA–CIO Puppet
> Flatheaded
> Lame-Brained
> Assassine
> Nincompoop
> Everlasting
> Retirement
> SOON!!!![5]

Most of the letters were favorable, however, and many applauded Flanders for raising an issue "that had to be raised." One letter reported "the common gossip among servicemen and others that Cohn is determined to keep Schine from going overseas . . . because they are homosexuals." Another letter, from the director of a girls' school in Vermont, said simply: "You are the first to put the spotlight on the sordid relationship behind this tragic scene, a relationship which must be evident to most people, but which, of course, can't be stated more specifically than you did . . ."[6]

Flanders did not raise the issue again, at least not in public. Privately, however, he maintained that Cohn and Schine were lovers, and that the hearings could be understood in no other terms. "It was an unsavory relationship," Flanders recalled. "I got evidence of that later in Europe. But that is all I'll say. . . . Am I liable for libel on that? Well, anybody with half an eye could see what was going on."[7]

━━━━━━

AT THE HEARINGS, meanwhile, Roy Cohn was in his fourth full day on the stand. At issue were the eleven memoranda that he, Carr, and McCarthy had "dictated" between October 2, 1953, and March 11, 1954 —the memoranda supporting their claim that the Army had used "blackmail" and "bribery" to halt the Monmouth investigation. Senator Potter wrote, "Of all the documents presented these were the most mysterious, the most important, the most unbelievable." They had been released to the press on March 12, 1954—the morning after the Adams Chronology had appeared. No one, save Cohn, Carr, and McCarthy, had been aware of their existence. They seemed to materialize out of thin air.[8]

Now, almost ten weeks later, these mysterious, important, unbelievable documents were finally read into the record.

MR. JENKINS: Where did you dictate them?

MR. COHN: In Senator McCarthy's office.

MR. JENKINS: To whom?

MR. COHN: Mary Driscoll.

MR. JENKINS: She is the senator's secretary?

MR. COHN: That is right.

MR. JENKINS: Mr. Cohn, would you consider it out of order if we asked you to step aside and called Mrs. Driscoll in and questioned her about these documents?

MR. COHN: It is not my judgment, sir. Whatever you say.

Mrs. Mary Driscoll, the sister of David Brinkley, the news commentator, had been McCarthy's personal secretary for almost six years. She was, by all accounts, a superb office manager—competent, intelligent, loyal to a fault. Her duties included everything from typing and filing to putting out the brush fires that Roy Cohn periodically ignited around the office. A few weeks earlier, for example, Cohn had circulated an oath of loyalty among the staffers, an oath to Roy Cohn and Joe McCarthy. Most of the staffers had signed it, although many were resentful. "These guys were a little scared of their jobs, you know, they had to make a living," recalled Ruth Watt, the subcommittee's chief clerk. "I had a husband to fall back on. . . . I said, 'This is not done on Capitol Hill, and I'm not signing anything.' " Watt took the letter to Mary Driscoll, who put it in her pocket. "And its not been seen since," Ruth Watt added. ". . . Mary destroyed the letter." *

On June 1, 1954—in front of eight senators, assorted staffers, a packed hearing room, and millions of television viewers—Mary Driscoll demonstrated her loyalty under fire, not on paper. She testified that the eleven memoranda were genuine items, typed by her on the dates they carried.

MR. JENKINS: Do you recall Mr. Cohn dictating any of these documents to you, Mrs. Driscoll?

MRS. DRISCOLL: I have no independent recollection of them, but I am sure that he dictated some of them to me. All of these that say from Mr. Cohn were obviously dictated by him. Otherwise I would not have put his name on the paper.[9]

Ray Jenkins was gentle but persistent. Did the witness recall the contents of the memoranda? "No, I couldn't. I take too much dictation." Did she keep her original shorthand notebooks? "No, I never keep shorthand notebooks." Did she place these memoranda in a single file before their release on March 12? "Yes. That is right." Did the file have any identification on it? "Yes. Investigations Committee."

MR. JENKINS: Well, it has nothing on it to indicate what the particular phase of investigation the committee was carrying out there?

MRS. DRISCOLL: That is right.

MR. JENKINS: How did you know where to go to look for that file, Mrs. Driscoll, when you were called upon to produce it?

MRS. DRISCOLL: I can't tell you that, Mr. Jenkins.

MR. JENKINS: How is that?

MRS. DRISCOLL: I can't tell you that. That is my way of filing. [Laughter]

* McCarthy knew nothing about the letter. He was out of town at the time. The letter was written by staffer Dan Buckley, the cousin of columnist William F. Buckley, and circulated by Buckley, Juliana, and Cohn. Their pitch to staffers: "It would mean a lot to Roy if you signed it." See *Ruth Watt Oral History*, pp. 121–24, Senate Historical Office, Washington, D.C.

Then Joe Welch took his turn. "Mr. Chairman," he said, "could I have the chair by the witness?" Roy Cohn objected, and with good reason. It was his chair that Welch wanted, the chair from which Cohn had been coaching Mrs. Driscoll and passing on the scribbled notes from Senator McCarthy.

SENATOR MUNDT: That would seem a bit unfair.

MR. WELCH: I thought it would be a convenience if I sat near her as I examined her. [Laughter]

Welch opened with a kindly confession: it was, he said, "somewhat awkward and difficult" for him "to cross-examine a lady." And for several minutes his questions were simple and routine—so simple, in fact, that Senator McCarthy turned away to read a press clipping that had been brought to the committee table. Suddenly, Joe interrupted. "Mr. Chairman, I have a question. . . . Senator Flanders this morning made a statement that the committee has not yet—I am reading from the press story —has not yet dug into the real heart of the mystery." Welch looked at Mundt, but the chairman did not try to intervene. "It is a vicious thing . . . a dishonest thing . . . dishonest beyond words. . . . I would like to ask the Chair to subpoena the Senator. . . . I would like to get it under oath. . . . That is the end of the question."

Mundt was relieved. "Mr. Welch, you have ten minutes," he said, and the Bostonian started again.

MR. WELCH: I think you have told us that you have more than one typewriter in your office. Is that right?

MRS. DRISCOLL: Yes.

The question was important, for Welch knew that the memoranda had been typed on at least three typewriters.

MR. WELCH: The one at your desk is an IBM, is that right?

MRS. DRISCOLL: There is an IBM at my desk now.

MR. WELCH: Was it there in October?

MRS. DRISCOLL: I don't recall. . . . A typewriter is a typewriter and I don't pay any attention to the type of typewriter.

Welch mocked the witness in his calm, weary way. "You are a paragon of virtue," he said. "My secretaries are always kicking about them and wanting a new one. You don't pay any attention to them."

MRS. DRISCOLL: No.

Welch pressed ahead, memo by memo, until he came to the final one, dated March 11, 1954. The key sentence said that Frank Carr, the memo's author, was "searching the files for the memoranda dictated concerning Schine." This was puzzling, for Mrs. Driscoll had testified that these memoranda were already together in a neat file marked "Investigations Committee."

MR. WELCH: Did you say to him, "Mr. Carr, look no further, I have got them all in the slickest little package you ever saw"?

MRS. DRISCOLL: Absolutely not.

MR. WELCH: Mrs. Driscoll, it is awfully simple. You had them all together, did you not?

MRS. DRISCOLL: Maybe I overlooked one.

MR. WELCH: . . . May I ask you this, Mrs. Driscoll: Did you ever find a single memorandum to add to this file after Frank Carr dictated that to you?

MRS. DRISCOLL: That question, Mr. Welch is—you are confusing me.

This was true, of course, and McCarthy cut in to prevent the confusion from spreading any further. He was appalled by the heckling, he said. It was one thing to heckle a man and quite another to heckle this "young lady." Welch replied that he had "nothing but admiration" for Mrs. Driscoll; it was the memoranda that disturbed him, "and I think I must now ask to have them . . . examined and expert opinion taken as to their authenticity."

The senator was furious. It had been a long, painful day, filled with attacks upon his underlings. He waved a finger at "this man Welch . . . this very, very clever little lawyer."* His voice spiraled up like a siren. "Let's have him take the stand. Let's have him take the oath. I want to cross-examine him." He paused—and called for lie detector tests all around. "I'll take the first one. . . . I have complete confidence in them. . . . We used them back in Wisconsin. . . . They are practically unbeatable."

When Joe had finished, the ever patient Mundt suggested that the committee forget about lie detectors and document experts and get on with the business at hand—the cross-examination of Roy Cohn. Welch agreed, reluctantly, because the Republican members were dead set against further delays. So the gavel fell, Mrs. Driscoll stepped down, and the authenticity of the eleven memoranda remained as elusive and mysterious as before.

---

* Welch was actually 6 feet, 3 inches, about four inches taller than McCarthy. And Mrs. Driscoll, the "young lady," was fiftyish and a grandmother.

―――

WERE THE MEMOS AUTHENTIC? The answer is no; they were not. They
were phonies, and Willard Edwards had witnessed their panicked production. Years later Edwards recalled that the release of the Adams
Chronology had put the McCarthy staff in a quandary. "The senator's
own lack of files was a handicap. His staff, relying on memory, had good
reason to suspect a distortion . . . of facts to support the Army's case. So
a decision was made to translate memories into typed memos, back-
dated. Carr, former FBI agent, advised on paper, etc. so that no check
could be made to question the authenticity of these exhibits."

Edwards added an interesting afterthought. He had always been puzzled, he said, by the certainty with which Joe Welch pursued the issue.
What made him so *sure* of his allegation? After the hearings ended,
Edwards ran into a prominent member of the Army's legal team at a
Washington party. "I asked him the question. A little under the weather,
he hesitated, then blurted out: 'We knew some of the McCarthy memos
were forgeries because they were responsive to memos that were forged
by the Army.'"

Surely, said Willard Edwards, "there are few parallels in congressional investigating history for a hearing in which one fake memo was
rebutted by a fake memo from the other side!"[10]

CHAPTER THIRTY-ONE

"So Reckless, So Cruel"

O F ALL THE INCIDENTS in the Army–McCarthy hearings, there is only one that people remember with any consistency. It took ten minutes, perhaps, but it revealed more about McCarthy and his style than anything that had been said or seen or written before. In these black minutes, the Wisconsin *State Journal* lamented, "McCarthy wrecked it all. He blew his angry head of steam and cast out an ugly, unsupportable, nonsensical smear on a young man who had absolutely no connection with the case. It was worse than reckless. It was worse than cruel. It was reprehensible." The young man was Frederick Fisher. His ordeal was painful—and generally misunderstood.[1]

It began on April 3, when Welch asked Fisher and James St. Clair to assist him with the Army's defense. Both men worked at Hale and Dorr, and both accepted the invitation at once. In Washington that evening they met Welch for dinner at the Carlton Hotel. Welch said to them, "Boys, we're in the kind of lawsuit that is different from anything you've known. Everything will go—even the lawyers will be on trial. If there is anything in any of your lives that might be embarrassing to you, it better come out now. . . . Jim, do you know of anything about yourself? How about you, Fred?"[2]

St. Clair did not see any problem, but Fisher did. In the 1940s, he said, he had belonged to the National Lawyers Guild, an organization that had been listed as "subversive" by the House Un-American Activities Committee. Furthermore, he had organized a Guild chapter with a man named Greenberg, who turned out to be an official of the Communist Party. Fisher insisted that he had never been a Communist himself. He said he had joined the Guild to meet other lawyers, many of whom were moderate and liberal in their politics, and some of whom were—like himself—members of the Republican Party. He had resigned from the Guild in 1950, he added, after learning about the link between the Boston chapter and the local Communist organization.

After dinner the three men returned to their suite at the hotel. They were joined by Struve Hensel and Fred Seaton, the Deputy Secretary of Defense. According to Fisher's recollection, "several bottles of whiskey were on hand, and we engaged in a discussion of the problem raised by my past associations. . . . Everyone agreed that the matter would certainly come out at the hearing. The only controversy was whether the damage to the Army's case would be more severe if I left than if I remained. . . . Jim, Joe and I believed that I should return to Boston as soon as possible, and both Jim and Joe asked to be relieved from trying the case."[3]

Hensel and Seaton both disagreed. They were uncertain about Fisher but adamant that Welch and St. Clair should remain on the case. Finally the men agreed to consult with James Hagerty and to abide by the decision he rendered. It was late, almost midnight, but another meeting was arranged at Hensel's Georgetown home. On the way over, Fisher recalled, "I remember Hensel saying that he had crawled on his knees to Senator McCarthy long enough and now he would stand up and walk. I believe Seaton said that never since the Civil War had the country been in greater danger, and that in the tradition of his Revolutionary ancestors he was ready to sacrifice all for his country's freedom."[4]

In Hagerty's presence, however, discretion got the better part of valor. Fred Fisher repeated his story about the Lawyers Guild. No problem, Hagerty replied. Fisher could count on a friend in the White House —"my boss, the President." Then Fisher brought up the Greenberg connection, and Hagerty let out a groan. That was "a different story," he said. That would "smear-up the Army's defense." Hagerty was sorry, he did not *want* to say this, but Fisher would have to return to Boston at once.[5]

On the way back to the hotel Welch joked that Fisher was lucky to be leaving, because no one could tell what might happen to those who remained. Then Welch winked and said, "What a case! A million dollars couldn't buy all the publicity."[6]

Still, Welch worried. He assumed that McCarthy would learn about the Fisher case and spring it at some future date. To prevent this, Welch broke *part* of the story himself. On April 16 the New York *Times* noted that Frederick Fisher, a second assistant counsel, had been relieved from duty "because of admitted previous membership in the National Lawyers Guild, referred to by Herbert Brownell, the attorney general, as 'the legal mouthpiece of the Communist Party.' " The article appeared on page 16. It seemed unimportant at the time.

In the following weeks, however, the senator would regularly approach Welch or St. Clair and threaten to tell "the Fisher story" on national TV. This was disturbing, for McCarthy did not say how much he knew about the case.* Assuming the worst—knowledge of the Greenberg connection—Joe Welch made three basic moves. He told Fisher to prepare for a full-scale attack on his past; he worked on a rebuttal of his own; and he let McCarthy know that the game of assassinating assistants could be played from both sides of the fence.

Welch had an ace in the hole—or so he thought. On June 4, a Friday, he showed the card and deftly pulled it back.

> MR. WELCH: Mr. Cohn, there have, I think, been some articles published about you and your draft status, of which you are probably aware, are you not?
>
> MR. COHN: Sir, I would say articles have been published about me on just about everything, yes, sir.

Welch did not pursue the matter that day. He said simply, "I hope before we go into that you will consult your file or bring it to the stand with you, so you can reel it off to us, what your whole story has been."

Cohn had reason for concern. His draft record looked suspicious indeed. He had turned eighteen during the final bloody months of World War II. Classified 1A, he had won a deferment when his congressman, a family friend, nominated him for the U.S. Military Academy at West Point. Then a roadblock appeared; the young man failed a physical test that included push-ups, sit-ups, and other such things. Still, Cohn persisted; he did not give up hope.† Reclassified 1A, he won renomination to West Point—and failed the same test again. By this time the war had ended and the nation had stopped drafting its young men.

The story did not end there. Cohn enlisted in the National Guard on June 22, 1948—two days before the *peacetime* draft became the law of

---

* McCarthy never did learn about the Greenberg connection. This is a bit surprising, for the FBI probably knew about it. According to FBI documents, the Bureau had placed a "confidential" informer (BOS-627) inside the Guild's Boston chapter.

† In his book Roy Cohn describes his nomination to West Point this way: "I had visited there many times with my parents and loved the place. I was, of course, overjoyed." But this comes on page 201, during his analysis of the Fred Fisher incident. There is no mention of West Point or a military career in the chapter on Cohn's formative years—or anywhere else in the book. As Cohn writes, again and again, "Law and politics fascinated me from the beginning. . . . At the age of eight I would sit entranced in the courtroom. . . . Already I had politics on the brain." See Roy Cohn, *McCarthy*, 1968, pp. 19–24, 201.

the land. This meant another deferment, because members of the Guard were not subject to the draft. While Cohn had done nothing illegal, he had managed to miss service in World War II and Korea. Rightly or wrongly, the image of the draft-dodger was certain to emerge.[7]

There is but one published account of what happened next—Roy Cohn's account.

> On June 7, two days before the Fisher blowup, the session adjourned at 5:40. . . . On the way out I fell into step with Mr. Welch.
>
> "There's a little matter I'd like to talk to you about sometime," Welch said. "I think you're the sort of person to whom I can talk off the record about it."
>
> "Coincidentally," I replied, "there is something I would like to talk to you about privately."
>
> "Well, then," he said, "let us make that sometime now."
>
> Down the hall, Welch spotted . . . an empty committee room. We entered and shut the door.[8]

In the discussion that followed, Welch promised to drop the draft-dodging issue and Cohn agreed to keep Fred Fisher out of the hearing. The two men shook hands. "That evening," Cohn recalled, "I went to Senator McCarthy's home and gave him a full account of my conversation with Welch and the agreement into which I had entered. *McCarthy approved the trade.*"[9]

This, of course, is Roy Cohn's version of the story—a story published after the death of Joseph Welch, who had planned to write a book about the hearings but never did. Welch left no written account of this incident; however, the unpublished notes of Fred Fisher do refer, indirectly, to the kind of agreement that Roy Cohn described. The notes read: "Toward the end of the hearings . . . the senator broke in and took the one weapon from his arsenal that all had agreed he should not use. He charged that Joe Welch had brought to Washington . . . a Communist lawyer."[10]

It happened the afternoon of June 9, 1954, while Roy Cohn was on the stand. Joe Welch was firing his questions, and tempers were rising on both sides.

> MR. WELCH: Mr. Cohn, if I told you now that we had a bad situation at Monmouth, you would want to cure it by sundown, if you could, wouldn't you?
>
> MR. COHN: I am sure I couldn't, sir.
>
> MR. WELCH: . . . Answer me. That must be right. It has to be right.
>
> MR. COHN: What I would like to do and what can be done are two different things.

MR. WELCH: Well, if you could be God and do anything you wished, you would cure it by sundown, wouldn't you?

MR. COHN: Yes, sir. . . .

MR. WELCH: And on September 7, when you first met Secretary Stevens, you had in your bosom this alarming situation about Monmouth, is that right?

MR. COHN: . . . Yes, sir.

MR. WELCH: And you didn't tug at his lapel and say, "Mr. Secretary, I know something about Monmouth that won't let me sleep nights"? You didn't, did you?[11]

Cohn couldn't remember. Probably not, he replied. "I know that on the 16th I did." This was hardly an earthshaking admission, but Welch —like Cohn himself—had a way of squeezing these things to death. "Mr. Cohn," he said, "tell me once more: Every time you learn of a Communist or a spy anywhere, is it your policy to get rid of them as fast as possible?"

MR. COHN: Surely, we want them out as fast as possible, sir.

MR. WELCH: And whenever you learn of them from now on, Mr. Cohn, I beg of you, will you tell somebody about them quick?

Now McCarthy broke in. "Mr. Chairman, in view of that question—"

SENATOR MUNDT: Have you a point of order?

SENATOR MCCARTHY: Not exactly, Mr. Chairman, but in view of Mr. Welch's request that the information be given once we know of anyone who might be performing any work for the Communist Party, I think we should tell him that he has in his law firm a young man named Fisher whom he recommended, incidentally, to do work on this committee, who has been for a number of years a member of an organization which was named, oh, years and years ago, as the legal bulwark of the Communist Party . . .

I am not asking you at this time to explain why you tried to foist him on this committee. Whether you knew he was a member of that Communist organization or not, I don't know. I assume you did not, Mr. Welch, because I get the impression that, while you are quite an actor, you play for a laugh, I don't think you have any conception of the danger of the Communist Party. I don't think you yourself would ever knowingly aid the Communist cause. I think you are unknowingly aiding it when you try to burlesque this hearing in which we are attempting to bring out the facts, however.

For once, Karl Mundt seemed genuinely upset. He looked at Cohn, who said nothing, and then at McCarthy.

SENATOR MUNDT: The Chair should say that he has no recognition or no memory of Mr. Welch's recommending either Mr. Fisher or anybody else as counsel for this committee. . . .

MR. WELCH: Mr. Chairman, under these circumstances I must have something approaching a personal privilege.

SENATOR MUNDT: You may have it, sir. It will not be taken out of your time.

Welch had prepared his remarks in advance, hoping he would not have to use them. He started to speak but McCarthy turned away.

MR. WELCH: . . . Senator, sometimes you say, "May I have your attention?"

SENATOR MCCARTHY: I am listening to you. I can listen with one ear.

MR. WELCH: This time I want you to listen with both.

SENATOR MCCARTHY: Yes.

MR. WELCH: Senator McCarthy, I think until this moment—

But McCarthy was not listening at all. He was talking to Jim Juliana, loudly instructing him to "get the news story on Fisher" for the record. It was rude, almost maddening, and Welch seemed close to tears. "You won't need anything in the record when I finish telling you this," he said. "Until this moment, Senator, I think I never really gauged your cruelty or your recklessness."

McCarthy was quiet now. He sat there, shuffling his papers, as Welch reviewed the events of April 3, when St. Clair and Fisher flew into town. Welch spoke of his warning at the dinner table: "Boys . . . if there is anything funny in the life of either one of you that would hurt anybody in this case you speak up quick." He said that Fisher had mentioned his membership in the Lawyers Guild, and that he (Welch) had replied: "Fred, I just don't think I am going to ask you to work on this case. If I do, one of these days that will come out and go over national television and it will hurt like the dickens." Welch did not mention the Greenberg connection or the meetings with Seaton, Hensel, and Hagerty. He said:

So, Senator, I asked him to go back to Boston. Little did I dream you could be so reckless and so cruel as to do an injury to that lad. It is true he is still with Hale and Dorr. It is true that he will continue to be with Hale and Dorr. It is, I regret to say, equally true that he shall always bear a scar needlessly inflicted by you. If it were in my power to forgive you for your reckless cruelty, I would do so. I like to think I am a gentleman, but your forgiveness will have to come from someone other than me.

This should have ended the matter. Welch had said his piece. He had wounded McCarthy, though not seriously, and he tried to move on. But the senator wouldn't let him. His mood darkened. He was furious—determined to get even now, to square accounts with the man who taunted and ridiculed his boys. "Mr. Welch talks about *this* being reckless and cruel," he exploded. What hypocrisy! "He's been baiting Mr. Cohn for hours. . . . I just give the man's record, and I want to say, Mr. Welch, that it has been labeled long before he became a member, as early as 1944—"

The sentence went unfinished. Welch interrupted, more in desperation than in anger. He seemed to be pleading with McCarthy.

MR. WELCH: Senator, may we not drop this? We know he belonged to the Lawyers Guild, and Mr. Cohn nods his head at me. I did you, I think, no personal injury, Mr. Cohn.

MR. COHN: No, sir.

MR. WELCH: I meant to do you no personal injury, and if I did, I beg your pardon.

Welch turned to McCarthy. "Let us not assassinate this lad further, Senator. You have done enough. Have you no sense of decency, sir, at long last? Have you left no sense of decency?"

McCarthy paused for a moment. "I know Mr. Cohn would rather not have me go into this," he replied. And he was absolutely correct. Roy Cohn could see what was happening. He sat there, eyes lowered, slowly shaking his head. He even scribbled a note to McCarthy: ". . . Please respect our agreement . . . because this is not going to do any good." But the senator was beyond this sort of persuasion. "I would like to finish this," he said, and off he went, blasting Welch, Fisher, and the Lawyers Guild. He stopped, briefly, but Karl Mundt set him off again.

SENATOR MUNDT: The Chair would like to repeat that he does not believe Mr. Welch recommended Mr. Fisher as counsel for this committee . . .

SENATOR MCCARTHY: Let me ask Mr. Welch. You brought him down, did you not, to act as your assistant?

MR. WELCH: Mr. McCarthy, I will not discuss this further with you. You have sat within six feet of me, and could have asked me about Fred Fisher. You have brought it out. If there is a God in heaven, it will do neither you nor your cause any good. I will not discuss it

further. I will not ask Mr. Cohn any more questions. You, Mr.
Chairman, may, if you will, call the next witness.

There was a second or two of silence, then a thunderous burst of
applause. Karl Mundt, who began each session with a stern warning
against "audible manifestations of approval or disapproval," made no
attempt to intervene. He waited for quiet, declared a recess, and quickly
left the room. Welch followed him out, looking weary and grim. "I never
saw such cruelty," he said. "I am close to tears." Then McCarthy appeared, looking grimmer still. He knew he had come off poorly, but he
did not seem to understand why. "What did I do?" he kept asking the
people around him. "What did I do?

THE REVIEWS WERE POURING IN NOW, and not many were kind to Mc-
Carthy. It wasn't the Fisher incident or any single mistake; it was rather
the cumulative impression of his day-to-day performance—his windy
speeches, his endless interruptions, his frightening outbursts, his crude
personal attacks. In Wisconsin newspapers long sympathetic to Mc-
Carthy were describing his behavior as "brutal" and "inexcusable." In
Washington Republican leaders were cutting his speaking engagements
and his role in the 1954 campaign. In New York his old friend Frederick
Woltman was preparing a "McCarthy Balance Sheet" for the Scripps–
Howard Chain. His opening sentence: "Senator Joseph R. McCarthy has
become a major liability to the cause of anti-Communism." [12]

Most Americans seemed to agree. According to the Gallup Poll,
McCarthy's "favorable" rating had dropped sharply since the beginning
of 1954.

	% Favorable	% Unfavorable	No Opinion
January 1954	50	29	21
March 1954	46	36	18
April 1954	38	46	16
May 1954	35	49	16
June 1954	34	45	21

SOURCE: Washington *Post*, November 12, 1954.

Furthermore, Gallup's unpublished findings showed that television
watching had a powerful effect upon the uncommitted, that McCarthy's
performance had lost him two people for every one he gained. But Gallup himself believed that no amount of television exposure could shake
the faith of the people who were still supporting the senator. After the
Fisher incident he wrote a friend: "My own guess is that McCarthy has
probably reached the bottom of his decline. The people who have not

been won to date probably cannot be won by any known tactics. Even if it were known that McCarthy had killed five innocent children, they would probably still go along with him." [13]

Gallup was right. The senator *had* reached bottom in terms of popularity. His favorable rating would remain around 30 percent for the rest of the year. But this was a dangerous number, especially for a politician who depended so heavily on the *appearance* of mass support. That had always been McCarthy's weapon—"Nobody Loves Joe but the People." That weapon was gone now, and gone for good.

———

ON JUNE 10 Senator McCarthy took the stand. His friends and staffers were petrified; some of them feared a complete physical collapse. In recent weeks McCarthy had been hit by excruciating headaches. He was eating poorly and suffering from insomnia. Observers found him "drinking before breakfast" and "drinking day and night." Senator Potter wondered about the effects of Joe's "liquid luncheons" at the Carroll Arms Hotel. Said Potter: "He always seems to make his worst mistakes in the afternoon."

The direct examination went smoothly, although the first, familiar questions from Ray Jenkins seemed to grate on the nerves.

MR. JENKINS: Your position on Communism, I take it, is well known. . . .

SENATOR MCCARTHY: I think so.

MR. JENKINS: You are not one of their fair-haired boys?

SENATOR MCCARTHY: You are right.

MR. JENKINS: You never have been tendered the nomination of the Communist Party for the presidency—is that what you mean?

SENATOR MCCARTHY: Not yet. [14]

There were groans from the audience as Jenkins asked McCarthy to describe "the set-up" of the American Communist Party. With that, the senator rose from his chair and approached a brightly colored map of the United States. Holding a large wooden pointer, he explained that the orders flowed "from Moscow . . . to the politburo . . . to the various districts . . . to the 25,000 members"—most of whom McCarthy seemed to mention by name. There was "Ben Carruthers, the Negro organizer, Eleanor Sachter, the steel organizer . . . Tom Fitzpatrick, the electrical organizer . . . Andrew Onda, Sid Taylor, Mike Russo, Leo Fisher, Tony Salopek, Sam Reed. . . . Am I taking too much time on this, Mr. Jenkins?"

Well, perhaps, Ray Jenkins replied, but how dangerous were these

Communists, anyway? "Dangerous?" said McCarthy. "They know exactly where to throw a log chain or a steel cable to cut off the electric power of any city in case of war with Russia. . . . They teach goon squads how to throw hand grenades, how in effect to commit murder. . . . This is no game at all."

Ray Jenkins agreed. The situation was no doubt alarming, and "I would like you to tell . . . what each individual American—man, woman, child—can do to . . . liquidate the Communist Party in this country."

The witness smiled a modest smile. The request was "rather unexpected," but he did have a few suggestions for the American people. First, they should support the Red-hunters in Washington, the patriots who "man the watchtowers of this nation." Second, they should guard against the Red hand in education, especially higher education, where a whole network of Communist professors was hiding behind the façade of academic freedom. This was a ticklish matter, McCarthy admitted, for the universities were also filled with "crackpots" and "screwballs" who posed no real threat to the nation's security. The people had to "be careful not to go off half-cocked . . . because they don't like what some teacher is teaching."

Ray Jenkins was impressed. Wouldn't it be wonderful, he mused, to teach America's children about "the dangers of Communism, say, around the hearthstone of the home, when their minds are young and pliable and impressionable?"

SENATOR McCARTHY: The gentleman has said that well.

MR. JENKINS: And carry it on to the school to which the first-grader goes . . . on to the upper classes and the colleges and universities of this nation.

SENATOR McCARTHY: I agree with you.

MR. JENKINS: And in civic organizations, the Rotaries, the Optimists, the Kiwanis, and then the churches, and through all the levels of life. . . .

SENATOR McCARTHY: You are very right, sir.

As the cross-examination began, a commotion developed in the back of the room. There, by the door, was Ralph Flanders, waving an envelope over his head. An aisle was cleared, and the cameras followed him to the long, gleaming table, where he confronted McCarthy and quickly turned away.

SENATOR McCARTHY: Will the chair ask Mr. Flanders to remain?

SENATOR MUNDT: Senator Flanders, Senator McCarthy is trying to get your attention.

SENATOR MCCARTHY: Mr. Flanders, you have just handed me a letter and I read it. . . . You say: "This is to inform you that I plan to make another speech concerning your activities. . . . If you so desire, I would be glad to have you present."[15]

Joe tossed the letter on the table. No, he replied, he would not come to listen to the speech. He had no interest in such drivel. However, if Flanders had something to say, something important, he could do "what I am doing now—take the oath, raise your right hand, let us cross-examine you. . . . I would be glad to step aside and have you testify."

At this even Karl Mundt protested. "The *committee* has control of these proceedings," he said. "We have to ask Senator Flanders to retire to the rear of the room. . . . I am sorry, we can't permit this kind of feuding to go on here." As Flanders walked away, Joe declared that he had "no feud" with his elderly colleague. On the contrary, he purred, "I have thought it was not the result of viciousness but perhaps senility that he is making these unfounded charges."

Flanders did not mind the insult. He had gotten what he wanted: televised publicity for his next move against McCarthy. And that afternoon, with the galleries well filled, he introduced Senate Resolution 231: "That Senator McCarthy be separated from the chairmanship of the Senate Committee on Government Operations and . . . any subcommittee thereof." When word reached the hearing room, McCarthy appeared to take it all in stride. He shrugged and said of Flanders, "I think they should get a net and take him to a good, quiet place."[16]

At the moment Joe had other problems on his mind. The Democrats, in cross-examination, were pressing him hard. To this point the damage had been done by Symington and McClellan; now "Scoop" Jackson took the lead, apparently convinced that some last-minute posturing would be politically useful—and perfectly safe. With Robert Kennedy feeding him questions from behind, the senator interrogated McCarthy about the qualifications of his unpaid assistant, G. David Schine.

SENATOR JACKSON: I think you have testified, Senator, that Mr. Schine had spent considerable time . . . dealing with the problems of psychological warfare.

SENATOR MCCARTHY: That is correct. It has been more or less his hobby. . . . He submitted a plan to the State Department. Roy says we have a copy of it here in case you would like to see it.[17]

Kennedy had read the Schine Plan. McCarthy had not. The plan said: "The broad battlefield is the globe and the contest is for men's souls. We can fill their bellies, as we must, but man does not live by bread alone. We require of the free peoples of the world, their hearts, their consciences, their voices, and their votes. How to do this?" Schine provided the answers in three single-spaced pages.[18]

The questions *were* amusing, and each one brought a burst of laughter from the hearing room crowd.

SENATOR JACKSON: Look under "Community Leaders." This is around the world. He has the Elks and the Knights of Columbus. Do we have an Elks Lodge in Pakistan? I belong to the Elks.

SENATOR MCCARTHY: Mr. Jackson, you apparently think this is amusing.

SENATOR JACKSON: Let's turn to "Periodicals." He has "Universal Appeal—pictures, cartoons, humor, pin-ups."

SENATOR MCCARTHY: . . . Mr. Jackson, pictures and cartoons can have an important place in any information program.

SENATOR JACKSON: I am directing the question to pin-ups.

SENATOR MCCARTHY: As to pin-ups, I don't know . . .

SENATOR JACKSON: We can all laugh on that one, I think, Senator.

McCarthy mumbled a few words in Schine's defense. It was late, almost 4:30, and Karl Mundt had the gavel in his hand.

MR. COHN: Mr. Chairman . . . Mr. Chairman . . . I would like . . . to ask some questions which might develop true facts about some of the things which Mr. Jackson said here this afternoon.

Mundt could see that Cohn was ready to explode. He did not want an incident—not after the Fisher fiasco and not at 4:30 on a Friday afternoon. He tried to pacify Cohn by placing his friend's document in a more favorable light: "I am sure the press will deal with it fairly. . . . I read it over. It has some worthwhile suggestions, Mr. Cohn, I agree to that."

The gavel fell. Cohn headed for Kennedy at the committee table. Their exchange went something like this:

COHN: Tell Jackson that we're going to get him on Monday. We've got letters he wrote to the White House on behalf of two known Communists.

KENNEDY: Tell him yourself. Don't threaten me. You've got a _____ nerve threatening me.

COHN: Do you want to fight right here?

Bystanders stepped between the men and no punches were thrown. "Since touch football and mountain climbing are not my long suits," Cohn recalled, "I was probably the gainer in the stopping of the fight." [19]

Roy Cohn did not "get" anyone the following Monday. He even

denied making the threat. But this was small comfort to Scoop Jackson, who spent a panicked weekend in search of two letters he could not remember writing. In his own way Cohn had evened the score. He had made the senator squirm.[20]

━━━━━━

THE HEARINGS DRAGGED ON. Frank Carr followed McCarthy to the witness stand and spent the next three days supporting the memos that his associates had concocted. There were moments of trouble and the usual notes and whispers from McCarthy and Cohn. But Carr did not arouse the passion—or even the interest—of his interrogators. Mr. Jenkens left the questioning to his assistant, Thomas Prewitt, and Mr. Welch bowed out in favor of Jim St. Clair.

There was one incident, however, and it spoke volumes about the downward direction of McCarthy's career. On the afternoon of June 14 Carr was asked about his clerical duties as director of the subcommittee staff. The questions came from Senator Symington, who was clearly spoiling for a fight.

> SENATOR SYMINGTON: Do you know what clearance each of your staff members have, that is each investigator, each stenographer, file clerk, and so forth?

Carr wasn't certain. He thought he did, but he couldn't vouch for them all.

> SENATOR SYMINGTON: It would be unfortunate if we had a subversive on our staff and he hadn't had clearance . . . and he got information which made it possible for him to betray the country.
>
> MR. CARR: It would be unfortunate and most unusual.
>
> SENATOR SYMINGTON: Klaus Fuchs was unusual, wasn't he?
>
> MR. CARR: He certainly was.*

McCarthy interrupted. His boys were again under attack. He demanded a "point of personal privilege"—and promptly accused Mc-Clellan (not Symington) of smearing the young patriots on his staff.

---

* Klaus Fuchs, a British scientist, had been jailed a few years earlier for passing atomic secrets to the Russians. Although the comparison with Fuchs was preposterous, Symington had just learned from sources inside the Administration that two of McCarthy's favorite subcommittee staffers, Don Surine and Thomas La Venia, had been denied clearance by the Department of Defense. The reasons were never made public, but Surine had been dismissed by the FBI in 1950 for allegedly having relations with a prostitute involved in a white slavery investigation (p. 117), and La Venia had once belonged to the American Law Students Association, the same group that McCarthy himself described as subversive in his earlier assault upon Philip Jessup (p. 212). A few days later McCarthy quietly transferred both men to his personal staff.

SENATOR McCLELLAN: Get your names straight!

SENATOR SYMINGTON: Mr. Chairman, may I proceed?

At this moment a bell rang summoning the members to a vote on the Senate floor. Symington got up to leave, but McCarthy challenged him to "name" the subversive or apologize to the staff. Angrily, Symington grabbed a microphone and said, "I think the files of what you call *my* staff, *my* director, *my* chief of staff, have been the sloppiest and most dangerously handled files that I have ever heard of since I have been in government."

The audience applauded and the room began to clear. Above the din McCarthy's voice could be heard: "You can run away if you like, Stu. You can run away if you like." The voice droned on: "You shouldn't *do* that, Mr. Symington. That is just *dishonest*. That is the same thing the Communist Party has been doing too long."

Joe remained in his chair as the members filed past him, smiling and shaking their heads. The stenographer rose to follow them out; McCarthy sputtered in protest. "Mr. Chairman. . . . Mr. Reporter, will you take this down, Mr. Reporter. . . . Mr. Symington. . . . He runs away. He won't answer the question. . . . That is the most dishonest, the most unfounded smear . . . I have ever seen."

The room was almost deserted. McCarthy stood up and packed his briefcase. His face was covered with sweat. "I guess," he said, "we must go vote now."[21]

———

ON JUNE 17, 1954—after 72 sessions, 35 witnesses, 42 exhibits, and 2,972 pages of testimony—the hearings were recessed *sine die*. One by one the members and the counsels made their final speeches and bade the cameras goodbye. Cheerfully denying reality, Senator Mundt described the process as Americanism in action, televised proof that freedom and self-government were alive and well in Washington. Senator Dirksen gushed his approval. The hearings had reached millions, he declared. They had rekindled the nation's interest in the crusade against Communism. For that he thanked God and the committee members; then he turned to Welch: "To my friend Mr. Boston, whose impish charm and wit always disarmed me somehow or other, may I say we have ploughed the long, hard furrow."[22]

Senator McClellan had a different view. Solemn and unsmiling, as always, he offered no congratulations, only a warning about the damage that these "deplorable events" had done to the dignity and prestige of the United States Senate. His words were devastating: "I would hate for the people of this nation to think that this is a fair sample of the proceedings . . . in the highest lawmaking body in the world. . . . I think this will be recognized and long remembered as one of the most disgraceful episodes in the history of our government."

Finally one player was left, the most gifted player of all. He rang down the curtain with the kind of folksy eloquence that had become his trademark. "I alone," he said, "I alone came into this room from deep obscurity. I alone will retire to obscurity. As it folds about me, softly as I hope it does quickly, the lady who listened and is called Judith Linden Welch will hear from me a long sigh of relief. I am sorry that this play had to take place in the fretful lightning and the ominous roll of noises from Indochina and around the world. It saddens me to think that my life has been lived so largely either in wars or turmoil. . . . I allow myself to hope that soon there will come a day when there will, in this lovely land of ours, be more simple laughter."[23]

———

BEFORE WELCH RETURNED TO BOSTON, Hagerty took him to meet the President in the Oval Office. There were handshakes all around and a rare compliment from Eisenhower on a job well done. Welch replied that, if nothing else, the hearings had kept McCarthy on television for thirty-six days, long enough for the people to observe him up close. The President agreed, of course. That had been his strategy all along.[24]

CHAPTER THIRTY-TWO

Censure

O<small>N JULY</small> 2, 1954, the President received a five-page, single-spaced letter from E. E. "Swede" Hazlett, a retired naval officer and a longtime friend. After praising Eisenhower, as he always did, Hazlett reviewed the Army–McCarthy hearings with a mixture of anger and dismay. "They were pretty nauseating," he began. "I suppose they had to be held, but they reflected no credit on the nation, the party, the Senate, or the Administration." Turning next to the participants, he added:

> How people of the calibre of McCarthy, Cohn, Dirksen, and Mundt work themselves into positions of responsibility in the most enlightened republic in the world I'll never know. . . . As for Mr. Stevens . . . I can't believe that your fine Army will continue to have confidence in him, a wishy-washy leader, and I hope he has the grace to resign as soon as the bad taste is out of our mouths.[1]

Hazlett was not alone, of course. His feelings were echoed in press reports, in public opinion polls, and by party leaders across the board. The Buffalo *Evening News* saw "no clearcut winners—only losers." The Kansas City *Star* claimed that "everyone involved in the hassle got hurt —most of all the country." The Louisville *Courier-Journal* said: "In this long, degrading travesty of the democratic process there have been no heroes. Senator McCarthy has shown himself to be evil and unmatched in malice. Secretary Stevens stands as a man of weak principle and little pride."[2]

There was truth in all of this. The hearings *were* degrading. There were no clear-cut winners, and almost everyone got hurt. If one spoke of heroes only Welch seemed to qualify (although many observers, including Dwight Eisenhower, agreed that McClellan had handled himself well.) Before long every one of the principals except McCarthy had resigned under fire. Roy Cohn joined a law firm in Manhattan; John Adams joined one in Washington, D.C. Frank Carr took a job with a trucking company in New England. And Robert Stevens returned to the family business, citing "compelling personal reasons."[3]

Cohn left in the summer of 1954. His departure followed an angry subcommittee meeting in which Senator Potter joined the Democratic members to demand an immediate shake-up of the staff. In the end that shake-up included Cohn, Carr, and the hapless Don Surine. As expected, Cohn did not leave quietly. "It has been a bitter lesson," he said, "to come to Washington and see a reputation, gained at some effort, torn to shreds because I was associated with Senator McCarthy, who has become a symbol of hatred for all who fear the exposure of Communism."[4]

A few weeks later the friends of Roy Cohn threw a banquet in his honor at New York's Astor Hotel. The guest list read like a Who's Who of the American Right: Westbrook Pegler, Alfred Kohlberg, Joe and Jean McCarthy, Fulton Lewis, Jr., William F. Buckley, and Rabbi Benjamin Schultz. There were delegations from the Catholic War Veterans, the Minute Women of America, and the "anti-Peress faction of the Parent Teachers' Association, PS 49." One speaker described Cohn as "the American Dreyfus." Others blamed his "ordeal" on Communists, New Dealers, Senator Lehman, Edward R. Murrow, and Eisenhower–Dewey Republicans. At the end toastmaster George Sokolsky praised the child-rearing habits of Judge and Mrs. Albert Cohn in remarkably ironic terms. "Your son," said Sokolsky, "represents something in American life that we did not know existed."[5]

Despite rumors to the contrary, Joe did not want Cohn to leave. He had come to rely on him for almost everything—contacts, information, ideas, scheduling, briefings, and political advice. Life after Cohn would not be easy, as the first hearing without him demonstrated all too well. One witness turned out to be the wrong man because nobody bothered to check his middle name. And Frank Carr's questioning proved so inept that McCarthy stormed out in disgust. Drew Pearson put it well: "Quiz Shows Joe's Need for Roy."[6]

━━━━━━

IN THE SENATE, meanwhile, Ralph Flanders was working to "separate" McCarthy from his committee chairmanships. His resolution (S. 231) was opposed by the Republican leadership; by Southern Democrats who worshiped the seniority principle; and by those who were running for reelection in 1954. Still, Flanders was not exactly alone. He could count on the support of longtime McCarthy opponents like Fulbright, Lehman, and Hennings. He knew from past experience that the media looked favorably upon those who challenged the Wisconsin senator. And, in a move that angered many Republicans, he decided to approach the liberal community for the help that he needed. Before long, groups like the National Committee for an Effective Congress (NCEC) were supplying him with money, research, publicity, and political advice.

The advice was rather simple: S. 231 had no chance of passage. Flanders had made a mistake by attempting to strip McCarthy of his chairmanships. The punishment was unprecedented. It would frighten away the Senate traditionalists. A better way of handling McCarthy would be to call for his censure. There *was* precedent in this approach, and it would not disturb the seniority system so dear to Southern hearts. Censure was a moral judgment—nothing more.

Flanders went along. In July he withdrew his resolution and substituted a new one (S. 301) in its place.

Resolved, that the conduct of the junior senator from Wisconsin is unbecoming a member of the United States Senate, is contrary to senatorial traditions, and tends to bring the Senate into disrepute, and such conduct is hereby condemned.[7]

The new resolution had at least a fighting chance. By late July the NCEC's head count showed thirty-one senators in favor, twenty opposed, and forty-five undecided. The last group included John Kennedy ("noncommittal"), Leverett Saltonstall ("on the fence"), and Stuart Symington ("all over the lot"). Saltonstall was running for reelection in 1954. He told Flanders: "If you call for a vote it will defeat me, for I'll have to support your resolution."[8]

On the Democratic side, the most important voice belonged to McClellan of Arkansas. Many saw him as the key to the undecided vote. McClellan had impeccable conservative credentials. He was well liked, politically astute, and apparently unafraid of McCarthy, who never dared to attack him in public. "John didn't lead many parades," a colleague recalled, "but when he joined them you knew they were safe." On July 18 William Fulbright arranged a meeting between McClellan and Flanders at a Washington hotel. The meeting went smoothly. McClellan expressed "interest" in the censure resolution, and Flanders agreed to postpone further action until after the Arkansas senatorial primary on July 27. Although McClellan had not committed himself, he did tell a friend: "I'm fond of Joe McCarthy, but he's getting out of hand, and we have to do something to control him."[9]

Flanders introduced his resolution on Friday evening, July 30. Ninety senators were present, and the galleries were jammed. "This matter is indeed a serious one," Flanders began. "The senator [McCarthy] has an habitual contempt for people. . . . Unrebuked, his behavior casts a blot upon the reputation of the Senate itself. It also makes plain the impossibility of controlling exhibitions of innate character by any change in the rules. The senator can break rules faster than we can make them."[10]

The opposition was formidable. Questions were raised about the lack of orderly procedure, the absence of formal charges, and the need for a special committee.* Senator Capehart warned that a vote for censure would be tantamount to political suicide. "We cannot condemn the one man who the American people think is trying to do something about Communism. . . . They are not going to stand for that." And Senator Dirksen, sounding just like McCarthy, lashed out at the Communists and liberals who had "climbed into bed" with the senator from Vermont:

> No conservative will be safe in this body . . . because all they need, if they disagree with you, is to get one man like Senator Flanders—honorable as he is—to put the brand upon you with a censure resolution. . . . Oh, the innuendo and sinister effect of it. God save the mark! I wish to say that I am distressed about this.[11]

After three days of debate the Senate accepted a "compromise" which referred S. 301 to a select six-man committee chosen by the Vice President. The tally was 75–12, with Flanders and Fulbright voting "nay" and McCarthy voting "present." Fulbright was clearly discouraged. He sensed that the moment had passed, that "Joe could buffalo any committee on earth." And McCarthy seemed to agree. "I am very happy," he said of the outcome. "This is good."[12]

━━━━━━━

THERE IS NO OFFICIAL DEFINITION of censure in the rules of the Senate. It carries no formal penalty. A censured member does not lose the right to vote or to sit on committees. His seniority is unaffected. Yet aside from outright expulsion, censure is the harshest punishment the Senate

---

* Flanders did provide a "bill of particulars" that night, but his charges were extremely vague. One of them, as noted above, was Joe's "habitual contempt for people." Senator Welker jumped to his feet. "I happen to know," he said, "that Senator McCarthy does not have contempt for people. He loves my child and my wife. . . . I will not allow that statement to go unchallenged."

In order to oblige these critics and to avoid the possibility of committee hearings, which some viewed as a "shelving maneuver," the NCEC provided Flanders with a list of thirty-three specific charges, which he introduced the following day. Fulbright submitted six more charges, and Wayne Morse added seven, for a grand total of forty-six. Although the introduction of these charges did not prevent the Senate from forming a select committee on censure, the committee members would rely heavily upon them in their later deliberations.

can levy. It carries the stigma of misconduct so serious as to bring the entire body into disrepute.

The symbolic power of censure is based largely upon its infrequent use. Before McCarthy there were but five cases in the history of the Senate. In 1810 Timothy Pickering of Massachusetts, an extremely unpopular member, was censured for releasing secret treaty information to the public. In 1844 Benjamin Tappan of Ohio was censured for the same offense, but Tappan apologized and the slate was wiped clean. In 1852 a special committee recommended the censure of Henry S. Foote of Mississippi after he pulled out a pistol and aimed it at the head of an approaching member. (The Senate, badly split between North and South, took no action against him.) In 1902 a special committee recommended the censure of South Carolina's two senators, John McLaurin and "Pitchfork Ben" Tillman, following their spirited fistfight on the Senate floor. (The recommendation was supported.) Finally, in 1929, the Senate censured Hiram Bingham of Connecticut for placing a lobbyist on his staff to assist in the writing of a tariff bill. Such behavior, the members agreed, was "contrary to the good morals and ethics of the Senate." *

There was a common theme in these cases. All of them, except Pickering's, involved a special committee; all of the committees recommended censure; and three of the four recommendations were accepted by the Senate. Put simply, the formation of a censure committee implied a strong presumption of guilt.

On August 5 Vice President Nixon released the names of the committee members to the press: Arthur Watkins (Republican, Utah), Frank Carlson (Republican, Kansas), Francis Case (Republican, South Dakota), Ed Johnson (Democrat, Colorado), John Stennis (Democrat, Mississippi), and Sam Ervin (Democrat, North Carolina). They had been hand-picked by William Knowland, the majority leader, and Lyndon Johnson, the minority leader, in a series of private meetings. There were no liberals in the group, no presidential contenders, no darlings of the press. Three of the members—Watkins, Stennis, and Ervin—were former judges, and all were from regions of the country where the McCarthy issue was not especially intense.[13]

The committee had other strengths as well. All of the members, except Case, belonged to the Senate's "Inner Club." They played by the rules and commanded respect inside the institution. This was important, for McCarthy's *real* crime was his utter indifference to the folkways of

---

* In its final report, the censure committee noted, incorrectly, that only three members (McLaurin, Tillman, and Bingham) had been censured previously by the Senate. This mistake was repeated by the press and by those who have written about McCarthy. For the best overview of the censure process, see Richard Hupman, *Senate Election, Expulsion and Censure Cases from 1793 to 1972*, Senate Document No. 92-7, Washington, D.C., 1972.

the Senate. He had transgressed the rules, written and unwritten, with an air of gleeful defiance. He was, in Bill Jenner's words, "the kid who came to the party and pee'd in the lemonade."[14]

The committee members were given a free hand in formulating their rules and procedures. They were determined to run an orderly hearing, and that meant keeping McCarthy in line. As Chairman Watkins explained, "We . . . were very much aware of what had happened at the recent Army–McCarthy hearings. . . . They revealed an almost total lack of orderly procedure. The shouting and name-calling were beyond belief. Senator McCarthy, it seemed to me, was the principal actor."[15]

The ground rules reflected these concerns. To prevent a media circus, the members barred television cameras from the hearing room. To head off an ugly confrontation, they decided to hear only firsthand testimony (thereby eliminating Flanders and Fulbright as witnesses). To limit the process of cross-examination, they agreed that Senator McCarthy and his counsel could not pursue the same line of inquiry. If one of them questioned a witness or raised an objection, the other would forfeit his right to be heard. The object, of course, was to take the cross-examination out of McCarthy's hands. The members *wanted* him to be represented by counsel. They even offered to pay for one out of committee funds.

The most difficult decisions concerned the charges themselves. Historically the Senate had distrusted its power to punish misdeeds committed during a previous Congress. It had only voted censure and expulsion for *specific current offenses*, such as breach of confidence, disorderly behavior, and assault. In McCarthy's case, however, the specific current offense seemed less important than the pattern of misconduct over the years. As Flanders wrote Watkins: "No one of the single actions with which Senator McCarthy is charged is as dangerous by itself as it is arrayed against the total sequence of his behavior."[16]

The committee members agreed. They assumed that the Senate *could* punish prior misconduct, and they followed a sequential approach by grouping the most serious charges into five general categories. They were: contempt of the Senate or a senatorial committee; encouragement of federal employees to break the law; receipt of classified documents from executive files; abuse of Senate colleagues; and abuse of General Zwicker.

Meanwhile, McCarthy got himself a lawyer—Edward Bennett Williams of Washington, D.C. This was a significant step, for it implied a deep concern about the charges and a belief that vindication was possible, that the verdict could go either way. Williams and McCarthy were personal friends. Williams had represented him in the past and would have done so at the Army hearings had not McCarthy insisted on cross-examining witnesses by himself. This time the senator agreed to let Williams run the defense. He promised to behave himself—no insults, no speeches, no interruptions. It didn't work out that way.*

———

THE HEARINGS BEGAN ON AUGUST 31. They were held in the Senate Caucus Room, though they hardly resembled the spectacle of a few months before. The cameras, the klieg lights, and the noisy crowds were gone. Smoking was forbidden by Arthur Watkins, the Mormon elder, and the seating arrangements told a story of their own. For one thing, the members sat at random, ignoring party lines. For another, McCarthy sat away from them, looking just like a defendant on trial.

The first session set the pattern to follow. McCarthy read a moderate opening statement written by L. Brent Bozell, a young Yale man who had just co-authored a favorable book on Joe's crusade with his brother-in-law, William F. Buckley, Jr.

> . . . I have carried on my part in the fight as best I know how. . . . It has been said that I am the cause of disunity in the country and in my party. There is disunity, and perhaps my activities have been part of the cause. . . . But it is now urged that I be censured. I would be untruthful if I agreed that my accusers were not affected by ulterior political considerations.[17]

There followed the reading of the charges, a long and boring formality made longer and more boring by the snail-like pace of committee counsel E. Wallace Chadwick, an elderly trial lawyer from Pennsylvania. Chadwick quoted every insult, every slur. He read the Zwicker transcript word by word. After several hours of this, Edward Bennett Williams suggested that perhaps the committee could save time by placing the exhibits into the record en masse. But the members rejected the idea. They were judging McCarthy, after all, and they wanted a public reading of his sins. Furthermore, they were genuinely uninterested in playing to the audience or the press. ("Let's get off the front pages and back among the obituaries," Watkins declared. "That will suit us just fine.") So the counsel droned on till his voice broke, and an assistant was called in to finish the chore.

Williams got nowhere that day. His opening argument, that a senator could not be punished for acts committed in a previous Congress, was curtly brushed aside. (Watkins advised him to submit a brief on precedents—if he could find them.) A bit later Williams questioned the impartiality of Ed Johnson, the ranking Democratic member. He produced a

---

* Williams worked on the censure case without compensation. He thought that the publicity would be compensation enough, but he may have been wrong. In 1956 the racketeer Frank Costello was looking for a lawyer to represent him at a deportation hearing. Someone suggested Williams. "Not that guy," snapped Costello. "Wasn't he the lawyer for McCarthy?" Costello eventually retained Williams, but only after every major trial lawyer in New York City had turned him down.

newspaper clipping which quoted Johnson as saying, "There isn't a Democrat in the Senate who doesn't loathe McCarthy." This was serious business, and Johnson asked to reply.

SENATOR JOHNSON: I have full faith in my ability to weigh the charges which have been made against Senator McCarthy, together with whatever evidence may be presented, without prejudice.

Williams persisted, to no avail. The members closed ranks.

SENATOR CASE: It occurs to me that this discussion is immaterial to the purposes of the inquiry.

THE CHAIRMAN: Senator Carlson.

SENATOR CARLSON: I confirm Senator Case's remarks, so far as this particular record is concerned.

McCarthy had been squirming for hours, trying his best to keep things inside. He interrupted, politely, but Watkins cut him off.

THE CHAIRMAN: Just a moment, Senator. Let us get this clear: . . . when your counsel speaks on a matter, that precludes you from addressing the Chair of the committee on the same matter.

This was too much for McCarthy. He grabbed the microphone from Williams.

SENATOR MCCARTHY: I should be entitled to know whether or not—

THE CHAIRMAN: The senator is out of order.

SENATOR MCCARTHY: Can't I get Mr. Johnson to tell me—

THE CHAIRMAN: The senator is out of order.

SENATOR MCCARTHY: —whether it is true or false.

Bang went the gavel. *"The senator is out of order. We will not be interrupted by these diversions. . . . The committee will be in recess."* With that, Joe pushed Williams aside and headed for the lobby, where the cameras and klieg lights were carefully in place. He seemed more astonished than angry at what had transpired. "This," he muttered to reporters, "is the most unheard-of thing I ever heard of."[18]

———

ON SEPTEMBER 15 the committee withdrew to write its final report. The process went quickly. There were no surprises, no holdouts, no angry debates. The members recommended censure on two counts and dismissed the other three. The report—40,000 words long—was completed in a week.

The most troublesome counts were those involving the receipt and use of classified information. For example: Were federal workers to be discouraged from supplying congressional committees with evidence about waste, corruption, and wrongdoing in their departments? Was McCarthy wrong in aggressively seeking this information? Was he wrong in charging that the Executive branch had too much power in determining what Congress should and should not receive in the area of government operations?

The members had to be careful. They were dealing with the right of Congress to investigate, to be fully informed. They did not want to set a precedent which might limit their own access to vital information. And they knew that other senators—Jenner, Mundt, and McCarran—were "guilty" of similar offenses, although no one but McCarthy had appealed for documents on national TV.

The result was predictable. The members fuzzed up the issues. They claimed that McCarthy's public statements were ambiguous—or "susceptible of alternative constructions." Put simply, they could not decide whether he had invited federal workers to send him routine information about wrongdoing or whether he had encouraged them to ransack the confidential files. The final report said:

> The committee, preferring to give Senator McCarthy the benefit of whatever doubts and uncertainties may have confused the issues in the past . . . does not feel justified in proposing his acts . . . as grounds for censure.[19]

The third count, abuse of senatorial colleagues, was based solely on McCarthy's remark about Flanders: "I think they should get a man with a net and take him to a good quiet place." * This one had no chance of passing. The Upper Chamber had never censured a member for name-calling or *verbal* abuse. Alben Barkley's famous rule—"If you think a colleague is stupid, address him as the able and distinguished senator; if you know he is stupid, address him as the *very* able and distinguished senator"—had been ignored by Barkley's closest friends, including Tom Connally of Texas, the quintessential Senate insider. Connally took great pride in tormenting his colleagues. He once described Burton Wheeler as a coward—and fired a book at his head. He called William Langer a "nut" and Homer Ferguson a "wretched man" covered with "the vomit of his spleen." Connally, said one Senate observer, "was—simply Connally; and who did not cherish the old man?"[20]

---

* McCarthy's "abuse" of Senator Hendrickson and members of the Gillette Committee was considered under the final count, contempt of a Senatorial committee. It is interesting that Flanders himself believed that McCarthy's remark was "so absurd as to be harmless." See Ralph Flanders to Arthur Watkins, September 10, 1954, *Arthur Watkins Papers,* Brigham Young University.

While few senators cherished Joe McCarthy, even fewer could ignore the Senate's long tradition of tolerance in this area. Furthermore, the issue was clouded by the provocative behavior of Senator Flanders, who had compared McCarthy to Hitler and raised the question of his "mysterious" sexual behavior. The report concluded:

> The remarks of Senator McCarthy were highly improper. The committee finds, however, that they were induced by Senator Flanders' conduct . . . and do not constitute a basis for censure.[21]

The members recommended censure on the final two counts: abuse of General Zwicker and contempt of a Senatorial committee. In the first instance, they confronted an issue that the Senate had carefully chosen to ignore: McCarthy's conduct as a committee chairman. The Zwicker case was "ideal" because it involved a witness with impeccable credentials. The members described him in glowing terms. They agreed that he had not been "intentionally evasive, irritating, and arrogant" on the stand. In short, there had been no provocation. McCarthy had acted "as critic and judge upon preconceived and prejudicial notions." His conduct warranted "censure by the Senate."[22]

The final count, contempt of the Gillette Committee, was the strongest by far. It involved McCarthy's failure to appear before that committee and his attacks upon the individual members. The most difficult issue— the fact that Joe had been asked to testify but never subpoenaed—was turned against him with telling effect.

> It is our opinion that when the personal honor and official conduct of a Senator of the United States are in question before a duly constituted committee of the Senate, the Senator involved owes a duty to himself, his State, and to the Senate, to appear promptly and cooperate fully. . . . This must be the rule if the dignity, honor, authority, and powers of the Senate are to be respected and maintained.[23]

The words jumped from the page: *duty, honor, dignity*. The report went on: "When persons in high places fail to set and meet high standards, the people lose faith. If our people lose faith, our form of government cannot long endure."

That left the other issue: the attacks upon individual committee members. There had been many of them, but the worst by far had been McCarthy's description of Senator Hendrickson: "a living miracle in that he is without question the only man in the world who has lived so long with neither brains nor guts." This attack went beyond simple namecalling. It impugned the "motives" of a Senate committee; it "obstructed" the legislative process; it had to be condemned.[24]

As a document on Joe McCarthy, the report left an awful lot unsaid. There was hardly a word about his anti-Communist crusade. J. Edgar

Hoover was mentioned once; Cohn and Schine were not mentioned at all. At the end of the report, in very fine print, were the charges the committee had chosen to discard. They included the payment from Lustron, the intimidation of reporters, the attacks on "citizens of good reputation," and the war wounds "which he did not, in fact, suffer." Put simply, the members hadn't judged McCarthy for offenses committed away from the Senate. They *had* judged him for transgressing the rules and the spirit of the club to which he belonged.

THE REPORT CAME OUT IN LATE SEPTEMBER, only six weeks before the election of 1954. This meant a sure delay in the censure process, for neither party relished a showdown at this point. The Democrats already had two powerful campaign issues: falling farm prices and rising unemployment. They expected to gain ground. And their Republican opponents, badly split on McCarthy, were fearful that a stand on censure *either way* would cost them dearly at the ballot box. As Senator Saltonstall remembered: "The issue was poison. One day I'd campaign in Pittsfield and the factory workers would plead with me to support McCarthy. The next day I'd drive down to Smith College and the audience would boo every mention of his name. I knew that I was going to vote against Joe, but I didn't dare say so in public. I told everybody that I would have to hear the debate before I made up my mind. A lot of others said that, too. And they weren't even from Massachusetts!"[25]

Unlike 1950 and 1952, Senator McCarthy took no part in the election campaign. His office explained that he had turned down hundreds of speaking engagements in order to spend more time on his committee chores. In fact, almost no one wanted his support. He had become a liability to his party and an embarrassment to all but his closest friends. On September 25 he entered the Bethesda Naval Hospital for treatment of the headaches that were now a regular—and excruciating—part of his life. "He was very quiet and very depressed," a newsman recalled. "He looked like he was about to collapse."[26]

The Republican strategy was directed by Richard Nixon and the White House staff. Essentially it called for a strong dose of McCarthyism without McCarthy. As the Vice President noted in a memorandum to Len Hall:

> Our handling of the McCarthy issue has gained us no new support. . . . We have lost considerably among Democrats whose reason for voting for us in '46, '50, and '52 was their distrust of the Truman administration on the handling of the domestic Communist issue. . . . We can remedy the situation . . . by ignoring McCarthy, emphasizing vigorously the Administration's anti-Communist record, and attacking the other side for its past and present softness on the issue.[27]

Nixon spearheaded the campaign by visiting ninety-five cities in thirty states. "We're kicking the Communists and fellow travelers and security risks out of government . . . by the thousands," he boasted. On the state level, Republican candidates questioned the loyalty of Estes Kefauver (Tennessee), Paul Douglas (Illinois), James E. Murray (Montana), and Joseph O'Mahoney (Wyoming), among others. (The most ingenious campaign flyer listed Murray as "Foreign Agent 783"—his registration number as the representative of Cuban sugar interests.) On election day the Democrats won control of both the House and the Senate, although their margin of victory was smaller than expected. Nevertheless, the *liberal* Democratic incumbents did rather well, while a host of Republican Red-hunters went down to defeat. In the words of one historian: "The meaning of the election was not entirely clear—the lessons of few elections are—but 1954 did seem to signal the end of the political dynamic which had supported McCarthy and the Communist issue."[28]

───────────

ON NOVEMBER 8 the Senate opened debate on the Watkins Report. There was an inevitability to the process that everyone understood. McCarthy would be censured. The vote would not be close. The debate would be very, very rough.

McCarthy showed up with his lawyer and his wife, looking better than he had for weeks. His stay in Bethesda had been a success. He was sober, well-rested, and realistic about his chances. "I can go fifteen rounds," he told reporters. "I'll be there at the end."

Watkins led off with a dry recitation of the findings. McCarthy responded with an angry statement, written by himself, which began, "I will be censured." The reason? As America's "symbol of resistance to Communist subversion," he had been targeted by the Reds and their dupes for political extinction. Even worse, these dupes included Ralph Flanders, "who was taken out of mothballs to advance his censure motion," and the members of the Watkins committee.

> I would have the American people recognize, and contemplate in dread, the fact that the Communist Party—a relatively small group of deadly conspirators—has now extended its tentacles to the most respected of American bodies, the United States Senate; that it has made a committee of the Senate its unwitting handmaiden.[29]

These were suicidal words, guaranteed to turn the uncommitted against him. But McCarthy didn't care. He knew that he had a *chance* of avoiding censure if he stood up and said: "I'm sorry. I've made some mistakes. I'll try to behave in the future." But these words were not in his vocabulary. He never apologized. He didn't believe he was wrong.

And he couldn't "behave" without consigning himself to the worst fate of all—a life of relative obscurity.

At first the debate was limited to the committee members, on the one side, and McCarthy's partisans, on the other. John Stennis declared that he could not approve "such slush and slime as a proper standard of senatorial conduct." Bill Jenner roared that McCarthy was right: "the strategy of censure was initiated by the Communist conspiracy." Then Arthur Watkins rose and spoke for an hour and a half. This alone was news, for Watkins had an ulcer condition which made standing and talking a very painful experience. At once, word passed to the cloakroom —the old man was on his feet and speaking like one possessed. He recalled how time after time McCarthy had turned honest debates into ugly gutter brawls; how he had impugned the integrity of the Senate and its duly constituted committees. At the end his voice broke as he said: "I am asking my colleagues in the Senate: 'What are you going to do about it?' " [30]

Watkins departed to thunderous applause. He found a couch in the cloakroom and literally collapsed. Wallace Bennett, the junior Republican from Utah, rushed in to console him. Bennett had been previously uncommitted on the censure issue. "Arthur," he said, "I want you to give me the privilege of moving to amend the censure resolution to include McCarthy's treatment of you." Watkins nodded in approval. "I would appreciate your doing it," he replied, "for I have decided that someone must do it . . . even if I have to do it myself." [31]

━━━━━━

BEHIND THE SCENES the Senate heavyweights were busy mapping strategy and counting heads. The Democrats, led by Lyndon Johnson, were quietly confident of their strength. Their main worry—the emergence of an outright champion for McCarthy within their ranks—had been eliminated by the death of Pat McCarran in October. At best, they figured that McCarthy could count on the support of one or two Southern conservatives and the neutrality of several Northern Catholics. As one insider noted: "Mike Mansfield is worried about the Catholic angle. He is glad that he and at least two other Catholics in the Senate will vote for censure. But he is very conscious of those nuns scattered throughout the gallery." [32]

The Democrats pursued a strategy of silence. They feared that their intervention would lengthen the debate, add a dangerous partisan element, and encourage some Democrats to stray beyond the findings of the Watkins Report. The pressure from LBJ was intense. He prowled the Senate floor, barking orders, twisting arms, and keeping the "hotheads" in line. "He is literally demanding that we refrain from rocking the boat," wrote an aide to Senator Lehman. "I hate to see the entire issue decided on as narrow a base as the Watkins Report establishes, but I am pretty well convinced that the size of the vote is more important than the arguments that are made."[33]

The supporters of McCarthy had their own strategy, designed to save the senator from himself. Mapped by Dirksen and Bridges, it went something like this: The dozen or so McCarthyites would reach out to an equal number of uncommitted Republicans. Senior members would work on junior members—Mundt on Francis Case, Bridges on Norris Cotton, and the like. With twenty-five votes in his pocket, Bridges could go to the rest of the Republicans and say, "Look, the party is split. Only the Democrats can win. We've got to work something out." If he could pick up ten more votes, he could then go to Lyndon Johnson and say, "You don't want this to become a party issue, do you? Let's compromise."[34]

What Dirksen and Bridges had in mind was the formation of a committee to draft a code of Senate behavior. Anyone who violated this code *in the future* would be punished. Furthermore, McCarthy would apologize to Hendrickson, and to Watkins as well.

Suddenly, on November 17, Joe dropped out of sight. Word reached the Senate that he had reentered the Bethesda Naval Hospital for treatment of an "elbow injury" he received while shaking hands with an overzealous admirer. The injury was diagnosed as "acute bursitis," and his doctor recommended "rest" and "physiotherapy" for a week and maybe more. Naturally, his supporters demanded an immediate recess. Everett Dirksen leaped to his feet: "This is a time for compassion. There is fever. There is pain."

And suspicion, too. Wayne Morse reminded his colleagues of the time he had been kicked by a horse. "I returned with my jaw wired, and I still made nine speeches." The Senate roared. Herbert Lehman said that he had campaigned successfully against Governor Dewey with a broken leg. And "Wild Bill" Langer called for a debate on whether to send "forget-me-nots, chrysanthemums, or roses." In the end, however, the members voted to adjourn for ten days, pending McCarthy's "recovery." They were not about to deny a colleague the right to defend himself in person.[35]

McCarthy was stalling, of course, but for reasons of his own.* He did not really care about a compromise; he was looking beyond the Senate to the public at large. His people were mobilizing. They were writing letters, holding rallies, planning big petition drives. He did not expect this activity to change many Senate votes, but that wasn't the point. He had begun to think in terms of a third party movement with Joe Mc-

---

* The senator did, in fact, suffer an elbow injury, though it hardly required ten days of hospitalization. Drew Pearson, who kept a "tail" on McCarthy, reported that Joe had slipped out of the hospital on several occasions to have dinner with friends.

Carthy as the presidential nominee. He wanted his enemies to see this groundswell, and he needed to see it himself.

━━━━━━━━

THE FAITHFUL RESPONDED, the people who had never doubted or faltered or drifted away. Rabbi Benjamin Schultz, director of the American Jewish League Against Communism, organized a rally for Joe at Washington's Constitution Hall. The crowd, about 3,000 strong, included a trainload of New Yorkers who came with "nets" to snare Ralph Flanders and with placards that read: "Why Did Hiss Want Trial in Vermont?" and "Moscow Hates McCarthy, Too!" On November 17—the day Joe entered the hospital—a group of superpatriots announced plans to gather 10 million signatures on petitions opposing censure. The group included a retired admiral, two retired generals, a handful of Hearst executives, and the president of the American Coalition of Patriotic Societies. Their message was simple: hidden forces inside the government were determined to destroy the man who had exposed their attempts to "Sovietize" America and the world. As Admiral John Crommelin told a rally of 13,000 McCarthyites at New York's Madison Square Garden: "We believe that the power of Congress to investigate the Executive is the first line of our internal defense against the HIDDEN FORCE. . . . Senator McCarthy is its prime target *not* because of his alleged contempt of the Senate. The HIDDEN FORCE must liquidate him for a much more practical reason. He is the *one* man left who —singlehanded—has been able to rouse the people of the United States to the menace of the HIDDEN FORCE in their government." *

Crommelin's message appeared again and again in the pro-McCarthy mail that poured into Congress. The common theme was the overwhelming belief in conspiracy and foul play. The letters frequently accused the Communists or the Zionists or the British of directing the censure movement. They claimed that a vote for censure was an *endorsement* of that conspiracy. And they demanded McCarthy's vindication in the name of God and the American people.

The percentage of hate mail and crank mail was higher than anyone on Capitol Hill could remember. According to Herbert Mack, the Senate

---

* The press devoted very little space to the petition drive. Interested students should check the *John F. Neylan Papers*, Bancroft Library, University of California. Neylan, a Hearst executive, was the West Coast director. On December 1, 1954, Admiral Crommelin delivered the petitions to Capitol Hill in an armored truck. After a short ceremony they were returned to New York City, where the counting began. The process was amusing, for Crommelin and his friends could have claimed any number they wanted. The petitions were not notarized, and the one making the rounds of the New York *Daily News*, a pro-McCarthy paper, had "Dr. Sam Sheppard" and "Irving Peress" opposed to censure. On the day the Senate voted, Crommelin modestly claimed a million signatures, with uncounted others "pouring in."

Postmaster, the names and addresses on the envelopes were so frequently distorted—"To the Anti-Christ from Utah" or "Dear Commie Senator from Vermont"—that he often felt he could not deliver them, although he knew full well for whom they were intended. Senator Watkins found the contents "disturbing" and "peculiar." So did Senator Fulbright, who read some of his letters into the *Record.*

> Red Skunk. You are not fit to clean Senator McCarthy's shoes. Hope you are struck by God.

> You English Louse. Go back to England with your British wife.

> I am an ex-marine who fought in the South Pacific, to open the gates of this Nation for the commie Jews that Hitler did not kill? You are one of the phony pinko punks connected with Lehman, Morse, Flanders and Bennett.[36]

One researcher analyzed all of Senator Flanders's constituent mail during 1954. He observed that the "educational quality" of the pro-Flanders and pro-McCarthy letters was fairly even at the beginning. As the year wore on, however, there was "an appreciable decline in the quality of the pro-McCarthy letters." Many of them were scribbled in pencil. The language was more abusive, more religious, more conspiratorial in tone. ("You have the Lord Against You." "I vomit at the mere sight of you." "I put horns and a tail on you and you look like Satan.") McCarthy still had his supporters, the researcher concluded. But his *range of support* had narrowed considerably. By November only the true believers remained.[37]

———

At BETHESDA, meanwhile, the "recovery" went well. Joe spent his time conferring with aides, chatting with Jeannie, and thanking supporters on the telephone. He also met with Barry Goldwater and Edward Bennett Williams, who used a back entrance to avoid reporters camped in the lobby. Williams handed McCarthy two letters of apology he had written for his signature—one to Senator Hendrickson, the other to Senator Watkins. The letters were mild; they conceded neither malice nor substantive error on McCarthy's part. Williams said that if Joe signed the letters (and particularly the one to Hendrickson) he had a chance of avoiding censure. If he didn't, he had no chance at all. At this, Goldwater recalled, McCarthy "threw the pen across the room, started swearing at both of us, and pounded the table." He yelled that he'd never apologize. He had done nothing wrong. His real friends understood this; they approved of what he had done, and they would stand by his side. "The commotion brought the floor nurse," Goldwater went on. "She called the doctor, who, in turn, called the admiral in charge of the hospital.

The admiral demanded to know what the hell we were doing . . . and threatened to have us arrested by the Shore Patrol."[38]

Another visitor followed—Everett McKinley Dirksen, who had been with Joe from the beginning. Dirksen brought his own letter of apology for McCarthy to sign. It read:

> Dear Bob (Hendrickson):
> You and I have always been friends. . . . I trust we shall always be friends.
> . . . I feel that in many particulars, the action of the Gillette Committee was wrong and required vigorous criticism. . . . But with reference to the statement I made about you to the press at that time, I freely concede that it was not a gentlemanly remark. I know, of course, that there is a certain dignity about the Senate and Senatorial conduct which is referred to as the tradition of the Senate. . . .
> In light of this, the remark which I did make should have been left unuttered no matter how deeply I felt about the whole matter . . . and therefore I tender you my regretful apology.[39]

Dirksen had brought a bottle of whisky with him. The two men drank and talked about the need for this apology in particular. Hendrickson had not provoked McCarthy. He had not compared him to Hitler or Dennis the Menace. He was a decent man who was leaving the Senate, and perhaps this apology would do some good. After much cajoling, Dirksen thought he had persuaded McCarthy to sign. But Joe replied: "No, I don't crawl. I learned to fight in an alley. That's all I know."[40]

———

WOULD AN APOLOGY HAVE BLUNTED the censure drive? The answer is by no means clear. Arthur Watkins said that he would have accepted "bona fide evidence of regret and repentance." But Watkins never defined what he meant by "bona fide evidence." Barry Goldwater claimed that the Southern Democrats would have welcomed an apology. But Goldwater's information came from Price Daniel of Texas, who wielded little influence in the Senate. Styles Bridges told reporters that the Republican moderates were enthusiastic about his compromise. But Bridges wrote a friend after the vote: "Certain Republicans were so fanatical in their determination to 'get their man' that no compromise was possible."[41]

Still, there were many senators who would have welcomed an apology, a compromise, or any maneuver designed to head off a final vote. Francis Case of South Dakota was a good example. As a member of the select committee, he came within an eyelash of repudiating his stand after home state Republicans threatened to run a McCarthy supporter against him in the next primary election. Other examples were Frank Carlson of Kansas, who feared that a vote for censure would alienate the forces least likely to forgive and forget; and Norris Cotton of New Hampshire, who received daily pep talks from Styles Bridges, publisher William Loeb, and Governor Hugh Gregg, all rabid McCarthyites.[42]

But the best examples by far were Wiley of Wisconsin and Kennedy of Massachusetts. Wiley, a moderate, was extremely unpopular with Tom Coleman and the state Republican leaders. He had offended them, as chairman of the Foreign Relations Committee, by supporting Chip Bohlen and opposing the Bricker Amendment. If he voted for censure, he would widen this dangerous rift; if he voted against it, he would lose much of his independent support. As a result Wiley avoided the censure debate, explaining that his "heavy duties in connection with the St. Lawrence Seaway" left him no time. In a letter to his constituents he said, simply: "I do NOT believe that any man should be penalized for his vigor in combating Communism; the cause of anti-Communism merits every patriot's continued support."[43]

Wiley was not known for his courage. After placing a phone call to John Foster Dulles, he was conveniently selected to represent the Administration at an economic conference in Brazil. (According to the summary of their monitored conversation, Wiley "wanted to go to Rio [because] it would be a nice way to get out of the McCarthy business.") Wiley left town without even pairing his vote. He solved his dilemma by simply running away.[44]

Kennedy's problems were rather well known. His father was a strong McCarthy supporter. His brother Bob was still fond of Joe, still willing to blame the mess on Cohn and Schine. And Massachusetts was . . . Massachusetts; the feelings hadn't changed. Senator Kennedy's political problem, an aide recalled, was one that faced all senators on different issues at different times. Lyndon Johnson didn't condemn the oil depletion allowance. William Fulbright didn't crusade against racial segregation. And John Kennedy didn't speak out against McCarthy.*

In fact, Kennedy had opposed Joe on a number of issues, including the Bohlen confirmation and the appointment of FCC Commissioner Robert E. Lee. It is possible, too, that Kennedy would have supported

---

* On one level Kennedy seemed to accept McCarthy for what he was, a family friend and a popular man in Massachusetts. But remarks about McCarthy made him edgy and defensive, as if his own family were on trial. Robert Amory, a friend, described the following incident at the 100th anniversary of a Harvard club in 1954: One of the guests "was talking about the spirit of Harvard and said he was glad that Harvard had never produced an Alger Hiss, although the law school had, . . . and doubly glad that neither had the college . . . produced a Joe McCarthy." Kennedy exploded. "He yelled, 'How dare you couple the name of a great American patriot with that of a traitor.' And a hushed silence fell upon the room and then all sorts of people tried to calm things down. But Kennedy was visibly mad and very short. He didn't right then walk out of the dinner but he left right at the end of dessert rather than waiting for the speeches."

Amory added that the story was known to some of the political writers in 1960, "but I, of course, never confirmed it. I thought it was a private matter. Now that he's dead, I say it for history." See *Robert Amory Oral Interview*, John F. Kennedy Presidential Library, Boston, Massachusetts.

censure if it had come to a vote on the evening of July 30, 1954. Kennedy had written a speech on the subject—which he pocketed, with obvious relief, when the Senate referred the matter to a select six-man committee. The speech went back to the files, forgotten but never destroyed. It recommended censure on the narrowest possible grounds: McCarthy's failure to control the "improper conduct" of his committee counsel, Roy Marcus Cohn.

In the fall of 1954 Kennedy underwent two serious spinal operations to repair a wound he had suffered during World War II. Heavily sedated, in constant pain, he spent eight weeks at a New York Hospital and four more at the family compound in Palm Beach. No one expected him to return to Washington for the debate or the vote on censure. In fact, he didn't have to. He could have paired his vote or recorded it with the Secretary of the Senate. But Kennedy did neither. His top aide, Theodore Sorensen, explained:

> The responsibility for recording or not recording him . . . fell on me. I knew, had he been present, that he would have voted for censure. . . . But I had been trained in the discipline of due process and civil liberties. An absent juror, who had not been present for the trial or even heard the indictment . . . should not have his predetermined position recorded. In all conscience, I could not ask the Secretary of the Senate to pair or record for censure.[45]

One can only wonder what Kennedy might have learned about McCarthy that he hadn't known before. He had been in the Senate for almost two years. He had sat with McCarthy on the Government Operations Committee. And he had been in Washington for the Watkins hearings and the release of the final report. If Kennedy was too ill to follow the censure debate, as Sorensen alleged, he certainly understood the symbolic importance of his vote to both sides in the controversy. In the end, it seemed, he could not bear to face the consequences of that vote. On the day he left for Florida his friend Charles Spalding was with him at the hospital. "He was sort of tapping his fingers on his teeth," Spalding recalled, "and he said, 'You know, when I get downstairs . . . those reporters are going to lean over my stretcher. There's going to be about 95 faces leaning over me, and every one of those guys will say, 'Now Senator, what about McCarthy?' And he said, 'Do you know what I'm going to do? I'm going to reach for my back and I'm going to yell, OOOW, and then I'm going to pull the sheet over my head and hope we can get out of there.' "[46]

Kennedy did support the censure of McCarthy—in 1958. He was a presidential contender then, and many liberals, including Eleanor Roosevelt, were using the "McCarthy issue" to question his fitness for higher office. The issue angered and embarrassed Kennedy, who believed he had no moral failing to account for. At the urging of friends and staffers, however, he stepped up his defense of civil liberties and repeated, again and again, that he would have voted for censure had he been on the Senate floor at that time. As Arthur Schlesinger, Jr. wrote him: "I would not, by the way, underestimate the importance of the kind of misgiving expressed by Mrs. R. You will really have to meet it effectively before 1960."[47]

THE SENATE VOTED ON DECEMBER 2, following three days of angry speeches and shouting matches on the floor. Jenner attacked Flanders, and Flanders struck back hard. Welker roamed the aisles muttering obscenities and struggling with difficult words. (He drew the biggest laugh by referring to "hyperbole" but pronouncing it "hyper-bowl.") Lyndon Johnson broke the Democratic silence by calling for censure. "Each of us must decide whether we approve or disapprove of certain actions as standards of Senatorial integrity," he declared. "I have made my decision."[48]

At the last moment, however, Johnson approached Senator Watkins and told him that the Zwicker charge would have to be dropped. At least a dozen Democrats were prepared to vote against it, he said, and others were straddling the fence. They believed that Zwicker had been evasive, and they worried about setting a precedent that might limit the vigorous examination of congressional witnesses in the future.[49]

Watkins gathered the committee members around his desk. Working quickly, they agreed to drop the Zwicker charge and to tack on the Bennett Amendment, which condemned McCarthy's abuse of the Select Committee in the previous weeks. The final resolution read:

> *Resolved.* That the Senator from Wisconsin, Mr. McCarthy, failed to cooperate with the [Gillette] Committee in clearing up matters referred to that committee which concerned his conduct as a Senator . . . and instead repeatedly abused the committee and its members who were trying to carry out assigned duties, thereby obstructing the constitutional processes of the Senate, and that this conduct . . . was contrary to Senatorial traditions and is hereby condemned.
>
> Sec. 2. The Senator from Wisconsin, Mr. McCarthy, in characterizing the [Select Committee] as the "unwitting handmaiden," "involuntary agent," and "attorneys in fact" of the Communist Party . . . acted contrary to senatorial ethics and tended to bring the Senate into dishonor and disrepute, to obstruct the constitutional processes of the Senate, and to impair its dignity; and such conduct is hereby condemned.

The resolution carried, 67–22. Lyndon Johnson delivered his Democrats—44 votes "yea." The Republicans were split down the middle, with moderate Easterners overwhelmingly in favor and the old Taft partisans overwhelmingly opposed. The Senate's lone independent, Morse of Oregon, voted "yea." Kennedy and Wiley were absent and unrecorded (the latter on "official Senate business"). McCarthy voted "present." *

In some ways, of course, the tally was deceiving. It did not reflect the doubts and misgivings of many who voted for censure, nor did it reflect the disproportionate power of those who voted against it. Among Senate Republican leaders, for example, only Leverett Saltonstall went with the majority. The others—Knowland, Bridges, Millikin, and Dirksen—were all in the minority column. Furthermore, the bitterness of the debate could hardly obscure the fact that censure had been voted on rather narrow grounds. Almost no one questioned McCarthy's "sincerity" or the excesses of his crusade. On the contrary, several Democrats praised his "good work" in this area, and others insisted that censure would have no effect on the "power" and the "willingness" of congressional committees to investigate Communism in the future. As Herbert Lehman put it, "We have condemned the individual, but we have not yet repudiated the 'ism.' " [50]

On the other hand, the size of the majority was impressive indeed. Sixty-seven members had gone on record against McCarthy. They had condemned him for obstructing the business of the Senate, impairing its dignity, and bringing the entire body into dishonor and disrepute. They had faced up to a *Senate* problem and moved to solve it in their own special way. McCarthy would remain in the Senate for three more years. He would retain his seniority, his right to speak, to vote, and to sit on committees. In the words of William S. White, however, "a door, quite unseen but quite heavy, had been shut before him. He might well remain a great power to a substantial minority in his party and elsewhere. But in the Institution he was a power no longer." [51]

DURING THE CENSURE DEBATE President Eisenhower had been an interested observer, nothing more. He had avoided all public comment—an Eisenhower trademark—as well as the backstage maneuvering that had characterized his behavior in the past. On the day after the vote, however, the President said to Hagerty: "Senator Watkins got quite a kicking around from McCarthy and his side. . . . I would like to do something to show . . . I am for him one hundred percent." [52]

On December 3 Eisenhower invited Watkins to the White House and congratulated him on a job well done. (He had congratulated Welch and

---

* After the roll call Senator Bridges noted that the word *censure* did not appear in the resolution. As a result Vice President Nixon, then presiding, struck the word from the title of the resolution while Jenner and Welker roared with laughter. In fact, the words *censure* and *condemn* were interchangeable in previous Senate resolutions, and William Fulbright ended this foolishness by calling for a dictionary and reading the definitions of both words aloud. McCarthy himself was undeceived. When asked by reporters for a comment he shrugged his shoulders and said, "Well, it wasn't exactly a vote of confidence."

Flanders, too, but those meetings had been private. This one was a media event, designed to highlight Ike's position on censure and his disgust with those who had voted against it.) Some reporters viewed the episode as typical Eisenhower—too little, too late. But others, recalling his reluctance to comment on any Senate matter, much less one relating to McCarthy, saw it as a very significant step.

McCarthy was furious. He already viewed Watkins as a hanging judge, a pawn of enemy forces, including the Administration. The meeting did not surprise him, but his anger grew as the days passed and no one stepped forward to condemn it. "It's vicious, slimy, back-door politics," he told his friends, "and nobody—not a soul—is saying anything!"

At a hearing of his subcommittee on December 7, McCarthy burst in late with a statement in his hand. Senator Mundt tried to calm him, but Joe would not be stopped. "They're shooting at me from the other end of the Avenue," he cried. "I've got to say something." And he did.

> During the Eisenhower campaign, I spoke from coast to coast promising the American people that if they would elect the Eisenhower administration that they could be assured of a vigorous, forceful drive against Communists in government. Unfortunately, in that I was mistaken. I find that the president, on the one hand, congratulates senators who hold up the work of our committee, and, on the other hand, urges that we be patient with the Communist hoodlums who as of this moment are torturing and brainwashing American uniformed men in Communist dungeons. . . . There has been considerable talk about an apology to the Senate for my fight against Communism. I feel that, instead, I should apologize to the American people for what was an unintentional deception upon them.

This was the last statement that he would make as chairman of the Subcommittee on Investigations. It would also be the last front-page McCarthy story (except for his death in 1957), and the last time he would cause his supporters or opponents much concern. In short order, his statement was repudiated by Knowland, Goldwater, and Mundt. Even General Van Fleet, a leader of the recent petition drive, issued a public rebuke. "Withdrawing all support," he wired McCarthy. "Shocked by your bitter personal attack on the President."

There was no shock at the White House, however. Upon reading the news of the attack, Hagerty rushed to the Oval Office with the ticker stories in his hand. He found Ike deeply engrossed in the *Encyclopaedia Britannica*, "looking up some information he wanted on the origin of the Jewish race." As Hagerty recalled: "The President . . . turned to me and said, 'Jim, I'm not at all sorry to see it come. I rather suspected as much, and it's all right with me.'" [53]

The President went on—and on. For too long, he said, he had wavered between two lines of action: the need to unite his party and the desire to redirect it toward "moderate progressive principles." He vowed that he was finished with "the McCarthys, the Welkers and people like that." He would fight them from now on. "I've had just about enough," he fumed. "If they want to leave the Republican Party . . . that's their business. . . . If they think they can nominate a Right Wing Old Guard Republican for the presidency, they've got another thought coming. I'll go up and down the country, campaigning against them. I'll fight them right down the line."

The President had been pacing back and forth. He returned to his desk and reopened the encyclopedia. "Jim," he chuckled, "you've heard this speech many times before. . . . Thank you for listening."

CHAPTER THIRTY-THREE

Final Years

In the life of Joe McCarthy there was no time for rest. His rise had been rapid, his great days very brief. And now, at forty-six, his life was disintegrating—quite literally—at a wicked rate of speed. In February 1954 the Senate had funded Joe's committee by a vote of 85–1. Eight months later it had condemned him by a vote of 67–22. And eight months after that it would crush his spirit—and what remained of his career—by a vote of 77–4. His fall has been well described by contemporaries, though not very well explained. It depended upon a number of circumstances, each important standing alone, and each flowing naturally into the others.

Although the censure obviously humiliated McCarthy, his physical decline had been obvious for years. Moreover, it was the Democratic victory in 1954, not censure, that stripped him of most of his power. He was no longer the chairman of Government Operations, which meant he no longer controlled the staff, the budget, or the targets to be probed. His position was that of an anti-Eisenhower Republican in a Democratic Congress. He was now a minority voice within the minority party—and a discredited voice at that.

On the other hand, the humiliation of censure was very real indeed. It had cost him many friends, and it had highlighted the obvious though painful realization that his influence in national affairs had virtually disappeared. When he rose to speak in the Senate, his colleagues would drift off the floor. When he entered the cloakroom, they would stiffly walk away. When he went to lunch, they would "finish their bean soup and sandwich and murmur an excuse about the need to return to their offices." Even his friends seemed uncomfortable in his presence. Everett Dirksen put it well: "I'd go crazy if I had another like him to defend."[1]

The worst snub came from 1600 Pennsylvania Avenue, where the Eisenhowers announced that Senator and Mrs. McCarthy had been stricken from the White House guest list for dinners and receptions. It was a petty gesture, but it hurt more than McCarthy let on. In 1956 the President invited every senator but one to a dinner dance at the White House. As Ruth Watt remembered: "We were having a hearing that day in the Caucus Room and Senator McCarthy kept calling me over and saying, 'Ruthy, go ask Mary Driscoll if I've heard from the White House yet, if I've gotten an invitation,' which I thought was kind of sad. He didn't get any invitation. I think it affected him greatly. I think it broke his heart, really."[2]

Politicians were not the only offenders. Even more heartbreaking, it seemed, was the studious inattention shown by the press. It was commonly believed by reporters who followed McCarthy that he wanted to be liked by everyone but that he would rather be hated than ignored. Following the censure vote he *was* ignored, almost without exception. Some reporters saw this as a natural development, entirely unplanned. "As far as the press is concerned," said George Reedy, "a good speech is a good speech . . . if it has some significance within the society. After the censure . . . it didn't matter how good the speech was. What difference did it make? Who cared?" But others, like Willard Edwards and Sam Shaffer of *Newsweek*, spoke of a press blackout—a *conscious* decision by editors and reporters that McCarthy was no longer news. "I wouldn't call it a conspiracy," said Edwards, "but I wouldn't call it a coincidence, either. Most reporters just refused to file McCarthy stories. And most papers would not have printed them anyway."[3]

There were several good examples of this blackout theory. In the spring of 1955 McCarthy offered the Milwaukee *Journal* a copy of a speech he was supposedly going to deliver to a group of supporters. The speech was on civil liberties. Joe told the reporter that he had been reading the works of Thomas Jefferson and Jefferson had convinced him that no man should be persecuted for his beliefs, no matter how subversive they might be. This was *interesting* news, to say the least, and the reporter wrote up the story. "It didn't turn up in the paper on Sunday," he recalled, "and when I came back to work on Tuesday I couldn't find anyone who knew about the decision not to use it. I remember feeling annoyed because [another reporter] said that McCarthy had offered to bet him that the *Journal* wouldn't use it, and I didn't like McCarthy to be proved right on anything about the *Journal*."[4]

EVEN IF THERE HAD BEEN NO CENSURE BATTLE, McCarthy's influence would have been severely curtailed by the easing of Cold War tensions at home and abroad. There were many signs inside America, though none was more significant or more bitterly opposed by congressional Red-hunters than the Supreme Court's dramatic return to libertarian values. In the 1955 term, and again in 1956, the Court reversed or modified a host of loyalty–security laws while reasserting its responsibility for the protection of political dissidents. In *Pennsylvania* v. *Nelson* it banned state sedition laws on the ground that federal legislation was "dominant" and "pervasive" in this field. In *Slochower* v. *Board of Higher Education* it invalidated the discharge of a college professor who had invoked the Fifth Amendment before a congressional committee. ("At the outset," wrote Justice Tom Clark, "we must condemn the practice of imputing a sinister meaning to the exercise of a person's constitutional right.") And in *Watkins* v. *United States* the Court held that the power of Congress to investigate was "inherent" though by no means unlimited. ("There is no congressional power to expose for the sake of exposure," wrote Chief Justice Earl Warren. "No inquiry is an end in itself; it must be related to or in furtherance of a legitimate task of Congress.")[5]

Combined with *Brown* v. *Board of Education,* these Cold War cases united a group of Southern Democrats and conservative Republicans behind the overlapping issues of states rights and militant anti-Communism. As one Alabama congressman asked: "How much longer will [we] continue to permit the Supreme Court to usurp the power of Congress, write the laws of this land, destroy states rights, and protect the Communist Party?" Senator McCarthy joined the fight, calling *Slochower* "a victory for the Communists" and *Watkins* "the most outrageous instance of judicial legislation that has ever come to my attention." Shunned by his own committee, he became an honorary member of the Internal Security Subcommittee, where Earl Warren–baiting was the favorite sport of the chairman, James Eastland of Mississippi.

SENATOR EASTLAND: What other explanation could there be except that a majority of the Court is being influenced by some secret, but very powerful Communist or pro-Communist influence?

SENATOR McCARTHY: It is impossible to explain it. Either incompetence beyond words, Mr. Chairman, I would say, or the type of influence you mentioned.

· · ·

SENATOR EASTLAND: You have heard one Communist after another come before this committee and take the position that the Communist Party was just another political party; in fact, that is the Communist line, is it not?

SENATOR MCCARTHY: That is strictly the Communist line.

SENATOR EASTLAND: Is that not the line that the Chief Justice of the United States takes?

SENATOR MCCARTHY: Unfortunately, yes, Mr. Chairman. . . . In their book Earl Warren is a hero. Now, I do not accuse Earl Warren of being a Communist, not even remotely. But there is something radically wrong with him. And I think it is extremely unfortunate that he was confirmed as Chief Justice.[6]

McCarthy continued his attacks upon Warren, calling him "a dreadful mistake" and "a good friend of Communists." The irony was that his relationship with Eastland had developed too late to allow either man to effectively aid the other. Their timing was off, though not by very much. Had the censure vote come a bit later, or the Cold War and civil rights cases a bit sooner, a formidable alliance of McCarthyites and Dixiecrats could easily have emerged.

━━━━━

IN FOREIGN AFFAIRS, too, the tensions and the rhetoric on both sides had begun to ease. In April 1955 the Russians announced their willingness to end the Austrian deadlock, long an American test of the Kremlin's good intentions. In May the Russians signed the Austrian State Treaty, ending nine years of oppressive occupation; then, at the United Nations Conference on Disarmament, they startled the Western delegates by proposing a reduction in conventional forces and a plan for the control and inspection of nuclear weapons. Whatever their intentions, the Soviets set the stage for the kind of "summit talks" that France and England had wanted, and America had resisted, for quite some time. In 1953 President Eisenhower had said: "I will not go to a Summit because of friendly words . . . by the men of the Kremlin; actual deeds . . . will have to be produced before I agree to such a meeting." In 1955, as the pressure for a summit became irresistible, Ike said he would "pick up and go from any place to Timbuktu to the North Pole to do something about this question of peace." After preliminary discussions the parties chose Geneva instead.[7]

Though public opinion polls showed widespread support for the summit talks, the Republican right was strongly opposed. Senator Bridges claimed that international conferences contained the seeds of "appeasement, compromise, and weakness"—a warning echoed by several Republican senators. In response the President assured his party that he did not intend to give anything away. Geneva, he said, was "not going to be another Yalta." This seemed to do the trick. It silenced everyone but McCarthy, who read an eloquent speech, written by Brent Bozell, which focused on the GOP's campaign pledge to liberate "captive peoples" from the yoke of "Godless terrorism." The speech was studiously ignored. As Willard Edwards remembered: "William S. White came out . . . and sat down beside me. 'You know,' he said, 'despite everything they say about Joe, he has just delivered a remarkable address. He is saying things that ought to be heard. I am going to give it a big play in the New York *Times* tomorrow.'

"I expressed some skepticism," Edwards went on, "but White insisted that his paper would not hesitate to give the speech publicity. . . . I looked with interest . . . in the next morning's *Times*. . . . His 1,500-word story appeared as a one-paragraph shirttail to another story on page 40. It did mention the unmentionable—that McCarthy was still alive and vocal and that was all."[8]

A few days later McCarthy went before the Foreign Relations Committee. He presented a resolution that read:

> Whereas the safety, peace, and independence of the United States can never be permanently secured . . . so long as certain areas of the world remain under Communist control. . . .
>
> *Resolved,* That it is the sense of the Senate that . . . the Secretary of State should secure the agreement of the Soviet Union, the United Kingdom, and France that the present and future status of the nations of Eastern Europe . . . now under Communist control *shall be a subject for discussion at such conference between the heads of state.*[9]

McCarthy knew that it had no chance of passage. His aim was to go on record against the talks and to embarrass the President as well. The Foreign Relations Committee opposed the resolution, as expected, but the matter did not end there. Led by Lyndon Johnson, the Democrats rushed the measure to the floor. "The issue is very simple," said LBJ. "It is whether the President of the United States shall be sent to Geneva with a gun at his head." But simple was hardly the word. The Republicans were outsmarted, outnumbered, and out of luck. They now had to choose between their President and their party platform. Lyndon Johnson—and McCarthy—had left them no choice.

The debate on the resolution was an old-fashioned McCarthy brawl. The only difference was that this time Joe was battling the Republican right. It began with an attack on Senator Knowland:

> I am not at all surprised at the position taken by the majority leader [Lyndon Johnson]. It is in accord with the long record of the Democratic Party to whine and whimper whenever the red-hot stove of Communist aggression is touched. . . .
>
> But I am surprised, shocked, and disappointed, I may say, at the position

that the Republican leader [William Knowland] takes. It is in complete opposition to the solemn pledges made in the Republican Party platform. It is
not the role of the Republican Party to backtrack, to appease, to whine, to
whimper. That is the position of the Democratic Party.[10]

Knowland was on his feet in a flash, shouting that no man could call
him a whiner or a whimperer and get away with it. "I'll place my record
in opposition to Communism against yours," he bellowed. "Not today,
you won't," snapped McCarthy.

Up rose Senator Hickenlooper to defend his *Democratic* friends. "I
do not agree that they are appeasers of Communism," he said, ". . . and
I do not suppose that the senator from Wisconsin meant that what he
said should be interpreted the way it sounded." This infuriated Mc-
Carthy, who replied that he meant every word he had said. The Democrats *were* appeasers. And so, for that matter, were Dulles and
Eisenhower and many senators on the floor. "The Korean surrender was
appeasement," he shouted. "Giving up the Tachen Islands was appeasement. Giving up northern Indochina was appeasement. And a further
example is what the Senate is encouraging today."

After five hours of this, the Senate rejected his resolution by a vote
of 77–4. McCarthy was joined by Langer, Jenner, and Malone, who
probably would have preferred a resolution declaring that Europe did
not exist. He was opposed by almost all of his former intimates: Bridges,
Butler, Dirksen, Welker, and Mundt. The irony, of course, was that
McCarthy had united his party behind Dwight Eisenhower as it had
never been united before.

The story did not end here. In the following months McCarthy condemned the Administration for "recognizing" the Communist satellites
in Europe, aiding Tito in Yugoslavia, and ignoring the freedom fighters
in Hungary:

> The Soviets are loading Hungarian patriots and their families into freight
> cars, then sealing the cars and shipping them east to Siberian slave-labor
> camps. . . .
> *What can we do? Make certain that those trainloads of women and children
> do not leave Hungary. How? By making bombers and bombs available to
> volunteer pilots from outside the Iron Curtain so that they may destroy the
> railroad bridges and rail lines and thus prevent this traffic in human slavery
> which has been set in motion by a new and infinitely crueler Genghis Khan.*

In each instance McCarthy suffered the worst punishment of all:
silence. He was completely ignored. "On my visits to the capital," Roy
Cohn remembered, "I would find him at home, sunk deep in his arm-
chair, staring into the fire." When the two men discussed the Communist
issue, McCarthy would rub his hands in despair. Continuing the battle,
he would say, was as futile as "shoveling shit against the tide."[11]

THIS WAS A TERRIBLE TIME FOR McCARTHY—a time when even his modest victories were seen as defeats. In 1955, for example, the Subcommittee on Investigations renewed its probe of *Army Personnel Actions Relating to Irving Peress*. Joe attended most of the hearings, though the days of intimidation were clearly in the past. If anything, the absence of deference—and fear—spoke volumes about his galloping decline.

SENATOR McCARTHY: Could I ask this? Is it the function of Mr. Brucker to object to questions and—

MR. BRUCKER: I have a right to counsel the witness.

SENATOR McCARTHY: Let me finish.

MR. BRUCKER: I thought you were finished. It is hard to tell. [12]

There was one memorable moment at these hearings, and it came with General Zwicker on the stand. The general had just quoted portions of a memo he had written in 1953:

The retention of Captain Peress is clearly not consistent with the interests of the national security. It is requested that immediate steps be taken to effect his relief from active duty.

McCarthy posed the obvious question: "Why did you not save yourself some grief by pointing this out at the original hearing?"

GENERAL ZWICKER: It was a security matter, sir.

SENATOR McCARTHY: I do not want to argue the point with you, but you can answer it today but you could not answer it then, and what happened in the meantime?

GENERAL ZWICKER: A great deal has happened since then, Mr. Senator.

SENATOR McCARTHY: I guess you are right. [13]

Although the hearings ended in the spring of 1955, the subcommittee's interest in General Zwicker continued for quite some time. Both the chairman, John McClellan, and the majority counsel, Robert Kennedy, believed that Zwicker had lied repeatedly on the stand. In April 1955 McClellan sent the transcript of the hearings to Attorney General Brownell. "It would be appreciated," he wrote privately, "if your office would advise whether there appears to be a violation of the perjury statute and what action your Department intends to pursue."

Brownell did exactly what Eisenhower expected him to do—nothing at all. Six months passed before McClellan wrote him again:

Reference is made to my letter of April 12, 1955, wherein I referred to you various material concerning Brigadier General Ralph W. Zwicker. . . . It would be appreciated if you would advise me as to the status of the case.

Another six months passed with no word from Brownell. Angrily, McClellan wrote him on June 13, 1956:

I am certainly surprised that your office has been unable to reach a decision in this case. . . . I would appreciate an answer within a week's time as to what action you intend to take. . . .

This brought an immediate reply from Warren Olney III, an Assistant Attorney General. Olney explained that "the questions involved are complicated" and "bound to take time." Eight more months passed before he forwarded the Department's finding to McClellan in a letter one paragraph long:

The complex legal and factual problems have been carefully considered. . . . As a result . . . it has been concluded that prosecution will not be undertaken. The case is being closed in the Criminal Division.[14]

The timing of Olney's letter was hardly accidental. Two weeks later Ralph Zwicker was promoted to the rank of major general.

———

THE COLLAPSE OF MCCARTHY'S INFLUENCE and support in Washington was matched, to a large degree, by the collapse of his influence and support in the nation as a whole. He still had his followers; he still drew cheers from the Catholic War Veterans and the DAR. But the crowds were smaller, the engagements fewer, the bookings minor league. In the spring of 1955 the city fathers of Boscobel, Wisconsin, predicted a turnout of 50,000 for a "McCarthy Day" celebration at a local park. Under clear blue skies the senator mounted the platform, spoke for a few minutes, and thanked the "vast turnout" of 1,500—many of whom were members of high school bands. The scene was repeated in Boston, where McCarthy delivered his "comeback address" on nuclear subversion from the ring of a downtown boxing arena. The sound system was poor and his voice reverberated against the thousands of empty seats. "When he began to speak," wrote one observer, "many complained that they could not hear him. This is understandable for the phrase 'sabotage of our intercontinental guided-ballistic missile program' is quite a mouthful for any orator and particularly for one who tends to mumble." * [15]

The realization that he could no longer make headlines or fill arenas was the worst blow of all. Sometimes Joe would cancel his engagements

___

* The comeback was sponsored by the "Friends of Senator McCarthy." They included Joseph Kennedy, publisher William Loeb, former Boston Mayor James Curley, and Cambridge candy manufacturer Robert Welch, who would later found the John Birch Society.

or fail to show up. Other times he would appear where he had not been invited and cause quite a stir. On one occasion—a campaign dinner for Richard Nixon at Milwaukee's Schroeder Hotel—the senator lurched into the ballroom, approached the dais, and took a seat at the end of the table. At this point, a newsman recalled, a dignitary asked Joe to leave— which he did, without saying a word. The newsman followed McCarthy outside. He found him sitting in an alley, weeping like a little boy.[16]

━━━━━━━

HIS LIFE BECAME A NIGHTMARE, shared by Jeannie and a few close friends. He lost interest in his senatorial duties, avoided his constituents, and skipped the Republican National Convention in 1956. More and more he focused on those who had "betrayed" him—Richard Nixon, Len Hall, Arthur Watkins, John Riedl of the Appleton *Post–Crescent,* and Roy Matson of the Wisconsin *State Journal.* "While I have not been either surprised or disturbed by the opposition of Bill Evjue and others," he wrote Matson in 1957, "I have been both surprised and disturbed by your sudden and apparent all-out opposition to me. I cannot understand this for the reason that my politics and policies are exactly the same now as when you were giving me all-out support." To which Matson replied: "You must be just catching up on your homework, and reading the back files. We haven't said anything very mean about you for quite a spell."[17]

A few weeks later Joe met a young Catholic missionary named Tom Dooley, whose charitable work had won him wide public acclaim. In a textbook case of projection, he told Dooley that the media would use him, attack him, and then discard him like yesterday's garbage. After- ward Dooley wrote his mother: "Senator McCarthy warned me of such an attack. . . . He says people like me have pretty brilliance for a while, and are heard from no more. . . . One reads of us in later years in the columns 'And where is . . . ?' "[18]

Early in 1956 Joe told friends that he had a year left to live. He spared them the details, but no one had to ask. He "was in pretty bad shape," Ruth Watt recalled, "and we knew he had cirrhosis of the liver."[19]

Always a heavy drinker in Washington, McCarthy had become a full- fledged alcoholic by 1954, a man who drank constantly and consumed a quart or more a day. His physical appearance shocked old friends and acquaintances like Ed Hart, who described him as "the town drunk in businessman's clothes." An observer at the Carroll Arms claimed that Joe "was in such bad condition that as he would pick up his drink and down it, some of it would dribble out of his mouth and down his suit." He sometimes appeared to be in a trance, unable to recognize familiar faces or to form intelligible words. "I ran into McCarthy and his wife in 1956," Bob Fleming remembered. "It was obvious he didn't know who I was. Jean said, 'Joe, it's Bob . . . Bob Fleming, the reporter.' He looked right through me; nothing registered upstairs. I just shook his hand and walked away."[20]

In December 1956 a reporter wrote William Evjue of the *Capital-Times:*

> A congressman tells me off the record that he twice ran into McCarthy in northern Wisconsin during the last few months and that both times Joe was drunk. . . . Like several others, the congressman is convinced that Joe is in the hospital for alcoholism—"taking the cure." A reporter who was once friendly with McCarthy and his wife—and who may still be—said that when Joe went to the hospital to sleep nights for several weeks last summer he did so because of terrible nightmares and tension at night that made him wake up screaming. That would be, in other words, the delirium tremens, or dt's.[21]

The report was correct. In the latter part of 1956 McCarthy was treated at the Bethesda Naval Hospital for a variety of ailments: hepatitis, cirrhosis, delirium tremens, and the removal of a fatty tumor from his leg. In between visits, his friends would plead with him to stop drinking, but to no avail. "I would scream at him," Van Susteren recalled. "I'd say, 'You're killing yourself, Goddamit.' And he'd say, 'Kiss my ass, Van.' And that was that."[*][22]

THROUGH IT ALL Jean remained at his side, nursing him, protecting him, and finding new ways to cheer him up. She framed his war medals and urged old friends to stop by when they could. There were many visitors in the final months—Alfred and Ida Kohlberg, Styles and Dolores Bridges, Louis and Margaret Budenz, and Bobby Kennedy, to name a few. Mrs. Kohlberg thought that Joe looked rather well. The only problem, she recalled, was that he stopped the conversation by yelling at no one in particular, "They're murdering me. They're killing me!" Young Kennedy was shaken by what he saw. He wrote that "Joe has been looking terribly. . . . Couldn't stand straight and often appeared to be in a trance."[23]

In January 1957 Jean tried a different kind of therapy. With help from Cardinal Spellman the McCarthys adopted a five-week-old girl from the New York Foundling Home. They named the child Tierney Elizabeth and brought her to Washington in a private railroad car donated by a family friend. Joe adored the infant and spoke frequently of adopting another. "I don't know very much about babies," he said, "but I'm crazy about this one."[24]

For a time his spirits soared and he looked eagerly to the future. He spoke about quitting politics and buying a ranch in Arizona, where it was

---

* There were rumors then—and later—that Joe became a drug addict, that he regularly used morphine to ease his hangovers. His friends insist that these rumors were false.

peaceful and warm. But here, too, his dream evaporated in typical McCarthy style. Always the plunger, he had invested heavily in a uranium company run by a friend from Green Bay. In 1957 the company folded and the friend fled to South America. McCarthy lost most of his savings. His nest egg was gone.

On April 28 he entered Bethesda for the last time. He was placed in a guarded room on the twelfth floor and allowed but one visitor, his wife, who gamely told reporters that Joe had a knee problem, nothing more. But Drew Pearson, who had contacts inside the hospital, wrote in his diary that "Senator McCarthy has been drinking heavily. . . . He is in an oxygen tent and has delirium tremens."[25]

By coincidence, Senator Prescott Bush was in Bethesda for a physical examination. He tried to visit Joe, without success, and eventually sent him a note through one of the floor nurses. "When I got back to my office," Bush recalled, ". . . I found a telephone message dictated by McCarthy . . . in which he thanked me very warmly for coming to see him, and he couldn't tell me how much he appreciated that."[26]

Joe died the following day—May 2, 1957—with his wife and a priest at his bedside. The official cause of death was listed as acute hepatitis— or inflammation of the liver. There was no mention of cirrhosis or delirium tremens, though the press hinted, correctly, that he drank himself to death.

There were dozens of front-page editorials—some neutral, some forgiving, some crying murder most foul.* William Loeb blamed the death on Eisenhower—"the stinking hypocrite in the White House." Others— like David Lawrence, the Brooklyn *Tablet*, and the Chicago *Tribune*— claimed that McCarthy had been "killed," "tortured," and "crucified" because of his political beliefs. On balance, however, the press responded with pity, not anger. From Washington, Eric Sevareid put it well:

> Senator McCarthy had a certain manic brilliance. . . . But his brilliance outran his knowledge, and his ambition outran them both. . . .
> Some say that things will not seem the same with Joe McCarthy gone. For his friends, this will be true; for Washington as a whole, it will not be true. McCarthy, the political force and symbol as distinct from McCarthy the human being, died three years ago when his fellow Senators formally passed their adverse judgment on his conduct.[27]

Those who had tangled with McCarthy had very little to say. General Zwicker refused all interviews. President Truman expressed his "sor-

---

* The New York *Times* chose to say nothing. Charles Merz, head of the editorial page, said: "I don't think we need an editorial on this. . . . Why dignify the bastard; let him pass from the scene without more attention." See Harrison Salisbury, *Without Fear or Favor*, 1980, p. 470.

row," as did Annie Lee Moss, who added that "death is something we've all got to do sooner or later." Dean Acheson offered the maxim: "Say nothing about the dead except good." And Joe Welch replied: ". . . I did not hate Senator McCarthy. If you quote me . . . please add that I'm not good at hating any man."[28]

At Jean's request, a requiem high mass was offered at St. Matthew's Cathedral, where the couple had been married in 1953. From there an honor guard of Marines escorted the body to a Capitol Hill service attended by Richard Nixon, Roy Cohn, J. Edgar Hoover, and seventy senators. The service took twenty minutes; there were prayers but no speeches. When it ended, the coffin was put on a military plane and flown to Green Bay, where huge crowds lined the airport and the highway leading south to Appleton. According to the *Post–Crescent*, all businesses, schools, and public buildings were closed for the day. "Men drifted out of taverns along the avenue. It was almost as if the city slowed down for a bit, waiting for Joe and standing for a moment as the hearse passed. Then a few looks, a few remarks—and more of the memories."[29]

They buried him beside his parents on a bluff overlooking the Fox River. Fighting back tears, Father Adam Grill said that Joe had "come to rest in an atmosphere of calm and peace such as he enjoyed only rarely in the closing years of the cycle that began in the ancient records of old St. Mary's." Then a rifle volley was fired and the sound of "taps" echoed across the graveyard. Joe was home at last.

━━━━━━━

IN THE FOLLOWING WEEKS, Jean McCarthy answered hundreds of letters of condolence. She thanked John Foster Dulles for his kindness. (Dulles had sent a one-line message of regret.) She told Styles and Dolores Bridges that "Tierney has sprouted two lower teeth since you've been here—without a whimper." And she wrote Louis and Margaret Budenz: "I only wish in some way I could comfort you, for we do indeed share a loss."[30]

In all of her letters Jean described her husband as a true believer, which undoubtedly was true. Befriended by J. Edgar Hoover, encouraged by Bridges and Taft, nourished by Kohlberg and Matthews, defended by Buckley and Bozell, the senator came to believe in the cause he had stumbled upon in 1950. His enemies never accepted this fact. *Their* Joe McCarthy was a cynic, a nihilist, a politician on the make. He believed in nothing, wrote Richard Rovere. "He could not comprehend true outrage, true indignation, true anything."

For the most part, historians have accepted this portrait of McCarthy. Some have even debunked his talents, calling him an "unimaginative opportunist" and a "second-rate politician." In doing so they have ignored the obvious questions: Why Joe McCarthy? Why did *he* dominate the era that carries his name? The answer is simple: McCarthy *was* unique. He had competitors but no equals. He was bolder than the Mundts and smarter than the Welkers. He knew how to use the media. He crafted a very effective public image. And he was adept at probing the weak spots of opponents.

Above all, the senator provided a simple explanation for America's "decline" in the world. He spoke of a massive internal conspiracy, directed by Communists and abetted by government officials who came to include the Republican President of the United States. He provided names, documents, and statistics—in short, the *appearance* of diligent research. And he understood intuitively that force, action, and virility were essential prerequisites in the Red-hunting crusade.

Yet, for all of this, McCarthy seemed curiously self-contained. He had no desire to lead a movement, to run for higher office, or to formulate a program that went beyond the simple exposure of Communists. His political skills were keen, but his reach was limited. And his ambition was too.

He was not a would-be dictator. He did not threaten our constitutional system, but he did hurt many who lived under it. He slandered dozens of prominent citizens. George Marshall, Anna Rosenberg, Dean Acheson, Charles Bohlen, Adlai Stevenson, John Carter Vincent—the list goes on and on. He played a role in chasing the China Hands out of government; as a result, he must bear some responsibility for America's disastrous Asian policy in later years. He terrorized witnesses who appeared before his committee. He had a devastating effect on government morale, and he made America look ridiculous—and frightening—in the eyes of much of the world. His investigations of the IIA and the Army Signal Corps were as destructive as any in recent memory. At his best, he produced evidence that the government's security procedures were sometimes remiss. But his critics were right: he never uncovered a Communist. He spent his days searching for the new Julius Rosenberg, the new Alger Hiss. He wound up settling for Owen Lattimore and Annie Lee Moss.

He could have been stopped rather quickly. Robert Taft, J. Edgar Hoover, Dwight D. Eisenhower—any of them could have halted McCarthy, but all of them had reasons for remaining supportive or simply aloof. Near the end the President played an important role in Joe's demise. But the *key* roles were played by others—by Roy Cohn, his scheming assistant, and by McCarthy himself.

In her letter to Dulles, Jean wrote: "God gave Joe the insight to grasp the central truth of our age. He equipped him with unfailing courage and with intellect. . . . With unswerving, uncompromising purpose, Joe served his God, his country, and his civilization." Millions believed these words in the 1950s. Some believe them today. A few still visit his grave.

Notes

CHAPTER ONE: BEGINNINGS (*pp. 1–20*)

1. Appleton *Post–Crescent*, May 7, 1975; interview with John Ellenbecker, January 19, 1977.

2. Western Historical Company, "History of Outagamie County," in *History of Northern Wisconsin*, 1881, pp. 667–90; William Raney, "Appleton," *The Wisconsin Magazine of History*, December, 1949, pp. 135–51.

3. Justille McDonald, *History of the Irish in Wisconsin in the Nineteenth Century*, 1954, pp. 245, 264–65, 273; Western Historical Company, "History of Outagamie County," p. 625; Theodore Roemer, *St. Joseph in Appleton*, 1943, pp. 1–16; interview with Henry Mortensen, January 19, 1977.

4. Thomas Ryan, *History of Outagamie County*, 1909, p. 1090; "Abstract Lands, Book 1," p. 109, Record Bureau, Outagamie County Courthouse, Appleton, Wis.

5. "Deed Book," 1896, #124698, p. 528, Outagamie County Courthouse, Appleton, Wis.

6. Interview with John Ellenbecker; interview with Urban Van Susteren, October 22, 1977; interview with Jim Heenan, October 22, 1977.

7. Interview with John Ellenbecker. The myth about Joe's shyness and his odd physical appearance began with Jack Anderson and Ronald May, *McCarthy*, 1952, pp. 6–10. They did a small amount of primary research but had no intentions of presenting this material objectively. Other biographers have simply used their stories and anecdotes, often word for word, without bothering to check their accuracy. See Fred Cook, *The Nightmare Decade*, 1971, pp. 78–79, and Lately Thomas, *When Even Angels Wept*, 1973, pp. 7–8.

8. Andrew Greeley, *That Most Distressful Nation*, 1972, pp. 108, 115.

9. Interview with John Ellenbecker; interview with Urban Van Susteren; interview with Jim Heenan; interview with Cliff Mullarkey, January 17, 1977.

10. Interview with Jim Heenan; interview with John Ellenbecker.

11. Anderson and May, *McCarthy*, p. 8.

12. Interview with Jim Heenan; interview with John Ellenbecker.

13. Portland *Oregonian*, April 11, 1954.

14. Interview with Jim Heenan; interview with John Ellenbecker; interview with Urban Van Susteren.

15. The idea of friction over Joe's career goals is most speculative. McCarthy's friends say it is possible that the parents disagreed but are unable to recall any specifics.

16. Portland *Oregonian*, April 11, 1954; Anderson and May, *McCarthy*, pp. 11–16.

17. Bob Schwartz, "The Junior Senator: Early Life," unpublished manuscript in the *Robert Fleming Papers*, Box 4, Manuscripts Division, Wisconsin State Historical Society. Schwartz, a *Time* reporter, interviewed scores of McCarthy's friends and family members for a piece *Time* did on the senator. His notes, which are unpublished, are invaluable to scholars of McCarthy's early career.

18. This story originated with Anderson and May, *McCarthy*, p. 12. Heenan, Ellenbecker, and Van Susteren, who all knew Bid McCarthy, say they simply do not believe it.

19. "Joe would always quote Bid's remark," says Van Susteren. "It seemed to mean a lot to him."

20. Anderson and May, *McCarthy*, p. 14.

21. Schwartz, "The Junior Senator: Early Life," p. 2.

22. Interview with Minnie Osterloth Rohde, January 18, 1977.

23. James Auer and Clark Kalvelage, "Joe McCarthy's School Days," unpublished manuscript, Manuscripts Division, Wisconsin State Historical Society.

24. *Ibid.*; interview with Ada Nye Nemshoff, January 18, 1977.

25. Auer and Kalvelage, "Joe McCarthy's School Days."

26. This story, again, originated with Anderson and May, *McCarthy*, p. 19; Hershberger's quote is in Auer and Kalvelage, "Joe McCarthy's School Days."

27. Interview with Melda Beckman Mortensen, January 18, 1977.

28. Auer and Kalvelage, "Joe McCarthy's School Days."

29. Interview with Minnie Osterloth Rohde.

30. Interview with Judge Richard Farrell, January 18, 1977.

31. Bob Byers, "How I Know Mr. McCarthy," unpublished manuscript, copy in author's possession; Donald Crosby, *God, Church, and Flag*, 1978, p. 34.

32. Anderson and May, *McCarthy*, pp. 25–26.

33. Interview with Thomas Korb, June 10, 1978.

34. *Ibid.* Also Michael O'Brien, *McCarthy and McCarthyism in Wisconsin*, 1980, pp. 8–9.

35. Interview with Clifford Mullarkey, January 17, 1977; interview with Charlie Middleton, January 17, 1977.

36. Interview with Charlie Middleton. The poker quote is in Bradley Taylor to Elaine Kretchman, June 3, 1954, Box 4, *Bradley Taylor Papers*, Manuscripts Division, Wisconsin State Historical Society.

37. Interview with Clifford Mullarkey; interview with Charlie Middleton.

38. Marquette *Tribune*, March 26, 1931; April 27, 1931.

39. *Ibid.*, May 5, 1932.

40. Interview with Thomas Korb.

41. Anderson and May, *McCarthy*, pp. 26–27.

42. See "Clinical Portrait of Senator McCarthy," in Public Relations File, Box 81, *Papers of the Americans for Democratic Action*, Manuscripts Division, Wisconsin State Historical Society.

43. Paul Douglas, *In the Fullness of Time*, 1971, p. 251; Richard Rovere, *Senator Joe McCarthy*, 1959, p. 60.

44. Interview with Francis Werner, January 20, 1977.

45. Interview with Dr. William Remmel, January 18, 1977.

46. Interview with Ed Hart, January 18, 1977; interview with Richard Brown, January 18, 1977.

47. Interview with Dr. William Remmel.

48. Interview with Ed Hart.

49. Interview with Irving Hanson, January 18, 1977; interview with Dr. William Remmel.

50. Interview with Ed Hart.

51. Interview with Clifford Mullarkey; interview with Dr. William Remmel.

52. Interview with Dr. William Remmel.

53. Waupaca County *Post*, February 20, 1936.

54. Shawano County *Journal*, July 1, August 1, 8, 1937; Shawano *Evening Leader*, April 14, 1937.

55. O'Brien, *McCarthy and McCarthyism in Wisconsin*, pp. 20–21.

56. "Campaign File, 1936, Senator Joseph R. McCarthy," Wisconsin State Historical Society.

57. Anderson and May, *McCarthy*, p. 36.

58. *Ibid.*, p. 37.

CHAPTER TWO: G.I. JUDGE *(pp. 21–35)*

1. Appleton *Post–Crescent*, March 31, 1939.

2. Interview with Richard Farrell, January 18, 1977.

3. Fred Cook, *The Nightmare Decade*, 1971, p. 81; interview with Francis Werner (no relation), January 20, 1977; interview with Clifford Mullarkey, January 17, 1977; interview with Ed Hart, January 18, 1977.

4. For the standard analysis of the McCarthy–Werner race, see Jack Anderson and Ronald May, *McCarthy*, 1952, pp. 37–43; Cook, *The Nightmare Decade*, pp. 81–82; Lately Thomas, *When Even Angels Wept*, 1973, pp. 14–17. The real problem with the Werner–McCarthy race, as with so much of Joe's early life, is that virtually no primary research has been done. Only Anderson and May bothered to read the local newspapers or to interview the people who were there during the campaign. Other biographers—Rovere, Cook, and Thomas—have simply used Anderson and May's work and paraphrased the relevant portions, sometimes almost word for word.

5. Richard Rovere, *Senator Joe McCarthy*, 1959, p. 88.

6. *Martindale–Hubbell Law Directory*, 1939, p. 1092; Appleton *Post–Crescent*, April 1, 1939.

7. Appleton *Post–Crescent*, April 1, 1939.

8. Interview with Richard Farrell; Guy Lorge interview in Anderson and May, "Rough Notes," in the *Files of the National Committee for an Effective Congress*, Washington, D.C.

9. Jack Alexander, "The Senate's Remarkable Upstart," *The Saturday Evening Post*, August 9, 1947, p. 16; Anderson and May, *McCarthy*, pp. 38–39.

10. Interview with John Ellenbecker, January 19, 1977.

11. Alexander, "The Senate's Remarkable Upstart," p. 16; interview with Clifford Mullarkey.

12. Dr. A. J. Werner to Robert Fleming, October 4, 1951, Box 3, *Robert Fleming Papers*, Manuscripts Division, Wisconsin State Historical Society.

13. Anderson and May, *McCarthy*, p. 45.

14. *Ibid.*, pp. 76–77.

15. Interview with Francis Werner.

16. An excellent summary of the case can be found in Michael O'Brien, *McCarthy and McCarthyism in Wisconsin*, 1980, pp. 34–39.

17. Interview with Clifford Mullarkey; interview with Richard Brown, January 18, 1977; the quote is from the interview with Francis Werner.

18. Interview with Clifford Mullarkey.

19. Both incidents are mentioned in Schwartz, "The Junior Senator," pp. 7–8.

20. *Ibid.*; Willard Edwards, "Notes on Joe McCarthy," unpublished manuscript in author's possession; interview with Willard Edwards, April 30, 1978.

21. Interview with Urban Van Susteren, October 22, 1977.

22. Schwartz, "The Junior Senator," p. 8.

23. *Ibid.*, p. 6.

24. Interview with Urban Van Susteren.

25. *Ibid.*

26. *Ibid.*

27. *Ibid.*; also, Gerald Jolin interview in Anderson and May, "Rough Notes," in *Files of the National Committee for an Effective Congress*, Washington, D.C.

28. Interview with Urban Van Susteren.

29. Quoted in Anderson and May, *McCarthy*, p. 54.

30. Quoted in "Bob?" to Robert Fleming, October 8, 1951, Box 4, *Robert Fleming Papers*.

31. Appleton *Post–Crescent*, November 15, 1943.

32. Quoted in Anderson and May, *McCarthy*, p. 61.

33. See especially Wisconsin *State Journal*, July 18, 1946; Appleton *Post–Crescent*, November 15, 1943; Anderson and May, *McCarthy*, pp. 58–66.

34. Captain Jack Canaan to William Evjue, December, 1949, *William Evjue Papers*, Manuscripts Division, Wisconsin State Historical Society.

35. "Bob?" to Robert Fleming, October 8, 1951.

36. *Ibid.*

37. Anderson and May, *McCarthy*, p. 63.

38. Robert Fleming to John Ferguson, October 4, 1951, Box 4, *Robert Fleming Papers*, Wisconsin State Historical Society; "Memorandum for Mr. Lloyd: Medical Record of Senator McCarthy," May 27, 1952, *Files of David Lloyd*, in the Harry S. Truman Presidential Library, Independence, Mo.

39. "Memo–McCarthy Claque," Box 2, *Robert Fleming Papers*, Wisconsin State Historical Society.

40. Roy Cohn, *McCarthy*, 1968, p. 16; James M. Burns interview and Abram Chayes interview, both in the *John F. Kennedy Oral History Project*, John F. Kennedy Presidential Library, Boston, Mass.

41. Quoted in Robert Griffith, *The Politics of Fear*, 1970, p. 6.

42. *Ibid.*; also, Sharon Coady, "The Wisconsin Press and Joseph McCarthy," unpublished master's thesis, University of Wisconsin, 1965, pp. 41–42.

43. Shawano *Evening Leader*, July 27, 1944.

44. Wisconsin *State Journal*, August 10, 1944. McCarthy was endorsed by newspapers in his home area, such as the Appleton *Post–Crescent*, and by the Wisconsin *State Journal*.

45. Madison *Capital–Times*, August 13, 1944; U.S. Congress, Senate, Report of the Subcommittee on Privileges and Elections to the Committee on Rules and Administration, *Investigation of Senators Joseph McCarthy and William Benton*, 1952, pp. 27–29.

46. *Ibid.*, p. 28.

47. Milwaukee *Journal*, May 25, 1947; Madison *Capital–Times*, February 14, July 31, 1947; Anderson and May, *McCarthy*, p. 254.

CHAPTER THREE: GUNNING FOR THE SENATE (*pp.* 36–52)

1. See Edward Doan, *The LaFollettes and the Wisconsin Idea*, 1947, pp. 37–176; Donald Young, *Adventure in Politics*, 1970, pp. vii–xvii.

2. Leon Epstein, *Politics in Washington*, 1958, pp. 36–38; Michael Rogin, *The Intellectuals and McCarthy*, 1967, pp. 59–80.

3. Young, *Adventure in Politics*, xi; Roger Johnson, *Robert M. LaFollette, Jr., and the Decline of the Progressive Party in Wisconsin*, 1964, p. 7.

4. The Lilienthal quote is in Young, *Adventure in Politics*, xiii; see also Karl Meyer, "The Politics of Loyalty: From LaFollette to McCarthy in Wisconsin, 1918–1952," unpublished doctoral dissertation, Princeton University, 1956, pp. 74–127.

5. Epstein, *Politics in Wisconsin*, p. 41; Young, *Adventure in Politics*, pp. 207–8.

6. Richard Haney, "A History of the Democratic Party in Wisconsin Since World War II," unpublished doctoral dissertation, University of Wisconsin, 1970, p. 13; William Leuchtenburg, *Franklin D. Roosevelt and the New Deal, 1932–40*, 1963, pp. 283–84; Russel Nye, *Midwestern Progressive Politics*, 1959, p. 341.

7. Thomas Amlie to Howard McMurray, October 10, 1947, *Thomas Amlie Papers*, Wisconsin State Historical Society.

8. See Fred Sheasby's column in the Milwaukee *Journal*, February 24, 1946.

9. Interview with George Haberman, former president, Wisconsin Federation of Labor, September 30, 1969; interview with George Hall, former secretary–treasurer, Wisconsin Federation of Labor, September 29, 1969; Richard Rovere, *Senator Joe McCarthy*, 1959, p. 100.

10. Haney, "A History of the Democratic Party in Wisconsin Since World War II," pp. 1–21.

11. Madison *Capital–Times*, February 12, March 14, 1946.

12. Johnson, *Robert M. LaFollette, Jr.*, pp. 124–27; John Steinke, "The Rise of McCarthyism," unpublished master's thesis, University of Wisconsin, 1960, pp. 29–45.

13. Alfred Bowman, "The Man Behind McCarthy: Coleman of Wisconsin," *The Nation*, March 20, 1954, pp. 236–37.

14. Aldric Revell, quoted in the Madison *Capital–Times*, February 28, 1946.

15. Thomas Amlie, quoted in *ibid.*, April 25, 1946; see also William Evjue's editorial in *ibid.*, March 18, 1946.

16. Aldric Revell, quoted in *ibid.*, April 25, 1946; see also Jack Anderson and Ronald May, *McCarthy*, 1952, pp. 78–91.

17. Michael O'Brien, *McCarthy and McCarthyism in Wisconsin*, 1980, p. 62.

18. Kohler's quote is in Bob Schwartz, "The Junior Senator: Early Life," unpublished manuscript in the *Robert Fleming Papers*, Box 4, Manuscripts Division, Wisconsin State Historical Society; Anderson and May, *McCarthy*, p. 83.

19. O'Brien, *McCarthy and McCarthyism in Wisconsin*, p. 61.

20. Aldric Revell, quoted in the Madison *Capital–Times*, May 7, 1946.

21. "Confidential Memorandum: Conference with Governor Goodland," April, 1946, *Thomas Coleman Papers*, Manuscripts Division, Wisconsin State Historical Society.

22. Milwaukee *Journal*, May 16, 1946; Madison *Capital–Times*, December 9, 1945.

23. Milwaukee *Journal*, October 25, 1946; Madison *Capital–Times*, October 23, 1946. One member of the Wisconsin Board of Bar Commissioners disputed McCarthy's contention and wrote to another member: "I observe from the public press that . . . McCarthy . . . denies that he is a member of the American Bar Association or the State Bar Association. I just ran across a copy of the proceedings of the State Bar Association for 1946 and I see there is a fellow named Joseph McCarthy, Appleton, Wisconsin, listed as a member. That must be 'Slippery Joe.' " See W. T. Doar to Edward Dempsey, July 10, 1949, *Edward Dempsey Papers*, Manuscripts Division, Wisconsin State Historical Society.

24. Edward Dempsey to R. T. Reinhardt, August 27, 1948; R. T. Reinhardt to Harlan Rogers, August 23, 1948, both in *Edward Dempsey Papers*, Manuscripts Division, Wisconsin State Historical Society.

25. Joe's "naughty boy" quote is in Robert Griffith, *The Politics of Fear*, 1970, p. 28; his call for the commissioners' resignations is in Anderson and May, *McCarthy*, p. 121.

26. O'Brien, *McCarthy and McCarthyism in Wisconsin*, p. 64.

27. For the primary campaign finances, see *Secretary of State of Wisconsin, Political Contributions of the 1946 Primary Elections*, Folder #2062, 4384, 4480. The LaFollette family contributed more than half of the $13,000 used by the incumbent. The brochure "The Newspapers Say" is on file at the Manuscripts Division, Wisconsin State Historical Society. The McCarthy quote to Van Susteren is in O'Brien, *McCarthy and McCarthyism in Wisconsin*, pp. 69–70.

28. Anderson and May, *McCarthy*, p. 85.

29. "Press Release: How Did Senator LaFollette Get All That Money?" June 27, 1946; "Press Release: No Regulation on LaFollette's Radio Station Profits," June 27, 1946, *Thomas Coleman Papers*, Manuscripts Division, Wisconsin State Historical Society.

30. Thomas Amlie to Howard McMurray, October 10, 1947, *Thomas Amlie Papers*, Manuscripts Division, Wisconsin State Historical Society.

31. Anderson and May, *McCarthy*, p. 93.

32. Wisconsin *State Journal*, April 27, 28, 1946; Eau Claire *Leader*, April 27, 1946.

33. Anderson and May, *McCarthy*, pp. 85–88.

34. Milwaukee *Journal*, July 26, 1946.

35. McCarthy's quote is in Anderson and May, *McCarthy* p. 91.

36. Johnson, *Robert M. LaFollette, Jr.*, p. 115.

37. David Oshinsky, *Senator Joseph McCarthy and the American Labor Movement*, 1976, pp. 20–21.

38. Racine *Labor*, July 12, 1946; *Wisconsin CIO News*, July 26, 1946; Kenosha *Labor*, July 25, August 8, 1946.

39. Anderson and May, *McCarthy*, p. 105; Fred Cook, *The Nightmare Decade*, 1971, p. 104.

40. *Wisconsin CIO News*, June 11, June 25, July 2, 1945.

41. Madison *Capital–Times*, April 10, 1946; Anderson and May, *McCarthy*, p. 104.

42. Milwaukee *Journal*, June 3, 1945; Wisconsin *State Journal*, June 4, 1945.

43. For a further explanation, see Oshinsky, *Senator Joseph McCarthy and the American Labor Movement*, pp. 30–33.

44. Thomas Amlie to Howard McMurray, October 10, 1947, *Thomas Amlie Papers*, Manuscripts Division, Wisconsin State Historical Society; Kenosha *Labor*, August 16, 1946.

45. Milton Mayer, "The People Lose," *The Progressive*, August 26, 1946, p. 5.

46. Aldric Revell, quoted in Madison *Capital–Times*, August 3, 1946; Eleanor LaFollette, "A Room of Our Own," *The Progressive*, August 26, 1946, p. 5; see also Young, *Adventure in Politics*, pp. 276–77.

47. U.S. Congress, *Congressional Record*, 1946, p. A 3441; Ronald Johnson, "The Communist Issue in Missouri," unpublished doctoral dissertation, University of Missouri, 1973, pp. 9–10; Milwaukee *Journal*, October 27, 1946; Superior *Evening Telegram*, November 3, 1946; the Hugh Butler quote is in Justis Paul, "The Political Career of Senator Hugh Butler," unpublished doctoral dissertation, University of Nebraska, 1966, p. 249; the Wherry quote is in H. A. Dahlstrom, "Kenneth S. Wherry," unpublished doctoral dissertation, University of Nebraska, 1965, p. 591.

48. See Anderson and May, *McCarthy*, pp. 111–15.

49. Green Bay *Press–Gazette*, September 6, 1946; Appleton *Post–Crescent*, September 6, 1946.

50. Milwaukee *Journal*, October 17, 1946.

51. Appleton *Post–Crescent*, October 25, 1946; Janesville *Daily Gazette*, October 30, 1946; Eau Claire *Leader*, October 17, 1946; Miles McMillin, quoted in the Madison *Capital–Times*, October 27, 1946.

52. Green Bay *Press–Gazette*, November 2, 1946; Waukesha *Daily Freeman*, November 4, 1946; Oshkosh *Daily Northwestern*, October 29, 1946; Appleton *Post–Crescent*, November 2, 1946.

53. Glen Roberts, quoted in Haney, "A History of the Democratic Party in Wisconsin Since World War II," p. 25.

54. Stevens Point *Daily Journal*, November 1, 1946.

Chapter Four: The Pepsi-Cola Kid (*pp. 53–71*)

1. "T.R.B.," in *The New Republic*, November 11, 1946, p. 615; William Manchester, *The Glory and the Dream*, 1973, p. 415.

2. See for example "The G.O.P. Mantle of Power," *Newsweek*, November 18, 1946, pp. 35–40; "The Election," *Time*, November 18, 1946, pp. 21–28.

3. Quoted in Jack Anderson and Ronald May, *McCarthy*, 1952, p. 115.

4. Jack Alexander, "The Senate's Remarkable Upstart," *The Saturday Evening Post*, August 9, 1947; *U.S. News*, November 15, 1946, p. 72; Anderson and May, *McCarthy*, p. 122.

5. Washington *Post*, November 24, 1946; January 19, 1947.

6. Interview with Urban Van Susteren, October 22, 1977.

7. Madison *Capital–Times*, October 18, 1951; Alexander, "The Senate's Remarkable Upstart," p. 16; Roy Cohn, *McCarthy*, 1968, p. 270; Tom Korb interview, in Anderson and May, "Rough Notes," in *Files of the National Committee for an Effective Congress*, Washington, D.C. (hereafter called *NCEC Files*).

8. Senator Prescott Bush interview, *Columbia Oral History Project*, Clinton Anderson, *Outsider in the Senate*, 1970, p. 101.

9. Anderson, *Outsider in the Senate*, pp. 101–2.

10. John Hanes interview, *Dulles Oral History Project*, Princeton, N.J.

11. *Ibid.*

12. Ronald May, in Anderson and May, "Rough Notes," *NCEC Files*.

13. Richard Rovere, *Senator Joe McCarthy*, 1959, p. 52; Bob Byers, "How I Know Mr. McCarthy" (n.d.), p. 4, Manuscripts Division, Wisconsin State Historical Society.

14. Quoted in Jim Watts, "Dress Rehearsal for Wheeling: Joseph R. McCarthy in the Senate, 1947–1949," unpublished paper in the author's possession, p. 19.

15. Interview with Ruth Watt, May 24, 1977.

16. Donald Crosby, *God, Church, and Flag*, 1978, p. 35.

17. Interview with Jack Anderson, September 9, 1977.

18. Interview with Ruth Watt; interview with Willard Edwards, April 30, 1978.

19. "Requests to See the President," December 3, 1946, Office File 337, *Harry S. Truman Papers*, Truman Library, Independence, Mo.

20. Washington *Post*, December 4, 1946; New York *Times*, December 6, 1946.

21. Manchester, *The Glory and the Dream*, p. 405; Anderson and May, *McCarthy*, p. 124.

22. U.S. Senate, 80th Cong., 1st sess., Committee on Expenditures in the Executive Departments, *Hearings on Senate Document #7: Aqueduct Near San Diego, California*, 1947, pp. 62–69, 112–13, 160–63, 168–69, 174–77.

23. U.S. Senate, 80th Cong., 1st sess., Committee on Expenditures in the Executive Departments, *Investigation of Expenditures in the Bureau of Customs*, 1947, pp. 83–84; U.S. Senate, 80th Cong., 1st sess., Committee on Expenditures in the Executive Departments, *Hearings on a Resolution Authorizing an Investigation of Surplus Property and Its Disposal, Basic Magnesium Plant, Henderson, Nevada*, 1947, pp. 12–29.

24. "Town Meeting: Bulletin of America's Town Meeting of the Air," April 3, 1947. Transcript on File at Widener Library, Cambridge, Mass.

25. See Drew Pearson, "Washington Merry Go Round," Washington *Post*, March 28, 1947; Anderson and May, *McCarthy*, pp. 128–37; U.S. Congress,

Senate, *Investigation of Senators Joseph R. McCarthy and William Benton*, 1952, pp. 38–39.

26. "Form Letter, Senator Joseph McCarthy to My Dear Senator," March 17, 1947, *Senator James Kem Papers*, Western Historical Manuscripts Collection, Columbia, Mo.

27. The entire sugar debate is in the *Congressional Record*, 80th Cong., 1st sess., 1947, pp. 2698–2707.

28. Robert Griffith, *The Politics of Fear*, 1970, p. 13.

29. Manchester, *The Glory and the Dream*, pp. 430–32; Richard Davies, *Housing Reform During the Truman Administration*, 1966, p. 43.

30. Davies, *Housing Reform During the Truman Administration*, pp. 40–49.

31. *Ibid.*, pp. 10–28.

32. See Drew Pearson, "Washington Merry Go Round," Washington *Post*, August 10, 1947.

33. *Ibid.*, Senator Joe McCarthy to Senator Charles Tobey, August 16, 1947, *Senator Charles Tobey Papers*, Dartmouth College Library, Hanover, N.H.

34. Washington *Post*, August 20, September 7, 1947; Anderson and May, *McCarthy*, p. 142.

35. Washington *Post*, August 20, 1947; Senator Joe McCarthy to Senator Charles Tobey, September 2, 1947, *Senator Charles Tobey Papers*, Dartmouth College Library, Hanover, N.H.

36. Elizabeth Hutson to Senator Charles Tobey, October 29, 1947, *Senator Charles Tobey Papers*, Dartmouth College Library, Hanover, N.H.

37. Anderson and May, *McCarthy*, pp. 145–46.

38. Byers, "How I Know Mr. McCarthy," p. 7.

39. Anderson and May, *McCarthy*, p. 150; Davies, *Housing Reform During the Truman Administration*, pp. 68–72.

40. New York *Times*, August 11, 1948.

41. Milwaukee *Journal*, March 1, 1949.

42. Anderson and May, "Rough Notes," Lustron File, *NCEC Files*.

43. *Investigation of Senators Joseph R. McCarthy and William Benton*, pp. 15–19.

44. *Ibid.*

Chapter Five: Rock Bottom (*pp. 72–84*)

1. *Milwaukee Journal*, November 6, 1946.

2. Drew Pearson column in the Washington *Post*, August 1, 1947; New York *Post*, September 4, 1951.

3. Senator Joe McCarthy to Senator Hugh Butler, January 7, 1949; Senator Joe McCarthy to Senator Robert Taft, January 7, 1949; both in Box 502, *Senator Robert A. Taft Papers*, Manuscripts Division, Library of Congress, Washington, D.C.

4. See David Oshinsky, *Senator Joseph McCarthy and the American Labor Movement*, 1976, pp. 82–86.

5. See U.S. Senate, Subcommittee of the Committee on Armed Services, *Malmedy Massacre Investigation*, 1949; Jack Anderson and Ronald May, *McCarthy*, 1952, pp. 158–59; Robert Griffith, *The Politics of Fear*, 1970, pp. 20–21.

6. See Michael Rogin, *The Intellectuals and McCarthy*, 1967, pp. 72–79; Anderson and May, *McCarthy*, pp. 163–64; Raymond Baldwin interview, *Columbia Oral History Project*, Columbia University Library, New York, N.Y.

7. Fred Cook, *The Nightmare Decade*, 1971, pp. 132–33; Miles McMillin to Abe Fortas, April 3, 1950, *William Evjue Papers*, Manuscripts Division, Wisconsin State Historical Society, Madison, Wis.; also, Milwaukee *Journal*, November 15, 1946, June 17, 1947, October 18, 1948, May 4, 1949.

8. Anderson and May, *McCarthy*, pp. 164, 255, 258; U.S. Congress, Senate, *Investigation of Senators Joseph R. McCarthy and William Benton*, 1952, pp. 248–52.

9. McCarthy to Taft, January 7, 1949, Box 502, *Taft Papers*.

10. Griffith, *The Politics of Fear*, pp. 23–24; for attendance figures, see *Malmedy Massacre Investigation*, pp. 1, 33, 71, 153, 223, 265, 321, 373, 441, 473, 555, 609, 655, 695, 731.

11. *Malmedy Massacre Investigation*, p. 102.

12. *Ibid.*, pp. 179, 239–40.

13. *Ibid.*, pp. 44, 214, 244, 263, 267, 269, 488, 631, 713. See Ernst von Weizsacker, *Memoirs*, 1951. William Shirer accurately described von Weizsacker as "the brains of the Foreign Office, a man who after the war made a great fuss of his alleged anti-Nazism but who served Hitler and Ribbentrop well almost to the end." Shirer, *The Rise and Fall of the Third Reich*, 1959, p. 381.

14. *Ibid.*, pp. 23, 27, 200, 224, 245.

15. *Ibid.*, pp. 247, 787–88.

16. *Ibid.*, pp. 630–39.

17. *Ibid.*, pp. 837–44.

18. Richard Rovere, *Senator Joe McCarthy*, 1959, pp. 112–17.

19. *Congressional Record*, 81st Cong., 1st sess., 1949, pp. 10160–75; Millard Tydings et al. to Senator Raymond Baldwin, August 16, 1949, "Malmedy File," *Files of the National Committee For an Effective Congress*, Washington, D.C.

20. "Robert Fleming Memo," November 1, 1951, Box 4, *Robert Fleming Papers*, Manuscripts Division, Wisconsin State Historical Society.

21. Madison *Capital–Times*, May 25, 1949.

22. *Ibid.*, October 1, 1949.

23. Senator Joe McCarthy to Roy Matson, December 3, 1948; Senator Joe McCarthy to V. I. Minahan, December 2, 1948; both in the unprocessed *Files of the Wisconsin State Journal*, Manuscripts Division, Wisconsin State

Historical Society; Senator Joe McCarthy to Karl Meyer, December 6, 1949, *William Evjue Papers*, Manuscripts Division, Wisconsin State Historical Society.

24. *Congressional Record*, 81st Cong., 1st sess., 1949, pp. 12877–79, 14507–8; the Magnuson exchange is in *ibid.*, 1947, pp. 4880–83.

25. "Town Meeting, Bulletin of America's Town Meeting of the Air," April 3, 1947, transcript on file at Widener Library, Cambridge, Mass.

26. For Taft's views, see James Patterson, *Mr. Republican*, 1972, pp. 383–87; McCarthy's views on NATO are expressed in a form letter he sent to constituents, March 22, 1949, in the unprocessed *Files of the Wisconsin State Journal*, Manuscripts Division, Wisconsin State Historical Society.

27. "Press Release from Senator Joe McCarthy, November 11, 1949," *William Evjue Papers*, Manuscripts Division, Wisconsin State Historical Society. I am indebted to Michael O'Brien for bringing the Parker episode to my attention.

28. See Michael O'Brien, "McCarthy and McCarthyism," in Robert Griffith and Athan Theoharis (eds.), *The Specter*, 1974, pp. 224–38.

Chapter Six: The Red Bogey in America, 1917–1950 (*pp. 85–102*)

1. Peter Filene, *Americans and the Soviet Experiment*, 1919–1933, 1961, p. 10.

2. *Ibid.*, p. 13.

3. *Ibid.*, p. 47; also Walter Lippmann and Charles Merz, "A Test of the News: An Examination of the News Reports in the New York *Times* on Aspects of the Russian Revolution of Special Importance to Americans," *The New Republic*, August 4, 1920, pp. 10–11.

4. Quoted in Leslie Adler, "The Red Image: American Attitudes Toward Communism in the Cold War," unpublished doctoral dissertation, University of California, Berkeley, 1970, p. 24.

5. Filene, *Americans and the Soviet Experiment*, p. 25; John Higham, *Strangers in the Land*, 1955, pp. 227–28; Rodney Minott, *Peerless Patriots: Organized Veterans and the Spirit of Americanism*, 1962, pp. 29–46.

6. Zechariah Chaffee, *Free Speech in the United States*, 1941, p. 241; Karl Schriftgiesser, *This Was Normalcy*, 1948, p. 61. A more realistic account of Palmer's motives appears in Stanley Coben, *A. Mitchell Palmer, Politician*, 1963, pp. 196–245.

7. *Congressional Record*, 57 (1919), 6865, 6869, 7063.

8. Coben, *A. Mitchell Palmer*, p. 196; Robert Murray, *Red Scare*, 1955, p. 194.

9. Murray, *Red Scare*, p. 213; Langtry's quote is in Paul Murphy, *The Meaning of Freedom of Speech*, 1972, p. 34.

10. Murray, *Red Scare*, p. 263; Colby is quoted in George Kennan, *Russia and the West Under Lenin and Stalin*, 1962, p. 197; see also Adler, "The Red Image," pp. 48–50.

11. William Preston, *Aliens and Dissenters*, 1966, pp. 240–46.

12. American Civil Liberties Union, *The Nation-Wide Spy System in the Department of Justice*, 1924, p. 6; American Civil Liberties Union, *The Police and the Radicals: What 88 Police Chiefs Think and Do About Radical Meetings*, 1924, p. 5.

13. Murphy, *The Meaning of Free Speech*, pp. 38–40, 198; American Civil Liberties Union, *The Gag on Teaching*, 1931, pp. 2–8; Adler, "The Red Image," p. 28; Ray Ginger, *Six Days or Forever*, 1958, p. 19.

14. Irving Howe and Lewis Coser, *The American Communist Party: A Critical History*, 1957, p. 341.

15. Quoted in *The Nation*, May 27, 1939, p. 603.

16. Earl Latham, *The Communist Controversy in Washington*, 1966, pp. 149–50.

17. See Richard Burkhardt, "The Teaching of the Soviet Union in American School Social Studies," unpublished doctoral dissertation, Harvard University, 1952, pp. 179–82.

18. Warren Walsh, "What the American People Think of Russia," *Public Opinion Quarterly*, Winter 1944, pp. 513–15.

19. Martin Dies, *The Trojan Horse in America*, 1940, p. 269; August Ogden, *The Dies Committee*, 1945, p. 48; Walter Goodman, *The Committee*, 1964, pp. 35–36.

20. Ogden, *The Dies Committee*, p. 60; New York *Times*, August 21, 22, 23, 1938.

21. Congressman Noah Mason, quoted in Goodman, *The Committee*, p. 73; Thomas Emerson and David Heldfeld, "Loyalty Among Government Employees," *Yale Law Journal*, December 1948, p. 14.

22. Robert Griffith, *The Politics of Fear*, 1970, p. 32.

23. Stewart Britt and Sheldon Menefee, "Did the Publicity of the Dies Committee in 1938 Influence Public Opinion?" *Public Opinion Quarterly*, July 1939, p. 457; New York *Times*, January 8, 1939; Goodman, *The Committee*, p. 55.

24. Eleanor Bontecou, *The Federal Loyalty-Security Program*, 1954, pp. 210–11; Harold Chase, *Security and Liberty: The Problem of Native Communists*, 1955, pp. 7–14; The Smith Act debate can be found in Robert Goldstein, *Political Repression in Modern America*, 1978, pp. 244–46.

25. "Stalin Spreads the War," *The New Republic*, December 13, 1939, p. 219.

26. Quoted in Richard Polenberg, *War and Society*, 1972, p. 40.

27. *Catholic World*, May 1942, p. 130, and September 1946, pp. 540–42; also Donald Crosby, *God, Church, and Flag*, 1978, pp. 8–9.

28. See Peter Filene (ed.), *American Views of Soviet Russia*, 1968, p. 162.

29. See Adler, "The Red Image," p. 59.

30. Latham, *The Communist Controversy in Washington*, pp. 203–16; R. Harris Smith, *OSS: The Secret History of America's First Central Intelligence Agency*, 1972, p. 277.

31. William Tanner and Robert Griffith, "Legislative Politics and McCarthyism," in Robert Griffith and Athan Theoharis (eds.), *The Specter*, 1974, pp. 178–79.

32. *Ibid.*

33. Richard Fired, *Men Against McCarthy*, 1976, pp. 23–24.

34. David Caute, *The Great Fear*, 1978, pp. 491–93.

35. On the Hiss case see Allen Weinstein, *Perjury: The Hiss–Chambers Case*, 1978; John C. Smith, *Alger Hiss: The True Story*, 1976. Weinstein believes that Hiss was guilty as charged; Smith takes the opposite position.

36. Weinstein, *Perjury*, p. 426.

37. Mrs. Roosevelt's quote is in Alonso Hamby, *Beyond the New Deal*, 1973, p. 384.

38. Eric Goldman, *The Crucial Decade—and After*, 1960, p. 113.

39. William Manchester, *The Glory and the Dream*, 1973, p. 488.

40. See Warren Cohen, *America's Response to China*, 1971, pp. 164–216.

41. Manchester, *The Glory and the Dream*, p. 488.

42. *Congressional Record* (83), 1949, p. 4372.

CHAPTER SEVEN: WHEELING (*pp. 103–14*)

1. Dean Acheson, *Present at the Creation*, 1969, pp. 355–58; Alonzo Hamby, *Beyond the New Deal*, 1973, pp. 368–70.

2. Washington *Post*, January 3, 5, 10, 12, 1950.

3. *Ibid.*, January 13, 30, February 8, 1950.

4. *Ibid.*, January 26, 1950; Acheson, *Present at the Creation*, p. 360.

5. Chicago *Tribune*, January 27, 1950; New York *Journal–American*, January 27, 1950; Baltimore *Sun*, January 26, 1950; Washington *Evening Star*, January 26, 1950. See also Manchester *Morning Union*, January 27, 1950; Los Angeles *Times*, January 27, 1950.

6. For anti-Acheson feelings in Congress, see Eric Goldman, *The Crucial Decade And After*, 1956, p. 125; William S. White's column in the New York *Times*, April 16, 1950; also Chicago *Tribune*, February 19, 1950. The Acheson–Maverick meeting is described in the *Drew Pearson Diaries*, 1974, p. 120.

7. See Cabell Phillips, *The Truman Presidency*, 1966, p. 20; Hamby, *Beyond the New Deal*, p. 394; "Act of Humiliation," *Time*, March 13, 1950, p. 17; Hugh Butler to Gilbert Brown, March 3, 1950, *Senator Hugh Butler Papers*, Nebraska State Historical Society.

8. *Congressional Record*, 81st Cong., 2nd sess., January 26, 1950, pp. 1002–8.

9. Walter Schneir and Miriam Schneir, *Invitation to an Inquest*, 1965, p. 57; Washington *Post*, February 1, 1950.

10. Schneir and Schneir, *Invitation to an Inquest*, pp. 59–69.

11. See Richard Fried, "Men Against McCarthy: Democratic Opposition to Senator Joseph R. McCarthy," unpublished doctoral dissertation, Columbia University, 1972, p. 66; Manchester *Morning Union*, February 14, 1950.

12. See especially Washington *Post*, February 7, 8, 9, 1950.

13. See for example Jack Anderson and Ronald May, *McCarthy*, 1952, pp. 172–73; Richard Rovere, *Senator Joe McCarthy*, 1959, pp. 122–23; Goldman, *The Crucial Decade*, pp. 137–45; Lately Thomas, *When Even Angels Wept*, 1973, pp. 85–86; Fred Cook, *The Nightmare Decade*, 1971, pp. 139–41.

14. Anderson and May, *McCarthy*, p. 173.

15. See, for example, Donald Crosby, *God, Church, and Flag*, 1978, pp. 47–52.

16. Washington *Post*, January 22, 27, February 7, 1950.

17. Willard Edwards, "Notes on McCarthy," unpublished manuscript in author's possession; interview with Willard Edwards, April 30, 1978.

18. Joseph McCarthy to Bradley Taylor, February 7, 1950, *Bradley Taylor Papers*, Wisconsin State Historical Society; Wheeling *News–Register*, February 8, 1950; Wheeling *Intelligencer*, January 31, 1950.

19. *Congressional Record*, 81st Cong., 2d sess., January 26, 1950, pp. 1002–8. A copy of the rough notes of McCarthy's speech can be found in the McCarthy File, *Theodore Green Papers*, Manuscripts Division, Library of Congress.

20. For a detailed account of McCarthy's early numbers game, see Alfred Friendly, "The Noble Crusade of Senator McCarthy," *Harper's*, August 1950, pp. 34–42.

21. Edwards, "Notes on McCarthy," *op. cit.*

22. *Ibid.*

23. Chicago *Tribune*, February 10, 1950; Denver *Post*, February 10, 11, 1950; St. Louis *Post–Dispatch*, February 10, 1950.

24. Salt Lake *Tribune*, February 11, 1950; *Deseret News*, February 11, 1950.

25. For a copy of the Lee List, see U.S. Congress, Senate, 81st Cong., 2d sess., Committee on Foreign Relations, *State Department Loyalty Investigation* (Tydings Subcommittee Hearings), 1950, pp. 1771–1813.

26. Joseph McCarthy to President Harry S. Truman, February 11, 1950, Official File 337, *Harry S. Truman Papers*, Truman Presidential Library, Independence, Mo.

27. Nevada *State Journal*, February 12, 1950; Thomas Miller to Bradley Taylor, February 17, 1950, *Bradley Taylor Papers*, Wisconsin State Historical Society.

28. George Elsey personal memorandum, February 14, 1950, *George Elsey Papers*, Truman Presidential Library.

29. Harry S. Truman to Joseph R. McCarthy (unsent), February 11[?], 1950, in Robert Ferrell, *Off the Record: The Private Papers of Harry S. Truman*, 1980, p. 172; also, Stephen Spingarn, "Memorandum for Mr. Murphy," February 15, 1950, *Stephen Spingarn Papers*, Truman Presidential Library.

30. *Congressional Record*, 81st Cong., 2d sess., February 20, 1950, pp. 1953–80.

31. *Ibid.*

CHAPTER EIGHT: BATTLE OF THE BILLYGOATS (*pp. 115–29*)

1. For Democratic attempts to neutralize McCarthy's charges, see Richard Fried, *Men Against McCarthy*, 1976, pp. 55–62.

2. *Congressional Record*, 81st Cong., 2d sess., February 22, 1950, pp. 2140–41; Robert Griffith, *The Politics of Fear*, 1970, pp. 58–60.

3. For McMahon's concern, see U.S. Congress, Senate, 81st Cong., 2d sess., Committee on Foreign Relations, *State Department Loyalty Investigation* (hereafter Tydings Subcommittee Hearings), Washington, D.C., G.P.O., 1950, p. 255.

4. New York *Times*, February 22, 1950; Washington *Post*, February 22, 23, 1950; Fried, *Men Against McCarthy*, p. 54.

5. William Leuchtenburg, *Franklin D. Roosevelt and the New Deal*, 1963, pp. 252–69; Griffith, *The Politics of Fear*, p. 65; "The Senate's Most Valuable Ten," *Time*, April 3, 1950, p. 20; Willard Edwards, "Memorandum" (n.d.), *Willard Edwards Papers*, copy in the author's possession.

6. Erwin Levine, *Theodore Francis Green: The Washington Years*, 1971, pp. 124–37; Lately Thomas, *When Even Angels Wept*, 1973, p. 358.

7. William S. White, "McMahon: Senator and Atomic Specialist," *New York Times Magazine*, February 12, 1950, p. 19; "Still Up in the Air," *Newsweek*, October 23, 1950, p. 34; Griffith, *The Politics of Fear*, p. 65.

8. Henry Cabot Lodge, Jr., "Modernize the G.O.P.," *The Atlantic Monthly*, March, 1950, pp. 23–28; "Lodge Defines the Minority Role," *New York Times Magazine*, September 17, 1950, p. 22.

9. "Charges Answered," *Newsweek*, June 13, 1949, pp. 20–21; "In the Floodlight," *Time*, June 6, 1949, pp. 17–18; Griffith, *The Politics of Fear*, p. 66.

10. "Recollections of Edward Morgan" (n.d.), Box 2, *Robert Fleming Papers*, Manuscripts Division, Wisconsin State Historical Society.

11. Interview with Jack Anderson, September 9, 1977; Howard Judd's warning to McCarthy is in the Minneapolis *Tribune*, April 19, 1950; for Nixon's admonition, see Earl Mazo and Stephen Hess, *Nixon*, 1968, p. 128; Griffith, *The Politics of Fear*, pp. 60–65.

12. Joseph Keeley, *The China Lobby Man*, 1969; Oliver Pilat, *Pegler: Angry Man of the Press*, 1963, pp. 219–44; Herbert Packer, *Ex-Communist Witnesses*, 1962, pp. 121–77; Jack Anderson and Ronald May, *McCarthy*, 1952, pp. 287–94; interview with Willard Edwards, April 30, 1978; interview with Robert Morris, April 29, 1978.

13. Interview with Robert Morris.

14. Walter Goodman, *The Committee*, 1964, p. 42.

15. John Thomas, *The Institute of Pacific Relations*, 1974, pp. 36–44.

16. Keeley, *The China Lobby Man*; Warren Cohen, "Who's Afraid of Alfred Kohlberg?" *Reviews in American History*, March, 1975, pp. 118–23.

17. *Oral Interview with Donald Hanson*, p. 31, Harry S. Truman Presidential Library, Independence, Mo.

18. Quoted in Keeley, *The China Lobby Man*, p. 3.

19. Tydings Subcommittee Hearings, pp. 4–8.

20. McCarthy's case against Kenyon is found in *ibid.*, pp. 16–32, 67–72.

21. Kenyon's rebuttal is in *ibid.*, pp. 176–214; see also "Faces in the News," *Life*, March 27, 1950, p. 34; "McCarthy at the Barricades," *Time*, March 27, 1950; Washington *Post*, March 13, 1950.

22. Interview with Willard Edwards; *Congressional Record*, 81st Cong., 2d sess., March 30, 1950, p. 4380.

23. See James Reston in the New York *Times*, March 9, 1950.

24. Bill Davidson, "The Surprising Mr. Jessup," *Collier's*, July 30, 1949, p. 67; "Russian for 'Hello,' " *Time*, May 16, 1949, p. 21; Anderson and May, *McCarthy*, p. 226.

25. Thomas, *The Institute of Pacific Relations*, pp. 42–43; William F. Buckley and L. Brent Bozell, *McCarthy and His Enemies*, 1954, pp. 97–124.

26. *Congressional Record*, 81st Cong., 2d sess., January 25, 1950, p. 904, and January 24, 1950, p. 817.

27. See "McCarthy at the Barricades," *Time*, March 27, 1950, p. 21.

28. For Jessup's testimony, see Tydings Subcommittee Hearings, pp. 215–75.

29. Buckley and Bozell, *McCarthy and His Enemies*, p. 99.

30. Griffith, *The Politics of Fear*, pp. 70–71.

31. For McCarthy's case against Brunnauer, see Tydings Subcommittee Hearings, pp. 84–91.

32. Goodman, *The Committee*, p. 187; Buckley and Bozell, *McCarthy and His Enemies*, p. 137; McCarthy's case against Shapley is found in the Tydings Subcommittee Hearings, pp. 126–27; against Schuman, pp. 142–43.

33. The best discussion of the Duran case is found in David Caute, *The Great Fear*, 1978, pp. 331–38.

34. Griffith, *The Politics of Fear*, p. 71.

35. McCarthy's case against Duran is found in Tydings Subcommittee Hearings, pp. 110–25.

36. Caute, *The Great Fear*, p. 338.

37. McCarthy's case against Hanson is found in Tydings Subcommittee Hearings, pp. 73–83.

38. Hanson's rebuttal is found in *ibid.*, pp. 347–71.

39. See Fred Cook, *The Nightmare Decade*, 1971, p. 270; Buckley and Bozell, *McCarthy and His Enemies*, p. 96.

40. Joseph Esherick (ed.), *Lost Chance in China*, 1974, p. xvi.

41. *Ibid.*, p. xix; Earl Latham, *The Communist Controversy in Washington*, 1966, pp. 203–16.

42. McCarthy's case against Service is found in Tydings Subcommittee Hearings, pp. 130–40.

Chapter Nine: Stand or Fall (*pp. 130–38*)

1. Interview with Urban Van Susteren, October 22, 1977.

2. Washington *Post*, August 5, 1951; "Fundamentalist Republican," *Time*, December 10, 1951, pp. 27–28.

3. Sidney Hyman, *The Lives of William Benton*, 1969, p. 419.

4. William S. White, "Portrait of a 'Fundamentalist,'" *New York Times Magazine*, January 15, 1950; Paul Healy, "Big Noise from Nebraska," *The Saturday Evening Post*, August 5, 1950, pp. 22–23, 76.

5. Bricker's remark is quoted in Fred Cook, *The Nightmare Decade*, 1971, p. 75.

6. Howard Rushmore, "The Gentleman from Indiana," *American Mercury*, July, 1954, pp. 55–58; "The Senate's Most Expendable," *Time*, March 20, 1950, p. 18; James Patterson, *Mr. Republican*, 1972, p. 440.

7. Washington *Post*, August 11, 1951; New York *Times*, August 11, 1951; Howard Rushmore, "The Senator from Moscow (Idaho)," *American Mercury*, July, 1955, pp. 141–43; Richard Rovere, *Senator Joe McCarthy*, 1960, p. 57.

8. Quoted in Patterson, *Mr. Republican*, p. 475.

9. *Ibid.*, pp. 444–49; for Taft's vehemence on the China issue, see Senator Robert Taft to Bernard LeVander, August 11, 1950, *Senator Robert Taft Papers*, Box 822, Manuscripts Division, Library of Congress, Washington, D.C.

10. Robert Griffith, *The Politics of Fear*, 1970, p. 73; Richard Fried, *Men Against McCarthy*, 1976, p. 68; Senator Robert Taft to Senator Joe McCarthy, May 2, 1950, *Senator Robert Taft Papers*, Box 814, Library of Congress.

11. "Doris Fleeson Memo," March 25, 1951, in *Joseph Pulitzer Papers*, Box 15, Library of Congress.

12. Interview with Robert Morris, April 29, 1978. Morris sat in on some of the strategy sessions.

13. "Trap for McCarthy," *Newsweek*, April 3, 1950, p. 19.

14. Interview with Henry Cabot Lodge, July 14, 1978; Senator Charles Tobey to Byron Waterman, April 5, 1950; Senator Charles Tobey to Allan Butler, April 5, 1950, in *Senator Charles Tobey Papers*, Box 53, Manuscripts Division, Dartmouth College Library, Hanover, N.H.

15. *H. Alexander Smith Personal Diary*, March 12, 13, 21, 1950, Manuscripts Division, Princeton University Library, Princeton, N.J.

16. *Ibid.*, March 26, 27, 1950.

17. *Congressional Record*, 81st Cong., 2d sess., March 27, 1950, pp. 4098–4106.

18. *Ibid.*, p. 4102.

19. *H. Alexander Smith Diary*, March 29, 30, 1950.

20. New York *Times*, March 24, 1959; Washington *Post*, March 23, 24, 1950.

21. Doris Fleeson is quoted in "Trap for McCarthy," *Newsweek*, April 3, 1950, p. 20; Anderson and May, *McCarthy*, 1952, p. 177; Tyler Abell (ed.), *Drew Pearson Diaries*, 1949–1959, p. 116.

22. Griffith, *The Politics of Fear*, p. 76; Earl Latham, *The Communist Controversy in Washington*, 1966, pp. 277–80; *Tydings Committee Report*, p. 72.

23. Sidney Hook, "Lattimore on the Moscow Trials," *The New Leader*, November 10, 1952, pp. 17–19; John Thomas, *The Institute of Pacific Relations*, 1974, pp. 20–21; Herbert Packer, *Ex-Communist Witnesses*, 1962, pp. 173–74.

24. Max Ascoli, Philip Horton, and Charles Wertenbaker, "The China Lobby," *Reporter*, April 15, 1952, pp. 2–24; *Congressional Record*, 81st Cong., 2d sess., March 2, 1950, p. 2642; *The Atlantic Monthly* carried Lattimore's controversial article (January 1950), "Rebuilding Our Policy in Asia."

25. Richard Rovere, *Senator Joe McCarthy*, 1959, p. 151; Joseph Keeley, *The China Lobby Man*, 1969, pp. 2–5.

26. Anderson and May, *McCarthy*, p. 197; Sam Shaffer, *On and Off the Floor*, 1980, pp. 26–27.

CHAPTER TEN: THE LATTIMORE CONNECTION (*pp. 139–57*)

1. K. L. Peterson to Senator James Kem, February 28, 1950, *Senator James Kem Papers*, Western Historical Manuscripts Collection, Columbia, Mo.

2. Washington *Post*, May 18, 26, 31, 1950; Cedric Belfrage, *The American Inquisition*, 1973, p. 122.

3. Milwaukee *Journal*, May 2, 1950.

4. David Caute, *The Great Fear*, 1978, p. 22; William Prendergast, "State Legislatures and Communism: The Current Scene," *American Political Science Review*, September 1950, p. 559; Walter Gellhorn, "A General View," in Gellhorn (ed.), *The States and Subversion*, 1952, p. 361.

5. Robert Cushman, "American Civil Liberties in Mid-Twentieth Century," *The Annals of the American Academy of Political and Social Science*, May 1951, pp. 4–5.

6. Chicago *Tribune*, June 2, 1950; Richard Fried, *Men Against McCarthy*, 1976, pp. 98–100.

7. Fried, *Men Against McCarthy*, pp. 96–97.

8. U.S. Senate, 81st Cong., 1st sess., Investigations Subcommittee of the Committee on Expenditures in the Executive Departments, *Hearings Pursuant to S. Res. 52, Influence in Government Procurement*, Washington, D.C., GPO, 1949, pp. 182–83.

9. *Ibid.*

10. Truman's letter is quoted in Fried, *Men Against McCarthy*, p. 155.

11. President Harry S. Truman to Senator Styles Bridges, March 26, 1950, *Harry S. Truman Papers*, Truman Presidential Library, Independence, Mo.

12. *Public Papers of the Presidents, Harry S. Truman*, 1950, pp. 234–36, 252, 258; New York *Times*, April 1, 1950.

13. New York *Times*, April 14, 15, 16, 1950.

14. McCarthy's speech is in the *Congressional Record*, 81st Cong., 2d sess., March 30, 1950, pp. 4375–93.

15. .See Lately Thomas, *When Even Angels Wept*, 1973, p. 140.

16. "McCarthy and the Past," *Life*, April 10, 1950, p. 32; "A Fool or a Knave," *Time*, April 17, 1950, p. 22.

17. See Robert Griffith, *The Politics of Fear*, 1970, p. 97.

18. Quoted in Fred Cook, *The Nightmare Decade*, 1971, p. 225.

19. New York *Times*, April 6, 7, 1950; "A Fool or a Knave," *Time*, April 17, 1950, p. 21.

20. Tydings Subcommittee Hearings, pp. 417–84; Cook, *The Nightmare Decade*, p. 236.

21. See Herbert Packer, *Ex-Communist Witnesses*, 1962, pp. 121–24; Louis Budenz, *This Is My Story*, 1947, pp. 162–63.

22. Packer, *Ex-Communist Witnesses*, p. 124; On March 20, 1956, Budenz wrote to McCarthy, "My checks can be continued to be sent to 26 Marshall Avenue . . . as they have been up to the present—until we get a permanent address." See Louis Budenz to Senator Joe McCarthy, March 20, 1956, *Louis Budenz Papers*, Providence College Library, Providence, R.I.

23. Bernard DeVoto, "The Ex-Communists," *The Atlantic Monthly*, February, 1951, p. 61; see also Hannah Arendt, "The Ex-Communists," *Commonweal*, March 20, 1953, pp. 595–99.

24. The Kersten incident is taken from Donald Crosby, "The Angry Catholics: Catholic Opinion of Senator Joseph R. McCarthy, 1950–57," unpublished doctoral dissertation, Brandeis University, 1973, p. 165.

25. "Of Cells and Onionskins," *Time*, May 1, 1950, p. 17; "Again, Who's Lying?" *Newsweek*, May 1, 1950, pp. 19–20. Interview with Robert Morris, April 19, 1978; interview with Urban Van Susteren, October 22, 1977.

26. Budenz's testimony is in Tydings Subcommittee Hearings, pp. 487–630.

27. Interview with Robert Morris.

28. New York *Times*, April 21, 22, 23, 1950.

29. Griffith, *The Politics of Fear*, p. 82.

30. Utley's quote on the Chinese Communists can be found in Freda Utley, *Odyssey of a Liberal*, 1970, p. 212; her feelings about Lattimore can be found in *ibid.*, pp. 125, 133, 213–14; her testimony is in Tydings Subcommittee Hearings, pp. 737–96.

31. Bella Dodd's testimony is in Tydings Subcommittee Hearings, pp. 631–59; Browder's is in *ibid.*, pp. 669–707.

32. On Huber, see Jack Anderson and Ronald May, *McCarthy*, 1952, p. 215; Griffith, *The Politics of Fear*, pp. 85–86; Packer, *Ex-Communist Witnesses*, pp. 147–52.

33. Robert Morris, *No Wonder We Are Losing*, 1958, p. 106; Sanford Unger, *FBI*, 1975, p. 42; Caute, *The Great Fear*, pp. 246–47.

34. Griffith, *The Politics of Fear*, pp. 96–97.

35. *Ibid.*; Bielaski's testimony is in Tydings Subcommittee Hearings, pp. 923–67.

36. The McCarthy quote to Wayne Morse is in Robert Fleming, "Memo—McCarthy Gossip" (n.d.), *Robert Fleming Papers*, Box 2, Manuscripts Division, Wisconsin State Historical Society.

37. See Fried, *Men Against McCarthy*, pp. 75–76.

38. "War Against McCarthy," *Newsweek*, May 15, 1950, pp. 24–26; Washington *Post*, May 10, 17, 1950.

39. *Congressional Record*, 81st Cong., 2d sess., May 9, 1950, pp. 6969–75.

40. Washington *Post*, May 13, 1950; "Address to the Midwest Council of Young Republicans," in *Congressional Record*, 81st Cong., 2d sess., May 9, 1950, pp. A 3426–28; "Address to the Sons of the American Revolution," in *ibid.*, May 19, 1950, pp. A 3786–89.

CHAPTER ELEVEN: DECLARATION OF CONSCIENCE (*pp. 158–78*)

1. The Gallup Poll is in the Washington *Post*, May 21, 1950; the Minnesota Poll is in the Minneapolis *Tribune*, April 30, 1950; the Gabrielson quote is in the Washington *Star*, June 23, 1950; see also the Thomas Stokes column in the Washington *Star*, June 26, 1950.

2. The incident with the cabbie is found in the Washington *Post*, June 25, 1950.

3. Interview with Urban Van Susteren, October 22, 1977.

4. Jess Barnett to Senator James Kem, June 22, 1950, *Senator James Kem Papers*, Western Historical Manuscripts Collection, Columbia, Mo.; Basil Brewer to Margaret Chase Smith, June 7, 1950, copy in the *Senator Robert Taft Papers*, Box 626, Manuscripts Division, Library of Congress. The unpublished song "Fall in Line with Joe McCarthy" was brought to my attention by Richard Tedlow of Brandeis University.

5. Jack Anderson and Ronald May, *McCarthy*, 1952, p. 262; interview with Willard Edwards; "Memorandum: IRS—Senator Joe McCarthy," February 17, 1954, *Thomas Coleman Papers*, Wisconsin State Historical Society; Subcommittee on Privileges and Elections to the Committee on Rules and Administration, *Investigation of Senators Joseph R. McCarthy and William Benton*, 1952, p. 35.

6. Washington *Post*, May 14, June 28, 1950; "Robert Fleming Memo—McCarthy Staff," Box 2, *Robert Fleming Papers*, Manuscripts Division, Wisconsin State Historical Society.

7. "McCarthy: Hero at Home," New York *Times*, June 9, 1950.

8. Thomas Coleman, "Report to the Strategy Committee of the Republican Party of Wisconsin, April 20, 1950," *Coleman Papers*; Coleman's quote is in Michael O'Brien, *McCarthy and McCarthyism in Wisconsin*, 1980, p. 102.

9. Zeidler is quoted in "Hoping Against Hope," *Time*, April 10, 1950, p. 19.

10. Robert Fleming, "Memo—McCarthy Tipsters," Box 2, *Robert Fleming Papers*.

11. Interview with Senator Milton Young, May 26, 1977; interview with Margaret Chase Smith, May 27, 1977; "McCarthy Gossip," Robert Fleming Memo, *Robert Fleming Papers*.

12. Richard Fried, *Men Against McCarthy*, 1976, p. 185.

13. Senator Ralph Flanders to Paul Hoffman, October 15, 1951, Box 105, *Senator Ralph Flanders Papers*, Manuscripts Division, Syracuse University Library.

14. Interview with Senator Leverett Saltonstall, April 27, 1978.

15. Margaret Chase Smith, *Declaration of Conscience*, 1972, pp. 4–5.

16. Interview with Margaret Chase Smith.

17. Smith, *Declaration of Conscience*, pp. 11–12.

18. The full text of Smith's address is in *ibid.*, pp. 12–18; Washington *Post*, June 1, 2, 1950.

19. Interview with Margaret Chase Smith.

20. Chicago *Tribune*, June 7, 1950; Senator Charles Tobey to Edwin Nichols, June 28, 1950, Box 53, *Senator Charles Tobey Papers*, Manuscripts Division, Dartmouth College Library, Hanover, N.H.

21. See for example William Manchester, *The Glory and the Dream*, 1973, pp. 530–38; Dean Acheson, *Present at the Creation*, 1969, pp. 402–25.

22. "The Washington Front," *The Nation*, July 8, 1950, p. 25.

23. Cabell Phillips, *The Truman Presidency*, 1966, pp. 294–304; Manchester, *The Glory and the Dream*, pp. 530–38.

24. William S. White, "Mood of Washington: Morale Gets Big Lift," New York *Times*, July 2, 1950.

25. Quoted in "Tydings on a Tear," *Newsweek*, July 31, 1950, p. 25.

26. Tom Coleman to Senator Joe McCarthy, July 7, 1950, *Thomas Coleman Papers*.

27. Senator Joe McCarthy to Tom Coleman, July 15, 1950, in *ibid.*

28. Senator Robert Taft to Bernard LeVander, August 11, 1950, Box 822, *Senator Robert Taft Papers*; Senator Kenneth Wherry to James Austin, August 18, 1950, Box 11, *Senator Kenneth Wherry Papers*, Manuscripts Division, Nebraska State Historical Society.

29. "Tydings Investigation," Robert Fleming Memo (n.d.), *Robert Fleming Papers*.

30. *Ibid.*

31. Tydings Subcommittee Report, pp. 154, 159–63, 167.

32. *Ibid.*

33. Quoted in Richard Fried, *Men Against McCarthy*, p. 86.

34. "Tydings on a Tear," *Newsweek*, July 31, 1950, p. 26; "Washington Wire," *The New Republic*, July 31, 1950, pp. 3–4.

35. *Ibid.*

36. For the entire debate, see *Congressional Record*, July 20, 1950, pp. 10686–10717; also New York *Times*, July 21, 1950; Washington *Post*, July 21, 1950.

37. See "Tydings on a Tear."

38. "Tydings Investigation," Fleming memo.

39. Baltimore *Sun*, July 19, 1950; Harold Ickes, "McCarthy Strips Himself," *The New Republic*, August 7, 1950, p. 17.

40. New York *Journal-American*, July 19, 1950; Chicago *Tribune*, July 19, 1950.

41. See Cedric Belfrage, *The American Inquisition*, 1973, pp. 133–34.

42. Fried, *Men Against McCarthy*, pp. 103–4; Belfrage, *The American Inquisition*, p. 231; New York *Times*, September 17, 1950.

43. See for example Leo Pfeffer, *This Honorable Court*, 1965, p. 362; William Tanner and Robert Griffith, "Legislative Politics and McCarthyism: The Internal Security Act of 1950," in Robert Griffith and Athan Theoharis (eds.), *The Specter*, 1974, pp. 174–89.

44. See Truman, quoted in the Chicago *Tribune*, June 9, 1950; also, Harry S. Truman to George Earle, February 28, 1947, Office File 263, *Harry S. Truman Papers*, Truman Presidential Library, Independence, Mo.

45. Tanner and Griffith, "Legislative Politics and McCarthyism," pp. 186–88; the Benton quote is in Robert Griffith, *The Politics of Fear*, 1970, p. 121.

46. See Phillips, *The Truman Presidency*, pp. 402–8.

47. The "mucking" quote is in "Washington," *The Atlantic Monthly*, July 1950, p. 9.

48. The first quote is in James Reston's column in the New York *Times*, May 19, 1950; the second is in Ernest Havemann, "War and Politics," *Life*, August 28, 1950, pp. 102–3.

49. McCarthy's friend is quoted in Anderson and May, *McCarthy*, p. 296.

50. See Hearings Before the Subcommittee on Privileges and Elections of the Committee on Rules and Administration, *Maryland Election Report*, 1951, p. 16; Murchison's quote is in Fred Cook, *The Nightmare Decade*, 1971, p. 305.

51. See especially Fried, *Men Against McCarthy*, pp. 122–53.

52. *Ibid.*

53. *Ibid.* Tydings's own feelings about his defeat are summarized in a letter from John Howe to Ken Birkhead, July 21, 1953, in the *William Benton Papers*.

54. See Griffith, *The Politics of Fear*, pp. 125–26; "Loss of Appetite," *Time*, November 20, 1950, p. 22.

55. "The Senate," *Time*, November 13, 1950, pp. 19–20.

56. "The Nixon Story," campaign book in the *Francis Keesling Papers*, Box 27, Manuscripts Division, University of California, Berkeley.

57. *Ibid.*

58. Interview with Senator J. William Fulbright, May 27, 1977.

CHAPTER TWELVE: THE FOURTH ESTATE (*pp.* 179–90)

1. Oliver Pilat, *Drew Pearson*, 1973, p. 26.

2. Interview with Jack Anderson, September 9, 1977.

3. Mary Jane Ferguson, "McCarthy vs. Pearson," unpublished master's thesis, University of Wisconsin, 1969, p. 47; Pilat, *Drew Pearson*, p. 26; Tyler Abell (ed.), *Drew Pearson Diaries*, 1974, p. 128.

4. Ferguson, "McCarthy vs. Pearson," pp. 47–50; Lately Thomas, *When Even Angels Wept*, 1973, p. 216; Earl Mazo and Stephen Hess, *Nixon*, 1959, p. 129.

5. Washington *Post*, December 15, 16, 1950; Ferguson, "McCarthy vs. Pearson," pp. 47–50.

6. *Congressional Record*, 81st Cong., 2d sess., pp. 16634–35, 16641.

7. Robert Fleming Memo, "McCarthy–Pearson" (n.d.), Box 2, *Robert Fleming Papers*, Wisconsin State Historical Society; the Watkins quote is in Thomas, *When Even Angels Wept*, p. 216.

8. *Congressional Record*, 81st Cong., 2d sess., p. 16641.

9. *Ibid.*; also Jack Anderson and Ronald May, *McCarthy*, p. 276.

10. Fleming Memo, "McCarthy–Pearson."

11. Jean Deaver, "A Study of Senator Joseph R. McCarthy and 'McCarthyism' as Influences upon the News Media . . . ," unpublished doctoral dissertation, University of Texas, 1970, p. 164.

12. The Arrowsmith incident is in Robert Fleming Memo, "Freedom of the Press" (n.d.) Box 2, *Robert Fleming Papers*, Wisconsin State Historical Society; see also Deaver, "Study of Senator Joseph R. McCarthy," p. 192.

13. Interview with Phil Potter, February 27, 1978; Deaver, "Study of Senator Joseph R. McCarthy," p. 191.

14. See especially Ferguson, "McCarthy vs. Pearson," pp. 20–29; Deaver, "Study of Senator Joseph R. McCarthy," pp. 144–89; Robert Griffith, *The Politics of Fear*, 1970, pp. 139–42.

15. Ronald May, "Is the Press Unfair to McCarthy?" *The New Republic*, April 5, 1953, pp. 10–11.

16. The *Journal* quote comes from its editorial of September 15, 1950.

17. McCarthy's quote is in Robert Fleming Memo, "Information from McCarthy" (n.d.), Box 3, *Robert Fleming Papers*.

18. Syracuse *Post–Standard*, October 19, 1952; on Greenspun, see New York *Times*, April 10, 1954, and Washington *Post*, April 18, 1955; on Sheboygan *Press* incident, see Michael O'Brien, *McCarthy and McCarthyism in Wisconsin*, 1980, p. 191.

19. New York *Times*, January 29, 1952; W. A. Swanberg, *Luce and His Empire*, 1972, p. 302; "How Come McCarthyism?" *Life*, September 8, 1952.

20. See Richard Rovere, *Senator Joe McCarthy*, 1959, p. 163.

21. See Douglas Cater, "The Captive Press," *The Reporter*, June 6, 1950, pp. 17–19; Deaver, "Study of Senator Joseph R. McCarthy," pp. 85–103.

22. Quoted in Deaver, "Study of Senator Joseph R. McCarthy," p. 91.

23. Elmer Davis, *But We Were Born Free*, 1952, p. 160.

24. Cater, "The Captive Press," pp. 17–19.

25. Lippmann is quoted in Rovere, *Senator Joe McCarthy*, p. 166; the Manhattan *Mercury–Chronicle* incident is in "How to Handle McCarthy," *Time*, October 24, 1954.

26. "Job for the Readers," *Time*, January 25, 1954, p. 79; Rovere, *Senator Joe McCarthy*, p. 166.

27. See "The Fetish of Objectivity," *Time*, May 4, 1953, p. 49; the *Journal's* editor is quoted in Deaver, "Study of Joseph R. McCarthy," p. 93.

28. Reedy is quoted in Deaver, "Study of Joseph R. McCarthy," p. 96.

29. Davis, *But We Were Born Free*, p. 163.

30. These quotes are in Deaver, "Study of Joseph R. McCarthy," pp. 19, 27, 189.

31. Interview with Robert Fleming.

32. Watkins is quoted in Deaver, "Study of Joseph R. McCarthy," p. 89; also Griffith, *Politics of Fear*, p. 142.

33. Deaver, "Study of Joseph R. McCarthy," p. 99.

Chapter Thirteen: "An Infamy So Black . . ." (*pp. 191–202*)

1. Arthur Schlesinger, Jr., and Richard Rovere, *The General and the President*, 1951, p. 139.

2. New York *Times*, November 3, 1950; John Spanier, *The Truman–MacArthur Controversy and the Korean War*, 1965, pp. 114–34.

3. Spanier, *Truman–MacArthur Controversy*, p. 137; William Manchester, *The Glory and the Dream*, 1973, p. 547; New York *Herald Tribune*, December 6, 1950.

4. See Spanier, *Truman–MacArthur Controversy*, pp. 137–64.

5. Bradley is quoted in *ibid.*, p. 247.

6. Taft's quote is in James Patterson, *Mr. Republican*, 1972, p. 488; Bridges in the Washington *Post*, January 5, 1951; McCarthy in the *Congressional Record*, 1950, pp. 16177–78.

7. Spanier, *Truman–MacArthur Controversy*, p. 1.

8. *Ibid.*, pp. 211–20: Schlesinger and Rovere, *The General and the President*, pp. 15–16.

9. Manchester, *The Glory and the Dream*, pp. 561–62.

10. Milwaukee *Journal*, April 12 and 13, 1951.

11. Interview with Urban Van Susteren, October 22, 1977.

12. *Ibid.*; also Chicago *Sun–Times*, April 13 and 14, 1950.

13. Milwaukee *Journal*, April 24 and 25, 1951.

14. See, for example, David McLellan, *Dean Acheson*, 1976, pp. 295–326.

15. *Congressional Record*, 1951, p. 5579.

16. Dean Acheson, *Present at the Creation*, 1969, p. 369; Washington *Post*, June 2, 1951.

17. Acheson, *Present at the Creation*, pp. 40–41; Richard Rovere, *Senator Joe McCarthy*, 1960, p. 172.

18. Walter Trohan, "The Tragedy of George Marshall," *The American Mercury*, March 1951, pp. 267–72.

19. New York *Times*, September 16, 1950; Robert Griffith, *The Politics of Fear*, 1970, p. 144.

20. Sidney Hyman, *The Lives of William Benton*, 1969, p. 457; Acheson, *Present at the Creation*, p. 424.

21. Marshall is quoted in Spanier, *Truman–MacArthur Controversy*, p. 12.

22. "Bob?" to Robert Fleming, Box 4, October 8, 1951, *Robert Fleming Papers*, Manuscripts Division, Wisconsin State Historical Society; Jack Anderson and Ronald May, *McCarthy*, 1952, pp. 235–36.

23. See Drew Pearson, "Washington Merry-Go-Round," Washington *Post*, June 19, 1951.

24. *Congressional Record*, 1951, pp. 6556–6603; Chicago *Tribune*, June 15, 1951.

25. Richard Rovere, *Senator Joe McCarthy*, p. 177; interview with Robert Morris, April 22, 1978.

26. New York *Herald Tribune*, June 16, 1951; Raleigh *News and Observer*, June 27, 1951; Youngstown *Vindicator*, June 16, 1951; "Why Not Spank Him?" *Collier's*, August 18, 1951, p. 74.

27. Richard Fried, *Men Against McCarthy*, 1976, p. 192; interview with Leverett Saltonstall, April 17, 1978; Washington *Post*, June 24, 1951.

28. The "Jezebel" quote is in Douglas Cater, "Is McCarthy Slipping?" *The Reporter*, September 18, 1951, pp. 25–26; the angry columnist was Alsop, "Matter of Fact," Washington *Post*, June 16, 1951. See also "Taft and McCarthy," *Life*, October 1, 1951, p. 32.

29. Patterson, *Mr. Republican*, p. 503.

30. See Robert Taft to Constituent, February 16, 1952, *Senator Robert A. Taft Papers*, Manuscripts Division, Library of Congress.

31. Cater, "Is McCarthy Slipping?"

Chapter Fourteen: "Slimy Creatures" (*pp. 203–13*)

1. "Busy Man," *Time*, October 8, 1951, p. 26.

2. See Arnold Forster and Benjamin Epstein, *The Troublemakers*, 1952, pp. 25–60.

3. *Ibid.*, p. 28; Robert Griffith, *The Politics of Fear*, 1970, p. 136.

4. Rankin's quote is in Forster and Epstein, *The Troublemakers*, p. 54.

5. *Ibid.*, pp. 51–52; Jack Anderson and Ronald May, *McCarthy*, 1952, pp. 309–13.

6. See 81st Cong., 1st sess., Committee on Armed Services, *Nomination of Anna M. Rosenberg to Be Assistant Secretary of Defense*, 1951, pp. 37–93.

7. *Ibid.*, p. 104.

8. E. J. Kahn, Jr., *The China Hands*, 1972, p. 214; Gary May, *China Scapegoat*, 1979, pp. 153–89.

9. Kahn, *The China Hands*, pp. 214–16; Anderson and May, *McCarthy*, pp. 199–201; May, *China Scapegoat*, pp. 180–84.

10. The Legion quote is in Wayne McKinley, "A Study of the American Right: Senator Joe McCarthy and the American Legion," unpublished master's thesis, University of Wisconsin, 1962, p. 112.

11. *Congressional Record*, 1950, A3426–27, A3786–87.

12. Alan Harper, *The Politics of Loyalty*, 1969, p. 219.

13. See Alfred Steinberg, "McCarran: Lone Wolf of the Senate," *Harper's*, November 1950, pp. 87–95.

14. "Interview with Senator McCarran," *U.S. News and World Report*, November 16, 1951, p. 29.

15. Interview with Robert Morris, April 22, 1978.

16. 82d Cong., 1st sess., Internal Security Subcommittee of the Committee on the Judiciary, *Hearings on the Institute of Pacific Relations*, 1951–52.

17. *Washington Post*, January 15, 1952.

18. Kahn, *China Hands*, pp. 12, 243; May, *China Scapegoat*, pp. 239–61; O. Edmund Clubb, *The Witness and I*, 1974, pp. 223–48; interview with Owen Lattimore.

19. Richard Fried, *Men Against McCarthy*, 1976, p. 173.

20. *Ibid.*, pp. 173–74; Anderson and May, *McCarthy*, pp. 409–10.

21. See Griffith, *The Politics of Fear*, p. 147; Fried, *Men Against McCarthy*, p. 188; "Periscope," *Newsweek*, October 8, 1951, p. 25.

22. 82d Cong., 1st sess., Committee on Foreign Relations, *Nomination of Philip Jessup to Be the United States Representative to the Sixth General Assembly of the United Nations*, 1951, pp. 2–142.

23. Interview with Senator William Fulbright, May 29, 1977.

24. New York *Times*, October 19, 1951; *The New Republic*, November 5, 1951, p. 17.

25. H. Alexander Smith Interview, *Columbia Oral History Project*, Columbia University, New York, p. 191.

26. "Jessup Backfire," *Newsweek*, October 22, 1951, p. 25.

CHAPTER FIFTEEN: TYDINGS'S REVENGE (*pp. 214–25*)

1. William S. White, in the New York *Times*, January 7, 1951.

2. Quoted in Drew Pearson, "Washington Merry-Go-Round," Washington *Post*, January 9, 1951.

3. Margaret Chase Smith, *Declaration of Conscience*, 1972, pp. 24–26; interview with Maurice Rosenblatt, December 23, 1976.

4. The Hennings quote is in Donald Kemper, *Decade of Fear*, 1965, p. 30.

5. Smith, *Declaration of Conscience*, pp. 21–22.

6. *Ibid.*, pp. 22–23.

7. 82d Cong., 1st sess., Committee on Rules and Administration, *Hearings on the Maryland Senatorial Election of 1950,* 1951.

8. See Marquis Childs column in the St. Louis *Post–Dispatch,* July 19, 1951; also Drew Pearson, "Washington Merry-Go-Round," Washington *Post,* July 5, 1951.

9. Robert Griffith, *The Politics of Fear,* 1970, p. 164.

10. *Congressional Record,* August 20, 1951, pp. 10319–37.

11. See especially Sidney Hyman, *The Lives of William Benton,* 1969, pp. 129–262.

12. Richard Fried, *Men Against McCarthy,* 1976, p. 199.

13. Quoted in Hyman, *Lives of William Benton,* p. 453.

14. *Ibid.,* p. 454.

15. *Congressional Record,* August 6, 1951, pp. 9498–9501.

16. *Ibid.*

17. Fried, *Men Against McCarthy,* p. 200; Smith, *Declaration of Conscience,* p. 28; Douglas Cater, "Is McCarthy Slipping?" *The Reporter,* September 18, 1951, p. 26.

18. Fried, *Men Against McCarthy,* p. 199; Subcommittee on Privileges and Elections to the Committee on Rules and Administration, *Investigation of Senators Joseph R. McCarthy and William Benton,* 1953, pp. 1–2; Hyman, *Lives of William Benton,* p. 455.

19. Quoted in Jack Anderson and Ronald May, *McCarthy,* 1952, pp. 316–17.

20. See especially William S. White in the New York *Times,* September 23, 1951.

21. Senator Joe McCarthy to Senator Guy Gillette, September 17, 1951, in *Investigation of Senators McCarthy and Benton,* p. 60.

22. The McCarthy letter is reprinted in the *Congressional Record,* 1951, p. 11857.

23. Hennings's reply is in *ibid.,* p. 11858.

24. *Ibid.,* pp. 11855–57.

25. White article, New York *Times,* September 23, 1951.

26. Senator Guy Gillette to Senator Joe McCarthy, September 25, 1951, in *Investigation of Senators McCarthy and Benton,* p. 61.

27. New York *Times,* September 29, 1951; Washington *Post,* September 29 and 30, 1951.

28. Senator Joe McCarthy to Senator Guy Gillette, October 4, 1951, in *Investigation of Senators McCarthy and Benton,* pp. 61–62.

29. "Confidential Memorandum from Ralph Mann to Senator Benton," Box 4, January 3, 1952, *Senator William Benton Papers,* Manuscripts Division, Wisconsin State Historical Society.

30. Hyman, *Lives of William Benton,* pp. 464–65; Senator William Benton to A. M. Gilbert, Box 4, August 14, September 9, 1952, *Benton Papers.*

31. Kemper, *Decade of Fear,* p. 57.

32. "Confidential Memorandum from Ralph Mann to Senator Benton."

33. Tyler Abell (ed.), *Drew Pearson Diaries*, January 16, 1952, p. 190.

34. *Ibid.*, p. 192.

35. Willard Shelton, "The Shame of the Senate," *The Progressive*, February 1953, p. 8.

36. Senator Joe McCarthy to Senator Guy Gillette, December 6, 1951, in *Investigation of Senators McCarthy and Benton*, p. 62.

37. Senator Guy Gillette to Senator Joe McCarthy, December 6, 1951, p. 63; Senator Joe McCarthy to Senator Guy Gillette, December 19, 1951, pp. 64–65, in *ibid.*

38. Hyman, *The Lives of William Benton*, p. 464; Senator Guy Gillette to Senator Carl Hayden, September 10, 1952, in *Investigation of Senators McCarthy and Benton*, p. 95.

39. Anderson and May, *McCarthy*, p. 322; Smith, *Declaration of Conscience*, pp. 32–33; Robert Hendrickson to Daniel Hendrickson, January 25, 1952, Box 21, *Senator Robert Hendrickson Papers*, Syracuse University Library, Syracuse, N.Y.

40. Smith, *Declaration of Conscience*, p. 32; New York *Times*, January 24, 1952.

41. Griffith, *The Politics of Fear*, p. 168.

Chapter Sixteen: Ike *(pp. 226–46)*

1. See Barton Bernstein, "Election of 1952," in Arthur Schlesinger, Jr. (ed.), *The Coming to Power*, 1971, pp. 385–436.

2. Walter Johnson (ed.), *The Papers of Adlai Stevenson*, vol. III, pp. 412–18.

3. Quoted in John B. Martin, *Adlai Stevenson of Illinois*, 1976, p. 471.

4. Bernstein, "Election of 1952," pp. 385–94.

5. Quoted in James Patterson, *Mr. Republican*, 1972, p. 489.

6. *Ibid.*, p. 530.

7. *Ibid.*

8. Herbert Parmet, *Eisenhower and the American Crusades*, 1972, p. 47.

9. *Ibid.*, pp. 49–50; Bernstein, "Election of 1952," p. 394.

10. Parmet, *Eisenhower and the American Crusades*, p. 60.

11. Washington *Post*, July 10, 11, 1952; Chicago *Tribune*, July 10, 1952; interview with Senator Leverett Saltonstall, April 24, 1978.

12. Senator Joe McCarthy to Tom Coleman, June 20, 1952, *Tom Coleman Papers*, Manuscripts Division, Wisconsin State Historical Society.

13. See especially Parmet, *Eisenhower and the American Crusades*, pp. 83–101; Richard Fried, *Men Against McCarthy*, 1976, pp. 222–25; Bernstein, "Election of 1952," p. 412.

14. *The Nation*, March 22, August 23, 1952; *The New Republic*, March 10, August 18, 1952; *Collier's*, November 24, 1951.

15. See John Wyngaard's column in the Green Bay *Press–Gazette*, November 11, 1952.

16. Interviews with Urban Van Susteren, October 22, 1977; Jack Anderson, September 9, 1977; Willard Edwards, April 30, 1978; also Sam Shaffer, *On and Off the Floor*, 1980, p. 43.

17. Michael O'Brien, *McCarthy and McCarthyism in Wisconsin*, 1980, p. 108; Alfred Steinberg, "Is This the Man to Beat McCarthy?" *Collier's*, November 24, 1951, p. 26.

18. See Graham Hovey, "Both McCarthy and His Foes Get Jolt," Washington *Post*, October 14, 1951.

19. Walter Kohler interview, p. 23, *Columbia Oral History Project*, Columbia University.

20. See "Schmitt vs. McCarthy," *The New Republic*, July 14, 1952, p. 9.

21. Quoted in Michael O'Brien, "The Anti-McCarthy Campaign in Wisconsin, 1951–52," *Wisconsin Magazine of History*, Winter 1972–73, p. 102.

22. *Ibid.* Interview with Urban Van Susteren, October 22, 1977.

23. Quoted in O'Brien, *McCarthy and McCarthyism*, pp. 185–86.

24. J. E. Hayes to Senator Frank Carlson, November 13, 1954; Lawrence Rittenhouse to Senator Frank Carlson, November 19, 1954, *Senator Frank Carlson Papers*, Kansas State Historical Society.

25. "Dear Friend" Letter from McCarthy Club, August 20, 1952, copy in author's possession; "The Truth About Senator Joe McCarthy," copy in author's possession.

26. John B. Oakes, "Report on McCarthy and McCarthyism," *New York Times Magazine*, November 2, 1952.

27. See especially Graham Hovey, "How McCarthy Sold Wisconsin," *The New Republic*, September 22, 1952, p. 10.

28. Thomas Amlie to Arthur Schlesinger, Jr., September 29, 1952, *Adlai Stevenson Papers*, Box 311, Manuscripts Division, Princeton University Library; Milwaukee *Sentinel*, September 11, 1952.

29. Interview with Tom Korb, June 9, 1978.

30. See Robert Griffith, *The Politics of Fear*, 1970, pp. 70, 103; Jack Anderson and Ronald May, *McCarthy*, 1952, p. 232.

31. New York *Times*, August 23, 1952.

32. General George Marshall to General Dwight Eisenhower, August 30, 1952, *Dwight D. Eisenhower Papers*, PPF 181, Box 935, Eisenhower Presidential Library.

33. "Jenner Grabs a Ride," in Murray Kempton, *America Comes of Middle Age*, 1963, pp. 243–45.

34. Parmet, *Eisenhower and the American Crusades*, p. 128; Emmet Hughes, *The Ordeal of Power*, 1963, p. 41.

35. Hughes, *Ordeal of Power*, pp. 41–42.

36. Charles Van Devander to Charles Murphy, October 3, 1952, *Philleo Nash Files*, White House Correspondence, Truman Presidential Library.

37. Sherman Adams, *First Hand Report*, 1961, pp. 30–31.

38. Walter Kohler interview, *Columbia Oral History Project*, p. 22.

39. Quoted in Robert Griffith, "The General and the Senator," *Wisconsin Magazine of History*, Autumn 1970, p. 27.

40. Milwaukee *Journal*, October 4, 1952.

41. Quoted in Hughes, *Ordeal of Power*, p. 43.

42. Interview with Charles Murphy, p. 149, *Truman Oral History Collection*, Truman Presidential Library.

43. Fried, *Men Against McCarthy*, p. 240.

44. Hartford *Courant*, October 14, 1952; interview with Jack Anderson, September 9, 1977.

45. Prescott Bush interview, p. 100, *Columbia Oral History Project*, Columbia University.

46. Donald Crosby, *God, Church, and Flag*, 1978, pp. 112–13.

47. Boston *Post*, December 6, 1953, November 29, 1953; "Information from Sargent Shriver," September 17, 1952, *Adlai Stevenson Papers*, Box 267, Manuscripts Division, Princeton University.

48. Roy Cohn, *McCarthy*, 1968, p. 66; Victor Lasky, *JFK: The Man and the Myth*, 1963, p. 143.

49. *Ibid.*, p. 141.

50. *Ibid.*, p. 142; see also Oliver Pilat, *Pegler*, 1963, pp. 20–23.

51. Senator John F. Kennedy to Westbrook Pegler, April 22, 1958, McCarthy File, *John F. Kennedy Papers*, Kennedy Presidential Library.

52. Interview with Henry Cabot Lodge, Jr., July 31, 1977.

53. Los Angeles *Times*, October 15, 1952; O'Brien, *McCarthy and McCarthyism*, p. 183.

54. See Alonso Hamby, *Beyond the New Deal*, 1973, pp. 497–98; *The Papers of Adlai E. Stevenson*, vol. 4, pp. 49–54.

55. Los Angeles *Times*, October 15, 1952; Fried, *Men Against McCarthy*, pp. 237–38.

56. Allen Matusow (ed.), *Joseph McCarthy*, 1970, pp. 60–64.

57. Fried, *Men Against McCarthy*, p. 234; Hamby, *Beyond the New Deal*, p. 496; Martin, *Adlai Stevenson of Illinois*, p. 744.

58. O'Brien, "The Anti-McCarthy Campaign," p. 106.

59. See David Oshinsky, *Senator Joseph McCarthy and the American Labor Movement*, 1976, pp. 135–55.

60. Louis Bean, *Influences in the 1954 Mid-Term Elections*, 1954, p. 18.

CHAPTER SEVENTEEN: GEARING FOR BATTLE (*pp. 247–64*)

1. Senator Joe McCarthy to Senator William Benton, March 18, 1952; Senator William Benton to Senator Joe McCarthy, March 18, 1952, both in *William Benton Papers*, Box 5, Manuscripts Division, Wisconsin State Historical Society.

2. See Benton to John Howe, April 2, 1952, in *ibid.*

3. New York *Times*, July 4, 1952; Richard Fried, *Men Against McCarthy*, 1976, p. 210.

4. U.S. Congress, Senate, Subcommittee on Privileges and Elections to the Committee on Rules and Administration, *Investigation of Senators Joseph R. McCarthy and William Benton*, 1952, pp. 94–95.

5. *Ibid.*, p. 103.

6. Tyler Abell (ed.), *Drew Pearson Diaries*, 1974, p. 240.

7. *Ibid.*, pp. 241, 245; Robert Griffith, *The Politics of Fear*, 1970, pp. 180–81; Fried, *Men Against McCarthy*, p. 213.

8. *Investigation of McCarthy and Benton*, p. 11.

9. *Drew Pearson Diaries*, p. 247.

10. New York *Times*, January 3, 1953; Griffith, *Politics of Fear*, p. 182.

11. Fried, *Men Against McCarthy*, p. 218.

12. *Ibid.*, p. 257; Howard Rushmore, "Pekin Farm Boy," *American Mercury*, April 1953, p. 82; Robert Donovan, *Eisenhower: The Inside Story*, 1956, p. 86.

13. Griffith, *The Politics of Fear*, pp. 207–12.

14. See Richard Rovere, *Senator Joe McCarthy*, 1960, pp. 197–98; William S. White, *The Taft Story*, 1954, pp. 218–20.

15. *Drew Pearson Diaries*, p. 253.

16. Fried, *Men Against McCarthy*, p. 263; Washington *Post*, January 13, 1953.

17. Griffith, *The Politics of Fear*, p. 208.

18. See Philip Horton, "Voices Within the Voice," *The Reporter*, July 21, 1953; James Wechsler, *The Age of Suspicion*, 1953, p. 251; "Rushmore v. Cohn," *Time*, November 1, 1954, p. 52.

19. Roy Cohn, *McCarthy*, 1968, p. 47; also interview with Robert Morris, April 22, 1978.

20. Cohn, *McCarthy*, p. 48.

21. *Ibid.*, pp. 21–24.

22. New York *Times*, January 3, 1953; Walter Winchell, *Winchell Exclusive*, 1975, p. 252.

23. "The Self-Infalted Target," *Time*, March 22, 1954.

24. *Ibid.*; Richard Rovere, "The Adventures of Cohn and Schine," *The Reporter*, July 21, 1953, p. 10.

25. See Cohn, *McCarthy*, pp. 249–50; Howard Rushmore, "Young Mr. Cohn," *American Mercury*, February 1953, pp. 67–74.

26. L. B. Nichols to Mr. Tolson, January 22, 1953, *Papers of the FBI*, Washington, D.C.

27. Interview with Urban Van Susteren, October 22, 1977.

28. See especially Cohn–Schine File, *Papers of The Reporter Magazine*, unprocessed, Manuscripts Division, Boston University Library.

29. Rovere, "The Adventures of Cohn and Schine," pp. 10–11; *The Harvard Crimson*, May 7, 1954; "Memo on G. D. Schine," Cohn–Schine File.

30. G. David Schine, "Definition of Communism," copy in the author's possession; James Rorty and Moshe Decter, *McCarthy and the Communists*, 1954, pp. 154–56.

31. "Cohn–Schine Memo, May 3, 1953," in Cohn–Schine File; interview with Willard Edwards, April 30, 1978.

32. See for example Rovere, *Senator Joe McCarthy*, pp. 25–27.

33. "Memorandum from L. B. Nichols to Staff," February 7, 1953, *Papers of the FBI*, Washington, D.C.

34. See Drew Pearson, "Washington Merry-Go-Round," Washington *Post*, March 2, 1953; Carey McWilliams, "Senator McCarthy's Sixth Column," *The Nation*, May 22, 1954, pp. 434–36; Marquis Childs's column in the Washington *Post*, December 15, 1953.

35. "Memo from Philip Horton to Richard Rovere," June 12, 1953, in *Richard Rovere Papers*, Manuscripts Division, Wisconsin State Historical Society; also W. W. Turner, *Hoover's FBI*, 1971, p. 176; "Ruth Watt Oral History," Senate Historical Office, Washington, D.C.

36. Senato Joe McCarthy to J. Edgar Hoover, July 30, 1952; J. Edgar Hoover to Senator McCarthy, August 6, 1952, both in the *Papers of the FBI*; also David Caute, *The Great Fear*, 1978, p. 114.

37. See Donald Lourie interview, *Dulles Oral History Collection*, Princeton University Library, p. 37; also interview with Robert Morris.

38. Earl Latham, *The Communist Controversy in Washington*, 1966, p. 400.

39. See Roscoe Drummond, "State of the Nation," *The Christian Science Monitor*, March 9, 1953; Fried, *Men Against McCarthy*, p. 254.

40. Dwight D. Eisenhower interview, *Dulles Oral History Collection*, pp. 11–14.

41. Dwight Eisenhower to William Robinson, March 23, 1954; Dwight Eisenhower to Paul Helms, March 9, 1954, both in the *Personal Papers of Dwight D. Eisenhower*, Eisenhower Library, Abilene, Kan.; also Griffith, *Politics of Fear*, pp. 196–207.

42. Eisenhower to Helms.

43. Eisenhower to Harry Bullis, March 18, 1953; Eisenhower to Robinson, March 23, 1954.

44. Arthur Larson, *The President Nobody Knew*, 1968, p. 12; Emmet Hughes, *The Ordeal of Power*, 1963, p. 92.

45. Hughes, *Ordeal of Power*, p. 92.

46. *Ibid.*, p. 66.

47. The Dulles letter is quoted in Michael Guhin, *John Foster Dulles*, 1972, pp. 188–89.

48. Richard Nixon to John Foster Dulles, January 14, 1952; John Foster Dulles to Richard Nixon, August 13, 1952, both in Box 62, *John Foster Dulles Papers*, Princeton University Library, Princeton, N.J.

49. Edward Corsi interview, *Dulles Oral History Collection*, pp. 21–25.

50. Joe McCarthy to John Foster Dulles, November 29, 1952, Box 62, *Dulles Papers*.

51. John Foster Dulles to Joe McCarthy, December 3, 1952; Joe McCarthy to John Foster Dulles, December 19, 1952, both in *ibid.*

52. James Reston interview, *Dulles Oral History Collection*, pp. 11–12.

53. William Hale, " 'Big Brother' in Foggy Bottom," *The Reporter*, August 17, 1954, pp. 10–16.

54. John Haines interview, *Dulles Oral History Collection*, pp. 81–82.

55. Charlotte Knight, "What Price Security?" *Collier's*, July 9, 1954, pp. 58–59.

56. *Ibid.*, pp. 67–68.

57. Guhin, *John Foster Dulles*, p. 193.

58. John Foster Dulles to Scott McLeod, December 28, 1953, Box 72, *Dulles Papers*.

Chapter Eighteen: Voices Within the Voice (*pp. 265–85*)

1. *Watkins* v. *United States*, 354 U.S. 178 (1957).

2. See especially Telford Taylor, *Grand Inquest*, 1955; James Hamilton, *The Power to Probe*, 1976.

3. Robert Elder, *The Information Machine*, 1968, pp. 32–44; John Henderson, *The United States Information Agency*, 1969, pp. 32–48; "Voice of America: The Problem," *U.S. News and World Report*, March 27, 1953, pp. 43–44.

4. Raymond Graham Swing, "VOA—A Survey of the Wreckage," *The Reporter*, July 21, 1953, pp. 30–33.

5. *Ibid.*

6. Senator Joe McCarthy to Thomas Coleman, June 28, 1950, *Thomas Coleman Papers*, Wisconsin State Historical Society; Don Surine to Ralph de Toledano, October 4, 1950, *Papers of The Reporter Magazine*, Boston University Library.

7. Martin Merson, *The Private Diary of a Public Servant*, 1955, p. 38.

8. "Telephone Conversation with Mr. Sokolsky," February 12, 1953; *John Foster Dulles Papers*, Princeton University Library.

9. "Telephone Conversation with Mr. Lourie," February 19, 1953, in *ibid.*

10. See Philip Horton, "Voices Within the Voice," *The Reporter*, July 21, 1953, pp. 25–29.

11. Hearings Before the Permanent Subcommittee on Investigations of the Committee on Government Operations, *State Department Information Program—Voice of America*, 1953. For McKesson's testimony, see pp. 1–11.

12. *Ibid.*, p. 361.

13. Wiesner is quoted in Frederick Woltman's article in the New York *World–Telegram and Sun*, July 16, 1954.

14. C. D. Jackson to John Foster Dulles, February 19, 1953, *Dulles Papers*.

15. *Christian Science Monitor*, March 7, 1953; New York *Times*, June 3, 1953.

16. *VOA Hearings*, pp. 164–77.

17. *Ibid.*, pp. 298–305.

18. *Ibid.*, pp. 307–8.

19. *Ibid.*, pp. 320–23.

20. *Ibid.*, p. 324.

21. *Ibid.*, pp. 190–211.

22. *Ibid.*, pp. 331–87; 495–520.

23. Merson, *Private Diary*, pp. 62–67.

24. "Notes on Cohn–Schine," *Papers of The Reporter Magazine.*

25. Merson, *Private Diary*, pp. 11–17; *VOA Hearings*, p. 131.

26. Eslanda C. D. Robeson, *African Journey*, 1945, p. 47.

27. Merson, *Private Diary*, pp. 14–15; Roy Cohn, *McCarthy*, 1968, pp. 75–92; Henderson, *The USIA*, p. 253.

28. Earl Latham, *The Communist Controversy in Washington*, 1966, p. 338.

29. "The Voice on TV," *Newsweek*, March 9, 1953, p. 20; Drew Pearson, "Washington Merry-Go-Round," Washington *Post*, March 2, 1953; Merson, *Private Diary*, pp. 17–19.

30. See especially *Bernard Shanley Diary*, June 17, 1953, Seton Hall University, East Orange, N.J.

31. Cohn, *McCarthy*, p. 81.

32. Theodore Achilles Interview, *Dulles Oral History Collection*, Princeton University.

33. Prescott Bush interview; Columbia Oral History Project, Columbia Univ.

34. See in its entirety Harvey Matusow, *False Witness*, 1955.

35. Hearings Before the Permanent Subcommittee on Investigations of the Committee on Government Operations, *State Department Information Program—Information Centers*, 1953, pp. 17–24.

36. *Ibid.*, pp. 25–39.

37. *Ibid.*, pp. 473–82.

38. *Ibid.*, pp. 115–29.

39. *Ibid.*, pp. 253–80.

40. *Ibid.*, pp. 41–59.

41. Quoted in Merson, *Private Diary*, pp. 132–33.

42. Interview with Jack Anderson, September 9, 1977.

CHAPTER NINETEEN: OF DIPLOMATS AND GREEK SHIPS
(*pp. 286–300*)

1. See especially James Rosenau, *The Nomination of Chip Bohlen*, 1958, pp. 1–2.

2. Charles E. Bohlen, *Witness to History*, 1973, pp. 4–6; "What Bohlen Can Do in Moscow," *U.S. News and World Report*, April 3, 1953, pp. 18–20; "The Expert at Ike's Elbow," *Newsweek*, July 18, 1955, p. 33.

3. Herbert Parmet, *Eisenhower and the American Crusades*, 1972, p. 97; Drew Pearson, "The Washington Merry-Go-Round," Washington *Post*, March 25, 1953.

4. Charles Bohlen interview, *Dulles Oral History Collection*, Princeton University Library.

5. Tyler Abell (ed.), *Drew Pearson Diaries*, 1974, p. 254; Joseph and Stewart Alsop, "Matter of Fact," Washington *Post*, May 27, 1953.

6. Committee on Foreign Relations, *Hearings on the Nomination of Charles E. Bohlen*, 1953, p. 34.

7. Taft is quoted in Rosenau, *The Nomination of Chip Bohlen*, p. 4.

8. *Hearings on the Nomination of Charles E. Bohlen*, pp. 101–12.

9. See Rosenau, *Nomination of Chip Bohlen*, p. 6.

10. Emmet Hughes, *The Ordeal of Power*, 1963, p. 85.

11. The entire Bohlen debate is found in the *Congressional Record*, 83d Cong., 1st sess., 1953, pp. 2187–2208, 2277–2300, 2374–92.

12. For Bogolepov's testimony, see Committee on the Judiciary, *Hearings on the Institute of Pacific Relations*, 1951, p. 4487.

13. "Ike's Victory with Bohlen Reduces McCarthy Influence," *Newsweek*, April 6, 1953, p. 21; Bohlen interview.

14. Hughes, *Ordeal of Power*, p. 93; confidential source.

15. "Ike's Victory with Bohlen"; "The Bohlen Affair," *The Nation*, April 4, 1953, p. 279; McCarthy's quote is in Joseph and Stewart Alsop, "Matter of Fact," Washington *Post*, April 1, 1953.

16. "Phony Greek Deal?" *Newsweek*, April 6, 1953, p. 26.

17. Patrick McMahon, "Ships and Greeks—and Senator Joe McCarthy," *The American Mercury*, May 1953, pp. 15–19; "The Greeks, the Senator, and the Slump," *Business Week*, April 11, 1953, p. 30.

18. Pearson, "Washington Merry-Go-Round," Washington *Post*, April 7, 1953.

19. McMahon, "Ships and Greeks—and Senator Joe McCarthy," p. 15.

20. Subcommittee on Investigations of the Committee on Government Operations, *Hearings on Control of Trade with the Soviet Bloc Nations*, 1953, p. 4.

21. *Ibid.*, p. 16.

22. *Ibid.*, p. 31.

23. Harold Stassen interview, *Dulles Oral History Collection*, Princeton University Library.

24. See "McCarthy and Greek Ships, 'Undermining' or 'Constructive'?" *Newsweek*, April 13, 1953, p. 39.

25. Pearson, "Washington Merry-Go-Round," Washington *Post*, April 10, 1953.

26. Quoted in Parmet, *Eisenhower and the American Crusades*, p. 252.

27. *Hearings on Control of Trade with the Soviet Bloc Nations*, p. 146.

28. The text of the letter is in Marquis Child's column, Washington *Post*, June 2, 1953.

29. *Ibid.*; also Sherman Adams, *Firsthand Report*, 1961, p. 141.

30. Washington *Post*, July 18, 1953; New York *Times*, July 19, 1953; Arthur M. Schlesinger, Jr., *Robert Kennedy and His Times*, 1978, p. 104.

31. Ralph Flanders interview, *Columbia Oral History Collection*, New York City; the Reuther quote is in Lately Thomas, *When Even Angels Wept*, 1973, p. 351; Stewart Alsop, "Matter of Fact," Washington *Post*, August 25, 1953; Rebecca West to Paul Hollister, copy in G.F. 172, Box 1272, *Dwight D. Eisenhower Papers*, Eisenhower Presidential Library.

32. *CIO News*, August 3, 1953.

33. Harry Bullis to Dwight Eisenhower, May 9, 1953, O.F. 99-R, *Eisenhower Papers*.

34. Dwight Eisenhower to Harry Bullis, May 18, 1953, in *ibid*.

CHAPTER TWENTY: FRIENDS AND ENEMIES (*pp. 301–14*)

1. Richard Wilson, "The Ring Around McCarthy," *Look*, December 1, 1953, pp. 29–33; the Longworth story is in William Miller, *Fishbait*, 1977, p. 161.

2. Albert Wedemeyer to Edmund Coblentz, June 10, 1953, CB 845, *Edmund Coblentz Papers*, Bancroft Library, Berkeley, California.

3. Wilson, "The Ring Around McCarthy," p. 30; New York *Daily News*, September 15, 1953.

4. Wilson, "The Ring Around McCarthy," p. 30.

5. See Jean F. Deaver, "A Study of Senator Joseph R. McCarthy and 'McCarthyism' as Influences Upon the News Media," unpublished doctoral dissertation, University of Texas, 1969, p. 44; *Ruth Watt Oral History*, Senate Historical Office, Washington, D.C.; Norman Ramsay interview, *Columbia Oral History Project*, Columbia University Library, New York City.

6. Quoted in Charles J. V. Murphy, "McCarthy and Texas Business," *Fortune*, May 1954, p. 101.

7. *Ibid.*, p. 214.

8. *Ibid.*, p. 100; Milwaukee *Journal*, March 15, 1953; David Oshinsky, *Senator Joseph McCarthy and the American Labor Movement*, 1976, p. 169.

9. Paul Dagget, "McCarthy in Texas," *The Nation*, August 22, 1953, pp. 147–49; "McCarthy, Hunt and Facts-Forum," *The Reporter*, February 16, 1954, pp. 19–27.

10. Charles J. V. Murphy, "McCarthy and the Businessman," *Fortune*, April 1954, pp. 156–92; Oshinsky, *McCarthy and the Labor Movement*, p. 167.

11. Seymour M. Lipset and Earl Raab, *The Politics of Unreason*, 1970, p. 226; Immanuel Wallerstein, "McCarthyism and the Conservatives," master's thesis, Columbia University, 1954, p. 34.

12. See Murphy, "McCarthy and the Businessman," pp. 184, 186, 190.

13. *Ibid.*, pp. 186, 188, 190.

14. New York *Times*, March 1, 1954.

15. See especially Donald Crosby, *God, Church, and Flag*, 1978, pp. 138–39, 158–60, 190. The *Tablet* quote is on p. 54. The *Tablet* is the official newspaper of the Archdiocese of Brooklyn.

16. *Ibid.*, pp. 81, 83, 165–67.

17. *Ibid.*, p. 243.

18. John Cogley, "Behind Many Faces," *Commonweal*, May 20, 1955, p. 182; *America*, December 13, 1952, p. 316.

19. The letter is quoted in Crosby, *God, Church, and Flag*, p. 184.

20. *Ibid.*

21. William F. Buckley, Jr., and L. Brent Bozell, *McCarthy and His Enemies*, 1954, pp. 4, 248.

22. Max Eastman, "The Necessity of Red-Baiting," *The Freeman*, June 1, 1953, p. 619.

23. Max Eastman, "Facts and Logic Re McCarthy," *The Freeman*, April 19, 1954, p. 532.

24. John T. Flynn, "What Is Joe McCarthy Really Trying to Do?" *The American Mercury*, March 1954, p. 69; William Schlamm, "Prologue," in *McCarthy and His Enemies*, xviii.

25. Whittaker Chambers to Henry Regnery, January 14, 1954, quoted in William F. Buckley, Jr., *Odyssey of a Friend*, 1956, p. 47.

26. Whittaker Chambers to William F. Buckley, Jr., February 7, 1954, in *ibid.*

27. See Jack Anderson, *Confessions of a Muckraker*, 1979, p. 26. Anderson's attempts to link McCarthy to organized crime can be found in rough notes for Anderson and May, *McCarthy*, located in the *Papers of the National Committee for an Effective Congress*, Washington, D.C. Anderson hints at his efforts in *Confessions*, p. 253. The Fleming memos are in Box 4 of the *Robert Fleming Papers*, Wisconsin State Historical Society.

28. Interview with Jack Anderson, September 9, 1977; Las Vegas *Sun*, October 25, 1952.

29. S. Davis to Adolph Silverstein, May 4, 1953. Box 39, *Papers of the Americans for Democratic Action*, Wisconsin State Historical Society; William Evjue to Drew Pearson, June 13, 1953, Box 81, *William Evjue Papers*, Wisconsin State Historical Society.

30. Philip Horton to P. Cronin, May 14, 1953; P. H. to C. C., May 27, 1953; Philip Horton to Dorothy Kahn, May 20, 1953; all in the Cohn–Schine File, *Papers of The Reporter Magazine*, Boston University Library.

31. The best article on the Hughes case is, "The Case of the Secret Informer," *National Review*, February 8, 1956, pp. 9–21; see also "The Hughes Case," *The Legal Aid Review*, Spring 1956, pp. 8–12.

32. "The Case of the Secret Informer," p. 15.

33. Interview with Thomas Bolan, April 17, 1979.

34. See Newark *Star–Ledger*, January 20, 1956.

35. Washington *Post*, February 4, 1956.

36. Rovere's letter is in the *National Review* issue of March 21, 1956.

CHAPTER TWENTY-ONE: A DISCOURAGING SUMMER (*pp. 315–29*)

1. U.S. Congress, Senate, Committee on Appropriations, *Hearings on the Supplemental Appropriations Bill*, 1954, pp. 620, 633.

2. Senator Charles Tobey to Sherman Adams, March 22, 1953, Box 76, *Senator Charles Tobey Papers*, Dartmouth College Library; interview with Senator Clifford Case, February 16, 1979.

3. Homer Ferguson interview, *Dulles Oral History Collection*, Princeton University Library; the Jenner quote is in Joseph Martin, *My First Fifty Years in Politics*, 1960, p. 237.

4. "Rushmore vs. Cohn," *Time*, November 1, 1954, p. 52; Washington *Post*, July 17, 1953; Karl Baarslag, "How to Spot a Communist," *Legion Magazine*, January 1947.

5. Kennedy's statement is in Arthur Schlesinger, Jr., *Robert Kennedy and His Times*, 1978, pp. 105–6.

6. Howard Rushmore, "Mr. Anti-Communist," *American Mercury*, June 1953, p. 79.

7. For the McCarthy–Matthews relationship, see Baltimore *Sun*, July 12, 1953; on the Matthews dinner, see Drew Pearson, "Washington Merry-Go-Round," Washington *Post*, July 11, 1953, and Fred Cook, *The Nightmare Decade*, 1971, pp. 426–27.

8. J. B. Matthews, "Reds and Our Churches," *American Mercury*, July 1953, p. 3.

9. New York *Times*, July 11, 1953.

10. *Ibid.* Also Washington *Evening Star*, July 10, 1953; New York *Herald–Tribune*, July 13, 1953.

11. New York *Post*, July 12, 1953; *Bernard Shanley Diary*, July 9, 1953, Seton Hall University Library.

12. *Shanley Diary*, July 9, 1953.

13. Quoted in Emmet Hughes, *The Ordeal of Power*, 1962, p. 96.

14. New York *Times*, July 11, 17, 1953.

15. *Ibid.*, July 12, 1953.

16. Washington *Post*, July 21, 1953.

17. The friend, John Wyngaard, is quoted in Michael O'Brien, *McCarthy and McCarthyism in Wisconsin*, 1980, p. 156.

18. The Pusey incident is well described in *ibid.*, pp. 149–50; also Appleton *Post–Crescent*, July 6, 1953.

19. *Ibid.*

20. Interview with Urban Van Susteren, October 22, 1977.

21. See R. Harris Smith, *OSS: The Secret History of America's First Central Intelligence Agency*, 1972, pp. 366–68.

22. Lyman Kirkpatrick, Jr., *The Real CIA*, 1968, pp. 135–36.

23. David Halberstam, *The Best and the Brightest*, 1969, pp. 480–81.

24. Senator Joe McCarthy to Allen Dulles, July 16, 1953, in the *Allen Dulles Papers* (unprocessed), Princeton University Library.

25. Allen Dulles to McCarthy, July 22, 1953, in *ibid.*; also Halberstam, *Best and Brightest*, p. 480.

26. See Leonard Mosley, *Dulles*, 1978, p. 319.

27. *Ibid.*, p. 320.

28. Telephone conversation with A. W. Dulles, July 10, 1953, *John Foster Dulles Papers*, Princeton University Library.

29. Richard Nixon, *Memoirs*, 1978, p. 140.

30. Washington *Post*, July 16, 1953; Alsop in *ibid.*, July 17, 1953.

31. Senator Joe McCarthy to Allen Dulles, August 3, 1953, *Allen Dulles Papers*.

32. New York *Times*, August 11, 12, 1953; Washington *Times–Herald*, August 12, 1953; Washington *Post*, August 11, 1953; Washington *Evening Star*, August 18, 1953; interview with Roy Cohn, March 21, 1979.

33. Washington *Post*, August 18, 19, 1953; New York *Times*, August 11, 19, 20, 1953.

34. Washington *Post*, August 30, 1953.

35. Roy Cohn, *McCarthy*, 1968, p. 53; Lately Thomas, *When Even Angels Wept*, 1973, p. 350; *Shanley Diary*, August 24, 1953.

36. Interview with Stanley Frosh, May 22, 1977.

37. Washington *Evening Star*, September 29, 30, 1953; "Pretty Researcher Marries Her Boss," *Life*, October 12, 1953, p. 65.

Chapter Twenty-Two: The Monmouth Hearings
(*pp. 330–44*)

1. Willard Edwards, "McCarthy's Record," reprinted from *Human Events*, November 10, 1954.

2. See Scientists Committee on Loyalty and Security, *Fort Monmouth*, 1954, pp. 11–33; Ralph Brown, *Loyalty and Security*, 1958, pp. 265–71; Arnold Forster and Benjamin Epstein, *Cross-Currents*, 1956, pp. 67–121.

3. Forster and Epstein, *Cross-Currents*, pp. 109, 113.

4. *Ibid.*, p. 120.

5. U.S. Senate, Subcommittee on Investigations of the Committee on Government Operations, *Communist Infiltration Among Army Civilian Workers*, 1953, pp. 3, 13.

6. *Ibid.*, pp. 9, 12, 16.

7. U.S. Senate, Subcommittee on Investigations of the Committee on Government Operations, *Communist Infiltration in the Army*, 1953, pp. 27, 37, 86, 101.

8. Interview with Willard Edwards, April 30, 1978; Roy Cohn, *McCarthy*, 1968, p. 168.

9. Chicago *Tribune*, October 15, 16, 1953; New York *Times*, October 17, 1953.

10. Chicago *Tribune*, October 20–27, 1953.

11. "Washington Merry-Go-Round," Washington *Post*, October 23, 1953.

12. See "The Accuser: Secretary Stevens . . . ," *Newsweek*, May 3, 1954, pp. 28–29; "Running the Army—An Education in Politics," *U.S. News and World Report*, March 26, 1954, pp. 81–82.

13. The telegram is quoted in *Communist Infiltration Among Army Civilian Workers*, pp. 2–3; see also Scientists Committee on Loyalty and Security, *Fort Monmouth*, p. 4.

14. Michael Straight, *Trial by Television*, 1954, p. 54; New York *Times*, October 21, 1953.

15. The article was the first of a four-part series. See Washington *Post*, November 9–12, 1953.

16. Washington *Post*, November 14, 1953; Straight, *Trial by Television*, p. 56.

17. U.S. Senate, Subcommittee on Investigations of the Committee on Government Operations, *Army Signal Corps: Subversion and Espionage*, pp. 36, 122, 218.

18. See Earl Latham, *The Communist Controversy in Washington*, 1966, pp. 381–84.

19. *Army Signal Corps: Subversion and Espionage*, p. 274.

20. *Ibid.*, pp. 171, 214.

21. One of the few summaries of the Coleman case is found in Scientists Committee on Loyalty and Security, *Fort Monmouth*. This interpretation, however, ignores most of the damaging evidence against Coleman.

22. *Army Signal Corps: Subversion and Espionage*, pp. 58, 61.

23. Reid's testimony is in *ibid.*, pp. 69–77.

24. Coleman's testimony is in *ibid.*, pp. 77–113.

25. *Ibid.*, p. 76.

CHAPTER TWENTY-THREE: WHITE HOUSE BLUES *(pp. 345–54)*

1. Richard Fried, *Men Against McCarthy*, 1976, p. 271; Peter Lyon, *Eisenhower*, 1974, p. 531.

2. Ronald Caridi, *The Korean War and American Politics*, 1968, pp. 246–81. The Jenner quote is on p. 275.

3. New York *Times*, October 16, 1953; Fried, *Men Against McCarthy*, pp. 277–78.

4. Sherman Adams, *Firsthand Report*, 1961, p. 137.

5. New York *Times*, November 7, 1953.

6. See Marquis Childs's column in the Washington *Post*, November 11, 1953; Alsops' column in the Washington *Post*, November 27, 1953; Drew Pearson's quote is in Tyler Abell (ed.), *Drew Pearson Diaries*, November 21, 1953, p. 286; Lippmann's quote is in the Louisville *Times*, November 22, 1953. The Truman–Velde battle is in the New York *Times*, November 6, 7, 1953.

7. *Public Papers of the Presidents*, Dwight D. Eisenhower, 1953, pp. 759–60, 762–63.

8. New York *Times*, November 17, 1953.

9. *Ibid.*, November 18, 19, 1953; *Drew Pearson Diaries*, November 18, 1953, p. 285.

10. New York *Times*, November 25, 1953.

11. Stewart Alsop, "Matter of Fact," New York *Herald–Tribune*, January 11, 1954.

12. See James Reston's front page article in the New York *Times*, November 26, 1953; also C. D. Jackson to Sherman Adams, November 25, 1953, *Dwight D. Eisenhower Papers*, Eisenhower Presidential Library.

13. *C. D. Jackson Diary*, November 29, 1953, Eisenhower Presidential Library.

14. *Ibid.*, November 30, 1953. In addition to Jackson, those present at the staff meeting included Press Secretary James Hagerty; Assistant Press Secretary Murray Snyder; Staff Secretary "Pete" Carroll; White House assistants I. Jack Martin and Bryce Harlow; and White House counsels Gerald Morgan and Bernard Shanley. Sherman Adams was out of town and Jerry Persons was home sick, although "pulling strings," according to Jackson. Shanley chaired the meeting. His diary entry for that day reads, in part, "The advocates of beat-McCarthy-over-the-head were pretty vociferous. Afterwards, Pete Carroll commended me for bringing peace and quiet back again because it had reached a point where it was pretty bitter." See *Bernard Shanley Diary*, Seton Hall University, pp. 1307–21. On December 1, Sherman Adams was briefed on the meeting by one of his staffers. "C. D.'s view is a minority one. But from what I gathered the opposed view is based on . . . the concept, as Jim Hagerty puts it, that for the President to react is to bring McCarthy up to his level. . . . This is patent nonsense. Ignoring the enemy can be a useful tactic but you can scarcely build a whole strategy around it." See J. M. Lambie, "Confidential Memo for Governor Adams," December 1, 1953, *DDE Presidential Papers*.

15. See Stewart Alsop, "Matter of Fact," Washington *Post*, December 4, 1953.

16. Washington *Post*, December 3, 1953; "Crackdown," *Time*, December 14, 1953, p. 26.

17. Washington *Post*, December 3, 1953; New York *Times*, December 3, 1953; Stewart Alsop, "Matter of Fact," Washington *Post*, December 4, 1953.

18. *C. D. Jackson Diary*, December 2, 1953.

19. New York *Times*, December 3, 4, 1953.

20. *C. D. Jackson Diary*, December 2, 1953.

21. Stewart Alsop, "Matter of Fact," Washington *Post*, December 4, 1953.

22. Drew Pearson, "Washington Merry-Go-Round," Washington *Post*, December 8, 1953; Stewart Alsop, "Matter of Fact," New York *Herald–Tribune*, January 11, 1954.

23. Washington *Post*, December 4, 1953.

24. *Ibid.*, December 5, 1953; Baltimore *Sun*, December 7, 8, 1953.

Chapter Twenty-Four: Who Promoted Peress? (*pp.* 355–71)

1. Dwight D. Eisenhower, personal diary, April 1, 1953, Dwight D. Eisenhower Presidential Library, Abilene, Kan.

2. Ralph Brown, *Loyalty and Security*, 1958, pp. 23, 32–33; U.S. Senate, *Internal Security Manual*, 1955, pp. 51–59; C. L. Sulzberger, *A Long Row of Candles*, 1969, pp. 921–22.

   As for *known* Communists in America, the President was out for blood. When an old friend wrote him to plead for clemency for the Rosenbergs, he responded: "What you did not suggest was the need for considering this kind of argument over and against the known convictions of Communist leaders that free governments—and especially the American government—are notoriously weak and fearful and that consequently subversive and other kind of activity can be conducted against them with no real fear of dire punishment on the part of the perpetrator. It is, of course, important to the Communists to have this contention sustained and justified." See Dwight Eisenhower to Clyde Miller, June 10, 1953, *Eisenhower Presidential Papers*, Eisenhower Library. After leaving office Eisenhower privately berated Chief Justice Earl Warren for the Supreme Court's lenient approach to the Communist problem. Warren explained that Communists had to be judged by the same rules that applied to everyone else. He then asked, "What would you do with Communists in America?" Ike replied, "I would kill the SOBs." See *The Memoirs of Chief Justice Earl Warren*, 1977, pp. 5–6.

3. George Gallup (ed.), *The Gallup Poll*, vol. 2, 1954, pp. 1194, 1201.

4. See Congressman Ralph Gwinn to Leonard Hall, November 18, 1953, and Hall's reply, November 23, 1953, both in the *Eisenhower Presidential Papers*, Eisenhower Library. The Simson quote is in Alsop's column in the Washington *Post*, March 1, 1954. In December 1953 a survey of several hundred senators and congressmen by *U.S. News and World Report* (December 18, 1953, pp. 30–32) showed most Republicans disputing Eisenhower's claim that "Communism in government" would not be a major issue in the 1954 campaign. In fact, they ranked it first.

5. Jenner is quoted in the *Congressional Record*, 1954, pp. 2125–26.

6. See Robert Griffith, *The Politics of Fear*, 1970, pp. 196–207. The Flanders quote is on page 197.

7. Eisenhower's quote is in *James Hagerty Diary*, May 20, 1954. A copy is on file at the Eisenhower Library.

8. Philip Reed to Dwight Eisenhower, June 8, 1953; Paul Hoffman to Dwight Eisenhower, March 24, 1954; both in *Eisenhower Presidential Papers*, Eisenhower Library.

9. Lippmann's quote is from his column in Washington *Post*, March 1, 1954.

10. Dwight Eisenhower to George N. Craig, March 26, 1954, Eisenhower Library.

11. See, for example, Robert Donovan, *Eisenhower: The Inside Story*, 1956, p. 247; Arthur Larson, *Eisenhower: The President Nobody Knew*, 1968, p. 13.

12. New York *Times*, December 18, 19, 1954; Washington *Post*, December 18, 19, 20, 1953.

13. Roy Cohn, *McCarthy*, 1968, pp. 111–12.

14. Richard Nixon, *Memoirs*, 1978, p. 140; New York *Times*, January 10, 1954.

15. Washington *Post*, January 6, 1954; New York *Times*, January 10, 17, 1954; *Newsweek*, January 11, 1954, p. 21.

16. Washington *Post*, January 2, 9, 1954; also U.S. Senate, *Annual Report of the Committee on Government Operations for 1953*, 1954.

17. Washington *Post*, January 9, 1954; New York *Times*, January 31, 1954.

18. Richard Fried, *Men Against McCarthy*, 1976, p. 276; Washington *Post*, January 7, 1954.

19. New York *Times*, January 31, 1954; Washington *Post*, January 7, 1954.

20. *Army–McCarthy Hearings*, 1954, p. 1057; also Michael Straight, *Trial by Television*, 1954, p. 103.

21. "Unflappable Bill Rogers," *Newsweek*, March 3, 1969, p. 21; Earl Mazo and Stephen Hess, *Nixon*, 1968, pp. 50, 111–25; Richard Wilson, "The Ring Around McCarthy," *Look*, December 1, 1953, pp. 29–33.

22. Drew Pearson, "Washington Merry-Go-Round," Washington *Post*, March 19, 1954.

23. Sherman Adams, *Firsthand Report*, 1961, pp. 143–44; Henry Cabot Lodge, *As It Was*, 1974, pp. 131–37; *Army–McCarthy Hearings*, p. 1059.

24. Drew Pearson, "Washington Merry-Go-Round," Washington *Post*, July 17, 1953.

25. *Ibid.*, November 22, December 22, 1953.

26. Jack Anderson, *Confessions of a Muckraker*, 1979, p. 265.

27. *Army–McCarthy Hearings*, pp. 1190.

28. *Ibid.*, pp. 1178, 1190.

29. The best (and most overlooked) sources on the Peress case are Lionel Lokos, *Who Promoted Peress?*, 1956; "Summary of the Case of Major Irving Peress, DC 1893643," in *Eisenhower Presidential Papers*, Eisenhower Library; and U.S. Senate, *Army Personnel Actions Relating to Irving Peress*, 1955.

30. Cohn, *McCarthy*, p. 99; anonymous to Senator Joe McCarthy, January 26, 1953, *FBI Papers*, Washington, D.C.

31. Zwicker's testimony is in *Army Personnel Actions Relating to Irving Peress*, pp. 389–92; Anastos's version is on pp. 529–52.

32. See U.S. Senate, Permanent Subcommittee on Investigations of the Committee on Government Operations, *Communist Infiltration in the Army*, 1954. The Peress testimony begins on p. 107.

33. McCarthy's letter is reproduced in *Army Personnel Actions Relating to Irving Peress*, pp. 423–24.

CHAPTER TWENTY-FIVE: THE CHICKEN LUNCHEON (*pp.* 372–89)

1. Richard Rovere, *Senator Joe McCarthy*, 1959, p. 39.

2. Lionel Lokos, *Who Promoted Peress?*, 1957, p. 169.

3. The Peress testimony can be found in Subcommittee on Investigations of the Committee on Government Operations, *Hearings on Communist Infiltration in the Army*, 1954, pp. 120–41.

4. See Senate Select Committee to Study Censure Charges, *Hearings on Senate Resolution 301*, 1954, pp. 177–79, 456.

5. "Confidential Affidavit of Captain William J. Woodward, February 20, 1954," copy on file at Dwight D. Eisenhower Presidential Library, Abilene, Kan.

6. *Hearings on Communist Infiltration in the Army.* Zwicker's testimony begins on p. 145.

7. See Joseph and Stewart Alsop, "Matter of Fact," Washington *Post*, February 25, 1954.

8. Theodore White, *In Search of History*, 1978, p. 378.

9. "Confidential Affidavit of General Ralph Zwicker," February 20, 1954, and "Memorandum for the Record," February 19, 1954, both in Eisenhower Library.

10. *Special Senate Investigation on Charges and Countercharges Involving Secretary of the Army Robert T. Stevens, John G. Adams, H. Struve Hensel and Senator Joe McCarthy, Roy M. Cohn, and Francis P. Carr* (Cited in subsequent chapters as *Army–McCarthy Hearings*), 1954, pp. 2155–56.

11. *Ibid.*, pp. 2120, 2136, 2144–45.

12. *Ibid.*, pp. 2090–95, 2136.

13. *Ibid.*, pp. 2144–45.

14. *Ibid.*, pp. 2019–23.

15. New York *Times*, February 22, 1954.

16. See "The Oak and the Ivy," *Time*, March 8, 1954, pp. 21–25; "McCarthy and Stevens—Behind the Scenes," *Newsweek*, March 8, 1954, pp. 19–24.

17. *Ibid.*

18. New York *Times*, February 21, 1954.

19. See Subcommittee on Investigations of the Committee on Government Operations, *Army Signal Corps—Espionage and Subversion*, 1954, p. 320.

20. Markward's testimony begins in *ibid.*, p. 309.

21. Richard Nixon, *Memoirs*, 1978, pp. 141–42; also "Private Interview with Vice President Nixon," February 26, 1954, in *Arthur Krock Papers*, Princeton University.

22. Nixon, *Memoirs*, p. 142.

23. For this session see *Army Signal Corps—Espionage and Subversion*, p. 331.

24. "The Oak and the Ivy"; "McCarthy and Stevens—Behind the Scenes."

25. *Ibid.* See also Joseph and Stewart Alsop, "Matter of Fact," Washington *Post*, February 25, 1954.

26. Washington *Post*, February 25, 1954; New York *Times*, February 25, 1954.

27. Nixon, *Memoirs*, p. 142.

28. "Private Interview with Vice President Nixon." Emphasis added.

29. Nixon, *Memoirs*, p. 142; *James Hagerty Diary*, February 24, 1954, copy at Eisenhower Library.

30. For a variety of opinions, see New York *Times*, February 25, 1954.

31. *Ibid.* Also Washington *Post*, February 25, 26, 1954; Philip Graham to Sherman Adams, February 26, 1954, Eisenhower Library.

32. "Presidential Phone Calls," *Whitman File*, February 25, 1954, Eisenhower Library.

33. Eisenhower made these remarks, privately, on at least two occasions. See "Legislative Leadership Meeting, Supplemental Notes, March 1, 1954," Eisenhower Library; also *Bernard Shanley Diary*, March 1, 1954, Seton Hall University.

34. "Private Interview with Vice President Nixon."

35. Washington *Post*, February 26, 1954.

36. *Ibid.*

CHAPTER TWENTY-SIX: "THE FAULT, DEAR BRUTUS"
(pp. 390–404)

1. Joseph and Stewart Alsop, "After Munich What?" Washington *Post*, March 3, 1954.

2. Washington *Post*, March 4, 9, 1954; *C. D. Jackson Diary*, February 26, 1954, copy at Dwight D. Eisenhower Presidential Library, Abilene, Kan.; New York *Times*, March 3, 4, 1954.

3. Presidential Phone Calls, *Whitman File*, March 2, 1954, Eisenhower Library; "Personal and Confidential Memorandum: Treatment of Government Personnel," March 5, 1954, Eisenhower Library.

4. Washington *Post*, March 4, 1954; New York *Times*, March 4, 1954.

5. Washington *Post*, March 4, 1954; the Alsop remark is in "Press Conference Notes," n.d., *Willard Edwards Papers*, copy in author's possession.

6. Washington *Post*, March 4, 1954; New York *Times*, March 4, 1954.

7. New York *Times*, March 4, 1954.

8. Edwards, "Press Conference Notes."

9. Washington *Post*, March 8, 9, 1954; New York *Times*, March 19, 1954; Lee's quote is in "The Scorched Air," *Newsweek*, March 22, 1954, p. 86.

10. Presidential Phone Calls, *Whitman File*, March 8, 1954; also *James Hagerty Diary*, March 9, 1954, copy at Eisenhower Library.

11. Richard Nixon, *Memoirs*, 1978, pp. 144–46; *James Hagerty Diary*, March 9, 1954.

12. New York *Times*, March 13, 14, 1954.

13. *Ibid*.

14. Joseph and Stewart Alsop, "The Sensible Senator," Washington *Post*, March 12, 1954; "Words from a Quiet Man," *Time*, March 22, 1954; Senator Flanders to Sherman Adams, July 30, 1952, *Senator Ralph E. Flanders Papers*, Syracuse University.

15. Flanders to Freeman Keith, March 12, 1951, *Flanders Papers*.

16. See Ralph E. Flanders, *Senator from Vermont*, 1961, p. 255.

17. Senator Ralph Flanders to Mrs. E. R. Archibald, February 15, 1954, *Flanders Papers*.

18. The entire speech is quoted in Flanders, *Senator from Vermont*, pp. 255–58; Ike's letter is in the Office File, March 9, 1954, Eisenhower Library.

19. The standard work on Murrow is Alexander Kendrick's *Prime Time*, 1969. Also excellent in discussing his impact are Eric Barnouw, *The Image Empire*, 1970, and David Halberstam, *The Powers That Be*, 1975.

20. Kendrick, *Prime Time*, pp. 37–39; Barnouw, *The Image Empire*, pp. 44–60.

21. Joseph Wershba, "Murrow vs. McCarthy: See It Now," *The New York Times Sunday Magazine*, March 4, 1979, p. 31.

22. *Ibid*.

23. John Cogley, "The Murrow Show," *The Commonweal*, March 26, 1954, p. 618; Gilbert Seldes, "Murrow, McCarthy and the Empty Formula," *The Saturday Review*, April 24, 1954, pp. 26–27. See also "The Scorched Air," *Newsweek*, March 22, 1954, p. 86.

24. Charles E. Potter, *Days of Shame*, 1965, p. 32.

25. *Ibid*., p. 30.

26. The Moss testimony can be found in Hearings Before the Subcommittee on Investigations of the Committee on Government Operations, *Army Signal Corps—Subversion and Espionage*, 1954, starting on page 443.

27. Presidential Phone Calls, *Whitman File*, March 12, 1954, Eisenhower Library.

28. The Adams Chronology can be found in the *Army–McCarthy Hearings*, 1954, pp. 135–42.

CHAPTER TWENTY-SEVEN: SETTING THE GROUND RULES
(*pp.* 405–15)

1. The eleven memos can be found in *Army–McCarthy Hearings*, 1954, pp. 1853–56.

2. New York *Times*, March 13, 14, 1954; Washington *Post*, March 13, 1954.

3. See "Minutes of the Executive Session of the Subcommittee on Investigations, March 16, 1954," in *Army–McCarthy Hearings*, pp. 1–26.

4. *James Hagerty Diary*, March 24, 1954, Dwight D. Eisenhower Presidential Library, Abilene, Kan.

5. Robert Griffith, *The Politics of Fear*, 1970, p. 253.
6. Interview with Ruth Watt, May 25, 1977; interview with Robert Morris, April 20, 1978. Also Karl Mundt to Joe McCarthy, June 17, 1950, and December 19, 1951, and Karl Mundt to Daniel Poling, December 18, 1951, all in *Senator Karl Mundt Papers*, Dakota State College, Madison, South Dakota.
7. See Charles Potter, *Days of Shame*, 1965, p. 26; Michael Straight, *Trial by Television*, 1954, pp. 156–57; "Investigators—Politicians—TV Actors," *U.S. News and World Report*, June 4, 1954, p. 70; "Seven Senators," *The New Yorker*, June 19, 1954, pp. 22–23.
8. Karl Mundt to "John, Ev, Charlie, Stu, and Scoop," April 2, 1954, *Mundt Papers*.
9. See "The Terror of Tellico Plains," *Time*, May 17, 1954, p. 26; Straight, *Trial by Television*, pp. 36–47; "The Men McCarthy Made Famous," *Life*, May 17, 1954, pp. 50–55.
10. The best biographical sketch of Welch is Fred Fisher, "Joseph N. Welch," unpublished manuscript in the author's possession. See also "That Sly Counselor—Welch," *Newsweek*, June 7, 1954, p. 27; "The Other Joe," *Time*, May 17, 1954, p. 27.
11. Chicago *Tribune*, March 18, 1954; New York *Times*, April 5, 1954; also Donald Crosby, *God, Flag, and Country*, 1978, pp. 147–60.
12. For the recall movement see Leroy Gore, *Joe Must Go*, 1954; David Thelen and Esther Thelen, "Joe Must Go: The Movement to Recall Senator Joe McCarthy," *The Wisconsin Magazine of History*, Spring 1966; Ted Cloak and Jane Cloak, "Joe Must Go: The Story of Dane County in the Recall," unpublished manuscript, Wisconsin State Historical Society.
13. Michael O'Brien, *McCarthy and McCarthyism in Wisconsin*, 1980, p. 166.
14. Karl Butler to James Green, December 7, 1954, and James Green to Karl Butler, n.d., both in the *John Hill Papers*, Wisconsin State Historical Society.
15. Interview with Jack Anderson, September 9, 1977; interview with Willard Edwards, April 30, 1978; interview with Robert Fleming, March 14, 1979.
16. Interview with Milton Young, May 26, 1977; interview with Willard Edwards; interview with Urban Van Susteren, October 22, 1977. Also Samuel Shaffer, *On and Off the Floor*, 1980, p. 43.
17. The Army's Bill of Particulars can be found in the *Army–McCarthy Hearings*, following page 99.
18. McCarthy's Bill of Particulars can be found in *ibid.*

CHAPTER TWENTY-EIGHT: THE HEARINGS BEGIN (*pp. 416–34*)

1. See G. D. Wiebe, "The Army–McCarthy Hearings and the Public Conscience," *Public Opinion Quarterly*, Winter 1958–59, pp. 490–502; Walter Lippmann, "Today and Tomorrow," Washington *Post*, March 25, 1954. Herblock had always been fascinated by McCarthy, but almost 40 percent of his cartoons on the senator appeared in the months between February and July 1954.

2. New York *Times*, April 23, 1954; Washington *Post*, April 23, 1954; Michael Straight, *Trial by Television*, 1954, pp. 3–6; Joseph N. Welch, "The Lawyer's Afterthoughts," *Life*, July 26, 1954, pp. 96–98.

3. Hearings Before the Special Subcommittee on Investigations of the Committee on Government Operations, *Special Senate Investigation on Charges and Countercharges Involving: Secretary of the Army Robert T. Stevens, John G. Adams, H. Struve Hensel, and Senator Joe McCarthy, Roy M. Cohn, and Francis P. Carr (Army–McCarthy Hearings)*, 1954, p. 31.

4. *Ibid.*, pp. 31–32.

5. *Ibid.*, p. 33.

6. General Reber's testimony is in *ibid.*, pp. 33–78.

7. *Ibid.*, p. 81.

8. *Ibid.*, pp. 89–99.

9. *Ibid.*, pp. 102–34.

10. The *Times* quote can be found in Roy Cohn, *McCarthy*, 1968, p. 134; see also "The Terror of Tellico Plains," *Time*, May 17, 1954, p. 26; "The Men McCarthy Made Famous," *Life*, May 17, 1954, pp. 50–55.

11. *Ibid.*, pp. 194–97.

12. Welch, "The Lawyer's Afterthoughts," pp. 96–98.

13. *Army–McCarthy Hearings*, pp. 255–56.

14. Cohn's testimony is in *ibid.*, p. 275.

15. Cohn, *McCarthy*, p. 183.

16. Juliana's testimony is in *Army–McCarthy Hearings*, pp. 523–51.

17. Interview with Urban Van Susteren, October 22, 1977.

18. Welch, "The Lawyer's Afterthoughts," pp. 96–98.

19. Cohn, *McCarthy*, p. 168.

20. *Army–McCarthy Hearings*, p. 703.

21. *Ibid.*, p. 705.

22. Collier's testimony begins in *ibid.*, p. 720.

23. *Ibid.*, p. 758.

24. "Memo for the Files," n.d., *Willard Edwards Papers*, copy in author's possession.

25. The Brownell letter appears in *Army–McCarthy Hearings*, pp. 820–21.

26. *Ibid.*, p. 830.

27. *Ibid.*, pp. 1573–75, 1787.

28. *James Hagerty Diary*, May 28, 1954, Eisenhower Library.

29. New York *Times*, May 28, 1954.

CHAPTER TWENTY-NINE: EXECUTIVE PRIVILEGE (*pp*. 435–45)

1. Presidential Phone Calls, March 18, 1954, *Whitman File*, Dwight D. Eisenhower Presidential Library, Abilene, Kan.

2. F. P. Heffelfinger to Karl Mundt, May 7, 1954, Central File, Eisenhower Library; George Stringfellow to Karl Mundt, May 7, 1954, and Alf Landon to Karl Mundt, May 8, 1954, both in the *Karl Mundt Papers*, Dakota State College, Madison, South Dakota.

3. *Army–McCarthy Hearings*, 1954, pp. 969–71.

4. *Ibid.*, pp. 978–84.

5. *James Hagerty Diary*, May 11, 12, 1954, Eisenhower Library.

6. *Army–McCarthy Hearings*, p. 1009.

7. Adams's testimony begins on pp. 1009–10.

8. Presidential Phone Calls, May 5, 1954, *Whitman File*; Henry Cabot Lodge, *As It Was*, 1972, p. 135.

9. *Army–McCarthy Hearings*, pp. 1198–99.

10. *James Hagerty Diary*, May 17, 1954.

11. *Army–McCarthy Hearings*, p. 1260.

12. *Ibid.*, pp. 1262–67.

13. *James Hagerty Diary*, May 14, 1954.

14. *Army–McCarthy Hearings*, p. 1296.

15. *Ibid.*, p. 1306.

CHAPTER THIRTY: THE ELEVEN MEMORANDA (*pp. 446–56*)

1. Roy Cohn, *McCarthy*, 1968, p. 184.

2. *Army-McCarthy Hearings*, 1954. Cohn's testimony begins on p. 1554.

3. *Ibid.*, pp. 1776–77.

4. *Congressional Record*, 83d Cong., 2d sess., June 1, 1954, p. 7389.

5. See Stanley Plog, "Flanders vs. McCarthy: A Study in Technique and Theory of Analyzing Constituent Mail," unpublished doctoral dissertation, Harvard University, 1961, pp. 96–97.

6. *Ibid.*, p. 94.

7. "Ralph E. Flanders Interview," *Columbia Oral History Project*, New York.

8. Charles E. Potter, *Days of Shame*, 1965, p. 231.

9. Mrs. Driscoll's testimony is in *Army–McCarthy Hearings*, beginning on p. 1816.

10. Willard Edwards, "Memo for the Files," *Willard Edwards Papers*, copy in author's possession.

CHAPTER THIRTY-ONE: "SO RECKLESS, SO CRUEL" (*pp. 457–71*)

1. Wisconsin *State Journal*, June 11, 1954.

2. Fred Fisher, "Joe Welch," unpublished manuscript in author's possession.

3. *Ibid.*

4. *Ibid.*

5. *Ibid.*; also *James Hagerty Diary*, April 2, 1954, Dwight D. Eisenhower Presidential Library, Abilene, Kan.

6. Fisher, "Joe Welch."

7. For a review of Cohn's draft problems, see New York *Times*, March 20, 24, 1954.

8. Roy Cohn, *McCarthy*, 1968, p. 200.

9. *Ibid.*, pp. 202–3. Emphasis in original.

10. Fisher, "Joe Welch."

11. The Fisher incident can be found in *Army–McCarthy Hearings*, 1954, pp. 2424–30.

12. See, for example, Janesville *Daily Gazette*, June 11, 1954; Racine *Journal–Times*, June 11, 1954. For Woltman's "Balance Sheet," see New York *World–Telegram and Sun*, week of July 10–16, 1954.

13. George Gallup to Gerard Ambert, June 14, 1954, copy in *John Foster Dulles Papers*, Princeton University, Princeton, New Jersey.

14. *Army–McCarthy Hearings*; McCarthy's testimony begins on p. 2431.

15. *Ibid.*, p. 2559.

16. *Congressional Record*, 83d Cong., 2d sess., June 11, 1954, pp. 8032–33; New York *Times*, June 12, 1954.

17. *Army–McCarthy Hearings*, p. 2590.

18. A copy of the document is in *ibid.*, pp. 2621–23.

19. Roy Cohn, *McCarthy*, 1968, p. 71; also Arthur Schlesinger, Jr., *Robert Kennedy and His Times*, 1978, p. 113; Michael Straight, *Trial by Television*, 1954, p. 192.

20. See Peter Ognibene, *Scoop: The Life and Politics of Henry M. Jackson*, 1975, pp. 51–55.

21. *Army–McCarthy Hearings*, pp. 2703–7.

22. *Ibid.*, pp. 2977–81.

23. *Ibid.*, p. 2984.

24. *James Hagerty Diary*, June 18, 1954.

Chapter Thirty-Two: Censure (*pp. 472–94*)

1. E. E. Hazlett to Dwight D. Eisenhower, June 30, 1954, *DDE Presidential Papers*, Dwight D. Eisenhower Presidential Library, Abilene,Kan.

2. For editorial reaction, see Lately Thomas, *When Even Angels Wept*, 1973, pp. 604–5.

3. New York *Times*, October 5, 1954, February 16 and March 17, 1955.

4. Roy Cohn, *McCarthy*, 1968, p. 219.

5. Frank Gibney, "After the Ball," *Commonweal*, September 3, 1954, pp. 531–35.

6. "Washington Merry-Go-Round," Washington *Post*, July 20, 1954.

7. See *Congressional Record*, 83d Cong., 2d sess., July 30, 1954, pp. 12729–42.

8. Robert Griffith, *The Politics of Fear*, 1970, pp. 284–91; Richard Fried, *Men Against McCarthy*, 1976, pp. 292–96; interview with Leverett Saltonstall, April 27, 1978.

9. *Ruth Watt Oral Interview*, Senate Historical Office, Washington, D.C.

10. *Congressional Record*, July 30, 1954, pp. 12729–42.

11. *Ibid.* Also pp. 12893–12927.

12. Arthur Watkins, *Enough Rope*, 1969, p. 31.

13. See William S. White, *Citadel*, 1956, pp. 128–33; Griffith, *Politics of Fear*, p. 295; Fried, *Men Against McCarthy*, pp. 297–98.

14. Cohn, *McCarthy*, p. 224.

15. Watkins, *Enough Rope*, p. 36.

16. Ralph Flanders to Arthur Watkins, September 11, 1954, *Arthur Watkins Papers*, Brigham Young University.

17. *Hearings Before a Select Committee to Study Censure Charges*, 1954, p. 7.

18. *Ibid.*, pp. 35–38; New York *Times*, September 8, 1954.

19. *Report of the Select Committee to Study Censure Charges*, 1954, pp. 37–39.

20. See, for example, White, *Citadel*, pp. 122–23; Ross Baker, *Friend and Foe in the U.S. Senate*, 1980, p. 241.

21. *Report of the Select Committee*, pp. 45–46.

22. *Ibid.*, pp. 57–58.

23. *Ibid.*, p. 27.

24. *Ibid.*, p. 31.

25. Interview with Leverett Saltonstall.

26. Interview with Willard Edwards, April 30, 1978.

27. Richard Nixon, *Memoirs*, 1978, p. 160.

28. Fried, *Men Against McCarthy*, pp. 305–7; Griffith, *Politics of Fear*, p. 306.

29. *Congressional Record*, 1954, pp. 15951–54.

30. *Ibid.*, pp. 15851, 15988–89, 16014, 16053.

31. Watkins, *Enough Rope*, p. 146.

32. John Howe to William Benton, November 24, 1954, Box 4, *William Benton Papers*, Wisconsin State Historical Society.

33. Julius Edelstein to Arthur Schlesinger, Jr., November 11, 1954, in *ibid*.

34. Howe to Benton, November 24, 1954, in *ibid*. The best arguments against censure can be found in "McCarthy Censure," a copy of which can be found in the *Styles Bridges Papers*, Henneker, New Hampshire.

35. New York *Times*, November 18, 19, 20, 1954.

36. See Watkins, *Enough Rope*, pp. 112–24; also Stanley Plog, "Flanders v. McCarthy: A Study in the Technique and Theory of Analyzing Constituent Mail," unpublished doctoral dissertation, Harvard University, 1961.

37. Plog, "Flanders v. McCarthy," pp. 106–16.

38. Edward Bennett Williams, *One Man's Freedom*, 1962, pp. 67–68; Barry Goldwater, *With No Apologies*, 1979, pp. 53–54.

39. A copy of this letter can be found in the unprocessed Papers of Everett Dirksen, Pekin, Illinois.

40. Neil McNeil, *Dirksen: Portrait of a Public Man*, 1970, pp. 125–26.

41. Watkins, *Enough Rope*, p. 80; Goldwater *With No Apologies*, p. 53; Styles Bridges to Richard Adams, December 9, 1954, *Bridges Papers*.

42. For the pressure on Carlson, see Ed Abels to Carlson, November 18, 1954, and Preston Dunn to Carlson, November 13, 1954, both in the *Frank Carlson Papers*, Kansas State Historical Society. For the pressure on Cotton, see Newport, N.H., *Times*, December 16, 1954; Concord, N.H., *Monitor*, December 28, 1954. The first article explains why Cotton voted for censure, the second is a vicious attack upon Cotton by Loeb.

43. "Form Letter to Constituents," November 11, 1954, *Alexander Wiley Papers*, Wisconsin State Historical Society.

44. "Telephone Conversation with Senator Wiley," November 1, 1954, *Dulles Papers*.

45. Theodore Sorensen, *Kennedy*, 1965, p. 54.

46. "Charles Spalding Interview," *Kennedy Oral History Project*, Kennedy Presidential Library.

47. Arthur Schlesinger, Jr., to John Kennedy, March 11, 1958, in *Kennedy Presidential Papers*.

48. *Congressional Record*, 1954, pp. 16292–93.

49. Watkins, *Enough Rope*, p. 149.

50. Fried, *Men Against McCarthy*, p. 310.

51. White, *Citadel*, p. 133.

52. *James Hagerty Diary*, December 3, 1954, Eisenhower Library.

53. *Ibid.*, December 7, 1954.

CHAPTER THIRTY-THREE: FINAL YEARS (*pp.* 495–507)

1. Arthur Watkins, *Enough Rope*, 1969, pp. 182–83.

2. *Ruth Watt Oral History*, Senate Historical Office, Washington, D.C.

3. Reedy's quote is in Jean Deaver, "A Study of Senator Joseph R. McCarthy and 'McCarthyism' as Influences Upon the News Media," unpublished doctoral dissertation, University of Texas, 1970, pp. 48–49; also interview with Willard Edwards, April 30, 1978; Sam Shaffer, *On and Off the Floor*, 1980, p. 46.

4. Edwin Bayley, *McCarthy and Press*, 1982, pp. 217–18.

5. *Pennsylvania* v. *Nelson*, (350 U.S. 497 (1956); *Sloehower* v. *Board of Higher Education*, 350 U.S. 551 (1956); *Watkins* v. *United States*, 354 U.S. 178 (1957).

6. See Walter Murphy, *Congress and the Court*, 1962, pp. 86–87, 89.

7. Ralph Levering, *The Cold War, 1945–1972*, 1982, p. 67; Robert Divine, *Eisenhower and the Cold War*, 1981, pp. 116–20.

8. Willard Edwards, "Post Censure Notes," *Willard Edwards Papers*, in author's possession.

9. *Congressional Record*, 1955, p. 8943. Emphasis added.

10. The debate is in *ibid.*, pp. 8938–60.

11. See Senator Joe McCarthy to Senator Karl Mundt, July 8, 1955, and Mundt to McCarthy, July 9, 1955; in *Senator Karl Mundt Papers*, Dakota State College, Madison, South Dakota; also Roy Cohn, *McCarthy*, 1968, p. 256.

12. Hearings Before the Permanent Subcommittee on Investigations of the Committee on Government Operations, *Army Personnel Actions Relating to Irving Peress*, 1955, p. 377.

13. *Ibid.*, p. 371.

14. The complete file of letters on the Zwicker case can be found in the *Mundt Papers*.

15. Madison *Capital–Times*, June 13, 1955; "Comeback Flop," *The Nation*, November 12, 1955, p. 414.

16. Interview with Phil Potter, February 27, 1978.

17. Senator Joe McCarthy to Roy Matson, January 9, 1957, and Matson to McCarthy, January 18, 1957, both in *Papers of the Wisconsin State Journal*, Wisconsin State Historical Society.

18. Tom Dooley to Mother, February 14, 1957, *Tom Dooley Papers*, Western Historical Manuscripts Collection, Columbia, Mo.

19. *Ruth Watt Oral History*.

20. Interview with Ed Hart, January 18, 1977; Frances Leighton, *Fishbait*, 1977, p. 158; interview with Robert Fleming, March 14, 1979.

21. Ron ? to William Evjue, December 23, 1956, *William Evjue Papers*, Wisconsin State Historical Society.

22. Interview with Urban Van Susteren, October 22, 1977.

23. Roy Cohn, *McCarthy*, p. 262; Arthur M. Schlesinger, Jr., *Robert Kennedy and His Times*, 1978, p. 173.

24. Willard Edwards, "Rough Notes," *Willard Edwards Papers*, in author's possession; Cohn, *McCarthy*, p. 261.

25. Tyler Abell (ed.), *Drew Pearson Diaries*, 1974, p. 379.

26. Prescott Bush Interview, *Columbia Oral History Collection*, New York City.

27. See David Lawrence's column in the New York *Herald–Tribune*, May 6, 1957; also Chicago *Tribune*, May 4, 1957; Donald Crosby, *God, Church and Flag*, 1978, p. 223; Eric Severeid, "Joseph R. McCarthy," *The Reporter*, May 16, 1957.

28. New York *Times*, May 3, 4, 5, 1957.

29. Appleton *Post–Crescent*, May 5, 6, 7, 1957.

30. Jean McCarthy to John Foster Dulles, June 4, 1957, *Dulles Papers*, Princeton University; Jean McCarthy to Styles and Dolores Bridges, May 22, 1957, *Bridges Papers*, Henneker, N.H.; Jean McCarthy to Louis and Margaret Budenz, June 4, 1957, *Budenz Papers*, Providence College, Providence, R.I.

Selective Bibliography

ORAL HISTORIES, DIARIES, AND PERSONAL INTERVIEWS

JACK ANDERSON, personal interview, September 9, 1977.

RAYMOND BALDWIN interview, *Columbia Oral History Project (COHP)*, Columbia University.

CHARLES BOHLEN interview, *John Foster Dulles Oral History Project (DOHP)*, Princeton University.

RICHARD BROWN, personal interview, January 18, 1977.

JAMES M. BURNS interview, *John F. Kennedy Oral History Project (KOHP)*, Kennedy Presidential Library.

PRESCOTT BUSH interview, *COHP*.

CLIFFORD CASE, personal interview, February 16, 1979.

ABRAM CHAYES interview, *KOHP*.

EDWARD CORSI interview, *DOHP*.

WILLARD EDWARDS, personal interview, April 30, 1978.

DWIGHT D. EISENHOWER, *Personal Diary*, Dwight D. Eisenhower Presidential Library.

DWIGHT D. EISENHOWER interview, *DOHP*.

JOHN ELLENBECKER, personal interview, January 19, 1977.

RICHARD FARRELL, personal interview, January 18, 1977.

HOMER FERGUSON interview, *DOHP*.

FRED FISHER, personal interview, July 6, 1980.

RALPH FLANDERS interview, *COHP*.

ROBERT FLEMING, personal interview, March 14, 1979.

STANLEY FROSH, personal interview, May 22, 1977.

WILLIAM FULBRIGHT, personal interview, May 27, 1977.

JAMES HAGERTY, *Personal Diary*, Eisenhower Library.

JOHN HAYNES interview, *DOHP*.

DONALD HANSON interview, *Harry S. Truman Oral History Project (TOHP)*.

IRVING HANSON, personal interview, January 18, 1977.

EDWARD HART, personal interview, January 18, 1977.

JIM HEENAN, personal interview, October 22, 1977.

C. D. JACKSON, *Personal Diary*, Eisenhower Library.

WALTER KOHLER interview, *COHP*.

THOMAS KORB, phone interview, June 10, 1978.

HENRY CABOT LODGE, personal interview, July 14, 1978.

DONALD LOURIE interview, *DOHC*.

CHARLES MIDDLETON, personal interview, January 19, 1977.

ROBERT MORRIS, personal interview, April 20, 1978.

HENRY MORTENSEN, personal interview, January 19, 1977.

MELDA BECKMAN MORTENSON, personal interview, January 19, 1977.

CLIFFORD MULLARKEY, personal interview, January 17, 1977.

CHARLES MURPHY interview, *TOHP*.

ADA NEMSHOFF, personal interview, January 18, 1977.

PHILIP POTTER, phone interview, February 27, 1978.

WILLIAM REMMEL, personal interview, January 18, 1977.

JAMES RESTON interview, *DOHP*.

MINNIE OSTERLOTHE RHODE, personal interview, January 18, 1977.

MAURICE ROSENBLATT, personal interview, December 23, 1976.

LEVERETT SALTONSTALL, personal interview, April 27, 1978.

BERNARD SHANLEY, *Personal Diary*, Seton Hall University.

H. ALEXANDER SMITH, *Personal Diary*, Princeton University.

MARGARET CHASE SMITH, phone interview, May 27, 1977.

HAROLD STASSEN interview, *DOHP*.

URBAN VAN SUSTEREN, personal interview, October 22, 1977.

RUTH WATT, personal interview, May 25, 1977.

Ruth Watt Oral History, Senate Historical Office, Washington, D.C.

FRANCIS WERNER, personal interview, January 20, 1977.

MILTON YOUNG, personal interview, May 26, 1977.

MANUSCRIPT COLLECTIONS

Americans for Democratic Action MSS, Wisconsin State Historical Society (WSHS).

THOMAS AMLIE MSS, WSHS.

WILLIAM BENTON MSS, WSHS.

STYLES BRIDGES MSS, Henneker, N.H.

LOUIS BUDENZ MSS, Providence College.

HUGH BUTLER MSS, Nebraska State Historical Society.

FRANK CARLSON MSS, Kansas State Historical Society.

THOMAS COLEMAN MSS, WSHS.

EDWARD DEMPSEY MSS, WSHS.

ALLEN DULLES MSS, Princeton University.

JOHN FOSTER DULLES MSS, Princeton University.

WILLARD EDWARDS MSS, in Mr. Edwards's and author's possession.

DWIGHT D. EISENHOWER MSS, Eisenhower Library.

GEORGE ELSEY MSS, Harry S. Truman Presidential Library.

WILLIAM EVJUE MSS, WSHS.

Papers of the FBI, Washington, D.C.

RALPH FLANDERS MSS, Syracuse University.

ROBERT FLEMING MSS, WSHS.

THEODORE GREEN MSS, Library of Congress.

THOMAS HENDRICKSON MSS, Syracuse University.

JOHN HILL MSS, WSHS.

FRANCIS KEESLING MSS, University of California, Berkeley.

JAMES KEM MSS, Western Historical Manuscripts Collection, Columbia, Mo.

JOHN F. KENNEDY MSS, Kennedy Library.

ARTHUR KROCK MSS, Princeton University.

DAVID LLOYD MSS, Truman Library.

KARL MUNDT MSS, Dakota State College.

PHILLEO NASH Files, Truman Library.

National Committee for an Effective Congress MSS, in the possession of Maurice Rosenblatt, Washington, D.C.

Papers of The Reporter Magazine, Boston University.

RICHARD ROVERE MSS, WSHS.

STEPHEN SPINGARN MSS, Truman Library.

ADLAI STEVENSON MSS, Princeton University.

ROBERT TAFT MSS, Library of Congress.

BRADLEY TAYLOR MSS, WSHS.

CHARLES TOBEY MSS, Dartmouth College.

HARRY S. TRUMAN MSS, Truman Library.

Papers of the Wisconsin State Journal, WSHS.

Unpublished Material

ADLER, LESLIE, "The Red Image: American Attitudes Towards Communism in the Cold War," Ph.D. dissertation, University of California, Berkeley, 1970.

AUER, JAMES, and CLARK KALVELAGE, "Joe McCarthy's School Days," unpublished MS., Wisconsin State Historical Society (WSHS).

BURKHARDT, RICHARD, "The Teaching of The Soviet Union in American School Social Studies," Ph.D. dissertation, Harvard University, 1952.

BYERS, BOB, "How I Know Mr. McCarthy," unpublished MS., WSHS.

CLOAK, TED, and JANE CLOAK, "Joe Must Go: The Story of Dane County in the Recall," unpublished MS., WSHS.

COADY, SHARON, "The Wisconsin Press and Joseph McCarthy," M.A. thesis, University of Wisconsin, 1965.

DAHLSTROM, H. A., "Kenneth S. Wherry," Ph.D. dissertation, University of Nebraska, 1965.

DEAVER, JEAN, "A Study of Senator Joseph R. McCarthy and 'McCarthyism' as Influences upon the News Media . . . ," Ph.D. dissertation, University of Texas, 1970.

FERGUSON, MARY JANE, "McCarthy vs. Pearson," M.A. thesis, University of Wisconsin, 1969.

FISHER, FRED, "Joseph N. Welch," unpublished MS. in author's possession.

HANEY, RICHARD, "A History of the Democratic Party in Wisconsin Since World War II," Ph.D. dissertation, University of Wisconsin, 1970.

JOHNSON, RONALD, "The Communist Issue in Missouri," Ph.D. dissertation, University of Missouri, 1973.

MCKINLEY, WAYNE, "A Study of the American Right: Senator Joe McCarthy and the American Legion," M.A. thesis, University of Wisconsin, 1962.

MEYER, KARL, "The Politics of Loyalth: From La Follette to McCarthy in Wisconsin, 1918–1952," Ph.D. dissertation, Princeton University, 1956.

PAUL, JUSTIS, "The Political Career of Senator Hugh Butler," Ph.D. dissertation, University of Nebraska, 1966.

PLOG, STANLEY, "Flanders vs. McCarthy: A Study in Technique and Theory of Analyzing Constituent Mail," Ph.D. dissertation, Harvard University, 1961.

SCHWARTZ, BOB, "The Junior Senator: Early Life," unpublished MS., WSHS.

STEINKE, JOHN, "The Rise of McCarthyism," M.A. thesis, University of Wisconsin, 1960.

WALLERSTEIN, IMMANUEL, "McCarthyism and the Conservatives," M.A. thesis, Columbia University, 1954.

WATTS, JIM, "Dress Rehearsal for Wheeling: Joseph R. McCarthy in the Senate, 1947–1949," unpublished MS. in author's possession.

Government Documents

U.S. Congress, *Congressional Record*, 1919–20, 1938, 1945–57.

U.S. Senate, Committee on Armed Services. *Malmedy Massacre Investigation*, 1949.

————, Committee on Armed Services. *Nomination of Anna M. Rosenberg to Be Assistant Secretary of Defense*, 1951.

————, Subcommittee of the Committee on Banking and Currency. *Study of the Reconstruction Finance Corporation*, 1951.

————, Committee on Expenditures in the Executive Departments. *Hearings on a Resolution Authorizing an Investigation of Surplus Property and its Disposal, Basic Magnesium Plant, Henderson, Nevada*, 1947.

————, Committee on Expenditures in the Executive Departments. *Hearings on Senate Document #7: Aqueduct Near San Diego, California*, 1947.

————, Subcommittee of the Committee on Foreign Relations. *Hearings on the Nomination of Charles E. Bohlen*, 1953.

————, Subcommittee of the Committee on Foreign Relations. *Nomination of Philip Jessup to be the United States Representative to the Sixth General Assembly of the United Nations*, 1953.

————, Subcommittee of the Committee on Foreign Relations. *State Department Employee Loyalty Investigation*, 1950.

————, Committee on Government Operations, Permanent Subcommittee on Investigations. *Annual Report*, 1954.

————, Committee on Government Operations, Permanent Subcommittee on Investigations. *Army Personnel Actions Relating to Irving Peress*, 1955.

————, Committee on Government Operations, Permanent Subcommittee on Investigations. *Army Signal Corps—Subversion and Espionage*, 1954.

————, Committee on Government Operations, Permanent Subcommittee on Investigations. *Communist Infiltration Among Army Civilian Workers*, 1953.

————, Committee on Government Operations, Permanent Subcommittee on Investigations. *Communist Infiltration in the Army*, 1953.

————, Committee on Government Operations, Permanent Subcommittee on Investigations. *Control of Trade with the Soviet Bloc*, 1953.

————, Committee on Government Operations, Permanent Subcommittee on Investigations. *Security—Government Printing Office*, 1953.

————, Committee on Government Operations, Permanent Subcommittee on Investigations. *State Department Information Program—Information Centers*, 1953.

————, Committee on Government Operations, Permanent Subcommittee on Investigations. *State Department Information Program—Voice of America*, 1953.

————, Committee on Government Operations, Special Subcommittee on Investigations. *Charges and Countercharges Involving Secretary of the Army*

Robert T. Stevens, John G. Adams. H. Struve Hensel, and Senator Joe Mc-
Carthy, Roy M. Cohn, and Francis P. Carr, 1954.

———, Committee on the Judiciary. *Hearings on the Institute of Pacific Relations*, 1951–52.

———, Committee on Rules and Administration, Subcommittee on Privileges
and Elections. *Investigation of Senators Joseph R. McCarthy and William
Benton*, 1952.

———, Committee on Rules and Administration, Subcommittee on Privileges
and Elections. *Maryland Senatorial Election of 1950*, 1951.

———, Joint Committee on Housing. *Study and Investigation of Housing*, 1948.

———, Select Committee to Study Censure Charges. *Hearings*, 1954.

BOOKS AND ARTICLES

ABELL, TYLER (ed.). *Drew Pearson Diaries, 1949–1959.* New York: Holt, Rinehart
& Winston, 1974.

ACHESON, DEAN. *Present at the Creation.* New York: Holt, Rinehart & Winston,
1959.

"Act of Humiliation," *Time*, March 13, 1950.

ADAMS, SHERMAN. *First Hand Report.* New York: Harper & Row, 1961.

"Again, Who's Lying?" *Newsweek*, May 1, 1950.

ALEXANDER, JACK. "The Senate's Remarkable Upstart," *The Saturday Evening
Post*, August 9, 1947.

American Civil Liberties Union. "The Police and the Radicals—What 88 Police
Chiefs Think and Do About Radical Meetings." New York: American Civil
Liberties Union, 1924.

ANDERSON, CLINTON. *Outsider in the Senate.* New York: World, 1970.

ANDERSON, JACK, and RONALD MAY. *McCarthy.* Boston: Beacon Press, 1952.

ARENDT, HANNAH. "The Ex-Communists," *The Commonweal*, March 20, 1953.

ASCOLI, MAX; PHILIP HORTON; and CHARLES WERTENBAKER. "The China Lobby,"
The Reporter, April 15, 1952.

BAARSLAG, KARL. "How to Spot a Communist." *Legion Magazine*, January, 1947.

BAKER, ROSS K. *Friend and Foe in the U.S. Senate.* New York: Free Press, 1980.

BAYLEY, EDWIN. *McCarthy and the Press.* Madison: University of Wisconsin
Press, 1981.

BEAN, LOUIS. *Influences in the 1954 Mid-Term Elections.* Washington, D.C.:
Public Affairs Institute, 1954.

BELFRAGE, CEDRIC. *The American Inquisition.* Indianapolis, Ind.: Bobbs-Merrill,
1973.

BELL, DANIEL (ed.). *The New American Right.* New York: Criterion Books, 1955.

"The Bohlen Affair," *The Nation*, April 4, 1953.

BOHLEN, CHARLES E. *Witness to History, 1929–1969.* New York: Norton, 1973.

BONTECOU, ELEANOR. *The Federal Loyalty–Security Program*. Ithaca, N.Y.: Cornell University Press, 1953.

BOWMAN, ALFRED. "The Man Behind McCarthy: Coleman of Wisconsin," *The Nation*, March 20, 1954.

BROWN, RALPH S. *Loyalty and Security*. New Haven, Conn.: Yale University Press, 1958.

BUCKLEY, WILLIAM F., and L. BRENT BOZELL. *McCarthy and His Enemies*. Chicago: Henry Regnery, 1954.

BUDENZ, LOUIS. *This Is My Story*. New York: McGraw-Hill, 1947.

"Busy Man," *Time*, October 8, 1951.

CATER, DOUGLAS. "The Captive Press," *The Reporter*, June 6, 1950.

———. "Is McCarthy Slipping?" *The Reporter*, September 8, 1951.

CAUTE, DAVID. *The Great Fear*. New York: Simon & Schuster, 1978.

CHAFFEE, ZECHARIAH. *Free Speech in the United States*. Cambridge, Mass.: Harvard University Press, 1941.

"Charges Unanswered," *Newsweek*, June 13, 1949.

COBEN, STANLEY. *A. Mitchell Palmer: Politician*. New York: Columbia University Press, 1963.

COGLEY, JOHN. "The Murrow Show," *The Commonweal*, March 26, 1954.

COHEN, WARREN. "Who's Afraid of Alfred Kohlberg?" *Reviews in American History*, March 1975.

COHN, ROY. *McCarthy*; New York: New American Library, 1968.

"Comeback Flop," *The Nation*, November 12, 1955.

COOK, FRED. *The Nightmare Decade*. New York: Random House, 1971.

CROSBY, DONALD. *God, Flag, and Country*; Chapel Hill: University of North Carolina Press, 1978.

CUSHMAN, ROBERT. "American Civil Liberties in Mid-Twentieth Century," *The Annals of the American Academy of Political and Social Science*, May 1951.

DAVIDSON, BILL. "The Surprising Mr. Jessup," *Collier's*, July 30, 1949.

DAVIES, RICHARD. *Housing Reform During the Truman Administration*. Columbia: University of Missouri Press, 1966.

DECTER, MOSHE, and JAMES RORTY. *McCarthy and the Communists*. Boston: Beacon Press, 1954.

DEVOTO, BERNARD. "The Ex-Communists," *The Atlantic Monthly*, February 1951.

DIVINE, ROBERT. *Eisenhower and the Cold War*. New York: Oxford University Press, 1981.

DOAN, EDWARD. *The La Follettes and the Wisconsin Idea*. New York: Rinehart, 1947.

DONOVAN, ROBERT. *Eisenhower: The Inside Story*. New York: Harper, 1956.

DOUGLAS, PAUL. *In the Fullness of Time*. New York: Harcourt Brace Jovanovich, 1972.

ELDER, ROBERT. *The Information Machine.* Syracuse, N.Y.: Syracuse University Press, 1968.

"The Election," *Time,* November 18, 1946.

EPSTEIN, LEON. *Politics in Wisconsin.* Madison: University of Wisconsin Press, 1958.

ESHERICK, JOHN (ed.). *Lost Chance in China.* New York: Random House, 1974.

EVANS, MATTHEW. *The Assassination of Joe McCarthy.* Boston: Western Islands, 1970.

"The Expert at Ike's Elbow," *Newsweek,* July 18, 1955.

"Faces in the News," *Life,* March 27, 1950.

FERRELL, ROBERT. *Off The Record: The Private Papers of Harry S. Truman.* New York: Harper & Row, 1980.

"The Fetish of Objectivity," *Time,* May 4, 1953.

FILENE, PETER. *America and the Soviet Experiment, 1917–1933.* Cambridge, Mass.: Harvard University Press, 1967.

FLANDERS, RALPH E. *Senator from Vermont.* Boston: Little, Brown, 1961.

"A Fool or a Knave," *Time,* April 17, 1950.

FORSTER, ARNOLD, and BENJAMIN EPSTEIN. *The Troublemakers.* Garden City, N.Y.: Doubleday, 1952.

FREELAND, RICHARD. *The Truman Doctrine and the Origins of McCarthyism.* New York: Knopf, 1972.

FRIED, RICHARD. *Men Against McCarthy.* New York: Columbia University Press, 1976.

FRIENDLY, ALFRED. "The Noble Crusade of Senator McCarthy," *Harper's,* August 1950.

"Fundamentalist Republican," *Time,* December 10, 1951.

GALLUP, GEORGE (ed.). *The Gallup Poll.* New York: Random House, 1972.

GELLHORN, WALTER. *The States and Subversion.* Ithaca, N.Y.: Cornell University Press, 1952.

GIBNEY, FRANK. "After the Ball," *The Commonweal,* September 3, 1954.

GOLDMAN, ERIC. *Rendezvous with Destiny.* New York: Knopf, 1952.

GOLDWATER, BARRY. *With No Apologies.* New York: Morrow, 1979.

GOODMAN, WALTER. *The Committee.* New York: Farrar, Straus & Giroux, 1964.

"The G.O.P. Mantle of Power," *Newsweek,* November 18, 1946.

GORE, LEROY. *Joe Must Go.* New York: J. Messner, 1954.

"The Greeks, the Senator, and the Slump," *Business Week,* April 11, 1953.

GREELEY, ANDREW. *That Most Distressful Nation.* Chicago: Quadrangle, 1972.

GRIFFITH, ROBERT. "The General and the Senator," *Wisconsin Magazine of History,* Autumn 1970.

———. *The Politics of Fear.* Lexington: University of Kentucky Press, 1970.

———, and ATHAN THEOHARIS (eds.). *The Specter.* New York: Franklin Watts, 1974.

GUHIN, MICHAEL. *John Foster Dulles*. New York: Columbia University Press, 1972.

HALBERSTAM, DAVID. *The Powers That Be*. New York: Knopf, 1978.

HALE, WILLIAM. " 'Big Brother' in Foggy Bottom," *The Reporter*, August 17, 1954.

HAMBY, ALONZO. *Beyond the New Deal*. New York: Columbia University Press, 1973.

HAMILTON, JAMES. *The Power to Probe*. New York: Random House, 1976.

HARPER, ALAN. *The Politics of Loyalty*. Westport, Conn.: Greenwood, 1969.

HAVEMANN, ERNEST. "War and Politics," *Life*, August 28, 1950.

HEALY, PAUL. "Big Noise from Nebraska," *The Saturday Evening Post*, August 5, 1950.

HENDERSON, JOHN. *The United States Information Agency*. New York: F. A. Praeger, 1969.

HIGHAM, JOHN. *Strangers in the Land*. New Brunswick, N.J.: Rutgers University Press, 1955.

HOOK, SIDNEY. "Lattimore on the Moscow Trail," *The New Leader*, November 10, 1952.

HOOPES, TOWNSEND. *The Devil and John Foster Dulles*. Boston: Little, Brown, 1973.

"Hoping Against Hope," *Time*, April 10, 1950.

HORTON, PHILIP. "Voices within the Voice," *The Reporter*, July 21, 1953.

HOVEY, GRAHAM. "Both McCarthy and His Foes Get Jolt," Washington *Post*, October 14, 1951.

―――. "How McCarthy Sold Wisconsin," *The New Republic*, September 22, 1952.

"How Come McCarthyism?" *Life*, September 8, 1952.

"How to Handle McCarthy," *Time*, October 24, 1954.

HOWE, IRVING, and LEWIS COSER. *The American Communist Party: A Critical History, 1919–1957*. Boston: Beacon Press, 1957.

HUGHES, EMMET. *The Ordeal of Power*. New York: Atheneum, 1963.

HYMAN, SIDNEY. *The Lives of William Benton*. Chicago: University of Chicago Press, 1969.

ICKES, HAROLD. "McCarthy Strips Himself," *The New Republic*, August 7, 1950.

"Ike's Victory with Bohlen Reduces McCarthy Influence," *Newsweek*, April 6. 1953.

"In the Floodlight," *Time*, June 6, 1949.

"Interview with Senator McCarran," *U.S. News and World Report*, November 16, 1951.

"Investigators—Politicians—TV Actors," *U.S. News and World Report*, June 4, 1954.

"Jessup Backfire," *Newsweek*, October 22, 1951.

"Job for the Readers," *Time*, January 25, 1954.

JOHNSON, ROGER. *Robert M. La Follette, Jr. and the Decline of the Progressive Party in Wisconsin.* Madison: State Historical Society of Wisconsin, 1964.

KAHN, E. J., JR. *The China Hands.* New York: Viking, 1972.

KEELEY, JOSEPH. *The China Lobby Man.* New Rochelle, N.Y.: Arlington House, 1969.

KEMPER, DONALD. *Decade of Fear.* Columbia: University of Missouri Press, 1965.

KEMPTON, MURRAY. *America Comes of Middle Age.* Boston: Little, Brown, 1963.

KENDRICK, ALEXANDER. *Prime Time.* Boston: Little, Brown, 1969.

KIRKPATRICK, LYMAN B., JR. *The Real CIA.* New York: Macmillan, 1968.

KNIGHT, CHARLOTTE. "What Price Security?" *Collier's,* July 9, 1954.

KOEN, ROSS Y. *The China Lobby in American Politics.* New York: Harper & Row, 1974.

LA FOLLETTE, ELEANOR. "A Room of Our Own," *The Progressive,* August 26, 1946.

LARSON, ARTHUR. *Eisenhower: The President Nobody Knew.* New York: Scribner's, 1968.

LASKY, VICTOR. *JFK: The Man and the Myth.* New York: Macmillan, 1963.

LATHAM, EARL. *The Communist Controversy in Washington from the New Deal to McCarthy.* Cambridge, Mass.: Harvard University Press, 1966.

LEIGHTON, FRANCES. *Fishbait: The Memoirs of the Congressional Doorkeeper.* Englewood Cliffs, N.J.: Prentice-Hall, 1977.

LEUCHTENBURG, WILLIAM. *Franklin D. Roosevelt and the New Deal, 1932–40.* New York: Harper & Row, 1963.

LEVERING, RALPH. *The Cold War, 1945–1972.* Arlington Heights, Ill.: H. Davidson, 1982.

LIPSET, SEYMOUR, and EARL RABB. *The Politics of Unreason.* New York: Harper & Row, 1970.

LODGE, HENRY CABOT. *As It Was.* New York: Norton, 1976.

———. "Modernize the G.O.P.," *The Atlantic Monthly,* March 1950.

"Lodge Defines the Minority Role," *The New York Times Magazine,* September 17, 1950.

"Loss of Appetite," *Time,* November 20, 1950.

MCAULIFFE, MARY SPERLING. *Crisis on the Left.* Amherst: University of Massachusetts Press, 1978.

"McCarthy and Greek Ships: 'Undermining' or 'Constructive'?" *Newsweek,* April 13, 1953.

"McCarthy and Stevens—Behind the Scenes," *Newsweek,* March 8, 1954.

"McCarthy and the Past," *Life,* April 10, 1950.

"McCarthy at the Barricades," *Time,* March 27, 1950.

"McCarthy: Hero at Home," *New York Times,* June 9, 1950.

MCDONALD, JUSTILLE. *History of the Irish in Wisconsin in the Nineteenth Century.* Washington, D.C.: Catholic University of America Press, 1954.

McLELLAN, DAVID. *Dean Acheson.* New York: Dodd, Mead, 1976.

McMAHON, PATRICK. "Ships and Greeks and Senator Joe McCarthy," *The American Mercury*, July 1953.

McNEIL, NEIL. *Dirksen: Portrait of a Public Man.* New York: World Publishing Co., 1970.

McWILLIAMS, CAREY. "Senator McCarthy's Sixth Column," *The Nation*, May 22, 1954.

MANCHESTER, WILLIAM. *The Glory and the Dream.* Boston: Little, Brown, 1973.

MARTIN, JOHN B. *Adlai Stevenson and the World.* New York: Doubleday, 1977.

MARTIN, JOSEPH. *My First Fifty Years in Politics.* New York: McGraw-Hill, 1960.

MATTHEWS, DONALD. *U.S. Senators and Their World.* Chapel Hill: University of North Carolina Press, 1960.

MATTHEWS, J. B., "Reds and Our Churches," *The American Mercury*, July 1953.

MATUSOW, ALLEN (ed.). *Joseph R. McCarthy.* Englewood Cliffs, N.J.: Prentice-Hall, 1970.

MATUSOW, HARVEY. *False Witness.* New York: Cameron & Kahn, 1955.

MAY, GARY. *China Scapegoat.* Washington, D.C.: New Republic Books, 1979.

MAY, RONALD. "Is The Press Unfair to McCarthy?" *The New Republic*, April 5, 1953.

MAYER, MILTON. "The People Lose," *The Progressive*, August 26, 1946.

MAZO, EARL, and STEPHEN HESS. *Nixon: A Political Portrait.* New York: Popular Library, 1968.

"The Men McCarthy Made Famous," *Life*, May 17, 1954.

MERSON, MARTIN. *The Private Diary of a Public Servant.* New York: Macmillan, 1955.

MINOTT, RODNEY. *Peerless Patriots: Organized Veterans and the Spirit of Americanism.* Washington, D.C.: Public Affairs Press, 1962.

MOSLEY, LEONARD. *Dulles.* New York: Dial Press, 1978.

MURPHY, PAUL. *The Meaning of Freedom of Speech: First Amendment Freedoms from Wilson to FDR.* Westport, Conn.: Greenwood, 1972.

MURPHY, WALTER. *Congress and the Court.* Chicago: University of Chicago Press, 1962.

MURRAY, ROBERT. *Red Scare: A Study in National Hysteria.* Minneapolis: University of Minnesota Press, 1955.

NAVASKY, VICTOR. *Naming Names.* New York: Viking, 1980.

NIXON, RICHARD. *Memoirs.* New York: Grosset & Dunlap, 1978.

NYE, RUSSEL. *Midwestern Progressive Politics.* East Lansing: Michigan State University Press, 1959.

OAKES, JOHN B. "Report on McCarthy and McCarthyism," *The New York Times Magazine*, November 2, 1952.

"The Oak and the Ivy," *Time*, March 8, 1954.

O'BRIEN, MICHAEL. "The Anti-McCarthy Campaign in Wisconsin, 1951–52," *Wisconsin Magazine of History*, Winter 1972–73.

————. *McCarthy and McCarthyism in Wisconsin.* Columbia: University of Missouri Press, 1980.

"Of Cells and Onion Skins," *Time,* May 1, 1950.

OGDEN, AUGUST. *The Dies Committee: A Study of the Special House Committee for Investigation of Un-American Activities, 1938–1944.* Washington, D.C.: Catholic University Press, 1945.

OSHINSKY, DAVID. *Senator Joseph McCarthy and the American Labor Movement.* Columbia: University of Missouri Press, 1976.

PACKER, HERBERT. *Ex-Communist Witnesses.* Stanford, Calif.: Stanford University Press, 1962.

PARMET, HERBERT S. *Eisenhower and the American Crusades.* New York: Macmillan, 1972.

PATTERSON, JAMES. *Mr. Republican.* Boston: Houghton Mifflin, 1972.

PEARSON, DREW. "Washington Merry-Go-Round," *Washington Post,* March 2, 1953.

"Periscope," *Newsweek,* October 8, 1951.

PFEFFER, LEO. *This Honorable Court.* Boston: Beacon Press, 1965.

PHILLIPS, CABELL. *The Truman Presidency.* New York: Macmillan, 1966.

"Phony Greek Deal?" *Newsweek,* April 6, 1953.

PILAT, OLIVER. *Drew Pearson.* New York: Harper's Magazine Press, 1973.

————. *Pegler, Angry Man of the Press.* Boston: Beacon Press, 1963.

POTTER, CHARLES. *Days of Shame.* New York: Coward-McCann, 1965.

POEMER, THEODORE. *St. Joseph in Appleton.* Appleton, Wis.: George Banta, 1943.

PRENDERGAST, WILLIAM. "State Legislatures and Communism: The Current Scene," *American Political Science Review,* September 1950.

"Pretty Researcher Marries Her Boss," *Life,* October 12, 1953.

ROBESON, ESLANDA C. D. *African Journey.* New York: John Day Co., 1945.

RANEY, WILLIAM. "Appleton," *Wisconsin Magazine of History,* December 1949.

ROGIN, MICHAEL. *The Intellectuals and McCarthy.* Cambridge, Mass.: MIT Press. 1967.

ROSENAU, JAMES. *The Nomination of Chip Bohlen.* New York: McGraw-Hill, 1958.

ROVERE, RICHARD. "The Adventures of Cohn and Shine," *The Reporter,* July 21, 1953.

————. *Senator Joe McCarthy.* Cleveland: World, 1959.

RUSHMORE, HOWARD. "Mr. Anti-Communist," *The American Mercury,* May 1953.

————. "Pekin Farm Boy," *The American Mercury,* July 1953.

————. "Young Mr. Cohn," *The American Mercury,* February 1953.

————. "The Gentleman from Indiana," *The American Mercury,* July 1954.

————. "The Senator from Moscow (Idaho)," *The American Mercury,* July 1955.

"Rushmore v. Cohn," *Time*, November 1, 1954.

"Russian for 'Hello'," *Time*, May 16, 1949.

RYAN, THOMAS. *History of Outgamie County.* Chicago: Goodspeed Historical Association, 1909.

SAUNDERS, D. A. "The Dies Committee: First Phase," *Public Opinion Quarterly*, April 1939.

SCHLESINGER, ARTHUR M., JR. *Robert Kennedy and His Times.* Boston: Houghton Mifflin, 1978.

———, and RICHARD ROVERE. *The General and the President.* New York: Farrar, Straus & Young, 1951.

"Schmitt vs. McCarthy," *The New Republic*, July 14, 1952.

"The Scorched Air," *Newsweek*, March 22, 1954.

SELDES, GILBERT. "Murrow, McCarthy and the Empty Formula," *The Saturday Review*, April 24, 1954.

"The Self-Inflated Target," *Time*, March 22, 1954.

"The Senate," *Time*, November 13, 1950.

"The Senate's Most Expendable," *Time*, March 20, 1950.

"The Senate's Most Valuable Ten," *Time*, April 3, 1950.

"Seven Senators," *The New Yorker*, June 19, 1954.

SEVEREID, ERIC. "Joseph R. McCarthy," *The Reporter*, May 16, 1957.

SHAFFER, SAMUEL. *On and Off the Floor;* New York: Newsweek Books, 1980.

SHELTON, WILLARD. "The Shame of the Senate," *The Progressive*, February 1953.

SMITH, MARGARET CHASE. *Declaration of Conscience.* Garden City, N.Y.: Doubleday, 1972.

SORENSON, THEODORE. *Kennedy.* New York: Harper & Row, 1965.

SPANIER, JOHN. *The Truman–McArthur Controversy and the Korean War.* Cambridge, Mass.: Belknap Press, 1965.

STAROBIN, JOSEPH. *American Communism in Crisis, 1943–1957.* Cambridge, Mass.: Harvard University Press, 1972.

STEINBERG, ALFRED. "Is This the Man to Beat McCarthy?" *Collier's*, November 24, 1951.

———. "McCarran: Lone Wolf of the Senate," *Harper's*, November 1950.

"Still Up in the Air," *Newsweek*, October 23, 1950.

STRAIGHT, MICHAEL. *Trial by Television.* Boston: Beacon Press, 1954.

SULZBERGER, C. L. *A Long Row of Candles.* New York: Macmillan, 1969.

SWANBERG, W. A. *Luce and His Empire.* New York: Scribner's, 1972.

SWING, RAYMOND. "VOA—A Survey of the Wreckage," *The Reporter*, July 21, 1953.

"Taft and McCarthy," *Life*, October 1, 1951.

TAYLOR, TELFORD. *Grand Inquest.* New York: Simon & Schuster, 1955.

"The Terror of Tellico Plains," *Time*, May 17, 1954.

"That Sly Counselor—Welch," *Newsweek*, June 7, 1954.

THELEN, DAVID, and ESTHER THELEN. "Joe Must Go: The Movement to Recall Senator Joe McCarthy," *Wisconsin Magazine of History*, Spring 1976.

THEOHARIS, ATHAN. *Seeds of Repression*. Chicago: Quadrangle, 1971.

THOMAS, JOHN. *The Institute of Pacific Relations*. Seattle: University of Washington Press, 1974.

THOMAS, LATELY. *When Even Angels Wept*. New York: Morrow, 1973.

"Trap for McCarthy," *Newsweek*, April 3, 1950.

"T.R.B.," *The New Republic*, November 11, 1946.

TROHAN, WALTER. "The Tragedy of George Marshall," *The American Mercury*, March 1951.

TURNER, W. W. *Hoover's FBI*. Los Angeles: Sherbourne Press, 1970.

"Tydings on a Tear," *Newsweek*, July 31, 1950.

"Unflappable Bill Rogers," *Newsweek*, March 3, 1969.

UNGER, SANFORD. *F.B.I.* Boston: Little, Brown, 1975.

UTLEY, FREDA. *The China Story*. Chicago: Henry Regnery, 1951.

"Voice of America: The Problem," *U.S. News and World Report*, March 27, 1953.

"The Voice on TV," *Newsweek*, March 9, 1953.

VON WEIZSACKER, ERNST. *Memoirs*. Chicago: Henry Regnery, 1951.

WALSH, WARREN. "What the American People Think of Russia," *Public Opinion Quarterly*, Winter 1944.

"War Against McCarthy," *Newsweek*, May 15, 1950.

WARREN, FRANK, III. *Liberals and Communism: The 'Red Decade' Revisited*. Bloomington: Indiana University Press, 1966.

"Washington," *The Atlantic Monthly*, July 1950.

"The Washington Front," *The Nation*, July 8, 1950.

"Washington Wire," *The New Republic*, July 31, 1950.

WATKINS, ARTHUR W. *Enough Rope*. Englewood Cliffs, N.J.: Prentice-Hall, 1969.

WECHSLER, JAMES. *The Age of Suspicion*. New York: Random House, 1953.

WELCH, JOSEPH N. "The Lawyer's Afterthoughts," *Life*, July 26, 1954.

WERSHBA, JOSEPH. "Murrow vs. McCarthy: See It Now," *The New York Times Magazine*, March 4, 1979.

"What Bohlen Can Do in Moscow," *U.S. News and World Report*, April 3, 1953.

WHITE, THEODORE. *In Search of History*. New York: Harper & Row, 1978.

WHITE, WILLIAM S. *Citadel*. Boston: Houghton Mifflin, 1968.

———. "McMahon: Senator and Atomic Specialist," *New York Times Magazine*, February 12, 1950.

———, "Mood of Washington: Morale Gets Big Lift," *New York Times*, July 2, 1950.

———, "Portrait of a 'Fundamentalist'," *The New York Times Magazine*, January 15, 1950.

"Why Not Spank Him?" *Collier's*, August 18, 1951.

WILLIAMS, EDWARD BENNETT. *One Man's Freedom*. New York: Atheneum, 1962.

WIEBE, G. D. "The Army–McCarthy Hearings and the Public Conscience," *Public Opinion Quarterly*, Winter 1958–59.

WILSON, RICHARD. "The Ring Around McCarthy," *Look*, December 1, 1953.

WINCHELL, WALTER. *Winchell Exclusive.* Englewood Cliffs, N.J.: Prentice-Hall, 1975.

"Words from a Quiet Man," *Time*, March 22, 1954.

YOUNG, DONALD (ed.). *Adventure in Politics: The Memoirs of Philip La Follette.* New York: Holt, Rinehart, 1970.

Index